Third Edition

D0128529

Contemporary Cultures and Societies of Latin America

A Reader in the
Social Anthropology of
Middle and South America

Dwight B. Heath

Brown University

WAVELAND

PRESS, INC.

Prospect Heights, Illinois

For information about this book, write or call:
 Waveland Press, Inc.
 P.O. Box 400
 Prospect Heights, Illinois 60070
 (847) 634-0081
 www.waveland.com

To

AMC

Sine qua non

Contents

PART IV — Identity and Ethnicity   245

PART V — Relations of Power   343

PART VI — Views of the World   **447**

Preface

It was a real challenge to revise a book that had been well known and widely used by two generations of students;[1] few textbooks survive that long, but colleagues asked for a new edition, the publisher liked the idea, and I saw it as an opportunity to learn more about what's being done by people whose work I hadn't known in detail. Earlier versions of this book served as an introduction to Latin America for many who care deeply about anthropology, and it provided an introduction to anthropology for many who have other interests in Latin America. Constructive feedback from both instructors and students—many of whom have become productive and influential practitioners, colleagues, and movers and shakers in various fields of endeavor—has helped to guide me in choosing papers that combine those interests and that reflect recent thinking in a time in which both fields of study are changing rapidly.

This is truly a new book,[2] but one that continues the original aim of including articles that contain substantive and theoretic relevance and that show a variety of approaches to both current concerns and long-term processes. The aim is to be both timely in terms of providing fresh insights about current events, and, in a sense, also timeless in offering helpful ways of looking at institutions, relationships, and patterns of belief and behavior anywhere and everywhere.

In the years since this book was first published, much has changed among contemporary cultures and societies of Latin America and among the interests, methods, and concerns of those who study them. In this book I have tried to provide a sampling of articles that are representative of both what's going on in Latin America and what matters in anthropology. In real terms, the emphasis is on mainland Latin America; other books deal with the Caribbean where cultural and historical diversity are very different. In disciplinary terms, the emphasis is on social and cultural anthropology, the contemporary ways of life of people living there. Most of the readings are new; many of the topics are new; and all of the viewpoints should be both interesting and helpful to any reader who wants to learn more about those broad subjects, both of which are developing rapidly in directions that were hardly imagined when Rick Adams and I first ventured to compile a reader in 1965.

There have indeed been changes that affect the daily lives of a great many of the people in Latin America. Rural-to-urban migration has accelerated to the point where more than half the population in most countries now lives in large urban rather than rural or small-town settings. Agriculture and mining, which used to focus on a single product in most countries, have largely given way to manufacturing, commerce, other services, and even remittances as principal sources of national income. Tourism has transformed some small areas, and wars have transformed others, often prompting local people to go abroad. Twentieth-century means of transportation and communication reach into regions that seemed relatively isolated just a generation ago, and it has become far more evident that the global economy impinges on almost everyone in various ways. To a remarkable degree, however, patterns of belief and behavior still vary from one population to another, and it is just such differences—and similarities—and interfaces between such bundles of patterns (which we call *cultures*) that concern most anthropologists.

At the same time, anthropology itself has not been static. To be sure, most anthropologists still have one foot in an academic setting, but anthropological perspectives increasingly are being recognized as relevant and useful in the workaday world, where practicing anthropology (analogous to what we used to call applied anthropology) has gained respect and recognition that were too long denied to this important source of understanding and problem solving.

The readings offered in this book still focus largely on what people think and do in their daily lives, how broader institutions impinge on them; how they react to those influences; and how they relate to other people, individually or collectively, and why. An attempt has been made to include both macroscopic and microscopic perspectives, inasmuch as the view from the grassroots level is as important to each person as the world-systems perspective must be to anyone who tries to plan or comprehend common markets, international trade, or the implications of the Internet.

So much has changed that it seemed apt to reorganize the contents of this book. In my experience, and in that of most colleagues with whom I have discussed it, students are generally reading less and in different ways than did their predecessors in the latter part of the last century. Social scientists have generally come to recognize that their reportage need not strive for total objectivity, but that some indication of their role in interactions often helps to clarify the meanings of their data in a broader context. Some of the topical areas that are of special interest today were largely ignored when this book was first published, such as gender studies or ethnicity, and others carry less weight than they used to, such as social structure or national character.

It goes without saying that any book on so broad a subject as contemporary cultures and societies of Latin America must deal as much with outsiders' views of the area as with insiders' views about all sorts of things. Although there has been a serious effort to reflect data and concepts from a range of academic and scientific disciplines, the focus is on an anthropological perspective. Just what that means will differ, depending on who's talking and when, but at the beginning of the twenty-first century in the United States, I speak for many anthropologists when I characterize our interests broadly as "the human experience."

As in earlier editions, I have also included here a number of papers written by people who do not think of themselves as anthropologists, in either the academic or the practicing sense. They include, for example, an astronomer, a climatologist, an ecologist, historians, a nurse, a political scientist, and a sociologist as well. The contributing authors are not only trained and practicing in the United States but also in Argentina, Brazil, Canada, Chile, England, France, Mexico, and the Netherlands, and they represent a wide range of political, economic, and social philosophies. Several of those whose work appears here were enthusiastic because they had "cut [our] teeth on the first edition." Others welcomed the opportunity to "be in such distinguished company," and some were simply surprised to be invited. It is important to note that nothing here is "written down" to students; most chapters are from books or scientific and professional journals in which colleagues communicate among themselves.

This book will probably most often be used as a complement to lectures and discussions, and in combination with various monographs that deal with specific regions or topics in greater detail. It would be unrealistic to suggest that any single anthology on such broad and controversial areas as anthropology and Latin America could satisfy everyone.[3] Although each contributor is knowledgeable and experienced, that does not mean that each chapter should be viewed as *the* authoritative statement on its subject matter. Readers will doubtless find that some articles provide fresh insights, while they may disagree with others.

The six parts of this book were named *after* most of the individual readings had been chosen. An array of papers was selected to reflect a variety of approaches to some of those topics that are currently important in the field. Each paper was judged to have some intrinsic interest for a number of readers, to be clear and readily understandable, to offer descriptive information that is not necessarily broadly known, and to make a point that not only lends more meaning to those data but that can also be applied to help illuminate other situations elsewhere.

The introductory sections to the various parts of the book are purposely brief, intended primarily to set the individual chapters into an historical and intellectual context. Each introduction offers a frankly subjective overview of why certain themes appear to be worth highlighting as important aspects of a social science approach to Latin America at this time. Another editor would probably have organized such a book very differently, and readers would do well to think about the logic of alternative approaches to this vast corpus of literature.

A list of suggestions for further reading follows each of the introductions to the six sections of this book. These suggestions by no means add up to a comprehensive bibliography on the topics discussed within the sections. They are intended as a guide, featuring a few key books and important authors, to illustrate a range of approaches and to provide a valuable starting point from which any student can further pursue his or her interests.

Although books are most often listed as suggested references, most if not all of the important points made by anthropologists can also be found, written earlier and amply outlined, in articles appearing in scientific or academic journals or periodicals. To access that vibrant and generally succinct literature, a number of guides are available, each with detailed indexing by authors' name, topic, tribe or country, and so forth. Those guides that are most salient for pertinent subjects and authors are briefly discussed in the Bibliographical Essay, which follows the final section of this book and should be helpful to any student who may wish to pursue a topic in greater depth.

In Part I, Latin America: Image and Reality, five readings deal successively with why Latin America is important, what a cultural perspective adds to that, the relevance for human rights and for ecological concerns, and a review of different kinds of research that have been conducted in one area over several decades.

Part II, The Anthropological Enterprise, shifts from a broadly regional focus to emphasize specifically what anthropologists do. Seven readings range from the nature of the fieldwork experience to ethnicity and international borders, an ethnographic survey retracing an early account by an insightful traveler, how anthropology directly contributes to development, the importance of preserving native languages, ethical dilemmas that grow out of service to the local community, and levels of truth and symbolism with reference to an Indian Nobel laureate.

Part III, Traditional and Modern Cultures, offers a sampling of ten case studies that nicely illustrate the diversity of contemporary ways of life throughout Latin America. One shows how indigenous organizations are bringing formerly disenfranchised First Nations (native peoples) into mainstream political and other participation, even at national and international levels; another describes a game in terms that highlight some unfamiliar basic premises. Culture shock and contrast in a tourist resort, and the plight of street-food vendors show different ways in which the global economy impacts at the grassroots level. Analyses of the meanings of the Zapatista rebellion, and of adaptive strategies of a penny-capitalist entrepreneur, show how an anthropological perspective complements those of political science and economics. Within a single country, changing drinking patterns show very different cultural meanings and interpretations of a commonplace activity; and a tribe strives, with help from anthropologists, to protect its autonomy and its territory. A handcraft that was traditionally important in women's clothing becomes an art form traded around the world, and a U.S. university as beneficent landlord helps peasants on a Peruvian hacienda to join the modern world on their own terms.

In Part IV, Identity and Ethnicity, eight readings focus on various ways in which individuals and groups find, assert, or are assigned different kinds of identification in relation to others. One paper outlines origins and distribution of Jews in Latin America; another emphasizes recently increasing attention paid to Afro-Latin Americans. Distinctive local women's dress undergoes rapid modernization in another study, and North American women are treated as bogeys in Guatemala. The lifestyle of gay males is cramped by traditional family ties, although *machismo* is shown not always to be the crudely assertive masculinity that the stereotype suggests. An ancient religious rite has evolved into a modern national symbol with Mexico's Day of the Dead, and Amazonian Indians shrewdly use modern media to gain international support for their cause.

Part V, Relations of Power, looks at variants of that key concept in nine readings that combine sociological, political, historical, and psychological viewpoints with anthropological observations. The dyadic contract and its associated complementarity of patronage and clientage provides a model for understanding how people relate to supernaturals as well as to each other. Bribery and small-scale corruption are shown to be integral parts of an ostensibly egalitarian bureaucratic system, and we see how housewives in Chile became politically vocal and active in just a few years, as did their sisters in Argentina, reacting to governmental abuses. An ethnographer wrestles with the contradictions of studying an apparent gentleman who has been labeled a monster, and Protestant missionaries make it look as if God were a North American. The controversial concept of a culture of poverty is considered, as is the plight of modern-day descendents of a colonial aristocracy. The idea of brokerage between cultures is offered as an analytic tool that allows us better to understand complex societies and how they evolve.

In Part VI, Views of the World, eight readings dramatically highlight the significance that worldviews have for easing—and for obstructing—understanding between peoples. The ostensibly culture-free process of arithmetic calculation is shown to be not at all straightforward and universal. The story of a local saint, caught in crosscurrents of liberation theology and political revolution, gives vivid meaning to patronage and clientage as dynamic principles in social relations. One scientist offers an overview of hallucinogenic plants in South America, and others demonstrate how the latest space-age technology proves the validity of traditional folk-wisdom that guided Andean farmers for centuries. Personal problems and individual choices are shown as bases for religious conversion, and it becomes clear why some mothers do not mourn the death of their infants. The impact of war on a peasant community and the impact of love in interpersonal relations are both sensitively portrayed in the context of ethnographic fieldwork.

Many of the readings in this book have been abridged by the editor. In most instances, this includes only minor changes in wording to smooth or advance the text or to do away with an allusion that would soon be outdated. In no instance does such editing significantly affect either the original content or intent of the author. A reader who is especially interested in any selection should go to the original before citing it and may well want to look up other works by the same author. Each reading is prefaced by a brief note from the editor indicating both the importance of that reading and some ways in which it relates to others, as well as brief identification of the author(s) and a credit-line indicating its source.

The editor is indebted to a number of people for varied contributions at all stages of the preparation of this book. Clyde Kluckhohn at Harvard first sparked my enthusiasm for anthropology and made it seem like a realistic and realizable venture. George P. Murdock, Floyd Lounsbury, and Eric R. Wolf at Yale provided some of the "nuts and bolts" in graduate school. Richard N. Adams was an effective and exciting co-editor and Random House a supportive publisher early on. At Waveland Press, Tom Curtin combined enthusiasm with remarkable patience, and Gayle Zawilla helped fit the many pieces together into a meaningful whole. In continuing recognition that a volume such as this represents essentially a collective effort, the contributing authors have volunteered their works, and I am again assigning royalties to further research, this time through Harvard University.

Dwight B. Heath
Providence, Rhode Island

Notes

[1] Heath, Dwight B., and Richard N. Adams (eds.), *Contemporary Cultures and Societies of Latin America: A Reader in the Social Anthropology of Middle and South America,* Random House, New York, 1965; Heath, Dwight B. (ed.), same title (second ed.), Random House, New York, 1974; Heath, Dwight B. (ed.), same title (with additional Preface), Waveland Press, Prospect Heights, IL, 1988.

[2] Any reader who is interested in the recent history of anthropology and Latin American studies may find it helpful to compare this book with the three previous printings. Each expressed the culture of the time, and collectively they reflect changes both in cultures throughout Latin America and in anthropological methods, concepts, and modes of interpretation.

[3] To my knowledge there is only one other book that essays to deal with these subjects in comparable breadth and depth: Whiteford, Michael B., and Scott Whiteford (eds.), *Crossing Currents: Continuity and Change in Latin America,* Prentice-Hall, Upper Saddle River, NJ, 1998. Many of the same authors and topics are represented there, and they have even used some of the chapters that I included in the previous edition of this book. Their organization more closely parallels that of an introductory course in anthropology; mine tends to reflect more on recent changes in what anthropologists are doing and writing about among their colleagues.

PART I

Latin America
Image and Reality

This section of the book considers the question of why Latin America deserves to be studied and how so large and diverse a region makes sense in terms of social science in the twenty-first century: It was about 50 years ago that a Mexican historian caught worldwide attention with a book provocatively titled *Does Latin America Exist?* (O'Gorman 1945). Recognizing that few people who live there consider themselves Latin Americans, and that many of the countries still have border disputes rather than seeking union or confederation, recent responses to O'Gorman's question have tended to be either tinged with bitter humor ("Yes, but only at institutes and universities in the rest of the world") or condescendingly, in stereotypes that are reminiscent of the Black Legend. (Although people rarely use the term today, vestiges of that way of thinking survive. From the seventeenth through the nineteenth centuries, a series of chroniclers characterized Spanish and Portuguese settlers of what we now call Latin America as nothing more than a gang of bloodthirsty, rapacious thugs, looking to live in leisure supported by Indian slaves—in contrast with the supposedly pacific and beneficent industrious and humanitarian family-oriented northern Europeans who settled in what is now Anglo-America. In recent decades, the Black Legend was generally discredited by historians as having been largely anti-Catholic propaganda, but some of the tone lives on in the popular mind of many North Americans.) Nevertheless, O'Gorman's eloquently simple and simply eloquent question still is pertinent for all of those who claim to be interested in Latin America, perhaps even more pertinent as rapidly increasing globalization in terms of economic and political activities, transportation, and communication could well negate the value of area studies that flourished briefly in the cultural awakening that followed World War II.

It may not be very helpful to recall that the term *Latin America* was introduced by Napoleon III when he was looking for a rationale to justify French imperial ambitions

1

in what had recently been Spanish and Portuguese territories, stressing the tenuous linguistic and cultural links to a common classical ancestry.

THE SETTING

This book limits treatment of Latin America to the mainland, excluding the Caribbean islands that are so varied in terms of their colonial history that most of them share little with the legal, political, and historical traditions of Mexico, Central, and South America. The "Latin tradition" is palpable despite regional variations, because Spain and Portugal were the dominant colonial powers throughout most of the region until the 1820s. Trade and administration had been centralized to a remarkable degree, the two languages predominated, and traditions of social organization, law, education, and attitudes all were strongly influenced by their European antecedents. Native or indigenous cultures have generally been ignored, except by anthropologists, until recent years.

Persistence to the twenty-first century is obvious in linguistic terms and, upon close inspection, in terms of a great many values, norms, and patterns of belief and behavior that are widespread—and that contrast with those in other parts of the world. Despite significant diversity, there are also major threads of continuity and similarity among the various nations, at least at the level of those communities that are outward looking and that strive to take part in the global system. To be sure, most of these same countries also contain relatively isolated refuge regions, or enclaves, where populations persist that did not willingly take part in the colonial way of life and that, in many instances, would still prefer to remain affected by the outside world only to the extent that they themselves would choose, perhaps in terms of tools, medications, or a few other conveniences.

For certain kinds of analysis, the ethnic minorities can accurately be viewed as relatively unimportant, having little economic impact and almost no influence on major cosmopolitan institutions. In anthropological terms, however, it is often those variant forms of social and cultural life that are the most interesting, engaging, and revealing as we try to understand sociocultural systems and how they work, sampling the range of human experience and looking at the world from the grassroots.

Latin America—land of contrasts! Although it has become popular as a catchy slogan to promote tourism, that characterization embodies a significant truth that has profoundly influenced the historical, economic, political, and other types of development for millennia. It is an area of extremes in both natural and social features, and often differences can be as dramatic within a country as they are between countries.

SOME GOVERNING IMAGES

A few geographical anomalies may pique the interest of a student who has never paid close attention to Latin America. For example, nearly all of the South American continent lies to the east of Miami, Florida, to the point where Recife is closer to some cities in Africa than it is to some towns along the Brazilian borders with Peru, Bolivia, or Colombia. Parts of Chile are closer to Antarctica than to the capital city, Santiago. In passing through the Panama Canal from the Pacific Ocean to the Caribbean and Atlantic, one sails from east to west. Most countries in Latin America are in the tropics, yet some have mountains that are perpetually snowcapped. The Amazon River and its tributaries carry fully half of the world's fresh water at any given time, although the Atacama Desert, stretching from Peru through much of Chile, has had no measurable rainfall in recorded history.

Such trivia are unimportant in themselves, but each has implications for the people who live there and for the ways in which they relate to the rest of the world. It matters that Brazil is half of the landmass of South America, similar in size to the 48 contiguous United States. It matters that Mexico City is both the largest and the most rapidly growing metropolis in the world. It matters that Bolivia, as big as Spain and France combined, has no seaport and lost fully half of its territory to its neighbors in a succession of disastrous wars. It matters that a similar portion of Mexico was lost to the United States little more than 150 years ago.

Well within living memory, there were several countries in Latin America where the predominant sector of the economy was agriculture, with 90 percent of the land held by a mere 10 percent of the landholders, vast tracts (latifundia) contrasted with tiny subsistence holdings (minifundia). Wealth and power were similarly polarized, and quasi-feudal regimes had landlords as virtual masters on their estates and tenant farmers as virtual serfs. While less than one-fourth of a nation's population lived in whatever that government chose to designate as cities, the remainder were often widely dispersed in homesteads or small bands in areas with neither easy transport nor sustained contact with the rest of the country.

Because anthropologists have been studying all kinds of communities throughout Latin America during the past 50 years, we have remarkably detailed documentation about a time of tremendous change that rarely replicates the history of Western Europe or North America, which has too often uncritically been taken as a model. In paying attention to the local setting in its own terms, anthropologists have given us a better understanding not only of how people relate to each other, but also of how some institutions grow and others die, how apparently entrenched elites can be displaced without violence, how violence as a tool of governing can backfire, and how individuals make different choices to shape their lives.

SOME CURRENT REALITIES

One small but fundamental change in recent years has been the overall reduction of births, still well above the rate of replacement in most areas but down markedly from what it was a generation ago when the Malthusian specter of a burgeoning population led to apocalyptic predictions. Agrarian reform in many countries broke the stranglehold that landed gentry had over the peasant masses, and those who ventured abroad have often been able to send remittances that are changing the face of their home communities. Manufacturing has grown, and tourism provides jobs and income in many regions that had neither.

Native populations and their cultures are gaining recognition and a voice in nations where previously they had been ignored or dismissed, even when their significant numbers sometimes evoked the image of a sleeping giant. Participant democracy is increasingly cited as a goal if not a reality, and both the church and the military have lost the presumption of justifiable predominance that they so long enjoyed. It is convenient and sometimes revealing to distinguish Latin American counterparts, as does the reading by Skidmore and Smith (chapter 1).

Levine (chapter 2) briefly touches on the historical links among countries throughout Latin America and their cultural similarities and differences. By tracing some currents in recent scholarship he demonstrates the fundamental importance of two basic concepts, culture (see Part III of this book) and power (see Part V), in better understanding the region and people within it.

For people everywhere the issue of basic human rights is important, and anthropologists have played major roles in promoting and promulgating both the idea and the reality of those rights on many fronts. Messer (chapter 3) reviews the spread of the human rights movement and emphasizes the special responsibility of its proponents to work on behalf of many who do not yet enjoy full realization of those rights, with special emphasis on Latin America.

Although it was long neglected as a mysterious and dangerous backwater, the Amazonian tropical forest that occupies the heart of South America has gained widespread attention for a series of disasters, some of them continuing: sporadic accounts of genocide against scattered native peoples, massive deforestation as agriculture and pastoralism invade on a grand scale, colonization as landless peasants from the drought-stricken northeast stream in as homesteaders, large-scale pollution as results of careless mining or cocaine production, and so forth. Sponsel (chapter 4) uses the problems of the Amazon as justification for calling on anthropologists to change their paradigms from academic and scientific detachment to active engagement in the interests of ecology.

Because of its proximity to the United States, its cultural diversity, and the congeniality of its people, Mexico has been home to more than one of the world's few novel experiments that involved long-term research (Foster, Scudder, Colson and Kemper 1979) by truly multidisciplinary and international teams of investigators, paying extensive and intensive attention to many aspects of culture and intercultural relations. One such study, the Harvard-Chiapas Project based at Harvard University, was focused on a mountainous region of southern Mexico known for colorful variation among its Maya-speaking inhabitants, long before it became globally famous as a focus of native insurrection against what had generally been portrayed as a beneficent national government (see Collier, chapter 17). Vogt (chapter 5) spent many years as director of that project and oversaw a truly outstanding sequence of studies, many of which have become major monographs in anthropology and other fields. His retrospective view provides what can be considered almost a microcosm of similar events, processes, and systems throughout Latin America.

In the abundant literature written in recent years about prospects and problems concerning contemporary Latin America, specious alternatives abound: tradition or change, evolution or revolution, conservatism or reform, continuity or chaos, dictatorship or anarchy, and so forth. When closely scrutinized these supposed choices are rarely mutually exclusive, and they probably in no instance actually exhaust the range of possibilities. The advantage of an anthropological perspective is that it helps reveal how tradition can provide directions for change; how local evolution can meet popular and supposedly revolutionary goals; how conservative people can reform institutions; and, in many other ways, how the alternatives that are contrasted in rhetoric can be reconciled in practice.

FOR FURTHER READING ON
LATIN AMERICA: IMAGE AND REALITY

Probably the best brief introduction to an anthropological perspective on Latin America is E. R. Wolf and E. C. Hanson, *The Human Condition in Latin America* (Oxford University Press, 1972), even though it may be slightly outdated in a few details. Earlier editions of *Contemporary Cultures and Societies of Latin America* (1st ed., D. B. Heath and R. N. Adams (eds.) [Random House 1965]; 2nd ed., D. B. Heath (ed.) [Random House 1974]) attempted to provide convenient compilations of the best anthropological research on the area to date and were well received by students and colleagues alike. To deal with major changes in both Latin American studies and anthropology, a revised reissue was done (Waveland, 1988). In a sense, these books trace the major currents of that time. Another book with similar aims and scope is M. B. Whiteford and S. Whiteford (eds.), *Crossing Currents: Continuity and Change in Latin America* (Prentice Hall, 1998).

An ambitious *Encyclopedia of Latin American History and Culture*, edited by B. Tenenbaum (C. Scribner's Sons, 5 vols. to date, 1996–) is a good place to start tracking down information on relatively well-known people, places, events, and institutions. Similar in scope is *The Encyclopedia of World Cultures*, edited by D. Levinson (G. K. Hall, 10 vols., 1991–1996); volume 7 deals with South America and volume 8 with Middle America and the Caribbean.

A student just beginning work in the social sciences may find it helpful to consult brief but authoritative articles about key concepts and other terms that are used with special meanings. *The International Encyclopedia of the Social Sciences* is just such a major source (edited by D. L. Sills, Macmillan and Free Press, 18 vols. to date, 1968–). More specialized is *The Encyclopedia of Cultural Anthropology* (4 vols.) edited by D. Levinson and M. Ember (H. Holt, 1996).

Although it was avidly discussed by scholars throughout the Americas, O'Gorman's quasi-ironic query about the existence (and, implicitly, importance) of Latin America appears never to have been translated to English (*Existe América Latina?* Fondo de Cultura Económica, 1945). The joke about Latin America existing in foreign institutes harks back to the heyday of area studies in the wake of World War II; the philosophy of that approach, which remains vital today, was laid out by J. H. Steward, *Area Studies, Theory and Practice* (Social Science Research Council, 1950).

Stereotypes about Latin American culture existed in academia as well as in popular culture. Some of the less objectionable (often found in books written by Latins) are by J. J. Arevalo, H. Bernstein, A. O. Hirschmann, C. Veliz, L. Zea, and others. The Black Legend has generally been discredited in recent years as exaggeration (sometimes of real atrocities) by anti-Catholic propagandists; see R. Gibson, *The Black Legend* (A.A. Knopf, 1971).

The idea of refuge areas was developed by G. Aguirre B., *Regions of Refuge* (trans. rev., Society for Applied Anthropology, 1979). The idea of a frontier as the movable interface between Western and non-Western peoples, although an ancient one, still has meaning in parts of Latin America. See I. Bowman, *The Pioneer Fringe* (American Geographical Society, 1931) and *Pioneer Settlement* (AGS, 1932); for current uses, see *Journal of Comparative Frontier Studies,* or L. Gill, *Peasants, Entrepreneurs and Social Change* (Westview, 1987), among others.

To learn more about those populations that have tried to stay apart from Western culture (often called tribals or Indians), an introductory guide may be helpful before one gets into the many detailed monographs. Two such multi-volume and multi-authored encyclopedias are J. H. Steward (ed.), *Handbook of South American Indians* (Smithsonian Institution Bureau of American Ethnology, 1946–51), and R. Wauchope (ed.), *Handbook of Middle American Indians* (University of Texas Press, 16 vols. to date, 1964–).

To get some flavor of the pervasive threat that demographers perceived in Latin America's high birthrate in the mid-twentieth century, see, e.g., J. M. Stycos, *Human Fertility in Latin America* (Cornell University Press, 1968); various works by D. Heath, W. Thiesenhusen, H. Landsberger, and others discuss agrarian reform.

On distinctive patterns of cultural change in Latin America, see various works by R. N. Adams, C. J. Erasmus, G. M. Foster, C. Furtado, J. H. Steward, C. Veliz, C. Wagley, and E. R. Wolf.

Human rights, especially with respect to indigenous populations and from an anthropological perspective, are a recurrent theme in several works by various authors. J. H. Bodley's *Anthropology and Contemporary Human Problems*, and *Victims of Progress* (both Cummings, 1976 and 1990) and his *Tribal Peoples and Development Issues* and *Cultural Anthropology* (both Mayfield, 1988 and 1997) are right on target; so is D. Maybury-Lewis, *Indigenous Peoples, Ethnic Groups, and the State* (Allyn & Bacon, 1997); G. Urban and J. Scherzer (eds.), *Nation-States and Indians in Latin America* (University of Texas Press, 1991); or D. L. van Cott, *Indigenous Peoples and Democracy in Latin America* (St. Martin's, 1994). Various organizations publish newsletters, occasional monographs, and other pertinent human rights-related material, including Cultural Survival, Survival International, and International Work Group on Indigenous Affairs. On the increasing voice and power of native peoples, an excellent summary volume is A. Brysk, *From Tribal Village to Global Village: Rights and International Relations in Latin America* (Stanford University Press, 2000).

For anthropological studies that focus on the Amazon, see other works by L. Sponsel, including *Indian Peoples and the Future of Amazonia* (University of Arizona Press, 1995) and *Tropical Deforestation: The Human Dimension* (Columbia University Press, 1996). For similar viewpoints see E. Moran, *The Dilemma of Amazonian Development* (Westview, 1983); and B. J. Meggers, *Amazonia: Man and Culture in a Counterfeit Paradise* (rev. ed., Smithsonian Press, 1996). Elaborating also on broader aspects of the ecological approach in anthropology are E. F. Moran, *Human Adaptability* (Westview, 1979); and L. Sponsel, *Human Ecology* (Mayfield, 2001).

The Harvard-Chiapas Project (like the Cornell-Peru Project, Doughty, chapter 22) is one of the world's few long-term, multidisciplinary studies and has resulted in a long and distinguished series of monographs by different authors and publishers on a wide range of subjects, many of which are important milestones. To appreciate the logic and variety of such projects, see G. M. Foster et al. (eds.), *Long-Term Research in Social Anthropology* (Academic, 1979).

The political importance of the Chiapas area and its highland Maya peoples (Collier, chapter 17) is more fully spelled out in G. Collier, *Basta! Land and the Zapatista Rebellion in Chiapas* (Institute for Food and Development Policy, 1994), works by J. Nash and others, and on the Zapatista website (http://flag.blackened.net/revolt/zapatista.html).

References

Foster, George M., Thayer Scudder, Elizabeth Colson, and Robert V. Kemper (eds.), 1979. *Long-Term Research in Social Anthropology.* New York: Academic Press.

O'Gorman, Edmundo, 1945. *Existe América Latina?* México, Fondo de Cultura Económica.

Thomas E. Skidmore is the Carlos Manuel de Céspedes Professor of Modern Latin American History, Professor of History and Portuguese and Brazilian Studies, and Director of the Center for Latin American Studies at Brown University. Among his more influential books are Black into White *(2 editions);* Cambridge Encyclopedia of Latin America and the Caribbean *(with S. Collier and H. Blackmore);* Brazil; Television, Politics, and the Transition to Democracy in Latin America *(2 editions); and* Modern Latin America *(5 editions, with P. H. Smith).*

Peter H. Smith is Simón Bolívar Professor of Latin American Studies, Professor of Political Science, and Director of the Center for Iberian and Latin American Studies at the University of California, San Diego. Among his more influential books are The Challenge of Integration: Europe and the Americas; Talons of the Eagle: Dynamics of U.S.–Latin American Relations; Latin America in Comparative Perspective; *and* Modern Latin America *(with T. E. Skidmore, 5 editions).*

In their book that focuses primarily on recent political and economic history of individual countries in Latin America, Skidmore and Smith also provide a concise summary of some of the main currents in social science thinking about the region and its institutions. Although this kind of macroscopic view may appear to be far removed from the workaday activities of individuals, it provides a context that is indispensable for understanding much of what happens in local communities and to their inhabitants. Compare Levine (chapter 2) for more comparisons and contrasts with Anglo-America.

Why Latin America?

Thomas E. Skidmore and Peter H. Smith

INTERPRETATIONS OF LATIN AMERICA

Most analysts of modern Latin America have stressed the area's political instability, marked frequently by dictatorship. North American and European observers have been especially fascinated with two questions: Why dictatorships? Why not democracy? This preoccupation is not recent. In 1930, for example, a U.S. economic geographer specializing in the region observed, "the years roll on and there arise the anxieties and disappointments of an ill-equipped people attempting to establish true republican forms of government." A year earlier an English scholar had noted that "the political history of the republics has been a record of alternating periods of liberty and despotism." Implicitly assuming or explicitly asserting that their style of democracy is superior to all other models of political organization, North American and European writers frequently asked what was "wrong" with Latin America. Or with Latin Americans themselves.

What passed for answers was for many years a jumble of racist epithets, psychological simplifications, geographical platitudes, and cultural distortions. According to such views, Latin America could not achieve democracy because dark-skinned peoples (Indians and blacks) were unsuited for it; because passionate Latin tempers would not stand it; because tropical climates somehow prevented it; or because Roman Catholic doctrines inhibited it.

Each charge has its refutation: dictatorial rule has flourished in predominantly white countries, such as Argentina, as well as among mixed-blood societies, such as Mexico; it has appeared in temperate climes, such as Chile, not only in the tropics, such as Cuba; it has gained support from non-Catholics and nonpracticing Catholics, while many fervent worshippers have fought for liberty; and, as shown by authoritarian regimes outside Latin America, such as Hitler's Germany or Stalinist Russia, dictatorship is not restricted to any single temperament. Such explanations not only failed to explain. When carried to extremes, they helped justify rapidly increasing U.S. and European penetration—financial, cultural, military—of the "backward" republics to the south.

The scholarly scene improved in the late 1950s and early 1960s, when North American social scientists formulated "modernization theory." As applied to Latin America, this theory held that economic growth would generate the social change that would in turn make possible more "developed" politics. The transition from a rural to an urban society would bring a change in values. People would begin to relate to and participate in the voluntary organizations that authentic democracy requires. Most important, a middle class would emerge—to play both a progressive and moderating role. Latin America and its citizenries were not so inherently "different" from Europe and North America. Instead they were simply "behind." Modernization adepts thought the historical record showed this process was well under way in Latin America.

Reality, however, proved harsher. Instead of spreading general prosperity, economic growth in the 1960s and 1970s (and it reached sustained high rates in Mexico and Brazil) generally made income distribution more unequal. The gap in living standards between city and countryside grew. Domestic capital's ability to compete with the huge transnational firms declined. Meanwhile, politics was hardly following the model predicted by many experts on modernization. The middle strata, relatively privileged, forged a sense of "class consciousness" which, in critical moments of decision, such as in Argentina in 1955 or 1976, Brazil in 1964, and Chile in 1973, led them to join the ruling classes in opposition to the popular masses. Politics took an authoritarian turn, producing military governments. And in stark contradiction of modernization theory, these patterns emerged in the most developed—and most rapidly developing—countries of the continent. What had gone wrong?

Two sets of answers came forth. One group of scholars focused on the cultural traditions of Latin America and their Spanish and Portuguese origins. These analysts argued, in effect, that antidemocratic politics was (and remains) a product of a Roman Catholic and Mediterranean world view that stressed the need for harmony, order, and the elimination of conflict. By failing to grasp these continuities in the Iberian experience, scholars had confused form with substance, rhetoric with reality. Latin America's constitutions were never as democratic as they appeared; party politics was not as representative as it might have looked. The North American and European academic community, afflicted by its own myopia and biases, had simply misread the social facts.

A second group of scholars accepted modernization theory's linking of socioeconomic causes with political outcomes but turned the answer upside down: Latin America's economic development was qualitatively different from that of North America and West Europe, and therefore it produced different political results. Specifically, these scholars argued, Latin America's experience was determined by the pervasive fact of its economic dependence. "By dependency," as one exponent of this viewpoint has explained,

we mean a situation in which the economy of certain countries is conditioned by the development and expansion of another economy to which the former is subjected. The relation of interdependence between two or more economies, and between these and world trade, assumes the form of dependence when some countries (the dominant ones) can expand and be self-sustaining, while other countries (the dependent ones) can do this only as a reflection of that expansion, which can have either a positive or a negative effect on their immediate development.

By its intrinsic character, "dependent development" generated inequities, allocating benefits to sectors participating in the world market and denying them to other groups. A typical case might involve a country whose economic growth relied on a single export crop, such as coffee or sugar. A national landowning elite, the planters, would collaborate with export-import merchants, often foreign, to sell the goods on an overseas market. Most profits would be restricted to those groups. The planters would use much of their money to import high-cost consumer goods from Europe or the United States, and the merchants (if foreign) would remit profits to their home countries. The export earnings would therefore provide precious little capital for diversifying the local economy, thus creating a situation that some observers have labeled "growth without development." Because of a labor surplus, field workers would continue to receive low wages; groups outside the export sector would get little benefit. Consequently, regional imbalances would intensify and income distribution would become more unequal than before. What growth occurred, moreover, would be subject to substantial risk. If the overseas market for coffee or sugar contracted, for whatever reason, then the entire economy would suffer. It would in this sense be "dependent" for its continued growth on decisions taken elsewhere and it would be, as our just-cited author says, "conditioned by the development and expansion of another economy."

The proponents of "*dependencia* theory," as it quickly came to be known, maintained that economic dependency leads to political authoritarianism. According to this view, "the dependent" location of Latin America's economics placed inherent limitations on the region's capacity for growth, especially in industry. The surest sign of this economic trouble is a crisis in the foreign accounts—the country's ability to pay for needed imports. Exports lag behind imports, and the difference can only be made up by capital inflow. But the foreign creditors—firms, banks, international agencies such as the World Bank—deny the necessary extra financing because they believe the government cannot impose the necessary "sacrifices." Backed against the wall, the country must take immediate steps to keep imports flowing in. Political strategy falls hostage to the need to convince the foreign creditors.

The most frequent solution in the 1960s and 1970s was a military coup. The resulting authoritarian government could then take its "hard" decisions, usually highly unpopular anti-inflation measures, such as increased public utility prices, cuts in real wages, and cuts in credit. Hardest hit are the lower classes. To carry out such policies therefore requires a heavy hand over the popular sectors. Thus, the coups and repressive authoritarian regimes that emerged in Brazil, Argentina, and Chile came about not in spite of Latin America's economic development, but because of it.

The 1980s replaced these authoritarian regimes with civilian leaders and elected governments. Explanations for this trend took many forms. Once thought to be dominant and monolithic, authoritarian regimes came to display a good deal of incoherence and fragility. Everyday citizens rose up in protest movements, formed civic organizations, and demanded popular elections. Confronted by severe economic crisis, people from Argentina and Chile to Central America sought to express their political rights. By the mid-1990s almost all countries of the region, with the conspicuous exception of Cuba, had elected governments. Whether or not these new regimes were fully "democratic," a point that led to much debate, they represented considerable improvement over the blatantly dictatorial patterns of the 1970s. Many observers expressed the optimistic hope that, at long last, Latin America was moving toward a democratic future.

Economic prospects brightened as well. Under pressure from international creditors throughout the 1980s, Latin American leaders imposed far-reaching measures designed to "liberalize" their national economies—reducing tariffs and other barriers to trade, selling state-supported companies to private investors, and curtailing deficit spending. Inflation declined and foreign investment increased. As a result, average growth in Latin America rose from a scant 1.5 percent per year in 1985–89 to 3.5 percent in the early 1990s.

Scholars approached these political and economic developments with intellectual caution. Instead of launching grand theories, such as modernization or dependency, political analysts stressed the role of beliefs, ideas, and human conviction. Some interpreted the turn toward democracy in Latin America and elsewhere as a global triumph of U.S. values, especially in light of the collapse of the Soviet Union. Others emphasized the importance of leadership and tactical maneuvers at the elite level. As for economics, some experts regarded the growth spurt of the early 1990s as vindication for pro-capitalist, free-market policy reforms. Others noted that the surge tended to reflect the ebb and flow of international investments, and that capital promptly vanished in the face of crisis—leaving Latin America just as "dependent" as before. Of continuing concern, for many, was the problematic relationship between economic and political transformation. Does economic liberalization lead to political democracy? Or might it be the other way around? Recent developments in Latin America thus raised new questions and posed new challenges for the scholarly community.

LATIN AMERICA'S CONTRIBUTION TO THE WORLD

Given its political and economic constraints, what is Latin America likely to contribute to the human experience? It has already made its mark in literature. Gabriel Garcia Márquez, Carlos Fuentes, Jorge Luis Borges, Jorge Amado—the "boom" in Latin American literature has led to its translation into major European languages. Mass paperback editions have facilitated wide distribution. More recently, Chile's Isabel Allende and the Mexican American Sandra Cisneros have won over many English-speaking readers.

In no realm has Latin America made a more powerful contribution than music. Latin Americans have also been conspicuous for their impressive contributions in athletics. In soccer, the most universally played sport, Brazil is the first country to win the World Cup four times. Argentina won the cup in 1978 and 1986. Even small Latin American countries such as Uruguay have taken home the World Cup. European soccer clubs bid into the millions of dollars to lure Latin American stars.

Latin America has also made a great contribution in the field of race relations. Notwithstanding persistent cruelty to those of non-European descent, Latin America has produced societies in which persons of mixed racial background have enjoyed considerable mobility. The *mestizos* of Mexico, Central America, and the Andean region represent a new social category born out of the mixture of European and Indian. Although racism still exists in many guises, mobility has been notable. The same can be said for the mulatto in Brazil, Cuba, Colombia, and the Caribbean nations. To find a contrast one need only look to North America. Of course, prejudice and discrimination still occur in Latin America, especially against the "pure blood" Indians and very dark-skinned people in general. Yet the relative social harmony is conspicuous, especially in light of the miserable record left by the Europeans in so many parts of today's developing world.

Finally, Latin America is increasingly influencing the United States, the country that for so long looked down on its southern neighbors. Cities such as New York, Chicago, and Los Angeles, not to speak of Miami, have burgeoning Spanish-speaking communities. Music, dance, and cuisine are being transformed even for the gringos. In 1992 salsa outsold ketchup for the first time in America. The Latino population has reached 30 million and is growing at a rate seven times that of the general population.

It is estimated that by 2050 Latinos will make up a quarter of the population, equal to half the white population. Such a change in America itself cannot fail to alter its beliefs about and attitude toward Latin America.

In the future, as in past centuries, the fate of Latin America will depend largely on its relationship to the centers of international power. In the meantime it must mobilize its own resources for sustained economic growth and seek a more equitable distribution of the results. The region will also have to continue to fight off the sense of despair engendered by the bitter experience of repression and economic failure. Meanwhile, outsiders will continue to be startled and fascinated by what Garcia Márquez called "the unearthly tidings of Latin America, that boundless realm of haunted men and historic women, whose unending obstinacy blurs into legend."

Daniel H. Levine teaches political science at the University of Michigan (Ann Arbor). Among his best-known books are Churches and Politics in Latin America, Religion and Popular Protest in Latin America *(with S. Mainwaring),* Popular Voices in Latin American Catholicism, *and* Constructing Culture and Power in Latin America.

A popular book of the nineteenth century was entitled Does Latin America Exist? *Here Levine suggests that, despite the enormous diversity that occurs in many respects, there are also common threads that make it meaningful for social scientists to examine various aspects of culture in that broader framework. In a sense, this chapter sets the stage for the rest of this book, which is made up largely of more micro-level case studies of culture and power.*

Constructing Culture and Power in Latin America

Daniel H. Levine

LATIN AMERICA AS A QUESTION

Latin America is a worthwhile subject because Latin American experience presents problems for analysis in ways that challenge conventional ways of thinking about culture and power. To frame the issues, it may be helpful to begin with a brief review of the kinds of elements relied upon over the years to justify talking about Latin America as a coherent entity. Is there any reality to Latin America? Is the expression anything more than a convenient but misleading shorthand? The mixed cultural and geographical sense of the name Latin America (as opposed, for example, to Anglo-America) rests on a common history with roots in the conquest and its heritage. Elements of language, economic and social structure, institutional formation, and overlapping networks (ecclesiastical, educational, literary, diplomatic, military, and migratory) make one section of the area or fragment of its history recognizable in another.

This conventional familiarity notwithstanding, it has never been easy to capture Latin America's identifying traits in any neat or simple formula. To Alexis de Tocqueville the region's identity and apparent difficulties constituted a difficult and demanding puzzle. The physical circumstances and conditions of Latin America were broadly equal to those of the North, but even by the 1840s the region already appeared mired in stagnation and oppression. Tocqueville found the decisive difference not in static conditions but, rather, in culture and mores, the practical ethos of peoples and leaders that made them engage the world in characteristic ways. The practical ethos of Anglo-Americans reflected and reinforced prevailing social equality, making them self-reliant and capable of sustained collective action. The practical ethos of Latin Americans exaggerated authority and dependence on it and made sustained collective action all but impossible. Tocqueville's view has been shared by generations of Latin America's liberal elite, who believed that Spain cursed the region at birth with a heritage of religious and political absolutism. The key to progress lay in discarding and/or at least marginalizing that heritage. Prescriptions intended to emulate North America and Western Europe followed: reshaping legislatures, forming constitutions, setting economic policy, and, tempered by the racism of the times, importing white settlers to "improve" the race.

This image of a Latin America crippled by inherited culture and institutions persists in varied forms to the present day. Even such otherwise different schools of thought as "Ibero-American cultural fragments" and modernization/development share this basic assumption. According to the first, Latin America is best understood as a fragment of Iberian culture implanted in the New World. Enduring themes in Iberian culture, crystallized in the Americas through institutions of religion and law and manifest in basic cultural norms about hierarchy, authority, and the use of power, are what make the region distinctive. The modernization/development school explains the particularities of Latin America in terms of lag, with cultural forms lagging (and also dragging) needed economic and institutional change. Only "development" could change things, by approximating regional patterns more closely to those of the already developed world. Each school depicts culture as something inherited from the past, controlled by elites who socialize new generations and emergent groups into its principles and practices. Latin Americans thus appear as captive of their culture. The kind of stability and progressive change envisioned and desired comes either by recognizing and adapting to the demands of the existing culture or as the aftereffect of deliberate promotion of value change through "modernization." In each case, the literature points ultimately to culture as the key to understanding Latin America, with cultural transformation depicted as necessary but exceptionally difficult.

In addition to viewing culture primarily as an inheritance from the past, both schools of thought privilege ties between culture and order, leaving little theoretical room for the analysis of culture and change. This is not the place for a detailed account of these positions or of the debate over alternatives. Suffice it to say that both came under growing attack in the late 1960s, with the result that culture was replaced at the heart of scholarly concern about Latin America with arguments about structures, manifest above all in resurgent concern for classical issues of political economy. The emergence of dependency theory did much to spur creative rethinking of state, class, and power in Latin America. Now the region's distinctiveness was seen to rest not on inherited traditions or lagged development in general but, rather, on specific relations with global systems of economic, political, and cultural power, which decisively shaped opportunities. Class formation, political coalitions, and the overall structure of power were cast in a new light. In brief, Latin America was the way it was because of ties with already developed nations. It was therefore misleading to expect development on the North Atlantic model: Latin American possibilities were decisively constrained by the prior existence of that model and the ubiquitous presence of economic and political forces it unleashed and controlled.

Long-standing conventions about what to study and where to look in Latin America ("Brazilian literature," "Venezuelan politics," "Argentine military elites," "Andean communities," "religion among the Tzotzil," and so forth) began to lose their sharpness and force of conviction. Efforts were made to cut across these lines, for example, in work on local manifestations of world system phenomena: media networks, investment and trade patterns, flows of migration and employment opportunities. Economic factors were privileged over culture, politics, law, and institutions. By the early 1960s identification with the Indian (*indigenismo*) and concentration on community studies began to lose their force of conviction as society urbanized and few unstudied communities remained.

> But just when a search for new directions and a turn to the city became urgent, a "cold wave" of Marxism engulfed us all. Structures now took precedence over actors, and attention went to the economic base, not the cultural superstructure. . . . The rich accumulation of anthropological monographs became little more than raw

material, with concern for usages, customs or values painted as superfluous, even frivolous, in light of the urgent need to grasp the scientific (read, economic) laws, essential for the advent and ultimate success of a revolution thought to be imminent. . . . Suffice it to say that life showed us that social actors don't let themselves be confined by laws that reduce them to epiphenomena of structures. Culture elbowed its way in, forcing us in many tangible ways to recognize how far it was from being merely a reflection, a superstructural frill. (De Gregori, Blondet, and Lynch, 1986:14–15)

As these authors suggest, categories derived from Marxist and dependency scholarship quickly ran into problems of their own. The subordination of change in Latin America to the impact of global economic formations obscured critical differences and made it hard to see changes arising from other sources. In particular, the widespread return to civilian politics combined with a surge of cultural innovation and new social movements throughout the 1980s to underscore the weaknesses of economic determinism (Levine 1988b; Remmer 1991; P. Smith 1991).

One of the central lines of scholarly response to these difficulties has been an effort (visible in many disciplines) to find units of analysis capable of linking global systems with nations, regions, communities, and ordinary routine. There is also concern to study how new ideals and organizational forms are created in encounters between institutions and their potential clients. Interest then turned to detailing the character of these linkages as lived experiences, through research on the construction of social roles and connecting structures. Analysis turns from abstractions like tradition, modernity, development, modernization, class, or even culture to a multifaceted portrait of encounters: urban migrants with city and with the state, peasants with new economic formations or with church or party organizers, encounters of men and women with family structures and gender roles in new circumstances, encounters with the new meaning of politics and with the openings literacy provides to the rest of the world. The "rest of the world" emerges more clearly then as a world constructed by people within parameters of power that they do not create but also do not accept passively.

In these ways the evolution of scholarship has directed attention to units of analysis that make it possible for observers to hear the voices emerging from everyday life and to specify the midlevel organizations being created on the ground throughout the region. There has been renewed concern to craft a phenomenological perspective, pointing research to work with cultural and organizational categories that make sense within a society. Doing so properly requires seeing these categories precisely as creations, making a space for change and for those who push it along. Phenomenological efforts at imaginative reconstruction therefore involve more than recreating the pattern of ideas: attention to the origins and history of these ideas, and to what makes them change, is also required. The issue is important if only because groups and individuals may follow rules that vary in systematic ways from what scholars expect. Class, for example, may be mediated by culture, both by gender or race, and so forth. In broad theoretical terms, working with a phenomenological approach substantially enriches understanding of why people act as they do.

The issue takes on added significance in scholarship on Latin America given the ambiguous relation of class to organization and identity. It is a sociological truism that class position does not translate in any direct way into collective action or shared identity. This general point is reinforced in Latin America by the emergence of a kind of self-image and identity that has drawn growing attention in the social sciences as it has in art, music, religion, and literature. At issue is the creation of an identity as members of "popular sectors." Popular music, art, religion, and literature were once widely viewed as products of ignorant and uninstructed individuals. But over the last few decades these cultural products spread into media and arenas once reserved to elites. In addition, they have increasingly been seen not as distortions requiring correction (for example, through education or evangelization) but, rather, as the expression of new and valid identities being created in these societies.

The emergence of "popular" as a widespread kind of identity affects how we understand the origins of social movements and grasp their likely impact on politics. To begin with, the pace and scale of social change has made the potential base of any movement much more heterogeneous, while the near-universal experience of personal and group transformation has spurred a powerful sense of equality of condition. Emergent popular identities thus combine a rough and ready egalitarianism with a claim to group autonomy and a disposition to assert rights that is new in the culture. This growing capacity for collective action often comes without stable ties to larger structures of power like political parties or the state. The lack of sustained connections can fragment political action: groups end up confined to local issues, easily manipulated, prone to splits and co-optation, and weak, with a barely defined "vocation for power" (Eckstein 1989; Portes 1989; Caldeira 1984; and De Gregori, Blondet, and Lynch 1986). But at the same time the whole effort is more widespread and flexible because it rests less on formally organized groups than on general wider currents of egalitarian belief and social capacity. The phenomenology of power and action visible here is not well understood in all-or-nothing terms. Instead, we find a repertoire of actions and understandings whose range underscores how much the effort to play the game can itself provide a means for creating and reinforcing new identities and confidence in oneself and one's community.

The preceding sketch differs from many overviews by its deliberate focus on problems rather than disciplines. There has, of course, been a regular flow of assessments of the state of the various disciplines working on Latin America. Work in this genre has oscillated between bouts of enthusiasm for new topics, and for the prospects of applying innovative theory, method, and collaborative, interdisciplinary strategies with laments about the continued marginalization of work on Latin America in the world scholarly community. An important recent effort came in the mid-1980s, with essays commissioned by the Latin American Studies Association on the state of research in history, political science, economics, sociology, anthropology, and literary studies (Mitchell 1988). The results are instructive.

Overall, the essays reveal that concern about the status of Latin America as a subject (i.e., does it mean anything? Is it as good as work on Europe?) has yielded to a focus on core scholarly problems such as culture, power, identity, ideology, change, and conflict. These are framed around a desire to see how Latin Americans interpret and grapple with their own situation. Expanded scholarly interaction between Latin and North Americans has reinforced this concern, and spurred the growth of a scholarship that is problem-focused and self-critical. In economics, for example, "competing economic ideologies have [thus] been a central part of the modern Latin American development experience. That debate currently continues under the impulse of the most severe downturn in economic activity since the Great Depression" (Fishlow 1988:110). In sociology and anthropology there has been a double effort to redefine the proper unit of inquiry: first, away from community (anthropology) or nation (sociology) to the world system; and then to interest in how the world system is manifested in and connected with ordinary life. One notable result, according to Portes (1988), is that there is now less concern with creating a general "sociology of development" than with using sociological theory to inform comparative and historical study of specific problems.

Some of the biggest swings and sharpest changes are visible in the study of politics. From beginnings in the study of law and institutions, political analysis moved quickly through fascination with modernization and its associated tool kit of concepts and methods to an equally intense affair with the analytical categories of dependency and the explanation of authoritarianism. Attention has lately returned to political institutions, which are now understood in a more dynamic and comparative way. Efforts have also been made to confront the challenge of how best to construct and maintain viable democracies (Remmer 1991; Valenzuela 1988; Levine 1988b; P. Smith 1991). History has also returned to the center of political analysis, for example, in work on state and labor, critical junctures, and the production and reproduction of historical legacies (Collier and Collier 1991).

The evolution of scholarship on Latin America has been marked by a seemingly endless search for paradigms and saviors: theories, methods, and critical social groups, which, it is hoped, will together provide a key to analysis and action. At present, there appears to be no consensus but, rather, analytical drift and eclecticism (Remmer 1991; P. Smith 1991). The solution is not to abandon theory or to give up the search for generalization and still less to opt for some "compromise" that includes elements from all schools. Rather than produce yet another review of changes in the disciplines, or even a collection of classic pieces on a given problem, the intention here is to reinforce the interchange already underway between central issues of intellectual work and the problematic that Latin America presents. It will be more fruitful to return to classic problems in social theory, using the literature to escape its bounds, while working on the enduring challenges it poses.

CENTRAL CHALLENGES

The central challenges arising from the literature on Latin America come in the effort to understand culture and power in ways that do justice to the values and efforts of those involved without getting lost in the minutiae of individual lives and small-scale settings. The response to this challenge constitutes a thread unifying the contributions to this volume, whatever their empirical focus. It is now appropriate, therefore, to alter voice and perspective, moving away from general discussions of scholarship on Latin America to close accounts of issues that inform the research collected in this volume.

References

Arizpe, L., Salinas, F., and Velásquez, M. 1987. "Effects of the Economic Crisis on the Living Conditions of Peasant Women in Mexico." In *The Invisible Adjustment: Poor Women and the Economic Crisis*. Santiago: UNICEF.

Barham, B., Clark, M., Katz, E., and Schurman, R. 1992. "Nontraditional Agricultural Exports in Latin America," *Latin American Research Review*, 27.

Bonilla, E. 1990. "Working Women in Latin America." In *Economic and Social Progress in Latin America: 1990 Report*. Washington, DC: Inter-American Development Bank.

ECLAC (Economic Commission on Latin America and the Caribbean) 1988a. *Latin American and Caribbean Women: Between Change and Crisis*. Santiago: United Nations.

———. 1988. *Women, Work and Crisis*. Santiago: United Nations.

———. 1992. *Economic Survey of Latin America and the Caribbean 1990*, Vol. 1. Santiago: United Nations.

García, A. I. and Gomáriz, E. 1989. *Mujeres Centroamericanas: Ante la Crisis, la Guerra y el Proceso de Paz*. San José: FLACSO/CSUCA/University para la Paz.

González de la Rocha, M. 1988. "Economic Crisis, Domestic Reorganization and Women's Work in Guadalajara, Mexico," *Bulletin of Latin American Research*, 7.

———. 1992. Familia Urbana y Pobreza en América Latina. Unpublished manuscript prepared for Economic Commission on Latin America and the Caribbean (ECLAC).

Mulhern, M. and Mauzé, S. 1992. "Gender and Trade and Investment in Latin America and the Caribbean." GENESYS, Special Studies No. 8. Prepared for United States Agency for International Development. Washington, DC: Office of Women in Development and Bureau for Latin America and the Caribbean.

Otero, M. 1989. "Rethinking the Informal Sector," *Grassroots Development*, 13.

Psacharopoulos, G. and Tzannatos, Z. 1992. *Women's Employment and Pay in Latin America: Overview and Methodology.* Washington, DC: World Bank.

Yudelman, S. 1994. "Women Farmers in Central America: Myths, Roles, and Reality," *Grassroots Development*, 17.

Ellen Messer is a free-lance anthropologist; while writing this paper, she was director of the Center for the Study of Hunger at Brown University, and she is currently a research fellow at the Woodrow Wilson International Center as well as visiting professor in nutrition science and policy at Tufts University.

Some anthropologists feel strongly that, regardless of academic or scientific interests, the discipline should focus on humanitarian political activism to promote and defend human rights everywhere. This imperative may be especially strong in Latin America, where violations of those rights have long been routine and often extreme. Messer outlines what is meant by human rights, why they are important, and how anthropologists can serve to foster them, even in the face of oppressive regimes.

Among the cases that she examines are Guatemala (cf. Stoll, chapter 12), Argentina (cf. Robben, chapter 35; and Feijoo and Gogna, chapter 34), and Chile (cf. Boyle, chapter 33). For specifically indigenous resistance, consider Chiapas in Mexico (Collier, chapter 17) and the emergence of native organizations (Stavenhagen, chapter 13). On relevance to developments in the Amazon, see Sponsel (chapter 4).

Anthropology and Human Rights in Latin America

Ellen Messer

LATIN AMERICAN ANTHROPOLOGY, HUMAN RIGHTS, AND GLOBAL CHANGE

Since 1988 the global community has experienced monumental changes in politics and human rights. These changes include the end of the cold war, the resolution of East-West conflict-fueled civil wars, and the expansion of free markets and trade liberalization through institutions such as the World Trade Organization (WTO) and the North American Free Trade Agreement (NAFTA) These forces of political-economic globalization have in turn been accompanied by widespread demands from the grassroots: for greater democratization, respect for human rights, and local control over land and resources. The international struggle for human rights, as articulated in the 1948 United Nations Universal Declaration of Human Rights, initially addressed basic civil liberties and to a lesser extent the essential social welfare rights of individuals. But it since has marked two watersheds: (1) the formulation and adoption of principles of development rights that call for a peaceful and just social and economic order that also protects the environment, and (2) the increasingly careful formulation of collective—especially indigenous—rights, which led to the 1994 Draft Declaration of the Rights of Indigenous Peoples. Increasingly, human-rights scholars and activists call for harmonization rather than prioritization of the so-called four generations of rights: civil-political, economic-social-cultural, development, and indigenous (Messer 1993:221–23).

Latin Americanists and the peoples whose lives and cultures they study also have been experiencing changes with respect to this evolving human-rights landscape. In 1988, the NGO Cultural Survival published *Human Rights and Anthropology* (Downing and Kushner 1988), which reviewed human-rights conceptualizations and violations and listed an extensive bibliography organized by Human Rights Internet. The essayists suggested that anthropologists working on human rights had exerted little

Written expressly for *Contemporary Cultures and Societies of Latin America*, Third Edition.

influence thus far but had much more to contribute. Doughty (1988) observed that anthropology appeared to be at a crossroads, especially in Latin America, where abuses of civil-political rights, violations of basic subsistence rights, and discrimination against indigenous peoples were already prominent concerns. Indeed, five of the book's chapters were authored by Latin Americanists, referred to Latin American ethnographic data, or dealt with Latin American themes. In addition to documenting widespread abuses (Doughty 1988), the authors addressed the ways human rights might be conceptualized (Downing 1988), the evolutionary significance of cultural survival (Barnett 1988), the limited rights of Mexican immigrant workers in the United States (Weaver 1988), and the limits of cultural relativism (Schirmer 1988).

That same year Stavenhagen and colleagues (1988) in Mexico published *Derecho Indígena y Derechos Humanos en América Latina* (Indigenous Law and Human Rights in Latin America). They reviewed the ideological and legal underpinnings of Latin American states' subjugation of indigenous peoples, indigenous peoples' struggles to achieve both individual and collective rights, national and international efforts on behalf of indigenous peoples, and the strengths and failings of existing international human rights concepts and instruments to protect the rights of indigenous peoples. Pressing for greater indigenous- and human-rights documentation, analysis, and advocacy by anthropologists, the authors concluded that violations of the individual and collective rights of indigenous peoples were unlikely to diminish until their collective rights were recognized in law and indigenous peoples were able to participate fully in the political process.

If Latin Americanists predominate in these and subsequent anthropological discussions of human rights, this is probably because violations appear to be so rooted in Latin American history, political economy, society, and culture. But in addition, the legal responses and cultural analyses by both indigenous and nonindigenous Latin Americans have been relentless (e.g., Stavenhagen et al. 1988; Stavenhagen 1989; Stavenhagen and Iturralde 1990; Chase-Sardi 1990). Most Latin American states, their ratifications of United Nations human-rights covenants notwithstanding, persistently violate rather than protect human rights, as the region continues to experience the legacy of colonial violence, terror, racism, and genocide that has characterized the state-building process (Bodley 1990; Declaration of Barbados III 1998; Sponsel 1997). Correspondingly, Latin American peoples and anthropologists have been at the forefront, documenting abuses and organizing for change. Country by country, case studies indicate that indigenous peoples and other subnational groups desiring control over resources and participation in political processes, are formulating their identities and entering the international arena via demands for human rights (Diskin 1991; Jackson 1995). As a result of these negative and positive historical currents, individuals and peoples in Latin America have grown accustomed to using human-rights instruments and rhetoric to protest abuses. In 1995 alone, eight of the twelve cases considered by the American Anthropological Association's (AAA) Committee for Human Rights (CfHR) were Latin American, and in 1998 one Chilean case of human-rights violations against Pehuenche people displaced by a river-management project dominated the CfHR's discussions. In addition, the AAA Society for Latin American Anthropology separately convenes its own Human Rights Committee.

Although most cases of human-rights violations consider indigenous rights or political violence, women's and children's rights advocates in Latin America also draw on this background. They appeal to human rights as a vehicle to organize and raise consciousness that violence against women and children is not permissible (Agosin 1993; Amnesty International 1991) and to press for solidarity on socioeconomic demands, including access to adequate food, fair wages, and health care (Messer 1993;

Safa 1990). Those advocating a human right to health and health care (e.g., Heggenhoughen 1995) decry discrimination, political-economic exploitation, and injustice against indigenous peoples. In the process, they elucidate the integral connections between access to land, health care, political violence, and lower life expectancies.

Through such wide-ranging human-rights activities, anthropologists demonstrate that a profound sense of social justice underlies their professional interests in the relationships of people to land and of ethnic entities to states. Like Latin America's sixteenth-century Franciscan ethnographers, they are conscientious heirs to Latin America's special legacy: its legal, philosophical, and religious inquiries into the questions, "Who is a human being?" and "What are rights?", which in 1550 pitted Las Casas against Sepulveda in a colonial setting rife with political violence and human rights abuses against indigenous peoples. As Las Casas's successors, Latin American anthropologists pressing for human rights have faced personal conflicts, incarceration and expulsion, and some have even lost their lives. Their activities are chronicled not only in academic books and articles but in the newsletters of national anthropological associations, indigenous sources, and in professional networking instruments such as the *Anthropology Resource Center, Cultural Survival* (Quarterly and Reports), the *Guatemalan Scholars Network News*, the *International Work Group for Indigenous Affairs Documents*, and the *North American Congress on Latin America Report on the Americas*. In the sections below are summarized the major human rights-related activities by Latin American anthropologists arranged under the international human-rights categories of civil-political, economic-social-cultural, development, and indigenous rights, plus cross-cutting issues of rights in conflict. A final section begins to answer the questions: "Why take a human rights approach?", "What do anthropologists have to contribute to human rights?", and "What does the human-rights framework have to contribute to anthropology?".

CIVIL-POLITICAL RIGHTS

Individual rights to personal security, freedom from arbitrary violence by the state, freedom of speech, freedom of religion, freedom of movement, and to self-determination are all among the basic rights and protections offered by the 1948 Universal Declaration of Human Rights and its supporting 1996 Covenant on Civil and Political Rights. In a separate legal convention outlawing the Crime of Genocide (1951), the United Nations also emphasizes that a state's political choices leading to extinction of an indigenous, ethnic, or religious people constitute a punishable crime against humanity. Anthropologists working in Latin America have drawn on the language of these and other human-rights agreements in seeking protections and redress of grievances for individuals and peoples suffering politically motivated violence ranging from terror, rape, and torture to involuntary public service, slavelike servitude in the private sector, and the quieter violence of hunger and neglect (Bodley 1990; Martinez 1996). They continue to attribute the sources of such abuse to political culture (Van den Berghe 1990; Schirmer 1998), oppressive socioeconomic structures (Crahan 1982) or both (MacDonald 1994) and to link basic subsistence and health violations to civil-political abuses (Heggenhoughen 1995; Messer 1996). They also assist the efforts of indigenous groups and their leadership, who increasingly adopt the rhetoric of human rights to protest civil-rights abuses, to press claims over land and resources, and to demand political autonomy.

Whereas no Latin American state is entirely innocent of violations, Guatemala probably illustrates most vividly the synergisms connecting political violence, socioeconomic marginalization, and cultural discrimination. In view of its long political history of violence and discrimination against indigenous people and the poor, anthropologists from inside and outside Guatemala sometimes question whether the state-building process can break free and move on toward pluralism, democracy, and market-led growth (Montejo 1994; Nagengast 1994; Van den Berghe 1990). Guatemala's political violence may build also on portrayals from indigenous folklore and social relations that communicate a sense of betrayal, reduce expectations of human decency, and fan social dysfunction (Warren 1993).

Fracturing cycles of rights violations and promoting democracy, as Timerman (1985) observed, will necessitate two complementary sets of activities. The first is documentation of abuses and punishment of the abusers to prevent repetition of such atrocities. The second is broad democratic education for everyone. Anthropologists contribute documentation by systematically analyzing the patterns of abuses (Arias 1990; Smith 1990) and also by bearing witness (Montejo 1987; Carmack 1988; Falla 1988, 1994). Increasingly, forensic anthropologists also offer technical skills to help expose the contexts of murder and state terror. Their efforts not only document the past but also may help prevent future violations. Forensic studies of massacres open political space for participation by survivors and provide undeniable lessons about atrocities committed in situations of limited democracy (Burns 1994; Binford 1996). A critical question remains how, in the face of such atrocities, individuals and communities retain standards of human decency and dignity, and prevent moral breakdown and hopelessness. It has been suggested that the concept of victimization may motivate human-rights concerns in the rest of society, as in Argentina (Brancaforte 1994). But anthropologists are also beginning to document how the bystanders, alongside the victims and victimizers, learn to "misremember" or misrepresent the past—at least to outsiders (Perera 1993; Dubois 1994).

Additional civil-political rights concerns surround refugees' and immigrants' rights. Political violence and discrimination trigger massive displacements, leaving individuals political strangers without rights anywhere. Even though welfare rights and entitlements may exist in the recipient state, that state (the United States a case in point) may deny eligibility to immigrants fleeing political or economic injustice and attempt to limit freedom of movement and the right to work (Weaver 1988; Nagengast, Stavenhagen, and Kearney 1992). Significantly, some studies have documented how Central American refugees in the United States have learned to use the language of international human rights to justify their asylum and the language of immigrants' rights to argue for citizenship and inclusion in economic and social entitlements. They then appeal to cultural rights to maintain their cultural difference (Coutin 1994; Flores 1994; Gonzales 1994). The experiences of repression and subsequent refugee status have also been credited with heightening awareness and forging of new senses of national identity (Menchú 1984; Falla 1994; Stoll 1999). But new political awareness and organization do not automatically resolve economic challenges and may create new lines of fission within and across communities and social movements. New and old cultural images and indigenous organizations among Guatemalan (Nelson 1999) and Chiapas, Mexican (Collier and Stephen 1997) Maya are but two examples.

ECONOMIC, SOCIAL, AND CULTURAL RIGHTS

Political violence impacts also on economic-social-cultural rights, which include every individual's right to a decent standard of living (including adequate food, health, and general welfare) (Universal Declaration of Human Rights [UDHR] 1948, art. 27 and Covenant on Economic-Social-Cultural Rights, art. 11). Additional protections surround the right to work, the right to a cultural identity, and the rights of women and children. Recent human-rights discourse contrasts rights- versus needs-based assessment of conditions; the former focusing on mobilization of potential beneficiaries, the latter measuring frameworks of "basic needs" and the impacts of public policies on the poor (Crahan 1982; Lernoux 1982), with statistics that tend to compare food intake, nutritional outcomes, or other health measures or development indicators among populations (Dore and Weeks 1982; Whiteford and Ferguson 1991; Heggenhougen 1995; see also Scheper-Hughes (1997) for a critique of the children's rights approach). Human-rights inquiries also cite as abuses unjust working conditions, including coercive recruitment, inadequate compensation, violence, and restricted freedom on the work site (especially lack of an exit option), as well as gender subordination and discrimination, and child labor (Martinez 1996). Political and economic demands coalesce as mothers organize protests over rising food prices in terms of the right to feed their families (Safa 1990). The Zapatista rebellion in eastern Chiapas provides a well-documented case study of the overlap between political repression and exclusion, which are violations of civil-political rights, and extreme poverty and economic underdevelopment, both economic rights concerns (Collier with Quaratiello 1994).

Across Latin America, no matter what the political system, the struggle for land tends to be the most pressing human-rights demand in rural areas (Barraclough 1989). Especially where indigenous peoples happen to reside over oil deposits or rich mineral reserves, or along river waters potentially tapped for hydroelectric power, governments rarely apply established legal principles, which are supposed to grant local autonomy and indigenous rights of control over local resources. Indigenous groups also confront private mining, timber, agricultural (especially cattle), and energy interests that seek to dispossess them. These may present additional damages, as in the poisoning of Yanomami by gold-mining activities and excess deaths stemming from pesticide contamination in Central America (Collier with Quaratiello 1994; Sponsel 1997), and signal multiple human-rights violations. Official manipulations of land rights increasingly press indigenous groups and/or communities into competition. In Guatemala in the early 1990s both the Ixil and K'iche (Maya) had legitimate claims that the military apparently played off against each other. The Guatemala Scholars Network presented multiple perspectives on this drama, which involved not only the indigenous communities but also the anthropologist David Stoll, the Center for Human Rights Legal Action, Peace Brigades International, and other anthropologists (Moors 1995). In another example, Communities of Peoples in Resistance, after suffering terrorization, restricted freedom of movement, and hunger, found themselves competing against neighboring communities for control over the land necessary for self-determination of their socioeconomic future (Falla, 1994). Strategically the military counts on such dissension among indigenous and human-rights communities to prevent indigenous unification against them.

Cultural Rights

The above concerns for community and cultural control over resources also center on interpretations of cultural rights of individuals and collectivities, whose interests sometimes clash. Historically, indigenous ways of life have experienced continuing violations by states, businesses (especially transnational corporations), missionaries, and NGOs, each seeking to control the resources and destinies of particular landed cultural groups. But cultures are dynamic. Especially in pluralistic state contexts, where indigenous groups are supposed to enjoy special protections, individuals and collectivities compete for the right to speak for their peoples and to chart an authentic cultural course toward autonomy, control, and self-determination over land, resources, and economic development. Constructions of (new) Indian identities, communities, and political-interest groups are influenced by international NGOs promoting human rights, as well as by the lessons of other indigenous groups, the Left, government, missionaries, and other NGOs. Indigenous cultural identity claims often prove to be flexible and more or less inclusive, as leaders seek to respond appropriately to different threats, such as loss of access to resources. Leaders may claim to represent parts or wholes of nationwide indigenous movement. Jackson (1995) has observed these developments in her case study of Colombia.

However, demands to protect the cultural rights of communities also raise troubling questions about the rights of individuals to choose their own cultural paths. In both Mexico and Guatemala, indigenous peoples continually are besieged by external political and religious agents who desire to transform them. In such contexts, the traditional leaders of distinctive Maya communities have been known to restrict an individual's religious freedom and choice of livelihood and to coerce community service. Ostensibly aimed at conserving culture and community, these actions protect the leadership's vested interests and power base. In Chiapas, some indigenous Maya communities in the 1970s and 1980s excluded and exiled non-conformists who threatened the status quo (Gossen 1994a).

Cultural rights also more than occasionally conflict with women's rights. New feminist demands for equal participation, access to resources, and protections for female individuals as human beings often clash with entrenched cultural values and mores dominated by males. Increasingly, women insist that their individual rights as human beings take precedence over cultural rights. They often resist appeals to alleged cultural rights, indigenous rights, or the rights of the community that exclude, marginalize, or permit violence against women (Carneiro da Cunha 1992; Tula 1994). As women present and organize educational, economic, ecological, and health ventures as human-rights-focused activities, their new assertiveness is also transforming culture (Stephen 1995). Conversely, women occasionally adopt and manipulate symbols of their subordination in cultural gender ideology to create a space for their larger public roles as defenders of human rights, as in the case of the *Madres de Plaza de Mayo* (Sarramea 1994).

DEVELOPMENT RIGHTS

Solidarity or development rights emphasize people's rights to a peaceful, just, environmentally sustainable and equitable socioeconomic order, which places human beings at the center of the development process. They also emphasize that all classes of rights are interconnected and should be indivisible. Good case studies are the communities of Chiapas, Mexico, which are struggling for land, equal access to the Mexican government's socioeconomic welfare programs, and guarantees of basic subsistence; and also freedom from violence and arbitrary arrest, and participation in fair and free elections. These demands show how civil-political and economic-social-cultural rights are interconnected and united under the demand for a right to development that would prevent extreme poverty, protect the environment, and not subject communities to the unbridled ravages of free-trade agreements (Collier with Quaratiello 1994; Nash 1993; Messer 1995:67).

Environmental rights comprise an additional dimension of the right to development. Environmentalists, business, state, indigenous, and other community interests increasingly draw on the language of environmental rights as they vie over who should control the earth and its resources—rainforests, waterways, and paths to development. Studying both the environmental and indigenous movements, anthropologists draw attention to the interconnections between cultural and environmental destruction, and the nonmarket values of both natural and cultural resources. Insisting that such resources must be protected, they try to demonstrate ways in which human rights and protection of the rights of indigenous minorities can serve multiple ends, including environmental protection and economic development. Ecotourism, conservation of biodiversity, and protection of intellectual property rights—all special topics treated at length in *Cultural Survival Quarterly*—raise complex questions about who should control development. Even allegedly successful alliances of environmentalist and indigenist interests may threaten to undercut individual indigenous group identity. More often, indigenous groups and environmentalists have conflicting agendas. The idea of a community of indigenous and global environmental interests appeals to a transnational audience but only partially masks the tension between indigenous goals of self-determination and control over resources and environmentalists' desire to protect the rainforest (Conklin and Graham 1995; Varese 1996). In Mexico, state and local community interests clash over who should control the rainforest, which may be classified as part of the nation's cultural resources because it contains archaeological sites (Arizpe 1993). Increasingly, anthropologists try to work with indigenous organizations to find innovative economic solutions that can generate income while protecting lands, rights, and resources. One example is *Cultural Survival*'s support of the candied-nut mixture, Rainforest Crunch. But these efforts too are controversial because they thrust indigenous peoples into a capitalist system and into world markets over which they have little control.

INDIGENOUS RIGHTS

Latin America has provided the focal point for organizing indigenous rights (Declaration of Barbados 1971; Declaration of Barbados III 1993; Wright and Ismaelillo 1982); documenting states' abuses against native peoples (Arias 1990; Smith 1990), and organizing to demand rights to land, culture, and self-determination in development (Messer 1993:230–31). Increasingly, indigenous voices, not anthropologists', speak for native peoples and organize their struggles for human rights (*Centro de Estudios de Cultura Maya*; Fischer and Brown 1995; Montejo 1987; Varese 1988). Anthropologists instead respond to requests for up-to-date legal information and access to channels of communication to expand international advocacy efforts. This pattern was illustrated in the Spring 1994 issue of *Cultural Survival* (devoted to the Zapatista rebellion in Chiapas, Mexico), which showcased the Clandestine Indigenous Revolutionary Committee's cry for "democracy" and the rights of "all the Indian and non-Indian peoples" alongside more conventional analyses of the ecological, political-economic, and religious roots of the rebellion, the significance of "Zapata" as a Mexican symbol, and transformations in ethnic-national identity (Cancian and Brown 1994; Earle 1994; Gossen 1994b; Nations 1994; Nigh 1994; Vogt 1994).

The recent history of "peoples" self-identifying and organizing to oppose brutality and demand human rights illustrates how the language of human rights, nationhood, and autonomy is being manipulated by indigenous (and other) Latin American peoples struggling for land and access to other resources (Diskin 1991; Jackson 1991). In Colombia, anthropologists observe the beginnings of a redefined tribal entity, of which the terms are "not so much about *being* Indian as *becoming* Indian" (Jackson 1991:131). As emergent identities prove to be far more self-conscious and politicized than traditional, anthropologists called by indigenous groups to assist them in negotiating and legitimating their identities and human-rights demands often find themselves caught in the middle: however critically they may wish to analyze indigenous claims, doing so risks jeopardizing future working relationships (see e.g., Jackson 1995; Stoll 1999; Nelson 1999).

Anthropologists' studies of indigenous rights, as of other rights, tend to focus on the roles of multiple peoples or nations in postcolonial state-building processes. In Nicaragua under the Sandinista government, Diskin (1991) noted that the Nicaraguan Costeños' self-identification as an "(Indian) nation" allowed them to demand autonomy and land rights along with other indigenous groups. At the same time, Miskito demands for rights over and against the Sandinista regime caused rifts between the Miskito and the international community that supported indigenous rights and the Sandinistas. In Chiapas, Mexico, as Zapatistas with composite Maya or purely peasant identity struggle for respect and self-determination, they exercise rights as indigenous but also as Mexican citizens in what they view as a multinational state (Collier and Stephen 1997). Although considerations of collective rights begin with notions of communities with customary law, in the case of the Zapatistas and some of the Guatemalan Maya groups, religious and economic transformation have removed the communitarian identities that characterized the *municipio* organization of the 1960s. Human-rights demands have been influenced not only by United Nations conventions, but by Marxism, the labor movement, Roman Catholic Liberation Theology, and Protestant egalitarianism as well. They are motivated also by local experiences of and response to limited economic options and oppression and exploitation of individuals by their own indigenous leaders as well as by state and local authorities. Appeals to indigenous rights address negative and positive rights concerns: protection from human-rights abuses, usually perpetrated by states but increasingly by drug, commercial, and environmentalist interests. These appeals demand fulfillment of (indigenous) peoples' rights to development, in which communities seek alliances in the name of human rights that will allow them to move into the future with intact identity but new options (see, e.g., Varese 1996). Drawing on the rules and rhetoric of international United Nations and other development organizations and agencies, pan-Indian multinational organizations are emerging from their fragmented histories of oppression, marginalization, and war and are negotiating with states for inclusion with full rights, or where opportune, sometimes bypassing states as they negotiate and defend their own subsistence base.

RIGHTS IN CONFLICT AND THE LIMITS OF CULTURAL RELATIVISM

Indigenous notions of rights and persons sometimes come into conflict with those formulating international norms, but customary and international legal systems have mutual lessons to teach regarding: (1) definitions and treatment of citizens versus noncitizens or strangers (in states); (2) special legal protections for minorities, women, children, or other marginalized groups; and (3) the specific contents of economic, social, and cultural rights.

The primary struggle is to bridge the gaps separating international human-rights guarantees, individual government definitions of who qualifies as a human being or person before the law, and community-level customary practice. Exclusions at the state level may involve native peoples, and, at the local level, full political participation or control over resources by women or non-native inhabitants. Old and new state constitutions that guarantee civil rights often deny them to members of indigenous communities, women and children, and other unprotected strangers or protect those guilty of crimes of genocide. In the case of Guatemala, former governments, which did not count indigenous individuals as full persons, violated their human rights; new civilian governments threaten to perpetuate cycles of violence by offering amnesty to violators and not insisting on accountability for crimes of genocide. Schirmer's (1988, 1998) interviews with Guatemalan (and also South American) military elites captured the rhetoric and rationale for such brutality: in the words of Guatemalan General Gramajo (executor of that country's 1980s "bullets and beans" strategy of repression and scorched earth), he too was protecting cultural sovereignty and national rights. Such claims elucidate the legal and cultural contexts of discrimination and violence, and flag the limits to cultural relativism. They also highlight the malappropriation of human rights and humanitarian rhetoric by the perpetrators of crimes against humanity. To paraphrase the general, the "bullets and beans" strategy, which involved killing 30 percent of indigenous individuals but provided food for the remaining 70 percent, constituted humanitarianism because the previous doctrine had promoted killing 100 percent! Schirmer is probably right to conclude that Guatemala's new constitutional democracy, built on such human-rights views and unpunished state violence, bodes ill for a future peace until the individuals responsible for killings have been brought to justice.

Women's individual rights to representation, to hold property, and to control resources (including their persons) are also subject to contestation at multiple levels. Women's participation constitutes one of the more contentious issues in indigenous and other political movements; the same indigenous leaders who seek collective rights vis-à-vis the state often seek to marginalize women's political voices within the community. In addition, a special tension exists between individual and collective notions of who has the right to decide how land is to be used (or disposed of), women's and children's rights to (health) care, and a woman's individual right not to be beaten. In the Peruvian Amazon, Urarina women exercise considerable household economic power but are excluded from positions of local, regional, or supraregional power; Dean (1999) does not expect this to change any time soon. Notwithstanding, within indigenous communities in both South America and Central America women are increasingly seeking leadership, as well as control over cultural conservation and construction, by attempting to acquire and manage their children's education. In addition, when faced with constraints or outright brutality, women who have been made aware of their rights may seek redress in civil courts for perceived injustices that in customary (community) terms may be viewed as ordinary or nonsanctionable behaviors.

WHY TAKE A HUMAN RIGHTS APPROACH?

The cases above illustrate many of the interconnections between civil, political, economic, social, and cultural rights. Clearly, in the modern states of Central America and in the Southern Cone, governments are not meeting basic human needs for subsistence or guaranteeing even minimal personal security. Notwithstanding the human-rights covenants they have signed, they collude in criminal behaviors that violate the physical security of communities and individuals and deprive them of land, livelihood, and life. But traditional cultural communities also violate human rights. Anthropologists are now challenged to learn how to represent peoples and their cultural interests at the same time that they defend individual human rights.

Such investigations suggest answers to some basic questions. Why take a human-rights approach? Because a human-rights approach demands that an anthropologist think about what it means to be human and indicates the connections linking political-economic abuses, civil-political inequalities, and sociocultural discrimination. A human-rights approach also gets beyond explanations framed only in terms of political-economic exploitation. Although such inequities are a significant part of the picture, it considers human well-being in a wider framework that insists every human being has a right to basic freedoms and a minimum standard of well-being. A human-rights approach also moves beyond misery research; beyond drawing on charitable response, such an approach insists the respondent consider the human issue of social justice.

For anthropologists, a human-rights approach also moves beyond applied anthropology, which helps improve the social and cultural appropriateness of nutrition, health services, or economic-development scheme. Instead, it engages policy makers and forces them to think about fundamental concerns, such as human dignity and freedom from want. Specifically, a human-rights approach takes anthropologists beyond technical scientific studies of the synergisms between nutrition and reproductive health, or women's education and children's nutrition, to consider sustainable solutions to fundamental social problems in terms of basic rights of individuals and collective rights of communities. As Amartya Sen (in view of Asia) and Alex DeWaal (in view of Africa) put it so well, where there is true democracy, there is a right not to starve (DeWaal 1997; Sen 1999). For Latin America also, a focus on democratic processes that can lead to a right not to starve might serve as a starting point for studies of political and economic rights, as well as of the rights of indigenous peoples.

In Latin America, the historical unfolding of human rights is also a history of social transformation. Latin Americanist anthropologists furthermore recognize that progress in human rights will determine the future of society at local to global levels. They contribute to this history, both directly and indirectly, in their writings and actions on behalf of, and sometimes in condemnation of, communities, states, and international organizations. They offer human rights activists and the rest of the world cogent analyses of the historical abuses of human rights in Latin American societies. They also strengthen the universal human-rights framework by making available a wealth of comparative data and ideas on cultural notions of human rights and a distinctive discourse demonstrating the implications of human rights for human dignity, security, and community development. Finally, in their organizational efforts and advocacy actions, Latin Americanist anthropologists have shown that academic anthropologists can and must make a difference. Defending and advancing human rights, and so ensuring the lives and societies central to anthropology's focus, is anthropology's mission.

References

Agosin, M. (Ed.). 1993. *Surviving Beyond Fear: Women, Children, and Human Rights in Latin America*. Fredonia, NY: White Pine Press.

Amnesty International. 1991. *Women in the Front Line: Human Rights Violations Against Women*. New York: Amnesty International.

Arias, A. 1990. Changing Indian Identity: Guatemala's Violent Transition to Modernity. In C. Smith (Ed.), *Guatemalan Indians and the State*, pp. 230–257. Austin: University of Texas Press.

Arizpe, L. 1993. Scale and International in Cultural Processes: Towards an Anthropological Perspective of Global Change. Paper presented at the ICAES, July 1993.

Barnett, C. 1988. Is There a Scientific Basis in Anthropology for the Ethics of Human Rights? In T. Downing and L. Kushener (Eds.), *Anthropology and Human Rights*, pp. 21–26. Cambridge, MA: Cultural Survival.

Barraclaugh, S. L. 1989. The Legacy of Latin American Land Reform. *Report on the Americas, 28*(3), 16–21.

Binford, L. 1996. *The El Mazote Massacre: Anthropology and Human Rights*. Tucson: University of Arizona Press.

Bodley, J. H. 1990. *Victims of Progress*. Mountain View, CA: Mayfield Publishing Company.

Brancaforte, D. 1994. Psychoanalytic Narratives and Human Rights Discourse in Post-Dictatorship Argentina. *Abstracts of the 934d Annual Meeting of the American Anthropological Association*, p. 88.

Burns, K. 1994. Forensic Anthropologists: Technical Resources for Human Rights Organizations. *Abstracts of the 93rd Annual Meeting of the American Anthropological Association*, p. 96.

Cancian, F., and P. Brown. 1994. Who Is Rebelling in Chiapas? *Cultural Survival Quarterly 18*(1) (Spring), 22–25.

Carmack, R. M. (Ed.). 1988. *Harvest of Violence: The Maya Indians and the Guatemala Crisis*. Norman: University of Oklahoma Press.

Carneiro da Cunha, M. 1992. Custom Is Not a Thing, It Is a Path: Reflections on the Brazilian Indian Case. In Ja'a' Nai'im (Ed.), *Human Rights in Cross-Cultural Perspective: A Quest for Consensus*. Philadelphia: University of Pennsylvania Press, pp. 276–294.

Chase-Sardi, M. 1990. *El Derecho Consuetudinario Indígena y Su Bibliografía Antropológica en el Paraguay*. CEADUC-Biblioteca Paraguaya de Antropología VI. Asunción, Paraguay.

Collier, G., with E. Quaratiello. 1994. *Basta! Land and the Zapatista Rebellion in Chiapas*. Oakland, CA: A Food First Book.

Collier, G., and L. Stephen (Eds.). 1997. Ethnicity, Identity, and Citizenship in the Wake of the Zapatista Rebellion. *Journal of Latin American Anthropology, 3*, 1.

Conklin, B., and L. Graham. 1995. The Shifting Middle Ground: Amazonian Indians and Ecopolitics. *American Anthropologist 97*(4), 695–721.

Coutin, S. 1994. Refining Legal Entities: Salvadoran Refugees and Immigrants in Los Angeles, California. *Abstracts of the 1994 Annual Meeting of the American Anthropological Association*, p. 113. Washington, DC.

Crahan, M. 1982. *Human Rights and Basic Needs in the Americas*. Washington, DC: Georgetown University Press.

Dean, B. 1999. Recognizing Rights and Engendering Power in Indigenous Amazonia. Paper presented at the 98th Annual Meeting of the American Anthropological Association, Chicago, Illinois, 19 November 1999.

Declaration of Barbados. 1971. IGWIA. Doc. 1. Copenhagen: International Work Group for Indigenous Affairs.

Declaration of Barbados III. 1993. Declaration of Barbados III. Rio de Janeiro, December 10, 1993.

DeWaal, A. 1997. *Famine Crimes: Politics and the Disaster Relief Industry in Africa*. Bloomington: University of Indiana Press.

Diskin, M. 1991. Ethnic Discourse and the Challenge to Anthropology: The Nicaraguan Case. In G. Urban and J. Sherzer (Eds.), *Nation-States and Indigenous Indians in Latin America*, pp. 156–180. Austin: University of Texas Press.

Dore, E., and J. Weeks. 1982. Economic Performance and Basic Needs: The Examples of Brazil, Chile, Mexico, Nicaragua, Peru, and Venezuela. In M. Crahan (Ed.), *Human Rights and Basic Needs in the Americas*, pp. 15–187. Washington, DC: Georgetown University Press.

Doughty, P. 1988. Crossroads for Anthropology: Human Rights in Latin America. In T. E. Downing and L. Kushner (Eds.), *Human Rights and Anthropology*, pp. 43–71. Cambridge, MA: Cultural Survival.

Downing, T. E. 1988. Human Rights Research: The Challenge for Anthropologists. In T. E. Downing and L. Kushner (Eds.), *Human Rights and Anthropology*, pp. 9–20. Cambridge, MA: Cultural Survival.

Downing, T. E., and G. Kushner (Eds.). 1988. *Human Rights and Anthropology*. Cambridge, MA: Cultural Survival.

Dubois, L. 1994. Contradictions of Dictatorship in Argentina. *Abstracts of the 93rd Annual Meeting of the American Anthropological Association,* p. 131.

Earle, D. 1994. Indigenous Identity at the Margin. *Cultural Survival Quarterly 18*(1) (Spring), 26–30.

Falla, R. 1988. Struggle for Survival in the Mountains: Hunger and Other Privations Inflicted on Internal Refugees from the Central Highlands. In R. Carmack (Ed.), *Harvest of Violence*, pp. 235–255. Norman: University of Oklahoma Press.

Falla, R. 1994. *Massacres in the Jungle: Ixcan, Guatemala 1975–82* (Julia Howland, Trans.). Boulder, CO: Westview Press.

Fischer, E., and R. M. Brown. 1995. *Maya Cultural Activism in Guatemala*. Austin: University of Texas Press.

Flores, W. V. 1994. Claiming Rights: Cultural Citizenship and Imagined Latino Communities. *Abstracts of the 1994 Annual Meeting of the American Anthropological Association*, p. 144. Washington, DC.

Gonzales, M. 1994. The Unrecognized Refugees: Fleeing Rural Power Struggles in Mexico. *Abstracts of the 1994 Annual Meeting of the American Anthropological Association*, p. 159. Washington, D.C.

Gossen, G. 1994a. Comments on the Zapatista Movement. *Cultural Survival Quarterly, 18*, 19–21.

Gossen, G. 1994b. From Olmecs to Zapatistas: A Once and Future History of Souls. *American Anthropologist, 96*, 553–70.

Heggenhoughen, K. 1995. The Epidemiology of Functional Apartheid and Human Rights Abuses. *Social Science and Medicine, 40*, 281–84.

Jackson, J. 1991. Being and Becoming Indian in the Vaupes. In G. Urban and J. Sherzer (Eds.), *Nation-States and Indigenous Indians in Latin America*, pp. 131–155. Austin: University of Texas Press.

Jackson, J. 1995. Culture: Genuine and Spurious: The Politics of Indianness in the Vaupes, Colombia. *American Anthropologist, 22*, 3–27.

Lernoux, P. 1982. Cry of the People: The Struggle For Human Rights in Latin America. *The Catholic Church in Conflict With U.S. Policy.* Baltimore: Penguin.

MacDonald, T. 1994. Some Essential, Not Simply "New," Approaches to Human Rights. *Cultural Survival Quarterly, 18* (1), 1.

Martinez, Samuel. 1996. Indifference with Indignation: Anthropology, Human Rights, and the Haitian Bracero. *American Anthropologist, 98*, 17–29.

Menchú, R. 1984. *I, Rigoberta Menchú: An Indian Woman in Guatemala.* Edited and introduced by E. Burgos-Weber (A. Wright, Trans.). London: Verso.

Messer, E. 1993. Anthropology and Human Rights. *Annual Review of Anthropology, 22*, 221–249.

Messer, E. 1995. Anthropology and Human Rights in Latin America. *Journal of Latin American Anthropology, 1*(1), 48–67.

Messer, E. 1996. Anthropology, Human Rights, and Social Transformation. In E. Moran (Ed.), *Transforming Societies, Transforming Anthropology*, pp. 165–210. Ann Arbor: University of Michigan Press.

Montejo, V. 1987. *Testimony: Death of a Guatemalan Village* (V. Perea, Ed., Trans.). Willamantic, CT: Curbstone Press.

Montejo, V. 1994. A History of Human Rights in Guatemala. *Abstracts of the 93rd Annual Meeting of the American Anthropological Association*, p. 254.

Moors, M. 1995. *Los Cimientos Packet.* Guatemala Scholars Network.

Nagengast, C. 1994. Violence, Terror, and the Crisis of the State. *Annual Review of Anthropology, 23*, 109–36.

Nagengast, C., R. Stavenhagen, and M. Kearney. 1992. *Human Rights and Indigenous Workers: The Mixtecs in Mexico and the U.S.* San Diego: University of California Center for U.S.-Mexican Studies.

Nash, J. (Ed.). 1993. Global Integration and Subsistence Insecurity. *American Anthropologist, 96*, 7–30.

Nations, James D. 1994. The Ecology of the Zapatista Revolt. *Cultural Survival Quarterly, 18*(1), 31–33.

Nigh, Ronald. 1994. Zapata Rose in 1994: The Indian Rebellion in Chiapas. *Cultural Survival Quarterly 18*(1), 9–13.

Nelson, D. 1999. *A Finger in the Wound: Body Politics in Quincentennial Guatemala.* Berkeley: University of California Press.

Perera, V. 1993. *Unfinished Conquest: The Guatemalan Tragedy.* Berkeley: University of California Press.

Pollock, D. 1994. The Forest People and the Politics of Environmentalism in Western Brazil. *Abstracts of the 93rd Annual Meeting of the American Anthropological Association*, p. 280.

Reed, R. 1994. Two Rights Do Not Make a Wrong: Conflicting Agendas of Paraguay's Indigenous Peoples and International Conservation Agencies. *Abstracts of the 93rd Annual Meeting of the American Anthropological Association*, p. 287.

Safa, H. 1990. Women's Social Movements in Latin America. *Gender Sociology, 4*, 354–69.

Sarramea, A. 1994. From the Kitchen to the Plaza de Mayo. *Abstracts of the 1994 Annual Meeting of the American Anthropological Association*, Washington, DC, p. 303.

Scheper-Hughes, N. 1997. Demography Without Numbers. In D. I. Kertzer and T. Fricke (Eds.), *Anthropological Demography: Toward a New Synthesis*, pp. 201–22. Chicago: University of Chicago Press.

Schirmer, J. 1988. The Dilemma of Cultural Diversity and Equivalency in Universal Human Rights Standards. In T. E. Downing and L. Kushner (Eds.), *Anthropology and Human Rights*, pp. 91–106. Cambridge, MA: Cultural Survival.

Schirmer, Jennifer. 1998. *The Guatemalan Military Project: A Violence Called Democracy.* Philadelphia: University of Pennsylvania Press.

Sen, A. 1999. *Development as Freedom.* New York: Routledge.

Smith, C. (Ed.) 1990. *Guatemalan Indians and the State.* Austin: University of Texas Press.

Smith, C. 1996. Development and the State: Issues for Anthropologists. In E. Moran (Ed.), *Transforming Societies, Transforming Anthropology*, pp. 25–56. Ann Arbor: University of Michigan Press.

Sponsel, L. 1997. The Master Thief: Gold Mining and Mercury Contamination. In B. Johnston (Ed.), *Life and Death Matters: Human Rights and the Environment at the End of the Millennium*, pp. 99–127. Walnut Creek, CA: Alta Mira Press.

Stavenhagen, R., with collaboration of Tania Carrasco and others. 1988. *Derecho Indígena y Derechos Humanos en América Latina* [Indigenous Law and Human Rights in Latin America]. México, D.F.: Instituto InterAmericano de Derechos Humanos: Colegio de México.

Stavenhagen, R. 1989. Indigenous Customary Laws in Latin America. *América Indígena, 49,* 223–43.

Stavenhagen, R. 1991. *The Ethnic Question: Conflict, Development, and Human Rights.* Tokyo: UNU Press.

Stavenhagen, R., and D. Iturralde. 1990. *Entre la Ley y la Costumbre: El Derecho Consuetudinario Indígena en América Latina.* Instituto Interamericano de Derechos Humanos—Instituto Indigenista Interamericano, México.

Stephen, L. 1995. Women's Rights are Human Rights: The Merging of Feminine and Feminist Interests Among El Salvador's Mothers of the Disappeared. *American Ethnologist, 22,* 807–27.

Stoll, D. 1999. *Rigoberta Menchú and the Story of All Poor Guatemalans.* Boulder, CO: Westview Press.

Timerman, J. 1985. Preface. In C. Brown (Ed.), *With Friends Like These: Americas Watch Report on Human Rights and U.S. Policy in Latin America.* New York: Pantheon.

Tula, M. T. 1994. *Hear My Testimony: Maria T. Tula, Human Rights Activist of El Salvador* (L. Stephen, Trans.). Boston, MA: South End Press.

Turner, T. 1997. Human Rights, Human Difference: Anthropology's Contribution to an Emancipatory Politics. *Journal of Anthropological Research, 53,* 273–91.

Van den Berghe, P. (Ed.) 1990. *State Violence and Ethnicity.* Niwot: University of Colorado Press.

Varese, S. 1988. Multiethnicity and Hegemonic Construction: Indian Plans and the Future. In R. Guidieri, F. Pellizzi, and S. Tambiah (Eds.), *Ethnicities and Nations. Processes of Interethnic Relations in Latin America, Southeast Asia, and the Pacific,* pp. 57–77. Houston, Texas: Rothco Chapel.

Varese, S. 1996. The New Environmentalist Movement of Latin American Indigenous People. In S. Brush and D. Stabinsky (Eds.), *Valuing Local Knowledge: Indigenous People and Intellectual Property Rights,* pp. 122–42. Washington: Island Press.

Vogt, E. Z. 1994. Possible Sacred Aspects of the Chiapas Rebellion. *Cultural Survival Quarterly 18*(1), (Spring), 34.

Warren, K. (Ed.) 1993. *The Violence Within: Cultural and Political Opposition in Divided Nations.* Boulder, CO: Westview Press.

Warren, K. 1996. Reading History as Resistance: Maya Public Intellectuals in Guatemala. In E. F. Fischer and R. McKennan Brown (Eds.), *Maya Cultural Activism in Guatemala,* pp. 89–106. Austin: University of Texas Press.

Weaver, T. 1988. The Human Rights of Undocumented Workers in the United States-Mexico Border Region. In T. Downing and M. Kusner (Eds.), *Anthropology and Human Rights,* pp. 73–90. Cambridge, MA: Cultural Survival.

Whiteford, S., and A. Ferguson (Eds.) 1991. *Harvest of Want: Hunger and Food Security in Central America and Mexico.* Boulder, CO: Westview Press.

Wright, R. M., and Ismaelillo. 1982. *Native Peoples in Struggle: Cases from the Fourth Russell Tribunal.* Bombay: Erin.

Leslie E. Sponsel teaches anthropology at University of Hawaii (Manoa); his books include Endangered Peoples of Southeast and East Asia; Tropical Deforestation: The Human Dimension; Indigenous Peoples and the Future of Amazonia; The Anthropology of Peace and Nonviolence; *and* Human Ecology.

The Amazon Basin has long been recognized as the world's major remaining pool of cultural, botanical, and zoological diversity, even while damage to each of those realms has progressed at an almost geometric rate throughout the past century. After briefly outlining the major kinds of harm that stem from massive deforestation and disruptive incursions on indigenous cultures, Sponsel sounds an urgent call to anthropologists that they also be activists in support of native peoples and the fragile ecology.

For more details on human rights, see Messer (chapter 3); for a small case study of cultural and environmental preservation fostered by anthropologists, see Stearman (chapter 20); for alternative views of development, contrast Durston (chapter 9).

Relationships among the World System, Indigenous Peoples, and Ecological Anthropology in the Endangered Amazon

Leslie E. Sponsel

Five hundred years ago Amazonia was not an endangered biome, even though indigenous peoples had already lived there for millennia. Although the destruction of the Amazon started with Western colonization centuries ago, only in recent decades has this destruction reached a level that increasingly endangers the entire region. Economic development has been achieved through deforestation and other forms of environmental degradation. It has also been achieved through the imposition of sudden and profound ecological, economic, and cultural changes on indigenous societies. In the process, many have become extinct, and many others are endangered. Some people euphemistically call these changes the advance of civilization and progress. Others honestly label it ecocide, ethnocide, and genocide.

Three things are now alarmingly clear. The futures of indigenes and ecosystems of the Amazon are intimately interrelated and increasingly influenced by Western society. The future of the Amazon is uncertain at best, especially if trends continue. And the future of the Amazon is likely to be determined within the next few decades, if it is not already too late to avoid disaster.

As it has in the past, so in the future, human adaptation in Amazonia will depend on the flexibility and resilience of indigenous populations, their cultures, and the ecosystems they inhabit. But the future of Amazonia also depends on the adaptability of Western society—its willingness to learn from indigenous knowledge and wisdom as well as from its own past mistakes in order to develop sustainable relationships with both ecosystems and indigenous societies. In turn, this adaptability depends on Western society's appreciating the intrinsic as well as the extrinsic value of indigenes and ecosystems, and on respecting and defending the basic human rights of indigenes.

Considering some of the historic occasions of the early 1990s—the Columbian quincentenary, the Earth Summit, the United Nations' International Year of Indigenous

Peoples—and the 1990s as the turning point for a new century and millennium, it is not only appropriate now but even vital to critically rethink Western society's relationship to the indigenous peoples and tropical forests of the world. This historical juncture also provides an opportunity and should serve as a catalyst for us to rethink the role of anthropologists, both individually and collectively. It is becoming increasingly clear that purely academic interests in the Amazon can no longer be maintained, considering the gravity and urgency of the growing crisis of combined ecocide, ethnocide, and genocide. There is also increasing concern among indigenous peoples about the role of anthropologists. For these and other reasons, the situation in the Amazon demands a paradigm shift in anthropological research on human ecology and other topics.

DEFORESTATION

Tropical deforestation threatens to diminish the quality of organic and human life on planet Earth as a whole because of the vital environmental services, economic resources (including medicines), and aesthetic value of forest ecosystems. Deforestation and extinction are nothing new, but their recent magnitudes are certainly reason for alarm and action (Grove 1992). Current rates of deforestation throughout the tropics exceed 30 hectares per minute (Repetto 1990). In recent years, deforestation rates were higher in Latin America than elsewhere both in absolute area and percentage of total forest area (Anderson 1990:4). The associated spasm of extinction resulting from habitat destruction in the tropics is rare if not unique in geological history (Jablonski 1991; Raup 1988). Wilson (1992) estimates that three species are becoming extinct each hour in the tropical rain forest. There is certainly no precedent in the prehistory and history of indigenous societies for the deforestation that has been occurring at an exponential rate in Amazonia since the 1980s.

Causes

Deforestation involves complicated phenomena and multiple causes. The specific combination of proximate causes varies in time and space from country to country, and even regionally within a country. But the ultimate causes are usually the same—the greed of outsiders and, to a much lesser extent if at all, the needs of locals. Sometimes the latter do not have any alternative for economic survival but to pursue activities that contribute to deforestation.

Contrary to popular belief, deforestation is not caused by shifting (swidden or slash-and-burn) horticulture. Traditional indigenous populations are low in density and fairly mobile, and they normally practice a rotational subsistence economy with polycropping, adequate fallow periods, and ample areas of forest held in reserve for future gardens (Carneiro 1988). In general, swidden farming is efficient, productive, and sustainable. It contributes to deforestation only when it is not practiced in traditional ways, when population pressure develops, and/or when cash crops are introduced for export in a market economy. Admittedly, one or more of these new conditions are rapidly developing in many areas of Amazonia.

Most population growth in Amazonian countries is taking place not so much in the forest as in boomtowns and especially in cities, but these in turn put pressure on the land and resources in adjacent forests (Godfrey 1990; Lugo 1991). The government of Brazil tried to relieve the population problem in the poverty- and drought-stricken arid northeast sector of the country by designing a scheme to relocate people along the Transamazon Highway, but the initiative was far from successful (Moran 1988; Smith 1978). Such *shifted* (in contrast to shifting) farmers usually do not know how to farm or in other ways adapt in the tropical forest, and so they become another factor contributing to deforestation in the Amazon. By far the most important cause of deforestation in Brazil, however, has been the conversion of forest to pasture that appears to be for cattle ranching but is really for profit from land speculation. About 85 percent of the deforestation in the Brazilian Amazon is caused by only some 500 ranches (Hecht 1989; Hecht and Cockburn 1989).

Forest conversion for establishing massive monocrop plantations for agricultural produce, timber, or paper pulp is another cause of deforestation (McNeil 1986; Margolis 1977)—but except for the infamous Jari project, this kind of activity has been fairly limited in the Amazon so far. Hydroelectric dams (Fearnside 1989a; Gribel 1990) and mining projects are other important causes of deforestation in Brazil. The timber in the lakes formed behind the dams is not cut but simply left to die and decompose, polluting the waters. The enormous Carajas iron mine smelts ore with the use of charcoal produced from the surrounding forest (Fearnside 1989b). Otherwise, commercial logging has not been a major cause of deforestation in Amazonia, although it could well become so in the future as Japan and other tropical timber importers turn to this region after depleting the forests of Southeast Asia and Melanesia. Even selective logging, where less than 10 percent of the trees are cut, can still damage more than half the trees in the forest (Myers 1992).

In Brazil, these and other schemes for economic development have been integral parts of the military's initiative to conquer its frontier, integrate the area economically and politically, and assimilate or exterminate the indigenes, all in the name of national security and economic progress. Much of this destruction is financed by international lending organizations, notably the World Bank. Such banks are supported partly by taxpayers in the United States and other developed countries (Buschbacher 1986; Guimaraes 1991; Hecht and Cockburn 1989; Katzman 1975; Moran 1983; Poelhekke 1986; Schmink and Wood 1992; Treece 1989).

Consequences

The consequences of deforestation are manifold—evolutionary, genetic, environmental, social, economic, medical, political, and aesthetic. They range from impacts on local people and wildlife to global warming and rising sea levels. In all aspects and at all scales they can be far reaching and even catastrophic (Bunyard 1987; Cook, Janetos, and Hinds 1990; Molion 1989; Myers 1992; Sioli 1987).

Species are unique, closed genetic units; species extinction is forever. In a few years, human activity can destroy millions of years of organic evolution. Moreover, the extinction of any species has a multiplier effect, influencing numerous other species because of the great diversity and complexity of the tropical forest ecosystem, which is characterized by multiple linkages and interdependencies between species. The erosion of biodiversity through habitat destruction and species extinction eliminates forever possibilities for future evolution, germ plasm for agriculture, food and pharmaceutical products, and industrial materials (Barrau 1982; Pimentel et al. 1992; Plotkin 1991; Smith and Schultes 1990; Smith et al. 1992; Wilson 1989).

In Amazonia, about half the rainfall circulates in the water cycle of the local ecosystem. Massive deforestation will disrupt this cycle and probably lead to increased aridity regionally and far beyond, with detrimental effects on agricultural activity and productivity (Salati 1987).

A neglected consequence of deforestation is disease. Transients and colonists introduce new diseases from the outside to local residents, some triggering devastating epidemics. Endemic diseases such as malaria are aggravated by changes in the forest ecology and are also contracted by colonists and transients (ICHI 1986).

Solutions

Also multiple and complex are any solutions for deforestation. Westerners have treated the forests as obstacles to development rather than as foundations for sustainable land and resource use. Governments, for example, often define colonists' claims and land improvements in terms of their converting forested land into farms and pastures, even providing financial incentives for their efforts in doing so. The future of the forests lies not in conservation alone, in the sense of mere preservation, but also in sustainable land and resource management of existing forests as well as regeneration of deforested areas where feasible (Anderson 1990; Barrett 1980; Clay 1988; Eden 1990; Fearnside 1990a; Foresta 1991; Gómez-Pompa, Whitmore, and Hadley 1991; Head and Heinzman 1990; Hecht and Cockburn 1989; Lugo, Clark, and Child 1987; Myers 1992; Ryan 1992).

If Westerners afford the forest itself any value, often it is only for logging. So-called minor, secondary, or nontimber forest products have been grossly undervalued and neglected. An economic assessment of one hectare of forest indicates its value for different uses: $1,000 if clear-cut for timber, $2,960 if converted to pasture, $3,184 if converted into a *Gmelina arborea* plantation for pulpwood and timber, and $6,820 if used for the extraction of fruit and latex and occasional selective logging. The exploitation of nontimber forest products can be a nonconsumptive and sustainable use of forest, and at the same time most profitable in comparison to other uses (Peters, Gentry, and Mendelsohn 1989; see also Godoy and Lubowski 1992). The hunting of wildlife for subsistence and/or commercial purposes by indigenes (traditional and acculturated), colonists, and others also needs to be carefully considered (Redford and Padoch 1992; Robinson and Redford 1991).

Other factors that need to be calculated include the environmental services provided by the forest, such as soil and moisture retention. One promising development is ecological economics, which seeks to expand the scope of neoclassical economics by integrating natural laws and natural resource constraints into analyses of costs, benefits, and values, and by considering the long term as well as the short term (Farnworth et al. 1983; Fearnside 1989c; Katzman and Cale 1990; Repetto 1987, 1992). (For a discussion of extractive industries and reserves, see Browder 1992; Bunker 1984; and Fearnside 1989d. Ehrlich and Ehrlich 1992 review the value of biodiversity.)

An important part of the solution to deforestation must be fundamental changes in the attitudes, values, and practices of the nonindigenous world, particularly the frontier mentality, materialism, and consumerism of Western society (Bodley 1990:6–7; Hvalkof 1989). Western exploitation of the Amazon has been predicated on ignorance, driven by greed, and operated for external interests rather than the benefit of locals. Environmental and social impact assessments need to be made as an integral and meaningful part of the planning, implementation, and monitoring phases of all economic development projects, instead of appealing to such assessments for public relations and damage control, usually after policy decisions have already been made and implementation begun (Fearnside 1986).

Frontier and Development

The Amazon is one of the last frontiers on planet Earth. Frontiers are peripheral to the centers of economic and political power in the world system. A frontier is generally viewed as a wilderness, unpopulated or underpopulated, unused or underused, and therefore rich in resources that are unlimited and free for anyone to exploit to make a quick profit (Dickenson 1989). Frontiers are usually rife with direct and indirect forms of violence, initially caused spontaneously by colonists, and largely beyond the control of the nation-state (Amnesty International 1992; Bodley 1990; Miller 1993). The national government gradually acquires control over the frontier through its military, administrators, missionaries, colonists, and other representatives. This government targets the frontier for integration for purposes of national security, economic development, modernization, and civilization, usually initially through missionization (Bodley 1990; Hecht and Cockburn 1989; Schmink and Wood 1992).

Most outsiders consider the indigenes on the frontier to be, variously, subhuman or barely human, wild, savage, prehistoric survivals, anachronistic, backward, primitive, simple, unsophisticated, inefficient, unproductive, lazy, wasteful, destructive, ignorant, and irrational. The conquest of the frontier rests on such racist and ethnocentric beliefs and values, as well as on their associated behavior, including missionization, warfare, administration, reservations, and other forms of direct and indirect violence. In the process of conquering and developing the frontier, social and economic justice, equity, and rights for the people of the forest are disregarded, as are the rights of future generations of humanity (Amnesty International 1992; Berwick 1992; Hecht and Cockburn 1989:193–209).

More often than not, the net effect on the indigenous societies is dispossession, displacement, depopulation, detribalization, dehumanization, demoralization, and dependence, or, at worst, ecocide, ethnocide, and genocide (Bodley 1988, 1990; Burger 1987; Hemming 1987; Miller 1993; Wolf 1982). In Brazil from 1900 to 1957, for example, the number of indigenous cultures declined through extinction from 230 to 87 (Ribeiro 1972). This horribly destructive process continued during the closing years of the twentieth century. In this respect, during 500 years Western civilization has made, morally, little progress.

Ultimately we face a matter of values: the gross failure of the West to recognize the intrinsic as well as extrinsic value of indigenes and their environment, combined with the myopic pursuits of a materialistic consumer society that considers only the benefits of resource exploitation and economic development and does not adequately assess their ecological, social, and psychological costs in both the short term and the long term (Bodley 1985; Crosby 1972; Myers 1993; Repetto 1992; Sponsel 1986; Wolf 1982). Western economic development and the consumer society are analogous to cancer—uncontrolled growth that eventually destroys the host. Unlike cancer, Western society is supposed to be rational, knowledgeable, humane, and civil. Yet it has been repeatedly demonstrated that Western society does not know how to develop Amazonia without destroying the environment and the indigenous inhabitants (Hecht and Cockburn 1989; Sponsel 1992a; Stone 1993). The loss of cultural and biological diversity, not to mention human lives, impoverishes the biosphere, humankind, and even future evolution and adaptation, given the immensity, diversity, richness, and fragility of Amazonia.

Economic development and modernization are partly rationalized as contributing to improvements in quality of life and other aspects of progress. Appell (1975:31) provides a reality check:

> Every act of development involves, of necessity, an act of destruction. This destruction—social, ecological, or both—is seldom accounted for in development projects, despite the fact that it may entail costs that far outweigh the benefits arising from the development. And I use the term development here to cover all those activities usually incorporated under such terms as economic, educational, and agricultural planning and development.

He goes on to provide a more accurate definition of development (also see Appell 1988):

> A development act is any act by an individual who is not a member of a local society that devalues or displaces the perception by the members of that society of their relationship with their natural and social world. By this definition we can include in

the act of development planning the local school teacher, the local doctor, as well as the economic, agricultural, and educational experts who work in the major centers of the developing country and who are ultimately responsible for the lower-level acts (Appell 1975:33).

THE INDIGENOUS WORLD

Clay (1989:1), who worked for many years with Cultural Survival, has observed:

Virtually all the world's tropical forests are populated, usually by indigenous peoples. In order for local, state or international interests to exploit forest resources, the rights of indigenous groups must be denied and the groups themselves displaced. It is no accident, therefore, that indigenous peoples are disappearing at an even faster rate than the tropical forests upon which they depend. Their own survival is intricately linked with that of their forests. They also represent our best first line of defense against the destruction of the forests.

Yanomami

Until recently the Yanomami were often described as the largest unacculturated indigenous society remaining in the Amazon. There are about 20,000 people in the Yanomami nation. Their territory straddles the border between the states of Brazil and Venezuela. Although archaeological research in their territory has been negligible, genetic and linguistic evidence indicates that the Yanomami have been a distinctive population for at least 2,000 years.

Although the Yanomami have experienced centuries of intermittent and diverse contact with representatives of Western society (Ferguson 1992), only in recent decades has this contact intensified to the point that Yanomami society is now threatened with extinction through the invasion of their territory first by road construction in the 1970s and then by gold miners in the 1980s. The road reduced some Yanomami to hunger, disease, beggary, alcoholism, and prostitution. Subsequently, an apparently spontaneous invasion of miners, which peaked in 1987, aggravated the situation, depleted game resources, and added mercury and other pollutants to the environment (Berwick 1992; Sponsel 1994).

In Venezuela, very near the border with Brazil, during late July of 1993, at least 16 Yanomami, including women, elderly people, children, and infants, were brutally massacred by Brazilian gold miners. Several were decapitated. Bodies were mutilated in other ways (Albert 1993). Again in Venezuela, this time in late November of 1993, at least 19 Yanomami were found dead, presumably of mercury poisoning, although details remain obscure at this writing. Thus the Columbian holocaust continues in the Amazon to this day, with the Yanomami being among the latest victims (Tierney 2000).

Yanomami have been subjects of research by some three dozen anthropologists from several countries for over a century. Yet proposals by Survival International for a Yanomami park in Brazil to protect their basic human rights and allow them gradually to adapt to Western society lacked such fundamental information as the amount of land necessary to sustain their traditional subsistence economy in the long term (i.e., carrying capacity requirements) (Fearnside 1990b; Ramos and Taylor 1979).

Decades of pressure from advocacy groups have finally, in recent years, forced the former presidents of Brazil and Venezuela to take some positive measures to protect the Yanomami. However, persistent political and economic crises in both countries, and other factors such as international economic interests, do not leave much room for optimism. The Yanomami continue to suffer and even die from the invasion of gold miners. An even greater number die from diseases, most of them preventable. To compound the tragedy of the situation, the impact of both diseases and illegal miners could be greatly reduced if the governments of Brazil and Venezuela would only assume their responsibilities toward indigenous residents and according to international agreements they have signed regarding health care and human rights (see Albert 1992; Arvelo-Jiménez and Cousins 1992; Chagnon 1992:207–246; Pallemaerts 1986; Sponsel 1979, 1981, 1993; Survival International 1991; Turner 1991). (The Yanomami are not the only indigenous society plagued by gold miners. There are more than half a million gold miners in Amazonia. The mercury they use in processing the gold is a major pollutant [Maim et al. 1990; Martinelli et al. 1988].)

Successes

Although many indigenous societies, like the Yanomami, are threatened with imminent extinction, others have avoided genocide and ethnocide, experienced a population rebound after initial depopulation by Western contact diseases, selectively accepted Western culture, and maintained their territorial integrity and ethnic identity (e.g., Hern 1992). Among such successful indigenous societies are the Shuar of Ecuador, Shipibo of Peru, Kayapó of Brazil, and Ye'kuana of Venezuela.

It is a myth that all indigenous peoples are inevitably destined to suffer extinction—biological or cultural (Bodley 1990). This is not to imply that culture is static. A major message of anthropology is about the dynamics of cultural and environmental systems in space and time. Change is inevitable, and it is what adaptation is all about (Steward 1955). Cultural extinction, however, is not inevitable, except in the minds of the so-called realists (Bodley 1990: chapter 10). But the rubric "realist" is a misnomer. The "realists" are unrealistic because they fail to confront their own involvement—at least indirect, if not direct—in change as an economic and political process, often a destructive one, induced by Western society in Amazonia and elsewhere. They also fail to recognize that conscious choices are actually made by economic and political actors to induce genocide, ethnocide, and ecocide, and they fail effectively to oppose such choices and their dire consequences.

Knowledge and Education

The Shuar (often called "Jívaro") nation of Ecuador has in large measure maintained its identity, self-determination, and territory. The Shuar have managed to control the schooling of their children by offering Western education through radio broadcasts to villages, instead of following the usual method of sending children away for most of the year to distant boarding schools, most of them run by missionaries. Radio broadcasts to villages allow children to grow up with family and community, thereby benefiting from both worlds—bicultural and bilingual education in the Western and the indigenous systems. Western education is necessary if people are to adapt to the outside world, although there is plenty of room in which to render it of more practical relevance to indigenes. Indigenous education is necessary to adapt to the indigenous world, including the forests and rivers.

Culture is socially learned and shared behavior, and therefore education is a cross-cultural universal, even though indigenous systems of education may be very different from Western ones. When children remain in their villages they continue to learn from the older members of their families and community in the indigenous system of education. This education includes the knowledge, technology, and skills needed for survival, subsistence, and adaptation in the forest and associated ecosystems. Children who are sent away from the village to boarding schools miss this indigenous education and grow up less competent in basic survival and subsistence skills than do children who remain in the village and benefit from its traditional educational system. Boarding school education is a situation that needs not only to be systematically documented but also urgently rectified as one of the main causes of ethnocide. The inherent racism and ethnocentrism of Western education in Amazonia must be challenged, while, simultaneously, indigenous culture, language, and education must be fully recognized and appreciated if these peoples and their ecosystems are to survive.

The importance of indigenous knowledge, technology, and skills is demonstrated by the fact that any colonists who have successfully settled in the forests and floodplains of Amazonia, regardless of their "racial" and cultural heritage, have survived by adopting indigenous ways. Indeed, this practice is the key to the success of the rubber tappers and other so-called *caboclos*, *ribereños*, mestizos, and criollos who live in the Amazon. These people number in the hundreds of thousands and make up a syncretic culture that emerged historically mainly in the riverine contact zone between the indigenous and Western worlds (Hecht and Cockburn 1989; Hiraoka 1985, 1989; Padoch 1988).

The significant contributions of indigenous societies to humanity are not sufficiently recognized and appreciated (Crosby 1972, 1986; Weatherford 1988). As just one example, consider manioc, or cassava, which was probably originally domesticated in the northwest Amazon. In recent centuries and decades it has been introduced throughout the tropical world from Africa to Asia to Oceania. It is the fourth most important source of energy in the tropics, providing food for humans and livestock (see Hawkes 1989; Mowat 1989).

Political Movements and Environmentalists

By far one of the more promising developments since the 1970s has been the political mobilization of indigenous communities through various regional organizations in Amazonia as well as larger associations such as the World Council of Indigenous Peoples (Bodley 1990: chapter 9, appendices D and E). In recent years this movement has even begun to be felt in the growing influence of indigenes in the United Nations. Another hopeful development is the joining of forces by rubber tappers and indigenes to call for the establishment of extractive reserves in the Brazilian Amazon (Allegretti 1990; Lutzenberger 1987; Schwartz 1989; Schwartzman 1989).

The Coordinating Body of the Indigenous Peoples' Organizations (COICA) issued a statement to environmentalists that is also relevant to ecological anthropologists. While applauding the efforts of environmentalists to conserve the Amazon forest, they express concern that indigenes not be neglected. They assert that indigenes are the original inhabitants, ecologists, and conservationists of Amazonia, and that these facts as well as their land rights and other human rights should be recognized. They call for active and effective collaboration between environmentalists and indigenes (COICA 1990).

Fortunately, there is growing recognition of the need for such collaboration by many environmentalists (Kempf 1993; McNeely and Pitt 1984; McNeely et al. 1990a, 1990b). This convergence of indigenous and environmentalist concerns appears to have been realized in Colombia, where President Barco's government in 1988 decided that the best way to conserve the forests of Amazonia was to entrust them to the indigenous peoples who depended on them for survival by officially recognizing their rights to ancestral lands (Bunyard 1989, 1993). The convergence of indigenous and environmentalist interests and political forces is a very promising development, but it is too recent to permit us to detect its ramifications (Clay 1991; COICA 1990; González 1992).

At the same time, it is troubling that some environmentalists have been rather careless in their criticisms of indigenes (e.g., Redford 1990, 1991, 1992; cf. Sponsel 1992a). Indigenes deserve special consideration, for not only are they the descendants of the original peoples of Amazonia, but in many ways they are also the ultimate artists, theologians, philosophers, scientists, librarians, engineers, and guardians of the forest. Furthermore, if anyone knows how to use natural resources sustainably, without irreversibly degrading or even completely destroying the forest ecosystem, it is most indigenous societies. Indeed, it can be argued that they have actually enhanced biodiversity through swidden cultivation, agroforestry, and other traditional practices. This is not to deny that indigenous societies have a significant impact on their forest habitat, but to recognize that their environmental impact, even cumulatively, is usually within the realm of natural disturbances such as gaps created by tree falls. This situation is in sharp contrast to the environmental impact of Western civilization in the Amazon (Sponsel 1992a). It is worth repeating that 500 years ago Amazonia was not an endangered biome, but it has increasingly become so with Western penetration, mostly within recent decades.

ANTHROPOLOGY

More than a century of anthropological research, publishing, and teaching have had surprisingly little effect in changing the colonial relationship between so-called civilization and so-called primitive peoples in frontier zones like the Amazon. The section on anthropology from the neglected but nonetheless historically important "Declaration of Barbados"—a document issued after a symposium on interethnic conflict in South America in which most participants were anthropologists from South America—provides some insight into this matter:

> Anthropology took form within and became an instrument of colonial domination, openly or surreptitiously; it has often rationalized and justified in scientific language the domination of some people by others. The discipline has continued to supply information and methods of action useful for maintaining, reaffirming, and disguising social relations of a colonial nature. Latin America has been and is no exception, and with growing frequency, we note nefarious Indian action programs and the dissemination of stereotypes and myths distorting and masking the Indian situation—all pretending to have their basis in alleged scientific anthropological research. A false awareness of this situation has led many anthropologists to adopt equivocal positions. These might be classed as the following types:
>
> 1. A scientism that negates any relationship between academic research and the future of people who form the object of the research, thus eschewing the political responsibility that the relationship contains;
> 2. A hypocrisy manifested in a rhetorical protestation based on first principles, which skillfully avoids any commitment to a concrete situation;
> 3. An opportunism that, although it may recognize the present painful situation of the Indian, at the same time rejects any possibility of transformative action by proposing the need "to do something" within the established order; this position only reaffirms and continues the system.
>
> The anthropology now required in Latin America is not that which relates to Indians as objects of study but rather that which perceives the colonial situation and commits itself to the struggle for liberation. In this context, we see anthropology providing, on the one hand, the colonized peoples with data and interpretations about both themselves and their colonizers that might be useful for their own fight for freedom and, on the other hand, redefinition of the distorted image of Indian communities extant in the national society, thereby unmasking its colonial nature and its supportive ideology (Dostal 1971:278–80).

Some additional points may be made in considering this matter. First, as I mentioned earlier, most anthropologists assume a "realist" position—that extinction of indigenes is inevitable, either biologically or through assimilation (Bodley 1990:179–207). Second, the values of cultural evolution*ism* and salvage ethnography have led most anthropologists to ignore or neglect cultural change (Fabian 1983; Gruber 1970; Pandian 1985; Sponsel 1985:95–98, 1989). Third, most anthropologists have avoided direct involvement in the change process under the fallacious pretense of preserving scientific objectivity through neutrality (Marquet 1964). Fourth, studies of cultural change and applied anthropology have never been valued by the profession as prestigious. When anthropologists have participated in the process of cultural change, it has usually been as consultants for a government or other external agents of change, perhaps with the hidden agenda of making the changes less painful and more humane for the indigenes.

A fifth point is that most anthropological field research is conceived, designed, and, after implementation, analyzed, reported, and published solely within the framework of academia. During the entire research process there is usually little, if any, consideration of the interests, priorities, problems, and issues of the local indigenous community in which the anthropologist is privileged to live and work. Rarely does the anthropologist report the results of the research to the local community. Instead, most publications are directed toward the intellectual entertainment of colleagues and students and more generally toward some sort of contribution to Western knowledge and science (Sponsel 1991, 1992b).

Sixth, except perhaps for reporting human rights abuses to appropriate government authorities, human rights organizations, and/or news media, most anthropologists are relatively powerless economically and politically, albeit not in comparison to the indigenous community. Anthropologists working in foreign countries are especially vulnerable because their visas and research permits can be readily revoked if they cause perceived problems or expose embarrassing violations of human rights (Sponsel 1990, 1991, 1992b). The anthropologist's previous research investment and continued career development naturally translate into a strong interest in maintaining access to an area for research, and this interest tends to preempt much if any involvement in the problems that confront the host community. Admittedly, dealing in the field with serious problems such as human rights can be dangerous personally for anthropologists as well as for members of the host community.

Finally, another factor that can easily become a rationale for procrastination is that the anthropologist must first understand the details and complexity of a situation before considering appropriate action. However, this factor does not prevent the design of basic research, and accordingly there is no reason why it should prevent the design of applied or advocacy research, especially if it is conducted in close collaboration with members of the host community as knowledgeable colleagues. In any field research, the anthropologist must proceed with special caution and sensitivity.

Advocacy and Human Rights

Seldom have anthropologists acted directly on behalf of the survival, rights, and other practical concerns of indigenous communities, although since the 1960s such action has progressively emerged as advocacy anthropology. It is practiced by a relatively small number of anthropologists and a few organizations such as Cultural Survival, Survival International, the International Work Group for Indigenous Affairs, Rainforest Action Network, and Rainforest Alliance (Hecht and Cockburn 1989:193–209; Miller 1993; Paine 1985; Rainforest Action Network 1990; Warry 1990; Wright 1988).

In this respect, several developments of the early 1990s are important; the Society for Applied Anthropology published a report on the relationship between human rights and the environment (Johnston 1993); the American Anthropological Association (AAA) established its Commission for Human Rights and made human rights the main theme for its 1994 annual convention (Alfredsson 1989; Sanders 1989); and the European Association of Social Anthropologists established its Network on Human Rights and Indigenous Peoples. Thus there appears to be a growing concern for human rights within the profession of anthropology.

The increased interest in human rights within the AAA would appear in part to be a natural development from its "Statement on Ethics: Principles of Professional Responsibility" (American Anthropological Association 1976:1), especially these points:

> In research, an anthropologist's paramount responsibility is to those he studies. When there is a conflict of interest, these individuals must come first. The anthropologist must do everything within his power to protect their physical, social, and psychological welfare and to honor their dignity and privacy.

In the modern world there is general agreement that all human beings and societies have certain basic rights that all nations should respect (Donnelly 1989). This international recognition of human rights has been a promising development in global politics and international law since World War II. However, there is less agreement on the specifics of human rights and on whether they should be narrowly or broadly defined. Human rights that are now part of international agreements approved by many countries include the following (also see Downing and Kushner 1988; Miller 1993):

1. The right to life and to personal integrity free from physical or psychological abuse
2. The right to a nationality
3. The right to freedom from genocide, torture, and slavery
4. The right to seek and enjoy in other countries asylum from persecution
5. The right to freedom from arbitrary arrest and imprisonment
6. The right to a fair trial in both civil and criminal matters
7. The right to freedom of movement, including the right to leave and return to one's own country
8. The right to privacy
9. The right to own property
10. The right to freedom of speech, religion, and assembly
11. The right of peoples to self-determination
12. The right to preserve culture, religion, and language
13. The right to adequate food, shelter, health care, and education (Indian Law Resource Center 1984:1–2).

Human rights offer anthropologists one very practical focus and set of priorities for a research agenda, whether their personal emphasis is on basic or applied work. For example, a little reflection will reveal that ecological anthropology and all 13 of these basic human rights are mutually relevant, at least indirectly. *The rights to life, movement, land, resources, food, shelter, health care, education, culture, language, religion, and self-determination are basic for the survival, adaptation, and welfare of indigenes in Amazonia.* Ecological anthropologists can help document, defend, and promote these needs in traditional and acculturated societies (e.g., Clay 1988:69–73; Messer 1993).

Paradigm Shift

Research in ecological anthropology in Amazonia needs to go far beyond the traditional approach; it must add and emphasize a whole new dimension—*indigenous adaptations to the new challenges of Western society's encroachment on their society and environment* (Table 1). Some of the frontiers for future research in ecological anthropology may be itemized as follows:

1. Basic considerations of territory, land, resources, nutrition, health, demography, education, language, and religion
2. Adaptations to spatial and temporal variation in natural ecosystems
3. Adaptations to Western society and the changes it causes in the indigenous society and environment
4. A more systematic, sustained, and vocal defense of the indigenous society, as well as a critique of Western society
5. Sociocultural restoration and revitalization of indigenous societies and their adaptations
6. The political as well as the economic, ecological, and sociocultural dynamics of the preceding items, including human rights issues
7. Relevant information provided directly to the leadership of indigenous communities and organizations for their own use, empowerment, and self-determination

Table 1
Paradigm Shift for Ecological Anthropology in Amazonia

Category	Past	Future
Ethics and politics	Covert	More overt and examined
Research emphasis	Knowledge as end in itself as good, i.e., basic research	Knowledge as means to an end; applied and advocacy research including systematic critique and lobby of government, missionaries, and other external change agents
Framework	Cultural evolutionism and salvage ethnography	Advocacy as well as ecology of adaptation: survival, well-being, identity, and self-determination
Environment	Static, pristine, homogeneous	Dynamic, heterogeneous, deforestation, indigenous environmental impact, historical ecology
Culture	Indigenous society as isolated, static, and pristine	Dynamic: interaction of indigenous and Western societies
Challenges	Uneven distribution and scarcity of natural resources; natural hazards	Western society and world system as hazards, in addition to natural resources and hazards
Focus	Subsistence economy as it influences culture in interplay with environment and population	Political economy and human rights; market as well as subsistence economy, economic alternatives; resource use, management, and conservation; relations with nutrition, health, and demography
Audience	Academia and Western society, including state government	Indigenous society for empowerment and enhanced adaptation

This paradigm shift does not necessarily require the abandonment of the previous concerns of ecological anthropology, but only the addition of new ones, together with a redefinition of priorities—including our priorities in terms of audience. For example, basic research in archaeology, ethnohistory, and ecological anthropology can provide valuable documentation for the land-rights claims of indigenous societies, as well as information for the anthropological profession and its general audience. It remains important to document the usually ecologically sound values, knowledge, and technology of indigenous peoples (Clay 1988; McNeely et al. 1990a, 1990b; Posey et al. 1990; Sponsel 1986, 1992a). It is important to document cases in which indigenes are influenced by and/or involved in deforestation, and also to help them develop alternative, nonconsumptive, sustainable economic activities such as the regulated ecotourism being conducted in the Manu Park in Peru (Anderson 1990b; Plotkin and Famolare 1992; Redford and Padoch 1992).

Information arising from anthropological research needs to be made available in meaningful ways directly to appropriate leaders of indigenous communities and organizations. An important element in this paradigm shift is the acknowledgment of indigenes as *colleagues* rather than simply as informants, and therefore the addition of indigenes to the team that designs, implements, reports, and uses the research (e.g., Warry 1990; Wax 1991). This is not a new idea, but it is potentially revolutionary in its consequences. The first International Congress of Ethnobiology (Posey et al. 1990:I:8), for example, published a document called *Declaration of Belém,* which, among other things relevant to ecological anthropology, recommends that:

> (1) henceforth, a substantial proportion of development aid be devoted to efforts aimed at ethnobiological inventory, conservation, and management programs;
>
> (2) mechanisms be established by which indigenous specialists are recognized as proper authorities and are consulted in all programs affecting them, their resources, and their environments . . .
>
> (4) procedures be developed to compensate native peoples for the utilization of their knowledge and their biological resources . . .
>
> (7) ethnobiologists make available the results of their research to the native peoples with whom they have worked, specially including dissemination in the native language;
>
> (8) exchange of information be promoted among indigenous and peasant peoples regarding conservation, management, and sustained utilization of resources.

A major challenge for ecological anthropologists in the future is to translate these ideas into practice. This will be accomplished by more creative and responsive research conducted in ways appropriate to the individual anthropologist and the particular situation. It will not be easy or without controversy. This paradigm shift recognizes the intrinsic as well as the extrinsic value of indigenes and environments. If this change is not made voluntarily, then it will be forced upon anthropologists by the circumstances of the increasing impact of Western society on indigenes and ecosystems and by the concerns and demands of indigenes themselves. Indeed, this sort of pressure is already being felt in many areas of the Amazon. In Venezuela, half the indigenous groups no longer welcome anthropological researchers. This shift can help promote the survival of indigenes and environments in the endangered world of Amazonia, although, of course, much more has to happen in other arenas as well. The shift will also promote ecological anthropology, among other things, through the mutual feedback between theory and practice. Obviously, ecological anthropology will not survive if its subject matter becomes extinct, except perhaps as a variant of archaeology and ethnohistory.

Perhaps the main criticism of the new paradigm is that it introduces morality and politics into science, which can remain objective only by preserving neutrality. But the myth that science is necessarily amoral and apolitical should have been dispelled long ago by the role of science in Nazi ideology and in medical experiments at death camps, and later, in another way, by the role of science, including anthropology, in the UNESCO *Statement on Race* and the UN *Declaration of Human Rights*, among other things.

The conflation of objectivity and neutrality is neither valid nor useful. Neutrality is elusive and not always desirable. A medical doctor applies science in an objective manner but is not neutral in dealing with disease and death. The persistent argument that science can only be objective by being neutral, and therefore amoral and apolitical, is either remarkably naive or purposefully deceptive. The "neutrality" many anthropologists express in the face of the continuing holocaust in the Amazon contributes, at least indirectly, to genocide, ethnocide, and ecocide. Such inaction is tantamount to complicity, even if the latter is inadvertent. If anthropology does not become more of the solution, then it will remain more of the problem in the holocaust in Amazonia. Political involvement of some kind is increasingly unavoidable for the ecological anthropologist, simply because indigenous societies and environmental concerns are increasingly political.

The proposed paradigm shift would also allow ecological anthropology to make a significant contribution as part of the broader and varied movement of radical ecology. This movement has been described by the respected environmental historian Merchant (1992:1):

> Radical ecology emerges from a sense of crisis in the industrialized world. It acts on a new perception that the domination of nature entails the domination of human beings along lines of race, class, and gender. Radical ecology confronts the illusion that people are free to exploit nature and to move in society at the expense of others, with a new consciousness of our responsibilities to the rest of nature and to other humans. It seeks a new ethic of the nurture of nature and the nurture of people. It empowers people to make changes in the world consistent with a new social vision and a new ethic.

CONCLUSIONS

To conclude this paper, I would reiterate that a paradigm shift is required in ecological anthropology to focus much more attention on the survival, well-being, identity, and self-determination of indigenous peoples as they adapt to the challenges of Western society in the contexts of political economy, human rights, and sustainable use of the unique tropical forest ecosystems of Amazonia. A new component—indigenous communities and organizations—is added to the team designing, implementing, and reporting this research, toward the end of contributing to indigenous people's information and thereby to their empowerment and self-determination. The significance and urgency of greater collaboration between indigenes and ecological anthropologists is underlined by the gravity of the deforestation crisis with all of its human, as well as biological, ramifications.

This paper was intentionally written to be provocative, but constructively so. I hope this review and its recommendations will provoke healthy individual introspection, along with collective retrospection, debate, and change in at least some, of the research and teaching being done by specialists on the anthropological aspects of the human ecology of Amazonia. And in doing so, perhaps it will make some contribution to advance indigenous causes. If there is any hope for the future of the Amazon, it lies with the descendants of the original people of the region. For millennia, these people have developed the land, generally in ways that used land and resources on a sustained basis without major, irreversible environmental degradation and destruction

(Sponsel 1992a). In Amazonia, in various ways, indigenes are to a large extent the key to environmental ethics, ecological knowledge, sustainable land and resource use and management, and the conservation of biodiversity, ecosystems, and wildlife. Anthropologists who develop more meaningful collaboration with indigenes may make some contribution toward the survival of the people and ecosystems of the increasingly endangered world of the Amazon.

References

Albert, Bruce. 1992. Indian Lands, Environmental Policy, and Military Geopolitics in the Development of the Brazilian Amazon: The Case of the Yanomami. *Development and Change* 23:35–70.

———. 1993. The Massacre of the Yanomami of Hashimu. *Folha de São Paulo* (Brazil), October 10.

Alfredsson, Gudmundur. 1989. The United Nations and the Rights of Indigenous Peoples. *Current Anthropology* 30(2):255–59.

Allegretti, M. H. 1990. Extractive Reserves: An Alternative for Reconciling Development and Environmental Conservation in Amazonia. In *Alternatives to Deforestation: Steps Toward Sustainable Use of the Amazon Rain Forest,* Anthony B. Anderson (ed.), pp. 252–64. New York: Columbia University Press.

American Anthropological Association. 1976. *Statement on Ethics: Principles of Professional Responsibility.* Washington, DC: American Anthropological Association.

Amnesty International. 1992. *Brazil, "We Are the Land": Indigenous Peoples' Struggle for Human Rights.* New York: Amnesty International.

Anderson, Anthony B. 1990. Deforestation in Amazonia: Dynamics, Causes, and Alternatives. In *Alternatives to Deforestation: Steps Toward Sustainable Use of the Amazon Rain Forest,* Anthony B. Anderson (ed.), pp. 3–23. New York: Columbia University Press.

Appell, George N. 1975. The Pernicious Effects of Development. *Fields Within Fields* 14:1–45.

———. 1988. Costing Social Change. In *The Real and Imagined Role of Culture in Development,* Michael R. Dove (ed.), pp. 271–84. Honolulu: University of Hawaii Press.

Arvelo-Jiménez, Nelly, and Andrew L. Cousins. 1992. False Promises: Venezuela Appears To Have Protected the Yanomami, But Appearances Can Be Deceiving. *Cultural Survival* 16 (1):10–13.

Barrau, Jacques. 1982. Plants and Men on the Threshold of the Twenty-First Century. *Social Science Information* 21(1):127–41.

Barrett, Suzanne W. 1980. Conservation in Amazonia. *Biological Conservation* 18:209–35.

Berwick, Dennison. 1992. *Savages: The Life and Killing of the Yanomami.* London: Hodder and Stoughton Ltd.

Bodley, John H. 1985. *Anthropology and Contemporary Human Problems.* Menlo Park, CA: Cummings.

———. 1990. *Victims of Progress.* Mountain View, CA: Mayfield Publishing Co.

Bodley, John H. (ed.). 1988. *Tribal Peoples and Development Issues: A Global Overview.* Mountain View, CA: Mayfield Publishing Co.

Browder, John O. 1992. The Limits of Extractivism. *BioScience* 42(3):174–82.

Bunker, Stephen G. 1984. Modes of Extraction, Unequal Exchange, and the Progressive Underdevelopment of an Extreme Periphery: The Brazilian Amazon 1600–1980. *American Journal of Sociology* 89(5):1017–64.

Bunyard, Peter. 1987. The Significance of the Amazon Basin for Global Climatic Equilibrium. *The Ecologist* 17 (4/5):139–41.

———. 1989. Guardians of the Forest: Indigenist Policies in the Colombian Amazon. *The Ecologist* 19(6):255–58.

Bunyard, Peter (ed.). 1993. *New Responsibilities: The Indigenous Peoples of the Colombian Amazon.* Cornwall, U.K.: Wadebridge Ecological Centre.

Burger, Julian. 1987. *Report from the Frontier: The State of the World's Indigenous Peoples.* Atlantic City, NJ: Zed Books, Ltd.

Buschbacher, Robert J. 1986. Tropical Deforestation and Pasture Development. *BioScience* 36(1):22–28.

Carneiro, Robert L. 1988. Indians of the Amazonian Forest. In *People of the Tropical Rain Forest,* Julie Sloan Denslow and Christine Padoch (eds.), pp. 73–86. Berkeley: University of California Press.

Chagnon, Napoleon A. 1992. *Yanomamo.* New York: Harcourt Brace Jovanovich College Publishers.

Clay, Jason W. 1988. *Indigenous Peoples and Tropical Forests: Models of Land Use and Management from Latin America.* Cambridge, MA: Cultural Survival, Inc.

————. 1989. Defending the Forests. *Cultural Survival Quarterly* 13(1):1.

————. 1991. Cultural Survival and Conservation: Lessons from the Past Twenty Years. In *Biodiversity: Culture, Conservation, and Ecodevelopment,* Margery L. Oldfield and Janis B. Alcorn (eds.), pp. 248–73. Boulder, CO: Westview Press.

COICA (Coordinating Body of the Indigenous Peoples' Organizations). 1990. We Are Concerned. *Orion Nature Quarterly* 9(3):36–37.

Cook, Allison G., Anthony C. Janetos, and W. Ted Hinds. 1990. Global Effects of Tropical Deforestation: Towards an Integrated Perspective. *Environmental Conservation* 17(3):201–12.

Crosby, Alfred W. 1972. *The Columbian Exchange: The Biological and Cultural Consequences of 1492.* Westport, CT: Greenwood Press.

————. 1986. *Ecological Imperialism: The Biological Expansion of Europe, 900–1900.* New York: Cambridge University Press.

Dickenson, J. P. 1989. Development in Brazilian Amazonia: Background to New Frontiers. *Revista Geográfica* 109:141–55.

Donnelly, Jack. 1989. *Universal Human Rights in Theory and Practice.* Ithaca, NY: Cornell University Press.

Dostal, W. (ed.). 1971. *The Situation of the Indian in South America.* Geneva, Switzerland: World Council of Churches.

Downing, Theodore E., and Gilbert Kushner (eds.). 1988. *Human Rights and Anthropology.* Cambridge, MA: Cultural Survival, Inc.

Eden, Michael J. 1990. *Ecology and Land Management in Amazonia.* New York: Belhaven Press.

Ehrlich, Paul R., and Anne H. Ehrlich. 1992. The Value of Biodiversity. *Ambio* 21(3):219–26.

Fabian, Johannes. 1983. *Time and the Other: How Anthropology Makes Its Object.* New York: Columbia University Press.

Farnworth, Edward G., Thomas H. Tidrick, Webb M. Smathers, Jr., and Carl E. Jordan. 1983. A Synthesis of Ecological and Economic Theory toward More Complex Valuation of Tropical Moist Forests. *International Journal of Environmental Studies* 21:11–28.

Fearnside, Philip M. 1986. Settlement in Rondonia and the Token Role of Science and Technology in Brazil's Amazonian Development Planning. *Interciencia* 11(5):229–36.

————. 1989a. Brazil's Balbina Dam: Environment Versus the Legacy of the Pharaohs in Amazonia. *Environmental Management* 13(4):401–23.

————. 1989b. The Charcoal of Carajas: A Threat to the Forests of Brazil's Eastern Amazon Region. *Ambio* 18(2):141–43.

————. 1989c. Forest Management in Amazonia: The Need for New Criteria in Evaluating Development Options. *Forest Ecology and Management* 27:61–79.

————. 1989d. Extractive Reserves in Brazilian Amazonia. *BioScience* 39(6):387–93.

————. 1990a. The Rate and Extent of Deforestation in Brazilian Amazonia. *Environmental Conservation* 17(3):213–26.

————. 1990b. Estimation of Human Carrying Capacity in Rainforest Areas. *Tree* 5(6):192–96.

Ferguson, R. Brian. 1992. A Savage Encounter: Western Contact and the Yanomami War Complex. In *War in the Tribal Zone: Expanding States and Indigenous Warfare,* R. Brian Ferguson and Neil L. Whitehead (eds.), pp. 199–227. Santa Fe, NM: School of American Research Press.

Foresta, Ronald A. 1991. *Amazon Conservation in the Age of Development: The Limits of Providence.* Gainesville, FL: University of Florida Press.

Godfrey, Brian J. 1990. Boom Towns of the Amazon. *The Geographical Review* 80(2):103–17.

Godoy, Ricardo, and Ruben Lubowski. 1992. Guidelines for the Economic Valuation of Nontimber Tropical-Forest Products. *Current Anthropology* 33(4):423–33.

Gómez-Pompa, A., T. C. Whitmore, and M. Hadley (eds.). 1991. *Rain Forest Regeneration and Management.* Park Ridge, NJ: Parthenon Publishing Group.

González, Nicanor. 1992. We Are Not Conservationists. *Cultural Survival Quarterly* 16(3):43–45.

Gribel, Rogerio. 1990. The Balbina Disaster: The Need to Ask Why? *The Ecologist* 20(4):133–35.

Grove, Richard H. 1992. Origins of Western Environmentalism. *Scientific American* 267(1):42–47.

Gruber, J. W. 1970. Ethnographic Salvage and the Shaping of Anthropology. *American Anthropologist* 72:1289–99.

Guimaraes, Roberto P. 1991. *The Ecopolitics of Development in the Third World: Politics and Environment in Brazil.* Boulder, CO: Lynne Rienner Publishers.

Hawkes, J. G. 1989. The Domestication of Roots and Tubers in the American Tropics. In *Foraging and Farming: The Evolution of Plant Exploitation,* D. R. Harris and G. C. Hillman (eds.), pp. 481–503. Boston: Unwin Hyman.

Head, Suzanne, and Robert Heinzman. 1990. *Lessons of the Forest.* San Francisco, CA: Sierra Club.

Hecht, Susanna B. 1989. The Sacred Cow in the Green Hell. *The Ecologist* 19(6):229–34.

Hecht, Susanna B., and Alexander Cockburn. 1989. *The Fate of the Forest: Developers, Destroyers and Defenders of the Amazon.* New York: Verso.

Hemming, John. 1987. *Amazon Frontier: The Defeat of the Brazilian Indians.* London: Macmillan.

Hern, Warren M. 1992. Family Planning, Amazon Style. *Natural History* 101(12):30–37.

Hiraoka, Mario. 1985. Mestizo Subsistence in Riparian Amazonia. *National Geographic Research* 1(2):236–46.

———. 1989. Agricultural Systems on the Floodplains of the Peruvian Amazon. In *Fragile Lands of Latin America: Strategies for Sustainable Development,* John O. Browder (ed.), pp. 75–101. Boulder, CO: Westview Press.

Hvalkof, Soren. 1989. The Nature of Development: Native and Settler Views in Gran Pajonal, Peruvian Amazon. *Folk* 31:125–50.

ICHI (Independent Commission on International Humanitarian Issues). 1986. *The Vanishing Forest: The Human Consequences of Deforestation.* London: Zed Books.

Indian Law Resource Center. 1984. *Indian Rights, Human Rights: Handbook for Indians on International Human Rights Complaint Procedures.* Washington, DC: Indian Law Resource Center.

Jablonski, David. 1991. Extinctions: A Paleontological Perspective. *Science* 253(5021):754–57.

Johnston, Barbara R. (ed.). 1993. *Who Pays the Price? Examining the Sociocultural Context of Environmental Crisis: A Society for Applied Anthropology Report on Human Rights and the Environment.* Oklahoma City: Society for Applied Anthropology.

Katzman, Martin T. 1975. The Brazilian Frontier in Comparative Perspective. *Comparative Studies in Society and History* 17(3):266–85.

Katzman, Martin T., and William G. Cale, Jr. 1990. Tropical Forest Preservation Using Economic Incentives. *BioScience* 40(11):827–32.

Kempf, Elizabeth. (ed.). 1993. *The Law of the Mother: Protecting Indigenous Peoples in Protected Areas.* San Francisco: Sierra Club Books.

Lugo, Ariel E. 1991. Cities in the Sustainable Development of Tropical Landscapes. *Nature Resources* 27(2):27–35.

Lugo, Ariel E., John R. Clark, and R. Dennis Child (eds.). 1987. *Ecological Development in the Humid Tropics: Guidelines for Planners.* Morrilton, Alaska: Winrock International.

Lutzenberger, Jose. 1987. Brazil's Amazonian Alliance. *The Ecologist* 17(4/5):190–91.

McNeely, Jeffrey A., Kenton R. Miller, Walter V. Reid, Russell A. Mittermeier, and Timothy B. Werner. 1990a. *Conserving the World's Biological Diversity.* Washington, DC: World Resources Institute.

———. 1990b. Strategies for Conserving Biodiversity. *Environment* 32(3):16–20, 36–40.

McNeely, Jeffrey A., and David Pitt (eds.). 1984. *Culture and Conservation: The Human Dimension in Environmental Planning.* New York: Croom and Helm.

McNeil, John R. 1986. Agriculture, Forests, and Ecological History: Brazil, 1500–1984. *Environmental History Review* 10(2):123–34.

Malm, O., C. P. Pfeiffer, C. M. M. Souza, and R. Reuter. 1990. Mercury Pollution Due to Gold Mining in the Madeira River Basin, Brazil. *Ambio* 19(1):11–15.

Margolis, M. 1977. Historical Perspectives on Frontier Agriculture as an Adaptive Strategy. *American Ethnologist* 4:42–64.

Marquet, J. 1964. Objectivity in Anthropology. *Current Anthropology* 5:47–55.

Martinelli, L. A., J. R. Ferreira, B. R. Fosberg, and R. L. Victoria. 1988. Mercury Contamination in the Amazon: A Gold Rush Consequence. *Ambio* 17(4):252–54.

Merchant, Carolyn. 1992. *Radical Ecology: The Search for a Livable World.* New York: Routledge.

Messer, Ellen. 1993. Anthropology and Human Rights. *Annual Review of Anthropology* 22:221–49.

Miller, Marc S. (ed.). 1993. *State of the Peoples: A Global Human Rights Report on Societies in Danger.* Boston: Beacon Press.

Molion, Luiz Carlos B. 1989. The Amazon Forests and Climate Stability. *The Ecologist* 19(6):211–13.

Moran, Emilio F. 1983. *The Dilemma of Amazonian Development.* Boulder, CO: Westview Press.

———. 1988. Following the Amazonian Highways. In *People of the Tropical Rain Forest,* Julie Sloan Denslow and Christine Padoch (eds.), pp. 155–62. Berkeley: University of California Press.

Mowat, Linda. 1989. *Cassava and Chicha: Bread and Beer of the Amazonian Indians.* Aylesbury, U.K.: Shire Publications.

Myers, Norman. 1992. *The Primary Source: Tropical Forests and Our Future.* New York: W. W. Norton.

Myers, Norman. (ed.). 1993. *Gaia: An Atlas of Planet Management.* Garden City, NY: Anchor Press.

Padoch, Christine. 1988. People of the Floodplain and Forest. In *People of the Tropical Rain Forest,* Julie Sloan Denslow and Christine Padoch (eds.), pp. 127–40. Berkeley: University of California Press.

Paine, Robert (ed.). 1985. *Advocacy and Anthropology.* St. Johns: University of Newfoundland Press.

Pallemaerts, Marc. 1986. Development, Conservation, and Indigenous Rights in Brazil. *Human Peace Quarterly* 8(3):374–400.

Pandian, Jacob. 1985. *Anthropology and the Western Tradition: Toward an Authentic Anthropology.* Prospect Heights, IL: Waveland Press.

Peters, Charles M., Alwyn H. Gentry, and Robert O. Mendelsohn. 1989. Valuation of an Amazonian Rainforest. *Nature* 339:655–56.

Pimentel, David, Ulrich Strachow, David A. Takacs, Hans W. Brubaker, Amy R. Dumas, John J. Meaney, John A. S. O'Neil, Douglas E. Onsi, and David B. Corzilius. 1992. Conserving Biological Diversity in Agricultural/Forestry Systems. *BioScience* 42(5):354–62.

Plotkin, Mark J. 1991. Traditional Knowledge of Medicinal Plants: The Search for New Jungle Medicines. In *The Conservation of Medicinal Plants,* Olayiwola Akerele, Vernon Heywood, and Hugh Synge (eds.), pp. 53–63. New York: Cambridge University Press.

Plotkin, Mark, and Lisa Famolare (eds.), 1992. *Sustainable Harvest and Marketing of Rain Forest Produce.* Washington, DC: Island Press.

Poelhekke, Fabio G. M. N. 1986. Fences in the Jungle: Cattle Raising and the Economic and Social Integration of the Amazon Region in Brazil. *Revista Geográfica* 104:33–43.

Posey, Darrell A., et al. (eds.). 1990. *Ethnobiology: Implications and Applications,* vols. 1–2. Proceedings of the First International Congress of Ethnobiology. Belém, Brazil: Museu Paraense Emilio Goeldi.

Rainforest Action Network. 1990. *Amazon Resource and Action Guide.* San Francisco: Rainforest Action Network.

Ramos, Alcida, and Kenneth Taylor. 1979. *The Yanomami in Brazil 1979.* Copenhagen: International Work Group for Indigenous Affairs, document 37.

Raup, David M. 1988. Diversity Crises in the Geological Past. In *Biodiversity,* E. O. Wilson and Francis M. Peter (eds.), pp. 51–57. Washington, DC: National Academy Press.

Redford, Kent H. 1990. The Ecologically Noble Savage. *Orion Nature Quarterly* 15(1):46–48.

———. 1991. The Ecologically Noble Savage. *Cultural Survival Quarterly* 9(l):41–44.

———. 1992. The Empty Forest, *BioScience* 42(6):412–22.

Redford, Kent H., and Christine Padoch (eds.). 1992. *Conservation of Neotropical Forests: Working from Traditional Resource Units.* New York: Columbia University Press.

Repetto, Robert. 1987. Creating Incentives for Sustainable Development. *Ambio* 16(2–3):94–99.

———. 1990. Deforestation in the Tropics. *Scientific American* 262(4):36–42.

———. 1992. Accounting for Environmental Assets. *Scientific American* 264(6):94–100.

Ribeiro, Darcy. 1972. *The Americas and Civilization.* New York: E. P Dutton.

Robinson, John G., and Kent H. Redford (eds.). 1991. *Neotropical Wildlife Use and Conservation.* Chicago: University of Chicago Press.

Ryan, John C. 1992. Conserving Biological Diversity. In *State of the World 1992,* Lester R. Brown (ed.), pp. 9–26. New York: W. W. Norton.

Sanders, Douglas. 1989. The U.N. Working Group on Indigenous Populations. *Human Rights Quarterly* 11:406–33.

Schmink, Marianne, and Charles H. Wood. 1992. *Contested Frontiers in Amazonia.* New York: Columbia University Press.

Schwartz, Tanya. 1989. The Brazilian Forest People's Movement. *The Ecologist* 19(6):245–47.

Schwartzman, Stephen. 1989. Extractive Reserves: The Rubber Tappers' Strategy for Sustainable Use of the Amazon Rainforest. In *Fragile Lands of Latin America: Strategies for Sustainable Development,* John O. Browder (ed.), pp. 150–65. Boulder, CO: Westview Press.

Sioli, Harald. 1987. The Effects of Deforestation in Amazonia. *The Ecologist* 17(4/5):134–38.

Smith, Nigel J. H. 1978. Agricultural Productivity Along Brazil's Transamazon Highway, *Agro-Ecosystem* 4:415–32.

Smith, Nigel J. H., and Richard Evans Schultes. 1990. Deforestation and Shrinking Crop Gene-Pools in Amazonia. *Environmental Conservation* 17(3):227–34.

Smith, Nigel J. H., J. T. Williams, Donald L. Plucknett, and Jennifer P. Talbot. 1992. *Tropical Forests and Their Crops.* Ithaca, NY: Cornell University Press.

Sponsel, Leslie E. 1979. A Note on the Urgency of Research Among the Yanomama of the Brazilian Amazon. *Review of Ethnology* 7(1–9):72.

———. 1981. Situación de los Yanomama y la civilización. *Boletín Indigenista Venezolano* 20(17):105–16.

———. 1985. Ecology, Anthropology, and Values in Amazonia. In *Cultural Values and Human Ecology in Southeast Asia,* Karl Hutterer, Terry Rambo and George Lovelace (eds.), pp. 77–122. Ann Arbor: University of Michigan Southeast Asia Studies Center.

———. 1986. Amazon Ecology and Adaptation. *Annual Review of Anthropology* 15:67–97.

———. 1989. Foraging and Farming: A Necessary Complementarity in Amazonia? In *Farmers as Hunters,* Susan Kent (ed.), pp. 37–45. New York: Cambridge University Press.

———. 1990. Does Anthropology Have Any Future? *Anthropology Newsletter* 31(3):32, 29. Washington, DC: American Anthropological Association.

———. 1991. Sobrevivirá la antropología al siglo XX? Reflexiones sobre la mutua relevancia entre indígenas y antropólogos. *Arinsana* 7(13):65–79.

———. 1992a. The Environmental History of Amazonia: Natural and Human Disturbances, and the Ecological Transition. In *Changing Tropical Forests: Historical Perspectives on Today's Challenges in Central and South America,* Harold K. Steen and Richard R Tucker (eds.), pp. 233–51. Durham, NC: Forest History Society.

———. 1992b. Information Asymmetry and the Democratization of Anthropology. *Human Organization* 51(3): 299–301.

———. 1993. The Yanomami. In *Who Pays the Price? Examining the Sociocultural Context of Environmental Crisis: A Society for Applied Anthropology Report on Human Rights and the Environment,* Barbara R. Johnston (ed.), pp. 163–72. Oklahoma City: Society for Applied Anthropology.

Steward, Julian H. 1955. *Theory of Culture Change: The Methodology of Multilinear Evolution.* Urbana: University of Illinois Press.

Stone, Roger D. 1993. *Dreams of Amazonia.* New York: Penguin Books.

Survival International. 1991. *Yanomami: Survival Campaign.* London: Survival International.

Tierney, Patrick. 2000. *Darkness in El Dorado: How Scientists and Journalists Devastated the Amazon.* New York: W. W. Norton.

Treece, Dave. 1989. The Militarization and Industrialization of Amazonia. *The Ecologist* 19(6):225–28.

Turner, Terry. 1991. Major Shift in Brazilian Yanomami Policy. *Anthropology Newsletter* 32(6):1, 46. Washington, DC: American Anthropological Association.

Warry, Wayne. 1990. Doing Unto Others: Applied Anthropology, Collaborative Research and Native Self-Determination. *Culture* 10(1):61–73.

Wax, Murray. 1991. The Ethics of Research in American Indian Communities. *American Indian Quarterly* 15(4):431–56.

Weatherford, Jack. 1988. *Indian Givers: How the Indians of the Americas Transformed the World.* New York: Fawcett Columbine.

Wilson, Edward O. 1989. Threats to Biodiversity. *Scientific American* 261(3):108–16.

———. 1992. *The Diversity of Life.* Cambridge, MA: Harvard University Press.

Wolf, Eric R. 1982. *Europe and the People without History.* Chicago: University of Chicago Press.

Wright, Robin. 1988. Anthropological Presuppositions of Indigenous Advocacy. *Annual Review of Anthropology* 17:365–90.

5

Evon Z. Vogt is a professor emeritus of anthropology at Harvard University and Honorary Curator of Middle American Ethnology at Harvard's Peabody Museum. His best-known books reflect the breadth of his research interests: Aerial Photography in Anthropological Field Research, Fieldwork among the Maya, Handbook of Middle American Indians *(with R. Wauchope, various volumes),* A Reader in Comparative Religion *(with W. A. Lessa, 3 editions),* Tortillas for the Gods, Water-Witching USA *(with R. Hyman), and* Zinacantán *(various editions).*

There is a very real sense in which the history of the Harvard-Chiapas Project reflects, in microcosm, the history of anthropology and of social science in Latin America during the same period. For that reason, this fairly extensive chronicle has implications far beyond the local situation or the academic base-institution. As long-term director of the project, Vogt shows how it grew out of the intellectual ferment of the 1950s, linked with Mexico's swelling community-development program, and integrated the then-new idea of non-Western societies as intimately conjoined with larger regional, national, and even international systems (compare Wolf, chapter 39).

Although each participant in the project made a contribution that can be appreciated on its own terms, this review of the monumental corpus of studies—some of them definitive monographs on their respective subjects—shows a degree of both integration and evolution in the overall program, with remarkable transdisciplinary collaboration as well as controversy, in what proved to be a major training ground for a generation of scholars. The project was distinctive in both scope and duration and also nicely shows how theoretic, academic, and scientific enterprises often complement more applied or participatory ventures. Readers should be aware that Chiapas is at the heart of recent demonstrations by self-styled Zapatistas who have focused the world's attention on native claims to land, justice, and social welfare (compare Collier, chapter 17).

A Retrospective View of the Harvard-Chiapas Project

Evon Z. Vogt

Without attempting to evaluate the scholarly results of thirty-five years of the Harvard Chiapas Project—these are contained in the existing and ongoing publication of many technical books and articles by the members of the project—I offer a brief retrospective look at what I consider we have accomplished in our field operations with special focus on (a) our strengths and advantages and (b) our weaknesses and difficulties.

STRENGTHS AND ADVANTAGES OF THE PROJECT

The major strengths I perceive were (1) the superb training of our students, (2) the high quality of the ethnography, (3) the first-rate research productivity, and (4) the development of long-term personal and intellectual relationships among the members of the project.

Our training program included prefield courses in Tzotzil and a seminar on selected problems and methods in Latin American ethnology; individual placement of students in Indian households in Chiapas; and field conferences in which students were expected to report on their research progress and be critiqued and advised by both the field leader and their student peers. I believe we produced better-trained stu-

Abridged, with permission of the author and publisher, from chapter 12, "Reflections," in his book *Fieldwork among the Maya: Reflections on the Harvard-Chiapas Project,* © 1990 University of New Mexico Press, Albuquerque.

dents than had previously been the case in Middle American studies. Our students (graduates and undergraduates) could get off the bus in San Cristóbal and be doing first-class, productive field ethnography within the first few days of arrival in Chiapas. The arriving students knew Spanish and as much Tzotzil as it was possible to learn in an intensive one-term course that included not only carefully prepared language materials and tapes, but experienced teachers and, whenever possible, a native Tzotzil speaker from Chiapas. They had read much of the published and unpublished ethnographic material on the Indian and Ladino cultures of highland Chiapas, and they had at least a preliminary notion of the research problem on which they would be focusing. Finally, when relevant, they brought along aerial photographs of the municipality and hamlets in which they would be working. The students who returned to Chiapas for additional seasons were even better trained and ready to engage in what I consider to have been some of the best ethnographic research in the history of anthropology.

Judging the quality of the ethnographic research an anthropologist does in another culture is always a complicated and somewhat subjective business, but some objective measures can be applied. Knowing the native language, learning and understanding the native patterns of behavior well enough to avoid serious breaches of etiquette, and having two or more observers agree to the basic correctness of ethnographic descriptions are all measures with considerable objectivity. These features of the ethnographic experience are maximized in long-range research projects in which multiple observers cope with understanding and analyzing recurring patterns of behavior in the various domains of the cultures under investigation over many successive years.

What a far cry from the traditional methods of doing ethnography when a single person (or, at most, a married couple) went out to a particular tribe or community, studied it for a year (or two, at the most) and then returned to publish their results! Those results were in turn processed into the Human Relations Area Files (and other archives of data) and became the "God's Truth" about the tribe or community. Often it was years, or decades, later before the field site was revisited, frequently by a different anthropologist, and the result was another celebrated controversy about the nature of the culture.

In our case, copies of the field data were normally deposited in the Harvard Chiapas Project Archives where they were—and still are—available to other members of the project with the understanding, of course, that proper credit be given to the original collector of the data. Each fieldworker also normally circulated manuscripts to other members of the project for comment and criticism in advance of publication. Although I sometimes find it maddening to have to revise an article or a book three or four times in response to sharp comments from my colleagues and former students, I am convinced the final products are better for it, both ethnographically and analytically (Vogt 1990:15).

For the most part, our field operations were focused on research in what the late Robert Redfield called "the little community." We were always aware of, and, indeed engaged in some field research on, Ladino culture in the city of San Cristóbal and in the various Indian ceremonial centers in which a number of Ladino families lived. We were also aware of the impact of the larger region upon the Indian communities. But the focus of the project operations was to understand the culture and the dynamics of change in Zinacantán and Chamula as towns and of the hamlets within those towns. In that respect, we managed to do a solid and perceptive job of ethnographic reporting and analysis at a level of detail never before reached in Mesoamerican studies.

The research productivity of a project is likewise somewhat subjective in a field like anthropology. One measure might be the number of Ph.D. dissertations (over twenty) and senior honors theses (more than thirty) to come out of the Chiapas Project. With respect to publication, I have never been one to simply count the number of books and articles published by an anthropologist as an operational measure of his or her productivity. We all know that some articles and some books have a much greater long-range impact on the development of anthropology than do others. Nevertheless, I have always been immensely proud of the publication record of the members of the Harvard Chiapas Project which, for what it is worth, has already published more than forty books, about 200 articles, and two novels, as well as produced two ethnographic films. For the most part, the books have been published by outstanding university presses, such as Harvard, Stanford, Texas, and Chicago, and the articles have appeared in all the mainline anthropological journals, such as the *American Anthropologist, Man, American Ethnologist, Journal of Anthropological Research*, and *Ethnology* (Vogt 1978).

Another measure of our effectiveness would be the production of professional anthropologists. We provided a field setting and intellectual community for graduate students, as well as many undergraduates, who had already selected anthropology as a career. And, as had been predicted, we also managed to recruit into anthropology a number of brilliant students who originally had a variety of other careers in mind. I calculate that of the 142 students we had doing field research in Chiapas from 1957 through 1980, 47 are now practicing, professional anthropologists, and another 17 are in closely related fields such as sociology, cognitive psychology, development economics, etc. Further, I believe history will demonstrate that the Chiapas field experience had an important educational impact (international understanding, knowledge of and respect for other cultures, and appreciation of the problems of underdeveloped countries) on the other seventy-eight who have gone on to a variety of careers. That they deeply appreciated the experience has been underscored by letters I have received from them over the years.

A fourth strength of the project is the enduring personal and intellectual relationships that have developed between fieldworkers of different generations and between anthropologists and informants/consultants, who, in the best of cases, become collaborators. A corollary of these long-term relationships is, of course, the collaboration and academic generosity that has characterized the Harvard Chiapas Project.

WEAKNESSES AND DIFFICULTIES OF THE PROJECT

The critical weaknesses and difficulties we encountered were (1) paradigm changes in anthropological research, (2) fewer new graduate students in the later stages of the project, (3) the emergence of overly dependent Indian informants, and (4) certain tensions arising from differences of concept and method among members of the project.

One of the weaknesses of the project was that we may not have responded quickly and fundamentally enough to the appearance of different anthropological paradigms during the course of our thirty-five years of research. The principal paradigms I refer to were: (a) the Marxist-inspired World-System theories that became all the rage in sociology, and, to some extent, in anthropology in the late 1960s and early 1970s; and (b) the postmodernism paradigm being promoted during the 1980s by the cultural critique school of James Clifford, George Marcus, Michael Fischer, et al.

Among the accompaniments of the counterculture movement, with its intellectual ferment and its student rebellions in Europe and North America in the 1960s and 1970s, was the appearance of a different and quite fashionable paradigm for anthropological research. Converts to this paradigm have leveled a number of criticisms at the work of the Harvard Chiapas Project. For example, W. R. Smith asserted that "society in Chiapas is a stratified regional organization, the basic feature of which, hidden under the colorful veneer of native costume and customs, is a grossly unegalitarian system of social class. The Harvard Chiapas Project has studied the region for almost two decades but has paid little attention to this overarching pattern of class and power" (1977:23) Hawkins argued that "the Hispanic center of San Cristóbal de Las Casas should be studied in relation to Zinacantán, and vice versa. Indeed, the principal criticism one can make of Vogt's impressive opus (1969, 1976) is that it is done without adequate relation to the surrounding Hispanic culture" (1984:407–8) And Hewitt de Alcantara added that

> during the roughly twenty years covered by the Harvard Chiapas Project the community as [an] object of anthropological interest had experienced a renaissance within an influential sector of American structural-functionalism, precisely at the time when a number of anthropologists within the functionalist—as well as the cultural ecologist, Marxist, and indigenista—paradigm were seriously questioning the utility of a community-study approach. (1984:58–59)

These quotes are typical examples of the critiques that faulted our project for focusing on the Tzotzil-Mayan Indian communities as a unit of study and for ignoring the Hispanic cultural and political presence during the colonial and modern periods as well as the contemporary forces of imperialistic capitalism in southeastern Mexico.

These critiques need to be placed in historical perspective. When my generation was in training in the late 1940s to engage in our first anthropological fieldwork, the focus on "community study" was in full bloom. The emphasis of my professors (Fred Eggan, Robert Redfield, Sol Tax, and W. Lloyd Warner) at the University of Chicago, and of my colleagues in social anthropology (Clyde Kluckhohn and Douglas Oliver) at Harvard was essentially on the study of social and cultural phenomena in a community or tribal unit—the Hopi Tribe of Arizona, the villages of Tepoztlán and Chan Kom in Mexico, the municipality of Panajachel in the highlands of Guatemala, Yankee City in Massachusetts, the Ramah Navaho, or the Solomon Islanders. Stemming, at least in large part, from the thinking of Radcliffe-Brown and Malinowski, all of these professors and colleagues were in some sense functionalists, or structural-functionalists, as some prefer to label this approach.

Earlier generations of anthropologists, we learned in graduate school, thought of culture as "a thing of shreds and patches" as they collected data on particular items like bows and arrows or folktales and studied how they developed or diffused from one tribe to another. But for my generation the important task of the anthropologist was to engage in field research with a view to understanding the structure and functioning of a whole community or whole tribe—these being the naturally occurring units in which most of humankind lived out their lives (Redfield 1955). Some careful attention was paid to the history of the community or tribe, especially by scholars like Eggan (1950), but this was secondary to the primary focus on understanding the community or tribe as a contemporary functioning unit.

On the larger theoretical front, most of us had studied Marx in our undergraduate courses. Marx was required reading in Social Sciences I in my college days at the University of Chicago. The Marxist approach was to be taken into consideration, but it was hardly regarded seriously as a total explanation of the complex phenomena encountered in the tribes and communities that anthropologists studied.

When I began my anthropological fieldwork I quite understandably focused on communities—the Ramah Navaho, a homesteader community in New Mexico, the *municipios* (municipalities) of Zinacantán and Chamula in the highlands of Chiapas. And I recall being particularly impressed with Tax's key article on the *municipio* as a unit of study in Guatemala (Tax 1937). Even though my colleagues and I were fully aware that each of our communities and tribes was significantly embedded in and related to the larger world, we were occasionally berated by an author who thought we should be focusing much more on at least the regional world beyond the local community (e.g., Starr 1954). It was our (largely unstated) view, however, that most anthropologists who wrote such articles had failed as field ethnographers, and that what they had to say was merely a second-class substitute for ethnographic truth of the kind we were getting with intensive fieldwork in communities and tribes.

When I initiated the Harvard Chiapas Project in the highlands of Chiapas in 1957, my research design was based on the framework of "controlled comparison" set out by Eggan in a classic paper (1954). The Chiapas highlands contained some thirty-four Tzotzil- and Tzeltal- speaking communities all derived within the past millennia from the proto-Tzotzil-Tzeltal Maya. They shared much in common but had variations that resulted, I postulated, from differences in their microecological niches, their historical experiences with the Spanish conquerors and their descendants in the colonial and modern period, and their encounters with the contemporary community development programs of the Mexican government, especially on the part of the *Instituto Nacional Indigenista* (National Indian Institute). My goal was to discover by close comparative study the crucial determinants of the processes of cultural variation and change that had occurred and were continuing among these contemporary Maya Indians in the highlands of Chiapas.

I believe in retrospect that we never ignored or overlooked the ways in which the *municipios* of Zinacantán and Chamula we studied were related to or embedded in the larger world of San Cristóbal Las Casas (the market town), of Tuxtla Gutierrez (the state capital), of Mexico City (the national capital), or of the imperialistic forces that sweep across the world. How could one ignore the ubiquitous bottles of Coca-Cola and Pepsi-Cola, the General Motors and Ford trucks, or the blaring Panasonic and Sony radios? Rather, we considered it our task to go beyond the easy work of interviewing in Spanish the government officials and business proprietors in major cities, or of reading reports and documents in the provincial or state historical archives, or of socializing with the latest group of visiting Mexican and French Marxist intellectuals in Chiapas. And, in any event, we assumed that those were tasks better done by political scientists, historians, economists, or philosophers of science. Our unique anthropological task was to describe, analyze, and understand the inner workings of the "little communities" of Zinacantán and Chamula, including their subsistence systems, their social structures, their ritual life, and their symbol systems. To do this we had to learn Tzotzil as fluently as possible, and we had to utilize the usual battery of field techniques, but especially participant observation of the flow of Indian life and the sustained interviewing of Indian informants.

Now, to be sure, Zinacantán and Chamula are not so little! Zinacantán had a population of eight thousand when we began fieldwork; it has now grown to more than twenty thousand. Chamula was about twenty-thousand strong in 1957 and now has upwards of forty-five thousand within the *municipio* boundaries, to say nothing of another fifty-five thousand in the outlying colonies established in the recent Chamula diaspora (Gossen 1983). But it was still possible to describe and analyze the social structures and cultures of these two *municipios* at a reasonably profound level of understanding.

While our focus was explicitly on the local Indian communities, there has been some useful publication since the beginning of the project on the relationships of the Tzotzil Indians to the Ladinos and to the larger world. For example, one of the first pieces of research undertaken by Barbara Metzger was to pull together all the available data on the history of Indian-Ladino relations in the highlands of Chiapas

(Metzger 1960). Colby (1966) also provided a general summary of ethnic relations in highland Chiapas, and Edel (1966) dealt with the *ejido* land reform program in Zinacantán. Frank Cancian's later books (1972, 1992) clearly deal with the larger world in which Zinacanteco maize farmers are involved. We have also had more than a dozen field studies of the Ladino culture and history of San Cristóbal (many of them unfortunately still unpublished).

We have also begun the process of detailed comparative study of Tzotzil and Tzeltal communities (Bricker 1973, 1981; Vogt 1973, 1992a, in press; McQuown and Pitt-Rivers 1970), but I do not believe these efforts will be completely successful until we have a larger corpus of solid ethnographic data on more communities than Zinacantán and Chamula.

The new paradigm that influenced the anthropological world in the 1960s and 1970s was clearly anticipated by Eric Wolf in the mid-1950s (see Wolf 1955, 1956, 1957). The new thrust came from such sources as Gunder-Frank (1967) and Wallerstein (1974, 1980) at the world-system level, and the publications of Stavenhagen (1969, 1970), Gonzalez Casanova (1969), Warman (1972, 1980), and Barta (1969, 1974) at the national-regional level in Mexico, and Adams (1970), W. R. Smith (1977), and C. A. Smith (1978) in Guatemala. All were based on the various brands of Marxist theory that direct attention to the critical role of the infrastructure and apply regional, national, or global analyses to explain what is going on in local rural communities. A balanced treatment of this general shift in paradigms on the Mexican scene is found in Hewitt de Alcantara (1984).

On the Chiapas scene the shift in paradigm influenced one of the University of Chicago students, Salovesh (1979), to urge that we look beyond the *municipio* to the region as a unit of study, and that we "study up" rather than merely focus on "studying down." He meant by these apt expressions that field ethnographers find it easier to cope with less powerful people in local communities than to study the more powerful economic and political elites of a region or country. Salovesh's interesting point is more applicable to a *municipio* like Venustiano Carranza, where he did his field research. This *municipio* has an Indian population that is concentrated in a town center rather than dispersed into a large number of scattered hamlets, as is the case in Zinacantán and Chamula. It would actually have been much easier for us to "study up" in San Cristóbal Las Casas and Tuxtla Gutierrez using only Spanish than it was for us to "study down," which required mastering Tzotzil and learning how to cope with the rigors of life—fleas, impure drinking water, monotonous food, lack of showers and toilets, sharing one room with large families—in Indian houses in remote mountain villages. I agree with Ortner's conclusion: "The attempt to view other systems from ground level is the basis, perhaps the only basis, of anthropology's distinctive contribution to the human sciences" (1984:143).

Recently, F. Cancian (1985) pointed out that while a world-system approach is useful in describing and analyzing the broad economic classes that have emerged in the modern world, a microanalysis is equally necessary in order to understand the social rank systems found in local communities. Similarly, Gossen (1986) has convincingly demonstrated how some of the central features of Tzotzil cosmology are local/regional manifestations of a set of persisting Mesoamerican ideas, whereas Collier (1989) showed how variations in the structure of Zinacanteco families reflect the vagaries of employment opportunities for them in southern Mexico.

Some of the most recent ethnographic work in highland Chiapas combines the insights and approaches of the macro- and microlevels of analysis in highly sophisticated and productive ways. In Chiapas we have, for example, the ecological analysis of G. Collier (1975), which clearly places Zinacantán in a regional context, and the work

of J. Collier (1973, 1976), which relates the legal procedures to social and political levels in Zinacantán and in the larger Ladino world of Chiapas. An even more recent
example is Gossen's study of the Chamula diaspora as the Chamulas have expanded
beyond their own *municipio* and have grown in numbers to more than one hundred
thousand; and we have had the papers of Haviland (e.g., 1986) in which detailed ethnographic data from a hamlet of Zinacantán is clearly placed in regional and national
economic and historical contexts. Indeed, Haviland argues:

> I take as given the general notion that the "cultural life" of peasant Indian commu-
> nities like Zinacantán is neither autonomous nor insulated, but rather constrained
> and shaped by the "material" forces of wider Chiapas (and Mexican) economic and
> political life. To give substance to such a perspective, to breathe into it ethnographic
> life, however, we must describe how these global or structural interconnections
> (between regional economic forces, say, and particular local social organization) are
> realized in detail. I think this is the heart of ethnography: to see how tangible, mate-
> rial forces are transformed, through the mediation of individual choice, conscious-
> ness, and understanding. (1986:4–5)

In sum, I agree that many of the recent macrolevel analyses undertaken by
anthropologists have proved to be illuminating for our understanding of the historical
and economic forces that have engulfed us all in the contemporary scene. But I would
like to make a strong case for the continuation also of the microlevel studies of the little communities of the world and for the kind of fine-grained ethnography that
emerges with full control of the indigenous language and the in-depth study of these
face-to-face communities in which most humans continue to live.

Microlevel studies of the small communities are what anthropologists do best, and
given the physical and psychological problems of field research in these communities,
anthropologists, with their driving curiosity about alien cultures and their deep motivations to escape from their own societies and enter into the life of another culture,
are the only scholars who are likely to continue this kind of research in the modern
world. Further, these microlevel studies are essential for an understanding of the
"inside view," for what is "inside the black boxes," at the local community or tribal
level. It could also be argued that most macro studies are better done by professional
historians, economists, sociologists, and political scientists who are especially trained
to cope with these problems.

The postmodernism paradigm grew, in part, out of the interpretive anthropology
of Geertz (1973, 1988) and became popular in the 1980s in theoretical writings such as
Clifford and Marcus (1986), Marcus and Fischer (1986), and Clifford (1988). Here the
view is that anthropologists have been living in a dream-world if they think they are
writing objective ethnographic descriptions of cultures based on the collection of
empirical data by the time-honored methods of participant observation and interviewing. Rather, ethnographic monographs are reports that reflect the time, place, and role
of the ethnographer in the unfolding interactions between conquerors and conquered
peoples, especially the evolving political and economic relationships between Europeans and the native peoples we study.

Perhaps the three most interesting and sensitive recent treatments of postmodernism to come to my attention have been those of Shweder and Tedlock. Shweder
(1991) has argued that there are what he calls "multiple objective worlds" on which
hard empirical data can be collected and analyzed. Tedlock (1991) makes a plea for the
co-production of ethnographic knowledge with a sensitive, two-way interaction
between the Self and the Other between the anthropologists and the natives they are
studying—as when members of the Harvard Chiapas Project have been teaching

Tzotzil-Mayas to read and write in Tzotzil since the early 1960s, and our Tzotzil colleagues have been writing texts both on their own culture and on the culture of the North Americans that they observed on journeys to the United States.

In my judgment the postmodernism paradigm had less impact on the Harvard Chiapas Project than it did on most other research enterprises in anthropology—in part because of its later arrival on the anthropological scene, in part because our field researchers were less inclined to take it seriously as the pivotal approach to our data. As I review the continuing publications of members of the Harvard Chiapas Project, I note with interest that those who chose to do their Ph.D. fieldwork elsewhere have been somewhat more influenced by postmodernism than have those who continued to work in Chiapas.

One might wonder if those of us who continue in Chiapas have merely maintained a stubborn mind-set against postmodernism as the pivotal paradigm for ethnography. Or whether, as I believe, our long-range studies with the double-checking of field data over long time periods and among quite disparate observers have convinced us that there is still hope for the writing of objective ethnographies.

A more serious weakness of the project developed in the late 1970s and 1980s: the inability of the project to recruit new graduate students to engage in the field research in Zinacantán, Chamula, and other neighboring Tzotzil *municipios*. The basic reason for this development is something I should have anticipated, but did not. Each year in my classes and seminars I conveyed to my students the enormous excitement of discovery I had during my early years in Chiapas when we knew next to nothing about the culture and were arriving for the first time in unstudied Indian hamlets. By the time the project research operations in Zinacantán and Chamula had gone on for more than twenty-five years, I began to discover that the best new graduate students readily absorbed my message and then, quite naturally, set out to find new, unstudied communities where they could be pioneers as I had been at the beginning of my project!

In a sense this trend began in the late 1960s, but the problem was exacerbated by the 1970s after even more research had been done in Chiapas.

I have nothing but admiration for students who went elsewhere and did excellent work, especially since they, in effect, followed in my footsteps. But it does make it tough for a long-term project to recruit able new graduate students who have the same inner motivations and impulses as their teachers—to go out and discover new, if not exactly virgin, territory for their Ph.D. fieldwork.

To consider overly dependent informants as a project weakness is perhaps too strong a statement. But I have become increasingly concerned about the long-range welfare of some of the Zinacantecos and Chamulas who have worked for the Chiapas Project for more than two decades. The effect of this employment, which has provided them with a reasonably steady income over the years, has been to pull them away from maize farming and other economic pursuits to the point where they no longer have the necessary stamina, knowledge, and skills to make a living in the traditional manner. But to consider this project employment in perspective, I should point out that by 1983 about 50 percent of the Zinacanteco males cultivated no corn and were making their living in a variety of other ways that had nothing to do with the project. In the case of the project informants, we have at least provided them with skills and knowledge, travel experience in the United States and learning to read and write (including touch-typing on typewriters or personal computers) in Tzotzil, as well as being able to serve as experienced informants for other anthropological projects at are initiated in Chiapas.

For some, these skills have been put to good use in their own *municipios*. Many of them are sought out to write documents for fellow Zinacantecos or Chamulas who need such assistance to borrow money from a bank, to manage time-payments on a new truck, etc. Two of them have served successful terms as *presidente municipal*; several others are now working for the Chiapas Writers' Cooperative, writing booklets about legends and history in Tzotzil and acting in one-act dramas based on traditional Tzotzil myths.

The family that has been most affected by the presence of the project is that of Romin Teratol, the first informant we employed full-time, beginning in 1959. Romin, who had disliked maize farming from the beginning, worked for the project for the ensuing eighteen years, until his death in 1976. Now his son, Shun (age thirty), who bore the brunt of the responsibility of supporting his mother and younger siblings after his father died, is a steady member of the Chiapas Writers' Cooperative. All is well, for the time being, as long as the cooperative continues to be supported with sufficient grants and donations from the United States. But should the situation change, Shun would have a difficult time adjusting to farming again, or to a manual labor job that is the fate of most Zinacantecos seeking employment outside the *municipio*.

Another form of dependence that developed was the perennial pattern of informants requesting loans of money from members of the project. For although the long-range relationships, and especially the *compadre* (personal kin) connections, we managed to develop with the Zinacantecos and Chamulas led to close rapport that greatly enhanced the quality of the ethnographic data, the multitude and magnitude of accumulated monetary debts became a problem. If a *compadre* managed to visit us and present a bottle of sugarcane liquor with all the proper etiquette, it was difficult to refuse a loan. At first these loans were minor in amount, compared to our research and fellowship grants, but they increased in magnitude and numbers as the young informants grew older and took more expensive positions in the ceremonial centers, had more children to support, and aspired to make more expensive purchases, such as chemical sprayers to kill the weeds in their fields or trucks to bring the sacks of maize home from their lowland fields.

We slowly learned more about how to collect these many loans. We discovered that the Indians themselves managed to delay payment of ordinary small loans by offering cane liquor to their creditors when they encountered them in the market in San Cristóbal or at a fiesta in the ceremonial centers, or even on the trail. Indeed, many of the small gatherings of men drinking together in these situations are debtors asking their creditors for more time to repay debts. When a Zinacanteco or Chamula reached a crisis point in his life, such as a forthcoming wedding or a cargo post coming up the following year, then the claim for repayment of loans or asking for new loans could be more insistent, even mandatory. Our fieldworkers adopted the same pattern. For example, one year when Bob Laughlin was leaving Chiapas to return to Washington, he visited all of his debtors in Zinacantán and told them that his airplane ticket home would cost ten thousand pesos and that he needed the money. He managed to collect five thousand pesos from his debtors in less than a week.

But over the long haul many of the debts were never paid, and never will be. I have a lengthy list of debts dating back to 1963, which I have given up trying to collect. For a time, the debtors either served me cane liquor when we met or tried to avoid me altogether, which was worse, especially when I was eager to talk to with them about other matters of life in Zinacantán. After a time I stopped pressing them about small debts and became more selective about the loans I made. But the requests never ceased, and I guess that we never really solved this debt problem, which is one of the inevitable facets of contact between anthropologists from the developed world working with informants in underdeveloped countries.

On a larger canvas I am often asked about the impact the Harvard Chiapas Project has had on the Tzotzil culture we were studying. Our influence has made itself felt on two levels: the immediate day-to-day relationships with the Maya families and communities and the more indirect effects stemming from our publications.

It is easy to exaggerate our day-to-day influence on the Indian cultures. For although we have been doing fieldwork involving a large number of researchers over the years, the communities we study are relatively large. Even with a field party of as many as fifteen students, we were never so conspicuous in the total Zinacanteco population of eight thousand to twenty thousand or the Chamula population of thirty thousand to one hundred thousand as a single anthropologist is in a tribe of two hundred people in the interior of Brazil. Further, we have never placed more than two fieldworkers in a hamlet, and in these cases the communities have populations of at least fifteen hundred (Vogt 1979:297). We have had an impact on selected Indian families as described above. But I doubt that our overall influence on the cultures has been nearly as significant as the countless other forces impinging on the Chiapas highlands during the last three decades: the rapid increase in population and consequent land shortage, which has led increasing numbers of Zinacantecos and Chamulas to seek a living in ways other than the traditional maize farming; the building of roads, even to remote hamlets, and the startling increase in automobiles owned by Indians; the large number of Mexican government programs to improve life in the native communities, etc.

Our publications have had some effects on the communities, although these effects are also difficult to assess. We have made it a practice to give copies of our publications (especially those that appear in Spanish or have many photographs) to our Tzotzil friends. They spend hours poring over the photographs and read selectively in the texts. Some of the books are proudly kept on household altars and brought out to show visitors. I suppose there is some small "Hawthorne effect" in this, insofar as it makes the Indians aware that they and their culture are important enough to be studied and written about. Perhaps somewhat more important are effects that stem from the reading of our books by government officials and travelers who come to visit highland Chiapas. We know that the governors have been personally handed copies of our books. One Chiapas governor promptly gave his copy of my monograph on Zinacantán to the president in Mexico City and wrote me requesting another copy. Whether any particular item of government policy was altered by what that governor (or any of the many INI officials who always received our books) read is unclear to me, except for the governor's insistence that government publications using Tzotzil words follow the orthography we were using. There is also some evidence that the establishment of the first radio station in San Cristóbal to broadcast in Tzotzil was influenced by our publications. This station might eventually have been established, but I am certain that it was put into operation years earlier than it might have been as a consequence of the governor's reading and acting upon one of the predictions in the final chapter of my monograph (Vogt 1969:611; Vogt 1979:299).

Our publications have also had some influence on tourist travel to the Chiapas highlands, but this impact is probably minuscule compared to the activities of tour companies in the United States, and more especially in France and Germany, which bring tour groups to San Cristóbal and bus them out to Chamula and Zinacantán.

On the whole the various members of the Harvard Chiapas Project have gotten along surprisingly well together considering the disparate nature of the group over the years. We have had no celebrated conflicts over which *municipio* or hamlet of Indians is whose for the purposes of field research, nor any of the usual fights over the field data we each collected in Chiapas. Many of us believe the liberty afforded students to pursue whatever line of research they wanted helped to create lifelong friendships, which were not only personally satisfying but resulted in a frequent, mutually fruitful sharing and interchange of knowledge.

The main lines of tension we had between members of the project have been twofold: the differences in concept and method between those scholars who are, or hope to be, hardheaded scientists and those who are more humanistic in their operations, and the arguments between the Marxist materialists and the symbolic structuralists.

These differences in basic concepts and methodology have not led to so much tension that the two types on the Harvard Chiapas Project have had serious difficulties in cooperating or communicating with one another. Rather, the arguments, mainly friendly, express varying modes for reaching ethnographic conclusions.

It is interesting that the Harvard Chiapas Project ran through the three decades of change in anthropological theory that were recently described by Ortner (1984): the 1960s when the major paradigms were symbolic anthropology, structuralism, and cultural ecology; the 1970s with structural Marxism and the political economy (i.e., world-systems analysis) of Wallerstein and Gunder-Frank; and the 1980s with postmodernism and the emphasis on practice (or history).

In retrospect, I believe that our coping with these various intellectual and practical complications that emerged especially in the later phases of the Chiapas Project were in the long run instructive for us all. In any event, they provided illuminating illustrations of some of the major problems faced by cultural anthropology in the past three decades.

References

Bricker, Victoria R. 1973. *Ritual Humor in Highland Chiapas.* Austin: University of Texas Press.

———. 1981. *The Indian Christ, The Indian King: The Historical Substrate of Maya Myth and Ritual.* Austin: University of Texas Press.

Cancian, Frank. 1972. *Change and Uncertainty in a Peasant Economy: The Maya Corn Farmers of Zinacantán.* Stanford: Stanford University Press.

———. 1985. "The Boundaries of Rural Stratification Systems." In *Micro and Macro Levels of Analysis in Anthropology: Issues in Theory and Research*, edited by Billie R. DeWalt and Pertti J. Pelto. Boulder, CO: Westview Press.

———. 1992. *The Decline of Community in Zinacantán: The Economy, Public Life, and Social Stratification, 1950 to 1987.* Stanford: Stanford University Press.

Clifford, James. 1988. *The Predicament of Culture: Twentieth-Century Ethnography, Literature, and Art.* Cambridge: Harvard University Press.

Clifford, James, and George Marcus. 1986. *Writing Culture.* Berkeley: University of California Press.

Colby, B. N. 1966. *Ethnic Relations in the Chiapas Highlands.* Santa Fe: Museum of New Mexico Press.

Collier, George A. 1975. *Fields of the Tzotzil: The Ecological Bases of Tradition in Highland Chiapas.* Austin: University of Texas Press.

———. 1989. "Changing Inequality in Zinacantán: The Generations of 1918 and 1942." In *Ethnographic Encounters in Southern Mesoamerica: Essays in Honor of Evon Z. Vogt, Jr.*, edited by Victoria R. Bricker and Gary H. Gossen, pp. 111–24. Austin: University of Texas Press.

Collier, Jane Fishburne. 1973. *Law and Social Change in Zinacantán.* Stanford: Stanford University Press.

———. 1976. "Political Leadership and Legal Change in Zinacantán." *Law and Society Review* II: 131–63.

Edel, Matthew D. 1966. "El Ejido en Zinacantán." In *Los Zinacantecos: Un Pueblo Tzotzil de los Altos de Chiapas*, edited by Evon Z. Vogt, pp. 163–82. Colección de Antropología Social, vol. 7. México: Instituto Nacional Indigenista.

Eggan, Fred. 1950. *Social Organization of the Western Pueblos.* Chicago: University of Chicago Press.

———. 1954. "Social Anthropology and the Method of Controlled Comparison." *American Anthropologist* 56(5):743–63.

Geertz, Clifford. 1973. *The Interpretation of Cultures.* New York: Basic Books.

———. 1988. *Works and Lives: The Anthropologist as Author.* Stanford: Stanford University Press.

Gonzalez Casanova, Pablo. 1969. *La Sociología de Explotación.* México: Siglo XXI.

Gossen, Gary H. 1983. "Una Diáspora Maya Moderna: Deplazamiento y Persisténcia Cultural de San Juan Chamula, Chiapas." *Mesoamérica* 5:253–76.

———. 1986. (ed.). *Symbol and Meaning Beyond the Closed Community: Essays in Mesoamerican Ideas.* Albany: Institute for Mesoamerican Studies, State University of New York.

Gunder-Frank, Andre. 1967. *Capitalism and Underdevelopment in Latin America.* New York: Monthly Review Press.

Haviland, John B. 1986. "Creating Ritual: Holy Week in the Lake of Thunder." Unpublished ms. Stanford: Center for Advanced Study in the Behavioral Sciences.

Hawkins, John. 1984. *Inverse Images: The Meaning of Culture, Ethnicity and Family in Postcolonial Guatemala.* Albuquerque: University of New Mexico Press.

Hewitt de Alcantara, Cynthia. 1984. *Anthropological Perspectives on Rural Mexico.* London: Routledge and Kegan Paul.

Marcus George, and Michael Fischer. 1986. *Anthropology as Cultural Critique: An Experimental Moment in the Human Sciences.* Chicago: University of Chicago Press.

McQuown, Norman A., and Julian Pitt-Rivers. 1970. *Ensayos de Antropología en la Zona Central de Chiapas.* México: Instituto Nacional Indigenista.

Metzger, Barbara. 1960. "Notes on the History of Indian-Ladino Relations in Chiapas." Unpublished ms., Harvard Chiapas Project, Peabody Museum, Harvard University.

Ortner, Sherry. 1984. "Theory in Anthropology Since the 1960s." *Comparative Studies in Society and History* 26:126–66.

Redfield, Robert. 1955. *The Little Community: Viewpoints for the Study of a Human Whole.* Chicago: University of Chicago Press.

Salovesh, Michael. 1979. "Looking Beyond the Municipio in Chiapas: Problems and Prospects in Studying Up." *Currents in Anthropology: Essays in Honor of Sol Tax*, edited by Robert Hinshaw. The Hague: Mouton.

Schweder, Richard A. 1991. *Thinking Through Cultures.* Cambridge: Harvard University Press.

Smith, Carol A. 1978. "Beyond Dependency Theory: National and Regional Patterns of Underdevelopment in Guatemala." *American Ethnologist* 5(3):574–617.

Smith, Waldemar R. 1977. *The Fiesta System and Economic Change.* New York: Columbia University Press.

Starr, Betty W. 1954. "Levels of Communal Relations." *The American Journal of Sociology* 60:125–35.

Stavenhagen, Rodolfo. 1969. *Las Clases Sociales en las Sociedades Agrárias.* México: Siglo XXI.

———. 1970. "Classes, Colonialism, and Acculturation: A System of Interethnic Relations in Mesoamerica." In *Masses in Latin America,* edited by Irving L. Horowitz. New York: Oxford University Press.

Tax, Sol. 1937. "The Municipios of the Midwestern Highlands of Guatemala." *American Anthropologist* 39(3):423–44.

Tedlock, Barbara. 1991. "Participant Observation to the Observation of Participation: The Emergence of Narrative Ethnography." *Journal of Anthropological Research* 47(1):69–94.

Vogt, Evon Z. 1969. *Zinacantán: A Maya Community in the Highlands of Chiapas.* Cambridge: Harvard University Press, Belknap Press.

———. 1973. "God and Politics in Zinacantán and Chamula." *Ethnology* 12(2):99–114.

———. 1976. *Tortillas for the Gods: A Symbolic Analysis of Zinacanteco Rituals.* Cambridge: Harvard University Press.

———. 1978. *Bibliography of the Harvard Chiapas Project: The First Twenty Years, 1957–1977.* Cambridge: Peabody Museum of Archaeology and Ethnology, Harvard University.

———. 1979. "The Harvard Chiapas Project: 1957–1975." In *Long-Term Field Research in Social Anthropology,* edited by George M. Foster, Thayer Scudder, Elizabeth Colson, and Robert V. Kemper, pp. 279–303. New York: Academic Press.

———. 1990. *The Zinacantecos of Mexico: A Modern Maya Way of Life, 2/E.* Ft. Worth: Holt, Rinehart and Winston.

———. 1992. "Cruces Indias y Bastones de Mando en Mesoamerica." In *De Palabra y Obra en el Nuevo Mundo 2: Encuentros Interétnicas,* Manuel Gutierrez Estevez, Miguel Leon-Portilla, Gary H. Gossen, and J. Jorge Klor de Alba (eds.), pp. 249–294. Madrid: Siglo XXI.

———. 1994. "On the Application of the Phylogenetic Model to the Maya." In *North American Indian Anthropology: Essays on Society and Culture,* Raymond J. DeMalt and Alfonso Ortiz (eds.), pp. 377–414. Norman: University of Oklahoma Press.

Wallerstein, Immanuel. 1974. *The Modern World-System I: Capitalist Agriculture and the Origins of the European World-Economy in the Sixteenth Century.* New York: Academic Press.

———. 1980. *The Modern World-System II: Mercantilism and the Consolidation of the European World-Economy, 1600–1750.* New York: Academic Press.

Wolf, Eric R. 1955. "Types of Latin American Peasantry: A Preliminary Discussion." *American Anthropologist* 57(3):452–71.

———. 1956. "Aspects of Group Relations in a Complex Society." *American Anthropologist* 58(6):1065–78.

———. 1957. "Closed Corporate Communities in Mesoamerica and Java." *Southwestern Journal of Anthropology* 13(1):1–18.

PART II

The Anthropological Enterprise

A basic purpose of this book is to introduce students to the nature and value of an anthropological perspective as a means of better understanding what people think and do, and why they act and think differently in various contexts. At the same time, using mainland Latin America as an array of case studies, some broad generalizations can be made about social groupings, values and attitudes, continuity and change, and other processes that must be taken into account when dealing with human behavior everywhere.

Because anthropologists are too often thought to be fossil diggers, grave robbers, or explorers, I find the term "people watchers" to be apt for those of us who focus our attention on social and cultural systems. In more didactic terms, the anthropological perspective explores various aspects of the interrelations among individuals, between individuals and the societies of which they are members, between specific data and general propositions, and between formal rules for behavior and the informal realities of workaday interaction.

ANTHROPOLOGY AS AN ACADEMIC DISCIPLINE

Although it is relatively new as an academic field of study, anthropology has flourished in the United States during most of the twentieth century as a small but vital discipline, ambitious in its having chosen nothing less than the understanding of humankind as its scope. Simultaneously the most humanistic of sciences and the most scientific of humanities, it is still the only academic field represented on the boards of the National Science Foundation (major research entity in the "hard" sciences), the Social Science Research Council (major research entity in the social sciences), and American Council of Learned Societies (major research entity in the humanities).

Such a broad perspective required that students pay attention to "the four fields": archaeology, focusing on the prehistoric (and, more recently, also historic) portions of the human experience; physical or biological anthropology, with an emphasis on the human animal in structural and biological terms from ancient times to the present; social, cultural, or sociocultural anthropology, focusing on the social and cultural aspects of human life; and linguistic anthropology, dealing with communication and the use of symbols as major features that long appeared to distinguish human beings from other animals.

There have been contrary currents within anthropology in recent years. The rapid growth of the field has afforded schools and individuals the luxury of greater specialization, so that each student is no longer expected to be competent in all of those four subdisciplines. One reaction to increased specialization among the growing numbers of anthropologists has been a movement calling for the traditional four fields to be supplemented by adding, for example, applied or practicing anthropology, the use of data and concepts beyond an academic context to influence policy, to solve practical problems, and so forth. Others would encourage us to pay more systematic attention to media or popular anthropology, efforts at more broadly disseminating our findings and attitudes among the public in extracurricular ways. There are already topical specialties such as gender studies, medical or legal anthropology, and ethnohistory, to name a few.

Those who still endorse the four-fields approach also tend to cherish the idea that anthropologists provide a holistic perspective (at least, more than do most others in the social and behavioral sciences), paying more attention to the broadest possible range of variables without prejudging what will be important in a given situation. That predominantly inductive approach contrasts dramatically with the currently fashionable emphasis on isolating a few dependent and independent variables, an approach that has scientific appeal but can result in keyhole vision.

In most of the anthropological enterprise, context is crucial: the meaning and function of any thought or action can be interpreted far more fruitfully and realistically if it is weighed in relation to who was involved, where, when, with whom, in what ways, and, insofar as it is possible to discern, why. This is always the case, whether we are dealing with a single utterance, a fight between two people, a wedding, a tool, a garment or a piece thereof, a large ceremony, a building, or, for that matter, a network of roads or the accumulation of noxious byproducts from manufacturing. Although this may seem like a truism, much that is done in the name of social science pays little attention to the many variables that are listed above as parts of context, and responses tend to be reported in aggregate ways that disallow anyone's distinguishing one individual from another. Whereas survey research forces a respondent to choose among a few pre-coded alternatives, most anthropologists prefer to allow an open-ended response, not knowing when an unexpected, very different, and telling bit of information may come to light.

ANTHROPOLOGY IN LATIN AMERICA

A major justification for compiling this book at this time is the fact that there have been many changes in the anthropological enterprise and in Latin American studies in recent years. In order to understand those intellectual currents it is helpful to review the evolution of such studies.

Precursors to Social Science

There is an abundant and varied body of information on the cultures and societies of Latin America that dates from long before anyone thought in terms of "social science," or even of "Latin America." In a sense, men and women in groups have left records of their ways of life ever since they crossed southward over what is now the Rio Grande, at least 12,000 years ago—not written records, but rather the fragmentary records that skilled archeologists can discern in tools, artifacts, and other remains, many of which were unintentionally left behind in the routine of daily living. From more recent millennia, carved and painted representations of native life still survive to give a vivid picture of patterns of dress, ornamentation, gesture, and other aspects of behavior that would otherwise be unknown. The oral tradition of most peoples—that which is often patronizingly dismissed as folklore or mythology—combines accounts of events and social processes in ways that are increasingly being substantiated, sometimes as consistent metaphor and sometimes even as historical fact. In a few limited areas, notably northern Mesoamerica, forms of writing were developed even before Europeans discovered what they arrogantly called "the New World."

Indigenismo

Early in the twentieth century, a few Latin American literati sparked the intellectual current of indigenism, something of a "noble savage" approach that exalted ancient civilizations and their descendants in the search for roots of national pride that extend beyond the then-discredited Spanish Empire. One of the ways in which nationalism was expressed during the Mexican Revolution, which preceded the Russian Revolution—as every Mexican fervently knows but many foreigners do not—was in an idealization of the pre-Columbian indigenous societies. To be sure, this does not mean that the intellectuals embraced the Indians. It is one thing to reject the bloody history of Spanish conquistadors as violent intruders in a remote, idyllic "golden age" of prehistory and quite another thing to go beyond expressions of sympathy for contemporary Indians whose dress, diet, language, and religion were totally alien. Nevertheless, a few people made a start in that direction and, although many of their contributions show little concern with methodology or with recent standards of contextual reporting, they introduced a new kind of awareness and also influenced a generation of students who shaped social anthropology.

To be sure, much of the indigenist quasi-sociological literature was based more on empathy than on understanding, just as the novels of social protest eloquently and forcefully denounced the miserable living conditions of peasants and miners although neither accurately describing nor even reflecting those conditions.

This is not to say that all *indigenistas* were armchair scholars or critics. Some were active in the Mexican Revolution and did what then passed for ethnographic fieldwork. Others in Peru were more familiar with Indian communities than most of their urban contemporaries, and they championed Indian cultures as vestiges of what they thought to be natural socialism. In short, a number of early indigenists contributed to what was then a very sparse body of scholarly literature, but even those who did not do so managed to have an impact on the developing field of anthropology if only because so few people were interested in native peoples at that time.

Early Cultural Anthropology

During the first half of the twentieth century, anthropological research in Latin America tended to emphasize archaeological excavation or attempts to identify the historical derivation of various individual cultural traits as they were encountered in Afro-Latin American enclaves or in what were then called "Hispanicized Indian" communities. The close and sustained contact with native peoples that became the hallmark of anthropology in Latin America came later, as did genuinely multidisciplinary research pioneered by the Carnegie Institution of Washington.

Recognizing major differences between many Latin American communities and those found in other parts of the world, a variety of new concepts and approaches developed, such as R. Redfield's effort to contrast "folk" and "urban" as types of societies, J. H. Steward's "levels of sociocultural integration," or S. Mintz's recognition of a rural proletariat. The pattern of restudy of a single community came to be acceptable. In some instances this involved another investigator, as in the case when O. Lewis appeared to find a very different ethos in Tepoztlán, Mexico, in contrast with what R. Redfield had found earlier. In other instances, restudy was the work of a single investigator whose successive returns to a community provided a sequential way of dealing with issues of continuity and change. Whatever shortcomings there may have been in terms of scientific paradigms, such efforts—supported by significant expansion of funding for research and a rapid growth in the number of college professors—made Latin America a major focus of attention for foreign scholars and made anthropology a dominant discipline among those who studied Latin America.

Applied or Action Anthropology

Even before many scientists came to accept that they had a moral obligation to try to put their knowledge to use in the resolution or minimization of problems, some of the countries that had large indigenous populations recognized that different cultures required their administrative approaches to be adjusted and that there was little hope of successfully incorporating their citizenry otherwise. A number of U.S. initiatives— from the Good Neighbor policy to Point Four; from the Alliance for Progress to the war on drugs; from Peace Corps to ill-fated political interventions; as well as diverse efforts to improve health, education, roads, and social welfare—all provided, for better or for worse, occasions for anthropological knowledge and concepts to be put to practical use. The Organization of American States and the United Nations, together with such institutions as World Bank, InterAmerican Development Bank, Rockefeller Foundation, and others occasionally pay attention to the grassroots concerns and human impact of projects they are considering.

In recent years, new groups have been established that focus on human rights and their abuses, especially with respect to native peoples. Those most active in Latin America include Cultural Survival, Survival International, and the International Work Group for Indigenous Affairs, each of which publishes occasional bulletins and monographs that combine ethnographic reporting with news about activities in the field.

Although it was not the case as recently as a generation ago, there is now no sharp division of labor between applied anthropology and academic anthropology with respect to Latin America. On the contrary, the same people have often achieved distinction in both kinds of work, and the publications that emerge often differ only slightly in terms of emphasis. While many consider this to be a good thing, there are still some who consider scientific objectivity to be incompatible with an ethic of social service, others who favor no change at all, and still others who scorn any effort short of violent revolution.

Other Currents

Standing on the shoulders of such giants, students who entered anthropology after the 1960s have done work that is increasingly sophisticated in many respects, some of which goes in new and exciting directions and some of which is even more penetrating than any previous efforts in terms of understanding or more humanistic in terms of revealing sentiments and motivations of the people that they study. Many of them are not reluctant, as their predecessors were, to discuss the roles that the investigator plays and to share with readers a glimpse of what fieldwork means and how it affected them.

Although no new distinctive types of studies characterize the anthropological enterprise in Latin America today, it remains a vital field of activity and inquiry. For example, the startling numbers of Protestant converts can better be understood when individual cases are examined. The ethos of traditional male dominance and the reality of many professionally active women is less paradoxical in the context of cultural meanings and alternatives. Some of the sources and impacts of local wars are vividly revealed by anthropologists who attend to insiders' views in ways that other reporters don't. The remarkable ecological adaptations of native peoples are being studied in terms of increasing production, protecting the environment, improving the quality of life, or a combination of all those things. Migrants, craftspersons, small-scale entrepreneurs, homesteaders in frontier regions, and others are being shown as vibrant human beings, independent actors whose personal decisions help to shape their nations, rather than merely as passive pawns subject to outside forces that are beyond their understanding or control. The discipline has grown and diversified so that there are few individuals who can be cited as significantly influencing the direction of Latin American anthropology in their time, even though their several contributions include excellent reports and analyses and though what they do for host populations continues to be constructive and appreciated.

In the selection of readings that follow, Kensinger's essay (chapter 6) well exemplifies the recent shift to reflexivity in ethnographic reporting, that is, showing the anthropologist as a participant rather than an anonymous "fly on the wall" as had previously been the custom. He reveals some of the often-ignored false steps that an ethnographer almost invariably makes when first confronted with the bewildering task of decoding an alien language and culture; he also shows the patient and good-natured ways in which one always hopes that the investigator and his or her informants (or subjects) interact during the long and difficult process of accommodating to and learning about each other.

In earlier days, the study of migrants and migration tended to focus on either the sending communities (why some individuals choose to leave and others don't) or on the receiving communities (how migrants adjust and adapt in new settings). More recently the process itself has come under scrutiny, with closer attention being paid to waystations; frequency of travel (so that some migrant laborers turn out to be long-term, long-distance commuters); and the changing social, political, and economic contexts in which all of this takes place. The work of Kearney (chapter 7) reflects this broader concern, placing it in an international framework that shows U.S. governmental employees as enabling accomplices even while their ostensible aim is the opposite. Kearney combines detailed ethnographic vignettes with an explication of why anthropology's traditional focus on "the other" now seems anachronistic and often inappropriate. He also shows that ethnicity is not just a means of social categorizing but is often mobilized as important to the self. His comments on the potential values of a more porous international border have been again broadened at a meeting between U.S. President Bush and Mexico's President Fox.

The traditional ethnographic focus on relatively isolated and homogeneous populations may have borne some relation to Rousseau's wishful image of the "noble savage," but the realities of workaday life in such communities rarely justifies the perpetuation of such a belief. Prins's (chapter 8) seems almost to admit that such a romantic vision was part of the motivation for his nostalgic retracing of the route that

C. Lévi-Strauss had taken and that provided the germ of what subsequently grew into modern structuralism, reshaping literary criticism more than it did anthropology. What little we do learn of the peoples revisited is a sad commentary on the impact of global civilization on tribal peoples.

Perhaps the most appropriate way to illustrate how anthropology has become recognized as pertinent even to an institution with global economic impact such as the InterAmerican Development Bank is to let an officer of that bank describe some of anthropology's contributions (Durston, chapter 9).

Language is a crucial aspect of culture, not only for communication but also for signaling identity and continuity. At a time when many of the world's languages are becoming extinct, some anthropologists have been active in their preservation, in their reinvigoration, and even in fostering their wider use. One who pioneered in such efforts (Bernard, chapter 10) explains why and how publication of previously unwritten languages is now feasible and is becoming a useful tool in sustaining the vitality of traditional cultures, especially in Latin America.

Like Kensinger (chapter 6), Ehrenreich (chapter 11) reflects the greater reflexivity and transparency in the anthropological enterprise that largely displaced an earlier implicit code of striving for scientific detachment in ethnographic reporting. He illustrates the complicated—and sometimes agonizing—ethical dilemmas of personal involvement that can arise from the relationship between an investigator and his or her key informants.

Most anthropologists who choose to be politically active speak out, often forcefully and effectively, in support of indigenous peoples and help them to interpret their cultures to the rest of the world. In one exceptional situation, however, an indigenous spokesperson had already gained a worldwide audience as winner of the Nobel Peace Prize, and an ethnographer who was familiar with the local situation felt constrained by his obligation to the truth to correct distortions in the record. Although some wonder whether Stoll's criticism of Rigoberta Menchú (chapter 12) was justified or was in poor taste, few challenge its accuracy, revealing another unorthodox part of the anthropological enterprise.

FOR FURTHER READING ON
THE ANTHROPOLOGICAL ENTERPRISE

A number of textbooks offer clear, concise, well-organized introductions to the field of anthropology, and a reader who has not taken a course on the subject would probably find any one of them helpful in defining key terms and showing how they relate to both data and concepts. Among those that have been popular with both students and faculty over successive revisions are several with the same title (*Anthropology*) by W. A. Haviland (8th ed., Harcourt, 2000), by M. Ember and C. Ember (8th ed., Allyn & Bacon, 1996), and by C. Kottak (7th ed., McGraw-Hill, 1996). Much the same can be said for books entitled *Cultural Anthropology* by those same authors and publishers, and also by S. Nanda and R. L. Warms (4th ed., Wadsworth, 2000), among others.

The controversy over the "four-fields" approach has taken place largely in articles and letters in the newsletter of the American Anthropological Association, which since the 1960s has been variously named *Fellow Newsletter*, *Anthropology Newsletter*, and *Anthropology News*. In much of Europe and elsewhere this issue is moot, with linguistics, human morphology, and archeology situated in other academic departments.

The early reciprocal importance of Latin America as a region and the North American style of anthropology is reflected in the number and variety of methodological and conceptual advances that were made there. In archeology, the fundamental importance of stratigraphy was first recognized and applied in Peru. Scholars doing fieldwork in Latin America developed most of the systems that are still used for classifying the world's languages. Ethnographers who spent longer stays there than were usual in other parts of the world recognized that individual communities could not be fully understood without reference to their regional and national linkages. The concept of peasantry, the discipline of urban studies, and the perception of migration as appropriate to anthropology—as well as the incorporation of such diverse approaches as economics and psychoanalysis—were pioneered in Latin America. U.S.-trained anthropologists whose research south of the border resulted in important contributions that affected the way anthropology is practiced and reported everywhere include A. L. Kroeber, M. Harris, R. Redfield, C. Wagley, J. H. Steward, and E. R. Wolf.

Indigenismo was perhaps more indicative of a literary movement than it was of the roots of social science in Latin America. Nevertheless, works by M. Gamio, G. Aguirre, A. Caso, and others in Mexico bridged the gap and introduced some modern social science approaches in Latin America; in Peru, the same is true of early works by H. Castro-Pozo and J. Mariátegui. A modern twist on early twentieth-century *indigenismo* is primitivism, critically examined in E. Camayo-Freixas and J. E. Gonzales (eds.), *Primitivism and Identity in Latin America* (University of Arizona Press, 2000).

The earlier studies of blacks in Latin America were largely devoted to identifying "Africanisms," styles and traits that had presumably survived despite the devastating effects of slavery; the works of M. J. Herskovits and R. Bastide predominated. In Mesoamerica and the Andes, ethnographers such as E. Parsons, S. Tax, C. Leslie, W. La Barre, and others paid attention to "Hispanicized Indians"—groups who spoke non-Western languages but also lived in settled communities, took part in Catholic rituals, handled national currency, and had a vague familiarity with law and other aspects of government. Often they wore homespun clothing of an archaic style and included some traditional elements in their own local variant of folk-Catholicism. The lasting impact of colonialism was evident in many aspects of their behavior, but they did not think of themselves as citizens of the country in which they lived, nor were they often so recognized by neighbors. The earlier image of cultures as isolated and self-contained was clearly inadequate to account for such syncretism and hybrid ways of life as are typically found there.

It was in such a setting that R. Redfield proposed the folk-urban continuum, and colleagues debated it for years (largely in the pages of the *American Anthropologist* and *Southwestern Journal of Anthropology* of the 1950s), and J. H. Steward's idea of distinguishing among levels of sociocultural integration was embraced as a convenient tool for describing and analyzing complexly layered societies. Essays by Redfield and Steward, as well as those of O. Lewis and E. R. Wolf, are revealing in this connection.

Anthropologists had long shown an almost proprietary concern for "their" people, and it was generally respected. O. Lewis's *Life in a Mexican Village* (University of Illinois Press, 1951) created a stir because he and a group of students described distrust and jealousy in the same village where R. Redfield, in *Tepoztlán: A Mexican Village* (University of Chicago, 1930), had found cordiality and warmth. Some agonized about how the observational methods of ethnography might not be scientifically rigorous to a sufficient degree, until the implication of a full generation having passed between the times of those two studies were recognized. With increasing numbers of working anthropologists and increasing interest in more topically focused research, restudies became acceptable. This was especially the case when it was the same investigator working in a community, dealing with a succession of topics or with cultural changes over time.

G. M. Foster's work in *Tzintzuntzán: Mexican Peasants in a Changing World* (Waveland, 1988) exemplified that pattern as well as an increasing willingness to be involved in nonacademic programs of applied or action anthropology. He and others consulted and worked with national governments, local groups, and both UN and nongovernmental agencies to promote social welfare, economic development, health, and education. The periodical *Human Organization* is an important source in this connection, as is G. M. Foster's *Traditional Societies and Technological Change* (2nd ed., Harper & Row 1973).

The concern for indigenous rights that has been a moral imperative for most anthropologists is well expressed in a series of books by J. H. Bodley and D. Maybury-Lewis. Periodic publications by such organizations as Cultural Survival, Survival International, and the International Work Group for Indigenous Affairs report worldwide activities that affect indigenous peoples, as outlined in more detail in Part IV of this book.

The increase of reflexivity and transparency in fieldwork of the 1960s is evidenced in many individual monographs. The intellectual impact of that shift from impersonal observer-reporter to ethnographer-participant and native-as-colleague can probably best be appreciated by comparing almost any of the books mentioned earlier with G. Berreman, *Behind Many Masks* (Society for Applied Anthropology, 1962) or with D. Maybury-Lewis, *The Savage and the Innocent* (World, 1965).

The border between the United States and Mexico was for a long period of time the only border between a superpower and a third-world country. As a result, activity across it, both licit and illicit, has attracted considerable attention from social scientists of all fields. The University of California at San Diego even has a Center for Border Studies that frequently publishes books and monographs; among them are two by M. Kearney that are pertinent in this context: *Causes and Effects of Agricultural Labor Migration from the Mixteca of Oaxaca to California* (1981) and *Human Rights and Indigenous Workers* (1992). He had earlier written about the area from which many migrant workers come in *The Winds of Ixtepeji* (Waveland, 1986).

C. Lévi-Strauss, probably the best-known anthropologist alive, has ironically done very little fieldwork, most of it in the area that Prins (chapter 8) nostalgically revisited. The French title *Tristes Tropiques* has been retained for the numerous English translations (various eds., Athenaeum, Random House, Simon & Schuster) of the unorthodox combination ethnography and travel journal that laid the groundwork for a series of interpretive volumes (largely on mythology) that sparked modern structuralism, a dynamic force more influential in literary analysis and criticism than in anthropology. See also Lévi-Strauss's *Elementary Structures of Kinship* (rev. trans., Beacon, 1969), and a series of four volumes with various titles all including the words *Science of Mythology* (trans., Harper & Row, 1969).

After having been criticized for paying too little attention to the human impact of many of their development projects, the World Bank got anthropologists involved and now publishes many reports and monographs that deal with irrigation, highways, and other public works at the grassroots level.

The value of native languages for preserving and sometimes even reinvigorating cultures is discussed in N. Hornberger (ed.), *Indigenous Literacies in the Americas* (De Gruyter, 1996) and illustrated in H. R. Bernard and J. Salinas P., *Native Ethnography* (Sage, 1989).

Ethical considerations in anthropological fieldwork have been a concern at least since the 1950s. R. L. Beals summarized *Politics of Social Research* (Aldine, 1969), G. N. Appell compiled a sampler of *Ethical Dilemmas in Anthropological Inquiry* (African Studies Association, 1978) and M. A. Rynkiewich and J. P. Spradley (eds.) anthologized several contributors in *Ethics and Anthropology* (J. Wiley & Sons, 1976). The newsletters of various professional organizations tend to carry lively discussions on this subject from time to time. A more recent view is C. Fleuhr-Lobban, *Ethics and the Profession of Anthropology* (University of Pennsylvania Press, 1991).

No one questions the general characterization of ethnic exploitation and the horrors of civil war as they were vividly portrayed in Rigoberta Menchú's supposedly autobiographical book *I, Rigoberta Menchú* (trans., Verso, 1998). D. Stoll had similarly reported on those conditions but challenged many specific details as relating to other people, in his *Rigoberta Menchú and the Story of All Poor Guatemalans* (Westview, 1999). Both views are weighed in G. Lovell, *A Beauty that Hurts: Life and Death in Guatemala* (University of Texas Press, 2001).

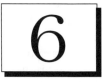

Kenneth M. Kensinger long taught at Bennington College before becoming an independent anthropologist in Roaring Springs, Pennsylvania. Unlike many anthropologists, he has devoted most of his professional career to better understanding, and helping the Cashinahua. His best-known books are The Cashinahua of Eastern Peru, The Gift of Birds: Featherwork of Native South American Peoples *(with R. E. Reina),* Marriage Practices in Lowland South America, *and* How Real People Ought to Live.

In this deceptively simple paper, the author quietly but forcefully describes the humbling and faltering process of becoming "like a child" in order to accommodate to a new language and a new sociocultural system. Such total immersion in an alien context forced earlier generations of ethnographers to confront the stark realities of cultural differences, including such fundamental aspects of life as time, relationships, what's edible and what's not, and so forth. Many spoke of fieldwork as a kind of initiation rite, a liminal state from which the anthropologist emerged as a gravely changed person, seeing the world through new eyes. But few who underwent the process were ready to admit just how ignorant they had been at the outset.

It should be stressed that, over ensuing decades of frequent close and intensive work among the Cashinahua, Kensinger not only learned to be at home with them but also they with him, resulting in a cumulative ethnographic effort that shed new light in an area that had been little known.

An Experiment in Cross-Cultural Communications

Kenneth M. Kensinger

The data obtained through ethnographic fieldwork are central to the development and testing of anthropological theory. An ethnographer's job is to observe, learn, understand, and report on the culture of a particular society. Through observation and participation, the ethnographer attempts to learn everything needed in order to behave properly in every context and the standards by which the members of the society judge their own and others' behavior to be appropriate. Thus, by its very nature, ethnographic fieldwork becomes an experiment in cross-cultural communication.

By *communication*, I mean the process of transmitting messages between individuals. Communication involves three stages: (1) the transmission of a message, verbal or nonverbal, by a sender; (2) the reception of the message; and (3) the acknowledgment of the message (feedback) by the receiver of the initial message. In order to have a satisfactory communicative act, the receiver of a message must understand the code or codes used by the sender and then be able to respond to the message if the exchange of information is to be completed.

This process can be complicated by the fact that each person is unique. No two people ever totally share the same life experiences. Thus, although they share a common linguistic or cultural code, they may not mean exactly the same thing even when they use the same words. For example, the word *marriage* may be interpreted in a variety of ways. If the person who receives a message containing the word *marriage* is a bride on her honeymoon, she responds quite differently from two people celebrating their fiftieth wedding anniversary. If a man who has just gone through a messy divorce hears the word, he is likely to respond in yet another way and so, too, a wife who feels that she is being isolated in the home and is unable to fulfill her potential as a woman. A single person may see marriage as a trap. Each person brings to the message his or her own experiences. At the same time, each person makes a guess about what the sender of the message means by the term. If the hearer knows the sender, his or her guess is likely to be more accurate.

The problem is magnified when the factors of totally different cultures and totally different languages are added to the equation. Just how difficult the problem is became painfully obvious to me during my fieldwork with the Cashinahua. When I arrived in one of their villages, I did not speak or understand a single word of their language, while they neither spoke nor understood any language I could use, and interpreters were not available.

I began by pointing at an object and asking what it was in English, Spanish, or Portuguese (the latter two being the trade languages of the area) and trying to write down what they would say. The responses were disappointing and confusing because they often seemed to sound similar, having a common base, *men*, with other syllables attached. Obviously, the Cashinahua did not understand me and I did not understand them. Some days later I learned that in Cashinahua you do not point with your finger, you point with your lower lip. This method of pointing is just as accurate as using a finger once you learn to follow from the curve of the lip to the object. In Cashinahua society, one points with a finger only when making a legal accusation, a very serious matter. The words they had given in response to my question were, "it is his finger" "his hand," "he is pointing," and so on, all of which contained the morpheme *men,* meaning "hand." Once I learned the question *hawamen* ("What is it?"),[1] I was able to collect the names of all kinds of objects, but I was not able to converse with them because I needed verbs: you cannot point at verbs, whether with your finger or your lip. More about eliciting verb forms later.

In collecting the names of objects, I became aware of sound contrasts such as *paka* (bamboo), *baka* (fish), *taka* (liver), *daka* (to rest), and *kaka* (basket). Many of the sounds used in Cashinahua are similar to those in English as in the words above. However, slight differences in sound often produce striking differences in meaning, as when I referred to a woman using the term *shanu,* which I thought meant "grandmother" or "old woman." She responded with anger because I had called her a rattlesnake (an insult sometimes used to refer to women who gossip). The correct term is very similar to *shanu;* the initial "sh" sound should have been made with the tip of the tongue turned back, thus, *xanu,* which does mean "grandmother."

Late one afternoon I was called to eat with the men. All of the men of the village had gathered, sitting in a circle around the bowls of food placed on the ground. I was a little slow responding to the invitation so that when I arrived, all the turtle shells, carved wood stools, and firewood used as seats were occupied and I was left with the option of squatting or sitting on the damp ground. I thought it would be better to use a palm leaf mat and turned to ask one of the women for one, but at the moment I could not remember the word. I knew that it was similar to the word for ribs, *pishi,* so I said in what I thought was good Cashinahua, *en pisi bikatsis ikai.* She stood up and went to get what I had requested, and I squatted down and started to eat. When two men across the circle started to smile, I turned to look for the source of their amusement just as something hit me between the shoulder blades. There was a popping sound, something wet and sticky ran down my back, and I was engulfed in a putrid cloud. Everybody started to shout *"pisi, pisi, min pisi haida"* at me. They spat and howled with glee. I had received what I had asked for, something foul smelling. The woman had gotten an egg that had been under a hen for six weeks without hatching. Because we were all contaminated by the fumes, dinner was adjourned while we went to the river for a bath. When we returned, the woman handed me a palm leaf mat and said,

"*Pisi maki, pishin*" (It isn't *pisi, pishin*). I was right; the word for "mat" is similar to "ribs." The only difference is that the final vowel of the word for "mat" is made with air passing through the nose and mouth simultaneously: that is, it is a nasalized vowel as opposed to the oral vowel, a distinction we do not use in English.

Verbs were more difficult to elicit than nouns. After various attempts to get them by acting out something—like "jumping"—without success, I found that it was easier to guess at the meaning of words used in situations involving actions. Someone would hand me a banana and say "*piwe*," or take me by the hand and lead me over to where food was being served, saying "*pinunwen*." I guessed that the *pi* might mean "to eat." They often gave added nonverbal clues, like putting food up to my mouth. Little by little, I was able to figure out the meaning of the parts of utterances. For example, in the following words based on the verb-stem *ka,* many recurrent forms are found: *kawe* (Go!), *kanunwen* (Let's go!), *enkai* (I am going), *kadiwe* (Go quickly!), *kaditanwen* (Go quickly, but return!), and *kapa* (May I go?).

Verbs were easier to elicit once I had learned the meaning and proper usage of *min hawa wai*. I had guessed that the form meant, "What are you doing?" However, when I responded to that form with a statement of what I was doing, they seemed to be insulted. When I asked a man who was sitting in his hammock, sharpening his arrows, "*Min hawa wai?*" he responded, "*En hawa maki*," the same response I got from his wife, who was grinding corn, and from his young daughter, who was playing. Several days later, I sat in my hammock watching two children playing a game of chase. One of them ran into the side of a large clay pot full of about five gallons of corn gruel. It cracked and spilled its contents onto the ground. The child's mother called out to the child, "*Min hawa wai?*" The response—"*En hawa maki*." The mother repeated her question, "*Min hawa wai?*" The child answered, "*En beyusai*" (I'm playing). (I knew this form). As I puzzled over this verbal exchange, I did not know what it all meant, but I guessed that my original hunch that "*Min hawa wai*" meant "What are you doing?" was correct.

A little later one of the men came into the house and said to me, "*Min hawa wai?*" to which I replied, "*En hawa maki*." He repeated his question, "*Min hawa wai?*" I replied, "*En disin dakai*" (I'm resting in the hammock). He whooped and laughed, running from the house only to return with his brother, who repeated the sequence: "*Min hawa wai?*" "*En hawa maki*." "*Min hawa wai?*" "*En disin dakai*." His response was the same, and more men were called to repeat the sequence. I was mystified, but they were happy. I had learned something important. But what?

Some time later, I realized what it all meant. "*Min hawa wai*" does mean "What are you doing?" and "*En hawa maki*" means "I'm not doing anything." However, the significance does not lie in the meaning of the words, but in the sequence and the cultural rules. The question is not asked in order to find out what a person is doing. One's actions are visible to the questioner. Rather, it is a query about one's mood. If the response to the initial question is a statement of one's activity, the implication is that the individual is busy and does not wish to be bothered or is not in the mood to be sociable. A response of "*En hawa maki*" (I'm not doing anything) implies "Pull up a turtle shell, sit down, and talk." This sequence is not unlike our "How are you," which usually calls for a response of "Fine, thank you. And how are you?" In general, only a doctor is looking for a detailed and accurate answer to "How are you?"

In the early months and years of my studies among the Cashinahua, I spent a great deal of time working with the men. This was necessary because I could determine the meaning of a word only if I knew the context to which it referred. Therefore, many of my days were spent hunting with one of the men. We would leave the village at daybreak and dogtrot into the jungle. The pace would slacken slightly once we were out of the area where the sounds of village life could be heard, but we would stop only to examine spoor or to prepare to stalk an animal. Occasionally my companion would pause to point out herbs used to treat illness or indications of the presence of *yushin* (spirits). He rarely spoke, and then only in a low voice or whisper. Unless we were lucky and killed a large animal like a tapir, deer or peccary, or several smaller animals, we would hunt all day, returning to the village by three o'clock in the afternoon. After a bath in the river, I would have my companion tell me about the day's events. My assumption was that since we had experienced the same things, I would be able to make more accurate guesses about the meaning of sentences. I was only partly right. His rehearsal of the facts did provide me with many sentences for which I could provide translations. However, while I remembered the difficulties of the hunt, the thickets of sharply barbed bamboo, the thorns, and the almost impenetrable jungle as well as the excitement of the chase, he went into great detail about the signs of animal movements, or spirit activities, or about a tree with nearly ripened fruit. He had seen and would speculate about the amount of honey in the hollow-tree home of stingless black bees. It was years before I learned the mechanics of moving quietly through the forest and began to see the jungle through Cashinahua eyes.

My participation in the hunt resulted in my learning an important lesson in nonverbal communication. Companions in a hunt share the results, and my success produced problems. I often returned with more than ten pounds of meat. With no refrigeration, I was only able to use part of the meat, so I followed the example of my companion and generously gave most of it away. In order to show no partiality, I carefully distributed meat to every family, giving it to the women of each household. I was unaware that the distribution of meat within the village follows strict rules. A man gives meat to his wife or wives, to his mother, his mother-in-law, his sisters, or his grandmothers. Meat given to other women constitutes a proposition and with the acceptance of the gift, the woman obligates herself to arrange for a sexual exchange. My generosity resulted in increasing friendliness from the women but suspicion, anger, and hostility from their husbands. The problem was resolved when the headman started to address me as "son," and his son (now my brother) told me to whom we could give meat without arousing suspicions.

Increased understanding of their language and culture led to an increased degree of communication with the Cashinahua. After several years, I found myself thinking and even dreaming in the language. Behavior patterns that had once been studiously performed became second nature. However, no matter how fluent I became in the language, I could never become a Cashinahua because I carried in my head a totally different cultural background that I could never fully communicate to them. Good communication was possible, perfect communication was not.

Perfect communication is only theoretically possible in a situation in which the parties are identical in every respect; something that never happens. Good communication does not demand that the parties share the same values, beliefs, experiences, etc. Rather, it results from a desire for mutual understanding based on mutual respect, and a lot of hard work.

Note

[1] The *men* in this utterance does not mean "hand," but rather indicates a question.

Michael Kearney teaches anthropology at University of California (Riverside). His major books include World View, The Winds of Ixtepeji: World View and Society in a Zapotec Town, Human Rights and Indigenous Workers *(with C. Nagengast and R. Stavenhagen), and* Reconceptualizing the Peasantry.

It used to be easy to say that "Latin America is that area south of the Rio Grande . . . ," but political borders rarely coincide with cultural ones, and that particular border has come dramatically into question in recent years. At a time when "globalization" is taken for granted as a general trend around the world, accelerated in some areas by specifically North American forces commonly derided as "Coca Colonization," it is somewhat ironic that large areas of the United States have simultaneously become dramatically Latinized.

Kearney's early fieldwork in southern Mexico forced him to recognize the immediacy of informal transnational linkages, and his subsequent work along the border may surprise some North Americans but fits nicely with proposals from Mexico's President Fox. This paper illustrates how an anthropological perspective can make new sense out of what look like faulty institutions, by revealing functions that run counter to what they are supposed to be (see also Aron-Schaar, chapter 32). It also underscores the practical relevance of social research when the investigator does not shy away from some thorny issues of status and power.

Borders and Boundaries of State and Self at the End of Empire

Michael Kearney

Do not ask who I am and do not ask me to remain the same: leave it to our bureaucrats and our police to see that our papers are in order. At least spare us their morality when we write.

—Michel Foucault, *The Archaeology of Knowledge*

The geopolitical wound called "the border" cannot stop the cultural undercurrents. The "artistic border" is artificial. It shouldn't be there, and it is up to us to erase it.

—Guillermo Gómez Peña, "A New Artistic Continent"

INTRODUCTION

This paper was stimulated by my ethnographic work on the United States/Mexico border. The immediate problem I encountered there was that of representing social and cultural forms of an indigenous people—namely, Mixtecs—who migrated in large and increasing numbers into this border area from their homeland, in the state of Oaxaca in southern Mexico. This task of ethnographic representation is made complex not only by the spatial extension of the Mixtec community into the border area but by the ambiguous nature of the border area itself, which has become a region where the culture, society, and state of the United States encounter the Third World in a zone of contested space, capital, and meanings. Furthermore, the problem of ethnographic representation of this community in this border region is made yet more problematic by a corresponding decomposition of what now can be seen as the "classic" epistemological relationship between the anthropological Self and the ethnographic Other. In other words, exploration of these themes is prompted by the need not only to make sense of the ethnographic subject that presents itself in this complex field, but also of the changing boundaries and constitution of anthropology itself, that is, its sociology, epistemology, and practice.

When I speak of anthropology as a "scientific field," I do so in Bourdieu's sense of scientific field not only as a field of study but also as a field of struggle—a point to which I shall return below (Bourdieu 1981). Also, with respect to terminology, I find it useful to distinguish between "boundaries" as legal spatial delimitations of nations (that is, boundary lines) as opposed to the "borders" of nations, which are geographic and cultural zones or spaces (that is, "border areas" that can vary independently of formal boundaries). The issues with which I am concerned here have to do with the lack of correspondence between the borders and boundaries of the nation-state.

Let me turn now to the question of changing boundaries and borders of the United States, which, due to the exigencies of exposition, I break into two periods, the first of which I call the modern, and which corresponds to the growth and maturation of the United States as a "colonial" nation-state.

THE COLONIAL NATION-STATE

The nation-state was a necessary form for the development of capitalism in the modern era. As Corrigan and Sayer have shown, the maturation of modern capitalism necessarily entailed the formation of the nation-state as a cultural revolution, which over the course of several centuries put in place not only the bureaucratic and intellectual but also the more general popular forms and practices that in their totality constituted the conditions for the development of capitalist society (Corrigan and Sayer 1985). Apart from these internal conditions, the modern nation-state is the product of two processes of global differentiation, one being the tension with other emergent absolute states, the second being the tension between the nation-state and its dependencies. Here, we are primarily concerned with the latter relationship.[1]

The modern period is thus coterminous with "the Age of Empire," in which the colonial powers, constituted as nation-states, are clearly differentiated from their colonies (Hobsbawm 1987). This external oppositional dimension of the modern nation-state was predicated on distinct spatial separation between it and its colonies, a structural feature that is integral to what elsewhere I call "the Colonial Situation," and that provides the basis for the cognitive distinction between the colonizer and the colonized. Just as the task of the state is to consolidate internal social differentiation as national unity, so must nationalism as a force in modern history effect the differentiation of peoples on a global scale. Globally, the modern age was thus coterminous with the power of capitalism to differentiate the world into developed, underdeveloped, and "de-developed" regions. And in this modern differentiation it is the nation-state that emerges as the supreme unit of order, a social, cultural, and political form that, as Anderson shows, is distinctive in having absolute geopolitical and social boundaries inscribed on territory and on persons, demarcating space and those who are members from those who are not (Anderson 1983). Thus, whereas absolute states achieved the consolidation of absolute power, it remained for the modern nation-state to construct absolute boundaries.

Since its inception, and until boundaries became fixed in the mid-nineteenth century, the United States enjoyed considerable territorial expansion at the expense of Mexico. During its period of territorial growth the United States rolled back Mexican society and sovereignty to its present southwestern border. During a period when passports were devised and required for entry from Europe and Asia, movement across the southwestern boundary was essentially unrestricted. Indeed, this lack of concern with demarcation of the border was a sign of its de facto categorical absoluteness born of military conquest: Anglo was "unitedstatesian" and Mexican was Other.[2]

A firm distinction between Anglo Self and Mexican Other was but one instance of a global system of distinction that was the fundamental structure of what I above refer to as the "Colonial Situation," which reached its apogee in the early twentieth century. This spatial and categorical distinction, this separation of a Western nation from its colonies, provided the poles along which an axis of extraction and accumulation was constructed such that net economic value flows from the latter to the former. It was onto this spatial and economic distinction that social and cultural differences were inscribed. Thus the structuring of the colonial situation depended on the spatial separation of peripheral production and extraction of value and knowledge as raw materials from their consumption and transformation in metropoles such that they could be reinvested back into the colonial project. It was within this systematic asymmetry that anthropology as a distinctive discipline assumed its "classic" modern form as an intellectual enterprise structured by and structuring the lineaments of the colonial situation, such that the collection and consumption of anthropological knowledge became a permutation of the extraction, transformation, and consumption of economic capital.[3]

As absolute boundaries become necessary for the construction of the modern nation-state, so does nationalism,[4] for a nationalism without borders and boundaries that can be defended and enlarged is impossible, as Anderson might say, "to imagine" (Anderson 1983). It is deemed "natural" therefore, that nationalism is the preeminent totemic sensibility of the modern age. And in no other nation did this distinctly modern sentiment have more power to offset other bases of collective identities than in the United States, with its power to dissolve the ethnicity of its immigrant masses and to reconstruct it as "American" and as, inter alia, race and racism.

A fundamental project of the state—the inward task of the modern nation-state—is to elaborate and resolve the contradiction of differentiation and unity. The disciplinary power of the state must facilitate the reproduction of social and cultural differentiation within the nation while at the same time perpetuating national unity. Thus, beyond the regulation (licensing, censusing, taxing) of the trades of the butcher, the baker, and the candlestick maker as they constitute a Durkheimian organic unity, the state must also ensure the reproduction of difference as social inequality, and this it does in large part by assuming responsibility for public education whereby it establishes a system of "good" and "poor" schools, and then "grades"—in both senses of the term—students such that they come to occupy the same social class position as their parents. We will return to this theme.

THE NATION-STATE AND ITS BORDERS
IN THE AGE OF TRANSNATIONALISM

What I propose—and this proposition is suggested by the ethnography of the border area—is that history has passed beyond the "modern age" as I have just described it with reference to boundaries of the nation-state as firm, absolute distinctions between national We and distant They and, by the same token, between anthropological Self and ethnographic Other—between those who write and those who are written about. Whereas the modern phase was socially and culturally predicated on the nation-state, the present state of the nation-state is aptly characterized as "transnational."

"Transnationalism" implies a blurring or, perhaps better said, a reordering of the binary cultural, social, and epistemological distinctions of the modern period—and as I'm using it here, it has two meanings. One is the conventional one having to do with forms of organization and identity that are not constrained by national boundaries, such as the transnational corporation. But I also wish to load onto the term the meaning of transnational as postnational in the sense that history and anthropology have entered a postnational age.

The Border: Scene I

Cañon Zapata is a deep north-south cleft between hills on the U.S.-Mexico Border where it runs along the edge of the city of Tijuana. Most of the canyon is on the California side of the border, but there are no tangible boundary markers except for an old monument and the broken strands of a wire fence on the hills to the east and west of the canyon. Down in the canyon there are no markers or wire at all. Up the canyon, well into the unitedstatesian side are small food stalls made of scrap wood, covered with old sheet metal or boards for a little shade, and equipped with butane or wood stoves. Venders of second-hand clothing and shoes have also set up their stalls. The canyon comes to life around three o'clock every afternoon as hundreds of people start to congregate, waiting until the right time to make an attempt to get to "the other side." They are of course already on the other side. What they must do, though, is get beyond agents of the Border Patrol who are on the hills overlooking the branches of the canyon above the town of San Ysidro. About a mile to the west of the canyon there is a large unitedstatesian customs facility which sits on the line between San Ysidro and Tijuana. This is the most heavily trafficked official international border crossing in the world. Cañon Zapata is certainly one of the most, possibly the most, heavily trafficked unofficial crossings.

As the afternoon shadows move into the canyon the migrants who have assembled eat their last taco, take a final swig of soda pop or beer, and possibly put on new shoes or a jacket that they have just bought. Then in groups of five or maybe ten or twelve, they start to head out, up the canyon, and into its side branches, They walk in single file, each little group led by its *coyote,* the smuggler that they are paying to lead them to a safe point and to perhaps arrange for transportation to somewhere yet farther north. Or perhaps there are experienced migrants in the group who have made the trip many times and no longer need the expensive services of a smuggler.

When the sun is low, Border Patrol agents, the *Migra,* are silhouetted on the hills above the canyon. They scurry about in jeeps and on motorcycles and horses, responding to the probings of different groups, some of which are serving as diversions to draw the patrols away from others. The *Migra* almost never come down into the base of the canyon where the migrants congregate, nor does the unitedstatesian government make any attempt to fence off or otherwise close or occupy this staging area.[5]

This same basic scenario is enacted at other sites where the border runs along the edge of Tijuana as well as many other places on its nearly 2,000 mile length between Mexico and the United States.

The Border: Scene II

A few days before Christmas, 1987, several green Border Patrol vehicles filled with agents swoop down into Cañon Zapata. The *ilegales* apprehensively move back towards the boundary line. Border Patrol agents pile out of the vehicles. One is dressed as Santa Claus and has a large bag of presents. The agents spread food and soft drinks on the hoods of their vehicles, and call to the *ilegales* to come and get them. The Santa Claus hands out presents and a "Christmas party" ensues. Then the *Migra* get back into their vehicles and drive away as the migrants prepare to attempt crossing "to the other side" by avoiding surveillance and capture.[6]

The Border: Scene III

It is a moonless night. Two sleepy Border Patrol agents sit in an observation post that resembles a gun emplacement. The post is just on the unitedstatesian side of the boundary line where it runs through hills near the Pacific Ocean. Just behind the observation post is a wire mesh fence that runs along the international boundary on the edge of Tijuana. The fence is old, bent, and festooned with rags and scraps of paper impaled on it by the wind. It has many gaping holes through which "illegal" border crossers come and go almost as freely as the wind. The Border Patrol agents scan the hills around them and the fields below them with infrared nightscopes. Peering through these devices they see dozens of human forms, bent over, clutching small bags, parcels and sometimes children, silently hurrying along well worn trails through the dry brush. Two days earlier, some eighty miles to the northeast, one of the agents had been sitting on a hilltop with binoculars scanning trails a two-day walk from the national boundary line.[7]

The nightscopes are but one component in a sophisticated high-tech surveillance program that also includes motion sensors, searchlights, television cameras, helicopters, spotter planes, and patrols in various kinds of boats and ground vehicles, all coordinated by computers and radio communication. The annual budget for this sector of the Border Patrol is millions of dollars, but no money has been allocated in recent years to repair the fence.

The basic thesis concerning transnationalism that I wish to advance is that it corresponds to the political economic and sociocultural ordering of late capitalism (Mandel 1975). Entailed in these new forms is a reordering of the capitalist nation-state. As a global phenomenon the beginning of transnationalism corresponds to a historic moment that might be characterized as "End of Empire."[8] This characterization is most literally apparent for Great Britain at the end of World War II, emerging as it did among the losers, or certainly as having lost its empire. Thus, the middle decades of the twentieth century saw the dismantling of the formal European colonial system and, with it, what had been in effect categorical distinctions between the Western nation-states, and between them and their colonies.

The modern age, the age of imperialism, was driven (according to Lenin, anyway) by the exporting of surplus capital from developed to underdeveloped areas of the world with subsequent destruction of noncapitalist economies and societies, processes that created wage labor, much of which was absorbed in these peripheral areas. The current transnational age is, however, characterized by a gross incapacity of peripheral economies to absorb the labor that is created in the periphery, with the result that it inexorably "flows" to the cores of the global capitalist economy (Kearney 1986). This "peripheralization of the core" is now well advanced in Great Britain, whose colonial chickens have come home to roost, so to speak (Sassen-Koob 1982). The same is also true of former European colonial powers, which are being "overwhelmed" by former colonial subjects who are now "guest workers": Algerians in France, Turks in Germany, Guatemalans and Africans in Spain, and so on.[9]

A similar process is well underway in the decline of the unitedstatesian empire, which is experiencing a comparable dissolution in the spatial and symbolic distinction between itself and its dependencies. Nowhere is this more apparent than in the southwestern border area and in the cities of this zone, which dramatically manifest a transnationalization of identity in the culture, economics, and politics of late capitalism.

In recent years the border area has, after a century of quiescence since the Mexican-American War of 1848, again become contested terrain. Now, however, it is not territory per se that is being contested, but personal identities and movements of persons, and cultural and political hegemony of peoples.[10] A Latino reconquest of much of the northern side has already taken place. But this Latino cultural and demographic ascendancy is not congruent with jural territorial realities that are still shaped by continued unitedstatesian police power. This incongruity of cultural and political spaces makes of the border area, aptly named as such, an ambiguous zone. It is in this border area that identities are assigned and taken, withheld and rejected. The state seeks a monopoly on the power to assign identities to those who enter this space. It stamps or refuses to stamp passports and papers, which are extensions of the person of the traveler who is "required" to pass through official ports of entry and exit. But every day thousands of undocumented persons successfully defy the state's power to control their movement into and through this space and in doing so contest not only space, but also control of their identity.

Within official policy-making circles of the state, discussion of transnational subaltern communities is elaborated within a discourse of "immigration policy" whereby the state attempts to regulate international migration. Rhetoric aside, and as noted above, the de facto immigration policy of the unitedstatesian government is *not* to make the U.S.-Mexican border impermeable to the passage of "illegal" entrants but rather to regulate their "flow," while at the same time maintaining the official distinctions between the "sending" and "receiving" nations—that is, between kinds of peoples—to constitute classes of peoples—classes in both the categorical and social sense.[11] Issues concerning "migrant labor" are indeed at the core of the ongoing immigration debate, and here a major contradiction in official immigration policy appears. This situation results from the special nature of labor as a commodity that is embodied in persons who have national identities. Foreign labor is desired, but the persons in whom it is embodied are not desired. The immigration policies of receiving nations can be seen as expressions of this contradiction and as attempts to resolve it. The task of effective immigration policy is to separate labor from the jural person within which it is embodied, that is, to disembody the labor from the migrant worker. Capitalism in general effects the alienation of labor from its owner, but immigration policy can be seen as a means to achieve a form of this alienation that increases greatly in the age of transnationalism, namely, the spatial separation of the site of the purchase and expenditure of labor from the sites of its reproduction, such that the loci of production and reproduction lie in two different national spaces. This structure of transnational labor migration distinguishes it from the prevalent modern capitalist mechanisms for the appropriation of labor from subaltern groups: namely, national labor markets, slavery, and internal colonialism. Only in transnational "labor migration" is there national separation of the sites of production and reproduction (see Burawoy 1976; Cohen 1987, Corrigan 1990a).

Modern capitalism has for several centuries relied in various degrees on transnational labor migration. But the point here is that transnational labor migration has now become a major structural feature of communities that have themselves become truly transnational. Official migration theory, informed by and in the service of the nation-state, is disposed to think of the sociology of migration in terms of "sending" and "receiving" communities, each of which is in its own national space. But what the ethnography of transnational migration suggests is that such communities are constituted transnationally and thus challenge the defining power of the nation-states they transcend.

Elsewhere, Nagengast and I characterize the greater Mixtec diaspora and other widely extended subaltern communities as comparable to the transnational corporation, and we accordingly refer to them as transnational communities (see Kearney and Nagengast 1989; cf. Rouse 1991). Both kinds of organizations engage in production orchestrated in two or more national spaces and so reproduce themselves. Thus, just as the transnational corporation in part transcends the Durkheimian power of the nation to impress itself as the basis of corporate identity, so do members of transnational communities similarly escape the power of the nation-state to shape their sense of collective identity.

To the degree that transnational corporations and transnational migrants escape the impress of the nation-state on their identity, so must the native, nonethnic "white citizens" avail themselves of the only totemic capital that they have available to form an identity from an inevitable dialectic of opposition with nonnationalist communities that are forming on and within their boundaries. And that totemic capital is, of course, nationalism (with strong dash of racism). In areas of California, European Americans have definitively lost control of much geographic space, of boundaries that have been "invaded" by "foreigners," by "aliens." But having lost control of geographic space in the border area, they have begun to take fallback positions, and we see a shift to defense of social and cultural spaces where the state still has power to legislate identities and practices. Thus, a major part of the discourse on immigration now centers on such issues as English as "the official language," now so legislated in California, Arizona, Colorado, and Florida.

These new forms of discipline correspond to a movement from an offensive jingoist nationalism to a nationalism on the defensive, a shift from a nationalism of expansion and domination to a nationalism concerned with loss of control of its borders. To the degree that the modern nation-state and its associated culture are becoming anachronistic in the age of transnationalism, there should be apparent expression of disease within the body politic—a concern with the integrity of its boundaries. As Gómez Peña aptly notes, "For the North American the border becomes a mythical notion of national security. The border is where the Third World begins. The U.S. media conceives [sic] the border as a kind of war zone. A place of conflict, of threat, of invasion" (Gómez Peña, quoted in Fusco 1989:55). The current national obsession with "foreign" drugs and "crime" that are "penetrating" into "our nation" are also forms of transnationalism that also threaten the categorical integrity of the modern nation-state.

> One only need go down to this border just a short distance south of us to see how wildly out of control it is. And when we speak of out of control, we're not just talking about a few folks wanting to come in to get a job, we're talking about a torrent of people flooding in here, bringing all kinds of criminal elements and terrorists and all the rest with them.[12]

Such nativist sentiments as expressed in this quotation are symptomatic of the loss of spatial separation between developed and de-developed poles of transnationalism. A major way in which this blurring of the "modern" and the "traditional" is effected is via the spatial relocation of Third World peoples into the core areas of the "modern" capitalist West.

THE TRANSNATIONAL BODY AND PERSON

The Border: Scene IV

Four Mixtec migrants are sitting around a table in the home of anthropologists having their first meal in several days. For the previous four days they have been walking through the rugged mountains of eastern San Diego County. They are exhausted from cold and lack of sleep and food. Part of their trek was through snow; all of them are wearing light cotton clothing and two of them wear tennis shoes. They are talking with a Paraguayan peasant leader now in political exile, who is living in the house and who is astounded at their manner of entry into the United States. They tell him that when they come through these mountains they try to sleep for part of the day and walk at night when it is too cold to sleep. But one night, they say, they became so cold that they had to stop and build a fire. One of them, the most articulate, says that he was thinking as they were huddled around the small fire, hoping that it would not attract the attention of the *Migra*. He was thinking, he says, that he felt like a criminal, like someone who had to hide because they were doing some bad thing. But, he says, he could not understand what bad thing he was doing for he is an honest man who comes to the United States only to work, to leave his sweat and earn some money. He says he is a father and husband and a good worker, and that is why his *patrones* always hire him. They do not think that he is criminal, but he says that he feels like he is a criminal and he cannot understand why. The other men agree that they feel the same when they are exposed to possible apprehension by the Border Patrol or by other police agents.[13]

As the above sketches reveal, the unitedstatesian-Mexican border is riddled not only with holes, but also contradictions. In this scene the Paraguayan, who is skilled in his own form of a pedagogy of the oppressed, proceeds to explain to the migrants why they feel like criminals, even though they know that they are honest productive workers. He startles them, he grabs their attention by telling them that they run and hide scared from the *Migra* and the police because, as he says to them, "You pay the *Migra* to chase and persecute you." "How is that possible?" they ask. He then proceeds to give them a crash course in the accumulation of surplus value in the California farm labor market. These men will seek work as orange pickers in Riverside. The Paraguayan assists them to calculate the approximate unit wage that they are paid for picking a pound of oranges. He then reminds them of the per pound price of oranges in local markets, which differs greatly from what they are paid. He then explains how the difference is apportioned into costs of production, taxes, and profits that are paid and earned by the grower. He then calls the men's attention to the taxes that the grower pays and how these taxes go toward the maintenance of the Border Patrol. Thus he proves his point that the migrants pay the *Migra* to pursue them like criminals. They of course then ask him why things are arranged this way, and by a Socratic questioning he elicits the answer from them: because they run scared all the time and are desperate to get work before they are apprehended and sent back to Mexico, they accept whatever wage is offered and then work like fiends and otherwise do what they can to satisfy their *patrón*. In short, in a lesson that might have been taken from Foucault, he brings them to understand that the surveillance activities of the Border Patrol are not intended to prevent their entry into the United States to work but instead are part of a number of ways of disciplining them to work hard and to accept low wages.

The contradiction in unitedstatesian immigration policy noted above is inscribed on the social person so constructed, the "alien." This "alien" is desired as a body or, more specifically, as labor power that is embodied in this person by employers and indirectly by all who benefit economically and socially from this cheaply bought "foreign" labor. But this alien as a legal person who might possess rights and prerogatives of a national, of a citizen of the nation, is the dimension of personhood that is denied. The ambiguity of the alien results from policy and policing that inscribe both of these identities—worker and alien—onto his person simultaneously.[14] Being neither fish nor fowl and yet both at the same time, the alien is a highly ambiguous person.

The frontier between the United States and Mexico is formally a line with no width. But it is also a social and cultural zone of indeterminate extent, and some might argue that it runs from deep in Mexico to Canada. It is by passage into but never completely through this transnational zone that the alien is marked as the ambiguous, stigmatized, vulnerable person that he or she is. This border area is a liminal region into which initiates pass via what Van Gennep might punningly have called *"raites* of passage," but from which they never emerge.[15] The alien exists in what appears to be the intersect of one of Edmund Leach's Venn diagrams (Leach 1964; cf. Turner 1964). And as we would expect from the anthropology of liminality, the initiate is reduced to a categorical state of nonhuman—in this case an "alien." In colloquial Mexican Spanish, "illegal" border crossers are *pollos* or *pollitos,* that is, "chickens" or "little chicks." This avian identity can be seen as a symbolism of initiation, of the twice born. Moreover, the *pollos* are also defenseless creatures vulnerable to the predators who prey upon them in the border zone. Indeed, the immediate border area is infested with predators who rob, rape, assault, murder, apprehend, extort, and swindle the vulnerable *pollos*, whose only advantage is their large numbers—most get through alive, although poorer.[16] And, as Leach and Turner might have predicted, the hero of this liminal border is the supremely ambiguous and contradictory trickster and cultural hero of indigenous Mexico and North America, *El Coyote* (Melendez 1982). Ironically, but of necessity, the *pollos* must put themselves in the care of the coyote who may either deliver them or eat them.

We now can return to the Mixtec and ask how they respond to existence in this liminal (transnational) border area. Denied permanent residence in their homeland by economic necessity and denied naturalization by the United States, Mixtec "alien" migrants construct a new identity out of the bricolage of their transnational existence. What form does this transnational identity take? It coalesces as *ethnicity,* as an ethnic consciousness, which is the supremely appropriate form for collective identity to take in the age of transnationalism. In our work we have observed how Mixtec ethnicity rises as an alternative to nationalist consciousness and as a medium to circumscribe not space but collective identity, precisely in those border areas where nationalist boundaries of territory and identity are most contested and ambiguous (Kearney 1988; Nagengast and Kearney 1990). This situation conforms to Varese's analysis of how under "normal" conditions the nation-state is able to suppress other possible nations within it: "Yet, sooner or later, it can no longer mask the development of the existing violent contradiction between the nations (that is the Indian ethnos) and the state" (Varese 1982:35).

As Comaroff notes, "ethnicity has its origins in the asymmetric incorporation of structurally dissimilar groupings into a single political economy" (1987:307). In this case, the single political economy is the transnational milieu of Mexico and the United States, where in both regions the Mixtec are construed as aliens. Denied their patrimony in Mexico, legally prejudiced in the United States, and otherwise used and abused in both nations, the Mixtec are marked as subaltern Other by the nations that reject them so as to exploit them. This transnational structured differentiation obviates the impress of nationalism as a basis for collective consciousness and thus opens the possibility for the ascendance into consciousness of ethnicity as a sign that marks difference, a sign that is recognized as such both by those who are marked, those who mark them.[17] Moreover, those marked persons also remark on and thus collaborate in the construction of this system of difference.[18] The most outwardly visible form of Mixtec self-differentiation is the formation of various kinds of grassroots organizations in the United States and in Mexico that seek to defend their members as workers, migrants, and "aliens."

As Mixtecs say, they come to the United States to leave sweat and take home some money. Sweat is a metaphor of *labor* which becomes disembodied from the "alien" and as such contrasts with *work.*[19] Sweating for others in the United States contrasts with sweating for oneself in his or her own community in Oaxaca. There, as it were, one's sweat falls onto their own land and makes it produce *for them,* not for others. The community in Oaxaca is precisely that, a community, which is to say a social body, one that retains, more or less, its own sweat, its own labor in the form of work. To be an "alien" is not only to experience the disembodiment of one's labor, but also to be socially disembodied, that is, to be removed from one's community to the degree that one's sweat, one's labor, and one's identity are soaked up in the United States. The individualized migrant is allowed into the unitedstatesian nation-state not as a citizen but as an "alien," not as someone to be incorporated into the social body but as someone to be devoured by it. Migration policy/policing and resistance to it is thus a struggle for the value contained within the personal and social body of the migrant. The individual migrant resorts to microstrategies invented and reinvented by workers throughout the history of capitalism to retain economic capital embodied in their persons and desired by the patrón. The worker seeks to be not just a machine or an "animal," but to be a human being.[20] And as the individual worker seeks to defend his person and its embodied economic capital, so in a parallel manner the community attempts to defend the body social and its collective capital. This it does by converting some of that embodied capital into symbolic capital; specifically, symbolic capital in the form of markers of collective identity, expressions of which are noted by the state and by anthropologists as "ethnicity."

The Mixtec migrants are seemingly paradoxical in that they elaborate what appear to be signs of traditionality under conditions of modernity. But such inconsistency is only a spurious artifact of the discourse of nationalism and its intrinsic component of modernity. In other words, as the borders of the modern nation-state dissolve under conditions of transnationalism so does the opposition between tradition and modernity self-deconstruct and give way, grudgingly, to ethnicity as the primary form of symbolic capital expended in the construction of community in the age of transnationalism.

DISINTEGRATION AND RECONSTRUCTION
OF DISCIPLINARY BOUNDARIES

Deterioration of the borders of the nation can be expected to provoke a reconstitution of the state and its components, among which are its disciplines. Among the official academic disciplines anthropology is unusual in the degree to which it has been assigned responsibility for articulating difference, and thus engaging in the intellectual/symbolic reproduction of differentiation, on a global scale, with respect to "less developed peoples" as compared with "us." The fundamental epistemological structure of this classic form of anthropology—classic compared to the baroque anthropology of the present—was its firm categorical separation of anthropological Self from ethnographic Other—of those who undertook to know and those who were to be studied, known and, by implication per Foucault, to be controlled. The modern period, as identified above and that comes to an end after World War II, corresponds with this age of classic ethnography/anthropology.[21]

Anthropology (far from unique among the social sciences) is predicated primarily on the study of the alien Other and has its own distinctive social epistemology of a knowing anthropological Self and a categorically distinct ethnographic Other that is to be known. This epistemological asymmetry of subject-object, of Self-Other, is a reflection of a political asymmetry in which power, like the knowledge being discovered and produced, is unevenly distributed. Moreover, this differential production of knowledge is a differentiating production of power. Within capitalist society the social construction of reality occurs within the structured relations of classes of persons—those who study and consume the knowledge produced and those who are the objects, the raw materials of the knowledge. The dualism of bourgeois epistemology is predicated on this social duality and as such is inherited by all social sciences that acquire it as a basic disposition. But, as noted above, anthropology has its own social basis for epistemological dualism given to it by the ethnographic distinction between Self and Other, which is so structured within the colonial situation and upon which colonial institutions erect parallel distinctions of class. Thus, given the double social origins of anthropology's epistemological dualism, it is, unlike that of, say, sociology, doubly determined.

As noted, the mission of classic (modern) anthropology was contradictory: it had to humanize while it differentiated. We are all human, but we are all different. This is parallel to the contradiction that the nation-state must resolve. We are all one, but we are internally differentiated into classes, genders, and races. In other words, the state states that we are all of one nation and that in this oneness we are all equal, but its policies and practices ensure that we shall remain differentiated along lines of class, race, gender, citizenship, and so on, such that some of us are more equal than others. Similarly, the historical mission of classic anthropology was to humanize while differentiating. In fulfilling this mission anthropology applied the categories given to it by the ordering of official knowledge, especially the categorical distinction between Self and Other. Anthropological categories were established in the modern era, which was associated with a robust nationalism. This classic official anthropology sought to represent an ethnographic Other that was categorically distinct from the national anthropological Self. In the transnational era, this dualistic construction of classic anthropology, in both its positivist and interpretive modes, is inappropriate for the global, transnational differentiation of late capitalism, in which the dualism of the colonial situation has been reconfigured into different spatial relationships. It is not that differentiation at the end of empire lessens, but that it involves a distinctly different spatial and temporal constellation of Self and Other and of the relationship between them. This reordering of anthropological Self and ethnographic Other is most visible spatially when they become interspersed, one in the geography of the other. Classic anthropology was conducted in communities of distinct Others; now, increasingly, the ethnographic Other is constituted in highly dispersed communities that are transnational in form.

With the collapse of the categorical distinction between imperial Self and colonial Other, the basis was laid for the erosion of the social foundation of the modern nationalism of the West and the emergence of new dimensions of global differentiation.[22] The imagining of this transnational condition has been reflected in several innovative "antidisciplines." They are antidisciplinarian in the double sense that they transcend the domains of the standard disciplines and in the sense that they have tended to form themselves outside of the official institutional body of the state and thus have escaped the necessity of official scholarship elaborated as a constituting component of the nation-state. It is this sort of antidisciplinary scholarship that has given us the vocabulary to understand transnationalism as global history.

Foucault's project, too, is an exemplar of antidisciplinary and antidisciplinarian scholarship. Foucault is the herald of the "death of man," of the death of the Western subject in the postmodern age, which is to say in the age of transnationalism. The modern subject, the individual "actor" of capitalist society, whose demise Foucault announced, was and is a cultural construction born of two distinctly modern conditions. One of these was the power of commodification to create "individuals" as distinct from the communities from which, by market forces, they were alienated and so formed. The other basis for the cultural construction of the modern individual was the modern distinction between colonial Self and colonized Other. The Western subject/ Self only exists in *relationship* to an Other,[23] and thus the collapse of the modern global categorical relationship between anthropological Self and ethnographic Other also occasions the "death of man," of the subject as it was constructed in the modern age. This disappearance of the subject/person of the classic social sciences and humanistic disciplines threatens the constitution of these disciplines as they have been classically constituted. Accordingly, the dissolution of the disciplines that discipline the person/ body can be assumed to correspond to a reconstitution of disciplines.

Foucault does not study the transnational age, focusing as he does on the modern age, but his method personifies it, based as it is on Marx, whose work was not, as is often observed, interdisciplinary, but transdisciplinary in both senses noted above. Unlike and more than Foucault, Marx's transdisciplinary method pointed the way to transnationalism, denoted in his discourse as an "internationalism," an idea that informed the subaltern counterpart of the transnational corporation, namely, "The International." *This* internationalism as a vision of global identity is a prescient sentiment that appeared in the mid-nineteenth century at the apogee of the modern age and foretells the dissolution of its necessary sociocultural form, the nation-state.

As the "alien" presents a challenge to the integrity of the unitedstatesian nation-state it has responded by developing new disciplines to control its territorial boundaries and the cultural constructions upon which they are predicated. This discourse of nations and their borders is manifest, for example, in the current debates on university campuses over "Western Civilization" and "Ethnic Studies" requirements. One can also note here the recent rise and institutionalization of programs of "Border Studies," which are in some ways the academic counterpart of the Border Patrol. Other homologues of this tension in the boundary of the nation-state are the official language laws noted above and the national debate on immigration policy, which was dramatically punctuated by the passage of the United States Immigration and Reform Control Act of 1986.

The dialectic of transnational exploitation and resistance takes place on the margins of nations and is both a symptom and cause of the progressive dissolution of the power of these nations to impress themselves as nationalities and as nationalisms on the subaltern peoples within their boundaries. One of the various dimensions of this challenge to the nation-state is the increasing refusal of transnational ethnic minorities to be the objects of study by the disciplines of the nation-state—it might be said that this is but one of a number of ways in which they refuse to be disciplined. As transnational subalterns increasingly penetrate into the cores of the world system, their presence there not only reorganizes the spatial differentiation of development and underdevelopment, but also challenges the epistemological basis of classical anthropology, predicated as it was on the "Colonial Situation" (see above), in which the collection and consumption of anthropological knowledge became a permutation of the extraction, transformation, and consumption of economic capital. One result of this reordering is an increasing refusal of former ethnographic Others to submit to being taken as objects of investigation by the standard disciplines and a corresponding insistence on writing and speaking for themselves.[24]

Just as the borders and boundaries of the modern nation-state have become contested terrain, so increasingly is the power of official anthropology to describe unilaterally peoples and form policies that affect them being challenged. In the case of Mixtecs this sensibility has manifested as a desire and efforts, among various spokespersons and groups, to develop an autochthonous social science that can inform "the community" about itself and its relationships with the powers that encompass it. This informing thus becomes literally part of the process of forming the ethnic community that is informed. In the Mixtec transnational community this indigenous anthropology thus becomes a constituent of that which it seeks to study.[25] Such an anthropology that is brought into being by the conditions of transnationalism, and all that this term implies for the constitution of subaltern communities apart from the impress of national forces and for the dissolution of the traditional disciplining disciplines, is aptly referred to as a "Practical Anthropology" (Kearney n.d.).

On the unitedstatesian side of the border, in California, the differentiating project of the state seems to have gotten "out of control." This is most apparent demographically, with Los Angeles being simultaneously the largest city in California and, as pundits ironically note, the second largest city in Mexico following Mexico City, the largest city in the world. And the second largest city on the Pacific Coast, following Los Angeles, is now Tijuana. Clearly, Latin America does not stop at the border: a Mexican-Latino corridor now extends from Tijuana on the border to deep within unitedstatesian territory, and here and beyond there is a large and growing archipelago of Latino peoples.[26]

Throughout this archipelago practices of differing from below, born of forms of survival and resistance, proceed apace with official differing from above and combine in a dialexis that defies modernism's ideology of the "melting pot" (Corrigan n.d.). For generations, until the late 1970s, one of the main results of this dialexis was "Chicano culture" in its various forms ranging from the more defiant and more or less conscious styles of resistance elaborated by *pachucos*, "low riders," and "home boys" with their distinctive argot to the persistence of more traditional forms of Mexican culture such as Mexican language, music, folk medicine, and cuisine. From the dominant European American perspective all of these "alien" ways were simply Mexican. But to Mexicans—"real Mexicans"—in Mexico, these things Mexican American were *pocho,* that is, ersatz and inferior. But in the late 1970s *el Chicano* was "discovered" by Mexican intellectuals and cultural brokers. No longer seen as a bastard son, the Chicano became an icon of a particular kind of "Mexican" creativity and resistance deep in the belly of the colossus to the north. In Mexican eyes the Chicano has gone from a *pocho* to a cultural hero living in a region of occupied Mexico.[27] The border has thus taken on a different meaning to Mexicans than it has to European Americans.

The dramatic revaluing of the Chicano and of Mexico's relation to the North in general that has taken place in recent years is doubtlessly related to the deep "crisis" that Mexico has been experiencing since the mid-1980s, in which real income of the middle and low sectors has decreased around 50 percent and foreign debt has grown significantly.[28] Under these conditions there is more pressure than ever for Mexicans to go to the United States to work. Were the Mexicans living and working in the United States to be repatriated into Mexico's supersaturated labor markets, all commentators agree that an impossible situation would result, aggravated by the loss of the sojourners' remittances, which are no doubt Mexico's second or third most important source of foreign exchange. There are thus in Mexico deep structural reasons affecting perception of the border. It has become more of an obstacle, a hindrance in getting to work and back, not unlike commuter problems elsewhere.

With respect to the necessity of the Mexican state to export jobs, a porous border is desirable. But as a modern nation-state, an assault on the integrity of its border is an assault on its power—its power to order and to differ. The border has thus become highly problematic for the Mexican state. And nowhere is this more apparent than in Tijuana, which is, as Gómez Peña notes:

> . . . a place where so-called Mexican identity breaks down—challenging the very myth of national identity. The Mexican government has constructed this myth, which is that we have a univocal identity, one that is monolithic and static, and that all Mexicans, from Cancún to Tijuana, from Matamoros to Oaxaca behave, act and think exactly the same. Of course this a very comfortable myth for them to justify their power. By homogenizing all Mexicans and saying that, for example, Mexicans have a hard time entering into modernity, the Mexican state can offer itself as a redemptor of Mexicans, and the one who is going to guide them by the hand into modernity. So Tijuana is a kind of challenge to the Mexican government (quoted from Fusco 1989:70).

Tijuana is in its own way as transnational a city as is Los Angeles, and, indeed, the two are inexorably fusing together into one transnational megalopolis spanning the border. Another variant of this transnationalism is the immense demographic, cultural, emotional, and very "illegal" unofficial transnational bridge now in place between urban areas such as Los Angeles and Central America. As a result of united-statesian interventions in Central America, hundreds of thousands of refugees from that troubled area now live in the liminal world of the "undocumented" who are in the United States but not of the United States. What has become apparent now is that imperial projects to differentiate the colonized Other promote indigestible differences within the colonizing Self.

CONCLUSION

The border area has become a liminal area where creative energies are released, creating signs and identities that are born outside of the national projects of the two nations which presume to control identities in this zone. This changing configuration of the border challenges the ability of the two nation-states involved to define legal and cultural identities of their border populations which transcend the official spatial and legal bounds. Two forms contributing to decay of the nationalist project are notable: one is inability—an inability born of contradictory desires—of the unitedstatesian state to "document" the "aliens" in its territory; the other is the "crisis of representation" in anthropology about which so much has been said. This is so because the epistemology of modern anthropology has been constructed as part of the dualism in the modern nation-state whereby it differentiates between its "modern" Self and "traditional" Other. In the border area this once spatial, categorical, and very political distinction is becoming increasingly blurred. Whereas the past histories of immigration into the United States have been one of assimilation, the ethnography of the border area suggests that future histories will be one of indigestion as the unity of national totemism gives way to the multiplicity of transnational ethnicity.

***

I wish to thank Paul Chace, John Comaroff, Philip Corrigan, Jean Lave, Carole Nagengast, Daniel Nugent, Mary O'Connor, Roger Rouse, and Jonathan Turner for helpful comments on an earlier version of this chapter.

***

Notes

[1] For an illuminating discussion of the "dialexis" of differentiation and dominance in general, see Corrigan 1990b, n.d.

[2] Since 1986, when English became by law the "official language of California," I began to speak a disruptive English. "Unitedstatesian" is drawn from the Spanish *estadounidense* and as such is a (syn)tactical violation of official speech acts. Thus, like Gómez Peña, "I am very interested in subverting English structures, infecting English with Spanish. Finding new possibilities of expression within the English language that English speaking people don't have" (quoted in Fusco 1989:74).

[3] Regarding economic capital and its transformations, see Bourdieu 1986.

[4] Following Marx's distinction it is useful to see bourgeois society as asserting itself outwardly as nationality and inwardly as state; see Corrigan and Sayer 1985:1.

[5] Observations made by the author on various occasions since 1985.

[6] Description and photos of this event were presented to the author by Jorge Bustamante, President of El Colegio de la Frontera Norte, Tijuana, Baja, California.

[7] Observations made by the author on various occasions in recent years.

[8] I have taken this term from a BBC Television documentary series of the same name.

[9] See Mandel (1989) for an illuminating discussion of the cultural politics of ethnicity and difference in the context of foreign labor migration in Europe.

[10] Heyman discusses and documents how "the overall trend of U.S. policy from 1940 to 1986 has been increased application of force at the border" (1991:41).

[11] Immigration policy is, as Cockcroft (1986) notes, in practice labor policy disguised as immigration policy. This interpretation of unitedstatesian policy regarding the unitedstatesian-Mexican border is supported by research of Bustamante (1983), who has found an inverse relationship between economic indicators of the health of the unitedstatesian economy and the rate of apprehensions of undocumented Mexican migrants. In other words, as the unitedstatesian economy enters periods of expansion, the "valve" is opened more, allowing a greater "flow" of Mexican labor; when the economy enters a recession associated with rising unemployment in the United States, the valve is partially closed to reduce the "flow."

[12] James Turnage, director of the Immigration and Naturalization Service in San Diego, quoted from Daniel Wolf 1988:2.

[13] Observed by the author in 1985.

[14] "But the body is also directly involved in a political field; power relations have an immediate hold upon it; they invest it, mark it, train it, torture it, force it to carry out tasks, to perform ceremonies, to emit signs. This political investment of the body is bound up, in accordance with complex reciprocal relations, with its economic use; it is largely as a force of production that the body is invested with relations of power and domination; but, on the other hand, its constitution as labour power is possible only if it is caught up in a system of subjection (in which need is also a political instrument meticulously prepared, calculated and used); the body becomes a useful force only if it is both a productive body and a subjected body" (Foucault 1977:25–26).

[15] *Raite* is a corruption of "ride" and is pronounced "rye-tay." One of the main services of coyotes is to arrange for *raites*, which are transportation to points north, or informal transportation in general. A person who provides such services is a *raitero*. Migrants sometimes punningly refer to raiteros as *rateros* (thieves).

[16] Regarding collaboration of police and coyotes, police extortion, and other human rights violations of Mexican migrants in the border area, see Nagengast et al. 1992.

[17] Regarding consciousness of the transnational, see Comaroff and Comaroff 1987.

[18] John Comaroff comments on this dialectic of ethnic formation: "The emergence of ethnic groups and the awakening of ethnic consciousness are . . . the product of historic forces which structure relations of inequality between discrete social entities. They are, in other words, the social and cultural correlates of a specific mode of articulation between groupings, in which one extends its dominance over another by some form of coercion, violent or otherwise; situates the latter as a bounded unit in a dependent and unique position within an inclusive division of labor; and, by removing from it final control over the means of production and/or reproduction, regulates the terms upon which value may be extracted from it. By virtue of so [doing], the dominant grouping constitutes both itself and the subordinate population as classes; whatever the prior sociological character of these aggregations, they are, in the process, actualized as groups *an sich*" (Comaroff 1987:308).

[19] Regarding the distinction between "work" and "labor," see Comaroff and Comaroff 1987:196–202.

[20] A frequent observation of Mixtec migrants in the United States is, "Here we live and work like beasts." And as one Mixtec farmworker recently remarked, "The bosses treat their animals better than they treat us. They give their dogs, horses, and chickens houses to sleep in. But us they leave out in the rain. They even have barns for their tractors, but not for us." The reference here is to the thousands of Mixtecs in California and Oregon who live outdoors in makeshift camps.

[21] The "classic" period of anthropology reached its apogee in the interwar period, when the "classic ethnographies" were written—for example, those of Malinowski, Evans-Pritchard, Firth, Radcliffe-Brown, and their Boasian counterparts in the United States.

[22] The rise of a differently constituted nationalism, a peripheral nationalism propelled by movements of "national liberation," are an important part of this global shift to transnationalism but cannot be dealt with here; see Chatterji 1986.

[23] Regarding the worldview universals of Self, Other, and relationship, see Kearney 1984.

[24] See Harlow 1987 and issues No. 70 and 71 (1991), of *Latin American Perspectives*, which are devoted to testimonial literature.

[25] Numerous comparable instances exist among other "traditional" groups that have recently assumed and been ascribed ethnicity; regarding the Kayapo, for example, see Terence Turner 1989.

[26] This image of Latin America as an archipelago is Gómez Peña's (Fusco 1989:73).

[27] Regarding *cholos*, *chavos*, and punks on the border, see Valenzuela 1988.

[28] The now chronic nature of the "crisis" has made it a contradiction in terms.

References

Anderson, Benedict. 1983. *Imagined Communities: Reflections on the Origin and Spread of Nationalism.* London: Verso.

Bourdieu, Pierre. 1981. "The Specificity of the Scientific Field." In *French Sociology: Rupture and Renewal since 1968.* Charles C. Lemert, editor, pp. 257–292. New York: Columbia University Press.

———. 1986. "The Forms of Capital." In *Handbook of Theory and Research for the Sociology of Education.* J. B. Richardson, editor, pp. 241–258. New York: Greenwood Press.

———. 1988. *Homo Academicus.* Stanford: Stanford University Press.

Burawoy, Michael. 1976. "The Functions and Reproduction of Migrant Labor: Comparative Material from Southern Africa and the United States." *American Journal of Sociology* 81:1050–1087.

Bustamante, Jorge A. 1983. "The Mexicans Are Coming: From Ideology to Labor Relations." *International Migration Review* 17:323–431.

Chatterji, Partha. 1986. *Nationalist Thought and the Colonial World.* London: Zed Press.

Cockcroft, James. 1986. *Outlaws in the Promised Land: Mexican Immigrant Workers and America's Future.* New York: Grove Press.

Cohen, Robin. 1987. *The New Helots: Migrants in the International Division of Labor.* Aldershot Hants, England: Avebury.

Comaroff, Jean, and John L. Comaroff. 1987. "The Madman and the Migrant: Work and Labor in the Historical Consciousness of a South African People." *American Ethnologist* 14(2):191–209.

Comaroff, John L. 1987. "Of Totemism and Ethnicity: Consciousness, Practice and the Signs of Inequality." *Ethnos* 52:301–323.

Corrigan, Philip. 1990a. "Feudal Relics or Capitalist Monuments? Notes on the Sociology of Unfree Labour." In *Social Forms / Human Capacities: Essays in Authority and Difference.* Philip Corrigan, editor, pp. 54–101. London: Routledge.

———. 1990b. *Social Forms / Human Capacities: Essays in Authority and Difference.* Philip Corrigan, editor. London: Routledge.

———. n.d. "Power/Difference." Unpublished manuscript, University of Exeter.

Corrigan, Philip, and Derek Sayer

———. 1985. *The Great Arch: English State Formation as Cultural Revolution.* London: Basil Blackwell.

Foucault, Michel. 1972. *The Archaeology of Knowledge.* New York: Harper.

———. 1977. *Discipline and Punish.* New York: Vintage.

Fusco, Coco. 1989. "The Border Art Workshop/Taller de Arte Fronterizo: Interview with Guillermo Gómez Peña and Emily Hicks." *Third Text* 7:53–76.

Gómez Peña, Guillermo. 1986. "A New Artistic Continent." *High Performance* 35:24–31.

Harlow, Barbara. 1987. *Resistance Literature.* New York: Methuen.

Heyman, Josiah. 1991. *Life and Labor on the Border: Working People of Northeastern Sonora, Mexico, 1886–1986.* Tucson: University of Arizona Press.

Hobsbawm, Eric. 1987. *The Age of Empire: 1875–1914.* New York: Pantheon.

Kearney, Michael. 1984. *World View.* Novato, CA: Chandler & Sharp.

———. 1986. "From the Invisible Hand to Visible Feet: Anthropological Studies of Migration and Development." *Annual Review of Anthropology* 15:331–361.

———. 1988. "Mixtec Political Consciousness: From Passive to Active Resistance." In *Rural Revolt in Mexico and U.S. Intervention.* Daniel Nugent, editor, pp. 113–124. San Diego: Center for U.S.-Mexican Studies, University of California Monograph Series, 27.

———. n.d. "Practical Ethnography/Practical Anthropology." Unpublished manuscript.

Kearney, Michael, and Carole Nagengast. 1989. *Anthropological Perspectives on Transnational Communities in Rural California.* Working Group on Farm Labor and Rural Poverty, Working Paper, 3. Davis, CA: California Institute for Rural Studies.

Leach, Edmund R. 1964. "Anthropological Aspects of Language: Animal Categories and Verbal Abuse." In *New Directions in the Study of Language.* E. H. Lenneberg, editor, pp. 23–63. Cambridge, MA: MIT Press.

Mandel, Ernest. 1975. *Late Capitalism.* London: New Left Books.

Mandel, Ruth. 1989. "Ethnicity and Identity among Migrant Guestworkers in West Berlin." In *Conflict, Migration, and the Expression of Ethnicity.* N. Gonzalez and C. McCommon, editors, pp. 60–74. Boulder, CO: Westview Press.

Melendez, Theresa. 1982. "Coyote: Towards a Definition." *Aztlan: International Journal of Chicano Studies Research* 13:295–307.

Nagengast, Carole, and Michael Kearney. 1990. "Mixtec Ethnicity: Social Identity, Political Consciousness, and Political Activism." *Latin American Research Review* 25:61–91.

Nagengast, Carole, Rodolfo Stavenhagen, and Michael Kearney. 1992. *Human Rights and Indigenous Workers: The Mixtecs in Mexico and the United States.* San Diego: Center for U.S.-Mexican Studies, University of California.

Rouse, Roger. 1991. "Mexican Migration and the Social Space of Postmodernism." *Diaspora: A Journal of Transnational Studies* 1(1):8–23.

Sassen-Koob, S. 1982. "Recomposition and Peripheralization at the Core." *Contemporary Marxism* 5:88–100.

Turner, Terrence. 1989. "Amazonian Indians Lead Fight to Save Their Forest World." *The Latin American Anthropology Review* 1(1):2–4.

Turner, Victor. 1964. "Betwixt and Between: The Liminal Period in Rites of Passage." In *Proceedings of the American Ethnological Society*, pp. 4–20. Seattle: University of Washington Press.

Valenzuela, José Manuel. 1988. *La brava ese.* Tijuana: El Colegio de la Frontera Norte.

Varese, Stefano. 1982. "Restoring Multiplicity: Indianities and the Civilizing Project in Latin America." *Latin American Perspectives* 9(2):29–41.

Wolf, Daniel. 1988. *Undocumented Aliens and Crime: The Case of San Diego County.* San Diego: Center for U.S.-Mexican Studies, University of California.

Harald E. L. Prins is a professor of anthropology at Kansas State University, and president of the Society for Visual Anthropology. In addition to filmmaking and serving as an advocate for native rights among many populations throughout the Americas, he has written or edited books including The Mi'kmaq: Resistance, Accommodation, and Cultural Survival, *and (with E. W. Baker)* American Beginnings: Exploration, Culture, and Cartography in the Land of Norumbega.

No matter how scientific an anthropological project may be—with rigorous methodology, elaborate quantification, sophisticated conceptualization and theorizing, and so forth—there may also be at least a trifling component of romanticism or exoticism related to location or degree of difference. The distinguished anthropologist Claude Lévi-Strauss started half a century ago with a travel journal that hints at the elaborate analyses of structuralism, for which he subsequently became famous. Prins's recent, almost whimsical, retracing of Lévi-Strauss's itinerary turned out to yield an unintentionally blurred portrait of those same evanescent (some would say "deculturated") tribes in the heartland of South America. The "noble savage"—if ever he or she existed—is a romantic ideal, rarely encountered in ethnographic investigations.

A Handful of Ashes
Reflections on *Tristes Tropiques*
Harald E. L. Prins

Can it be that I . . . am the only one to have brought back nothing but a handful of ashes. Is mine the only voice to bear witness to the impossibility of escapism? (Claude Lévi-Strauss 1955:41)

My badly damaged and waterstained paperback copy of *Tristes Tropiques* (Lévi-Strauss 1955) has just weathered a three-month voyage through the Chaco and Mato Grosso. Early in 1997, about to embark on a footloose journey through the tropical heartland of South America, I stumbled on this book while checking some travel guides in the local public library. I hoped to experience once more the primitive glory of that continent's remnant wilderness and indigenous inhabitants—before all is bulldozed into civilization.

Leafing through *Tristes Tropiques*, I realized that Lévi-Strauss was inspired by a similar dream when he trekked through this region about sixty years ago. Intrigued by the coincidence, I decided to buy my own copy of the book. This was how, packed in my old blue rucksack, Claude Lévi-Strauss became my fellow-traveler. I confess, the title was familiar. Twenty-five years ago, as a young student at a Dutch university, I first read this text by the French anthropologist. It was and remains his most famous book, but I could only remember that it was long, confusing (particularly because we had to read the French original), and that it offered too little about what really interested me: ethnographic detail on South American Indians. Although it has long been listed as part of the anthropological canon, I suspect that many readers have a similar blurry memory.

My own journey began in Asunción, Paraguay, where I revisited a group of Ma'ka Indians. When I first met them, their small island village in the Rio Paraguay had become a tourist attraction just outside the city: now they are languishing in a filthy suburban slum, too remote from nature to hunt or gather edible food and too distant

Originally published in the German, "Eine Handvoll Asche: Überlegungen zu 'Traurige Tropen'" (pp. 113–123), in Kapfer, van de Loo, Petermann & Reinhart (Eds.), *Wegmarken: Eine Bibliothek der Ethnologischen Imagination*. Edition Trickster im Peter Hammer Verlag, Wuppertal, Germany. Copyright © 1998 Harald E. L. Prins. Reprinted with permission. All rights reserved.

from the urban center to make money off gawking tourists. Leaving the Ma'ka behind, I drove through the marsh and shrublands of the central Chaco where I met a group of Sanapana: landless Indians, they are about to be expelled from their hamlet by the *estanciero* (landlord), who views them as troublemakers on his cattle ranch.

Moving on, I stayed for a while with German-speaking Mennonites and made several excursions to surrounding Chaco Indian reserves inhabited by largely acculturated Angaite, Enthlit (Lengua), and Nivacle (Chulupi): most are poor peasants and many perform casual labor for their Mennonite neighbors. I then crossed into the deep jungles of eastern Bolivia. There I spent some time in an Ayoreo Indian community near the Rio Zapocos: since gratis commodities seduced these fierce forest nomads to settle down at a Protestant mission post, their culture has decayed—even their once-strong teeth are now either rotting or missing.

After trekking through cool Andean highlands, I entered the sweltering lowlands of the Rio Beni area. Pressing northwards into Brazil, I took a boat down the Rio Madeira, one of the Amazon's great tributaries, and disembarked at Porto Velho. Next, setting out for the Mato Grosso plateau, I drove to the new frontier town of Comodoro. Eager to leave this aggressive settlement of mixed-blood hucksters, barkeepers, and visiting loggers and cowboys, I turned on a red-dirt track leading to the vast Nambikwara Indian reservation (over one million hectares). Abruptly, the pesticidal green of irrigated farmland changed into the natural mottle of savannah. Although Lévi-Strauss had traveled through this region in 1938 and described the same Indian people, I was unwilling to have his thoughts guide my eyes and influence my thinking.[1] So, I left his book untouched in my backpack.

After I had traveled some thirty kilometers through tall grass and shrub, a large *maloca* suddenly caught my eye. Covered with dry palm-fronds, the conical hut rose almost ten meters into the blue sky. Soon afterwards, the Nambikwara village came into view and I saw that the splendid *maloca* was its ceremonial center. Located near a fresh stream running clean into the Rio Juina, this village is Zapezal, home of those Nambikwaras known as Halotesu.[2] For one enchanted week, I made this my home too. One day, as I wandered across the savannah, I chanced upon a small party of Nambikwara hunters. Muscular men armed with bows and arrows, their lean brown bodies were smeared bright red with *urucu* (annatto). Some were adorned with a feather sticking through their pierced nose; others made do with a little piece of green bamboo. Oldest among them was Manu, a handsome tribesman in his sixties, holding a young *coati* pet in his arms. A few days later, during a lashing rainstorm, I found shelter in Manu's camp near the Rio Juina. Joining other Nambikwaras huddling around his fire, I felt warm. That I could not speak their language did not matter. Soon thereafter, I reflected on our encounter in my notebook:

> Manu, the quintessential "savage," the naked hunter, the embodiment of the "primitive." I am surprised to realize that all this talk about "the Other" does not refer to him at all. To the contrary, he represents something of the self that has been repressed, forgotten, or no longer understood. But when I saw him, I felt I did know him, as some kind of primordial alter-ego. I realized very quickly, after the first surprise, that he was not a strange man at all! What he is, I think, is a dream we don't live.

The following morning, I wished my Nambikwara friends farewell. Just before crossing the reservation boundary, I noticed toxic garbage (herbicide and pesticide containers and other junk) dumped on Indian lands—welcome to civilization! After passing the sources of the Rio Tapajos, I finally reached the São Lourenco River. Although I had planned to visit Kejara, the Bororo village described in *Tristes Tropiques,* I found out that it no longer exists: an epidemic killed most of its inhabitants and the few survivors abandoned their once-beautiful village, which has probably eroded into an archaeological site. Instead, I went to Gorogedupauru (or Corriego Grande) on the Bororo reservation at Gomes Carneiro. Situated near the bank of the São Lourenco, a fast-flowing stream which runs into the Upper Paraguay River, this Bororo village still has its traditional structure—a wide circle of palm-leaf clan houses with the *baito* (men's house) in the center.

It was here, on a cold and rainy morning with little else to do but gaze at the muddy-brown river outside my shack, that I finally reached for *Tristes Tropiques*. Lying in my cotton hammock (with a text whose title matched my mood), I began thumbing through the chapters on the Bororo and looked at the images. A few days later, I showed the book to some Bororo men who seemed fascinated by its photographs and drawings; I could only guess what they were saying. The morning of my last day in Gorogedupauru, I wrote in my notebook:

> Thinking of the Bororos visited by Lévi-Strauss, I'm struck by the fact that they still exist. How precariously close to extinction have they come. A few decades ago, when the invasion of the Mato Grosso began in full blast, they had been reduced to only 500 people, total! Of the three villages in the Rio Vermelho group mentioned by Lévi-Strauss, namely Kejara, Pobori, and Jarudoriq, only the second still exists, but with just 37 inhabitants. Kejara, described by Lévi-Strauss as "one of the last strongholds of independence" was the first to vanish, probably in the late 1940s, followed by Jarudori around 1980, when *fazendeiros* [ranchers] invaded the reserve surrounding the *aldeia* [village].

After a short week on the forested river bank of the São Lourenco, I left the Bororo village and went hiking through the vast wetlands of the Pantanal, among the world's greatest remaining wildlife preserves. Later, aboard an old wooden boat sailing down the Rio Paraguay and passing long stretches of inundated Chaco marshland, I continued reading *Tristes Tropiques*.

When we docked in the harbor of Asunción, my three-month voyage had come to an end. As I flew away from South America, I looked at the darkened Chaco beneath the flame-coloured western sky and thought of the small band of Ayoreo Indians (perhaps twenty people) camping in the bush: unwilling to give up their traditional life, these nomadic foragers still refuse to be contacted and use spears and arrows to drive their point home.

Back home in the Great Plains of North America, I slung my hammock to finish reading *Tristes Tropiques*. Because I had traveled in geographic opposition to Lévi-Strauss, it seemed only natural that I digest his chapters in reverse order. Now, having read the book, I think about the man. Prior to my journey I considered the erudite structuralist, forty-three years my senior, a bit too cerebral, perhaps too logical for me. Now I see a thirty-year old French *gringo* trekking down an Amazon forest trail to visit a remote Indian village: composing short poems to forget his fatigue. He limps because a young monkey clings to his left boot, "just above the foot, with all four limbs, from morning till night. This position was tolerable on horseback and perfectly acceptable in a canoe. But traveling on foot was another matter, since every thorn, low branch or swampy patch drew piercing cries from Lucinda" (Lévi-Strauss 1955:342).

But what were the difficult voyages described in *Tristes Tropiques* all about? And what about my own journey? Were they mere adventures, romantic escapes from the temporary hold that civilization has on us? (cf. Lévi-Strauss 1955:40–41). Lévi-Strauss opens his complex narrative with a paradox, telling us: "I hate traveling and explorers. Yet here I am proposing to tell the story of my expeditions" (1955:17). Why? Only towards the end of his long and winding narrative goes he disclose his driving force: Jean-Jacques Rousseau, the eighteenth-century French philosopher. Lévi-Strauss calls him "our master and brother . . . to whom every page of this book could have been dedicated, had the homage been worthy of his great memory" (Lévi-Strauss 1955:390).

Rousseau published his *Discours sur les origines et les fondements de l'inégalité parmi les hommes"* (1755) precisely two hundred years before Lévi-Strauss completed *Tristes Tropiques.* In his early critique of Western civilization, Rousseau reproached philosophers for not traveling abroad: only observation and description of far-flung peoples—in particular tribal savages of the New World—can teach us about ourselves, he said. Having been insulated from "world history" (until their recent discovery), American Indians had avoided the pitfall of Progress. Consequently, Rousseau imagined these "noble savages" as the uncorrupted youth of humankind (cf. Lemaire 1980:214–15; 1986:234–237).

Heeding Rousseau's exhortation, Lévi-Strauss began his expeditions in search of the primitive, "to look for what Rousseau calls 'the almost imperceptible stages of man's beginnings'" (Lévi-Strauss 1955:316). But, the quest left him disappointed. Having gone "as far as the earth allows one to go," he discovered that what he had been looking for was already beyond reach. Now only able to chase "after the vestiges of a vanished reality," he laments: "I wished I had lived in the days of the *real* journeys, when it was still possible to see the full splendour of a spectacle that had not yet been blighted, polluted and spoilt" (Lévi-Strauss 1955:43, cf. 316).

How well do I understand his nostalgia! A few months ago, fifteen years after my last extensive journey through South America, comfortable as a university professor in the United States, I reflected on my life—forty-five years old, I yearned for the abandon with which I once trekked through forests, mountains, and pampas, working on horseback with Gauchos and visiting Indians by canoe. Lévi-Strauss felt a similar itch in 1954, when he was about my age now: "A few weeks ago, after a lapse of fifteen years I was toying with the idea of recapturing my youth by revisiting Brazil in the same way . . ." (Lévi-Strauss 1955:22). Instead of leaving his study, he embarked on a different sort of voyage—a twenty-four week writing binge resulting in two-hundred thousand words, organized in forty chapters, grouped in nine parts, the book he titled *Tristes Tropiques.*[3]

Intrigued by the Ayoreo who still range free in the Chaco wilderness, but are now so precariously close to the fangs of civilization, I can well imagine Lévi-Strauss' Elysian fascination when he encountered a band of twenty-five Munde Indians,[4] "authentic savages" living in a "fantastic garden" on the Pimento Bueno River: "Already in 1938," he writes, "this supreme reward could only be obtained in a few regions of the world—few enough indeed to be counted on the fingers of one hand. Since then, the possibilities have diminished still further" (Lévi-Strauss 1955:334).

Although Lévi-Strauss duly grieves about Western civilization crushing the Amazonian wilderness into extinction, *Tristes Tropiques* is not a naive primitivist plea for a return to a supposed original state of nature. Nor does he completely disparage the idea of progress (Lévi-Strauss 1955:390–91; cf. Lemaire 1976:258–60). But, he is sharply critical of modern civilization's self-satisfaction and argues that something went profoundly wrong a long time ago.

Since *Tristes Tropiques* was first published in 1955, vast tracts of Brazil's virgin forests have been ruthlessly destroyed and many streams are now polluted with mercury. In much of the Mato Grosso, zebu cattle graze in pastures where once jaguars hunted in dark woods. Only a few still isolated Indian bands pursue their ancient way of life in the last remaining unspoiled forests of the northern Guapore drainage area. But their precious survival is now threatened by hungry hordes of *garimpeiros* (goldpanners) and *madereiros* (loggers) about to invade their domains. Powerful *fazen-*

deiros (big landowners), getting wind of Indians on lands they claim as private property, employ *jaguncos* (professional killers) to destroy these indigenous inhabitants and their hamlets. Genocide happened in 1938 and still occurs today.

What will be the future of all those Indian tribes I just visited a short while ago? Will they be doomed to end their days in filthy slums like the Ma'ka? As landless peasants like the Sanapana? As wage laborers like the Enthlit and Nivacle? Or will their lives be threatened like the Nambikwara? Is all they can expect a marginal existence on some small reserve like the Bororo? And what about those Ayoreos still roaming free in the northern Chaco? Will they be wiped out like the Beicos de Pau, who became victims of a devastating epidemic in the late 1960s? Or will they be murdered like the relatives of the few surviving Kanoe Indians hiding in the Rio Omere valley? How long can they hold out, where can they flee? Is there no refuge?

It has been said that Lévi-Strauss never really stayed anywhere long enough for "real fieldwork" (cf. Clifford 1988:245). While this may be true, I find his narrative far more interesting than most contemporary anthropological accounts. As an observer of the human condition, he has an acute eye and reveals a poetic soul. His eloquent descriptions of bone-weary excursions into the tropical wilderness reflect the exquisite mind of an aesthete. He can sketch what a forest looks like, how it actually smells, sounds, tastes, feels, and how it stressed his nerves.

Some anthropologists recently pronounced *Tristes Tropiques* to have been a "marginal" disturbance (Clifford & Marcus 1986:13), "destined to be taught in literature classes as a model of *belles lettres*" (Marcus and Fischer 1986:34). A model of belles lettres? The book, as I now read it, is a *tour de force* in reflexive anthropology; vivid with sensual detail, it blurs genres and foreshadows postmodernism (but, without its tortured jargon). *Bricolage,* it is part memoir, ethnography, confession, travelogue, philosophy, lament, and historical account. A brilliant rejoinder to Rousseau, *Tristes Tropiques* is myth—a modern intellectual version of an ancient aboriginal *songline.*

Notes

[1] According to Lévi-Strauss, Candido Rondon misapplied the ethnonym "Nambikwara" to the people now carrying that tribal name. Although he is correct about that, he is mistaken about its meaning. Lévi-Strauss (1946:140) states that it is a Tupi word for "big ears," but it really means "pierced earlobe" (Gigi dos Santos, personal communication).

[2] Lévi-Strauss writes the name Halotesu as Wakletocu, which means "savannah people."

[3] Now, I am surprised how much more I seem to have in common with Lévi-Strauss. For instance, we both first traveled to South America on a freighter and disembarked in Brazil's old seaport Santos (he as a young French visiting professor at the University of São Paulo in 1934 and I, in 1973, a Dutch doctoral student); both revisited the continent several times, although neither was initially interested in the region; both our lives took a definite turn as a result of our personal encounters with South America's Indians (he grew dissatisfied with philosophy, I with prehistoric archaeology); and both went to the New School for Social Research in New York City (he as visiting professor, 1942–1944, I as List Fellow, 1978–80).

[4] Lévi-Strauss states in *Tristes Tropiques* (331): "These Indians, who referred to themselves as Munde, had never been mentioned in any anthropological study." However, according to Brazilian indigenist Marcello dos Santos, Lévi-Strauss erred in his identification: these Tupi-speaking Indians are Salamai, and Munde was their headman's name (personal communication, 1997).

References

Clifford, James. 1988. *The Predicament of Culture: Twentieth-Century Ethnography, Literature, and Art.* Cambridge: Harvard University Press.

Clifford, James, and George E. Marcus (Eds.). 1986. *Writing Culture: The Poetics and Politics of Ethnography.* Berkeley: University of California Press.

Lemaire, Ton. 1980. *Het Vertoog Over de Ongelijkheid van Jean-Jacques Rousseau.* Baarn (Netherlands): Ambo.

———. 1986. *De Indiaan in ons Bewustziin: De Ontmoeting van de Oude met de Nieuwe Wereld.* Baarn (Netherlands): Ambo.

Lévi-Strauss, Claude. 1946. The Name of the Nambikwara. *American Anthropologist,* vol. 48, pp. 139–140.

———. 1955. *Tristes Tropiques.* Translated from the French by John and Doreen Weightman. Harmondsworth: Penguin Books.

———. 1963. *Structural Anthropology.* Harmondsworth: Penguin Books.

Marcus, George E., and Michael M. J. Fischer. 1986. *Anthropology as Cultural Critique: An Experimental Moment in the Human Sciences.* Chicago: The University of Chicago Press.

Rousseau, Jean-Jacques. 1964. Discours sur l'Origine et les Fondements de l'Inégalité parmi les Hommes (1755). In *Oeuvres Completes.* Paris: Editions de la Pleiade, III (1755).

John Durston is a social anthropologist working in the Social Development Division of the United Nations' Economic Commission for Latin America and the Caribbean. He has recently written an article for CEPAL Review (No. 69, 1999) entitled Building Community Social Capital.

The World Bank, International Monetary Fund, and certain member countries of the United Nations have often been demonized as oversized, anonymous, and too-powerful multinational institutions bent on imposing Western ways in the name of fostering global development, with little attention to traditional or local variations in values and ways of doing things. In recent years, more attention has been paid to the grassroots impact of their programs and projects, sometimes on the basis of sound understanding and sometimes on the basis of what Durston here discounts as "anthropological myths." An anthropologist on the staff of the UN's Economic Commission for Latin America and the Caribbean, he addresses "the nonanthropological staff" of such agencies by explaining how a few key concepts, together with close attention to empirical realities of local situations, can help assure that development projects better serve to promote social welfare and justice for those whose voices often are not heard nor adequately attended to. Readers should pay close attention to how this practicing (or "applied") anthropologist grounds his realistic and practical recommendations on the work of academic (or "theoretic") anthropologists. Compare Foster (chapter 31), to which he specifically refers, and also Bernard (chapter 10) and Sponsel (chapter 4), for other examples of linkage between the discipline in academia and, increasingly, in "the real world."

The Contributions of Applied Anthropology to Peasant Development

John Durston

The present surge of interest in participative rural development projects based on peasant communities differs from similar past experiences in that it forms part of a broader tendency to decentralize social management, to enhance the role of the beneficiaries of social policies, and to give them a bigger say in their implementation. In order to avoid repeating the failures of past decades in programs designed to reduce rural poverty, it is necessary to incorporate elements of modern applied anthropology in programs for the training of extension workers and in the explanatory models of specialists formulating rural development projects. The practical contribution that applied anthropology can make stems not only from the experience of anthropologists in development projects but also, and above all, from a knowledge of the empirical reality revealed by academic anthropology. Although some anthropological concepts are already being used in some other disciplines, they usually correspond to outmoded theories already discarded by many anthropologists. This article identifies some of these "anthropological myths" and explores ways in which the new perceptions of anthropology could be applied to some of the commonest components of rural development projects. The concepts used in this dual task include the development cycle of peasant households, kinship as a reserve of mutual aid, the community as a referent of prestige, and ethnic identity as a social resource.

INTRODUCTION

Various Latin American governments and the international agencies which deal with the reduction of poverty are displaying considerable interest in community-based

Slightly abridged, with permission of the author and publisher, from an article with the same title in *CEPAL Review* 60:99–114, 1996.

participative rural development. This is perfectly natural, since in spite of the high degree of urbanization, poverty in twelve Latin American countries is still a predominantly rural phenomenon (World Bank Group, 1996; Valdés and Wiens, 1996). Neither structural reforms, nor the growth of the product, nor the functioning of the market have been able to bring about a significant reduction in poverty in this sector.

At the same time, there is a long history of defeats in the war against rural poverty, and it is interesting to note that proposals for social investment to resume the struggle are being made once again after the lengthy withdrawal from such efforts that followed the meager results obtained in the 1970s from the big integrated rural development projects.

The new participative rural development projects centered around communities of small farmers are in no sense "the mixture as before":[1] they only retain a few elements of those integrated projects, because it is considered from the start that the excessive centralization and technocratic nature of the latter raised their cost and adversely affected feedback and the motivation of the beneficiaries (Errázuriz, 1986; Durston, 1988; FAO, 1988).

Nowadays, emphasis is placed on the fact that support programs for small rural producers must be participative and community-based (World Bank Group, 1996; Banuri and others, 1996). It may be recalled that the few successful integrated rural development programs shared the common feature of displaying a high degree of real participation of their beneficiaries (Lacroix, 1985).

Although the present proposals may not seem completely new—participative development was in vogue on a number of previous occasions, beginning with the "community development" of the 1960s and attaining more sophisticated expressions in the late 1970s and early 1980s (Coombs, 1980)—what *is* new is that they now form part of a new general model for the fight against poverty.

Such proposals form part of a more general tendency towards broad and sustainable decentralized management of local resource systems in order to give all the interested parties a chance to participate (World Bank Group, 1996). The concept of participation is now both more complex and more concrete than the optimistic ideological formulations of past eras, and it usually means greater decision-making power—empowerment—for the beneficiaries, greater negotiating capacity, and accountability: the right for them to demand reports (Durston, in press). This scheme is quite novel because it means that programs must be propelled and managed mainly by the beneficiaries themselves, rather than by the central government or technicians (Ashby and Sperling, 1992).

The experience of past decades made it clear some time ago that generating and organizing community involvement is much more complicated than many advocates of community participation believe (Coombs, 1980, p. 23). In most rural villages resources and power are concentrated in a few hands, there are few truly democratic institutions, and there are rival factions. Good intentions are not enough to ensure the success of interventions from outside: it is also necessary to take into account the attitudes, sociology, cultural traditions, politics and economic aspects of the community (Coombs, 1980, p. 24).

To be more specific, changes are needed in the local and regional environment to permit the democratization of development and the strengthening of excluded groups as social actors (Fox, 1995), as well as the training of planners and extension workers in the sociocultural dynamics of peasant society. In particular, it is necessary to understand the social organization and priorities and strategies of the peasants, which may be very different from the schemes proposed by members of urban, developed, "modern" societies.

The anthropological theory of social organization (Firth, 1961) deals with this elusive reality that lies between the individual and macro levels (DeWalt and DeWalt, 1992); thus, it offers explanatory and potentially prescriptive contributions which are highly relevant to the new approaches that place the social actors at the center of proposals for participation (Cernea, 1996, pp. 340–352).

Such proposals make it clear that, in order to be able to help the rural poor to organize themselves, to understand the policy options before them and to formulate their demands, it is necessary to incorporate into the strategies the recommendations made on the basis of research into social relations (World Bank Group, 1996, p. 34). Anthropological research, in particular, has created a body of knowledge on Latin American peasant communities which goes back for more than half a century (from Redfield, 1930, through Foster, 1948, Tax, 1953 and others) and has been enhanced over the years by new findings and scientific debate.

It is quite true that most of this body of ethnographic description, analysis and development of theories is of an academic nature and only indirectly touches upon the practical problems of rural development programs. Nevertheless, this store of knowledge and theory allows anthropologists to gain access to a wide range of analytical tools and comparative examples which, taken together, enable them to appreciate the complex empirical reality of the peasant world that lies beneath superficial impressions (Cernea, 1996, pp. 340–352).

Thus, it shows up once again the falsity of the alleged dichotomy between academic or analytical work, on the one hand, and practical or operational work on the other. The understanding of the realities of poor rural communities made possible by the theoretical models and accumulated knowledge of anthropology cannot be replaced by experience in the field, because on its own this usually merely strengthens a perception of simple models that claim to represent the complex peasant reality. Although professionals in other fields are usually familiar with basic anthropological concepts, these tend to be of an elementary nature and correspond in many cases to outmoded theories already discarded by modern anthropology. Until quite recently, many agronomists and economists dealing with agricultural issues opposed the incorporation of anthropologists into the rural poverty debate, except in respect of a few limited topics, but it is increasingly clear that the new proposals require that extension workers in the field and experts formulating programs to combat rural poverty should incorporate into their models and approaches some basic—but not oversimplified—elements of anthropology (Cernea, 1996, pp. 340–352).

In particular, there is an increasing awareness of the need to change the approach of agricultural extension activities aimed at peasants. The idea is to get away from the tendency—which is predominant in the traditional academic training of extension workers and planners—to think in terms of a simple one-way transfer of information and techniques to producers who have no knowledge of them or have completely mistaken ideas. This traditional view also assumes that the beneficiaries live in a simple, standard social environment which is the same everywhere and does not warrant much analysis by the experts who seek to increase peasants' productivity.

Although there is an awareness of the shortcomings of this approach and it is known that social and cultural variables can determine the success or failure of a project, there is not such a clear awareness of what those variables are, how they can be identified in detail, and what adjustments they call for in the activities of an actual project.

Here, we have considered some shared perceptions: that we should gain a deeper knowledge of the conditions we aim to change; that the sociocultural realities of peasant society do not only represent problems and obstacles for the transfer of the productive know-how of the experts, but also strengths and opportunities which should be exploited and strengthened, and that there are abstract elements which are common to the varying cultures and situations of peasants from different parts of Latin America. These common elements make it possible to prepare a common framework for guiding the construction of more complex models reflecting the particular circumstances of each project and each rural community. Some of these elements refer primarily to cultures of indigenous origin, but the processes of syncretism between the original and the Spanish cultures (in the cases of both present-day indigenous peoples and nonindigenous peasants) allow them to be extended to every peasant community in Latin America, as a general framework, for the purpose of analyzing each specific situation.

The following sections will try to give a brief definition of the relevant theoretical concepts of social and cultural anthropology: i) the development cycle of the household unit; ii) the community as a referent of prestige; iii) kinship as a reserve of mutual aid, and iv) ethnic identity as a social resource. They will also seek to correct some common anthropological myths in this respect which are based on outmoded theories already discarded by anthropologists, to link up these concepts within a coherent theoretical framework that can serve as a guide in the analysis, of actual situations arising in participative development projects for small producers, and to set forth some practical connotations of this framework for certain components of participative rural development projects, especially those concerned with organization, extension activities, credit and marketing.

THE ANTHROPOLOGICAL APPROACH: SOME FUNDAMENTAL CONCEPTS

Their culture and their informal social organization[2] are factors that determine people's decisions and their relations with larger organizations.

The term "culture" has been incorporated into the modern vocabulary with rather a vague meaning. It is important to develop the concept behind this word more fully from the standpoint of modern anthropology. Every culture has two main components: on the one hand, a view of the world—i.e., a coherent set of beliefs about reality—and on the other an ethical view: that is to say, a scale of values that determine attitudes to good and evil and a set of rules for people's "proper" behavior. In order to become a culture, this dual view—of what is real and what is correct or proper—must be shared and transmitted within specific, concrete groups of persons, through a common language. Modern anthropology tends to make an analytical distinction between the concept of culture (an abstract system of ideas) and the concept of social structure (the practices, customs, regular interactions and institutions which exist and are observable in real everyday life).

It has long been accepted that every specialist should have an "open mind" regarding what is taking place in intellectual fields outside the "closed system" of his own specialty (Gluckman, 1964). Even so, there is a problem of communication among the different professions which stems above all from the frequent fact that even those specialists who have acquired elementary notions of another discipline—such as anthropological theory, for example—usually learn (either from teachers working in their own specialty or from textbooks) outmoded theories which have already been left behind in fast-evolving fields of knowledge. In the following sections we shall summarize and explain some of these "anthropological myths": that is to say, these beliefs which are widely held but whose bases have been greatly weakened in modern anthropology.[3]

> Anthropological myth: The cultural systems and informal institutions of indigenous and peasant societies are ancestral traditions which have remained unchanged throughout the centuries; contact with the modern economy and society, the mass media, etc. means the destruction of these age-old cultures and institutions.

This belief appears to be the result of the first hypotheses developed almost a century ago by the functionalist school of anthropology. Now, however, we know that, while intercultural encounters always mean tensions on both sides (and in extreme cases may lead to the disappearance of a culture), cultures have much greater capacity to adapt to changes in the material environment and in the sphere of ideas than they were formerly credited with.

Culture is not, however, a simple and immutable set of rules that can be summed up in a few words. Many anthropologists believe that those rules, as well as being expressed through a language, actually *function* as languages or programs, comparable with those of a computer in that they are mutable and contain sentences and routines that remain latent and manifest themselves only in the right circumstances. Cultures are constantly changing and adapting their beliefs and rules in response to the changes that are taking place every day in the social, economic and intellectual environment. In this sense, there are no traditional cultures: there is no culture in the world which is the same today as it was a generation ago, or even a year ago. A culture, like a silent language, is constantly evolving as people change the way they use it.

The most novel theoretical proposals put forward an even more dynamic idea of cultures. They see cultures—like ecosystems—as adaptive systems which are in a constant process of change, generated by the co-evolution of the strategies applied by the individual agents of the populations making up the societies involved (Cowan and others, 1995, various articles).

Among the most salient aspects of cultures analyzed below are mutual aid and the values of prestige and social status; among the institutional forms of social organization, special emphasis will be placed on the difference between household and family and the development cycle of the household; on kinship and kindred; on "dyadic contracts"; on mutual support groups connected with the clientage of the so-called "big men"; and on the community as referent of prestige and as the context for the taking of decisions.

The Development Cycle of the Household and the Life-Strategy of the Head of Household in the Management of Peasant Holdings

Contributions and Limits of the Approach Based on Systems of Production

Let us start out from the assumption that rural development projects are based on a view of the peasant holding which is rather special in terms of economic theory because it differentiates this type of holding from a conventional capitalist agricultural enterprise. In other words, let us assume that the readers of this article share the view that the main object of decision-making in the peasant economy—the family farm—combines an income-oriented logic with a consumption-oriented one, since its labor force are also the owners of the enterprise. Unlike a capitalist enterprise, the management aim in the family farm is not to reduce the cost of its own labor force, and neither can it lay off staff when labor needs go down.

> Anthropological myth: For some theoreticians of agricultural economics, the peasant unit follows a special rationale whose sole aim is reproduction and not accumulation of capital; consequently, once the basic needs for the social reproduction of the household have been satisfied, peasants will not keep on producing in order to accumulate capital, especially if this means taking risks. This view of peasants as being reluctant to participate in agricultural development is further strengthened by the first anthropological myth, referred to earlier, which considers peasant culture to be an immutable ancestral system and sees peasants as lacking in entrepreneurial spirit, averse to taking risks, and generally "resistant to change."

This image of peasants appears to stem from a mistaken reading of the Russian rural sociologist Chayanov, although it also concurs with stereotypes deeply rooted for many decades past. It is also strengthened by fragmentary and anecdotic observations of the behavior of some peasants. Thus, it is quite true that many poor peasants are averse to taking risks, many slacken the pace of family labor if their basic needs have been satisfied, and many are resistant to change, but these forms of behavior are circumstantial and are not essential features of peasant culture.

For example, many anthropologists consider that nowadays a tendency to give priority to mere subsistence appears to be due largely to the need to minimize risks in the poorest households when their physical survival itself is in the balance (Durston and Crivelli, 1984). In many of these communities, however, there are "rich peasants" who have made some progress in a process of sustained accumulation. Reduction of the pace of family labor takes place when it has been possible to overcome a situation of excessive self-exploitation, after which the demands on the labor of the smallest children can be reduced and usual standards for the sexual division of labor can be applied.

Resistance to change and innovation, for its part, is almost always due to some older peasants, for the younger ones are usually very open to new ideas. For many years this has been interpreted as evidence of the recent penetration of "modern" culture in the new generation. However, the repetition of this phenomenon in successive generations of young peasants supports the hypothesis that it is rather a question of the typical characteristics of different stages in life (Durston, 1996) and that old peasants who stick to rigid formulas today do so because they are old: when they were young they may have been rebels and innovators, sometimes imposing formulas which were new in those days but are now unsuited to present-day conditions.

Whether for reasons of survival or of accumulation, peasant units apply various "systems of production" which combine multiple purposes and products. A basic error in rural development programs is to treat the various family farms of a community or region as if they were homogeneous, instead of differentiating them into a manageable number of types or models of production systems (see DeWalt, 1985; Van Alphen, 1994).

In the following pages we shall analyze the question of the multiple objectives— especially the non-economic ones—which guide the taking of decisions in the management of peasant family enterprises and of the social resources that such enterprises mobilize in their strategies, which are both economic and social.

From an analysis of systems of production, it may be concluded that formal multipurpose organizations (cooperatives and committees) are useful for coordinating self-help efforts to overcome rural poverty, but the fundamental decision-making units are the family farms. As these farms have quite varied types of systems of production (for ecological or social reasons, or for reasons connected with the life-cycle of the head of household), their objectives do not always coincide. The level of participation in the pursuit of a given common production objective, even when this has been decided upon democratically in the organization, is bound to be low in the case of farms whose systems of production do not include that objective in their strategies. Consequently, for certain specific objectives it is better to encourage the spontaneous emergence of interest groups among farms with the same type of system of production (Van Alphen, 1994). To a large extent, then, work with such groups must be flexible in terms of time, must fit in with the demands formulated by the peasants themselves, and must seek to encourage the formation of interest groups corresponding to the various systems of production.

One of the limitations of the approach based on systems of production is that the analysis usually only includes the economic objectives of the farm. Research and the formation of theories along anthropological lines can make some of their most important contributions in this field by revealing how social objectives strongly condition decision-making in peasant households.

Social Factors in Peasant Decision Making

There are various levels of definition of the "decision-making unit" in peasant society, ranging from the individual, through the nuclear household, the extended family and informal mutual support groups, to the community itself. All these "units" of different levels of aggregation influence each other in their decisions. Another of the contributions of the approach based on systems of production is that it has corrected the traditional practice of considering the "farmer"—that is to say, the head of the family—as the only interlocutor. Today, the other members of the household are beginning to come forward out of the shadows: nowadays, studies take into account the farmer's wife and, to an incipient extent, young people too (Durston, 1996).

Nevertheless, at the minimum level of decision making—that of the individual—it is the head of the household (usually male) who interests us most in this analysis, because in Latin American peasant society it is his objectives (material and social) which predominate in the economic strategy of the household. This is "the other side of the sex-based approach": the current efforts to overcome the traditional "invisibility" of peasant women (Campaña, 1994) must not lead us to neglect the due analysis of male roles and their incorporation in the planning of development project activities.

In reality, there is no equality of the sexes in decision making in peasant culture: neither in indigenous culture nor, even less, in nonindigenous peasant life. The head of the household is the dominant actor in defining the objectives of the family enterprise, which are usually also accepted by the other members. Unlike what happens in a truly commercial enterprise, the social objectives of the head of household—fulfilling religious duties, financing the studies of the children, providing a good dowry for a daughter, leaving the children something to inherit and, above all, amassing social prestige in the community and the area—are just as important as increasing profitability or capital, if not more so.

Although the objectives of the head of household are processed through negotiation with the other members of the household, and although they derive partly from his affective relationship with them, it is the head of household who represents his farm, not only for traditional planners but also for society; he is also the figure who represents his whole nuclear family in the social hierarchy of the community. Consequently, the productive activities of the family farm and the participation of each family member in them are aimed largely at achieving the personal objectives—whether material or symbolic—of the head of household.

What is a "Family"?

It is extremely important to distinguish between two terms which are very often used as though they were synonyms: family and household. However, household is not the same thing as family: whereas "household" is a unit of residence and consumption in which there is usually only a single consumption budget and all its members normally prepare and eat the same meal, "family" is a broader concept which overlaps in everyday language with the idea of "household" but actually has less clearly marked limits. The picture becomes even more complicated when we note that both households and families are very often described as being "nuclear" or "extended." Even social science publications do not use these terms in an agreed, standard manner, so that each author should really make it clear what definition of them he is using.

Anthropological myth: Social scientists who are not themselves anthropologists very often use a simplistic scheme in which the extended family and household are equated with "tradition" and with indigenous culture and rurality, while the nuclear family and household are seen as typical institutions of modern, urban Western culture.

The first danger involved in this scheme is that of confusing the concept of family (as a group of related persons) with the idea of household (as a domestic and residential unit). It is the latter institution which is registered by censuses and household surveys: indeed, the statistics almost always speak of households and not of families.

The second point is that the simple dichotomy posited by this myth does not correspond to reality. In many countries of the region there is a higher proportion of extended households in urban areas than in rural ones, due to the higher cost of urban housing.

Furthermore, the extended household—the residential unit which includes, in addition to the nuclear household, other relatives of the head of household, usually daughters-in-law and grandchildren, aged parents or in-laws—is less common than the nuclear household in rural areas of Latin America. This is not because rural society has become more "urbanized" or "modern," but because the extended household represents a stage or phase in the long normal development cycle of the household, in which children of the head of household have got married and are temporarily living with their parents until they have enough income and savings to obtain a home of their own. Ethnographic studies carried out in a large number of traditional peasant communities all over Latin America more than half a century ago registered a majority of nuclear households, just like today.

Consequently, the fact that most of the households in a peasant community are nuclear does not mean that that community is losing its traditional culture. By the same token, it is likewise not true that the extended family is now disappearing from peasant society: mutual aid among close relatives continues to be important, even though they may not live in the same household, but it takes different forms from those of yesteryear. The most accurate term for referring to this abstract concept of "family" or "parents" is kinship, and as we shall see below, kinship is the main foundation of the relations between persons on which mutual aid is based.

Here, we have preferred to associate the concept of household with that of the farm, with a head of household who is the farmer "managing" the farm. In view of the importance for the household of the life cycle of this personage, we are particularly interested in analyzing the nuclear unit: that is to say, the head of household and his wife and children. The term family will be used here to refer to close relatives who usually aid each other because of their links of common descent or matrimony. The practical connotations of these definitions may be appreciated from the following diagram; (the nuclear household always exists, but in order to avoid confusion we shall refer to the nuclear family, since in practice it coincides with the nuclear household):

Life cycle of the head of household and development cycle of the household

	Household	Family
Nuclear	Always exists	Abstract concept
Extended	Temporary phase in the life cycle	Always exists

It is worth emphasizing how important the age factor is in this context—i.e., the ages of the persons involved and the economic and social changes associated with their evolution—as this variable is almost always omitted from the conceptual frameworks of rural development projects (Durston, 1996). Thus, solely with regard to the question before us at this moment—the strategy of the head of household—we may say that as the head of household advances in his life cycle there is normally an increase in his capacity for autonomous decision making, in the ratio between the active labor force and dependents, and in the resources accumulated by the head.

Because of the high degree of identity between the objectives of the peasant farm—the "enterprise"—and the personal objectives of the head of household, there is a similarly close correlation between his life cycle and the development cycle of the household.[4] In other words, we can describe this latter cycle in relation to the age of the head of household.

Strictly speaking, the most important thing here is not the chronological age of the head of household, but the sequence of stages in the normal life cycle of male peasants: dependent childhood, the stage of going to school, the stage of acting as the father's helper in productive tasks, the stage of partial economic independence, and the stages of newly-married man, father of young children, head of an adolescent family labor force, head of an extended household, the stage of increasing loss of control over the work of sons who are now grown-up, the stage of giving land to the sons as a gift or advance legacy, and finally the stage of dependent old man.

Any of these stages can take place at different ages or simply not take place at all in particular cases; there are only statistical trends pointing to a common age cycle for all, although these trends may be strongly marked in a given peasant community or regional culture. In operational terms, it may be more exact to take the age at which the head of household got married, or his age when his first child was born, as the starting point for the development cycle of the household.

As a dominant trend, as the life cycle of the head of household advances, so too there is a gradual increase, in the development cycle of the household, in both the number of members and the ratio of active workers to dependents and to the area of land owned. The values of these display similar curves, with peaks at points between 40 and 60 years of age of the head of household. Finally, "demographic differentiation" puts an end to the potential social inequality involved in this concentration of resources, through the division of the capital among several children by inheritance.

SOCIAL PRESTIGE, THE COMMUNITY, AND CHANGES IN THE PROBABLE LEVELS OF PRIORITY OF OBJECTIVES

The Prestige of the Head, as an Objective of the Household

The economic approach to peasant farms acknowledges that they establish a scale of priorities for the various economic and family objectives that guide their production decisions. Studying the development cycle of the household helps to understand how the non-economic or "family" objectives change with the different stages in that cycle. The priorities laid down by the head of household evolve from the top-priority objective of subsistence/consumption in the case of a young head, via the objective of accumulation or expansion of capital under a middle-aged head, to the aim—when the head is of advanced age—of maximizing his own prestige by a combination of wealth, generosity and service.

The importance of prestige in peasant communities is generally underestimated in rural development projects, partly because it is a non-economic objective, but probably also because the planners of such projects have accepted the stereotype of peasants who are essentially equal to each other—that is to say, equally poor. At the same time, a technician or professional, looking down from a higher social position, may underestimate the degree of respect and admiration that a peasant may enjoy among his peers. Finally, the scale of values determining an individual's prestige is different from one cultural context to another, although the three factors mentioned in the preceding paragraph are essentially universal.

The Rural Community as Referent of Prestige

In poor peasant areas of the Andes, Mexico and greater Central America, prestige and status (the social rank resulting from the prestige won by an individual) have traditionally been associated with the fulfillment of a number of civic and/or religious "offices" which demand a great deal of material resources and time from the head of household.

> Anthropological myth: A hypothesis put forward in early anthropological studies which turned out to be false in many cases was that expenditure on parties and other social events had the effect of leveling out personal wealth, by demanding bigger expenditure from men who had managed to begin an accumulation process that could result in their social differentiation (leveling mechanisms).

We now see, on the contrary, that the expenditure of both money and time served as investments in prestige and undefined mutual aid (see below) which paid subsequent economic dividends: the expenses associated with the "offices" (officer of a fraternity, leader or member of some community group, etc.) did not in fact bring the holder down to the common level of poverty. Although a household's capital and level of consumption might go down in the year following expenditure on some civic or religious office, in the long run the head of household would increase his prestige and material fortune.

These traditional formal posts of honor, whose occupation used to be the most visible sign of the prestige of a head of household, have undergone great changes in recent decades, as for example in western Guatemala. In that country (except for some formal political posts whose importance has continued and increased), two new formal institutions have increased their presence in this field: evangelical sects, and international development or aid projects. Many of the activities of the old syncretic civic/religious system which, half a century ago, allowed a head of household (with sufficient land, grown-up children and savings) to show his spending power and his devotion to his fellow-men, have now been supplanted by the occupation of posts in evangelical movements, in the new Catholic lay organizations, or, increasingly, as committee chairmen, promoters, or in other capacities in connection with international development aid projects. According to some analysts (Stall, 1993), these posts—which also hold out the hope of clientage benefits—are now emerging as the new "offices" for giving community prestige to heads of peasant households.[5]

MUTUAL AID AND THE EGO-CENTERED NETWORK OF KINSFOLK AS SOCIAL RESOURCES

Mutual Aid: The Main Social Resource of the Household

In addition to its own material and human resources, the household/farm has an important class of social resources which consists essentially of the ties that strengthen cooperation. Unlike other social media, and in contrast with some stereotypes of peasant cooperation, these resources are based not so much on impersonal solidarity in a broad context as on interpersonal ties of concrete, specific individuals.

Perhaps the most important concept for understanding peasant culture better and going deeper than outside appearances is the concept of nondefined mutual aid. Although mutual aid is a form of exchange, it is not so much an economic transaction as a repeated exchange of gifts and favors without any immediate or well-defined compensation (that is to say, "nondefined"), in which each expression of aid reaffirms and strengthens the mutual confidence between the two persons involved.

This brings us to another important aspect of peasant mutual aid: this is not a group relationship (or if it is, it is a group relationship only through a set of individual relationships), but a relationship based on a standing implicit accord between two persons: what Foster called a "dyadic contract"—a completely informal contract which is "dyadic" because it is between two parties (Foster, 1961, pp. 1172–1192). These nonexplicit contracts between two persons to help each other in times of need and in economic ventures where there is an element of risk are to be found above all in environments where the law has only a feeble presence and where some personal assurance of good faith or confidence in the solidarity of the other person is needed. In all cultures, but especially in peasant culture, the shared ethics give rise to a strong sense of duty to aid relatives (especially close relatives of common descent) and to be honest and self-sacrificing with them. This nondefined mutual aid is strongest among relatives, but it also extends to friends of many years' standing, where it is formalized and strengthened in religious terms by acting as godfather, best man, etc., at christenings, weddings, and the like.[6]

> Anthropological myth: The institution of nondefined mutual aid prevents a peasant who manages to save from investing and building up capital in order to grow as a family enterprise. The demands of his duty to provide mutual aid to his relatives oblige a hard-working peasant to immediately share his savings with his less fortunate relatives.

In order to refute this old belief, which underrates the self-development capacity of the family farm, we must go more deeply into the nature of the mutual aid networks among Latin American peasants.

The Kinship Network: A Reserve of Social Resources

Although the strongest and most reliable stable mutual aid relationships that an individual can have are those with his relatives, not all relatives are active participants in "dyadic" relationships with a given individual (in anthropological jargon, an "Ego"). On the contrary, the known and recognized relatives of an Ego are no more than a potential reserve of mutual aid relationships: interaction with many relatives is only sporadic and casual, and the relationships with some of them are conflictive and rule out stable mutual aid, with its positive affective charge. Moreover, as the set of people who occupy the roles of relatives (brothers, uncles, brothers-in-law, etc.) is objectively different for different individuals, this network of potential social relationships is "Ego-centered": each Ego is at the center of a web of relatives disposed in concentric circles, which overlaps and intersects with the networks of relatives of the other Egos in the same community.

Kinship Groups, Support Groups, and "Big Men"

Out of this abstract network of potential relationships (to which must be added neighbors, friends and members of the same generation as the Ego), each head of a peasant family maintains active relations of nondefined mutual aid with a much smaller Ego-centered network. At the same time, he naturally participates in the Ego-centered networks of his relatives. These networks of real exchange relations among relatives have been termed "kinship groups." The fact that these kinship groups overlap with each other in a dense web of mutual aid relationships, with constant exchanges of aid, is what gives a kind of invisible solidarity to the community which is much stronger than that which could be provided by an abstract sense of common social interests vis-à-vis the rest of the world.

Kinship groups are not "social groups" in the strict sense of anthropological and sociological theory, because this latter concept denotes something more than a dispersed network or a mere category of similar persons: a social group is a set of people with stable interaction relations which has clearly perceptible frontiers that distinguish its members from other persons who are not members of the group. Consequently, Ego-centered kinship groups have been called "quasi-groups" (Mayer, 1966).

Very often, however, kinship groups form the basis for true social groups, whose presence has important implications for any attempt to intervene in a peasant community where such groups exist. These "real," though informal, social groups are support groups for specific notable individuals who in some cultures (such as Andean communities, for example) are called "big men" or something similar. These quasi-groups, in contrast with the myth that there is social pressure to share any savings, help peasant households to accumulate capital and grow as enterprises, through the contributions of labor of the mutual aid network. In return, the younger or less enterprising relatives enjoy the certainty that the "big man" will give help at times of need.

> Anthropological myth: Mutual-aid relations in peasant or indigenous societies are all horizontal, i.e., among equals.

As we have seen, the prevailing tendency is for older heads of households to have more resources and higher status than young people in general, which gives rise to "vertical" or patron-client mutual relations. In western Guatemala, mutual aid between unequal persons is also based on a sometimes very strong form of social stratification within the indigenous community, with abundant goods and high status being bequeathed by some fathers to their sons.

In the final analysis, many "big men" run relatively stable and well-defined support groups, based on their own kinship groups but expanded by godfather-type relationships with various nonrelatives. These groups act as expanded economic enterprises and as factions or cliques that support a particular man in the competition for prestige within the community. As their members cannot at the same time be members of the kinship groups of rival prestige-seeking men,[7] it is conceptually valid to speak of true social groups in these cases. In some communities there is only one "big man," who has stood out over the others. In other communities, there may be two or more, all with their respective support groups based on horizontal and vertical mutual aid, thus giving rise to conflicts between factions in the economic, political and organizational fields. Moreover, in many cases there is the paradoxical situation that, in order to strengthen commercial links, there may be godfather-type relationships with outsiders from nonpeasant social strata, who are sometimes the same people who have robbed the community of land or the proceeds of produce sales.

ETHNIC IDENTITY AS A SOCIAL RESOURCE

There can be no doubt that ethnic differences of identity and culture strongly condition any attempt to modify the situation of indigenous peasants. The most obvious importance of the differences between indigenous and nonindigenous peasants lies in the fact that both their interpersonal relations and the views of reality and scales of values that guide the individual behavior of these two groups follow profoundly different specific patterns. At the same time, however, it may be noted that "indigenous" status is the result of lumping together a wide variety of original peoples and relegating them all to a status below that of the "Spanish," "criollo" and "mestizo" colonial strata.

Ethnic Identity and Social Organization

The influence of indigenous culture and social organization is clearly important for participative development projects, and it is usually manifested in difficulties in setting projects in motion in what have been called closed corporative indigenous communities, which operate as defense mechanisms against the economic inroads of the dominant society, sometimes in veritable isolated regional strongholds.

Attention to special ethnic aspects should not be limited, however, to anthropological prescriptions which might be given for overcoming resistance to the presence of a project or to the adoption of the innovations it seeks to promote. In many cases, reluctance to go along with innovations is based on realities which the project itself will be obliged to identify and understand in order to modify its own proposed innovations; in other cases, it reflects well-founded caution about changes which may jeopardize the very survival of the community.

However, the most tightly closed indigenous communities are usually highly corporative, in the sense of forming a true "body" in which collective action is very effective. In such cases, it is important to become familiar with the informal organizations (in the strict sense) and their religious and mutual-aid-linked bases, in order to stimulate the real leadership of the community in the right direction with suitable support from the project.

There are other elements of ethnic differences which it is even more necessary to analyze in a peasant development project: interethnic relations, and ethnic and cultural identity. In all societies of the world there is some degree of ethnic-based prejudice and discrimination; even where ethnic frontiers are blurred indigenous peoples are affected by a dominant alien culture which, as well as depriving them of access to material resources (IFAD, 1993), also bombards them with messages about their alleged inferiority.

Ethnic Identity and Development

In development projects, then, there are two aspects connected with ethnic issues which it is difficult but very necessary to tackle. Firstly, the project takes place within an ethnically unequal power structure which makes it harder to achieve its higher objectives, and moreover most of the officials of the project belong to the dominant ethnic group and speak only the language of that group.

Secondly, the dominant culture transmits to the indigenous culture its perception that the latter is inferior, either in a frankly racist manner, or by taking an "enlightened" attitude which assumes that Western knowledge has a monopoly of the enlightened truth, while the indigenous culture is implicitly seen as a stronghold of ignorance and superstition. The danger is that implicit attitudes which reflect the innermost views of some extension workers or other officials may give the impression that the project claims to offer "superior" forms of knowledge and power and that indigenous groups are seen as ignorant. This attitude, which is sometimes quite unconscious, has its worst effects when it is internalized and accepted by indigenous persons themselves, who end up denying their own ethnic identity (Adams, 1990, pp. 197–224).[8]

A clear sense of identity is a basic human need as important as food itself. A positive self-image which includes a sense of belonging to a sector of humankind perceived as worthwhile is essential as a motive for self-esteem, particularly in the adolescent phase of formation of the adult personality. Fortunately, all over Latin America there is a recent trend towards the formation of positive self-images based on indigenous ethnic identity. As the problem is still very real, however, a development strategy which ignores it would jeopardize the attainment of the project's objectives (Kleymeyer, 1993; Partridge and others, 1996).

For the full application of an analysis of ethnic issues, it is also necessary to develop objectives aimed at strengthening the local culture and promoting indigenous self-management, but these subjects are outside the scope of the present paper, which is of an introductory nature.[9]

SOME PRACTICAL CONNOTATIONS

Some of the anthropological concepts summarized in this article may be important for specific areas of the practical activities of community-centered participative rural development projects: for example, for classifying households or farms, for analyzing probable systemic impacts of project activities, for forming organized groups and, as we shall see below, especially for those project components connected with organization, extension, credit and marketing.

The concept of the life cycle is particularly useful in practical terms for the *organization* and *training* components of the projects in question. Young adults who have more schooling and are easier to train rarely have a high level of authority, prestige or power. They can be trained as technicians, and it is important to give support to their medium-term training, as possible future leaders. But they are also the kind of young people most likely to migrate, because they have fewer possibilities of managing local resources at this stage of their life cycle.

With regard to the *credit* component, men aged around 35 to 45 are those most interested in investing. It is hard for young people to do this because they are poorer, they are concerned primarily with survival, or they prefer to migrate. However, making credit available to young people may stimulate advance inheritance in order to procure more resources for the household. The mere hint of possibilities for investment through a project can cause migrants to return. As young people have new ideas on consumption and independence, they are most likely to be interested in proposals for generating new local sources of income rather than emigrating.

Furthermore, the prestige of a post associated with the project can be a powerful asset of the *participation* component, if properly analyzed and exploited.

Familiarity with the informal social *organization* is essential for working with a participative approach in each specific community to reduce rural poverty, because specific relations cannot be predicted exactly on the basis of a conceptual framework or knowledge of similar communities. It is a positive factor for the project's activities when the potential for cooperation goes beyond the interest group based on farm systems and the support group, kinship relations and vertical mutual aid all lead to multifaceted forms of cooperation which go beyond the limits of a single production model.

It must be borne in mind, however, that the dynamics of cooperation on a scale larger than that of the mutual support quasi-group involve other criteria for consolidation. Cooperation among people with no prior mutual aid relations calls for the constant repetition of joint actions in order to test and strengthen the confidence in members of other (rival) mutual-aid groups as well as to confirm (through repeated tests) the faith in the aims of the project and the capacity of its staff.

In the *organization* component, it is important to remember that the selection of young people by the community as leading officials of organizations promoted from outside is no guarantee that they really have the authority that their posts would appear to give them. The men with the highest prestige often do not hold formal posts in the community: young people may enjoy their support because of their knowledge of the nonpeasant world, but they may be merely "ambassadors" or "foreign ministers" of the real, informal rulers of the community, who are often not familiar with the language of the dominant culture.

The *marketing* component is of key importance for the success of projects to combat rural poverty, because it has the potential to secure a significant improvement in the prices received for crops even in the first year of activity of the project. However, the formation and functioning of marketing committees raises a number of complications for whose solution the anthropological concepts of kinship, quasi-groups and patron-client mutual aid may be of key importance.

Thus, for example, when a group of peasants start their own marketing activities under the auspices of the project, this may break the relations of dependence and exploitation which existed with intermediaries who took advantage of mutual-aid links for that purpose. The main challenge is to establish mutual confidence among the peasants involved, because they will have to entrust their products to some of the members of the marketing committee who are responsible for delivering them to a reception center and finalizing the sale. Clearly, kinship groups provide a basis for such confidence, but usually not all the members of a kinship group produce and market the same crops. Consequently, marketing is an ideal activity for trying to extend the cooperation typical of kinship relations to broader interest groups.

Marketing can also be fertile ground for helping to reduce to some extent the total predominance of the life strategy of the male head of household compared with that of the women. In many peasant cultures, retail commerce (selling small amounts of produce to consumers at regularly-held fairs and markets) is a traditional activity of adult women. Moreover, generally speaking their own production of small livestock, vegetables, handicraft articles, etc., belongs to them personally, as do the proceeds of its sale. Thus, the formation of marketing committees made up of women, as well as "women's banks" organized around these production activities, is already culturally sanctioned as something traditional and acceptable.

Finally, with regard to the *extension* component, the key anthropological concepts set forth in this article must be assimilated by the extension workers, but something which is even more important is that they should accustom themselves to think like researchers, cultivate a sense of curiosity to learn more, try to understand peasant life better, and not merely limit themselves to transferring technical know-how. This involves collecting data, improving and enriching their own models, of production systems, and being conscious of their ambivalent role: as nonindigenous public officials, usually quite young, their prestige—in a post obtained despite their relative youth, and independently of their professional knowledge—will depend on their spirit of service and the power of the project vis-à-vis the State apparatus.

FINAL COMMENTS

It is hoped that these notes may be useful for participative rural development projects, because the planning of production itself, and especially the analysis of the difficulties which are inevitable in the operation of any project, demand that the analysis should not be limited to a standard "small producer" model but should cover the special sociocultural conditions of Latin American peasants. The main objective in drafting this paper has been to help to develop the analytical capacity of nonanthropological staff of rural development projects—especially among the extension workers, who are the key human factor in any rural project and to stimulate among them a concern to develop more sophisticated models of the actual conditions they seek to change.

It does not seem overly ambitious, however, to think in terms of also developing the capacity for analysis of the beneficiaries of rural projects themselves. They will need this capacity when outside support is withdrawn and the specific system of production, credit organization and marketing that a project leaves behind it begins to falter because of the changes which will sooner or later take place in the environment and which will oblige the peasants to review their approach in a hurry. It does not seem at all utopian to believe that the peasants of today—indigenous and nonindigenous—will be able to carry out the necessary analysis and management actions if the know-how transferred to them is not limited to purely technical matters but also includes training in management and the taking of decisions in a changing context.

Notes

[1] "This is not business as usual!", World Bank Group, 1996, p. 15.

[2] The term "informal social organization" has a connotation in anthropology which is totally different from that used in many development projects, where it means any organization that does not have recognized legal status. Anthropologists, however, apply this term to the stable social relationships among persons which are not always even given formal names but which constitute the social fabric that gives its strength to the peasant community (Firth, 1961; Barth, 1966; Durston, 1992).

[3] Truth to tell, almost all the ideas which we have called "anthropological myths" in this article, in order to liven up the analysis a little, still have their supporters among anthropologists themselves, for anthropology, like all sciences, is a battlefield of warring theories. The interpretations favored in this article are simply the hypotheses that the author himself supports, without losing sight of the fact that today's "truths" may very likely be changed in the future.

[4] For more details on the development cycle of the household, see Goody (ed.), 1958.

[5] This is only one of various recent past changes that must be taken into account by project personnel, not as a mere background to the present situation but as dynamics of social changes which are under way. Another element is population growth during the last generation, which, because of its effect on the population burden on productive land, has changed (among other things) both gerontocratic authority in the household and the political relations in the area. Because of their ongoing effects in the economic and social sphere, these past processes still affect the work of staff in the field, who must be familiar with their evolution in the recent past in order to understand them properly.

[6] These bases for mutual aid are so closely assimilated to blood relationships that godfathers, best men, etc. have been called "pseudo-relatives."

[7] Prestige, unlike capital (which can be generated or created) and more so than in the case of land, is an "absolutely limited good," since only one person can be the man with the highest prestige in a given community.

[8] As Adams points out—in keeping with the definition of culture given at the beginning of the present article—cultural change does not necessarily mean the loss of indigenous identity.

[9] For a diagnostic study and proposal regarding the IFAD projects with indigenous peoples, see Helms, 1994.

References

Adams, R. (1990). Algunas observaciones sobre el cambio étnico en Guatemala, *Anales de la Academia de Geografía e Historia de Guatemala,* vol. LXIV, Guatemala.

Ashby, J. and L. Sperling. (1992). Institutionalizing participatory, client-driven research and development. Paper presented at the Meeting of Social Scientists, Consultative Group on International Agricultural Research (CGIAR), The Hague, Netherlands, 17–20 August, *mimeo.*

Banuri, T. and others. (1996). *Desarrollo humano sostenible: de la teoría a la práctica,* New York, United Nations Development Program (UNDP).

Barth, F. (1966). *Models of Social Organization.* Glasgow: Glasgow University Press.

Campaña, P. (1994). *Informe, Consultoría sobre género en desarrollo*, Proyecto de Desarrollo Rural de la Sierra de las Cuchumatanes, Chiantla, Guatemala, *mimeo.*

Cernea, M. (1996). *Social Organization and Development Anthropology: The 1995 Malinowski Award Lecture,* Environmentally Sustainable Development Studies and Monographs Series, No. 6. Washington, DC: World Bank.

Coombs, P. (ed.). (1980). *Meeting the Basic Needs of the Rural Poor: The Integrated Community-Based Approach.* New York: Pergamon Press.

Cowan, O. and others. (1995). *Complexity: Metaphors, Models, and Reality.* Santa Fe, NM: Santa Fe Institute.

DeWalt, B. (1985). Anthropology, sociology, and farming systems research, *Human Organization,* vol. 44, No. 2, University of New Mexico.

DeWalt, K. and B. DeWalt. (1992). Agrarian reform and the food crisis in Mexico: Microlevel and macrolevel processes, in J. J. Poggie, Jr. and others (eds.), *Anthropological Research: Process and Application.* New York: SUNY.

Durston, J. (1998). Rural social policy in a strategy of sustained development, *CEPAL Review,* No. 36, LC/G.1537-P, Santiago, Chile, ECLAC.

——— (1992). *Organización social de los mercados campesinos en el Centro de Michoacán,* 2nd ed. Mexico City: Presencias/National Institute of Indigenous Affairs (INI).

—— (1993). Indigenous peoples and modernity, *CEPAL Review*, No. 51, LC/G.1792-P, Santiago, Chile, ECLAC.

—— (1996). Estratégias de vida de la juventud rural, *Juventud rural, modernidad y democracia en América Latina,* Santiago, Chile, ECLAC/United Nations Children's Fund (UNICEF)/Ibero-American Youth Organization.

—— (In press). La participación comunitaria en la gestión de la escuela rural, *mimeo.*

Durston, J., and A. Crivelli. (1984). Diferenciación campesina en la sierra ecuatoriana: análisis estadístico de cinco comunidades en Cotopaxi y Chimborazo, in M. Chiriboga and others, *Estratégias de supervivencia en la comunidad andina.* Quito: Centro Andino de Acción Popular (CAAP).

ECLAC (Economic Commission for Latin America and the Caribbean). (1994). *Social Panorama of Latin America 1994,* LC/G.1844, Santiago, Chile.

Errázuriz. M. M. (1986). Las insuficiencias del desarrollo rural, *El crecimiento productivo y la heterogenidad agrícola,* LC/L.396, Santiago, Chile, ECLAC/Food and Agriculture Organization of the United Nations (FAO).

FAO. (1988). *Potentials for Agricultural and Rural Development in Latin America and the Caribbean,* Rome.

Firth, R. (1961). *Elements of Social Organization,* 3rd. ed. Boston: Beacon Press.

Foster, G. (1948). *Empire's Children: The People of Tzintzuntzán.* Washington, DC: Smithsonian Institution.

——. (1961). The dyadic contract: a model for the social structure of a Mexican peasant village, *American Anthropologist,* vol. 63, Washington, DC.

Fox, J. (1995). Governance and rural development in Mexico, State intervention and public accountability, *The Journal of Development Studies,* vol. 342, No. 1.

Gluckman, M. (ed.). (1964). *Closed Systems and Open Minds.* Chicago: Aldine.

Goody, J. (ed.). (1958). *The Developmental Cycle in Domestic Groups,* Cambridge Papers in Anthropology, No. 1, Cambridge, U. K., Cambridge University.

Helms, B. (1994). *Indigenous Peoples in Latin America and the Caribbean: IFAD Policies and Projects,* Rome, IFAD.

IFAD (International Fund for Agricultural Development). (1993). *El estado de la pobreza rural en el mundo: la situación en América Latina,* Rome.

Kleymeyer, C. (1993). Introduction, in C. Kleymeyer (ed.), *Cultural Expression and Grassroots Development.* London: Rienner.

Lacroix, R. (1985). *Integrated Rural Development in Latin America,* Working Paper No. 716, Washington DC, World Bank.

Mayer, A. (1966). The significance of quasi-groups in the study of complex societies, in M. Banton (comp.), *The Social Anthropology of Complex Societies.* London: Tavistock.

Partridge, W. and others. (1996). *Inclusión de los excluídos: el etnodesarrollo en América Latina,* paper presented at Segunda Conferencia del Banco Mundial para el Desarrollo en América Latina y el Caribe, Bogotá, 30 June–2 July, *mimeo.*

Redfield, R. (1930). *Tepoztlán: A Mexican Village.* Chicago: University of Chicago Press.

Stoll, D. (1993). *Between Two Armies in the Ixil Towns of Guatemala.* New York: Columbia University Press.

Tax, S. (1953). *Penny Capitalism: A Guatemalan Indian Economy.* Washington DC: Smithsonian Institution.

Valdés, A. and T. Wiens. (1996). *Pobreza rural en América Latina y el Caribe,* paper presented at Segunda Conferencia del Banco Mundial para el Desarrollo en América Latina y el Caribe, Bogotá, 30 June–2 July, *mimeo.*

Van Alphen, R. (1994). *Propuesta de análisis de encuesta de base y estudio y uso de sistemas de producción,* Proyecto de Desarrollo de la Sierra de los Cuchumatanes, Chinantla, Guatemala, *mimeo.*

World Bank Group. (1996). *From Vision to Action in the Rural Sector,* Washington DC, World Bank, March.

Dr. H. Russell Bernard is a professor of anthropology at University of Florida. Among his most recent books are: Social Research Methods *(Newbury Park, CA: Sage Publications, 2000);* Research Methods in Anthropology *(Walnut Creek, CA: Altimira Press, 1994); and, with Jesús Salinas Pedraza,* Native Ethnography: A Mexican Indian Describes His Culture *(Newbury Park, CA: Sage Publications, 1989).*

Within a single generation, anthropologists have changed their positions from considering "nonliterate languages" to be the defining characteristic of "primitive" peoples to serving in the vanguard of an imaginative effort to render all languages literate, with the special advantages that such an effort offers for communicating across time and space. This movement runs counter to a rapidly accelerating trend toward the extinction of languages that some saw as an inevitable concomitant of the supposed globalization of Western culture. The interplay of ever-larger organizations, rapid and inexpensive communications, and the very human concern for some continuity of tradition and self-identification may take some unexpected turns in the twenty-first century, as illustrated in Bernard's unorthodox— but logical—account of language preservation through publishing.

Language Preservation and Publishing

H. Russell Bernard

There is increasing awareness that languages are vanishing and that they must be preserved. Many papers and anthologies attest to this interest (Hill 1979, 1989; Dressler 1981; Elmendorf 1981; Bernard 1985; Dorian 1989; Robins-Uhlenbeck 1991; Garzon 1992; Hale 1992; Krauss 1992); in 1992, the journal *Language* devoted an entire section to a series of articles on the topic; and there have been global discussions about endangered languages on the Internet.[1]

There is some debate, however, as to whether vanishing languages *should* be preserved, and if they should, then what might be the best contributions of professional linguists and anthropologists. In this essay I lay out reasons why we must take decisive action and why part of that decisive action is to publish books in previously nonliterary languages.

THE POLITICAL ARGUMENT

The most prominent discussion of whether linguists should work to preserve vanishing languages was initiated by Hale (1992), who asked a group of colleagues to write essays on various aspects of language preservation, and the set was published as lead article in *Language*.

The key fact is stated by Krauss in his contribution: at least 50% of the 6,000 languages still in the world will become extinct in the next century. If we include languages that have at least 100,000 speakers in the "safe" category, then just 600, or 10%, are safe from extinction. Krauss points out that even this assumption may be optimistic. Breton had a million speakers early in this century but is now struggling for survival; Navajo had over 100,000 speakers a generation ago and now faces an uncertain future (1992:6).

Krauss is right. There were at least 7,000 languages in the world in A.D. 1500 (when European nations began the era of colonial expansion), and there are about 6,000 languages today. This 15% reduction in linguistic diversity is just the beginning. In just the last few decades, the pace of extinction has quickened. Several hundred languages have vanished (their last speakers having died), and hundreds more are on the brink of extinction (their last speakers being old and no children being taught the language).

In 1962, Chafe listed 51 American Indian languages as having ten or fewer speakers. A generation later, those 51 languages are probably extinct, according to Zapeda and Hill (1991:136). In 1992, the *Ethnologue* (Grimes 1992) lists some 70 American Indian languages with fewer than 200 speakers. In another generation, those languages will be extinct or beyond recovery. The same story is being played out in Australia, South America, New Guinea, and Africa. The circumstances beg linguists to do something.

Not all linguists agree. Writing in *Language* later in 1992, Ladefoged says that the views expressed by Hale and colleagues "are contrary to those held by many responsible linguists" (1992:809). It would not be appropriate in places like Tanzania, he says, for linguists to help preserve language diversity. In Tanzania, the authorities see local languages as a source of tribalism and encourage the spread of Swahili at the expense of local languages, as a means to build the nation.

Ladefoged reports an encounter with a linguistic informant who speaks Dahalo. The informant was proud of the fact that his teenage sons did not speak the language. "Who am I to say that he was wrong?" asks Ladefoged. For linguists working in Tanzania, says Ladefoged, "it would not be acting responsibly to do anything which might seem, at least superficially, to aid in" the preservation of tribalism (Ladefoged 1992:809).

In her response to Ladefoged, Dorian (1993) agrees that responsible linguists ought not foment rebellion against authorities who are determined to eliminate language and cultural diversity. On the other hand, she says, the death of a language does not occur only under these circumstances. Much of it is taking place in democracies where economic, not political, exigencies operate to discourage people from teaching their ancestral language to their children. In those countries it is not a dangerous political act to work for language diversity.[2]

There are, of course, millions of speakers of local languages in democracies like the United States, Canada, and Australia who, like Ladefoged's Dahalo informant, proudly renounce their language. There are many millions more who do so without making any fuss about it. Those people, though, don't speak for everyone. There are speakers of small languages who do not want those languages to disappear and who are anxious to work actively for language preservation. Bilingual education is almost everywhere inimical to language preservation, but I have met bilingual educators from Mexico, Cameroon, Ecuador, and other countries who are looking for ways to stem the erosion of their indigenous languages.

Linguists interested in promoting language diversity need not work with people who are against it. We can easily find native-speaker colleagues in many countries with whom to mount effective language preservation programs. The people with whom I work in Mexico on the CELIAC project (about which more below; and see Salinas (1996) and González (1996)) are all bilingual school teachers and native speakers of indigenous languages. They all report that there are people in their villages who reflect the sentiment of Ladefoged's Dahalo informant. And none of these schoolteachers is willing to let those people carry the day.

LANGUAGE PRESERVATION:
THE EVOLUTIONARY PERSPECTIVE

Hale asserts that we should ask whether there is a danger in the loss of language diversity that is analogous to the loss of biodiversity (1992). Elsewhere, I have also drawn attention to the analogy of cultural/linguistic and biological diversity (Bernard

1992). Krauss (1992) makes the analogy explicit. There are, he notes, 326 of 4,400 mammal species, or 7.4% of mammals, on the endangered and threatened list. Next come the birds, with 231 of 8,600 species, or 2.7% listed as endangered or threatened.

Even such a relatively small number of extinctions, says Krauss, is considered a catastrophe in the making. There are, he notes, international and national bureaucracies, plus private organizations by the hundreds devoted to bioconservation. "Should we mourn the loss of Eyak or Ubkyh," asks Krauss, "any less than the loss of the panda or the California condor?" (1992:8).

The problem with all our analogies is that they are based on speculation, not on empirical observation or on theoretical grounds. Biologists have empirical evidence that biodiversity is good for life on the planet in general. They have strong theoretical models for the mutual dependence of diverse species. They have case studies that show the adaptive success of hybrid vigor. For all we know, there is really no comparison to be made between biodiversity and cultural diversity. For all we know, one language and one culture might be just fine.

I think we *can* make the evolutionary case for linguistic and cultural diversity. For 40,000 years, since the beginning of modern Homo sapiens, we humans have been an evolutionary success story. From perhaps half a million individuals (Kates 1994:94) living in just a few spots, we have expanded to 6 billion individuals occupying every ecological niche on the globe, including deserts, tundra, and high mountains. This spectacular case of adaptive biological radiation was characterized by an expansion of knowledge about survival in various environments, and that knowledge was stored in all the languages that developed during the radiation. And now those languages are vanishing.

It is not necessary to argue that language diversity *caused* the evolutionary success of humans. We need only recognize that the knowledge generated by all those successfully adapting cultural groups over the millennia is stored in all those thousands of languages now spoken around the world. Of the 6,000 spoken today, 276 of them comprise more than 5 billion speakers.[3] All the rest of the languages, 95% of them, are spoken by just 300 million people. Just 5% of the people in the world speak 95% of the world's languages.

Turn these numbers around to see the problem: 95% of the cultural heterogeneity of the planet—95% of the *differences* in ways of seeing the world—is vested in under 5% of the people, and the problem gets worse each year.

One could argue, of course, that language die-off is just part of natural evolution, something that should be neither fretted over nor tampered with. After all, the absorption of cultures into larger states has been going on since the late Neolithic, and with that absorption many languages have disappeared. Nothing catastrophic seems to have happened, so why worry now?

This is a high-risk approach because the pace of language extinction is rapid today. There would be lower risk to humanity if we had 26 or 30 Earth-like planets, unlimited time, and god-like power to test whether language diversity was really good for human evolutionary success. On some planets we could ordain that language diversity remain high, while on others it would decline toward zero. Then (over a few millennia perhaps), we might learn whether the decline in diversity placed the survival of humanity on any planet at risk.

In the course of this experiment, we might also learn whether knowledge in any modern human language can be translated perfectly into any other such language. If it can, then a program to rescue *knowledge*, rather than *languages*, would be sufficient to rescue humanity from the ill effects of diminishing language diversity.

In fact, we are conducting the experiment to find out if eliminating language diversity is harmful to our survival as a species. With no planets to fall back on, it's truly a reckless experiment. It should be stopped now.

How to Preserve Languages

Those committed to preserving language diversity engage in many activities toward this end. I think it's helpful to talk *of archiving* (or documenting) activities and *vitalizing* activities rather than simply preservation activities. Making dictionaries, writing grammars, and recording speakers all help to archive a language. Teaching children to speak a language makes the language vital. Both kinds of effort, archiving and vitalizing, can be said to help preserve a language.

I don't mean to create any hierarchy here. Vitalizing activities are not to be preferred over archiving activities. It's a matter of what, finally, can be done with the human and financial resources available. The tapes, grammars, and texts recorded by linguists are the only record we have of (too many) languages that have already died.[4] Training speakers of indigenous languages to be linguists extends greatly the accurate archiving of those languages (Hale 1969, 1972, 1976). And, as I will argue later, so does training indigenous authors to write books in their native languages.

Linguists can archive languages, but truly vitalizing programs must be in the hands of speakers themselves, and not in the hands of linguists. Programs like the one at Peach Springs School in Arizona for Hualapai (Watahomigie & Yamamoto 1988) and the preschool total immersion (or language-nest) programs for Maori in New Zealand and for Hawaiian in Hawaii (Zepeda & Hill 1991) are creating new, fully fluent young speakers of those languages. Few children were learning those languages before the programs were put in place.

Linguists can suggest new language vitalizing programs. We can help find financial support for and be advisors to those programs. I have suggested, for example, that in the United States, Canada, and Australia, some communities might provide working mothers of infant and toddler children with paid day-care by native-fluent elders who would speak only the local language to those children. Working mothers would get needed day care; elderly women and men would get needed income doing jobs that only they can do; children would get the requisite training for becoming bilingual speakers of the local and the national languages. But while linguists initiate such programs, in the end, the main responsibility for vitalizing the vanishing languages of the world is with the speakers of those languages.

Publishing and the Preservation of Languages

For those linguists who want to help preserve language diversity, there are, in my view, two best things to do. One is to help native people develop more language-nest programs (including day-care programs like the one I've suggested). The other is to help native people develop publishing houses.

I want to make clear that I am talking about real publishing of books that are sold on an aggressively sought market. And I want to make equally clear that bilingual education and teaching people to write their previously nonliterary languages is not, by itself, a solution.

I use the term "nonliterary" rather than "nonwritten" because many languages of the world have been written, often by linguists but sometimes even by native speakers, without developing a literary tradition. Tuvaluan, for example, is spoken by about 9,000 people in Tuvalu (the former Ellice Islands) of the South Pacific. Nearly all speakers of Tuvalu are literate, but there is practically no written literature available. Besnier (1991) studied how the people of Nukulaelae Atoll used their literacy skills and found that most people wrote letters to one another, a few people wrote sermons for delivery in church, and not much more.

Bilingual education programs for indigenous children almost universally involve teaching those children to read and write their ancestral language. But bilingual education for indigenous children is also almost universally understood to be transitional education.

For example, children who come to school as monolingual Eskimo speakers are introduced to schooling via Yup'ik, which is abandoned after the third grade. The official purpose of the program is to "wean students away from the need for their own language." This is not just local policy; it reflects "federal models of what bilingual education is to accomplish." That is, the programs are "designed to make [the children's] Eskimo language largely useless" (Iutzi-Mitchell 1992:9).[5]

This model is found across the world. Children who come to school at the age of five or six without competence in their national language (English, French, Spanish, etc.) are taught in their ancestral language as a transition to the national language (see de Bravo Ahuja 1992 for a discussion of the policy in Mexico).

This is not an argument against bilingual education. It is essential that indigenous children everywhere control their national language. If they don't, they will never be able to vote, to engage in commerce, to go into the professions, or to otherwise participate in the national economy and body politic. There is absolutely nothing to be said for avoiding full competence, including a high level of literacy, in a national language, just as there is nothing to be said for being poor. Most bilingual education, however, is based on the false choice between becoming monolingual in a national language and being poor.

A feature common to many transitional programs is the use of primers and readers written in the so-called vernacular language. (In the United States, in fact, indigenous-language publishing is limited almost entirely to primary school textbooks [Zepeda & Hill 1991:140].) This implies that an orthography has been developed and that some professional work has been done on the grammar.

In fact, most of the small languages of the world have an orthography developed by missionaries or linguists or both. There may be a translation of the Old and New Testaments, a formal grammar, and a small dictionary. What these languages do not have is a literary tradition—the kind that produces indigenous written works of poetry, fiction, biography, history, ethnography, and so on. Most of the languages of the world are still essentially oral, and their literature (poetry, biography, etc.) is oral.

There is disagreement about the effects of writing on thought (see Finnegan 1988 and Ong 1982 for opposing views), but it is my thesis that *if oral languages do not develop a written literary tradition, most of them will soon die.* One of the last Ainu speakers told Stephen Wurm that Ainu would disappear because, unlike Japanese, it could not be written. "An indigenous language with no traditional writing system tends to yield," said Wurm, to a language that has a written literary tradition (1991:8).

A written literary tradition means establishing a publishing industry in each such language—an industry that goes beyond the production of school primers. It may not be sufficient to establish publishing industries, but history shows clearly that printing and publishing greatly facilitate the development of literary traditions (Eisenstein 1979, Davis 1981).

ORTHOGRAPHIES AND DICTIONARIES

Across the world, a lot of effort goes into arguing about the relative merits of this or that orthography for previously nonliterary languages. The situation in Trinidad and Tobago is typical. According to Winer (1990), "a considerable amount of writing in Creole is now being done by people whose concern is not whether to write Creole, but how to spell it" (cited in Brown 1993).

The best way to establish orthographies is to publish and sell books using any orthography that people will pay to read. Among the major world languages, standard orthographies have emerged only recently, and in no case were they established by linguists. Rather, they were established by publishers. Books published in English just 200 years ago exhibit an amusing lack of orthographic consistency. The shape of letters, spelling conventions, punctuation conventions, paragraph conventions, and all the other components of the English orthography emerged in the context of commercial and government publishing.

The process is ongoing. Not very long ago, publishers in the United States used the character œ in the word "œdipus." Now the word is spelled "oedipus," and the diphthong is gone from American orthography. The circumflex accent over the "o" in 'rôle" is gone, too, as is the ç in "façade" (now spelled simply "facade"). The æ in the word "archæology" has become "ae" but early in this century the diphthong was dropped in U.S. government publications and many publishers now spell the word "archeology". Eventually, one spelling will emerge the winner, and linguists will have had little or nothing to do with the outcome.[6]

Dictionaries of the major languages of the world were not compiled by fieldworking linguists from oral text. The dictionaries were compiled from words taken out of printed literature. The first dictionary of English published in the United States was a very slim volume compared to the monumental dictionaries being produced these days because lexicographers now have so much more printed material than they did 200 years ago.

If a language has no literary tradition, then making a dictionary can only come from taking down oral text and combing that text for words and usages. Under the circumstances, the efforts of some linguists have been nothing less than heroic. After 26 years of fieldwork on Dyirbal in Australia, Dixon (1991:200) reports having developed a dictionary of "five or six thousand words." Nater's (1990) dictionary of Nuxalk (a Salishan language in Canada) contains 2,000 entries, after many years of work.

A literary tradition changes things radically. In 1989 I taught five speakers of Kom, a language spoken by 127,000 people in North West Province of Cameroon, to write their language with a word processor. In two weeks, the five had produced over 25,000 words of free-flowing text: a schoolteacher wrote about the local environment; another teacher wrote out 103 proverbs and was well into annotating those proverbs when the two-week training period ended; a Catholic priest (a native speaker of Kom) wrote about religious syncretism; an anthropology student at the university wrote about local medical practices; and a lawyer wrote about local marriage contracts.

Note that all of these people were bilingual speakers of English, and all of them were educated. Learning to write fluently in Kom did not require that they learn the skills of literacy. It meant only transferring those skills from English to Kom, which they did in a matter of hours. There was (and remains) disagreement about the best orthography for Kom. If we had focused on that disagreement we would have done nothing. Every educated speaker of English knows that there are more rational ways to write that language than the hodge-podge writing system we now have. It is simply not necessary to find the perfect orthography to begin developing a literary corpus.

Kinkade (1991:165) attributes the lack of published dictionaries for indigenous languages to high printing costs and small markets. Since publishers are unwilling to put out dictionaries in native languages, linguists are reluctant to compile them, he says. The 25,000-word corpus of Kom produced over 2,600 unique words. Many of these words were forms of underlying verbs and nouns, but the Kom project still produced the corpus for a context-sensitive dictionary of at least a thousand words in two weeks.

The insights of professional linguists about the workings of languages are unlikely to be generated by amateurs. But note that the 25,000-word corpus of Kom is now as available to linguists working in that region as it is to native speakers who may wish to read it for content and to native speakers who happen also to be professional linguists (there is at least one).

In other words, building dictionaries, like establishing orthographies, is best done by developing very large corpora of written text. And when texts are written on word processors, they can be studied for their grammar with all the power of computer-based tools. Teaching highly educated native speakers of nonliterary languages to use computers for writing large texts in those languages is thus the fastest, and most accurate, way to get data for studying the grammar of a language.

Of course, a dictionary based on written text will have different content than one based on oral text. A thorough description of a literary language obviously requires a dictionary that accounts for usage in speech as well as in written text. Until very recently, though, the only dictionaries of literary languages were based on the literary corpus, while speech-based dictionaries were made only for languages that did not have a literary tradition.

In 1994, Longman, a British publishing house, had 150 volunteers walk around for two weeks with tape recorders tied to their waists. The tapes were transcribed to produce a corpus of about ten million words. This corpus is published on CD-ROM by Oxford University and will greatly enhance our ability to study and analyze English. For example, we have already learned that the most common use of the word "like" is not as a verb but as a preposition ("he eats like a pig") (Nurden 1994:22).

Dictionaries based entirely on written text do not reveal this kind of language artifact. Similarly, the addition of computer-based corpora of written text will enhance our ability to study and analyze the majority of the world's languages. This should be reason enough for linguists to want to help people across the world develop native publishing houses.

But publishing does more than help us make dictionaries and acquire corpora for studying the grammar of a language. It increases immensely the archive of a culture, and it produces pride in the language. "The very existence of a book on a shelf," says Krauss, ". . . can be of crucial symbolic value" in the effort to preserve a dying language (1992:8, and see González 1996).

CELIAC

My comments on the means and motives for preserving languages brings us to CELIAC, the *Centro Editorial de Literatura Indígena, Asociación Civil*, in Oaxaca, Mexico. (*Asociación Civil* means "not-for-profit corporation" in Mexico.)

The charter of CELIAC is to promote the preservation of native languages and cultures in Mexico through the publishing of books in those languages. At CELIAC, prospective Indian authors from Mexico and elsewhere in Latin America learn to use computers to write books in their native languages. So far, 121 people have been through the Program. Instruction is in Spanish and is done by other Indians. The leaders of CELIAC are Jesús Salinas and Josefa González, both of whom have written articles on the subject.

Books written by indigenous authors at CELIAC are published and sold in Mexico and on the international market. Many speakers of Mexican Indian languages cannot afford to purchase these books. Our hope is that sales beyond the indigenous communities will make the publishing of indigenous-languages books self-supporting and that profits will pay for the distribution of books to speakers of indigenous languages in towns and villages.

CELIAC now has a list of books that have been published and a list of books in preparation,[7] but it remains to be seen whether sales will support the continuation of the effort. The risk is clear. Five hundred years into the Gutenberg revolution, 95% of the world's languages remain untouched by it because, so far at least, no one has been able to turn a profit by publishing in those languages. The economies of desktop publishing dare us all to take another try.

CELIAC is a not-for-profit publishing house, but like all corporations it must cover its costs, which include salaries, electricity, telephone, advertising, insurance, and so on. Until now, most of the costs have been covered by the project's association with various Mexican and international government organizations (Salinas 1996).

For example, until 1993, the project (known as the Oaxaca Native Literacy Project in English and as the *Proyecto en Literatura Indígena* in Spanish) was part of the Oaxaca branch of CIESAS (the *Centro de Investigaciones y Estudios Superiores en Antropología Social*), a Mexican government research group. CIESAS provided housing for the project in Oaxaca and, in cooperation with the government of the state of Oaxaca, published the first books that came out of the project.

The support of government agencies was thus crucial to the development of the project and will continue to be a factor. In late 1993, however, CELIAC became an independent organization, and in 1994 the project moved into its own building. Purchase and renovation of the building were covered by a grant from the Jessie Ball Du Pont Foundation, as are the current costs of book production. Eventually, CELIAC (and the many CELIAC-type organizations we hope will follow around the world) needs to cover the costs of book production and distribution on its own.

COMMODITIZING NONLITERARY LANGUAGES

This implies commoditizing nonliterary languages—turning them into things for sale. Can it be done? Should it be done?

It takes about a month for a prospective author to train at CELIAC and another several months to produce a draft of a document. It takes the author another three or four months to develop the book, and it takes CELIAC personnel another three months to do the formatting and production—all in all, about a year. It will take a few years, but eventually CELIAC should be able to produce six books a year. If the books sell 200 or 300 copies at a reasonable price (say, $30 each in 1995 dollars), the gross would not be nearly enough to cover the real costs of keeping a building, paying salaries, paying the per diem of authors in residence at CELIAC, advertising and distributing books, and paying royalties to authors.

On the other hand, CELIAC is not limited to publishing just books. They also now publish disks of the texts produced. Not every prospective author who trains at CELIAC produces a book. But the published disks can include texts that are not printed as books as well as texts that are. In 1995, CELIAC will install a small recording studio. The authors who work at CELIAC will record their texts on high-quality tape. Again, those whose texts are not published in book form, as well as those whose work is eventually published, may record their work on audiotape. As texts accumulate in a language (Mixtec, for example), CELIAC will publish corpora on CD-ROM.

Who will buy these products? Linguists and anthropologists (and the libraries with which they are associated), missionaries, and several other constituencies comprise an intensely interested and completely unserved market for texts in previously nonliterary languages—particularly for machine-readable texts accompanied by clear voice renditions on tape or on CD-ROM. The corpus of Nähñu (Otomí) text produced by Jesús Salinas since 1971 is well over 250,000 words. What I wouldn't have given for that corpus (in print, on disk, and on tape) in 1962, when I began as a graduate student to work with Jesús!

CELIAC'S FUTURE

But are there even 200 or 300 potential sales in the world for books, disks, and tapes in indigenous languages? Again, it remains to be seen if linguists and others are sufficiently interested in having access to a continuing supply of text in the indigenous languages of the world. In the near term, CELIAC could not survive if it had to depend only on publishing, but CELIAC is not limited to publishing. CELIAC is already branching out, taking on new functions. I will discuss two of them, each an example of commoditization of local culture and language.

In 1994, CELIAC received its first contract from a Mexican government agency. The national social security administration was conducting a public health survey on home remedies for infantile diarrhea. The leader of the project, Dr. Homero Martínez, recognized that hit-and-run surveys in Spanish had produced data of dubious quality in previous studies and asked CELIAC to collect the data in open-ended interviews. The interviews would be conducted with mothers of young children—in the native languages of the communities where the study was being done.

Graduates of CELIAC training conducted the interviews in Highland Mixtec, Coastal Mixtec, Isthmus Zapotec, Highland Zapotec, Mazatec, and Chinantec, the six most widely spoken of the native languages of Oaxaca. The interviewers transcribed the data and wrote up reports for the project. The reports will be published, in the local languages and in Spanish, jointly by the *Secretaría de Salubridad y Asistencia* and CELIAC.

Also in 1994, CELIAC received from Colorado College in the United States a contract to house 12 students for a month. There are dozens of fine programs in Mexico where U.S. college students can study Spanish and learn about Mexican culture, often by staying with Mexican families. Dr. Mario Montaño of Colorado College takes students regularly to Mexico for this kind of direct cultural contact. He thought that a one-month course at CELIAC would be unique because the students would be exposed to indigenous cultures.

Publishing indigenous language books; offering foreign students an opportunity to learn about indigenous cultures firsthand; collecting ethnographic data in the indigenous languages—these activities have one important thing in common: they represent commoditization of native languages by native people. Some people may be uncomfortable with the commercialism of this approach. In my opinion, the faster native languages and cultures become salable commodities the better chance they have of not disappearing.

The reason people *say* they give up speaking their native languages is that the languages offer no economic and/or social benefits. I used to try arguing the case: all cultures are ethnic groups, embedded as they are in nation states; maintaining one's language is an excellent way to maintain one's ethnic identity in a plural society; in democracies, people who keep their identity have a more legitimate claim on parts of the common weal. And so on.

Good arguments, but not good enough to combat national language policy and the legions of bilingual school teachers who carry the assimilationist message. If people want to abandon their language for economic reasons, then economic reasons must be found to make them want to keep their language. The way to preserve languages is to make languages economically and/or politically paying operations, even if only for a few people, like indigenous authors and indigenous publishers.

The sale of indigenous culture is nothing new among speakers of nonliterary languages. People sell native foods, native costumes, native jewelry, ceramics, tapestries, cloth, and other material artifacts. Native music and dance is sold (the Mexican National *Ballet Folklórico* is an example). Native people, however, have not participated directly in the sale of their languages. That has been the province of linguists, anthropologists, government functionaries, and missionaries. At CELIAC, Indians are selling their own intellectual property and their own skills in writing, interviewing, and teaching.

Commoditization of language and culture may seem crass. I don't think it is. After all, I make my own living as a university professor selling what I know. Some of what I know was acquired through contact with colleagues at CELIAC and elsewhere in other parts of the world. When I sell what I know—when I negotiate my salary with a university—I do not stress the primary cultural and linguistic knowledge I've acquired. No one knows that primary material better than the people with whom I've studied. I stress the value that I've added to the primary cultural material—my analyses of the data, my testing of certain hypotheses, and so on. It is the value-added that makes what I know, my culture, worth paying for.

It is the same for my colleagues at CELIAC. It is not simply that they know how to speak Mixtec, Zapotec, Nähñu, or some other indigenous language. What makes that knowledge economically valuable is its value-added packaging between the covers of a book, its packaging as a course for college students, its packaging as skill in interviewing and writing up ethnographic reports.

In my view, then, the commoditization of language and culture by indigenous people is a vehicle for the economic development of indigenous people. In the end, it is this development that will make it possible for indigenous languages to thrive.

***

This chapter was written while I was on leave from the University of Florida and in residence at the University of Cologne. My sincere thanks to the Alexander von Humboldt Foundation, the University of Cologne Institut für Völderkunde, and the College of Arts and Sciences at the University of Florida for support during this time. My thanks also to William H. Adams, Nancy Dorian, Kenneth Hale, Marvin Harris, Jane Hill, George Mbeh, Isaac Nyamongo, and Oswald Werner for their helpful comments on an earlier draft of this chapter.

***

Notes

[1] The most important discussions have taken place on Linguist-L (linguist@tam2000.tamu.edu), Nat-Lang (nat-lang@gnosys.svle.ma.us), and Endangered-Languages-L (endangered-languages-L@coombs.anu.edu.au).

[2] Moreover, language differences do not cause tribalism and imposing a common language does not by itself eliminate tribalism, if by tribalism one means the (often violent) conflict among ethnic groups. Competition for land may erupt in violent confrontations, and when the combatants vilify one another's language, it is easy to imagine that the conflict is about the hegemony of the languages themselves. Many Bosnians, Serbs, and Croats speak the same language yet were long locked in violent conflict over control of land. The conflict between Israelis and Palestinians is also about land and would not go away if both sides adopted a common language.

Isaac Nyamongo, a Kenyan anthropologist, points out that making people speak Swahili will not by itself conceal a person's ethnic origins. "In Kenya," he says, "I can tell a person's ethnic affiliation just by listening to the way they speak English. I can tell who is Kikuyu, Luo, Kamba, Gusii, Luhyia, and Kalenjin." If speaking English does not obliterate ethnic accents, he points out, then we should not expect speaking Swahili to do the job (personal communication).

[3] I am indebted to Barbara Grimes (personal communication) for the data on which this calculation is based. See Grimes 1988 for further information.

[4] According to Dimmendaal (1989:20), we know of a language in northeastern Uganda called Dorobo only because of a word list published by E. J. Wayland in 1931. The language was spoken by a now extinct group of hunter-gatherers.

[5] Oswald Werner (personal communication) reports visiting a Navajo-English, bilingual-education kindergarten 20 years ago where the reward for speaking English was to be allowed to play in the English corner of the room. "In that corner," he says, "were toy trucks, little stoves, and other trappings of middle-class American life. The Navajo corner had sheep corrals, and other trappings of Navajo life that even the kids considered either quaint or boring."

[6] I am indebted to William H. Adams and Jerald Milanich for information about this example.

[7] For a full list of available titles, contact CELIAC at CELIAC, 1107 Avenida Ejército Mexicano, Oaxaca 68020, Oaxaca, Mexico. Phone/fax: 52-951-59725/59729. E-mail: CELIAC@laneta.apc.org

References

Bernard, H. Russell. 1985. "The power of print: The role of literacy in preserving native cultures," *Human Organization* 44: 88–92.

——. 1992. "Preserving language diversity," *Cultural Survival* (Sept.).

Besnier, Niko. 1991. "Literacy and the notion of person on Nukulaelae Atoll," *American Anthropologist* 93: 570–587.

Brown, Becky. 1993. "The social consequences of writing Louisiana French," *Language in Society* 22: 67–101.

Chafe, Wallace. 1962. "Estimates regarding the present speakers of North American Indian languages," *International Journal of American Linguistics* 28: 162–171.

Davis, N. Z. 1981. "Printing and the people," in: H. J. Graff (ed.), *Literacy and social development in the West.* Cambridge: Cambridge University Press.

de Bravo Ahuja, Gloria. 1992. "The process of bilingualism in a multiethnic context," *International Journal of the Sociology of Language* 96: 45–52.

Dimmendaal, Gerrit J. 1989. "On language death in eastern Africa," in Nancy Dorian (ed.), *Investigating obsolescence: Studies in language contraction and death.* Cambridge: Cambridge University Press, 13–31.

Dixon, R. M. W. 1991. "A changing language situation: The decline of Dyirbal, 1963–1989," *Language in Society* 20: 183–200.

Dorian, Nancy C. (ed.). 1989. *Investigating obsolescence: Studies in language contraction and death.* Cambridge: Cambridge University Press.

Dorian, Nancy C. 1993. "A response to Ladefoged's other view of endangered languages," *Language* 69: 575–579.

Dressler, W. 1981. "Language shift and language death—a protean challenge for the linguist," *Folia Linguistica* 15: 5–27.

Eisenstein, E. 1979. *The printing press as an agent of change: Communications and Cultural Transformations in Early Modern Europe.* 2 vols. Cambridge: Cambridge University Press.

Elmendorf, W. W. 1981. "Last speakers and language change: Two California cases," *Anthropological Linguistics* 23 (1): 36–49.

Garzon, Susan. 1992. "The process of language death in a Mayan community in southern Mexico," *International Journal of the Sociology of Language* 93: 53–66.

González, Ventura, & Josefa Leonard. 1996. "Experiences in the development of a writing system for Ñuu Savi," in Nancy H. Hornberger (ed.), *Indigenous Literacies in the Americas.* New York: Mouton de Gruyter, 171–187.

Grimes, Barbara. 1988. "Area norms of language size," in Benjamin F. Elson (ed.), *Language in global perspective.* Dallas: Summer Institute of Linguistics.

Grimes, Barbara (ed.). 1992. *The Ethnologue.* Dallas: Summer Institute of Linguistics.

Hale, Kenneth. 1969. "American Indians in Linguistics," *The Indian Historian*, No. 2.

——. 1972. "A new perspective on American Indian linguistics," in Alfonso Ortiz (ed.), *New perspectives on the Pueblos.* Albuquerque: University of New Mexico Press, 87–133.

——. 1976. "Theoretical linguistics in relation to American Indian communities." In W. L. Chafe (ed.), *American Indian languages and American linguistics.* Lisse: Peter de Ridder Press, 35–50.

——. 1992. "Endangered languages," *Language* 68: 1–42.

Hill, Jane H. 1979. "Language death, language contact, and language evolution," in S. A. Wurm & W. McCormack (eds.), *Approaches to Language.* The Hague: Mouton, 45–73.

——. 1989. "The social functions of relativization in obsolescent and nonobsolescent languages," in Nancy Dorian (ed.), 149–166.

Iutzi-Mitchell, Roy D. 1992. Bilingualism and educational language policy in the far north: Framing the issues. Paper presented at the "Language and Education in the North" conference, University of California, Berkeley.

Kates, Robert W. 1994. "Sustaining life on the earth," *Scientific American* 271(4): 92–99 (October).

Kinkade, M. Dale. 1991. "The decline of Native languages in Canada," in Robins & Uhlenbeck (eds.), 157–176.

Krauss, Michael. 1992. "The world's languages in crisis, "*Language* 68: 1–42.

Ladefoged, Peter. 1992. "Another view of endangered languages," *Language* 68: 809–811.

Nater, H. F. 1990. A *concise Nuxalk-English dictionary*. Hull, Quebec: Canadian Museum of Civilization.

Nurden, Robert. 1994. "Spoken corpus comes to life," *The European*. October 28–November 3, 22.

Robins, Robert H. & Eugenius M. Uhlenbeck (eds.). 1991. *Endangered languages*. Oxford: Berg.

Salinas Pedraza, Jesús. 1996. "Saving and strengthening indigenous Mexican languages: The CELIAC experience," in Nancy H. Hornberger (ed.), *Indigenous Literacies in the Americas*. New York: Mouton de Gruyter, 171–187.

Watahomigie, L. J. & C. Y. Yamamoto. 1988. "Linguistics in action: The Hualapai bilingual/bicultural education program," in D. D. Stull & J. J. Schensul (eds.), *Collaborative research and social change: Applied anthropology in action*. Boulder: Westview Press, 77–98.

Wayland, E. J. 1931. "Preliminary studies of the tribes of Karamoja," *Journal of the Royal Anthropological Institute* 61: 187–230.

Winer, Lise. 1990. "Orthographic standardization for Trinidad and Tobago: Linguistic and sociopolitical considerations in an English Creole community," *Language Problems and Language Planning* 14: 237–268.

Wurm, Stephen A. 1991. "Language death and disappearance," in Robins & Uhlenbeck (eds.), 1–18.

Zepeda, Ofelia & Jane Hill. 1991. "The condition of Native American languages in the United States," in Robins & Ulenbeck (eds.), 135–155.

Jeffrey D. Ehrenreich teaches anthropology and chairs that department at University of New Orleans. A long-term editor of The Latin American Anthropology Review *and the* Society for Latin American Anthropology Publication Series, *his best-known books include* Healing and the Body Politic *(with J. Chernela),* Reading the Social Body *(with C. Burroughs), and* Political Anthropology of Ecuador.

Idealism and pragmatism both play important roles in the lives and daily decisions of most anthropologists, but sometimes those values—or habits—come into conflict. A colorful event during fieldwork among the Ecuadorian Awá has prompted retrospective soul searching on the part of this enthusiastic and imaginative ethnographer. Ehrenreich dabbled in being a shaman, juggling different cultural views about health and symbols in a way that people of goodwill could disagree about as being either hypocritical or sympathetic. A professional code of ethics, no matter how well formulated, leaves ample room for different actions and reactions in unforeseen situations, and a very special aspect of anthropology as a science is the often complex relationships that investigators develop in relation to their subjects.

Worms, Witchcraft and Wild Incantations
The Case of the Chicken Soup Cure
Jeffrey David Ehrenreich

. . . one cannot discuss lies merely by claiming that they don't matter. More often than not, they do matter, even where looked at in simple terms of harm and benefit (Sissela Bok 1978:71).

. . . What are the problems of practicing backwoods medicine? There are dangers to the patients in doing so. The medical establishment has a simple rule: First of all, do no harm. With the best of intentions, untrained medical care providers can allow their ambition to outrun their ability and harm patients . . . (Nancy Howell 1990:180).

ANTHROPOLOGISTS, MEDICINE, AND FIELDWORK

Speaking philosophically about native American peoples, Deloria has remarked that "[i]nto each life . . . some rain must fall. . . . But Indians have been cursed above all other people in history. Indians have anthropologists" (1969:78). His arguments directed at anthropologists, perhaps tongue in cheek, perhaps not, were essentially political, not ethical, in nature. Ethical questions concerning the process of doing anthropology, however, have become increasingly important as anthropologists have grown more critical and reflexive concerning the enterprise of fieldwork. The question of anthropologists' engaging in medical or health care delivery in the field and their presumed right to do so, along with corollary questions centered around where responsibility lies in the event some harm is done to "patients," seem to me to be, relatively speaking, a most urgent and neglected issue.

A few years ago Howell published a report through the American Anthropological Association entitled *Surviving Fieldwork* (1990), in which she outlined some of the dangers incurred by anthropologists working in the field (for example, snakebite, hepatitis, malaria, diarrhea, falling off a cliff, drowning, auto accidents). To state the obvious, fieldwork can indeed be dangerous to anthropologists, especially for ethnographers working in remote and isolated areas far from the facilities of "Western medicine." Howell's superb report briefly addressed (pp. 176–181) the issue of "practicing medicine in the field," primarily from the vantage point of a sociological questionnaire survey conducted among a sample of anthropologists. Her report indicates, at least from an emic perspective, that anthropologists "frequently feel that they used their skill to save a life, and rarely feel that any mistake they made caused someone to get worse" (p. 180). Yet, as Howell also suggests, we must surely question whether some harm occasionally occurs when anthropologists engage in what might be labeled "witch doctoring" in the field. I am aware of no attempt on the part of anthropologists to address seriously or systematically questions about the dangers of ethnographic fieldwork to natives with reference to the common practice of "witch doctoring" by anthropologists. This article is about such issues in the broadest sense. More specifically, it is concerned with not only the everyday ethical dilemmas of practicing medicine in the field without license or training, but also with a case in which fake doctors commit yet another major sham among the Awá-Coaiquer of Ecuador.

Fieldwork and the Awá of Ecuador

The Awá are an egalitarian horticultural people located in the rainforest of the wet littoral coastal region of Ecuador (see Ehrenreich 1985, 1990; Kempf 1985). In our first moments among the Awá-Coaiquer during a preliminary trip in 1977 into their territory, the Awá made direct appeals for medical help from Judith Kempf and me. As we were trying to decide whether or not to work among them, the Awá were immediately establishing exactly what they wanted from us if we did. They were open to our living with them only if we could provide them with medical services and drugs. They had had previous experience with "Western" medicine and care, and they were impressed.

Upon our return to do long-term fieldwork shortly thereafter, we set up a "clinic" in a section of the house that was to be the center of our activities in the widely dispersed Awá territory. Neither of us had any previous experience or training as doctors or nurses, except perhaps as children playing that time-honored game. We did, like other anthropologists before us, make real efforts before arriving in Ecuador to be as well informed as possible about doctoring in the field. To that end we consulted with medical doctors who had relevant experience and appreciate their guidance and help. Kempf, in fact, had genuine research interests in health, botanical, and medical issues, while my own interests in "doctoring" were nil. I neither liked doctors very much (out of a personal fear of them) nor did I feel especially comfortable medically or ethically in the role of delivering health care services to anyone in the field. From a "political" perspective, however, giving something back to the people with whom we worked seemed to us a responsibility. For better or worse, we were resigned to "practice medicine" among the Awá because they requested it. To this end, we brought to the field a Merck manual, eventually a copy of the book *Donde no hay doctor*, lots of aspirin and antibiotics, lots of vitamins (our standard placebo), and a full array of emergency pharmaceuticals and paraphernalia, ranging from thermometers to snake-bite kits. As with those proverbial boy scouts, we were prepared. For the record, our approach to medicine and "witch doctoring" in the field was simple: do as little as possible as infrequently as possible; be as conservative as possible; and never do anything that would cause harm. So much for our standards and credo.

With our guidelines in place, we proceeded as ethnographers and as witch doctors. In our "practice" we "treated" a full array of problems, ranging from headaches and stomachaches, colds, fevers, cuts, bruises, wounds, snakebites, skin rashes. We also took one woman to a hospital four travel days away and recommended that others make the same trip whenever we felt out of our depths medically, a fairly frequent occurrence.

WORMS AND WITCHCRAFT

About a year into our fieldwork word came to Kempf and me that a woman named Rosa had been carried for five days on her husband's back specifically to see us. She was very sick and, in fact, a number of people told us she was dying. According to our informants, all the traditional measures had already been taken—a number of *chutun* (shamanic curing) ceremonies had been held for her to rid her of *chutun* spirits (that is, the spirits that cause illness), and herbal remedies had been exhaustively tried, all to no avail. Up to this time those Awá who knew us best saw us as relatively powerful and effective "shamans" in their terms. Our guarded use of antibiotics, aspirin, and other drugs had certainly enhanced our reputations. We were also "cheap." In fact, we charged nothing for our services, although people paid us anyway in the traditional way with the gift of plantains and carefully wrapped eggs. On these bases we were seen as Rosa's last realistic hope for survival, a last but slim hope at best.

At our house Rosa seemed to be in really dire shape. We unceremoniously gave her some milk and soup but she hardly ate anything. Tension was high and it was quickly decided that Rosa, who was frightened, should be moved to her son-in-law's house and that we would visit later with some medicines. When we arrived a little later in the day, Rosa was lying on the floor of the house whimpering. She had already vomited the little food we had given to her earlier.

Her husband Ishmael also told us that the *chutun* ceremonies held for her had failed to cure her and that a sorcerer or witch (*brujo*) was killing her through witchcraft. Some time back, Ishmael said, he was walking in the forest and came across a distant neighbor. The man was aggressive (*bravo*) with him and so Ishmael responded in kind. Later, the man had a similar run-in with Rosa. In simple social terms, from his own perspective Ishmael had broken the standard code of etiquette and proper Awá behavior. He now believed that this man was a witch and that he was killing Rosa in revenge for Ishmael's lack of manners (see Ehrenreich 1985, 1990; and Kempf 1985 for further details concerning witchcraft among the Awá).

Rosa was both sick and extremely frightened. Because the food we gave her had caused her to vomit, she was not feeling much trust towards us, and our presence was disquieting to her. Her fear and trembling were of real concern to us. We believed that, from our etic perspective, we could help her. From what we had observed and learned in our conversation with Ishmael, we believed that, whatever else was wrong, Rosa had a severe case of parasitic infection (probably roundworms) and that her loss of appetite was causing her steadily to starve to death. Notably, such illness was pervasive throughout the Awá population with whom we worked. In addition, her panic about being bewitched was compounding the situation. The notion that her death was impending, regardless of the supposed cause, was reinforced further by the fact that people had started to visit in order to say their last goodbyes to her. From this perspective the solution seemed clear to us—Rosa needed nutrition that she could hold down, medicines to purge the parasites from her body, and relief from the ordeal of being bewitched.

The solution, however, was complicated by the fact that, based on our interactions to that moment, Rosa did not believe we were shamans powerful enough to help her. Nor, for that matter, had we ever stepped out of the bounds of administering medicine in any but a Western fashion. So she rejected our offers of help. Kempf and I conferred and decided that the only way to get Rosa to take the medicines and (the proverbial) chicken soup (the nutrition we believed she needed) was to convince her that, in her terms, we really knew what we were doing. We needed to give the appearance of powerful shamans. We came to believe that we had to treat Rosa's worms, her starvation, and also her beliefs and fears of witchcraft simultaneously.

WILD INCANTATIONS AND CHICKEN SOUP

Kempf and I decided to ritualize our curing techniques in the hope that Rosa might be more cooperative and trusting. And thus, the show commenced. I thought some strange incantations might help us accomplish our goals, so I began to sing Hebrew prayers I remembered from my childhood. As I prepared chicken soup, the traditional cure-all of Jewish folklore, I sang: *"Baruch aiah Adonai Eloheinu melech ha-olam, borei paree ha gafen."* This, for those who are not familiar with Hebrew ritual, is the traditional blessing said over wine, not chicken soup.

In order to induce Rosa to eat, I sang another prayer recalled from my youth: *"Ma nishtanah halailah hazeh, mikol halaiot; sheb'chol halailot anu ochlin, chametz u'matzah, halailah hazeh, kulo matzah . . ."* (This passage is the first of the four questions asked at the Passover Seder before eating the ritual meal.)

Kempf, herself a *shiksa*, made three tiny wooden crosses and placed them around the patient. In the days that followed, she burned the crosses, which ostensibly had become receptacles for the evil causing illness, in order to symbolize the removal of Rosa's bewitchment. Kempf also set up a mini-altar with the queen of hearts card as the centerpiece. The altar was placed in Rosa's line of vision. Kempf rubbed the card over Rosa's stomach as she comforted her in her pain.

For days we performed these mini-rites aimed at getting food and medicine into our reluctant patient. We were simultaneously concerned with saving Rosa's life and worried about any consequences of possible failure. Though not motivated by it, we were also conscious of the fact that our reputations as shamans and our position among the Awá would be considerably enhanced if we were successful.

There were certainly ironies in all this. As anthropologists among the Awá, we conjured up our own shunned heritages in order to succeed as witch doctors in the field. The religious training we had endured and rejected as children had turned out to be useful after all. The emptiness we had perceived in our own traditions did not prevent us from grasping the significance of ritualizing our secular cure in order make it work. In a sense, the one fraud for me (namely, religion) became the foundation upon which our own fraud had been constructed. To my mind, the chicken soup cure was duplicitous, and it left me feeling forever compromised.

CONCLUSIONS: "WITCH DOCTORING," ETHICS, AND ANTHROPOLOGY

What is it that is still so troubling to me? After all, the patient recovered. She believed she was fully cured of both the physical symptoms and the witchcraft that had brought her to the brink of death. She was even grudgingly grateful to Kempf and me for having saved her life. From a medical perspective we had done no harm and had undoubtedly saved a life. What harm, then, had been done?

From the moment we decided to put on a show for Rosa, we crossed what I believe to be a critically significant line in our activities as doctors in the field. Until then we had practiced medicine with the informed consent of our patients. They knew our limitations and no deception of any kind had occurred (notwithstanding the broader question of the right of any medically uncredentialed anthropologist to practice medicine in the field). But now we had manipulated the situation through a calculated sham in order to get an Awá patient to accept, on false premises, what we "knew" or thought to be the solution to her medical/spiritual problems. As all such rationalizations suggest, we had "done it for her own good." As philosopher Bok has suggested, "The paternalistic assumption of superiority to patients . . . carries great dangers for physicians [and presumably witch doctors] themselves—it risks turning to contempt" (1978: 227).

The rationale that we saved a life is, of course, very powerful. Yet, how is this reasoning different from what fanatical missionaries claim for their enterprises? The evangelist who believes that only by the act of the conscious embrace of Jesus can the human soul be "saved," is, from this assumption, operating ethically for the obvious good of others when engaged in any acts of proselytizing. The reasoning offered by some missionaries that causing the death of indigenous tribal people via the introduction of disease in the material world is an acceptable price to pay if just one soul (convert) is "saved" is not essentially different from the argument that medically saving a life justifies paternalistic intervention accomplished via deceit. Such reasoning rests on assumptions of power and superiority veiled in self-conceit and arrogance. Notably, anthropologists, including myself, have argued vehemently against this kind of "the-end-justifies-the-means" ethics as employed by missionaries, government officials, and even applied anthropologists. It is interesting that shortly after Ishmael and a cured Rosa left for home, an Awá man who had previously been disdainful of our presence in the area sent us a significant offering of food in order to stay in our favor. The message of our asserted "power" during the course of treating Rosa was surely not lost on him.

The case of the chicken soup cure was immediately understood and felt by me to be a major "transcendental" event of my fieldwork. Although I would act no differently if I had it to do again, my personal sense of compromise remains for me a particularly heavy personal burden. As in the case of a pacifist who is situationally forced to take a life for some greater good (for example, to save an innocent child's life or in self-defense), the justification itself does not ameliorate the impact on the principal now shattered, nor does it relieve the contradictions now created. It is not a question of guilt (personal or cultural) or a doubt about whether I was right to do what I did. When confronted with a situation in which I could either save a life or not act at all, I chose to act without hesitation, even as I was required to engage in a self-defined sham that violated my personal and professional code of ethics. My personal sense of humanity overrode my sense of professional purity and responsibility. However, I will always feel the loss of this ethical ideal which had always informed my work as an anthropologist. None of the reasoning offered from students and friends to whom I have told this story over the years has allowed me to differentiate my actions from those of other intruders—missionaries, government officials and politicians, land developers, colonists—who believe that they know what is best for members of other cultures such as the Awá, and that they therefore have the right to act out of their own convictions. For all intents and purposes, I must admit that my actions finally were, no matter how justified, rationalized or humane, just like theirs. I must therefore reluctantly extend to them my understanding, if not my approval. I have also come to see—painful though the insight may be—that I am more like them than I would ever care to be.

When I visited the Awá after a decade's absence, there was great disappointment that I had come with no medicines for them. Perhaps, in their terms, they believed that I had lost my medical or shamanic power through the years. In my terms, perhaps they were right.

***

The fieldwork for this article was supported by research grants from the Center for the Study of Man, Smithsonian Institution, and the Instituto Otavaleño de Antropología. My thinking on the events described here was first stimulated during an NEH Research Seminar in which I participated, at Cornell University, in the summer of 1988 (directed by Sander L. Gilman). An earlier version of this work was then presented at the 89th American Anthropological Association Meetings, held in New Orleans, 1990, in a symposium entitled "The Anthropologist as Healer: Ethical

Dilemmas of 'Witchdoctoring' Among the Indigenous Peoples of South America," which I orga-nized. I want to thank Samual Stanley, Hernon Crespo-Toral, Plutarco Cisneros A., Judith Kempf, and Janet Chernela for their roles in my work with the Awá.

***

References

Bok, Sissela 1978. *Lying: Moral choice in public and private life.* New York: Vintage Books (Random House).

Deloria, Vine, Jr. 1969. *Custer died for your sins: An Indian manifesto.* New York: The Macmillan Company.

Ehrenreich, Jeffrey David. 1985. Isolation, retreat, and secrecy: Dissembling behavior among the Coaiquer Indians of Ecuador. In *Political anthropology in Ecuador: Perspectives from indigenous cultures,* ed. Jeffrey Ehrenreich, Albany NY: The Center for the Caribbean and Latin America of the State University of New York and the Society for Latin American Anthropology.

————. 1990. Shame, witchcraft, and social control: The case of an Awá-Coaiquer interloper. *Cultural Anthropology,* 5(3): 338–345.

Howell, Nancy. 1990. *Surviving fieldwork: A report of the Advisory Panel on Health and Safety in Fieldwork, American Anthropological Association.* Special Publication of the American Anthro-pological Association, No. 26, Washington DC; American Anthropological Association.

Kempf, Judith. 1985. The politics of curing among the Coaiquer Indians, In *Political anthropology in Ecuador: Perspectives from indigenous cultures,* ed. Jeffrey Ehrenreich. Albany, NY: The Center for the Caribbean and Latin America of the State University of New York and the Society for Latin American Anthropology.

David M. Stoll teaches anthropology at Middlebury College. His books include Fishers of Men or Founders of Empire?, Is Latin America Turning Protestant?, Re-Thinking Protestantism in Latin America *(with V. Garrard-Burnett),* Rigoberta Menchú and the Story of All Poor Guatemalans, *and* Between Two Armies in the Ixil Towns of Guatemala.

Some of Stoll's critics depreciate his effort as "yellow journalism," a sordid exposé that besmirches a true folk hero on the basis of trivial caviling details. Others praise the dogged research in which he brought approaches from social science to bear on what has become almost a modern myth, in which a "politically correct" stance became difficult to distinguish (or more highly valued) as contrasted with more objective data.

It matters little for the popular image of Rigoberta Menchú which perspective is "true." Her story and her efforts to put a human face on the vast suffering of the Guatemalan people—especially rural peasant farmers—evidently helped bring the world's attention to bear in shortening that horrific internecine war.

No one's judgment about this emotionally laden controversy should rest solely on this brief extract; Stoll's book contains crucial evidence about life and death in that tormented time and place. But the relevance of native peoples and of ethnographic investigation has rarely been shown to be so closely linked to the greater academic community and popular public opinion. In a broader sense, both books shed light on social organization, attitudes, values, beliefs, and behavior among a population who have long been treated as a "minority" within a nation where they dominate numerically. In this increasingly interrelated world system, the Nobel Peace Prize must sometimes be recognized as among the "outside influences" that impact local communities and even individuals.

Rigoberta Menchú and the Story of All Poor Guatemalans

David M. Stoll

In 1992 a Guatemalan peasant won the Nobel Peace Prize. Except for people interested in Latin America or indigenous rights, the usual reaction was, "Rigoberta who?" Even for some acquainted with her name, Rigoberta Menchú was an unlikely peace laureate. Neither she nor anyone else had been able to end the civil war afflicting Guatemala since she was a child. Her public career had begun only a decade before, when she told an anthropologist in Paris the story of her life to the age of twenty-three. Born in a K'iche' Maya village, Rigoberta never went to school and had learned to speak Spanish only recently. She told of working on plantations as a child, being evicted by landlords, and learning how to organize. Then she told what soldiers and police had done to her family, terrible stories of death by torture and fire. The book created from the tape-recorded interviews, *I, Rigoberta Menchú* (1983), propelled her into a position of astonishing prominence for a person of her background. She became the best-known representative of the indigenous peoples of the Americas, a figure who could call on the pope, presidents of important countries, and the UN secretary-general.

What if much of Rigoberta's story is not true? This is an awkward question, especially for someone like myself who thinks the Nobel award was a good idea. Still, I decided that it must be asked. While interviewing survivors of political violence in the

Abridged, with permission of the author and publisher, from "Preface," "Rigoberta and Redemption" (chapter 17), and "Epitaph for an Eyewitness Account" (chapter 20) in David M. Stoll, *Rigoberta Menchú and the Story of All Poor Guatemalans.* © 1999 Westview Press, Boulder, CO (a member of Perseus Books, L.L.C.). Reprinted with permission. All rights reserved.

135

late 1980s, I began to come across significant problems in the life story she told at the start of her career. There is no doubt about the most important points: that a dictatorship massacred thousands of indigenous peasants, that the victims included half of Rigoberta's immediate family, that she fled to Mexico to save her life, and that she joined a revolutionary movement to liberate her country. On these points, Rigoberta's account is beyond challenge and deserves the attention it receives. But in other respects, such as the situation of her family and village before the war, other survivors gave me a rather different picture, which is borne out by the available records.

If part of the laureate's famous story is not true, does it matter? Perhaps not. Rigoberta won the peace prize on the five hundredth anniversary of the European colonization of the Americas. She has been the first to acknowledge that she received it not for her own accomplishments but because she stands for a wider group of people who deserve international support. Whatever the facts of her particular life, the prize was intended to dramatize the historical debt owed to the native people of the Western Hemisphere. The prize was also intended to encourage peace talks in her homeland of Guatemala. Although Rigoberta's village background is an interesting issue, it is not the most important one.

Despite Rigoberta's merits as a Nobel laureate, I decided that the problems with her 1982 account should be brought to wider attention. To some readers, a critical examination of *I, Rigoberta Menchú* will not be welcome. It sounds like giving ammunition to the enemy—in this case the army that has dominated Guatemala's political life for decades and still has much for which to answer. If Rigoberta is fundamentally right about what the army did, why dissect a personal account that is inevitably selective, like any human memory of anything? If her story expresses a larger truth, surely a sympathetic anthropologist should not challenge its credibility. As a colleague reasoned with me: "Maybe it's the fault of the French anthropologist who edited her testimony. Maybe the accuracy of her memory was impaired by trauma. Maybe Mayan oral tradition is not grounded in the same definition of fact as a Western journalist's. It's not like she lied in court. She spent a week talking to someone in Paris! Maybe she was tired, maybe there were communications problems, maybe she was just doing what advocates always do—exaggerating a little."

EPITAPH FOR AN EYEWITNESS ACCOUNT

I agree that it would be naive to challenge Rigoberta's account just because it is not a model of exactitude. Obviously, stories can be true even if they are selective in what they report. Indicting a Nobel laureate for inaccuracy is not the point of what follows. Even though Rigoberta is a genuine survivor of human rights violations, even though this makes her a symbol for victims of such abuses, the question remains: Why did such a catastrophe befall her family and village?

This is an issue meriting close examination, especially now that the war has ended, exhumation teams are digging up massacre victims, and truth commissions are publishing their findings. Where the contradictions between Rigoberta's version of events, that of neighbors, and the documentary record put her story into a different light is the problem of why the killing began locally. The most obvious answer—the well-attested brutality of the Guatemalan security forces—does not suffice as the only one. An underlying issue is far from settled. Was the guerrilla movement defeated in the early 1980s a popular struggle expressing the deepest aspirations of Rigoberta's people? Was it an inevitable reaction to grinding oppression, by people who felt they had no other choice?

On this question *I, Rigoberta Menchú* carries great authority, more than it deserves in my judgment. Although the laureate's views have changed over the years, in 1982 she presented herself as an eyewitness to the mobilization of her people. There is no stronger claim to authority, and most readers have taken her at her word in a way that matters beyond the confines of her own country. For some of my colleagues, dissecting the legacy of guerrilla warfare is like beating a dead horse. It is indeed a strategy that much of the Latin American left would appear to have repudiated. But it continues to be romanticized, as illustrated by the aura surrounding Che Guevara, and it has hardly disappeared, as demonstrated by news reports from Colombia, Peru, and Mexico.

What I discovered in Rigoberta's hometown is not very surprising in view of how celebrities and movements mythologize themselves. When the future Nobel laureate told her story in 1982, she drastically revised the prewar experience of her village to suit the needs of the revolutionary organization she had joined. In her telling, a tragic convergence of military moves and local vendettas became a popular movement that, at least in her area, probably never existed. Rigoberta told her story well enough that it became invested with all the authority that a story of terrible suffering can assume. From the unquestionable atrocities of the Guatemalan army, her credibility stretched farther than it should have, into the murkier background question of why the violence occurred. The result was to mystify the conditions facing peasants, what they thought their problems were, how the killing started, and how they reacted to it.

That a valuable symbol can also be misleading is the paradox that obliged me to write my book. The problem does not exist simply on the level of what did and did not happen in one corner of Guatemala. It also extends into the international apparatus for reporting human rights violations, reacting to them, and interpreting their implications for the future—the world of human rights activism, journalism, and scholarship. In a world swayed by the mass media, in which nations and peoples live or die by their ability to catch international attention, how do the gatekeepers of communication deal with the mixture of truth and falsehood in any movement's portrayal of itself, including those we feel morally obliged to support? Must we resign ourselves to be apologists for one side or the other?

In Guatemala I learned that it was impossible to discuss political violence without trespassing upon powerful symbols that assume what needs to be discussed, cloaking the debatable with the mantle of unquestionability. Like any symbol of sacrificial commitment, Rigoberta's image commands loyalty by fusing together a great deal of experience, feeling, and conviction. The destruction of her family stands for the deaths of thousands of others for whom justice could never be done. This was Rigoberta's purpose in telling her story the way that she did: It enabled her to focus international condemnation on an institution that deserved it, the Guatemalan army. But the condensing power of such a symbol comes at a cost.

When a person becomes a symbol for a cause, the complexity of a particular life is concealed in order to turn it into a representative life. So is the complexity of the situation being represented. Sooner or later, in one form or another, what the legend conceals will force its way back to our attention. The contradictions glossed over by a heroic figure will not go away because we wish to ignore them. In Guatemala much of what needs to be debated about the last half century of revolution and counterrevolution, bloodshed and peacemaking, is still wrapped up in symbols that prevent frank discussion. What was filtered out of *I, Rigoberta Menchú,* and what often gets filtered out of discussions about Guatemala, is the subject of this book.

Not at issue is Rigoberta's choice as a Nobel laureate or the larger truth she told about the violence. Unfortunately, such distinctions do not mean much to Rigoberta and some of her supporters, who regard challenges to her version of events as racist. In 1997 she produced a new book about her life, especially the fifteen years since the last one. *Crossing Borders* was, according to rumor, going to correct factual problems with the previous account. As it turns out, the new book is revealing but not revelatory. Although Rigoberta diverges from her earlier story in interesting ways, she makes no retractions.

In 1982 a young woman told a story that focused international attention on one of the most repressive regimes in Latin America. Her success took everyone by surprise, and it is quite an accomplishment. On the left, the story she created in 1982 with the help of Elisabeth Burgos has become a classic text for debating the relation between indigenous peoples and social transformation. Even if it is not the eyewitness account it claims to be, that does not detract from its significance. Her story has helped shift perceptions of indigenous people from hapless victims to men and women fighting for their rights. The recognition she has won is helping Mayas become conscious of themselves as historical actors.

To many ladinos as well as Mayas, Rigoberta is a national symbol and will continue to be one, however many vicissitudes she suffers because she is a living one. In Guatemalan intellectual life, she is a Mayan voice attempting to transcend the ladino-*indígena* dichotomy at the root of struggles over national identity. By pointing toward a more equitable relation between the two great ethnic groups in Guatemalan history, her book is a national epic. The key passage in *I, Rigoberta Menchú is* the first one: that "my story is the story of all poor Guatemalans." Even if the life told is not particularly her own, even if it is a heavily fictionalized heroic life, she achieved what she intended in a way that one person's actual life never could.

Certainly Rigoberta was a representative of her people, but hiding behind that was a more partisan role, as a representative of the revolutionary movement, and hiding behind that was an even more unsettling possibility: that she represented the audiences whose assumptions about *indígenas* she mirrored so effectively. I believe this is why it was so indecent of me to question her claims. Exposing problems in Rigoberta's story was to expose how supporters have subliminally used it to clothe their own contradictions, in a Durkheimian case of society worshiping itself. Here was an *indígena* who represented the unknowable other, yet she talked a language of protest with which the Western left could identify. She protected revolutionary sympathizers from the knowledge that the revolutionary movement was a bloody failure. Her iconic status concealed a costly political agenda that, by the time her story was becoming known, had more appeal in universities than among the people she was supposed to represent.

I suspect that Rigoberta has carried iconic authority for the same reason that many of my fellow graduate students said they were studying "resistance." As I heard this term again and again, I came to think of Prometheus chained to a rock—eternally bound, eternally defiant. The preoccupation with resistance assumed the same kind of Prometheus figure, the undying Western individual fighting for rights against oppression. Rigoberta was a Prometheus figure who justified the projection of Western identity drives into the situations we study.[1]

GUATEMALAN SCAPEGOAT, *GRINGO* SAINT

I, Rigoberta Menchú was an echo in Paris of the Guerrilla Army of the Poor. It was also the story of a young woman who "tried to turn my own experience into something which was common to a whole people."[2] For foreigners responding to a human rights emergency, a single story came to personify a nation in crisis, giving it an aura of representivity and significance that it otherwise would not have had. The result was mythic in two senses. In a narrow sense, part of her story was untrue. In a wider sense, her story became a mythic charter, a way for different groups of people to understand who they are and what they should do next. But a charter for whom and for what? Foreigners and Guatemalans have brought different needs to Rigoberta's odyssey, as becomes evident when we look at differences in how they perceive it.

What staggers Rigoberta's old neighbors is that a schoolgirl could become an international celebrity. Most Uspantanos hear her story through oral transmission, which washes out details to which they might object, leaving a sequence of persecution, survival, and denunciation with which many can identify. The same holds for a much wider Guatemalan public. Rigoberta was not known to most *indígenas* until the left began to publicize her as a Nobel candidate in 1991. Many warmed to the idea that a Maya was being honored internationally for what her people had suffered. Her story also appealed to the many ladinos who have had similar experiences. If poetic truth is good enough for you, this is the part of her story that is all too true.

Paradoxically, although Rigoberta has not faced much incredulity over her version of events, she is the butt of criticism from almost every corner of Guatemalan society, including her own disappointed supporters. This should not be a surprise: Contradictory feelings toward celebrities are integral to their power in the public imagination. As living symbols of the good, the bad, and the inevitable; of the tremendous role of luck in human affairs; and of the unfairness of it all, they exist to be adored one moment and envied the next, damned today and forgiven tomorrow. The same is true of Rigoberta, whose story has become a way for an entire country to reflect on its contradictions. By presenting herself as an everywoman, she has tried to be all things to all people in a way no individual could be. As Nobel laureate, she has bestowed her symbolic authority on the building of bridges between *indígenas* and ladinos, *indígenas* in the guerrilla movement and those opposed to it, and the political establishment and the majority of Guatemalans who are disillusioned with it. The peace process has implicated her in compromises that are bound to offend her supporters but are probably not going to convince her adversaries.

International adulation for Rigoberta has brought out the Guatemalan penchant for backbiting.[3] But there has been little interest in challenging the factuality of her narrative. For many Guatemalans, the simple thread of persecution, exile, and vindication is enough to validate her for the purpose intended by the Nobel committee, as a symbol for all who have suffered. Factual issues could seem insignificant because the atrocities she was trying to dramatize are so unquestionable. As Nobel laureate she has come to occupy a position similar to American presidents and British royals, whose symbolic importance is larger than any individual's ability to play the part. Ridicule of such figures can even protect an underlying respect for the office by preserving it from the shortcomings of the occupant. Scorned one moment, they can become a national rallying point the next.

Sometimes Rigoberta's last supporters seem to be the Europeans and North Americans who first responded to her story and set her on the path to fame. This reflects the outsize role that international opinion has played in the Guatemalan civil war—in the 1980s to help the guerrillas prolong a war they had lost, and in the 1990s to end a war that they and the army would otherwise have continued. Abroad it is the published version of Rigoberta's story that prevails, not the oral one, so foreign admirers have put their faith in a more detailed, problematic version of Rigoberta's story. Moreover, they have a different set of needs than Guatemalans do. For most Guatemalans, their moral solidarity with victims of the violence is not at issue—they are the victims. Guatemalans are also less likely to feel the need to vindicate the left's tradition of armed struggle, just as few of them wish to justify the Guatemalan right's history of repression. Instead, they tend to view the two sides as partners in a dance of destruction.

Rigoberta's foreign supporters are in a different position. Some continue using her story to prove that the guerrilla movement had deep popular roots and was an inevitable response to oppression. They want to defend the Latin American left's history of armed struggle, or at least show that it was not a complete disaster. For a wider circle of human rights activists, who regard themselves as pacifists but unknowingly have absorbed a guerrillaphile perspective, respect for Rigoberta's story is a test of solidarity with the oppressed. By believing in her story, they demonstrate their commitment. For scholars, meanwhile, believing in Rigoberta's story has helped us deal with a professional but very personal moral dilemma, over our legitimacy as observers of people who are so much less fortunate than we.

Since the 1980s a theoretical literature indicting Western knowledge as inherently colonialist has acquired considerable prestige in North American universities.[4] In parts of the humanities and the social sciences, its exponents look like the new establishment. Under various headings, such as cultural studies and postmodernism, much of this literature carries on the self-critical, empirical tradition in Western thought. But the new theories can also be used to shut down investigation and debate, by reducing intellectual discourse to relations of power and dismissing opposed points of view as reactionary.[5]

Here is how what purports to be critical thinking degenerates into dogmatism: If any empirical portrait of a sensitive subject reflects ethnocentric or bourgeois assumptions (e.g., my wish to approximate the facts), there is not much sense in debating the fine points, such as whether Vicente Menchú belonged to the Committee for *Campesino* Unity or even whether Rigoberta gave us a reliable account of her village before the war. Instead, what matters is the "metanarrative"—the discourse of power lurking behind a text. In the case of the book you hold in your hands, a white male anthropologist is accusing an indigenous woman of making up part of her story. The important issue is not whether she did or not. Instead, it is Western domination, which I am obviously perpetrating. Reasoning like this enables Rigoberta's story to be removed from the field of testable propositions, to instead become a proof-text that foreigners can use to validate themselves.

But how do we decide to which victims to listen? When I began to question Rigoberta's 1982 story, I learned that the testimony of victims can be used to discourage unwelcome questions. Not all victims are enshrined in this manner—just the ones who serve our purposes, because enshrining certain claims to victimhood involves rejecting others. What results are stereotypes reducing the complexities of history, inequality, and ambition to melodramas populated by stock characters, who will always meet our expectations because we disqualify evidence that they do not. The intellectual climate that results has consequences for the kind of work that young scholars do, for what is encouraged and discouraged, for what does and does not get published.

For scholars insecure about their moral right to depict "the Other," *testimonio* and related appeals to the native voice have been a godsend. By incorporating native voice into the syllabus and deferring to it on occasion, we validate our authority by claiming to abdicate it. This is not necessarily a bad thing—anthropology and Latin American studies are hard to imagine without it. But in an era of truth commissions, when there is a public demand to establish facts, privileging one version of a history of land conflict and homicide will not do. What if, on comparing the most hallowed *testimonio* with others, we find that it is not reliable in certain important ways? Then we would have to acknowledge that there is no substitute for our capacity to judge competing versions of events, to exercise our authority as scholars. That would unravel a generation of efforts to revalidate ourselves through idealized imaginings of the Other.

Notes

[1] As "the icon of testimonio writing," according to Gugelberger (1996:1), *I, Rigoberta Menchú* has been assimilated into the canon of university-assigned literature and become "merely another commodity" or "fetish," that is, a symbol covering up something that cannot be acknowledged. What is being covered up, according to Williams (1996) in the same collection, are "fantasies of cultural exchange"—the wish to resolve one's contradictions by identifying with the oppressed. Although Gugelberger and Beverley distinguish between icons in the mass media, see Horrocks (1995:17) and Simpson (1993–47–48), who defines the iconography of a blonde Brazilian pop star as "a symbolic pathway connecting each individual fulfillment."

[2] Burgos-Debray 1984:118.

[3] For example, Trejo 1996.

[4] As Nordstrom and Robben (1995:11) put it, anthropologists "depart for the field bowing under the weight of our own culture, propped up and propelled by Western assumptions we seldom question, shielded from the blaze of complex cultural diversity by a carefully crafted lens of cultural belief that determines as much as clarifies what we see. When we purport to speak for others, we carry the Western enterprise into the mouths of other people."

[5] Ellis 1997.

References

Burgos, Elisabeth. N.D. (Original edition 1983). *Me llamo Rigoberta Menchú y así me nació la conciencia*. Guatemala City: Arcoiris.

Burgos-Debray, Elisabeth. 1984. *I, Rigoberta Menchú: An Indian Woman in Guatemala* (trans.). London: Verso.

Ellis, John M. 1997. *Literature Lost: Social Agendas and the Corruption of the Humanities*. New Haven: Yale University Press.

Gugelberger, Georg M. (ed.). 1996. *The Real Thing: Testimonial Discourse and Latin America*. Durham, NC: Duke University Press.

Horrocks, Roger. 1995. *Male Myths and Icons: Masculinity in Popular Culture*. New York: St. Martin's Press.

Menchú, Rigoberta, with Dante Liano and Gianni Miná. 1998. *Rigoberta: La nieta de los Mayas*. Madrid: Aguilar [English ed., *Crossing Borders*. New York: Verso].

Nordstrom, Carolyn, and Antonius C. G. M. Robben (eds.). 1995. *Fieldwork under Fire: Contemporary Studies of Violence and Survival*. Berkeley: University of California Press.

Simpson, Amelia. 1993. *Xuxa: The Mega-Marketing of Gender, Race, and Modernity*. Philadelphia: Temple University Press.

Trejo, Alba. 1996. "A cuatro años del Nobel quién es la verdadera Rigoberta?" *Magazine 21 (Siglo Veintiuno)*, Septem___ ___ ___ ___.

Williams, Gareth. 1996 ___ ___ ___ ___ ___ an Subaltern Studies." In Georg M. Guge___ ___ ___ ___ nd Latin America, pp. 225–253. Durham, ___

by taking away the validity of Menchus story, we take away the possibility of judging "bad" events.

- disqualification of Menchus = ratification of white supremacy.

PART III

Traditional and Modern Cultures

This section provides a brief introduction to the enormous variety of cultures that can be found in Latin America today. It is beneficial to think hard about the concept of culture, and even to play with it a little, testing its relevance and utility in relation to a wide range of usages that, rightly or wrongly, have been popular at various times. Space does not allow for inclusion of even a single ethnographic vignette from every country or even each region, nor is there an attempt here to summarize the most widespread or best-documented ways of life. Rather, these readings have been selected to introduce a few of the actors and to show that traditional and modern cultures may not be so different as one might expect.

WHY CULTURE MATTERS

For this anthropologist, culture is one of the key concepts that help make sense of the bewildering variety of beliefs and practices that we find throughout history and across the vast range of human experience. Although the term has become popularized in recent years, its applications are not always faithful to the usages that have predominated in anthropology for 50 years, even while controversies, sometimes heated and substantial, have occupied our attention.

Some people think that culture is just something that other people have or do—especially those who live far away or who constitute a disadvantaged "minority." Quaint and curious customs characterizing "backward" people in exotic places were long thought to be the stock-in-trade of anthropology. But everyone participates in (or "has") a culture, if by that we mean a *system of patterns of beliefs and behavior*, a worldview together with guidelines about how to manage that world.

The "system" part of our definition recognizes that the whole is more than the sum of its parts, as in any clock or other machine. The parts relate to each other in such complex ways that they cannot be isolated easily, and the system functions differently if any part is significantly changed. The "patterns" part of our definition relates to the fact that beliefs and behavior are not so much discrete units as they are clusters or types, many of which have approximate equivalence in terms of propriety or acceptability, and that people recognize them as related even when unfamiliar with them in detail. "Beliefs" and "behaviors" are specific elements of action that collectively shape our daily lives. When the Roman dramatist Terence said *Nihil humanum mihi alienum est* (Nothing human is alien to me), he was getting at the heart of cultural differences. It is not that there is a single "human nature" that defines what is good, bad, or indifferent in a universal sense, but that there are many "human natures" that define what is good, bad, or indifferent in different cultures. Although many anthropologists during the past half-century have been working in terms of such a view, it appears to have escaped many scientists in other fields as well as laypeople until recently articulated anew by a few political scientists and students of formal organizations.

It is often convenient to think of a culture as a grammar for attitudes and actions. In language, the rules of grammar are such that we can easily tell sensible speech from nonsense and even distinguish "correct" from "incorrect" utterances. But this does not imply that the rules of grammar are like a straitjacket, restricting us to a limited field of discourse or resulting in stilted, constant repetition of a narrow repertory in which everyone says the same things all the time. Every day and every time we open our mouths, set pen to paper, or use a keyboard to input words, each one of us invents unique sentences that we have never heard before and may never again. A five-year-old child, with minimal reflection and with absolutely no formal recognition of the rules, can easily make, understand, and respond to a novel grammatical utterance and reject or question another that breaks the rules. Similarly, those who share a culture are not automatons stamped from a punch press and doomed to lockstep uniformity in terms of all they do or think. A culture, like a grammar, offers a broad range of possibilities from which individuals can choose many alternatives, invent spontaneously or hew closely to conventions, or develop a distinctive personal style, all without being seen as inappropriate or odd.

Similarly, the idea that factors other than those that are normally thought of as economic could be important in shaping the directions of development, or in posing obstacles to such a process, has long been generally accepted in anthropology. Only recently was it perceived and reported by some distinguished social scientists in other disciplines. To be sure, there is a controversy within anthropology on the subject. Few remain who are comfortable referring to culture as a sort of "black box" that, in some vaguely deterministic sense, can be invoked to account for events not easily explained by other concepts that enjoy currency in the social sciences. There are some who chafe under the widespread and simplistic use of the term with its connotations of predestination, as if a culture somehow caused some things to happen, disallowed others, and facilitated or obstructed some range in between, so that individual human beings had little choice but to follow the dictates of the culture in which they were reared and socialized (or enculturated, to use a more anthropological term). It seems more fruitful to view culture not as a restrictive cause but as an enabling toolkit that includes some familiar ready-made solutions to frequently encountered situations and also, more usefully, contains a range of alternatives with differing degrees of feasibility or acceptability, among which one may choose for adjusting to less familiar situations.

TYPES AND STEREOTYPES

When cultures were first discussed at the inception of anthropology as a field of study, it was usually not in terms of specific local minutiae that made each system unique but rather in terms of gross characteristics that marked types (or supposed stages) in the global evolution of humankind. One of the most famous of such schemes distinguished savagery from barbarism (by the introduction of pottery), and then civilization (by the development of agriculture). Each stage supposedly had low, middle, and upper substages within it, each defined by a specific trait that was said to represent a significant marker in terms of progress. This classification system allowed an approximate ranking of cultures and justified the Victorian view of the urban industrialized West as the culmination of some grand scheme through all of prehistory and history. But even such an elaborate scheme did little to help in understanding the variation that was to be encountered in the real world where, incidentally, traits tended too often to occur out of that sequence, and patterns of beliefs and behaviors did not correlate closely with the postulated types.

On the basis of anthropological fieldwork in Mexico, R. Redfield identified what came to be called the folk-urban continuum, which took into account not only material traits but also ecology (relative isolation), social organization (relative homogeneity), and other factors that appeared to relate not only to changes through which a culture passed historically but also to its openness to change as an ongoing system. The presence of plantations that operated like a factory-in-the-field for sugarcane, coffee, bananas and some other nonsubsistence crops prompted talk about a rural proletariat. Focusing on aspects of social organization, Wagley and Harris spelled out an elaborate typology of Latin American subcultures as an aid to ordering and comparing data from diverse areas.

Considerable attention was paid in the mid-1900s to determining what was meant by the term "peasant," again with heavy reliance on reports about the reality of different parts of Latin America as studied by anthropologists. As the anthropological enterprise itself evolved, with a simultaneous rapid increase in number of practitioners and greater concern for hypothesis-testing and scientific precision in specifying independent and dependent variables in individual studies, the earlier concern about classification waned and unique ethnographic descriptions proliferated.

Neither *Chicha* nor Lemonade

In much of Latin America, the phrase *ni chicha ni limonada* is used with some frequency to refer to something that defies easy classification or categorization; perhaps the closest analog in colloquial English would be "neither fish, flesh, nor fowl." We all recognize, at one level, the futility of naming and treating diverse entities as if they were identical or homogenous. Yet we also recognize the need to use some groupings in an ongoing effort to simplify the ways in which we deal with the booming, buzzing confusion that is the reality of almost infinite variation among many of the things that we attend to. This anthropologist strongly believes that cultures, like almost any other things that we think about, can usefully be grouped in terms of some common denominator(s), but that the bases for such groupings should be specified differently depending on the question one is asking or the purpose that one has in mind. The degree of generalization or specificity must reflect real similarities and differences to the extent that they are pertinent in understanding the organization or process being examined.

For this reason, "traditional" and "modern" cultures are discussed here without any further delineation of what is meant by those two terms. This can be viewed as a deliberate effort on the part of the editor to nudge the reader into thinking a little harder about the very process of classification and coming up with his or her own criteria for distinguishing the types. Or it can be viewed as a way to talk about cultures of Latin America with a view toward alerting readers to the great variety that is to be found there, while simultaneously emphasizing that differences in content and detail do not necessarily imply differences in access or outlook.

To begin, for example, we should recognize that speaking a non-Western language, wearing "exotic" dress or adornment, hunting with a bow and arrow or blowgun, or farming by the messy but efficient method of swidden (slash-and-burn agriculture) no longer implies that a group is on the fringes of the money economy or of the national polity, nor that its members are ignorant or unconcerned about what is happening elsewhere.

One of the most striking developments in recent Latin American history is the emergence of indigenous populations and groups that represent them as actors to be reckoned with both nationally and often on the international stage. A dramatic illustration of how this happens and is craftily used by politically savvy native peoples is Conklin (chapter 30); a broad view of the process is offered by Stavenhagen (chapter 13). A remarkably thorough and exciting account of such progress throughout the entire region is offered by Brysk (2000). Often deprecated as less than human, speaking "only a dialect and not a language," descendants of indigenous people throughout Latin America long remained disfranchised or even ignored by the urban, cosmopolitan governing segments of the population even when, as in Bolivia and Guatemala, their numbers were so disproportionately large as to constitute a literal majority. It is largely through the efforts of anthropologists that traditional cultures have been made known to outsiders, and sometimes that they have been preserved or resurrected for the people themselves (who are still generally referred to by Columbus's inaccurate term "Indians" (*indios*).

Another recent development in ethnology is reportage by some individuals as insightful and articulate spokespersons for their own cultures. The reading by Mares (chapter 14), incorporating a few interpretive notes by translator Burgess, shows to good advantage how new understandings can emerge from such a description. The ball game of the Tarahumara (an "outsider" name for the people who call themselves Rarámuri) had been characterized in general terms by outside observers for more than a century, but some of the subjective meanings and subtle interpersonal relationships have come to light only in this insider's account. Intimately linked to such ethno-ethnology is the innovative work that Bernard (chapter 10) has done in devising novel orthographic systems for non-Western languages and teaching native people to record and write about their own ways of life. It is difficult to imagine any other gift from an outsider that could have nearly so broad and so deep an impact as that of literacy.

Tourism is a vast and rapidly growing business, now among the major industries in the world. For example, it is already the major source of foreign currency in Costa Rica and Mexico. For much of the developing world that produces little of value for export, or that produces considerable amounts of raw materials that still add up to little value, the alluring combination of sand, sun, and imagery have become a valuable commodity. There is, of course, considerable debate about the balance of costs and benefits, especially when the consumption of resources is compounded, the impact of pollution soars, major portions of the profits go elsewhere, and servile jobs do not provide the income or mobility that local people had hoped for.

Others point to relative economic gains and increased opportunities as providing a win-win outcome for both tourists and their hosts. The beach resort of Cancun, Mexico, epitomizes the new economy and philosophy of tourism; it did not exist a generation ago and is now a major destination for large numbers of travelers from far and wide. Re Cruz (chapter 15) takes us backstage to reveal a little about the Cancun that tourists rarely see. At the same time she shows us some of the ways in which "cultural baggage" brought by U.S. student ethnographers interfered with their understanding or appreciating much of what they encountered in the lives of local Mexicans, a world that is alien in only a few (but important) respects.

In a small way, the plight of market vendors in southern Mexico is a reflection of the more general problems that many small businesses have of surviving in a world that is increasingly dominated by fewer and larger businesses. Chiñas (chapter 16) puts a human face on some of the risks and costs of globalization in a way that cannot be denied.

The Maya-speaking Indians of highland Chiapas in Mexico (cf. Vogt, chapter 5) epitomize the relatively new phenomenon of native peoples as forcefully active and outspoken players on the global stage. When their peaceful demonstrations were met with armed resistance by national troops, they began what has become a multi-year standoff. They have been joined by other native peoples who are also claiming land and protesting human rights abuses in the name of Mexico's revolutionary hero, Zapata. Collier (chapter 17) briefly chronicles the early stages of mobilization and the clever use of media that has gained support from many foreigners in all walks of life. Confrontation and passive resistance are both tools that some of those in traditional cultures have used to keep modern cultures from displacing or incorporating them, and it is interesting to see novel approaches to resolving this age-old problem (also compare Conklin, chapter 30).

Economists often mistakenly construe "the informal sector" as an important index of underdevelopment, whereas Buechler (chapter 18) clearly shows that, in the Bolivian instance, it is often a crucial bridge between more traditional activities (handicrafts) and export to the worldwide market. That same chapter shows how the tradition of relying on an extensive and far-flung network of kin and friends supports transactions in the city by a woman who has little formal schooling but is knowledgeable and adaptable in terms of making a living for herself and her family. One may well wonder which parts of her diverse enterprise are modern and which traditional— or, for that matter, whether such a dichotomy is useful, or for what purposes it may be.

When historians contrast traditional and modern ways of life, they are often dealing with changes over centuries or at least generations. By contrast, anthropologists sometimes have opportunities to observe meaningful developments in the course of a decade or less, and so are able to understand processes of choice and change, with a finely tuned attention to various parts of the context. While paying attention to the relatively inconsequential activity of drinking in five different cultures scattered throughout Bolivia, Heath (chapter 19) was able to document changes, relate them to simultaneous changes in the social organization of each community, and derive a warning that some of the theories proposed for studying such behavior may be grossly misleading if they do not attend to local variation. This may be a rare instance in which the anthropological approach yields an insight that is even more important to sociologists and historians than to fellow anthropologists.

We have already mentioned that native peoples are increasingly vocal and politically mobilized in asserting their ethnicity and identity (Stavenhagen, chapter 13; Conklin, chapter 30), but it is not always clear that anthropologists are often active allies if not leaders in such movements. A small but striking example of ethnodevelopment that extends to include preservation of the natural environment as well as way of life is the case of the Yuquí, here reported by Stearman (chapter 20), who played a major role as counselor and broker (Wolf, chapter 39) in dealing with national and international institutions. It is only during the past few decades that such applied, or practicing, anthropology has been widely accepted as an appropriate complement to academic or scientific research, often embodied in the same person(s) and project(s). In a somewhat broader sense, the entire Cornell-Vicos Project (Doughty, chapter 23) can be seen as another approach to ethnodevelopment, including a huge cast of characters over a long period of time and resulting in changes that no one could have foreseen at the outset.

Women's dress is one of the aspects of culture that tends to remain relatively constant over time, especially when it is handmade in and distinctive of the local community. A case study in Panama (Tice, chapter 21) deftly interweaves facts and attitudes about blouses that the Kuna women make and wear, with some insights into how they became important trade goods for a truly global market and what that change has meant in terms of the economic and gender relations in their still tight-knit community.

Although there may be a few cultures that most people would judge to be traditional and a few others that most would consider modern, it should be evident that these polar types do not easily reflect reality. A serious reader may revisit my earlier suggestion to think long and hard about what those terms mean, whether in Latin America or elsewhere.

FOR FURTHER READING ON TRADITIONAL AND MODERN CULTURES

The nature of culture was exhaustively appraised by A. L. Kroeber and C. Kluckhohn, *Culture: A Critical Review of Concepts and Definitions* (Peabody Museum of Harvard University, 1952). Cultural anthropology as a major subdiscipline that focuses on understanding different ways of life is conveniently outlined in a number of texts: W. A. Haviland, *Cultural Anthropology* (9th ed., Harcourt, 2000); S. Nanda and R. L. Warms, *Cultural Anthropology* (6th ed., Wadsworth, 1998); C. P. Kottak, *Mirror for Humanity* (8th ed., McGraw-Hill, 2000); or A. Rosman and P. G. Rubel, *The Tapestry of Culture* (7th ed., McGraw-Hill, 2001), for example.

Works reflecting the recent popularity of the concept of culture in nonanthropological contexts include S. P. Huntington and L. E. Harrison (eds.), *Culture Matters* (Basic, 2000); and T. Hamada and W. E. Sibley (eds.), *Anthropological Perspectives on Organizational Culture* (University Press of America, 1994). The plurality of human natures is an old concept in anthropology but has gained new popularity from E. O. Wilson, *Consilience: The Unity of Knowledge* (A. A. Knopf, 1998).

Early uses of the term culture in relation to the long history of human evolution were insightful, although outdated in detail. Outstanding examples were L. H. Morgan, *Ancient Society* (World, 1877) and E. B. Taylor, *Primitive Culture* (J. Murray, 1871).

The folk-urban continuum was suggested by R. Redfield on the basis of his *Folk Culture of Yucatan* (University of Chicago Press, 1951); it was debated in many professional journal articles for a decade. S. Mintz proposed that we attend to rural proletariat in those areas of Latin America with mining and monocrop agriculture; the Wagley and Harris typology was reprinted in earlier editions of *Contemporary Cultures and Societies of Latin America*.

On peasantry, R. Redfield wrote *Peasant Society and Culture* (University of Chicago Press, 1956). Many colleagues added various perspectives over the years, and M. Kearney's *Reconceptualizing the Peasantry* (Westview, 1996) reviews how meanings and usages changed. Closely related is our concern for indigenous peoples as actors. R. Stavenhagen, *Ethnic Conflict and the Nation-State* (St. Martin's, 1996) and *Agrarian Problems and Peasant Movements in Latin America* (Doubleday, 1970) should be added to those sources discussed in earlier sections of this book.

An excellent example of autoethnography, a penetrating and insightful account of one's own culture by a non-Westerner, is H. R. Bernard and J. Salinas P., *Native Ethnography: A Mexican Indian Describes His Culture* (Sage, 1989). Other advantages of

Indigenous Literacies in the Americas are discussed in N. Hornberger (ed.) (Mouton De Gruyter, 1996)

The Anthropology of Tourism is a brief introduction by D. Nash (Pergamon, 1996). A more current treatment is provided by E. Chambers, *Native Tours: The Anthropology of Travel and Tourism* (Waveland, 2000). *Annals of Tourism Research* is a multidisciplinary journal that deals with many pros and cons, as do D. G. Pearce and R. W. Butler (eds.), *Contemporary Issues in Tourism Development* (Routledge, 1999). The remarkably consistent imagery of a popular magazine has done much to perpetuate idealization of traditional cultures around the world; see C. Lutz and J. Collins, *Reading National Geographic* (University of Chicago Press, 1993).

The Maya-speaking Indians of highland Chiapas are discussed by Vogt (chapter 5). Other sources on their present condition are indicated in Part II of this book.

Global protests by native peoples are increasing both in numbers and in impact. See Part II of this book, but see also A. Brysk, *From Tribal Village to Global Village* (Stanford University Press, 2000); and G. H. Cornwell and E. W. Stoddard (eds.), *Global Multiculturalism: Comparative Perspectives on Ethnicity, Race, and Nation* (Rowman & Littlefield, 2000).

To a remarkable degree, alcohol provides an illuminating window on every culture where it is known (even if the people do not drink.). To understand better its many, often contradictory, and sometimes controversial roles, see D. B. Heath, *Drinking Occasions: Comparative Perspectives on Alcohol and Culture* (Brunner/Mazell, 2000); his *International Handbook on Alcohol and Culture* (Greenwood, 1995); or M. Marshall (ed.), *Beliefs, Behaviors and Alcoholic Beverages* (University, of Michigan Press, 1979).

The Cornell-Peru Project, like the Harvard-Chiapas Project (Vogt, chapter 5), is unusual in its long-term and multidisciplinary aspects. It was famous at the time as a supposedly ideal model for economic development and cultural change in developing regions. The long-term director, A. Holmberg, liked to refer to the method as participant-intervention (a take-off on ethnography's vaunted method of participant-observation), proudly noting that there was no conflict between action or applied work "in the real world" and academic or conceptual work furthering the discipline in academia. Works by A. Holmberg, P. Doughty, H. Dobyns, M. Vázquez, W. Mangin, and others describe various aspects of the Vicos adventure.

Kuna (or Cuna) *molas* are dealt with in detail by K. Tice in *Kuna Crafts, Gender, and the Global Economy* (University of Texas Press, 1995). The changing roles of *Women in the Latin American Development Process* are described by C. E. Bose and E. Acosta-Belen (eds.) (Temple University Press, 1995).

Rodolfo Stavenhagen is a sociologist and international public servant who teaches at El Colegio de México and the National Autonomous University of Mexico. His best-known books include Agrarian Problems and Peasant Movements in Latin America, Between Underdevelopment and Revolution, Ethnic Conflicts and the Nation-State, Social Classes in Agrarian Societies, *and* The Ethnic Question.

As part of the colonial heritage in most of Latin America, indigenous peoples often had little to do with the countries in which they lived—or with many other populations, for that matter. As mass media, transportation, communication, and exploitation of natural resources increasingly impinge upon them, however, they are being rapidly drawn—ready or not—into participation in the world system. Stavenhagen's paper examines both how this is happening and how they are adapting, in novel and imaginative ways. Regional and other "intertribal" organizations that were unthinkable a generation ago are becoming valuable corporate entities that represent the interests of large groups of people who might otherwise disappear, leaving little more than scattered anthropological accounts of their patrimony as integral parts of the human experience. For a case study of how some anthropologists are active participants in this process, see Stearman (chapter 20).

Indigenous Organizations

Rising Actors in Latin America

Rodolfo Stavenhagen

INTRODUCTION

In recent years, the indigenous peoples have emerged as new political and social actors in Latin America: they are becoming active subjects instead of continuing as passive objects of the course of history. Something has changed in the living circumstances of indigenous people, and something is changing in the relationship between the State and such peoples. Old claims and new demands have joined together to forge new identities; new ideologies are competing with old, long-standing paradigms; the theories of social change, modernization and nation building are being rethought in the light of the so-called "ethnic question" which was ignored and looked down upon for so long, and finally, the manner of practicing politics in connection with indigenous problems has changed too.[1]

Perhaps the best starting point for our analysis would be the formal initiation of a continent-wide policy on indigenous matters (known as indigenism) at the First Inter-American Indigenist Congress, held in Mexico City in 1940. At this congress, government delegates from many countries of the continent decided to put into effect policies to improve the living conditions of indigenous people, mainly through a process of assimilation or integration into so-called "national society." This dominant national society, reflecting the nationalist ideology of the white and mestizo urban middle class, however, completely rejected the indigenous components of national culture and simply did not envisage any future for them, except in an idealization of the past mainly represented in museums and, more recently, as a way of earning foreign exchange from tourism and the sale of handicraft products.

The policies adopted with regard to indigenous peoples, though well-meaning, turned out in fact to be ethnocidal and rather ineffective even in terms of their own

Slightly abridged, with permission of the author and publisher, from an article with the same title in *CEPAL Review*, vol. 62: 63–75, 1998. Reprinted with permission. All rights reserved.

declared objectives. At subsequent periodic inter-American indigenist congresses (the eleventh congress was held in Nicaragua in December 1993) the government delegates consistently deplored the lamentable conditions of the indigenous peoples of the continent, but while governments reported on their development programs and projects, often in a self-admiring manner, the economic and social situation of the indigenous peoples, which were often allowed only a symbolic presence at these congresses, visibly deteriorated. A recent World Bank study concludes that poverty among the indigenous peoples of Latin America is severe and persistent. It also considers that the living conditions of those peoples linked with poverty are, generally speaking, abysmally bad (Psacharopoulos and Patrinos, 1994).

WHO ARE THE INDIGENOUS PEOPLE OF LATIN AMERICA, AND HOW NUMEROUS ARE THEY?

Although the criteria used in the definitions vary from country to country and the available census data are not reliable, it is estimated that there are over 400 identifiable groups, with a total population of around 40 million, ranging from numerically insignificant and almost extinct bands of natives in the Amazon jungles to Andean peasant societies numbering millions of people. Mexico has the most numerous indigenous population in Latin America, amounting to some 10 million people, but they only represent between 12% and 15% of the total population. In contrast, the indigenous populations of Guatemala and Bolivia form the majority of the national population, and in Peru and Ecuador they form almost half of it. In Brazil, they represent less than 2% of the total population, but as they are the original inhabitants of Amazonia they have played an important part in resisting the depredation of their territories, demanding territorial rights and political representation, fighting for the preservation of the Amazonian environment, and securing the incorporation of this objective in the new Brazilian Constitution adopted in 1988 (see González, 1994; CELADE, 1994).

INDIGENISM AND THE INDIGENOUS MOVEMENT

The Latin American countries have a long and complicated history of indigenist legislation, in which the indigenous populations were generally put at a disadvantage with respect to the rest of society, although many of the laws were protective and tutelary. Although the right to formal citizenship was granted to almost the whole of the national population in the years following political independence, indigenous inhabitants continued to be treated as minors and as legally incompetent in many countries until very recently. It was only in the last few decades that the basic laws of Latin America were modified in this respect, as part of a wave of constitutional reforms which include not only rules regarding indigenous languages and cultures but also in some cases indigenous communities and their territories, as a specific form of social organization. Constitutional reforms of this type have been carried out in recent years in Argentina, Bolivia, Brazil, Colombia, Ecuador, Guatemala, Mexico, Nicaragua, Panama, Paraguay and Peru. Some observers see this restructuring as part of the wave of democratization that swept over Latin America in the 1970s and 1980s. Others, however, recognize the active role that the indigenous organizations have played in giving rise to these changes.

The emergence of indigenous organizations in past decades may be viewed as both cause and effect of the changes that have taken place in the public sphere with regard to indigenous peoples. Back in the 1960s, there were only a handful of formal organizations set up and run by indigenous people to pursue objectives that were of interest to the indigenous peoples as such. In the mid-1990s, however, there are hundreds of associations of all types with the most varied purposes: local-level organizations, intercommunity and regional associations, formally constituted interest groups, national federations, leagues and unions, and transnational alliances and coalitions with well-developed international contacts and activities. It can justly be said that indigenous organizations, their leaders, objectives, activities and emerging ideologies make up a new type of social and political movement in present-day Latin America whose detailed history and analysis have yet to be prepared.

One of the first organizations, often mentioned as the prototype for others, is the Shuar Federation, established in the 1960s to protect the interests of the various Shuar communities in the Amazonian lowlands of eastern Ecuador. The Shuars decided to form this federation in order to defend their territory from the invasions of settlers from outside and various commercial interests, and in the process they discovered that the struggle for land rights could not be divorced from the question of their survival as an ethnically distinctive people, with their own traditions and cultural identity. They also discovered—as so many other oppressed peoples have done in the course of history—that they could only attain their objective by building up their strength and joining forces. Although motivated by economic and social considerations (preservation of the lands of their ancestors and access to productive resources), the Shuars' struggle cannot be described simply as a class struggle, unlike the agrarian conflicts between peasants and landowners which took place more or less at the same time on the altiplano. Since the Shuars and other lowland indigenous peoples did not fit clearly within an agrarian class structure, their organization took on a more communal and ethnic nature than the more class-oriented movements of indigenous peasants in other parts of Latin America (Salazar, 1981; Descola, 1988; Ibarra, 1987).

Organizations similar to that of the Shuars sprang up during the 1970s in several other countries and further consolidated their activities during the 1980s. They soon managed to break out of the constraints of the community-level activities to which State development projects often limited them. Although community development projects, some of them financed by multilateral agencies and non-governmental organizations, did manage to generate growing participation by the local population, it soon became clear to the emerging indigenous elites that local-level activity was very limited from the political point of view. Like the Shuars, they managed to construct a trans-community indigenous identity, incorporating a growing number of local communities and making ethnic identity a unifying link and mobilizing agent. Thus, several ethnic organizations entered on the political scene, with leaders who spoke for their ethnic group as a whole rather than merely representing one or another rural community. These organizations were very soon followed by regional associations which included a number of ethnic groups, such as the Confederation of Indigenous Nationalities of Ecuadorian Amazonia (CONFENIAE), the Indigenous Association of the Peruvian Selva (AIDESEP), the Cauca Regional Indigenous Council (CRIC) in Colombia, the Eastern Bolivia Indigenous Confederation (CIDOB) and many others. All of them organized congresses, published manifestos and declarations, sent petitions to state and national governments as well as to the international community, and frequently organized militant actions—such as protest marches, manifestations, sit-ins, occupation of land, or other forms of active resistance—or embarked on legal proceedings and lobbied legislatures and public officials to achieve their various objectives.

A more recent form of organization is the national-level indigenous confederation. Once again, the Confederation of Indigenous Nationalities of Ecuador (CONAIE) led the way in political activity when it organized two massive peaceful indigenous uprisings in Ecuador in 1990 and 1993, which practically paralyzed the country and obliged the government to negotiate with the indigenous people on agrarian and other problems. The National Union of Indians (UNI) of Brazil, which brings together numerous Amazonian tribes, was very active in the political discussions on the new Brazilian Constitution in 1988, as also was the National Indigenous Organization of Colombia (ONIC) in 1991 (Guerrero, 1993).

Indigenous organizations have also expanded beyond their national frontiers to take part in international activities. In Central and South America, indigenous activists have attempted, with different degrees of success, to establish transnational regional organizations. Since the second half of the 1980s, various international meetings of regional and continental scope have been held in connection with the activities to commemorate the Encounter of Two Worlds (or rather 500 years of indigenous and popular resistance) and the International Year of Indigenous Populations (1993) and the International Decade of Indigenous Populations (which began in 1995), both proclaimed by the United Nations. Indigenous representatives of Latin America have also taken an active part in the discussions of the United Nations Working Group on Indigenous Populations, which is preparing a draft declaration on the rights of indigenous peoples for consideration by the General Assembly, and they have participated in the debates prior to the adoption by the International Labour Organisation of its Convention 169 on Indigenous and Tribal Peoples. Indigenous representatives are also present in the governing bodies of the Fund for the Development of the Indigenous Peoples of Latin America and the Caribbean, set up by the Second Ibero-American Conference of Heads of State and Government (Madrid, July 1992) and they are taking part in the consultations currently being held by the Inter-American Human Rights Commission of the Organization of American States on a future inter-American legal instrument on indigenous rights.

Through these activities, the representatives of the indigenous peoples of Latin America have made contact with representatives from other parts of the world and have become familiar with international law and the mechanisms and procedures for the protection of human rights in the international system: a relationship which both furthers their own cause and helps them to improve their political negotiating capacity in their own countries (Brysk, 1994).

A detailed analysis of the declarations, resolutions and proclamations of these various organizations and congresses (which is of course outside the scope of this article) would reveal a clear progression of ideas and sequence of items of concern to their members over the years. In the first few years, the indigenous manifestos reminded the public in general of the historical subordination of their peoples and their long-standing poverty, and called upon governments to grant some kind of compensation and justice for the wrongs of the past. At the same time, many of these documents idealized the pre-colonial indigenous past, sometimes described as a kind of Golden Age in which there was no exploitation, discrimination or conflict, while the pre-Columbian indigenous cultures were perceived as being morally superior to so-called Western civilization.

In later years, the demands posed by the indigenous organizations have been aimed more at specific problems such as access to land, agricultural credit, education, health, technical cooperation, investments in infrastructure, etc., whose solution they see as being the responsibility of governments. More recently, in addition to concrete economic and social demands they have also called for autonomy and self-determination. Ethnic identity has become a central issue for many of these organizations; concern with the environment is also an item of prime importance, especially in the case of the Amazonian lowlands, and there are increasingly frequent demands for changes in legislation and the fulfillment of recent international legal instruments, such as Convention 169 of the ILO and the draft United Nations declaration on the rights of indigenous peoples (Stavenhagen, 1988).

Indigenous organizations do not only hold meetings and spread their programs and ideas: they also negotiate with the public authorities, send representatives to international conferences, and often receive financial aid from international agencies for specific purposes. But whom do these organizations really represent, and how representative are they of the indigenous population? This matter is often raised by governments when they want to question the "authenticity" of indigenous representation at the national and international levels, or by rival factions and groups competing for official recognition or access to resources. It is true that in many cases the existing indigenous organizations were constructed from the top down and are made up of indigenous intellectual elites which do not have an authentic "popular" base, but such indigenous organizations are increasingly being constructed from the bottom up, through a laborious process of mobilization and organization which gives rise to a new leadership with popular bases and which expresses the true concerns of members.

THE INDIGENOUS LEADERSHIP

The question of representation will assuredly continue to be raised for some time to come. The traditional community-level leadership is generally carried out by an older generation of local authorities who, although steeped in the culture of their group, are not always well prepared to meet the challenges of "modern" organizations and political negotiations. These traditional authorities are gradually being displaced by a younger generation of indigenous activists, many of them professionals who have lived and matched their skills in a nonindigenous environment. Although tensions may arise between these two generations, their roles are often complementary: the traditional authorities made up of older people take care of community matters, while the younger leaders devote their efforts to building organizations and alliances and dealing with the outside world.

As more and more young indigenous people pass through the formal educational system and obtain professional positions as agronomists, teachers, doctors, lawyers, etc., an indigenous intellectual elite has been growing up in a number of Latin American countries that is becoming the lifeblood of the new organizations. Indigenous intellectuals are actively engaged in developing the "new indigenous discourse" which gives these organizations their distinctive identities. Not only do they devote their efforts to formulating the political agenda of their movements but they are also rediscovering their historical roots, concerning themselves with indigenous languages, culture and cosmology, and playing an active part in "inventing traditions" and constructing new "imagined communities." And in proportion as the new indigenous intelligentsia participates in national and international networks and succeeds in spreading its message to other sectors of the population, and as it proves capable of mobilizing resources and obtaining a certain amount of "collective goods" (material and political resources, public and legal recognition, etc.), so the indigenous intellectuals have been developing into indispensable links in the process of organization and mobilization. At the same time, the indigenous leadership is also succeeding in winning the support of the grassroots elements of the community, the local activists who are fighting against violations of human rights or struggling for land rights or protection of the environment: matters in which indigenous women are often particularly active. There sometimes seems to be some tension between local activists and the intellectuals, however, because the former deal with more immediate issues and seek concrete solutions, whereas the latter are more involved in building up institutions in the medium and long term. Furthermore, while indigenous intellectuals are helping to develop an "indigenist" ideology and *Weltanschauung* and are also sometimes involved in discussions with different ideological trends in Latin America (nationalism, Marxism, the theology of liberation, the Christian Democrat movement, evangelical Protestantism, etc.), local activists do not have much patience with these intellectual debates and are more interested in negotiating solutions for specific problems with the existing powers rather than pursuing ideological purity or coherence. These different approaches, along with other factors, have led to quite a few disputes over questions of organization, strategy and tactics which sometimes give the impression that the indigenous movement is seriously fragmented and split into factions.

ALLIANCES

As most of the indigenous communities in Latin America consist of rural peasant societies, indigenous demands have much to do with the concerns of all peasants over such matters as their rights to water and land, agrarian reform, agricultural credit, technical assistance, access to markets, agricultural prices and subsidies, etc. These questions have been particularly urgent on the Altiplano, as in other parts, since the 1960s, when numerous militant peasant movements sprang up in Latin America. Although indigenous organizations are very aware of their identity and independence, they also know that their impact and scope will be limited if they cut themselves off from other social movements. They have therefore had to cope with two interrelated types of problems: the role of indigenous movements in the framework of the conflicts and coordination of interests within their own national society, and the crucial issue of the building of strategic alliances with other organizations.

With regard to the first of these points, I will not waste time here with the outworn debates, common in the nineteenth and the early part of the twentieth century, about the alleged inferiority of the indigenous "races" in Latin America, nor with the national elites' objective of eliminating the indigenous "barbarians" who were endangering the survival of civilization. Instead, the debates in more recent decades have centered on two alternative concepts. On the one hand, there is the idea that indigenous cultures are not integrated into national culture and that national integration calls for the rapid incorporation of indigenous populations, which would mean their disappearance as such. This model presents indigenous organizations with the options of accepting the assimilationist policies of the State, while negotiating their terms; rejecting them out of hand; or putting forward other possible alternatives. Each of these three stances has been adopted at some time by one or another of the indigenous organizations.

ETHNICITY AND CLASS

On the other hand, extensive debates have been held since the 1930s about whether the indigenous peoples should be considered as an example of a subordinate and exploited social class (subsistence peasants, agricultural laborers) or as culturally different, oppressed peoples (nationalities) which in fact can also be internally differentiated in economic and social respects. This is the debate on ethnicity or class which has been heard so frequently in academic circles and which has various different connotations for the objectives and strategies of indigenous and other social movements.

If indigenous populations are to be considered simply as a segment of the exploited peasantry, then the solution to their problems may be found in the class struggle and organization (peasant unions; agrarian reform); from this standpoint, emphasis on ethnic identity would dilute their class consciousness and their corresponding political attitudes.

If indigenous identity is considered to be of fundamental importance, however, then matters connected with the class situation will be relegated to a secondary plane.

It would appear that in recent years indigenous organizations have mostly opted for the second of these positions. Without denying or ignoring considerations of class, they have emphasized their ethnic identity and the "ethnico-national" aspects of their struggles, which has also given them some prominence both at home and abroad. One of the reasons why they have adopted this position is the rather prejudiced attitude that traditional left-wing political parties have taken in Latin America to the "indigenous question." For many years, these parties promoted a conventional "classist" attitude to social conflicts, thereby alienating many potential indigenous allies who did not feel that their own concerns were reflected in the Marxist discourse of many of these political parties. Examples of these tensions may be seen in the conflict between the Sandinistas and the Miskitos in Nicaragua in the 1980s and the evolution of revolutionary ideology and armed conflict in Guatemala over the last thirty years (Díaz-Polanco, 1985; Arias, 1990; LeBot, 1995).

The debate on class versus ethnicity also has broader implications with regard to political strategy and tactics, because it concerns the possibility that indigenous movements may make alliances with other social and political organizations. From the very beginning of their process of organization and mobilization, indigenous activists realized that in order to achieve their broader objectives and avoid being left in watertight compartments they must seek alliances with other sectors of society, especially trade unions, peasant organizations, students and urban intellectuals, as well as with established institutions such as the Catholic Church (or at least with some of its current trends, such as the promoters of the theology of liberation) and, in certain circumstances, with some political parties.

Some indigenous organizations started off as branches of some political party. In Mexico, the Institutional Revolutionary Party (PRI) tried to organize and control some indigenous organizations in the 1970s, and in Bolivia the various political parties had, and some of them still have, indigenous branches: a clearly indigenous party, the Tupac Katari Indigenous Movement, or "Kataristas," openly competed for political power and their long-standing Presidential candidate, the Aymara Víctor Hugo Cárdenas, was Vice-President of Bolivia from 1993 to 1997 in a coalition government. Usually, however, indigenous organizations (though not their individual members) have avoided linking up with any specific political party, and their leaders generally reject the offers of political parties to incorporate or co-opt them into the established party structures (Albó, 1994).

Indigenous leaders realize, however, that they need to establish tactical alliances with other social organizations, especially when they share the same social objectives, such as the defense of human rights under repressive regimes (like the successive military dictatorships in Guatemala). The question of alliances has been publicly raised at some international congresses attended by indigenous organizations, where participants held that broad popular mobilization will have a bigger political impact than isolated actions by smaller, fragmented groups. On the other hand, indigenous leaders say that their specific interests (ethnic identity, recognition of the historical rights of indigenous peoples) are easily lost sight of and subordinated to the more general concerns of broad popular organizations. They generally fear (perhaps quite rightly) that indigenous organizations may come to be minor players in a game dominated by the established mestizo organizations and that they will run the risk of being manipulated by the more experienced nonindigenous politicians.

EXTERNAL SUPPORT

Indigenous organizations would not have progressed as much as they have done in all these years without external support. Indeed, many organizations originally started with the aid of outside agents who still often maintain their influence over them. Catholic and Protestant missions helped some of the Amazonian indigenous associations to organize their activities in the 1960s and 1970s, and the organization of the indigenous movement has also been aided at various times by teachers, government agronomists, anthropologists from academic institutions, health workers, and other nonindigenous professionals, as well as activists from different kinds of political groups. Many of these organizations now receive financial aid or subsidies from the many international agencies and different kinds of nongovernmental organizations that have been established in Latin America.

PROSPECTS OF THE INDIGENOUS MOVEMENT

Is the emergence of the indigenous movement a passing phenomenon, or is it a permanent element that represents some profound change in Latin American society? Only time will tell, but at the moment it is clear, at least for the writer, that the indigenous movement expresses fundamental social forces that are behind some of the changes that have been taking place in the continent during the last 30 years.

There are various factors that can account for the emergence of indigenous awareness and of these new social movements on the public scene. First, there is the general disenchantment with the failure of the traditional developmentalist policies assiduously applied by national governments and multilateral organizations since the end of the Second World War. "Economic development" was the magic expression, used by generations of official planners and academics, which was supposed to bring better standards of living and higher incomes to the poor, the marginalized, and the underprivileged people of Latin America. This promise was not fulfilled, however, as is shown by the "lost decade" of the 1980s. The indigenous peoples were indeed incorporated into the modern sector of the economy through the market mechanisms, labor migrations, and the expansion of the transport and communications infrastructure, but they saw that the benefits of growth went, as always, to the elites. Except in the case of a few experimental projects, the indigenous peoples witnessed the deterioration of their situation during this period, as they steadily lost their autonomy and means of subsistence and became increasingly dependent on market capitalism.

In this process of unequal development, the indigenous populations were everywhere victims rather than beneficiaries: the most vulnerable and fragile population groups, caught up in a maelstrom of rapid and unstable economic and social changes. This did not go unnoticed by the emergent indigenous intelligentsia, who quickly became skeptical of the optimistic economic projections and promises of their governments and the predictions that they were on the threshold of progress and civilization. Thus, their disillusionment was just as great as their hopes had once been (Davis, 1977).

Another factor, connected with the foregoing, was the increasing awareness of the emergent indigenous intelligentsia that the modern nation-state that the mestizo ruling elite had been building so diligently since the nineteenth century was flawed in its very foundations. Instead of being an integrative State it was exclusive: indigenous cultures were denied and "Indians" were victims of overt or covert racism and discrimination, and the indigenous peoples—even when they were the majority population groups in the nation as a whole, as in Bolivia and Guatemala, or in many subnational regions in the other countries—were excluded from economic well-being, social equality, political decision-making processes, and access to justice through the legal system. Indians saw no place for themselves in the prevailing model of the nation-state as constructed by the mestizo or white elites of the ruling class (mestizo elites came to power in some countries such as Mexico, but the traditional racial-cultural elites dominated by the locally born descendants of the Spanish colonists or other Europeans continued to prevail until well into the twentieth century in the other countries).

Latin America's indigenous roots were long considered a painful burden by the "European" elites, and the assimilation-oriented indigenist policies of their governments clearly indicated that indigenous cultures had no future in the modern nation-state. In spite of having received formal citizenship rights in most Latin American countries, the indigenous peoples have often been treated as second-class citizens, if not completely deprived of their rights as citizens (in some countries they were treated as minors, wards of the State, or legally incapable). Representative democracy, institutional political participation, equality before the law, due process, respect for their languages, cultures, religions and traditions, and the dignity accorded to the rest of national society were simply not for the Indians, many of whom reluctantly accepted the stereotypes and stigmas imposed on them by the dominant sectors and gave in to self-negation and self-denigration in order to be accepted by non-Indians. Others developed a "culture of resistance," becoming more introverted and avoiding contact with the outside world as much as possible (a reaction which has been increasingly difficult to maintain in recent years). Still others, conscious of the fact that the existing model of nation-state denies them their identity and their possibility of survival as viable cultures, have begun to question the prevailing idea of the nation and to propose alternative concepts of a multicultural and polyethnic State. This is one of the demands that the new indigenous movement has been putting forward in recent years.

There can be no doubt that the indigenous movement has also been inspired by the anti-colonial independence struggles of the post-war years. Indigenous intellectuals have identified themselves with the national liberation movements, often considering that their own struggles are also anti-colonial, because their peoples were victims of an earlier form of colonialism that became domestic colonialism after Independence. When they saw the achievements of the anti-colonial and national liberation movements, they probably asked themselves "And why not us too?". Indeed, in the many indigenous manifestos and proclamations the Indian peoples of Latin America are presented as the victims of colonialism, and their struggle is seen as an anti-colonial resistance movement. This was expressed and repeated very clearly at many national and international meetings in 1992, on the occasion of the 500th anniversary of the Meeting of Two Worlds: a celebration which further stimulated the establishment of indigenous organizations in the continent.

TOWARD A NEW APPROACH

The emergence of indigenous organizations also reflects the emergence of an indigenous or "Indianist" *Weltanschauung* which does not yet constitute a structured and coherent political ideology but does contain elements of such an attitude that clearly distinguish it from other ideologies which have permeated social thinking for many decades. It would seem that the emergent indigenous intelligentsia rejected the leading ideologies of the time because they did not tackle the problems of the indigenous population and the nation-state satisfactorily, deciding instead to formulate their own ideological texts.

A concept closely linked with the ideas of economic development and nation building is that of modernization, which was once put forward as a universalizing social process that would eventually embrace all the traditional, backward or pre-modern forms of society. It was considered that these forms were typical of indigenous communities and cultures and were therefore doomed to disappear. Modernization policies, touted as a remedy for underdevelopment and poverty, were designed to accelerate this process, which was felt by many to be both inevitable and desirable. The modernization paradigm, still proudly maintained by national leaders as a synonym of progress and hence morally legitimate, is now considered by many indigenous activists and their sympathizers as something tantamount to ethnocide. The emergent "Indianist" ideology finds little support in this paradigm and does not support it in its turn. On the contrary, in many cases it explicitly rejects modernization as a viable objective for the indigenous peoples. This tension is clearly expressed in the conflicts over ecological changes, particularly in tropical rainforest areas. In these areas, modernization is often identified with vast ecological changes that destroy the bio-resources of the tropical forests, which are the habitat of many indigenous groups.

The theory of modernization (one of the intellectual modes associated with the sociology of development) also asserted the need for profound changes in the cultural values of "backward" and "traditional" population groups. Various schools of "applied social scientists" used their skills to inform the indigenous populations of the world that their lifestyles were morally wrong (the missionary approach) or dysfunctional to the modern world (the technocratic approach). Indigenous peoples who accepted these arguments very soon found themselves morally dispossessed, culturally impoverished and materially devastated. The current indigenous (or Indianist) ideology therefore condemns the modernization paradigm as irrelevant in the best of cases and often potentially destructive of indigenous values.

For decades, the modernization approach to social and cultural changes competed among indigenous peoples with the Marxist view of the world, which served not only as a cognoscible map of the "real world" in which the indigenous peoples lived but also as a revolutionary guide for action and for changing the course of history. The various currents of Marxist political groups (communists, Trotskyites, Maoists, Castroists, etc.) sometimes had their own "indigenist" platforms (when they thought of the indigenous peoples, which was not very often). This generally meant inviting these peoples to give up their indigenous identities to join in the class struggle as poor and exploited peasants. Sometimes, however, it meant simply rejecting the indigenous peoples as being too primitive to understand the class struggle and concentrating instead on fomenting the revolution of the "advanced" classes of Latin America, especially the urban proletariat. It was claimed that once the battle was won, an enlightened revolutionary government would bring progress to the "backward" indigenous groups.

Indigenous intellectuals perceived the orthodox Marxist view of the "indigenous problem" as being not very different from that of the advocates of "modernization" mentioned earlier. Some of them rejected both approaches because they considered them to be products of the colonialist West. Indigenous skepticism increased still further when they saw how some indigenous groups were literally in the middle of the crossfire between leftist guerrilla movements and repressive armed forces under various Latin American governments (Bolivia, Colombia, Guatemala, Peru) during the 1970s and 1980s, while in Nicaragua they were caught between a leftist revolutionary government and the United States-organized "Contras" (Vilas, 1992).

Thus, the "Indianist" ideology arose as an alternative to the ideological vacuum displayed by the main political philosophies (both liberal and Marxist) with regard to the indigenous peoples. Although it would be hard to talk at present of a perfected, structured and coherent Indianist ideology (indeed, this could never exist), there are a number of issues and lines of thought which persistently appear in the various currents of

"Indianism," as reflected in the documentation of indigenous organizations, groups, seminars, conferences, workshops, reviews and periodicals. These issues, which are usually associated with specific demands made mainly to governments but also sometimes to society as a whole, may be grouped under the following five main headings.

Definition and Legal Status

While bureaucrats, legal experts and anthropologists, as well as the occasional missionary, have racked their brains over the question of who is or is not an Indian (or what qualifies as "indigenous"), since the definition and quantification of the indigenous peoples of Latin America is an ambiguous matter, the right to self-definition is one of the recurrent demands of indigenous organizations. This has become a question of cultural identity and often a matter of honor (independently of such "objective" criteria as the language or style of dress used, or active participation in community life). Rather than seeing this as a matter of individual choice, many organizations call for official recognition of indigenous groups and collective identities. When being an indigenous person was a source of social stigma there was little incentive for self-identification, but as times are changing, self-identification as an indigenous person has become a political instrument in a disputed social space.

Since social and cultural labels often imply a specific legal status, and the attribution of such status has typically been a prerogative of governments, indigenous organizations which claim the right to self-definition (now considered as a fundamental human right) also question the authority of governments to impose this status unilaterally (which is what actually occurred right from the start). The indigenous movement claims a new status for indigenous peoples within a democratic society: a demand that has been reflected in recent years in the legislative and constitutional changes mentioned at the beginning of this article.

The Right to Land

Although land rights—from which the agrarian reform question stems—no longer receive much attention in this era of economic globalization, they are of fundamental importance for the survival of the indigenous peoples of Latin America and form one of their main demands. Loss of their lands (which are essential for their lifestyle) has been a constant feature of the history of the indigenous peoples of Latin America, and the struggle to preserve or recover their land tenure rights lies at the root of many recent attempts by the indigenous peoples to organize themselves. Land and its various resources (forests, water, animals and even minerals) are viewed mainly as collective, communal goods, although the notion of individual property rights has made some headway among indigenous communities after decades of capitalist expansion. There have been struggles for land tenure rights by the Mapuches of Chile, the inhabitants of the Altiplano in Peru and Ecuador and the Mayas of Guatemala, and they also lie at the root of social conflicts in Mexico, including the 1994 indigenous uprising in Chiapas. For the indigenous peasants of Latin America, the land tenure question is far from being solved, and the neglect of this by governments—after the wave of agrarian reform measures during the 1960s as part of the program of the Alliance for Progress—is a heavy burden for the indigenous peoples to bear.

Although land tenure rights in the strict sense refer to production resources, the indigenous peoples insistently lay claim to their territorial rights, that is to say, the recognition and legal delimitation of ancestral territories occupied continuously by an indigenous group for time immemorial, which generally represent the geographic space needed for the cultural and social reproduction of the group. Indigenous territories have suffered serious losses as the result of colonization from outside or expropriations decreed by governments, and there is a general consensus that, without their own territory, the social and cultural survival of the indigenous peoples is seriously threatened.

Cultural Identity

Spontaneous cultural change and the process of acculturation, as well as State policies of assimilation of indigenous peoples, have been considered to represent a form of ethnocide: that is to say, they endanger the survival of indigenous cultures. Through a passive culture of resistance, many indigenous peoples have managed to preserve elements of their culture and keep alive their ethnic identity: efforts which have been strengthened in recent years by the conscious cultural rebirth promoted by the indigenous elites and cultural militants. Thus, for example, the Mayan culture is being actively promoted in Guatemala by numerous indigenous organizations (furthermore, in highly repressive environments purely cultural activity is somewhat less dangerous than openly political actions). The Quechua and Aymara languages and traditions have been revived in the Andean countries, and in Mexico an organization of indigenous writers and intellectuals is promoting indigenous literature. Sometimes these activities receive government support, but they are generally dependent on their own resources, with perhaps some aid from a sympathetic non-governmental organization.

Back in the nineteenth century, Spanish was declared to be the official and national language of the Spanish-speaking States of Latin America, and in the best of cases the indigenous languages were dismissed as dialects that did not deserve to be preserved. Consequently, formal and private (generally missionary) education imposed the State language on indigenous groups, and the use of indigenous languages was often even forbidden in public activities such as legal proceedings, municipal administration, etc. With such a disadvantage imposed on them in respect to the use of their own languages, the rights of the indigenous peoples were easily and systematically destroyed. In recent years, however, as the result of indigenous demands and the reappraisal of indigenist policies by teachers and social scientists, some governments have applied bilingual education programs in indigenous areas. The indigenous organizations now demand educational services in their own languages, teachers' training programs for their own people, and curricula that take the indigenous cultures into account. In some States (such as Peru) indigenous languages are now recognized as national languages, while in others members of the indigenous population are officially allowed to use their own language in administrative and legal matters that affect them.

Social Organization and Legal Customs

Indigenous community life, and hence the viability of indigenous cultures, depends on the vitality of the group's social organization and in many cases on the active use of local legal customs. In recent years this has become an important demand of indigenous organizations, since failure by the State legal system and the public administration to recognize the local form of social organization and legal customs is yet another factor contributing to the weakening and possible disappearance of indigenous cultures.

No Latin American State formally recognizes multiple legal systems, but there has always been some degree of tolerance for local "usages and customs" (in Colonial times, a special legal system was established by the Crown for the "Indian Republics"). Many indigenous organizations have now adopted the objective of securing formal recognition of legal customs, traditional forms of local authority and settlement of disputes, practices regarding inheritance and patrimony, rules on land use and communal resources, etc. These represent political demands that are often expressed in the indigenous population's objective of achieving a higher degree of political participation.

Political Participation

The indigenous organizations are now not only claiming greater political representation in government institutions (municipal councils, state legislatures, national congresses) but are also trying to win the right to self-determination (guaranteed in international law), as expressed in local and regional autonomy and self-government. Many States are still fearful of these demands because they see them as a step toward secession and fragmentation of the nation-state, but indigenous organizations generally insist that all they want is internal self-determination and greater participation in national politics, not as an excluded minority but as descendants of the first inhabitants of the country and hence "authentic" representatives of the "nation."

Various countries, including Brazil, Nicaragua and Panama, have adopted statutes giving autonomy to indigenous regions, while others are considering doing so. This is a matter that will undoubtedly give rise to much controversy in the future.[2]

The progress made in recent years at the international level in the field of indigenous rights has strongly influenced the position and evolution of the indigenous organizations of Latin America, and may also have influenced the evolution of governments' positions. The United Nations Working Group on Indigenous Populations has been preparing a draft declaration of indigenous rights since 1982. To begin with, Latin American governments paid little attention to these efforts, but as time has gone by they have been showing greater interest. At first, few representatives of the Latin American indigenous population participated in this work, but in recent years more and more indigenous organizations of the region have taken part in the annual debates of the Working Group in Geneva. Attending these meetings gives many indigenous leaders the chance to get to know the international environment, make contact with their opposite numbers in other countries, and thus strengthen their own domestic organizational work. Whatever the final result of the draft declaration (the United Nations General Assembly may adopt it in an amended form), the indigenous organizations already consider its various articles (though still only provisional, of course) as a necessary point of reference in their own political discourse. This is so, for example, in the case of the assertion that the indigenous peoples, just like all other peoples, have the right to self-determination.

On the other hand, there were few indigenous representatives at the debates leading up to the adoption of ILO Convention 169 in 1989. The indigenous points of view were mainly expressed by the workers' delegates, who were not always very familiar with these matters. Since Convention 169 has been ratified by a number of Latin American countries, the indigenous organizations rightly see it as one of the existing legal instruments that are binding on governments, and they are consequently actively promoting its ratification by the remaining countries.

As international law on indigenous rights grows up, the indigenous organizations of Latin America will use it for both legal and political purposes.

The indigenous discourse stands at the crossroads between matters of human rights, democracy, development and the environment. It has become increasingly clear that indigenous demands are not just of interest to the indigenous peoples themselves but also involve the whole of the respective national societies. The indigenous peoples are not just calling for more and better democracy, better application of the mechanisms for the defense and protection of human rights, or a bigger share in the supposed benefits of development programs. What they are really doing is questioning and challenging the basic assumptions on which the Nation-State has been built up in Latin America for almost two centuries past.

Notes

[1] With regard to the ethnic question, see Stavenhagen (1990); with regard to ethnocide and ethnodevelopment, see Bonfil and others (1982).

[2] For an earlier study of these questions, see Stavenhagen, 1992, pp. 63–118.

Bibliography

Albó, X. 1994. And from Kataristas to MNRistas? The surprising and bold alliance between Aymaras and neoliberals in Bolivia, in D. Lee van Cott (ed.), *Indigenous Peoples and Democracy in Latin America,* New York, St. Martin's Press.

Arias, A. 1990. Changing Indian identity: Guatemala's violent transition to modernity, in C. A. Smith (ed.), *Guatemalan Indians and the State,* Austin, Texas University Press.

Bonfil, G. and others. 1982. *América Latina: Etnodesarrollo y Etnocidio,* San José, Costa Rica, Latin American Faculty of Social Sciences (FLACSO).

Brysk, A. 1994. Acting globally: Indian rights and international politics in Latin America, in D. Lee van Cott (ed.), *Indigenous Peoples and Democracy in Latin America,* New York, St. Martin's Press.

CELADE (Latin American Demographic Center). 1994. *Estudios sociodemográficos de pueblos indígenas,* LC/DEM/G.146, Santiago, Chile.

Davis, S. 1977. *Victims of the Miracle: Development and the Indians of Brazil,* Cambridge, MA, Cambridge University Press.

Descola, P. 1988. Etnicidad y desarrollo económico: el caso de la Federación de Centros Shuar, in *Indianidad, etnocidio, indigenismo en América Latina,* Mexico City, Instituto Indigenista Interamericano (III)/Centro de Estudios Mexicanos y Centroamericanos (CEMCA).

Díaz-Polanco, H. 1985. *La cuestión étnico-nacional,* Mexico City, Editorial Línea.

González, M. L. 1994. How many indigenous people? in G. Psacharopoulos and H. A. Patrinos (eds.), *Indigenous People and Poverty in Latin America: An Empirical Analysis,* Washington, DC, World Bank.

Guerrero, A. 1993. De sujetos indios a ciudadanos étnicos: de la manifestación de 1961 al levantamiento indígena de 1990, in *Democracia, Etnicidad y Violencia Política en los Países Andinos,* Lima, Instituto de Estudios Peruanos (IEP)/Instituto Francés de Estudios Andinos.

Ibarra, A. 1987. *Los Indígenas y el Estado en el Ecuador,* Quito, Ediciones Abya-Yala.

LeBot, Y. 1995. *La Guerra en Tierras Mayas: Comunidad, Violencia y Modernidad en Guatemala (1970–1992),* Mexico City, Fondo de Cultura Económica (FCE).

Psacharopoulos, G., and H. A. Patrinos (eds.). 1994. *Indigenous People and Poverty in Latin America: An Empirical Analysis.* Washington, DC, World Bank.

Salazar, E. 1981. La Federación Shuar y la frontera de la colonización, in N. E. Whitten, Jr. (ed.), *Amazonia Ecuatoriana: La Otra Cara del Progreso,* Quito, Mundo Shuar.

Stavenhagen, R. 1988. *Derecho Indígena y Derechos Humanos en América Latina.* Mexico City, El Colegio de México/Inter-American Institute of Human Rights (IIHR).

———. 1990. *The Ethnic Question: Development, Conflicts and Human Rights.* Tokyo, United Nations University, Publications Unit.

———. 1992. La situación y los derechos de los pueblos indígenas de América Latina, *América Indígena,* vol. LII, Nos. 1–2, Mexico City, January–June.

Villas, C. M. 1992. *Estado, Clase y Etnicidad: La Costa Atlántica de Nicaragua,* Mexico City, FCE.

Albino Mares is a Rarámuri who has played ra'chuela *since boyhood; he has served as a native-language broadcaster and writes schoolbooks in Rarámuri for the Department of Education of the state of Chihuahua. Don Burgess is a linguist who often works with the Escuela Nacional de Antropología e Historia, Unidad Chihuahua.*

Detailed ethnographic studies are increasingly being recognized as collaborative efforts between Western-trained academics and members of other populations. In this instance, Mares, a monolingual Rarámuri, gives an "insider's view" of their traditional stick-ball game, briefly annotated by his translator, Burgess. With no didactic pretensions, the paper vividly demonstrates how very different are basic premises (even unarticulated) and cultural expectations about preparations for a game, how long it may last, the choosing of teams, rules, and even festive celebrations afterward. Contrasting a game that you know well, consider this as not just a batch of quaint and curious customs but as a tiny insight into a vastly different worldview.

Hit and Run
The Stick-and-Ball Game as an
Integral Part of *Rarámuri* Culture
Albino Mares
(Translated and annotated by Don Burgess)

Before 1900, traditional forms of field hockey, or shinny, were among the most popular games played by Native American groups in the western United States and northwestern Mexico. Today they are seldom played except among some Rarámuri *(also known as the* Tarahumara*) and Guarojío who live in southwestern Chihuahua State, Mexico. The* Rarámuri *version, known as* ra'chuela, *may involve as many as two hundred players and is sometimes played over the course of several Sundays. Only men participate (they say that if a woman plays, she will start acting like a man). Women have their own game, in which they throw a hoop with a stick.*

Rarámuri runners have long been known for their athletic endurance. In the 1890s anthropologist Carl Lumholtz recorded a Rarámuri *man making a round-trip on foot to the city of Chihuahua and back in five days, a distance of about six hundred miles. Because the* Rarámuri *live scattered over their rugged mountain-and-canyon homeland,* ra'chuela *and long-distance races, along with fiestas and communal work, offer important opportunities for social interaction.*

The author of the account below, Albino Mares, is a Rarámuri *who grew up in an isolated area about two days' walk from the nearest road. We met more than twenty-five years ago, during the Easter wrestling matches (another popular local event), when we were on opposite sides and had to wrestle each other. Shortly afterward, we began to work together writing books in the* Rarámuri *language about Albino's native culture.*

He is still an excellent player of ra'chuela. —*D. Burgess*

We Rarámuri of Chihuahua, Mexico, are known for our endurance in long races. In one of our races, each of two teams has a wooden ball, which the runners toss with their feet. Such races can cover one hundred miles and last more than twenty hours. For a team to win, the player who takes the ball over the finish line must have covered the entire distance himself, but other players help him by tossing the ball along the way.

Reprinted and abridged with permission of the publisher and author from his article "Hit and Run," in *Natural History,* vol. 108, no. 7, pp. 50–55, 1999. A map and several photographs have been omitted here; Don Burgess translated the original paper from Rarámuri (known as *"Tarahumara"* to outsiders) and provided some annotative notes (which are set off in squared brackets and italics before and after Mares' text).

I thought about running when I was just a small boy. My parents would wake me when the sun was about to come over the mountains so that I could run around the house three times, tossing a wooden ball with my feet, then face the rising sun to ask God to give me the desire and strength to be a good runner.

The sport I enjoy most is called *ra'chuela,* or, in Spanish, *palillo.* It is played only among groups in the western part of our tribe's territory. You use a stick with a spoon-like end to scoop a wooden ball up into the air and hit it. When I was young, I used to carry my *ra'chuela* stick everywhere I went, scooping up rocks and hitting them as far as I could.

Ra'chuela is played with a large number of people and requires a good deal of preparation. One person may suggest a game to another, who replies, "Let's do it! Can you give me what you are going to bet?" These men will be the captains. Both of them offer an item they want to bet—a peso, a kerchief, a mirror. The two captains do not match each other's bets; rather, each takes his opponent's bet back to his potential teammates, one of whom matches it with something of equal value. If the bet has great value—such as a goat or a cow—several players can pool their resources. This is how we invite players to be on our side, by showing them the bet, although a player does not have to bet in order to play. Other bets are added and matched, up to the time the game begins.

Ra'chuela is played from late September to May. They say that playing it in the rainy season (July through mid-September) will cause hail to fall. Games must be on a Sunday. That is the day of rest.

Before the game, each player must prepare some good sticks, two or three of them, so that if one breaks he can quickly grab another (his extra sticks will be carried along by a supporter who is watching the game). We prefer the wood of a tree we call *wahía* or of one we call *usá*—both are light and will not split. The same wood can be used for the ball, which is very round and about the size of a chicken egg. A light ball is better in case the game goes through a creek, because it will not sink. If the game is going to be played in a very dry place, this does not matter, and a heavy hall is preferred because it travels far when hit. We have to make several balls, in case one breaks or is lost.

Anyone can play, even if he was not invited to join a team. He takes his stick to whichever side he wants to play on. The sticks are placed in the middle of the field, where the game will begin. A stick from one side is placed touching a stick from the other side. Each must have an opponent. Also, the ball is buried a little under the dirt, just barely covered. Meanwhile, people who are not playing may continue to make bets.

The place where the game is played can be as much as a mile or two long, with a goal at each end; a goal might be a waterfall, a fence, or any other landmark. The players determine how a team will win and when play will be stopped. Sometimes the game is played until the ball crosses one of the goals. Sometimes the game ends when the shade reaches a certain place, even if neither goal has been crossed.

Once the sticks are all lined up and the betting is done, the game can begin. Each player picks up his stick, and the two captains begin fighting for the buried ball. At any time during the game, there are usually several players fighting over the ball, perhaps seven or eight, while the others stay back watching until the ball is hit in their direction. A player will not let an opponent be on his own, for if he is by himself and the ball reaches him, he could easily toss it up with his stick and hit it toward the goal.

A good player is one who most often can get the ball out from among a group of players and advance it. When the sticks are being given out before the game, the captains must make sure that an equal number of good players are on each team. Then the game may go on for hours in just one spot, and sometimes it gets dark while they are still there. When one team has a majority of the good players, you cannot have a good game.

The spectators watch from a distance, because if someone gets too close, it can be very dangerous. With so many sticks being swung at the ball, someone can get hit very hard. Players can be hit in the head and lose a lot of blood. A leg bone can get broken, or an eye hit, or a tooth broken, or a finger. When some people get mad, they hit the ball right at another player. If someone does that, the captain must reprimand him. If it happens again, that player must be put out of the game. Another can take his place, but if there is no substitute, then a player from the other side must drop out so that the teams remain even. [*The local government has prohibited the game in some areas where it was being used to take out grievances; one person was actually struck and killed with a stick.*—D. Burgess]

If the game is supposed to end when the ball crosses a goal and this does not happen before dark, the game will be continued the following Sunday, beginning where it left off. Occasionally it will continue over three Sundays. Often, however, the game ends when it gets late or dark. Victory is then declared based on which team's goal is closest when play is halted.

To help a team win, a ceremony called a *giholi* may be held to cure, or purify, the players. This takes place where the captain lives, on the Saturday night before the game. The person in charge is a healer called the *gihome*, who gives speeches that are like sermons or prayers. He asks the god Riosi to help them with the game. [*Some* Rarámuri *think of Riosi as the sun, others as the god who created the universe. The name may come from the Spanish* dios*. The more native word* Onorúgame *(the one who is father) is also used*—D. Burgess]. A cross is set up next to which the players place the sticks, the balls, and the items they have bet, along with special medicines. Musicians play the guitar and violin, and incense is burned. The god Riosi is said to eat the smoke of the incense. Besides giving speeches, the *gihome* also smokes tobacco, which enables him to know what the healer on the other side is doing.

A lot of corn beer must be prepared for the ceremony. The *gihome* and the musicians drink throughout Saturday night, but the players themselves drink very little. Sunday at dawn the players stand near the cross with their sticks. The *gihome* gives a speech to ask Riosi's help, then sprinkles the players with water in which certain plants have been soaked. These medicines protect the players from being struck by some sickness sent by the healer on the other side. The *gihome* also goes around all day during the game, thinking and smoking and drinking corn beer so that the players will not get lazy or sleepy, and so bad things will happen to the opponents.

Sometimes a *gihome* will use a human skull or bone to hex the opponents, although exactly how he goes about this is not generally known. Some men say that when a *gihome* is going to invite a skull to help, he talks to it as if it were alive so that it will allow him to carry it to the place where it will be used, and he also offers it food or drink, especially corn beer. It is said that the skull is buried where the game is played. The *gihome* can ask the skull to do whatever he wants, and it does as he asks. It causes the opponents to be unable to hit the ball and to become lazy, while enabling the *gihome*'s side never to miss and to gain strength and thus win. When the skull is no longer being used, it must be returned to the place from which it was taken. It is thanked for having helped so beautifully, and food or drink is left for it. Incense is burned so the skull will be happy, without bad feelings.

After the game ends and the bets have been divided up, the captain invites all his players to his house to eat and drink. This is a type of payment that is given for helping to will the game—and even if they did not win, because the corn beer is ready and must be drunk. But first the *gihome* gives a speech to thank Riosi for helping them win. He also advises them all to drink in tranquility, without fighting, since some of the youths get angry when they drink.

A large fire is made for people to warm themselves. When people begin to get drunk, the musicians begin to play and one person dances the *bascola*. This can go on until dawn if there is enough corn beer. Usually several households prepare corn beer for the players, and when all the beer at one house has been drunk, they move on to another one. When the corn beer in all the houses has been drunk, people return to their own homes.

This is how the Rarámuri who live in this world play the game of *ra'chuela*.

[Along with the ruggedness of their traditional homeland, the fact that it lay outside the major trade routes helped the Rarámuri *preserve their sports and their stamina. With the somewhat recent advent of contact with the wider world—through the railroad, roads, logging, schools, and tourism—diet and work habits are changing for many of the people, and the future of their athletics hangs in the balance. Efforts to encourage* Rarámuri *sports have increased in the last few years. Once a year, usually in May, the lowland* Rarámuri *(those who live in the tribe's western territory) gather to perform traditional dances and sports. Mexico's Instituto Nacional Indigenista has been arranging sports events in the region, and* Rarámuri *dancers, musicians, craftsmen, and athletes have also traveled to places outside their territory, including Mexico City and Tucson. In 1993* Rarámuri *runners were taken to the Leadville Trail hundred-mile race in Colorado, where they won first, second, and fifth places. Since then, they have won other races, including the 1998 twelfth annual Angeles Crest hundred-mile race near Los Angeles.—D. Burgess]*

Further Readings

Games of the North American Indians, by Stewart Culin (Dover, 1975).

Tarahumara of the Sierra Madre: Survivors on the Canyon's Edge, by John G. Kennedy (Asilomar Press, 1996).

Indian Running: Native American History and Tradition, by Peter Nabokov (Ancient City Press, 1987).

American Indian Lacrosse: Little Brother of War, by Thomas Vennun Jr. (Smithsonian Institution Press, 1994).

Alicia Re Cruz teaches anthropology at University of North Texas. Her best-known book is The Two Milpas of Cham Kom.

Although it didn't exist when the author was born, the city of Cancún, Mexico, has become a world-famous tourist resort in recent years—an interesting case study of economic development and globalization. Its explosive growth, dominated by the service industry, has resulted in some tensions between the workaday lives of residents and the face that is presented to the rapidly changing public of outsiders. Unusual insights into that contrast and the distressing phenomenon of culture shock are offered in this account of an ethnographic training program. Not all students are prepared for the peculiar roles that an anthropologist must sometimes fill in an alien culture (contrast Ehrenreich, chapter 11).

Fortunes and Misfortunes of a Field School in "the Other Cancún"

Alicia Re Cruz

This paper is a report on the experience of being an anthropologist while conducting an ethnographic school in the field. My aim is to emphasize the anthropologist's role in becoming a simultaneous cultural translator for the actors and institutions involved in the ethnographic field experience, and to reflect on the status of ethnographic fieldwork based on the prevailing theoretical and methodological debates of our discipline which are highly stimulated by the current global world trends. Current expressions and terms in the anthropological literature such as "trans-local or trans-national communities" (Kearney 1991, Rose 1992), the "Implosion of the Third World into the First" (Rosaldo, 1989), among others, are pointing to this global reconstruction, which affects not only the geopolitical order but the practical and theoretical fundamentals of our discipline. Postmodernism is the anthropological vein that deals with the understanding of the fragmentation and space-time disjunctured nature of today's world (Weiner 1995), within the globalizing glaze of late capitalism (Jameson 1991). This field project for undergraduate students was conceived within this postmodern anthropological perspective that emerges from current world global trends.

The ethnographic field school was designed as a summer course with a three-week field experience in Cancún, the tourist international emporium, located on the eastern coast of the Yucatán Peninsula in southern Mexico. The group consisted of twelve undergraduate students, one of them a mother of a six-month-old baby. Eight students were majors in anthropology; one was a major in sociology; two were majors in criminal justice, and one recently graduated with a bachelor's degree in emergency management. None had prior fieldwork experience.

The location of the field school was in the *Región 101* of Cancún, an area on the periphery of Cancún, where migrants from different regions of the nation settle in the territory, attracted by the job possibilities that the tourism industry of Cancún offers. The project was developed as a collaborative enterprise between the Mexican Red Cross and the Institute of Anthropology of the University of North Texas. The course was conceived as both an academic and a community service project. Academically, the students were exposed to actual field conditions. They had to face the aspect of practicing anthropology while making sense of the social reality, utilizing the notions and

Abridged, with permission of the author, from an article with the same title in *Teaching Anthropology* (Spring/Summer, 1996): 17–21. Copyright © American Anthropological Association.

anthropological concepts learned in the classroom—learning anthropology through practicing it. Students had to live in a socioeconomic and cultural context with which they were unfamiliar. As participants in this context, at first strange and unusual, they were pushed to understand it by using anthropological tools and techniques.

On the service angle, the purpose of the project was to involve the students in the community activities and programs that the Red Cross center developed in the *Región 101*. This center faced the challenge of dealing with a multi-ethnic population which mostly comprises Yucatec Mayas, but it also includes Mayas from Chiapas and Guatemala, and migrants from Michoacán, Guerrero, Veracruz and other Mexican regions. Some of the community projects undertaken in the area alerted the Red Cross to the need to understand better the social dynamics of a multicultural community of migrants. Based on the culturally diverse condition of the community, the field school aimed at promoting students' research activities that could provide a general view of a "global" community of migrants characterized by a broad spectrum of socioeconomic and cultural perspectives.

An important aspect of my doctoral research was the understanding of the migrant life when the peasants move to Cancún from the rural Maya communities. For six months in 1990, I lived with a Maya family from Chan Kom, a Maya peasant community (see Re Cruz 1992) that settled in the *Región 101* of Cancún. To share everyday life with the migrants in this neighborhood was a continuous social irony. Overcrowded areas of poverty and over-luxurious hotels with shopping malls were separated by just a few miles. These few miles seemed to constitute a clear border between the workplace, which is mostly located in the hotel area, and the living-place for the migrant-worker, the *barrios*. However, this border becomes invisible for the tourists of the hotel area from whom the *areas populares* or *barrios* are hidden. Through ethnographic analysis I discovered the intimate connections between the migrants' nurturing of the urban informal economy and their role as nurturers of the capitalist-consumption apparatus of Cancún's economy. The development and characteristics of the migrants' settlements are intimately connected to the Mexican Government's efforts to lessen international debt through a policy of high investments in tourism.

The high economic revenues of Cancún as a tourist enterprise come from the current international gusto for "the exotic." The paradise-like beaches and the presence of major ancient Maya archaeological sites, flavored by the existence of the living Maya people exposed in restaurants and hotels—waiters, waitresses, tortilla-makers—certainly contributes to the satisfaction of this international demand for "the exotic" (see Re Cruz, 1992). The intricate connections between the regional, national and international issues involved in the understanding of the Maya migrants living in the *barrios* of Cancún, brought me to contextualize the ethnographic discussion within a postmodern frame (see Re Cruz 1996).

By "postmodern" I am referring to the ethnographic style that allows the ethnographer to explain the complexities embedded in the current world global trends. To understand Cancún today, for instance, because of its international economic and social connections via tourism, we need to go beyond the national borders. Because of the peasant attachments to urban Cancún via the migrant labor needed to develop its tourism empire, we must also go beyond the rural/urban border.

GETTING PREPARED FOR THE FIELD

The ethnographic course started with introductory information about anthropology and the cultural and social setting of the field. This first part of the course took place at the University of North Texas for one week. The students were divided into four groups, each of them led by one student who could speak Spanish at a conversational level. Each group had a different research agenda: family patterns, religion, economy and transformation of women's roles in Cancún. Although it had not been confirmed, the students were supposed to live with families in the area. The living conditions in the *Región 101* of Cancún are close to the North American standard of "poverty" (e.g., lack of running water, sanitary services and electricity).

This first week of the course was devoted to reading ethnographic information and to watching visual material (slides and videos) depicting the *barrios* life in Cancún. Students were also required to read about basic field methods and techniques (Pelto & Pelto 1978, Bernard 1988, Spradley 1980). The following three weeks of the course were in the field, at Cancún.

THE FIELDWORK, GETTING STARTED

A general stage of bewilderment and confusion seized the students once they arrived at the *Región 101*, after being picked up by Red Cross ambulances at the airport. The social worker working at the Red Cross center in the *Región 101* welcomed us. However, she brought the news that I had feared: there would not be enough host-group families for the students. The bumping, unpaved streets, wooden-stick-wall and cardboard-roof houses, surrounded by an avalanche of children attracted by the novelty of having *gringos* in the *barrio*, were the first images welcoming the students. Two social workers, other members of the Red Cross center and some women from the community prepared a short reception for the group. The blue-eyed and light-skinned baby became the focus of attraction and attention, particularly for women. Looking at the baby, one of them advised me that, because of the intense heat, we should not bathe the baby with cold water. The woman's concern for the baby's health instantly moved me to ask her about the possibility of hosting the student with the baby. The woman accepted. Since nurturing a baby while conducting fieldwork would be hard work, another member of the team and the mother agreed to room together.

There was a high school located in the *Región 101*. Students from different neighborhoods, from the migrant low-income *areas populares* to middle-class areas, were attending this school. Among this student population, there were four families that expressed their willingness to host only female students. The male students did not have any option but to stay at the Red Cross center, joined by two other female students, and myself.

The Red Cross center was a large building that included a reception hall, a small doctor's office with bathroom, two small rooms and one big meeting room. With calculated precision this room was subdivided into six spaces for a cot and a chair for luggage, clothes and books. Independent from the main building, there were three structures used as classrooms where different types of activities for the community were scheduled during mornings and evenings. Courses on beauty, manicure, sewing, adult education and such were offered in these classrooms. With the installation of a gas pipe and a gas stove, we used the room as the cooking and meeting area for the group.

Next to our kitchen there was a bathroom with a toilet and a small sink. It was used by the community people who attended the adult education courses offered at the center. Upon our arrival, the water pipe was extended and transformed into a shower. That would be the bathroom for the boys. The girls' bathroom was off the doctor's office. Compared to the male students, the females were privileged because their toilet had the cover seat. "How should I sit?", one of them wondered. The Red Cross center was transformed into a hostel for the students. However, the water pipes could not stand the tension of meeting the demands of so many foreigners in tropical weather. The pipes stopped working on the third day of our arrival. As a result, we ended up obtaining water from the communal neighborhood pipe. The rest of our students, "adopted" by the high school students' families, were living in other residential neighborhoods with socioeconomic characteristics closer to middle class. In sum, the students were exposed to a broad range of socioeconomic living conditions.

ORGANIZING THE EVERYDAY ACTIVITIES

Once student housing was resolved, the next step in the field school program was to implement the daily academic, research and recreational activities for the students. The English lessons that the students would conduct at the center for the *Región 101* people had been advertised prior to our arrival. Our first sunrise at the center was followed by the noisy presence of a group of children anxiously waiting for the "real *gringos*" to teach them English. Most of the morning time was devoted to English classes.

Since we were going to handle the cooking for all the group at the "improvised kitchen," we needed to organize a rotation system of students who could assist in the kitchen with one of the social workers who volunteered to be the cook for lunch. We had to help ourselves for breakfast and dinner. Breakfast ended up being a source of culinary creativity. Once, a student was craving gravy but we did not have flour. Someone had the brilliant idea of improvising the gravy with flour for pancakes. Unanimously we call the new recipe "the Postmodern gravy."

We tried to convert lunchtime into a "family-community-event." The social workers, nurse and the Red Cross assistant were all invited. This was a time when we could share our anecdotes, adventures and misfortunes in the field. Right after lunch, twice a week, we held a general meeting. During the first one, either on Tuesdays or Thursdays, the leaders of each group gave us a report of their research. The goal was that all the students could learn from the information and research analysis of other groups in order to get a more holistic view of the community. The second meeting, generally held on Fridays, was aimed at engaging the entire group in a brainstorming discussion on their own perspectives, comments and ideas emerging from their gradual understanding of the community.

The Red Cross was developing a program of different activities offered for the community. *Madrinas de leche* (milk godmothers) was a program to assist the mothers whose babies appeared undernourished. Those who needed it were given milk and other products to overcome their economic deficiencies. A general "family education" class was also offered Thursday mornings. In this, the women received advice regarding family behavior patterns. Furthermore, courses on hair styling, cosmetology and sewing were offered. This broad range of scheduled programs became an important source of information for the students, and provided them opportunities to exercise their participant-observation skills.

Students were required to keep a journal. Their daily activities during weekdays were structured as follows. First, the waking up was earlier than expected:

> I woke this morning at 5:30 A.M. again. I walked outside to investigate the day. There were no sounds. The streets were empty except for an older man who walked with a slight gimp on his right leg. He wore sandals and dark green khaki style pants; no shirt. On his head he wore a dirty, worn baseball cap and he was carrying *tortillas*. I was struck with tranquility. [Marc]

Students gathered at the center around 7:30 A.M. where we had breakfast together. The handy pastry store around the corner provided us with early morning delights. Then, the group conducted English classes. Groups of two or three, headed by a Spanish-speaking student, handled a group of six or seven community children. That resulted in an extremely effective reciprocal-teaching system, in which the American students improved their Spanish skills while teaching community students the rudiments of the English language. After an hour and a half or two hours of teaching, the students got involved in their particular research activities. Some of them decided to walk around the neighborhood to arrange their interviews with possible informants, or just to have a "taste" of community life. Some of them preferred to take advantage of the activities held at the center and selected that avenue to talk to the people. Lunch was scheduled around 1:00 P.M. This was the time for the "community-family reunion."

Twice during the first week a general meeting with the doctor and his team was scheduled following lunch. For the second meeting, the doctor brought a Maya midwife who talked about *empacho* and other intestinal ailments related to her interpretation of the human body composition, which is intimately connected to the Maya cosmic vision. She focused her presentation on the *tipte'*, which is the "center" of the human body. When this center is moved or displaced, the disjointed body structure becomes unbalanced, promoting health disturbances. This was one of the exhilarating moments of the field school for me, for it was a privileged opportunity to open the students' minds to the operationalization of a cultural system that I had discussed in my courses on the ancient and contemporary living Maya. In this case, the students could exercise the quadripartite cosmovision principle of ancient Meso America, adopted by contemporary living Mayas in the way they perceive the human body and health.

Not only that, but the students were witnesses to this phenomenon contextualized in the *barrios* of the international tourist Cancún. I asked the midwife to show the group how to undertake the *sobao*, a type of massage around the stomach area to identify the movement of the *tipte'* in order to bring it to the center and re-establish balance in the human organism. One of the male students volunteered for the *sobao*. The diagnosis was that his *tipte'* was not in its place. A student records this event in the following terms:

> She (the midwife) used Tom to show us how. He laid on the floor and she began to press on his stomach and soon found a gas spot on his intestines. I am not sure what she did but Tom had a bowel movement soon after that. What was so funny was that Tom had kind of been disbelieving of her remedies in the beginning. I guess he is a believer now. [Marc]

During the afternoons, the students had the choice either to stay at the center and participate in the Red Cross programs for the community, or to exercise the field techniques for information-gathering around the community. The teacher of cosmetology requested some models for her students to practice the lesson on *maquillaje de fiesta* (makeup for parties). A group of six female students agreed. That was the first time that the students interacted closely with members of the community. Being "models" for them facilitated their interaction with some women who became their key informants. Moreover, seeing the *gringo* faces as a clown, a cat, or just ready for a Christmas party was a unanimous source of laughter and attraction for the kids, and a source of pride for the artists.

A thirty-five-year-old student, a recent graduate with high expectations for working with refugees in South Asia, wanted to take advantage of the field school as a practical way of obtaining knowledge and experience for his career. He did not master Spanish but he challenged himself to become a teacher in English for evening adult education classes during the entire three weeks. He developed a particular method of teaching through which he also was receiving lessons in Spanish from the students. In just one week he had become so successful and popular that people from other regions solicited permission to attend his classes at the center. He became known as *el maestro*. This is the way he writes about the experience:

> My class, my class, my class! I love my night English class! . . . Sometimes when things are very quiet, I will intentionally misspell a word just to see if they are paying attention or if my lecture has become "*aburrimiento*" (boring). So far they laugh and correct me every time. They are scared to death to speak English. So I first try to get them to speak as a group, then individually. I think it is important to speak to them in as much English as they can understand. It is equally important to make them laugh. [Marc]

In a letter addressed to the directors and managers of some hotels at the beach area, the director of the Red Cross asked their cooperation in allowing the students the use of their facilities, at least once a week. For such a heavy dose of fieldwork, particularly for first-time undergraduate fieldworkers, we agreed on leaving a day in the middle of the week, Wednesday, for a break from their research, academic and field responsibilities. On Wednesday morning, the group met at the center and conducted their English classes for the community children who avidly started arriving at 7:00 A.M. After their English classes, the students had the day free. Some of them decided to explore the "tourist culture" of Cancún by becoming active participants and escaping to nearby Cozumel, for instance. Others preferred to stay in the neighborhood and rest. I noticed that while students were at first attracted to "tourist culture," those living at the Red Cross center especially expressed their reaction against the "tourist world" of the hotel area. Certainly, these students appreciate the drastic psychological move that people in the *areas populares* or *barrios* have to get used to when sharing their own social reality with the social reality of their work setting. The following is an anecdote one of my students told me:

> On the way home tonight we boarded our usual R-2/R-94 bus to get back home and discovered some American tourists on the bus. This was highly unusual at this point of the bus' path. We asked them where they were going and they looked completely relieved to hear English. One set was a family with two children, the other a couple. They asked us if they were on the right bus for the hotel district. We looked at each other as we tried to fight off the ensuing laughter. We told them "no," that they were headed for the *barrios*. The couple behind them said nothing. When we entered the *barrios* and the character of the plush hotel and central district diminished into ragged streets and shanties, I began to explain to them what to do to get back and

that I would tell the driver for them in Spanish what they wanted. All of a sudden the woman broke out and started yelling, "I want to go back to civilization, I cannot believe that the bus would take us into the middle of nowhere. Where the hell am I, in some Godforsaken slum?" She was so caught up in her world of vanity that she couldn't do us the courtesy of at least not insulting the people of the *barrio* in their own neighborhood. [Tom]

During the weekends, some recreational activities were scheduled. We visited archeological sites *Tulum* and *Xel-ha* the first Saturday and the next day, Sunday, the group enjoyed *X-Caret*. The monumental *Chichen Itzá* was left for the second weekend. With *Tulum* and *Chichen Itzá* the students encountered ancient Maya architectonic remnants from which the Maya worldview still speaks. The past of the Maya people is stamped in the ancient urban designs, engraved in the figures and signs in the stones, and hidden in the temple, pyramids, ball-game and other structures. Students discovered certain Maya cultural trends which they could trace, from the Maya past, to the *Región 101* lifestyle.

The significance of the four corners, a Maya worldview principle that encompasses the quadripartite composition of the skies, the four corners of the *milpa* (the corn field), and the four divisions of the human body, was clearly identified in the urban structure of those major archaeological sites. The ancient quatripartite Maya axiom was similarly ingrained in the current Maya midwives' perception of the human body as divided in four, balanced by the *tipte'* or center. The overrepresentation of corn and the corn-god symbol in the ancient Maya walls activated the students' comparative method as well.

The everyday consumption of corn tortillas, the long waiting-line at the *tortillería* in the *Región 101* of Cancún just before lunchtime, gave a new level of community understanding by interweaving the past and present cultural features of the Maya people. The rural connection and peasant background, particularly within the Maya migrant families living in the *Región 101*, was more clearly understood as a characteristic of the urban community.

Some students expressed surprise when they discovered that some migrant households were still strongly connected to their peasant communities, particularly through their *milpas*, or corn fields, which they still cultivated. It is the maintenance of *milpas* that keeps Mayas attached to their peasant roots even while being migrants in the urban Cancún. When the migrant cannot work his *milpa* directly, he uses part of his urban wages to pay a peasant. The students could exercise the analysis and understanding of the rural-urban economic articulation of peasant economy in a capitalist system:

> The Tulum trip was better than I had imagined. . . . Then, we went to Xel-ha. The ruins are definitely part of the new ecotourism. The entire world is now into this kind of tourism: visiting nature and culture. But it is apparent here that the Maya are taking advantage of this opportunity to make money. The replacement of the traditional *milpa* (beans/corn) for the new *milpa* (ecotourism, working in resorts). [Jennifer]

THE FINAL STEP, REFLECTION AT WORK

The field school experience was topped off by a meeting with a group of graduate students from the University of Florida. These students were enrolled in an academic program that Dr. Allan Burns directs and conducts every summer at the Central University in Mérida (UADY). The two groups of students meet in one of the classrooms at the University of Mérida. It was the first day in the academic experience for Dr. Burns's students. For our group, it was the culmination of their fieldwork adventure. The encounter between the two groups resulted in an enlightening experience for both. Our group was forced to answer the questions issued by Dr. Burns's students. This was the starting reflective point on the impact of their practicing anthropological adventure in the *Región 101* of Cancún in their lives and world-views, a process that probably will never end.

CONCLUSION, THE TEACHINGS

Certainly the existence of the *areas populares* in Cancún exemplifies how inoperative the notions of Third and First Worlds are when overcrowding and poverty exist hand in hand with the First World of the luxurious hotel area. At the same time, the rural background of most of the migrants in the *areas populares*, ideologically stamped in the habits, customs and performance of some rituals, is enmeshed with the consumerism and urban life of Cancún.

In sum, the presentation of the type of socioeconomic and cultural contexts that the students encountered became an exercise of the Postmodern mood in the current anthropological debate. Once in the field, students were exposed to the rural-peasant, urban, national, international fragmentation of the *areas populares*, which they had to approach from the analysis of different research topics. Overwhelmed and confused by such a fragmented world at first, the field experience in the practice of anthropology demonstrated to the students that the complex and confusing nature of the social phenomena can be rendered understandable.

References

Bernard, H. Russell. 1988. *Research Methods in Cultural Anthropology*. Newbury Park, CA: Sage.

Harvey, David. 1990. *The Condition of Postmodernity*. Cambridge: Basil Blackwell Ltd.

Jameson, Frederic. 1991. *Postmodernism, or The Cultural Logic of Capitalism*. Durham, NC: Duke University Press.

Kearney, Michael. 1991. "Borders and Boundaries of State and Self at the End of Empire." *Journal of Historical Sociology*, 4(1)52–74.

Pelto, Perti J., and Gretal H. Pelto. 1978. *Anthropological Research: The Structure of Inquiry*. New York: Cambridge University Press.

Re Cruz, Alicia. 1992. *The Two Milpas of Chan Kom: A Study of Socioeconomic and Political Transformations in a Maya Community*. Unpublished PhD dissertation, Department of Anthropology, State University of New York at Albany.

———. 1996. *The Two Milpas of Chan Kom: Scenarios of a Maya Village Life*. Albany: State University of New York.

Rose, Roger. 1992. "Making Sense of Settlement: Class Transformation, Cultural Struggle and Transnationalism Among Mexican Migrants in the United States." in N. Glick Schiller, L. Basch and C. Blanc-Szanton (eds.), *Towards a Transnational Perspective on Migration*. New York: New York Academy of Sciences, pp. 25–52.

Weiner, Annette B. 1995. "Culture and our Discontents." *American Anthropologist* 97(1)14–40.

Beverly N. Chiñas is a professor emerita of anthropology at California State University, Chico. Her best-known books are La Zandunga *and* The Isthmus Zapotecs: A Matrifocal Culture in Southern Mexico.

From individual case studies, a knowledgeable friend of local market women offers practical recommendations for how to survive the enormous economic impact of the North American Free Trade Association, and the modernization of young people's taste in street foods. As is so often the case, globalization appears to benefit some (especially those who were already more powerful and economically dominant) and to hurt others (often those who were more vulnerable beforehand). Recognizing that "junk foods" from multinational corporations are coming to dominate a market niche that had traditionally supported female cook-vendors who lack other sources of income, Chiñas offers specific suggestions based on cross-cultural comparisons from halfway around the world that may be helpful to those who helped her when she was learning about their way of life. It would be distressing if women's political gains (see chapters 33 and 34) were to be undercut by losses in the economic realm.

Market Vendors vs. Multinationals
David and Goliath Revisited
Beverly N. Chiñas

In many areas of Mexico, just as in Aztec times, women are still able to earn money, sometimes the bulk of the family income, by preparing and selling food. Except for some areas where crafts are still practiced, it is usually the only salable skill a provincial woman has. Yet the so-called "casual" food sellers have received no encouragement from government economic development agencies to continue this type of business. On the contrary, they are usually harassed with restrictive laws, ordinances, and taxes by national, state, and local authorities that too often view such food-selling practices as "unsanitary" and embarrassingly reminiscent of an "undeveloped" economy.

CRAFTS VS. PREPARED FOODS

The Mexican government, recognizing the need for extra income among the millions of unskilled Mexican citizens, has placed a great emphasis in recent years on reintroducing crafts where they had all but died out, and on developing broader markets for traditional crafts where they remained vital. The purpose of this emphasis on crafts has been to capture the tourist dollar and the export market on the one hand and to increase family income of some of the lower-class, unskilled populace on the other. Has this program been successful?

As far as production of crafts is concerned, it has been an unqualified success in such places as the Valley of Oaxaca, where weaving and embroidery have expanded considerably. The textile markets of Oaxaca are glutted with goods, indicating the willingness on the part of the producers to devote their time, skill, and effort to the program. However, each time I visit the Oaxaca markets I am struck by how little tourists seem to buy and how hard they bargain. The reason is that the tourist and export craft market is unstable and unreliable, presumably because the products rep-

Written expressly for *Contemporary Cultures and Societies of Latin America*, Third Edition, based on her article, "Is there life for women's business after the multinationals invade?" in *Practicing Anthropology*, vol. 2, nos. 5 & 6, 1980.

resent luxuries and superfluous frivolities for the buyers, who do not really need them. This is the fallacy of underdeveloped economies relying on tourist and exotic markets for craft products: the producer must have income from the time he invests, but the products are not necessities for the purchasers. Thus, this imbalance will always act as a depressant on prices of craft products, the buyer having the discretion of buying at ridiculously cheap prices or not buying at all, while the producer has to take what she can get for the investment of her time.

The food-selling market, on the contrary, is far more stable and reliable—everyone needs food, not just tourists—and, while competitive, it is also more flexible and more responsive to customer demand. A poor product or a misjudgment in what will sell represents less than a day's investment of time, not weeks and months as with craft products. Furthermore, the consumers are not just outsiders who are only seasonally present but also are local people, one's neighbors, farmers, merchants, and wage earners. In the food market, women can earn by investing a small amount of money and a fair amount of time in preparing and selling a product everyone needs every day. This is why I believe women's food selling should be encouraged and aided with technological advice and easy credit.

ENTERPRISING WOMEN

Although there are women in the food business in Mexico who are only occasional sellers, there are many who are experts in their specialties, women who have devoted years to developing their expertise in processing and selling foods. Where they are inexpert is in predicting how change will affect them and in being able to realize ways to defend and expand their economic niches in the face of economic changes and developmental trends. Let us consider just four of these experienced women and their enterprises.

Alfonsa, age 50, has been trading between San Mateo (a small coastal village) and Oaxaca de Juarez (the state capital), as well as other urban markets, for nearly twenty-five years. She spends two days each week buying fresh fish and shrimp and selling to the coastal people the fruits and vegetables from the temperate interior. She dries, salts, and cooks coastal products as required for preservation, then takes them to city markets. Oaxaca trips require two nights' travel by bus. Her husband farms a few hectares of land, but it is widely recognized that Alfonsa's energetic trading is what has made this family prosperous and respected in the community for their contributions and sponsorships of the religious fiesta system.

A Mexican government project for the coastal people with whom she trades has tried to encourage those women to do their own trading in the city markets and has been hostile to Zapotec women such as Alfonsa, who are viewed by the development workers as sharp traders. When I asked Alfonsa how the project was going and if it had cut into her business, she laughed and said no, it had no effect, because coastal women were not cut out to be traders. In other words, beginning traders who are only mildly motivated are no match for the energetic, aggressive Zapotec women like her with years of experience in the business. Alfonsa's business is constantly harassed by more and more taxes and regulations, such as the ban on trade in sea-turtle eggs, but thus far corporations have not affected this particular type of trade.

Juanita is a 35-year-old divorced mother of a 12-year-old daughter, whom she has raised alone since infancy. Juanita has some land, which she works with hired labor, but it is not enough to support her and her daughter. About 1971 she began experimenting with curing a local plum-like fruit (*biadxi* in Zapotec), a traditional Zapotec sweet, but one she had never made before. The first year she made only 2,000 and sold them wholesale to street-vending neighbors. She experimented until she had a very superior product in both taste and visual appeal. The second year she made 5,000 and sold half of them at retail, during fiestas in her home community, and in surrounding small communities. Soon she was making about 20,000 per year and selling about half of them retail, half wholesale. Her *biadxi* business contributed at least half of the yearly household income, and in years of poor crops considerably more.

However, she finds that she must choose her selling places with care. *Biadxi* do not sell well in the major towns, probably because people there have abundant supplies of readily available commercial beverages and sweets that compete with her product. She finds sales best in small, isolated communities where commercial sweets are scarce and expensive.

Francisca, age 37, sells prepared foods daily in the local street markets. For several years she supported her entire family of six children and her husband almost single-handedly by selling prepared foods on a daily basis. Her husband finally got a permanent job as a guard in a new oil refinery nearby. It is true that the family were just barely able to exist on what Francisca could earn by working long and strenuously. Nonetheless, they did manage to survive while she produced another child every two years. On several occasions she and several of the children traveled to isolated mountain communities for a week at a time to sell food during religious fiesta days, in order to earn extra money; prices are higher during religious fiestas. She has not quit selling daily since her husband began working but instead has worked as steadily as before in order to improve their house, furnishings, and garden plot.

A last example of a Zapotec businesswoman is Aurelia, about 60 years old, who has sold tacos and tamales in local street markets for many years. Once when her husband had to spend an extended time in Mexico City seeking medical care for advanced diabetes, she helped pay their expenses by selling tacos on the streets in the neighborhood where they were staying with their son and family. At first her tacos did not sell well because they were different from those favored in Mexico City. She purchased a taco here, another there from other sellers, tasted and examined them, and imitated these types. In a short time, her tacos were selling out daily. Her major problem now is finding enough time to make and sell more.

CORPORATIONS AND THE SNACK MARKET

Traditionally, Mexico has been a nation of snackers, snack foods having been purchased from women in doorways, on street corners, and in the marketplace. Snacks consisted of such foods as slices of raw fruit, vegetables, and hundreds of variations of tacos, tamales, and sweet cakes based on maize as well as all sorts of cured, pickled, and candied fruits and vegetables. Commercially produced, prepackaged sweet cakes and cookies, jams, jellies, and candies increasingly have come into the market, especially in urban areas, but they have not found much favor with traditional populations, perhaps because of their high price and, for baked goods, lack of freshness. Since approximately 1975, however, national and multinational companies such as Pepsico, Frito-Lay, and Sabritas have made a massive attempt to create a market for their prepackaged salted snack products. These include corn chips, potato chips, parched corn, and various types of imitation products such as *chicharrones* (artificial pork cracklings) made of wheat flour. Within a year, these products were to be found at virtually every bottled beverage stand, in stores and market booths, and in most of the tiny *tienditas* (front-room shops) in houses throughout the Zapotec region. The products are manufactured of maize, wheat flour, or potatoes, oil, salt, and sometimes chile. Pepsico uses the familiar trademarks of Fritos, Ruffles, and Doritos for their products, while Sabritas has invented local names (Sabritas, Churrumais, and Sabritones) for very similar products. All these items are attractively packaged in individual portions, and Sabritas includes a tiny plastic toy as an extra inducement to children. When the price of a small package of Fritos containing 38 grams of maize was about 2 pesos, a peasant selling maize for 1.8 pesos per liter (approximately 700 grams) might see his children buying it back in the form of Fritos for 37 pesos per liter (more than 20 times the price he got as producer). It is obvious that corporations are able to charge very dearly for processing, packaging, and selling essentially the same products that lower-class Mexican citizens eat daily in their own homes.

In spite of the price, these "new" snacks are cutting deep into women's traditional snack market in southern Mexico. All the local sources tend to sell out on major holidays, and there is nothing available in any of the market towns for a week until the bright yellow Sabritas panel truck reappears, with the familiar logo of the smiling circle face and the slogan: "*A que no puedes comer solo una*" (I'll bet you can't eat just one).

SAVING AND RECLAIMING WOMEN'S TRADITIONAL BUSINESS: THE SNACK MARKET

How can women reclaim and retain their traditional rights to the food and snack market? First, women could be made aware of what is happening to the market, of the tremendous gap between what they sell maize for and what the corporations charge them as consumers. Second, women could profit from expert advice on improving snack and food products and on marketing techniques. Third, women food sellers need ready credit at low interest. Mexico, of course, has had small-business credit for years but, at least in southern Mexico, very few women apply for credit for their food-selling operations. Although they probably are not actively discouraged from applying for credit, nonliterate *humilde* (humble) women (as they call themselves) tend to be intimidated by the personnel in the credit agencies and banks (mestizo middle-class males for the most part) and by the paperwork that is required.

An agency geared more toward the needs of the food sellers—one perhaps modeled after the successful Self-Employed Women's Association (SEWA) of Ahmedabad, India organized by Ela Bhatt (1976) and associates (Jain 1975)—could be effective in revitalizing women's food selling. SEWA's goals are to improve the economic and living conditions of self-employed women such as food sellers, used-clothing dealers, cart pullers, and seamstresses. SEWA runs a cooperative women's bank, which the self-employed woman may join by purchasing one or more shares of stock for less than $1 U.S.—approximately two days' earnings. A share in the bank entitles a woman to borrow money at low interest rates for up to twenty months. Members are encouraged to use the loans to improve their ability to earn in their occupation, but loans are not restricted to such purposes. Women also are encouraged to save. An important part of SEWA's job is to offer expert advice in improving products and finding markets. SEWA's staff is unique in that all are women and the procedures are geared to nonliterate women with little or no experience in dealing with bureaucracy. The staff stresses the cooperative, self-ownership aspects of SEWA and tries to instill in members the idea of cooperative ownership as self-help. SEWA's progress has been rapid. In the first two years, 9,000 women had established savings and 6,400 women had taken loans. In addition, in cooperation with the Indian government SEWA had introduced a new, more efficient handcart for women cart pullers and had sold them to the women at reasonable prices through SEWA loans. Formerly many of these women had to rent their handcarts from merchants at an exploitative rate.

Would a similar SEWA work in Mexico? I think so, and I think it is needed to encourage women to remain in and expand their food businesses, to permit them to compete on a more equitable basis with national and international corporations who invade the markets with attractively packaged junk foods that lure customers away from traditional home-prepared foods.

References

Bhatt, Ela. 1976. *Profiles of Self-Employed Women.* Ahmedabad, India, n.p.
Jain, Devaki. 1975. *From Dissociation to Rehabilitation.* New Delhi: Allied Publishers.

George A. Collier is a research anthropologist who long taught at Stanford University. His best-known books are Fields of the Tzotzil (with J. Collier), Socialists of Rural Andalusia, Land Inheritance and Land Use in a Modern Maya Community, and Basta! Land and the Zapatista Rebellion in Chiapas.

The state of a nation's economy can have major impacts at the regional and local levels, and even that macrosystem is subject to the larger forces of international finance and trade. The emergence of a generally nonviolent rebellion in southern Mexico in recent years shows how intimately interwoven are law, politics, ethnicity, access to wealth, and even an historical figure from far away (Zapata). It is noteworthy that the self-designated "peasants" (campesinos) chose the beginning date of the North American Free Trade Agreement for their initial demonstration, and have cannily used the Internet to communicate their concerns around the world in ensuing years. Collier's clear and concise analysis of complex competing forces at different levels lays bare both strengths and weaknesses in that country's ways of dealing with ethnic minorities, and with fascinating emergences at the "grassroots" level.

Restructuring Ethnicity in Chiapas and the World

George A. Collier

Two events underscore subtle but important shifts in the ethnicity of indigenous populations in Chiapas. On March 19, 1995, several thousand people from dozens of diverse indigenous communities, among them Protestants and Catholics who have often been in conflict with one another, joined in the demonstration in support of liberation theologian Bishop of San Cristóbal de Las Casas, Samuel Ruiz. Barely a month later, on the April 19th eve of the scheduled renewal of peace talks between the Mexican government and the Ejército Zapatista de Liberación Nacional (EZLN, Zapatista Army of National Liberation), an equally diverse gathering of representatives of distinct indigenous communities and sometimes competing indigenous organizations from throughout the region converged on San Andrés Larraínzar to demonstrate support for the Zapatistas.

Ethnic identity once *divided* indigenous communities from one another in the Chiapas central highlands. Both recent events underscore a transformation: in the wake of the Zapatista rebellion, peoples of diverse indigenous background now are emphasizing what they *share* with one another in revindication of economic, social, and political exploitation.

How has this shift in indigenous identity come about? This article argues that the transformation reflects changes in Mexican rural society stemming from fundamental redirections of Mexico's policies for national society and its place in the world order, marking the ending of an era of Mexican social policy and statescraft.

For decades, Mexico effectively managed peasants and Indians as distinct sectors within its "institutionalized revolution," along with workers, ranchers, merchants, and industrialists, all under policies fostering development of a sheltered national economy. Mexico's all-embracing *Partido Revolucionario Institucional* (PRI, Institutional Revolutionary Party) used a corporatist approach of giving each sector a role in sheltered national development as well as corresponding rewards. As the government developed rural programs, it focused on communities, using agrarian reform to shape them sepa-

Prepared expressly for *Contemporary Cultures and Societies of Latin America,* Third Edition, based on the author's article in *Indigenous Affairs* 3:22–27, July–September 1995, IWGIA, International Work Group for Indigenous Affairs, Copenhagen.

rately, and Indianist policies that tended to "naturalize" ethnic differences among indigenous communities while distinguishing them from those of nonindigenous peasants.

But in the past twenty years, Mexico's national leaders have reoriented Mexican development to global commodity markets and international high finance. More generally, national planners have embraced the philosophy of structural adjustment that governments throughout the world are using to shuck off social responsibilities to the poor. In Mexico, leaders have set aside the nation's social contracts with the peasantry and indigenous people, abandoning long-standing programs of agrarian reform—uniting peasants and Indians in opposition to the national state.

As the reorientation ripples through the Mexican countryside, the gap has grown between the better-off and the poor, the powerful and the powerless, and the old structures of community that once framed ethnicity have eroded, making way for a new and evocative indigenous discourse voiced by the Zapatistas on behalf of Mexico's poor. The Zapatistas, furthermore, speak out from the position of indigenous peoples' historic subordination to protest problems that beset poor Mexicans everywhere, blurring the lines between indigenous, peasant, rural, and urban poor. To borrow a metaphor, we might say that the rebellion is recrafting ethnicity as an ecumenical rather than parochial discourse, evoked from and spanning society's base rather than being articulated from on high.[1]

Oil Development and the Crisis in Mexican Agriculture

The Zapatistas chose January 1, 1994—the inauguration of NAFTA (North American Free Trade Association)—to rebel as a way of protesting the government's "selling out" of Mexico to foreign interests. But NAFTA was only the last link of a chain leading back to Mexico's decision, after the OPEC crisis of 1973, to sell oil into global markets, unexpectedly transforming and destabilizing Mexican agriculture and ultimately removing its insulation and protection from the global economy.

For decades after President Lázaro Cárdenas nationalized foreign firms' oil holdings in 1938, Mexico reserved petroleum as a resource to tap for the internal needs of the national economy through a state-run petrochemical industry. To help the depression-era economy recover, Cárdenas subsidized Mexican industry and commerce, keeping the price of oil low and erecting tariffs and restricting imports to protect nascent businesses from foreign competition. Cárdenas stepped up agrarian reform so that peasant and indigenous farming could produce inexpensive foods, enabling workers to get by on low wages favorable to developing Mexican businesses. Those relationships among oil production, peasant and indigenous agriculture, commerce, and industry in the sheltered economy of "import substitution industrialization" sustained Mexico through several decades of growth.

After the OPEC crisis raised world petroleum prices in 1973, Mexico's decision to export oil distorted these relationships. To produce oil for export and not just for internal consumption, Mexico borrowed massively from the world banking system, glutted at the time with petrodollars from the mid-East and eager to place loans. Mexico used credits to finance new oil exploration—especially in the state of Tabasco and along the coast of the Gulf of Mexico—and to build new infrastructure throughout the country. In Chiapas, the government discovered oil reserves under what has become the heartland of the Zapatista rebellion. It also constructed hundreds of miles of roads and completed three major hydroelectric dams along the Grijalva River that now supply the country with about half of its hydroelectric power.

The resulting boom drew labor into construction, commerce, and transport and began to undercut and transform agriculture. Agriculture declined from about 14% of GDP in 1965 to about 7% of GDP by 1980. In addition, farmers sought to cut labor costs by shifting to chemical inputs—fertilizers and herbicides—that reduced labor while intensifying production but that also made producers dependent on credits and subsidies. Responding to the crisis in agriculture in the late 1970s, the government extended credits, subsidies, and marketing assistance in an attempt to revive agriculture through President López Portillo's *Sistema Alimentario Mexicano* (SAM, Mexican Foodstuffs System). Planners worried that the country had become too dependent on corn imported from the United States, a threat to Mexico's sovereignty at a time when U.S. politicians spoke of using grains as tools or weapons of foreign policy.

But the 1982 debt crisis shattered Mexico's development boom and the ability of the government to subsidize the transformed agriculture. Collapse of world petroleum prices left Mexico unable to service U.S. $96 billion of external debt, mostly borrowed on the unfulfilled promise of oil exports. The international banking system forced austerity on the Mexican budget. Credits, subsidies, and market supports began to dry up during the Miguel de la Madrid presidency. Six years later, President Salinas de Gortari embraced policies of liberal restructuring under which Mexico began to sell off or dissolve state-controlled enterprise in various sectors. Salinas targeted peasant agriculture as inefficient, removing remaining supports for peasant production, and redrafting the agrarian code to bring agrarian reform to a halt while allowing privatization and sale of indigenous and peasant lands that the code once protected.

RESTRUCTURING OF PEASANT AND INDIGENOUS LANDSCAPES

Throughout Mexico, these changes plunged peasant and indigenous agriculture into crisis. Poorer peasants who lacked capital or access to credits needed to purchase fertilizer and herbicides abandoned their land or rented it to wealthier compatriots. In many areas of central Mexico, peasants and indigenous people gave up farming and migrated to seek work in the urban peripheries or in the United States.

In Chiapas, reliance on chemical inputs began to differentiate the poor from the better-off *within* indigenous communities, often pitting wealthier indigenous elites of the *cabeceras* (municipal centers) against the poor of the outlying *parajes* or *aldeas* (hamlets) and breaking down community ethnic solidarities. Many of the poor were driven out of their ethnic homelands or left to seek their fortunes in the frontier colonies of eastern Chiapas and in squatter settlements around the city of San Cristóbal de Las Casas. Others took up employment as unskilled workers in construction in oil and hydroelectric development. After the 1982 debt crisis, when austerity curtailed construction, unskilled workers who returned to Chiapas's agrarian economy no longer could find employment, swelling the ranks of the impoverished.

As a result, ethnic populations that once had been community-based began to spread across the geographic and social landscapes of southeastern Mexico, intermingling with different indigenous and non-indigenous rural and urban poor, sometimes even in new livelihoods and new kinds of communities. Many of those marginalized from Chiapas's highland indigenous communities joined Indians and peasants from other states flowing into the tropical forest frontier lands of eastern Chiapas from which the Zapatista rebellion has since emerged. While some retained identities of ethnic origin, others turned to religion to consolidate frontier settlements, establishing them as communities of diverse worship—Presbyterian, Baptist, Seventh Day Adventist, Mormon, or as Catholic-linked Christian-based communities.

Even as oil development redeployed people and identities in this supposedly remote area, it left them vulnerable to dependency on credits, subsidies, and the marketing mechanisms of INMECAFE, the Mexican Coffee Institute. Eastern Chiapas's colonists (or homesteaders) allocated one-third of their production to coffee as a cash crop, another third to livestock, and the remainder to subsistence crops such as corn and beans. When austerity and restructuring set in, colonists might have been able to weather the shift in economic tides had not the world price of coffee also plummeted in 1989, further devastating peasant producers who had invested in coffee as their principal cash crop. The collapse of coffee prices coincided with Salinas's abrogation of agrarian reform, dashing colonists' unfulfilled quests for land.

Zapatista condemnation of NAFTA thus implicitly protests the trade liberalization and structural adjustment that began a decade earlier with Mexico's decision to enter global petroleum markets. Oil-led development threw agriculture into crisis; it undermined the solidarity of indigenous and peasant communities by differentiating people within them; it impoverished those made vulnerable to the collapse of credits and markets needed to survive in a transforming rural economy. Little wonder, then, that Chiapas's rural poor, no longer protected by the solidarities of old ethnic communities, should embrace the protest voiced by the Zapatista rebellion.

FROM GOVERNING BY PACT TO EXCLUSION

The restructuring of ethnic identities in Chiapas responds as well to a fundamental shift of the Mexican government away from social policies that drew pacts among and support from the various different sectors of Mexican society. Increasingly, the government and its ruling party, the PRI, have opted for policies that favor only the "modernizing" sector linked to international high finance, with waning commitment to other sectors. Many Mexicans, including most of those in peasant and indigenous communities, now feel excluded from the government's social contract. Some have joined parties and organizations opposed to the ruling party.

For decades, beginning with the 1934–40 presidency of Lázaro Cárdenas, the ruling party successfully managed public policy to give different sectors of society a sense that each had a voice in a political system that would mediate their sometimes-conflicting interests. In the countryside, the ruling party gave political access to peasants and Indians as well as to ranchers and commercial farmers; urban labor and industry also could count on being heeded. The government claimed to sustain a social contract acknowledging the legitimacy and needs of each sector. Mexico's relative social peace, and the willingness of the people to allow the endorsement of ruling party candidates in decade after decade of managed elections, reflected the success of government by pact.

Pacting reached into agrarian landscapes and evoked a style of indigenous and peasant leadership in which, for the most part, local leaders worked through the framework of municipal institutions and through those of the ruling party, the PRI, to help extract state resources for their followers in return for delivering the vote for ruling party candidates. The success of agrarian reform and Indianist policies in conforming ethnicity to municipal institutions matched the relatively strong loyalties of peasant and indigenous leaders to the government's ruling party.

Austerity, forced on Mexico by the world banking community after the 1982 crisis of debt, undercut the government's ability to sustain its social contract and sectoral pacts. Then, as modernizers within the PRI embraced the ideology of structural adjustment, the government cut subsidies for peasant agriculture and social programs for the burgeoning urban populace living in poverty.

As a result, the hegemonic success of the PRI eroded. In the 1988 presidential elections, the PRI faced its first serious electoral opposition from the *Partido de Acción Nacional* (PAN, National Action Party) and from supporters of Cuauhtémoc Cárdenas, many of them PRI defectors who opposed the policies of structural adjustment promised by Carlos Salinas de Gortari. Under Salinas, government policy ceased to represent all sectors of society. Programs such as Solidarity, ostensibly intended to assist the poor, channeled funding behind the scenes to PRI supporters, to the exclusion of those in the growing opposition.

Peasant and indigenous leadership shifted in style, meanwhile, as rural production concentrated in the hands of PRI-affiliated powerholders who controlled the capital and scarce credits needed to farm with chemical inputs. Elites who had established themselves in power by winning rewards for their followers in return for delivering the vote for the PRI began to monopolize government resources for themselves, using them to capitalize their own production in the transformed agrarian economy. As they no longer needed the labor of poorer compatriots in agrarian production, power-holding elites could cast off economic and political responsibilities to the growing numbers of expendable laborers in their own communities. The organic leaders of yesteryear thus transformed themselves into the *caciques* (roughly, bosses) of contemporary times.

As support for the ruling party eroded, and as marginalized peasants and Indians began to affiliate with the opposition parties, the PRI resorted increasingly to coercive tactics to hold onto the peasant vote, withholding funds and services from those whose loyalties were suspect. Even in indigenous hamlets, authorities withheld the benefits of government programs from those who did not support the PRI. Such practices further fractured rural communities, sharpening the divisions between powerful elites and marginalized poor. Increasingly, as a result, organic leadership among rank-and-file peasants and indigenous populations has coalesced around *opposition* to the PRI, in coalition with political parties of the opposition, with independent organizations, and now with the Zapatistas. Finally, in 2000, PRI lost the presidency.

UNITING AGAINST ARBITRARY AGRARIAN POLICIES

Extremely diverse ethnic and religious affiliation marked the colonization that flowed into eastern Chiapas in response to the restructuring of the agrarian economy in the 1970s. What brought people together in a movement that now spans ethnic and religious diversity was resistance to the arbitrariness of government agrarian policy in the region.

During the 1970s, President Luis Echeverría opened up eastern Chiapas to long-distance colonization by modifying the agrarian code to permit peasants to relocate far from their homes, even across state lines. Yet as colonists settled frontier areas, the government decreed huge tracts of the colonized land off-limits to them as "bioreserves." The huge Montes Azul Bioreserve, which encompassed dozens of new frontier settlements, was "reserved," it turned out, for government timbering.

Agrarian authorities ordered colonists in the bioreserves to relocate, but most refused. Attempts by the PRI to coopt peasants in eastern Chiapas and to divide followers from dissidents only heightened antagonisms. As colonists resisted continued pressure to relocate during the 1980s, most of them aligned with opposition to the PRI. When the government claimed overwhelming electoral support in 1988 from eastern Chiapas for the PRI's presidential candidate, Salinas de Gortari, colonists knew the elections had been rigged.

Upon taking office, Salinas rewarded colonists allied with the PRI in the Montes Azul Bioreserve by legitimating their land claims—while denying the claims of dissidents and opponents. Shortly thereafter, Salinas announced legislation to "reform" Article 27 of the Constitution, bringing agrarian reform to a halt. In effect, Salinas broke the nation's historic covenant with the peasantry to honor the hope, if not always the reality, of legal agrarian reform. For the first time the Zapatistas, present in small numbers since 1983 and advocating armed resistance to the national state, won recruits among colonists who believed that they had lost legal recourse to their lands claims.

These arbitrary and contradictory government agrarian policies unified dissident colonists across lines of ethnic and religious difference, while forging links to agrarian activists of other regions in Mexico's south. The Zapatista movement has helped generalize the alliances to span indigenous and non-indigenous peasants throughout and beyond the area of frontier colonization in eastern Chiapas.

NEW ECUMENISM IN INDIGENOUS DISCOURSE IN CHIAPAS

There is a new ecumenism in the ethnicity that is emerging in Chiapas as a result of the Zapatista rebellion—ecumenism with respect to religious difference as well as other kinds of difference.

The joining together of Protestants with Catholics among the indigenous groups who have been demonstrating solidarity with Bishop Ruiz's role as intermediary between the government and the Zapatistas in recent negotiations is an important development because religious difference had been a significant axis of conflict among indigenous groups in Chiapas in recent decades. I believe that the Zapatista rebellion furthered the evolution of such ecumenism.

Many analysts believe that the 1974 Indigenous Congress, organized by Bishop Ruiz at the request of the government of Chiapas to commemorate Fray Bartolomé de Las Casas, laid the foundation for the indigenous movement that has coalesced in the Zapatista rebellion. The Congress pulled together indigenous representatives from various linguistic and "tribal" groups, as well as various regions of Chiapas, including the colonizing region of eastern Chiapas, allowing them for the first time to articulate common demands for social change. In the wake of the Congress, independent organizing of indigenous and peasant communities in eastern Chiapas built upon the networks and channels of communication established in the Congress.

One must remember that the 1974 Indigenous Congress built on the catechist networks established by Bishop Ruiz in part to counter the spread of Protestant and evangelical churches in eastern Chiapas, where new religions afforded solidarities needed to consolidate frontier communities. Even though Liberation Theology galvanized indigenous alliances in the 1974 Congress, non-Catholic religious affiliation continued to grow, encompassing up to 40% of the frontier population by the 1990s. In this context, independent organizers had the advantage over religious organizers of being able to embrace groups of different religious persuasion into their movements. The Zapatistas built an inclusive movement in part by disavowing religious affiliation while affirming religious tolerance, epitomizing an ecumenism that has since become more prominent even in Bishop Ruiz's own church efforts.

More generally, the Zapatista movement has adopted what one might characterize as an ecumenical stance with respect to differences of political persuasion by welcoming diverse groups of civil society into a broad-based movement seeking reforms of Mexican society as a whole. As a result, diverse indigenous and peasant organizations have coalesced in organizations such as the *Consejo Estatal de Organizaciones Indígenas y Campesinas* (CEOIC, State Council of Indigenous and *Campesino* Organizations) that echo and reinforce the Zapatistas' challenges to the national state.

THE TRANSNATIONAL CONTEXT OF NEW REGIONAL MOVEMENTS

The shift of ethnicity in Chiapas to transcend, yet embrace difference parallels the emergence of new regional movements in many parts of the world where "borderlands" bring distinct cultures together in interaction without necessarily erasing their differences. Global development moves production "offshore" and circulates people, goods, money, and information in new kinds of translocational spaces shaped by economic restructuring. Peoples drawn together in new ways confront ambiguities of identity and polyvalent senses and possibilities of being. They experiment with guises and roles, and sometimes they forge, reformulate, and mobilize ethnic identity to hail new sympathizers—as the Zapatistas' faceless indigenous visages have appealed to those who project their own identities onto those imagined behind the Zapatista masks.

Contemporary Chiapas illustrates how alliances can span heterogenous peoples in borderlands without necessarily dissolving their differences. Oil-led development transformed southeastern Mexico, drawing the ethnically distinctive Indians out from Chiapas's agrarian economy and thrusting them together with non-indigenous peasants, workers, independent organizers, and even evangelizers, into work, politics, and religions not previously open to Indians. New alignments of wealth and power surfaced and sharpened the basis for a regional indigenous identity that emerged as the reversals of Mexico's energy development thrust the region into crisis. The Zapatistas tapped the discontent and consolidated a movement that elevated indigenous identity out of its old parochial loyalties, linked to patronage and protection of the corporate state, into something new, the shared identity of those whom politicians had spurned in pursuit of neo-liberal modernizing.

There are other ways in which encompassing transnational political and economic systems reshape and sometimes consolidate loyalties and identities drawn from ethnic landscapes. A new pan-"Mixtec" identity, for example, has spanned the primary loyalties to township that Mixtec speakers once held in the state of Oaxaca. It grows from Mixtec migrants' shared experience of border camps in Tijuana and work in the tomato fields of California, Oregon, Florida, and other parts of the United States where transnational agri-business has brought those seasonally migrant workers from Oaxaca together in new collective identity.

Regional identities and subnational popular movements also gain support from one another—much as the Zapatistas have tapped support from within Mexican civil society, from organizations of Native Americans ("Indians") and their supporters throughout the continent, from the Chicano movement, and from sympathizers as far away as Catalunya. They draw support from independent organizations that challenge the state and from non-governmental organizations whose resources and constituencies transcend national controls. While contemporary nation-states are in many instances struggling to reassert their primary claims on citizenship and identity, they are no longer the only game in town in the post cold-war and increasingly transnational order, which is giving rise to new, multivocal solidarities and alliances.

Notes

[1] For an analysis of the roots of the Zapatista rebellion, see *BASTA! Land and the Zapatista Rebellion in Chiapas* by George A. Collier and Elizabeth Lowery Quaratiello (Food First Books, 1994).

[2] Even Mexico's oil sovereignty is falling victim to restructuring as the Ernesto Zedillo government contemplates privatization of the state-run petrochemical industry after having pledged oil revenues to U.S. banks to guarantee repayment of the Clinton administration bailout.

Hans C. Buechler is a professor of anthropology at Syracuse University who has done fieldwork in Europe as well as Latin America. Among his books are The Masked Media; Women and Economic Change *(with A. Milnes);* The Bolivian Aymara; Migrants in Europe; Manufacturing against the Odds; *and* The World of Sofía Velásquez: Autobiography of a Bolivian Market-Vendor *(all with J.-M. Buechler).*

The "informal sector" of a nation's economy, consisting of relatively small, generally unregulated businesses, used to be viewed as anywhere from quaint to archaic, a conservative nuisance, or a drag on development in the formal economy. In recent years, however, especially in poorer nations, it has been recognized as an increasingly important adaptive alternative, flexible and responsive in ways that larger and more capital-intensive institutions rarely are, providing employment and income when both are decreasing in the formal sector. Because it builds upon unschooled entrepreneurship, fills needs that are not fully recognized in the formal sector, and mobilizes skills and labor on a quickly changing ad-hoc basis, the informal economy provides significant opportunities for those who recognize and use them, letting unos cuantos vivos *(a few sharp characters) like Doña Flora make a good living; help kin, friends and neighbors; and provide goods and services at many levels. Much of what really matters in terms of how an economic system works is only poorly reflected in national statistics, charts, or tables of organization, and it takes grassroots analysis to understand such uncharted networks and unreported production.*

Brief sections of this reading touch on points previously made in the author's chapter in George Gmelch and Walter Zenner (eds.), Urban Life: Readings in Urban Anthropology *(3rd ed.) (1996, Waveland Press); and in his book (co-authored with Judith-Marie Buechler)* Manufacturing against the Odds: Small-Scale Producers in an Andean City *(1992, Westview).*

Doña Flora and the "Informal Sector" Debate

Entrepreneurial Strategies in a Bolivian Enterprise

Hans Buechler

In recent years interest in small-scale enterprises has risen exponentially all over the world. An increasing number of economists as well as development agencies, and, to a lesser extent, government agencies in Third World countries have become disillusioned with models of development based on "trickle-down" mechanisms. The debt crisis in many of these countries, which, in part, resulted from blindly conceding government-guaranteed loans to corporations, has led to a revaluation of the wisdom of staking all hopes on larger enterprises.

A second look at the practical role of small enterprises is beginning to lead to a rethinking of the theoretical assumptions underlying economic programs, many of which had been accepted as articles of faith. And the argument that economies of scale must invariably lead to the demise of smaller units of production can no longer be accepted as a given.

One of the major theoretical problems with the rethinking of economic categories has been a tendency to employ traditional rubrics as a base. One such concept is the concept of "the informal sector" or "informal economy." First proposed in the early 1970s,[1]

Written expressly for *Contemporary Cultures and Societies of Latin America*, Third Edition. Brief sections of this reading touch on points previously made in the author's chapter in George Gmelch and Walter Zenner (eds.), *Urban Life: Readings in Urban Anthropology* (3rd ed.) (1996, Waveland Press), and in his book (co-authored with Judith-Marie Buechler), *Manufacturing against the Odds: Small-Scale Producers in an Andean City* (1992, Westview).

this concept came to dominate the discourse about small-scale productive, commercial, and service activities, particularly in Third World countries. It continues to enjoy considerable currency (see, for example, Rakowski, 1994; Wilson, 1998). The term has all but replaced the related concept of "dual economy" that implied the existence of two different economies, one "traditional" and one "modern," or the concept of "marginality" that wedded the concepts of "traditional sector" and that of "culture of poverty" acclaiming the self-perpetuation of poverty through cultural transmission of negative traits into a single framework (Perlman 1976). Both concepts came under sharp criticism in the 1970s.

Neither of these earlier dualisms took into consideration the systemic interlinkage of economic phenomena. The modern/traditional dichotomy relegated the "traditional" to the past and therefore regarded it as not worthy of serious consideration as a part of a working system. It was considered to affect the present only by posing obstacles to be overcome. The mainstream/marginal dichotomy did not even concede historical value to the "marginal." And if any interdependency was recognized at all, it was formulated in terms of a putative threat or drain that "marginals" presented to the "mainstream."

The term "informal" has meant very different things depending on the geographical area of investigation and the ideology of the investigator. Sometimes small size, "low capital, meager physical facilities, easy and frequent entry and exit, reliance on kinship or other contractual working relations and lack of written records" (Clark 1988:3) are considered adequate indicators of informality, regardless of legality. At other times, the exclusion or inclusion in official statistics is stressed. At still other times, the illegal character of "informal" economic activities, e.g., lack of licensing or failure to pay taxes, is emphasized, irrespective of the size of the economic unit. In general, the second definition is more commonly applied in industrialized countries, and the first definition is prevalent in the description of Third World economies. Particularly in Latin America, the "informal sector" was defined principally in terms of the size and capitalization of the firms involved, making it, in practice, into a synonym of "microenterprise." However, some Third World studies have applied the second definition as well, thereby leading to further confusion (Hart 1973). Often the two approaches are combined, resulting in the definition of the informal sector in terms of a list of traits, some of which were derived from the very different definitions of the sector.

The fact that small scale, or at least very small scale (for which the term microenterprise has been coined) is often confused or dealt with in the same breath as informality, particularly in the study of Third World situations, has detrimental repercussions on the manner in which they are viewed by social scientists and government agencies alike. Small scale is frequently regarded essentially as a means of competing with "legitimate" and "economically sound" larger enterprises by circumventing taxation and labor laws. It thereby receives a connotation of illegality and residualness. Acceptance of residualness leads to the treatment of small-scale industries as welfare beneficiaries at best rather than as full contributors to the national economy. In contrast, similar support to larger firms continues to be regarded as an appropriate means of securing a country's economic future.

In spite of the advantages of the formal/informal distinction over the earlier dichotomies, at least in its more systems-oriented version that included the "informal sector" as a part of a capitalist economy (whether legal or not) and recognized the overlap of the actors involved, it became apparent even to its proponents that the concept had serious flaws. First, it became obvious that not only the personnel, but also the economic activities themselves were interlinked. Whereas at first (and to a large extent still) the informal sector was seen as a residual category destined to disappear as the "modern sector progressed" (note the frequent use of "formal" and "modern" as synonyms even though "modern" now is no longer generally opposed to "traditional"), it has become apparent that, at least for the time being, the "informal sector" is on the increase, often at the cost of the "formal sector." This phenomenon is viewed negatively by Marxists who consider it "disguised wage labor" (i.e., a technique employed by capital to reduce social costs), and positively by neoliberals who see in it a font of new entrepreneurial talent or economic flexibility.

Second, the heterogeneity of the linkages between the two sectors came to be appreciated. Third, it came to be understood that the informal sector itself was internally differentiated according to the nature of activities and the position of individuals within a firm. It emerged, for example, that owners of firms in the "informal sector" often had incomes roughly equivalent to those of workers engaged in similar activities in the "formal sector." And fourth, the manifold movements between the two sectors, e.g., the frequent movement of "formal workers" into self-employment and as heads of small (informal) firms, became more apparent.

With the refinement of the concept, the weaknesses of the dichotomy have, if anything, become even more salient and more difficult to paper over. The resilience and growth of the sector, and the realization that the equation of informality with poverty or with a reserve labor force is untenable, have led to a shift from the definition of informality as economic marginality to an emphasis on illegality. As a result, the category of informal sector has become even more heterogeneous.

A few of the more successful proponents of the concepts have managed to continue their use of the dichotomy mainly because they fail to adhere strictly to their own definition of "informality," shifting its meaning as the need arises. However, if the dichotomy has so many problems and a discussion of "informality" is successful only when authors disregard their own definitions, then why not throw the concept out? I contend that the formal/informal dichotomy, while perhaps still useful to analyze issues of legality and illegality in specific cultural and historical contexts, has outlived its utility as a tool for distinguishing major differences in economic behavior cross-culturally. Such behavior is more appropriately analyzed in terms of operationizable sequences of behavior than in terms of murky typologies. I would emphasize the need to discover regularities of economic behavior (defined broadly) engaged in by individuals and collectivities within the context of social networks defining and linking inclusive levels of sociocultural integration from households and/or interdomestic clusters (such as collaborating kinfolk) to communities, states and transnational complexes.

We must also broaden our definition of "the economic" to include many kinds of behavior that are usually not included in economic analyses. "Social and political capital," for example, may constitute a major determinant of a firm's success. Even the very notion of what constitutes a "firm" and hence what constitutes success or failure of such an entity may require revision.

I suggest that small size, flexibility both in size and in the nature of the work-relationships, and low indebtedness are among the strategies that have enabled many firms to survive the economic crises of the 1980s in Bolivia. And further, these strategies probably involve cooperation as well as conflict between members of different social classes. Social class may, in fact, be equally context-dependent as "informality" and may be experienced differently depending on gender, place in the family, and background (e.g., rural or urban origin and ethnic identification).

A CASE STUDY

The history of a firm that my wife and I followed over two decades will serve to show both the complexity of small-scale firms in Bolivia and the vagaries of their trajectories over time, dependent on changing configurations of the kin network, health of the owner, and the changes in both the national and international economy. This is an interesting example for several reasons: it is characteristic of the blossoming urban entrepreneurship among second-generation rural-urban migrants; it illustrates the dominant role of women in small-scale commerce; it involves a wide range of individuals; it illustrates both upward and downward mobility within entrepreneurial families; and it shows the dependence of such families on individuals occupying different class positions and positioned differently in the national and world economies. Most importantly, in this context it shows the futility of separating the "formal" from the "informal." Depending on the time-period and the particularities of her enterprise, Doña Flora's firm could sometimes be considered "formal," e.g., when it involved dozens of individuals, worked closely with government agencies, and engaged in business transactions involving several thousand U.S. dollars. Then, too, it could be considered "informal" when it shrank in size to a mere handful of workers, to the extent it engaged workers without conceding them legal social security benefits, or to the extent it engaged in illegal circumvention of duties on exports.

An understanding of Doña Flora's enterprise requires a knowledge of the functioning of her firm at different points in its history and the manner in which it integrates with the local, regional, national and international economies, the human resources she is able to tap at various times, her own skills, her changing health, and her changing needs and those of her family. In addition, I examine the decisions directly associated with the running of her enterprise with other economic choices such as the education of her children, their strategic placement in jobs, subsidiary economic activities, and some real estate transactions, all of which in turn influence decisions made regarding her principal enterprise(s).

Doña Flora is the daughter of a rural-born miner who later moved to La Paz and worked as a porter in a brewery. When her husband, a bus owner/operator, was still living, she sold shawls in a street market. She did much of the weaving and stitching but also sold goods made by others. When her husband died and she had to feed their six children on her own in the late 1960s, she switched to making woolen ponchos and sweaters, which was more lucrative. "I didn't have any money," she explained. "I would buy a pound or so of wool and would spin it myself; then I would buy two pounds and then three." She sent one son to live with her parents in her rural community of origin so that there would be one less mouth to feed; her other children assisted her in the morning before they went to school. Her daughter, Ricarda, began working when she was ten years old. At that time there was little competition, and Doña Flora was soon selling to foreigners who asked her to provide the merchandise in large quantities. Soon she was sending shipments of 150 to 250 pieces to Germany and Canada, then 800 ponchos to London, and finally as many as 2,500 in a single shipment.

Doña Flora's son entered an apprenticeship as a mechanic, first working for a year without pay and then for a token 30 pesos a week for two additional years. She had to give him 10 pesos just so he could eat. "Now he is a full-fledged mechanic and earns well," Ricarda explained, "but he no longer has much strength. He is spent, because he had to go to work when he was small. He was only 16 when he started."

Doña Flora's enterprise got a boost when Ricarda married a man with a university education who worked as a shipping agent in the firm Doña Flora used to handle her overseas shipping. The firm's growth also coincided with a boom created through large inflows of capital in the 1970s, when Bolivia was considered an oil-rich country and a good place to invest.

At the time we first interviewed Doña Flora, when she was 45 years old, she was engaged in a wide range of economic activities combining manufacturing, wholesaling and retailing that entailed manifold commercial ties and labor relations. Bolivia in

1981 was entering what was to be called the "lost decade" in Latin America, a period of increasing national debt, decreasing production, and increasing unemployment in many countries. Politically, Bolivia was in turmoil. In 1979, the eight-year dictatorship of President Banzer had ended. It was followed by a rapid succession of democratic and military governments. During our stay in 1981, when another dictator, General Meza, was in power, unhappiness with the regime's repressive measures and its inability to cope with the economy resulted in no fewer than a dozen attempted coups. However, compared with what was to come, firms like that of Doña Flora were still relatively successful and were just beginning to feel the drop of internal demand for their goods, the drop in tourism due to political turmoil, and increasing inflation.

When Doña Flora branched out into the manufacture of jackets, the extended family to whom she had put out the sewing was able to make direct contact with her major foreign client, a buyer from London, and began working for him directly. The experience had been particularly galling, since it was the very same client who in 1973 had encouraged her to diversify from sweaters and ponchos into tailored garments.

Doña Flora's trouble with those workers led her to make changes that illustrate a pattern many employers followed, of shifting between work arrangements that entailed different degrees of dependence and intensity. The workers she lost sewed in their own homes. She would bring the work to them and pick it up when it was ready. In 1978, Doña Flora expanded her workshop and hired workers to work there permanently.

Doña Flora's seamstresses were just one part of an enterprise, the complexity of which became increasingly apparent to us as we observed her at work and interviewed various members of her workforce. For example, Doña Flora generally purchased alpaca wool from producer-vendors who came to the city to sell it. However, when she had large orders, this source often proved insufficient, forcing her to travel to distant markets to buy wool directly from the alpaca herders. She then paid elderly women who worked at home in the suburb of El Alto to spin the wool into thread on wooden spindles. She herself also engaged in this traditional activity occasionally. In addition, Doña Flora purchased machine-spun wool from the would-be state monopoly, and later, when the price the monopoly charged became prohibitive, she bought from a factory that produced it clandestinely.

The preparation of the warp on a loom is indicative of the low degree of technology involved in Doña Flora's operation, requiring an inordinate amount of travel and preparation, and the involvement of quite a few helpers, recruited in various manners. The task entailed the combination of different natural colors of both hand- and factory-spun yarn. This was a laborious task done with the assistance of anyone who happened to be available: her youngest teenage son, her mother on periodic visits from the Lake Titicaca community where she and her husband had returned after he retired, and sometimes an additional worker or two. Her preferred spot for this activity, which requires an area as long as the cloth to be woven, was a level plot she owns outside the city. On the day we accompanied her, two young women neighbors who had recently migrated from the altiplano came out to watch and help her disentangle the yarn, in the hopes of learning an aspect of a new trade. With but a few iron pegs and two metal basins, it took four persons six hours to prepare the 200-vara (180-yard) warp, not counting the hour spent by the two neighbors unraveling an unruly ball of yarn and the hour's travel-time. That day, Doña Flora took advantage of our presence (and jeep) to take the warps to a rural community 15 kilometers away; otherwise she would have had to go by bus or prevail on her younger brother to take her there in his ancient pickup truck. The community enjoys bus service twice a week from La Paz. One of the dairy-farm families in the rural community—a widower, his two daughters and four sons—weaves for Doña Flora. The family was introduced to her by a former weaver and *compadre* (ritual kinsman) who gave up his trade for a factory job. On occasion, the family has worked with as many as four looms at a time, some provided by Doña Flora, but during our visit only one was in operation. Although the family could have also prepared the warp, they preferred to handle only the actual weaving. Doña Flora had her own ideas about the pattern of stripes, and besides (according to Doña Flora), the weavers were afraid that she might suspect them of cheating by using less yarn or substituting yarn of inferior quality.

Then she engaged another weaver to work full-time on her own patio. A peasant from Lake Titicaca, this man (with whom Doña Flora has also established ties of ritual kinship) had, in the past, furnished her with cloth when she was selling goods to tourists in a street market.

After the cloth was woven, Doña Flora and her two daughters washed it in a river half an hour away by bus, and carded it to give it a smoother appearance. Then they handed it over to the four workers we have already encountered, who cut it, sewed jackets and made appliqué designs on pillowcases and wall hangings, using the shop's two sewing machines.

Doña Flora's second major line of craft goods was alpaca sweaters and ponchos. Her principal source of sweaters was a kin group (not related to her) in Huarina; ponchos were knitted for her by unrelated women in the Cochabamba area with alpaca wool she provided. She, her daughter and a neighbor spent a great deal of time mending small imperfections in the alpaca sweaters. When a large shipment had to be prepared, her cousin's son would come after school to help. Often he stayed overnight, repairing ponchos and sweaters and packing them for export. Doña Flora also had machine-knitted alpaca sweaters made in her own shop, and she traveled regularly to Cochabamba to sell them and other goods made out of artificial fibers that she purchased in La Paz. The two-way nature of this productive and commercial venture made the expense and time involved in the 500-kilometer trip well worth her while.

Although Doña Flora made most of the crucial decisions regarding her enterprise herself, she also obtained managerial advice and help from various others. Assistance with the paperwork was particularly important, because Doña Flora is illiterate. Her son-in-law, Indalecio, was in charge of the paperwork involved in exporting and shipping. Indalecio—who lived with Ricarda and their children in a separate part of Doña Flora's compound and generally shared meals with Doña Flora—had learned these aspects of the business when he was working for a major dispatching firm. He and Ricarda entered into a partnership with Doña Flora. In addition to Indalecio's managerial assistance, Doña Flora received advice from buyers and hired an outside accountant to go over the accounts with her.

Besides these two major lines of business, Doña Flora (as well as Ricarda) engaged in other subsidiary ones, the relative importance of which waxed and waned according to the health of their manufacturing enterprise. Both had market stalls in a biweekly street market, where, among other things, they sold clothing purchased in El Alto and "Laura Ingalls bonnets" (of the kind Bolivians see on television in the dubbed *Little House on the Prairie* series) made by Doña Flora's younger daughter. The two daughters-in-law who lived in La Paz engaged in similar marketing activities. A final source of income was transportation. At one time or another, both Doña Flora and her older daughter owned buses. In 1981, this was true only of Indalecio and Ricarda, who operated their bus on one of the regular city bus lines. When he had the time (and the bus was in working condition), Indalecio drove the bus himself. At other times, Doña Flora's younger brother took over.

Some of Doña Flora's economic decisions have no direct relationship to her firm nor to her subsidiary economic ventures. However, as we shall see later, they shape her enterprises indirectly. This was the case for her strategic placement of some of her children in positions that had the effect of providing long-term security to herself and her children. She encouraged one of her sons to emigrate to Australia, her bachelor brother to work as a porter in Washington, D.C., and her younger son to obtain a job in the U.S. Embassy in La Paz.

ANALYSIS

The work relationships in Doña Flora's firm are representative of both the range of ties required in the day-to-day operation of an artisan firm and the mutability of the work relationships over time necessary for the survival of both owners and workers.

Work Relationships with Kin

Work relationships with kin in Doña Flora's firm included the unremunerated collaboration of household members, partnerships with close kin living in semidependent households, the companionship and/or collaboration of siblings and more distantly related kin, and various other transactions such as the sale of products made by kin and the contracting of a kinsman to transport goods to distant localities in return for the payment of his bus fare and a small variable bonus.

One of the major advantages of kin ties lies in their potential multiplexity. Individuals are tied to their kin through other kin in a variety of ways, creating a system with considerable feedback. As a result, a firm owner rapidly learns if a kinsman or kinswoman is available to undertake some urgent task or to fill a more permanent position. Kin may thus become part-time or even full-time collaborators at one time, companions at another.

On the negative side, a kinsman who is available and nearby may not be equally suited for all the roles he is called upon to play by a more successful member of his kin network. Doña Flora's brother was probably a good companion on her trips to Cochabamba, but when it came to collecting a debt in Lima, he did not have the clout necessary to settle the matter. It later took the more astute Doña Flora and Indalecio only a day or two to do so. Similarly, this brother did not make an ideal driver. But he was available and needed the work. Also his limitations, unlike those of a stranger, were known. As the saying goes: *"Mejor es el mal conocido que el bien por conocer"* (Known evil is better than unknown good).

Attaching close kin to a firm has its limitations. During an economic downturn, an overreliance on a single major source of income by all members of an extended household may, in fact, be detrimental to their economic well-being. The need for economic diversification was among the reasons why Doña Flora encouraged some of her kin to find jobs abroad. The occasional order for goods from Australia as well as the possible option of following her son there, the generous remittances from Washington, D.C., and the regular income from the Embassy were soon to become more important to Doña Flora than the direct involvement of those kin in her firm would have been.

Conversely, Doña Flora may not have acted in her long-term interest when she insisted that her son-in-law join the firm rather than using his talents as a shipping agent in a more indirect or intermittent manner. For example, by urging Indalecio to join her firm rather than continue working in Santa Cruz she risked burdening the extended family with underemployment if or when the fortunes of the firm took a turn for the worse.

Work Relationships with Non-Kin

Arrangements with non-kin are equally variable. At the lowest level of intensity are one-time sales to customers in the market. But producers/intermediaries attempt to cultivate and consolidate ties that could potentially develop into longer-term relationships involving repetitive transactions. By looking at Doña Flora's activities, we can see some of the ways these ties were cultivated. For example, she invited a German buyer who bought from her regularly to dinner when he came to discuss a new shipment. She purchased sweaters from the same producer for many years, thereby assuring a relatively stable source of good-quality products, and she established *casera* (preferred-customer) relationships with some knitters and stall owners in Cochabamba. Particularly valuable ties were consolidated through bonds of ritual kinship. Both the mother of Doña Flora's in-house workers and the weaver from Huarina became her *compadres*, or ritual kin. So did the in-house weaver mentioned earlier who, upon his entry into a factory, introduced Doña Flora to the family of altiplano weavers to whom she put out work and from whom she, on occasion, bought knitted gloves. We, too, became her *compadres*.

These relationships with non-kin may be intensified over time as confidence builds and/or the need arises. The Latin American who took one of Doña Flora's sons along to Australia was a long-time client. Conversely, such long-term ties may become deactivated or even severed. The latter frequently occurs when one party disappoints the other and sometimes occurs when a worker becomes independent or is no longer needed. In the latter case, however, the relationship may simply become dormant or it may be downgraded and only one of its components continued.

Doña Flora seems to have relied quite heavily on chance encounters to establish her network of work relations with non-kin, although in at least one instance—the weaver family near El Alto—she was aided by an outgoing worker. In addition, she re-engaged at least one person with whom she had a previous work relationship in a new capacity.

Spatial Dimensions of Work Relationships

The ties necessary to succeed in craft production of the kind in which Doña Flora engages cut across local, regional and national boundaries. Within the city, she had ties with her urban kin, clients, shipping agents, and sundry officials. Her spinners lived in nearby El Alto, where she herself also owned a parcel of land and where she purchased goods from wholesalers to sell in La Paz proper. But for many reasons, her ties had to extend beyond the city. Rural artisans can charge less for their labor because they have additional income—often their principal source—from their land. Migrants, like Doña Flora's weaver, with strong ties to their communities of origin, are not forced to switch to another economic activity when business is slack but can return to their home communities to farm while continuing the relationship with crafts firms on a part-time basis. Women in Cochabamba, with their special skills and lower wage demands, also constituted an essential component of Doña Flora's network.

The most important ties of all were those with foreign buyers, for only they could open up such large (albeit very fickle) markets. Participation in international fairs in cities as distant as Caracas and Bogotá served the same purpose. Finally, encouraging kin to emigrate to Washington and Australia opened new sources of remittances and potential economic alternative sources, the value of which increase as Bolivia's economy deteriorates.

The spatial expansion of small-scale enterprises is, of course, not a universal phenomenon. Many enterprises operate on a strictly local basis. Although interregional expansion of the kind exhibited by Doña Flora's firm tends to be associated with somewhat larger firms, the operation of even small workshops may entail frequent travels that may include remote locations.

Social Class Interaction

The network of individuals on whom Doña Flora relied to produce and distribute her goods also cuts across class boundaries. At a social level well beneath her own, Doña Flora had ties with herders/market vendors who provided her with wool, and with the elderly women on El Alto who spin for her. These ties were clearly of long duration.

They were also multiplex; for example, the women who spin for her had previously sold her shawls when she had a stall in a tourist market. The women had requested the change. Even though spinning is one of the lowliest and least paid occupations, the spinners may have preferred a stable relationship with a successful producer to a less certain one involving sales on consignment to a stall- or shop-owner. From Doña Flora's vantage point, a special relationship with spinners was equally important. To give someone wool to spin entails a degree of trust. Besides, she needed to ensure that her spinners would be available when their services were required. In sum, personal relationships must be established with all workers regardless of wage levels.

The knitters from whom Doña Flora purchased sweaters are among the most poorly paid artisans. Possessing skills that are widely disseminated and popular among women because they can be undertaken at home and without interfering much with regular household duties, they are at the mercy of unscrupulous and aggressive middlewomen and store owners, who often pay them little more than their costs and, at least in the case of the latter, take their goods only on consignment. Long delays in securing payment are all too common; knitters often have to make several visits to the store owner before they are finally paid.

Doña Flora's ties with individuals whom she would consider her social superiors were associated principally with her role as an exporter.

Doña Flora's Commercial Roles

Doña Flora's success with exporting knitted goods from both sources depended in part on her ability to accumulate sufficient quantities (up to several thousand sweaters at a time) but also depended on her ability to maintain strict quality control. Her clients were well aware that quality control was one of the major problems in the crafts trade. Some had learned the hard way. One client had amassed 10,000 sweaters through agents who purchased whatever they could find in El Alto, but he was forced to throw most of the sweaters away when they arrived at their destination because they were poorly made. In contrast, Doña Flora did not hesitate to reject sweaters that failed to meet her standards.

However, the export of artisan goods is cutthroat indeed. Shipping agents are frequently approached by producers with promises of money if they direct foreign buyers to their firms. Doña Flora was not immune to this tactic; she had benefited from it on earlier occasions when her son-in-law was still working as a dispatcher.

The export business requires a network of connections including links with government officials, bureaucrats, and other middle-class and/or upper-class individuals. For producers with lower-class backgrounds, the establishment of such links can be particularly difficult, and hence they nourish the ones they already have with particular care. Some have been remarkably successful in this endeavor. The manner in which Doña Flora established ties with foreign buyers is ample proof that she could successfully defend her interests vis-à-vis her social superiors. In this, she is representative of the veteran La Paz market vendors who instill respect among the lower classes and the elite alike. However, she frequently sought brokers to assist her in this task. We saw her visit an agent of the Bolivian Institute for Small-Scale Industry and Artisanry (IMBOPIA) without the accompaniment of a broker. But she never traveled to international fairs by herself. In part, this may have been because she felt the need for a male companion, but it was also because the transactions at such fairs required literacy and she could neither read nor write.

Her son-in-law became Doña Flora's principal broker. She felt that her daughter Ricarda's marriage was one of the most important links she had to the middle class.

Ricarda had met Indalecio when she was sending goods to other countries. At first, the couple had moved to Santa Cruz, where Indalecio was put in charge of reorganizing the branch office of the shipping firm for which he had worked in La Paz. However, Doña Flora succeeded in persuading him to return to La Paz and join her firm. They shared the profits according to the amount of capital each had invested and labor each had contributed. She tried hard to keep the marriage together despite Indalecio's sexual escapades. His education—he was only a year away from obtaining a university degree in economics—and his experience with shipping could not fail to be an asset to the firm.

Doña Flora's Relationship to the State

As we have seen, Doña Flora's major involvement with government agencies was associated with her export activities. This meant that her firm was officially recognized as a legitimate enterprise. However, like many entrepreneurs, irrespective of the size of their firms, Doña Flora often circumvented legal requirements. Thus, she regularly had her export clients sign two invoices, one for her own records and one with a lower figure to show the authorities, thereby making some tax savings. This practice was not without risk. Not only could she have gotten into trouble with the authorities, but, on more than one occasion, a client wrote a bad check and then produced the invoice with the lower figure when Doña Flora took legal action against him.

DOÑA FLORA'S FIRM BETWEEN 1981 AND 1998

When we recently returned to Bolivia, the economy which had already been deteriorating significantly during our first stay had declined precipitously. While the country had a democratic government, installed in 1984, the peso was in a free-fall, while the government, anxious to mitigate the social effects of the crisis, was still reluctant to make drastic cuts in spending.

Since our last visit, the marriage with Ricarda had broken up and Doña Flora was less positive about Indalecio's contribution to the firm. Had he not mixed up two shipments to Spain and England, the firm might not have lost two good clients. She also accused him of misspending her money so that she lost a large store. Whatever the case may be, Indalecio also took one of Doña Flora's best clients with him when he opened his own two stores with his new wife. Indeed, her export business was reduced substantially and she was selling mainly goods produced by others, including wood carvings and musical instruments (the latter from a cooperative set up by migrants from a community specializing in the craft). While, in theory, the rate of inflation should have fostered exports, the government had mandated that all foreign currencies earned abroad had to be deposited at the low official exchange rate, making exports unattractive for most companies unless they could go around the rules (as Indalecio seemed to be able to do). With exports artificially constrained, foreign intermediaries could come to Bolivia and purchase goods at bargain rates. Doña Flora's brother, who continued to live in the United States, was sending her money. Her son in Australia had become well established, taken on the surname of the family that had brought him there, become an Australian citizen, and was "earning three salaries." "We imagine that he earns a lot of money; he calls us every week for more than half an hour." He suggested bringing Doña Flora and Ricarda to Australia to work in agriculture.

In 1984, Doña Flora's most important upward link appeared to be with her accountant, who was assisting her in her attempt to move into the leather industry. As with the Ecuadorian who took her son to Australia, she had succeeded in creating a multipurpose link. Earlier, the accountant helped her with the arithmetic and kept an eye on her interests vis-à-vis her son-in-law. Now, as an experienced manager of a leather-goods firm, she hoped that he would be able to assist her in an entirely new role.[2] She had already purchased some sewing machines for up to $1,000 apiece, which were, however, standing idle and she had no workers except for one who was working part-time for her. While some of her workers had become independent producers, others had gone back to work in their rural community to work the land. One of them who had kept some cattle even while he was working for her remarked, "Thank God that I did not give up my animals. What would I have done here with my children?" Even Doña Flora herself was planning to return to her parents' community of origin to cultivate the land, for she could always count on her father to cede her a plot for the year. As she said, "Even a small plot helps." In addition, she planned to purchase three hectares of land near Cochabamba. Doña Flora still ordered sweaters from knitters in the rural community of Huarina. And Ricarda continued to travel between Cochabamba and La Paz, now taking wooden carvings and gilt silver jewelry and bringing back ponchos and blankets.

Doubtlessly, ill health must have contributed to the turn in Doña Flora's fortune. A year earlier she had almost died from diabetes and credits herbal teas for the improvement in her health. She had heard about the cure from a man who had gone to the United States to be cured and when, after three years, he had not regained his health he returned to Bolivia and had learned about the herbal cure from a vendor of jackets from Tarabuco.

While Doña Flora's family did not have to go hungry, thanks to continued diverse economic activity and contributions from their migrant kin, the family of one of her former outworkers who had recently died was reduced to serving meatless meals, a real comedown.

On a more recent visit to Bolivia, the economic situation in the country had stabilized, at least as far as the national economic indicators were concerned. The Bolivian currency was considered among the more stable in Latin America and larger firms were beginning to reinvest in the country. However, stabilization came at a considerable social cost, with cuts in welfare benefits including the elimination of subsidies for such staples as bread, creating hardship for the poor. For artisans like Doña Flora, the stabilization of the *boliviano* was a mixed blessing. Although they no longer had to fear that inflation would eliminate their capital if they did not immediately invest it in goods or real estate, the fact that Peru continued to have a high rate of inflation made prices for foreign importers more attractive there. Doña Flora herself had imported goods from Peru for resale in Bolivia until the border was closed to imports, which presumably would have meant engaging in the more risky contraband, and she was not well enough to travel to Peru herself.

Doña Flora's health continued to affect her business. Ricarda, who in the meantime had remarried, had to sell her minibus to pay for the costs of healthcare. Ill health also forced Doña Flora to abandon her plans for making leather goods. In view of this situation, her accountant/partner first continued on his own, but soon went bankrupt and turned to operating a small bus. Ricarda and her fellow vendors also spent large sums for legal fees attempting to retain access to their market sites when the city wanted to evict them. She continued to travel to Cochabamba with silver- and gold-plated jewelry but had suffered losses from selling goods in Peru, where she was defrauded of $4,000, and from a trip to Spain, where she had not been able to make any sales but had spent $6,000, another large loss. Also, debts on equipment had doubled in two years.

Doña Flora's brother, who had remained a bachelor, had come back from the United States after his visa expired and she was hoping to work with him. She was also doing business with a daughter-in-law who wove garments for her. "She is family," Doña Flora explained. "I no longer work with those men. They take the designs with them [when they leave], which harms my business. That's why I only work with members of the family now." In addition, Doña Flora still owned a small bus and Ricarda's new husband was operating his parents' bus.

By 1998, our most recent visit to Bolivia, the economy had further stabilized. The major problem had become an excess of competition fostered both by the improved economic situation and by easier access to loans through nongovernmental organizations including a formally recognized bank, BancoSol, geared entirely towards making loans to small businesses (see Buechlers 1997). Indeed, many of Doña Flora's former workers had become independent and those who had gone to live in the country were working in their former trade again. Doña Flora believes that her earnings decreased by 50% in four years.

Doña Flora's health continued to drain her resources. She explained, "Last year I was in the hospital with diabetes. I was seized by shaking fits some fifty times a day. They say that I was dead. I don't remember anything. They sacrificed guinea pigs on my behalf and cured me." She had sold her two small buses and had spent some U.S. $12,000 to be treated in Lima. She figures that during the 17 years that she has suffered from diabetes she has spent a total of $40,000. Her major source of income appeared to be leather goods that she produced in her own workshop with two workers and sold from a small but centrally located sidewalk stall. She and Ricarda were also exporting to other parts of Bolivia, including Cochabamba and Santa Cruz, and Ricarda was planning to make another trip to an artisan fair in Portugal. Doña Flora was also doing business with her brother who made leather goods in Santa Cruz and often helped by leaving his pickup truck in La Paz so that one of her sons could take her around. Since both her parents were now dead, she was thinking of hiring a caretaker and raising angora rabbits at her country home and commuting there for weekends. She says she would also like to found a cooperative there and have the peasants engage in weaving. However, she has little hope for success, since members of the community are engaged in fishing and may have little interest in producing craft goods. Some of the members of the family have become upwardly mobile. The son in Australia studied computer science and has a doctorate in economics. "He exhibited llamas," she explained, "and they gave him a fellowship. I didn't have to spend anything." Arturo, the cousin once-removed who had assisted Doña Flora in the early 1980s was also upwardly mobile. By 1984 their work relationship had ended, and in 1988 Arturo had finished his studies and was working at the university library. Finally, one grandson is studying business administration at the state university in La Paz, and a second grandson is also studying at the university.[3]

The family had also lost some opportunities. Ricarda's son had a fellowship to study in the United States through the intermediary of Doña Flora's brother. However, after two years, Ricarda forced him to return to Bolivia. "She was really stupid," Doña Flora explained. "Now she cries about it. She did it without any reason. He has become unmanageable. But he still studies." So that she does not have to live alone, Doña Flora is raising a teenage granddaughter. But the granddaughter hopes that after studying in Bolivia for three years or so, Doña Flora will have enough money to send her to study in Australia.

CONCLUSION

In conclusion, the workings of the enterprise of Doña Flora over time show how inadequate our traditional categories are to do justice to the complex processes involved.

In order to understand her actions, one cannot separate her activities as the head of an enterprise from the specific interpersonal resources at her disposal. As those change, her tactics change with them. But there are also long-term continuities. The brother, who in 1981 appeared to be more of a dead weight in terms of the progress of

Deutsch 102　　　　　grammar check

Viviana Cardoso

Switch subjects and objects

1. Er sieht sie (sgl)　　Sie sieht ihn

2. Ich liebe dich　　　　du liebst mich

3. Wir rufen ihn an　　　Er ruft uns an

4. Ihr besucht sie (pl)　　Sie besuchen euch
   usit

5. Du suchst uns　　　　Wir suchen dich

Supply the personal pronouns

1. Sie waschen das Auto　Sie waschen es

2. Ich kaufe die Schuhe　　Ich kaufe sie

3. Wir sehen den Turm　　Wir sehen er ihn

4. Du rufst die Polizei an　Du rufst sie an

5. Er kennt den Professor　Er kennt ihn

$\frac{9}{10}$ A-

den = ihn

the firm, turned out to be a long-term reliable asset, not least because he remained a bachelor and was therefore more likely to want to collaborate with close consanguineal kin. In contrast, the daughter's divorce led to the loss of an extremely valuable asset from which the firm was never able to recover.

Doña Flora's entrepreneurial strategies must also be seen in conjunction with the options she has created for herself outside the confines of the enterprise per se. Placing a son in a secure position in the American embassy gives the extended family a potential resource should everything else fail. More importantly, the son in Australia could always be counted on for material support should it be needed, perhaps providing one explanation for Doña Flora's present relatively modest aims for her firm.

Doña Flora's interpersonal resources are not confined to individuals engaged in similar enterprises; rather, it is important for a person to have access to economic resources with very different characteristics: access to farm land for the most dire emergencies but also for recreation and even for new entrepreneurial options, a son with a low-paid but secure embassy job, hopefully less subject to the vagaries of the national economy, or one outside of the local economy altogether. Hers is certainly a "family business," but the nature of her reliance on kin varies over time and she also engages non-kin in various capacities at all times.

An analysis of Doña Flora's firm must also take into consideration the ravages of ill health, particularly in Third World countries, even for an individual who is far from the bottom of the economic ladder. Interestingly, it also shows that Doña Flora's ethnic background was as important as her access to modern medicines in influencing her medical choices. She is by no means the only one of our long-term informants whose economic standing has been influenced by large expenditures for medical treatment.

National and international economic trends are also of crucial importance to the workings of Doña Flora's firm. Her firm was established and grew during the relatively prosperous period of the 1970s. The subsequent vagaries of the Bolivian economy outlined earlier also affected her opportunities and the decisions she made, but she has not been well enough (and has, perhaps, also not felt the need) to take advantage of the renewed opportunities—albeit in a very competitive economic climate—the last few years. Yet she, like many of our informants from all social classes, is still full of ideas about new entrepreneurial possibilities.

I would suggest that, rather than viewing Doña Flora's entrepreneurial activities as characteristic of a particular sector of the economy, such as the "informal sector," or of a particular social class, we view them as one keen individual's adaptations to the vagaries of the economies of Third World nations, employing whatever resources are at hand including traditional skills but also encompassing resources spanning the world from the United States to Australia.

***

I wish to thank Judith-Maria Buechler, who shared much of the gathering and analysis of the data. Fieldwork in Bolivia was supported by the National Science Foundation, Hobart and William Smith Colleges, and Syracuse University.

***

Notes

[1] Clark (1988) credits Keith Hart with introducing the term in 1971 at a conference on urban employment in Africa held at the University of Sussex (see Hart 1973).

[2] Just what benefit the accountant expected to derive from this latter role could not be determined.

[3] For a discussion of upward mobility of children of small-scale entrepreneurs see MacEwen 1994:181–182.

References

Buechler, H. 1988. "Doña Flora's Network: Work Relations in Small Industries in La Paz, Bolivia." In *Urban Life: Readings in Urban Anthropology* (2nd ed.). George Gmelch and Walter Zenner, eds., pp. 369–380. Prospect Heights, IL: Waveland Press.

———. 1989. "Apprenticeship and Transmission of Knowledge in La Paz, Bolivia." In *Apprenticeship: From Theory to Method and Back*. Michael Coy, ed., pp. 31–50. Albany: State University of New York at Albany Press.

Buechler, H. & J.-M. 1992. *Manufacturing Against the Odds: Small-scale Production, Gender, Class and Crises in La Paz, Bolivia*. Boulder: Westview Press.

———. 1996. *The World of Sofía Velásquez: The Autobiography of a Bolivian Market Vendor*. New York: Columbia University Press.

Buechler, H., J.-M., S., & S. 1998. "Financing Small-Scale Enterprises in Bolivia." (with Judith-Maria Buechler, Simone Buechler and Stephanie Buechler). In *The Third Wave of Modernization in Latin America: Cultural Perspectives on Neoliberalism*. Lynne Phillips, ed. Wilmington (DE): SR Books, Jaguar Books series No. 16.

Clark, G. (ed.). 1988. *Traders Versus the State: Anthropological Approaches to Unofficial Economies*. Boulder: Westview Press.

Hart, K. 1973. "Informal Income Opportunities and Urban Employment in Ghana." *Journal of Modern African Studies* 11:61–89.

MacEwen, Scott A. 1994. *Divisions and Solidarities: Gender, Class and Employment in Latin America*. London: Routledge.

Perlman, J. 1976. *The Myth of Marginality: Urban Poverty and Politics in Rio de Janeiro*. Berkeley: University of California Press.

Piore, M. and C. Sabel. 1984. *The Second Industrial Divide: Possibilities for Prosperity*. New York: Basic Books.

Portes, A., M. Castells & L. Benton. 1989. *The Informal Economy: Studies in Advanced and Less Developed Countries*. Baltimore: Johns Hopkins University Press.

Portes, A. & J. Walton. 1981. *Labor, Class, and the International System*. New York: Academic Press.

Rakowski, C. (ed.). 1994. *Contrapunto: The Informal Sector Debate in Latin America*. New York: State University of New York Press.

Wilson, T., issue coordinator. 1998. *The Urban Informal Sector*. Issue 99, *Latin American Perspectives 25(2)*.

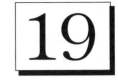

Dwight B. Heath is a professor of anthropology (research) at Brown University. His best-known books include A Journal of the Pilgrims at Plymouth, Land Reform and Social Revolution in Bolivia *(with C. J. Erasmus and H. C. Buechler),* Cross-Cultural Approaches to the Study of Alcohol *(with M. J. Everett and J. O. Waddell),* Contemporary Cultures and Societies of Latin America *(various editions, one with R. N. Adams),* The International Handbook on Alcohol and Culture, *and* Drinking Occasions: Comparative Perspectives on Alcohol and Culture.

The drinking of beverage alcohol is an ancient and widespread aspect of culture that has vastly different meanings, forms, and outcomes in various contexts around the world. This author has, for several years, used drinking as a kind of window on culture, comparing patterns of belief, behavior, and attitudes, with an eye toward regularities, the explanation of differences, implications for personal and public health, and social welfare, as well as practical policy implications.

In the multidisciplinary field of "alcohol studies," however, those who are not well grounded in the social sciences often labor under the misapprehension that a "culture" is congruent with a nation-state, that drinking patterns are peculiarly resistant to change, or that the history of alcohol use and its outcomes can be simplistically understood in terms of long cycles of alternating love and hate. By examining the drinking patterns of five distinct populations within the small country of Bolivia, we not only see intranational culture variations, but we also see how quickly—within living memory—they change, sometimes in diametrically contrasting ways. If social science is to be predictive, close attention must be paid to particular details of the local situation and how they relate to each other.

Another example of how alcohol provides a window on culture is Gutmann (chapter 28); other illustrations of how cultures change over time are Prins (chapter 8) and Doughty (chapter 22).

Changes in Drinking Patterns
in Five Bolivian Cultures
A Cautionary Tale about Historical Approaches
Dwight B. Heath

INTRODUCTION

Unlike many studies of changes in drinking patterns over the long-term, in which evidence has been garnered from travellers' accounts, novels, secondary analyses of local history, reprints of comments by classical authors, and similarly quasi-historical sources, these case studies are all contemporary and relate to changes that have occurred within a single generation. Not only did they all take place within the memory span of human beings who are still alive, but most were observed by a single social scientist and were reported originally in fairly detailed ethnographic context, with explicit linkages to political, economic, and other concurrent events that may have been relevant. In this sense, they provide a microscopic view of what some assume to be macroscopic processes: how drinking patterns change in various cultures. These cultural case studies also collectively provide a cautionary tale about the dangers of overgeneralizing from any single case to formulate or test propositions that might be applied as if they were universally applicable.

On the one hand, I will be briefly tracing at least a small part of the evolutionary trajectory of continuity and change among both the drinking patterns and associated consequences among various culturally distinctive populations within a relatively

Revised, with permission of author and publisher, from *Addiction Research*, vol. 2, pp. 307–318. Copyright © 1995 OPA (Overseas Publishers Association), N.V. Reprinted with permission from Gordon and Breach Publishers.

small nation-state. Size, of course, is a relative matter. The Republic of Bolivia today is only about half as large as it was at its founding, less than two centuries ago. A number of ill-fated wars with most of its neighbors have deprived this nation of its seacoast, large oil-rich areas in the south, and considerable forested expanses to the north and east. Like many other Latin American countries, it still has a few minor border disputes unsettled. Even if they were all resolved in favor of Bolivia, however, the total population would still be less than 7 million (lower than many cities elsewhere) and the land area would probably not exceed 425,000 square miles (or about 1,650,000 sq. km, the size of Spain and France combined, or of Texas and California).

It seems superfluous in this context to reiterate at length concerns that I have already expressed in print about the careless use of the term "culture" that characterizes many well-intentioned efforts at comparative social science in recent years. Those who are especially interested may want to consult my original reminder that countries are rarely congruent with cultures (Heath, 1986). Elsewhere, I have also offered another reminder that even anthropologists should be more careful to specify which usage, among so many, they are choosing to apply to any given corpus of data about "culture" (Heath, 1987). Throughout this paper, I am using "culture" in the sense of a social heritage or tradition (Group B among the Historical types of some 169 definitions critically assessed by Kroeber and Kluckhohn (1952) in their still-definitive monograph on the nature of culture).

Few nations around the world are as homogeneous as the alcohol literature would suggest. Whether we speak of "ethnic groups," "minorities," "societies," "subcultures," "socioeconomic classes," or other socially significant reference groups (Heath, 1991a), drinking patterns and associated attitudes, values, expectations, epidemiology, etc., are probably nowhere near so uniform or "typical" as is implied frequently when writers use national-level statistical data as if they were representative of some unitary "mainstream" national "culture" (e.g., Babor, 1986; Davies & Walsh, 1983; Mäkelä, et al. 1981). To be sure, not all nations are so culturally pluralistic as is Bolivia. Language is by no means coterminous with culture, but they tend to be closely linked, and it is a vivid reflection of diversity to note that Spanish, Aymara, Quechua, and Guaraní have all been treated simultaneously as official languages in Bolivia in recent years. Beyond that, linguists have identified more than 100 different languages still spoken by contemporary populations there, and villages only a few miles apart sometimes retain distinctive styles of dress, pantheons of gods and spirits, beliefs in powerful places, senses of self-identity, and other features that tend to distinguish one culture from another.

The various Bolivian sociocultural systems that are examined here include the Sirionó hunter-foragers in the Amazonian rainforest; Camba horticulturalists who live just south of there, where the jungle meets the grassy plains in the eastern lowlands; and Aymara villagers, Mestizo townspeople, and outsiders, all in the coca-growing highland valleys of *yungas* near La Paz. In each instance, a unique combination of ecological, economic, interethnic, religious, and technological factors will be considered as they seem relevant to changes in drinking patterns. No unifying historical theory has emerged from these studies, but they let us partially test a number of ideas that have been put forth about environmental factors at the level of sociocultural systems, and force us to consider some guidelines for ethnographic and historical approaches.

THE SIRIONÓ:
DISASTROUS DEVELOPMENT IN THE RAINFOREST

The story of changing drinking patterns among the Sirionó is a sad chronicle of development that went sour. It is a classic case of unforeseen harmful consequences of what originated as a well-intentioned, slightly paternalistic, efficiency-oriented material innovation, but that resulted in creating social problems that far outweighed the value of the human physical energy that was saved. The "obvious superiority" of an axe made of steel in comparison with an axe made of stone is often cited by those who boast of "bearing the white man's burden," and claim that the "civilized" or "highly developed" peoples of the world should offer our technology to the so-called "primitive" (or, as popular thinking has become progressively more liberal in this respect, "underdeveloped" or "developing" or even "differently developed") peoples. A straighter, sharper edge, easier to keep honed, heavier, and quicker in cutting down a tree, is self-evidently better for the job—ideology need play no role in such an evaluation, and there is no need for further discussion. Or, at least, that is how most people thought about such things in the 1940s, before anthropologists raised serious questions on exactly the subject of trading steel axes for stone, first among Australian Aborigines (Sharp, 1952), then among the Sirionó (Holmberg, 1954), and later among some other tribes in the Amazonian rainforest and elsewhere (Métraux, 1959).

When the Sirionó were first described (Holmberg, 1950), they appeared to be an unusually small group, far more isolated than most, with no clothes, few tools, an exceptionally rudimentary kinship system, minimal elaboration in philosophical, religious, mythological, or recreational terms, lacking even the dog and fire-making skills, which are almost universal. All in all, theirs was one of the least complex and heterogeneous cultures that had been encountered—rather like an earlier analogue to the Tasaday, but without the media coverage that made instant celebrities of the supposed Philippine cave dwellers. It was only academics who heard or cared about the Sirionó, and even in that small circle, far more attention was paid to their habits of eating than to their drinking. (Insofar as the Sirionó had a claim to fame on the world stage, it was on the basis of the fact that they contradicted Freud—they didn't dream about sex but about food; they didn't become jealous over sex, but over food; and so forth.)

In the Sirionó hunting and foraging lifeway, in bands of fewer than 20 individuals, drinking parties were rare but enjoyable occasions. Wild honey was the basis of the homebrew they made, and it was a painful and time-consuming job to cut a bees' nest from a tree. But when someone did, it was an occasion for joyous convivial drinking, in which wild drunkenness seemed to enhance sociability, make jokes funnier, and provide everyone with a welcome time of relaxation and enjoyment, with no evidence of any consequent problems.

Enter the anthropologist, bright-eyed and crew-cut, working on his doctoral dissertation, half-blind and helpless for much of his stay, but dogged in collecting data and flushed with the liberal ideal of helping people to help themselves. Along with pencils and pads of paper, he also brought in fishhooks, needles, a few chickens, watermelon seed, and a shotgun, as well as several machetes and steel axes. This is not an appropriate context in which to trace out in excruciating detail the tragic comedy-of-errors that followed. Incidentally, it was not some jealous latecoming anthropologist who discredited the noble efforts made by Holmberg, but rather he himself, sadly reflecting some years later on the ways in which he had unwittingly hurt the people he most wanted to help.

To make a long story short, the steel axes and machetes did, in fact, quickly prove to be far more efficient and effective than had been the traditional tools made of chipped stone, monkey teeth, or palm thorns. More honey flowed into the community, and it was promptly converted to beer. More beer meant more parties—and that meant less hunting. Meat, which was always in short supply, became especially scarce in that year of combined drought (in terms of rain) and superfluity (in terms of homebrew). Tempers grew short, with people exhorting each other to go out hunting, but with each hunter preferring to enjoy a prolonged drinking binge. There is no indication that anyone became "dependent" or "addicted," except in the narrow sense that the quest for drink interfered with some other important activities.

To hear Holmberg tell it, harsh words began to fly—as never before—and after that, actual fights broke out—which had been unknown before. It is difficult to evaluate who fought whom, what words or events precipitated aggression, or any of the microscopic details that would help us better to understand and evaluate the changes. He wrote in the modal/normative terms that predominated in ethnographic descriptions of the time (Holmberg, 1954). But, for all the lack of quantitative precision, there appears little reason to doubt the validity or reliability of his observations. The Sirionó are certainly a striking case where "modernization" appears to have brought some alcohol-related problems in its wake.

For a whole combination of reasons, most of which have nothing to do with alcohol, the Sirionó were progressively driven out of their jungle refuge, until what appeared to be the last wandering band were lured to settle in a missionary compound where they were recently learning to speak Spanish, to sing hymns, and to scorn "the old ways" as backward and ungodly (Stearman, 1984, 1987). Part of the price they pay— or perhaps some would say, part of the blessings they have received—in exchanging their independent way of life for the more secure but restricted life at the mission is strictly enforced universal abstinence. No one seems seriously to suffer from it, although a few old men occasionally reminisce fondly about their earlier way of life, replete with the adventures of hunting and the joys of drinking.

THE CAMBA: PROGRESS AND A PENDULUM-SWING

A very different sequence of events has characterized the Camba during the same period. Already speaking a lilting variant of Spanish (basically, sixteenth-century Castilian, with an admixture of words from a dozen nearby Indian languages), wearing cheap factory-made clothes of vaguely Western cut, and cultivating such imported crops as sugarcane, coffee, and bananas, among other things, the Camba might impressionistically be characterized as more nearly "Mestizo" than Indian (Stearman, 1985). But many Camba individuals grew up speaking Guaraní, Itatín, Chiriguano, Chiquitano, Izozeño, Chama, or other indigenous languages, and their handicrafts, houses, folk-medicine, and many other aspects of culture are closer to those of neighboring tribes than they are to medieval Spanish peasants, much less, to contemporary Europeans.

Sometime in the 1920s a Belgian immigrant brought with him the technology and know-how to distill sugarcane juice into very potent rum—178 proof by U.S. standards (i.e., 89% ethanol by volume). Sealed in metal cans that are painted shocking pink, such alcohol was eagerly accepted throughout the Andes, where, watered by about half, it became the poor man's *aguardiente*. The local Camba, however, some of whom were tenant farmers on his *hacienda* and others of whom were small-scale independent homesteaders or tenants on other *haciendas*, drank it undiluted. Whether they were taught to do so on the job, as is sometimes reported in quasi-feudal and otherwise tightly controlled caste-like labor situations, is unclear, but there is no uncertainty about their having come to pride themselves on drinking it neat, and joking about others who dilute it. This is not to say that they savor and enjoy it—they say it burns their throat just as it did mine, and their gestures and facial expressions make that appear to be true. And drink it they do, by the tumbler full (i.e., some 250 cc. of ethanol in a draft), in a strictly ritualized exchange of toasting, but only within the context of episodic communal drinking parties. Such parties are linked to the Roman Catholic calendar of saints' and other holy days, to the calendar of state and national holidays, and to the rhythm of a five-day workweek (leaving a sixty-hour weekend for celebration).

This description is written in the "ethnographic present," using the present tense for what was happening in the mid-1950s when the classic ethnographic description afforded us a clear and detailed "snapshot" of Camba culture (Heath, 1958); subsequent accounts dealt with successive decades of change (Heath, 1965, 1971, 1991b). Although (or perhaps, because) I had no academic knowledge of alcohol at the time, I paid attention to it only tangentially, as a commodity important in the lives of the people; my own interests were focused much more on land tenure, social organization, and political socialization in the wake of a real revolution (Heath, Erasmus & Buechler, 1969). Many readers are already familiar with those parties, in the most comfortable manner, having read about how they went on constantly, night and day, with those who were still sober stepping gingerly over or around their friends and neighbors who lay passed out among them. In an early paper, I took some pains to answer all of the questions that, at that time, had been raised about drinking in any tribal society, and was struck by the degree to which such fiestas seemed to complement the Cambas' unusually loose and unintegrated social organization. I concluded that "fiestas provide occasions for intense interaction, and drinking groups constitute primary reference groups which are lacking in other phases of Camba life" (Heath, 1958:504), in which "alcohol serves to facilitate rapport between individuals who are normally isolated and introverted" (ibid.:507). Another point that struck me at the time was the fact that, during all the drinking and drunkenness I saw, and all that I inquired about, there was no indication that any person among them had suffered any psychological, physical, social, or other harm or problem in connection with alcohol.

The Camba soon became famous—or infamous—for their prodigious thirst, and scientists were interested enough in the absence of problems so that some weighed in with elaborations and alternative interpretations of Camba drinking (e.g., Mandelbaum, 1965; MacAndrew and Edgerton, 1969). For this reason, it was all the more helpful that I was able to chronicle, during the ensuing ten years or so, a striking change in their drinking patterns (Heath, 1965). As the Camba region ceased to be an untamed frontier area and came under effective government control, many other things were also happening. The land reform broke up some of the large and traditional latifundia (of the quasi-feudal subsistence *hacienda* type) and encouraged new entrepreneurs to establish similarly large but more commercial and less paternalistic latifundia (of the market-oriented plantation type). The opening of a road and two railroads brought a flood of migrants to the region, some from densely populated and ethnically different Bolivian highlands, and many from other countries (Stearman, 1985). Peasant leagues that were established as both channels for political patronage and corporate petitioners for land allocations gave the Camba both primary reference groups and a variety of activities and demanding commitments such as they had never known before (Heath, 1972). By the mid-1960s, those *sindicatos* had virtually displaced traditional drinking parties as sociable pastimes for many of the Camba, although that hardy minority who continued to be homesteaders, moving every few years to stay on "the pioneer fringe" beyond advancing settlement, kept the old pattern alive.

A counterrevolutionary military coup succeeded to power in 1974 and was able to roll back a few of the gains that peasants had won. Contrary to expectations, the land reform was not reversed but the *sindicatos* were banned and many of the leaders killed or exiled, a drastic but effective measure toward weakening grassroots opposition to the new oligarchy. Many of the military officers in positions of political power became rich, and bought or stole large tracts of land, making themselves *hacendados* reminiscent of the pre-revolutionary quasi-feudal system. Others collaborated with local entrepreneurs who were becoming involved in the lucrative international drug trade (Gill, 1991). Converting the traditional crop of coca (high bulk with low value) to cocaine paste (low bulk with high value) requires only a few easily available chemicals, a little unskilled labor, and virtually no technological know-how, and yet the value added is enormous. Frequent flights took the paste to Colombia, where it was further refined to yield cocaine hydrochloride for the U.S. and European markets. Apart from the pervasive malaise that came from being "occupied" by what they considered an "alien" military force (most of whom are darker skinned and speak the very different Quechua language), the Camba were also subjected to a general sense of lawlessness and galloping economic inflation (in which they had no access to the flood of incoming dollars). The jungle that had been so important in their lives—providing housing, food, medicine, and many other necessities—was fast disappearing. The tide of immigrants continued to rise, and the newcomers quickly came to dominate the markets, for a combination of reasons. All in all, the Camba of the late 1980s felt displaced, disgusted, disoriented, and the incipient social organization that had emerged a few years earlier had disintegrated.

Drinking parties very like those I first encountered a quarter of a century earlier were again commonplace when I was there in 1989, and again there appeared to be no harmful consequences to anyone (Heath, 1991b).

AYMARA VILLAGERS, MESTIZO TOWNSPEOPLE, AND GRINGO BUYERS: ETHNICITY IN A TOPSY-TURVEY SITUATION

In the *yungas* region, there are many communities that are distinctly Aymara and others that are distinctly Mestizo ("mixed," reflecting both Spanish and indigenous aspects of their heritage). But because they live in such close economic symbiosis, it is difficult to discuss either in isolation from the other. This is the lush semitropical region of deep valleys in the eastern slopes of the Andes, where coca has been the dominant crop for at least 1,000 years. The revolution of 1952 and the subsequent military counterrevolution impacted this area in very different ways; perhaps most important for our discussion are two facts. First, Aymara social organization had long been remarkably cohesive—they are the one population that the Incas were not able to Quechua-ize in their vast pre-Columbian empire—and they remain distinctive five centuries later. Second, growing coca for sale had been the dominant activity for centuries, and it remains so. To be sure, the buyers are different people now, and they come to the source rather than requiring the *yungueños* to truck it to them along the perilous twisting dirt road that connects them with the capital city. But the old rhythm of farming, harvesting, drying and baling the leaves, with four harvests in a good year, is little changed.

The quasi-feudal paternalism of the Mestizo landlords did change in the wake of the revolution, although they still enjoy higher social status than the Aymara. There is still a caste-like separation, in which locals pay attention to height, skin color, surname, language (or accent, if Spanish is spoken), and (of rapidly decreasing importance) dress as characteristics that mark the boundaries between ethnic groups. The Mestizos have nearly all retreated to the commercial and administrative centers (the largest town has about 2,500 people), leaving the villages of under 500, scattered homesteads, and decaying ex-*haciendas* to the Aymara, many of whom used to be their tenant farmers (Heath, 1972).

Aymara drinking traditionally occurred only in binges, with both men and women hoping and expecting to become intoxicated in the course of periodic fiestas. The parties were geared to the Roman Catholic and indigenous religious calendars, and drinking usually occurred only in a group, and only in a formally patterned ritualized exchange of toasts (Carter, 1977). The beverage was *chicha*, a homebrew fermented from maize to about 4–6% ethanol; or, if one wished to display one's wealth, *aguardiente*, sugarcane rum watered to about 30–40%. Commercially bottled wine sometimes appeared, but not as a beverage to be drunk by the people who are present, so much as an offering to supernaturals, or poured on the ground at crucial times and with appropriate invocations, as part of any complex ritual (such as accompanied the first plowing, a child's first haircut, the blessing of a new house or other building, various kinds of curing, and so forth).

All of what I have described as the traditional pattern persists to this day. A small—but symbolically important—change occurred shortly after the revolution in terms of that narrow realm of action, interethnic drinking (Heath, 1971), however. Until that time, there had been no occasions when Aymaras and Mestizos drank together. Social distance was scrupulously maintained in most contexts, and the special combination of sociability and vulnerability that the Aymaras associate with intoxication was seen as not appropriate in the company of members of any other population. When the Aymaras took over the ex-*haciendas* but had no way of getting crops to market, the dispossessed ex-*hacendados* (former landlords) recognized a unique economic opportunity and many became middlemen, brokers who toured the countryside to buy produce which they trucked into the city at a dual profit—both marking up the value of the goods, and using differently advantageous systems of weights and measures when buying and when selling. In a context where both cultures emphasize personalistic relationships, with buying and selling preferably between individuals known to each other rather than strangers, the ex-*hacendados* who were trying to become produce brokers set out to cultivate special links with Aymara peasants whom they had formerly scorned as "brute Indians." One of the quickest and easiest ways to do that was to volunteer as *padrino* (godfather) in a ceremonial pseudo-kin relationship.

The Aymaras choose a different *padrino* for each child at birth, first haircut, baptism, confirmation, marriage, and on various other occasions, and it is advantageous to them to have a wealthier townsperson, fluent in Spanish, willing to buy the appropriate gifts or to sponsor the appropriate costs of a fiesta. The person who accepts the responsibility of serving as such a *padrino*-to-something thereby simultaneously becomes *compadre* (co-parent) to the child's parent, the owner of the building, or whatever, and owes a long-term debt of reciprocity. One way in which a peasant can reciprocate is in promising to sell his crops only to his *compadre*, thereby assuring an ongoing source of profit in exchange for relatively small and infrequent gifts. In substance, this kind of *padrinazgo/compadrazgo* relationship is well known throughout the Mediterranean Basin and the broader world of Catholic and Eastern Orthodox religions. A special twist that it took in the Bolivian *yungas* was that such occasions became the first and only ones in which Aymara villagers and Mestizo townspeople exchanged toasts, usually with *aguardiente*, but sometimes with whiskey or factory-bottled beer provided by the Mestizo in his role as *padrino*. This may sound like a minor degree of fraternization, but in view of the longstanding and deep animosity that had marked those interethnic relations, it was a striking innovation.

During the most recent 15–20 years, another group has been arriving in the area, entrepreneurs from the eastern lowlands and from abroad (collectively identified as "Gringos"). Unlike the Mestizos, many of whom the Aymaras have personally known for years, the Gringos share little more in common than being new to the area. The fact that a single term is used to label such a diverse category demonstrates effectively that "race" or "ethnicity"—as used by local people—has more to do with social and cultural factors than it has with biological or genetic ones. (Gringos may have Japanese surnames, sallow complexions, straight black hair, and narrow lips; or they may have English names, blue-black complexions, curly black hair, and thick lips; Hispanic names, light pink complexions, thin blonde hair, and medium lips; or any of several other combinations of characteristics.) They are eager to buy coca to be processed into cocaine paste. For them, coca is not just another agricultural product on which they can make a small margin by trucking to La Paz; it is the raw material of the international drug trade, on which they can make huge profits. They have brought so much money that the ex-*hacendados*, even with their *compadre* relationships, were quickly cut out of the market. Nevertheless, even the coca buyers hold to some of the niceties of exchange that are traditional in Andean cultures, and offer a drink when it is time to "seal a bargain" or to "close a deal." They usually carry non-traditional drinks, such as bottled beer (barley-based lager, manufactured in large modern breweries) or whisky (usually Scotch whiskey, drunk neat). Even when dealing with narcotraffickers, an Aymara peasant will be careful always to "*ch'allar*" before drinking—that is, to spill a little on the ground as an explicit offering to *Pachamama*, "the great Earth-Mother," just as they would with homemade *chicha* or with *aguardiente* during a religious or curing ceremony.

The traditional patterns of drinking among the Aymaras remain virtually unchanged, as does the conviction that occasional drunkenness is a good thing, even sometimes a sacred duty. In dealing with Mestizo and Gringo outsiders, however, beer appears rapidly to be displacing *chicha*, a change which may have long-term harmful effects on the status of women. It is the women who make *chicha*, who proudly boast of the quality of their particular product, and who pocket the profits for their own use. (Even when they spend it on household expenses such as food, fuel, or clothing for the children, women consider it important that they earn and control the money.) Buying beer sends money irretrievably away from the local community to the metropole, in contrast with buying *chicha*, which served as a kind of redistributive mechanism, recycling money within the local community. If drinkers were now to adopt the metropole's preference for cold beer, the whole question of refrigeration could become an important economic factor, and other possible implications are almost endless.

WHY THIS IS A CAUTIONARY TALE: IMPLICATIONS FROM FIVE CULTURES IN BOLIVIA

The preceding brief sketches of continuity and change in drinking patterns in different cultures within one nation raise a number of issues that deserve to be noted by historians and anthropologists, as well as other students of contemporary alcohol use.

The Sirionó case illustrates the wisdom of an old English proverb, "The road to Hell is paved with good intentions." That has long been known to many of us who toil in the field of development and international or transcultural relief and assistance, but it is often lost sight of by planners who know few of the details of workaday life in remote places, or whose pride and faith in "progress" obscures attempts at anticipating what will be the deleterious consequences of change in another cultural system. It is also a vivid exception to the generalization that social drinking, with traditional beverages of relatively low alcoholic content, tends to be trouble free. It is rare to find so much additional drinking and disruption in so short a time without being able to identify a commercial dealer, from a large and more powerful culture, who has much to gain from selling it. The recent shift to abstinence shows that societies, like individuals, are by no means caught in a progressive accumulation of difficulties, even after they have reached a point where drinking is sometimes problematic for themselves and for others who are close to them.

The Camba case could be seen, at one level, as a telling illustration of the fact that cultural systems are closely integrated, and that many parts tend to change concurrently and coordinately. But if we focus on the outcomes rather than the process, it could equally be seen as demonstrating that similar drinking patterns can occur in very different political, economic, ecological, and social contexts. The fact that they drink so heavily now, much as they did in the 1950s, despite an intervening period of light and infrequent drinking, might almost look like a pendulum-swing in drinking customs—but there is not enough evidence to warrant any guesses about whether this is part of a recurrent cycle, or "long wave" of change that might recur at other times in history. Now, as was the case many years ago, the Camba again appear to be the population who drink more, more often, of a higher-proof beverage, than any other in the world—and do so with no apparent deleterious consequences, whether in social, psychological, legal, physical, or other terms. They seem to be one of the more important exceptions to the widely accepted linked hypotheses that harm from drinking is dose-related, and that control of availability is the most appropriate approach to preventing alcohol-related problems.

The Aymara case fits with others elsewhere in which observers have noted that drinking patterns tend to be additive, rather than substitutive. In contrast with the other populations described in this paper, most of their drinking has been remarkably constant, in terms of who, what, where, when, how, and even why. But that special realm of interethnic drinking-as-an-adjunct-to-business, however small it may be in terms of time and quantity in relation to other patterns of Aymara drinking-with-friends, is highly visible and it is emotionally charged. It is a reminder of the obvious—but often overlooked—fact that social context can be crucial in terms of drinking, and that meanings and consequences of drinking are often shaped as much by psychology and intention as by pharmacology and biochemistry. We don't know enough about other patterns of drinking among the Mestizo villagers or diverse Gringos to make any comments on continuity or change, except that we know these specific patterns of interethnic drinking, with Aymara peasants and as an accompaniment to commercial transactions, are new, presumably based on their business dealings elsewhere, with other kinds of people. Ethnic segregation of drinking groups is not nearly so strict as some might believe.

In aggregate, these Bolivian case studies underscore cultural variation, in drinking patterns as well as in other terms, within a single nation. That is, they demonstrate, simply but vividly, that it is sometimes fallacious to treat the nation-state as if it were a single "culture," as is often done in alcohol studies and in other fields of comparative research. They also show how the study of alcohol can serve as a window upon cultures, revealing some of the complex interrelations of patterns of belief and behavior among a wide range of populations who see themselves as very different from each other.

What some consider a burning issue, that of cycles in history, finds little support in these data. To be sure, the time frame is quite limited, so we have no basis for saying that some sort of cycles are unlikely to emerge. We simply don't have much indication that they would, or if so, what would be the nature or periodicity of them. The Camba pendulum-swing from binge parties to relative sobriety and back to binge parties appears (at least to me) to be so intimately linked with changes in social organization that it hardly seems necessary to look for other explanations. Nevertheless, a strong case could be made for anomie (in the sense of collective depression with the loss of status and other values), stress, psychic escape, or some such mechanism as a "cause" for the recent heavy drinking. As an anthropologist, I must confess: the more I know about the details of a given situation, the less likely I am to lend much weight to more general forces. Particularity about details instills confidence about linkages within cultures, whereas it is easier to generalize in broad terms when one is ignorant of many specific details. Furthermore, we must never lose sight of the fact that, even when cycles do appear they are merely descriptive, and not explanatory.

The impact of outside cultures—especially those of the urban complex, industrial, Western world—in each instance had some negative effects on these populations. But the nature of the contact was not always one of political subordination, economic exploitation, or other hegemonic relationship. Neither was the nature of the negative effect similar, much less identical. Approaches that emphasize center-periphery or metropole-dependency have relevance in terms of many aspects of the relationship, but not necessarily in terms of drinking.

Beer and spirits are clearly and importantly differentiated in most of these cultures, but their meanings and uses are not always significantly different. For that matter, "native" as contrasted with "foreign-introduced" beverages are not consistently treated in different ways.

National policy is totally irrelevant in terms of the patterns discussed here. So are advertising, education, treatment facilities, prevention programs, or any of the other institutional variables that are often cited in comparing drinking patterns among nation-states. Each of the cultures dealt with here is unusually homogeneous in terms of occupations, social status, education, and patterns of belief and behavior. Nevertheless, male-female differences are significant, and women—although normatively permitted to drink in ways like the men—normally do not do so in quite the same quantities. That is, women go through the same gestures, with the same quantities of beverages, but routinely spill or spit out enough so that they stay sober longer than their male associates. We need to learn more about how they learn this, why they do it, and what drinking, drunkenness, and drunken comportment mean to women.

A few of the Mestizos are joked about as alcoholics, said to be "addicted" and "worthless," but are kept within their families in the status of slightly dotty or helplessly sick members. None of the other cultures discussed here has any people who drink "too often" or at culturally "inappropriate" times.

Verbal and physical aggression sometimes accompanied drinking in the latter days among the Sirionó, and it often happens among the Aymara, when there is a preexisting grudge between individuals. Mestizos tend to become boastful or boisterous, in ways that are socially acceptable and unproblematic. The Camba remain striking in the apparent absence of anything that might be characterized as an "alcohol-related problem."

I have simply tried to raise a few of the more obvious questions that arise from these case studies. I hope that similar and expanded cross-cultural studies may eventually reveal some regularities, or patterned differences, in ways that will further illuminate a number of concepts, theories, processual assumptions, and other factors in alcohol studies. Easy generalizations based on a few cross-cultural similarities or differences with respect to generalized drinking patterns (as if a nation were characterized by only one) can easily be misleading, and context is crucial in appreciating historical trends, whether in terms of continuity or change. Practical implications in terms of policies for public health and social welfare are not definitive, except that "the sociocultural model" seems more apt than "the control model" (Heath, 1988).

***

I would like to thank A. M. Cooper, who shared with me the research on which this paper is based.

***

References

Babor, T. F. (Ed.) (1986) *Alcohol and Culture: Comparative Perspectives from Europe and Americas* (Annals of the New York Academy of Sciences, 472) (New York, New York Academy of Sciences).

Carter, W. E. (1977) Ritual, the Aymara, and the role of alcohol in human society, in du Toit, B. M. (Ed.), *Drugs, Rituals, and Altered States of Consciousness*, pp. 101–110 (Rotterdam, A. A. Halkema).

Davies, P. and Walsh, D. (1983) *Alcohol Problems and Alcohol in Europe* (London, Croom Helm).

Gill, L. (1991) *Peasants, Entrepreneurs, and Social Change: Frontier Development in Lowland Bolivia* (Boulder, CO, Westview).

Heath, D. B. (1958) Drinking patterns of the Bolivian Camba, *Quarterly Journal of Studies on Alcohol, 19*, pp. 491–508.

Heath, D. B. (1965) Comment, *Current Anthropology, 6*, pp. 289–290.

Heath, D. B. (1971) Peasant revolution, and drinking: Interethnic drinking patterns in two Bolivian communities, *Human Organization, 30* (2), pp. 179–186.

Heath, D. B. (1972) New patrons for old: Changing patron-client relationships in the Bolivian yungas, in Strickon, A. & Greenfield, S. M. (Eds.), *Structure and Process in Latin America: Patronage, Clientage and Power Systems*, pp. 101–137 (Albuquerque, University of New Mexico Press).

Heath, D. B. (1986) Concluding remarks, in Babor, T. (Ed.), *Alcohol and Culture: Comparative Perspectives from Europe and Americas* (Annals of the New York Academy of Sciences, 472), pp. 234–237 (New York, New York Academy of Sciences).

Heath, D. B. (1987) Cultural studies on drinking: Definitional problems, in Paakanen, P. & Sulkunen, P. (Eds.), *Cultural Studies on Drinking Problems: Report of a Conference* (Social Research Institute of Alcohol Studies, 176), pp. 177–180 (Helsinki, Social Research Institute of Alcohol Studies).

Heath, D. B. (1988) Emerging anthropological theory and models of alcohol use and alcoholism, in Chaudron, C. D. & Wilkinson. D. A. (Eds.), *Theories on Alcoholism*, pp. 353–410 (Toronto, Addiction Research Foundation).

Heath, D. B. (1991a) Uses and misuses of the concept of ethnicity in alcohol studies: An essay in deconstruction, *International Journal of the Addictions, 25(5A/6A)*, pp. 609–630.

Heath, D. B. (1991b) Continuity and change in drinking patterns of the Bolivian Camba, in Pittman, D. J. & White, H. R. (Eds.), *Society, Culture, and Drinking Patterns Re-examined*, pp. 78–86 (New Brunswick, NJ, Rutgers Center of Alcohol Studies).

Heath, D. B., Erasmus, C. J. & Buechler, H. C. (1969) *Land Reform and Social Revolution in Bolivia* (New York, Frederick A. Praeger).

Holmberg, A. R. (1950) *Nomads of the Long Bow: The Sirionó of Eastern Bolivia* (Institute of Social Anthropology Publication, 10) (Washington, Smithsonian Institution).

Holmberg, A. R. (1954) Adventures in culture change, in Spencer, R. F. (Ed.), *Method and Perspective in Anthropology*, pp. 103–113 (Minneapolis, University of Minnesota Press).

Kroeber, A. L. & Kluckhohn, C. (1952) *Culture: A Critical Review of Concepts and Definitions* (Papers of the Peabody Museum of American Archaeology and Ethnology, Harvard University, 47(1)) (Cambridge, MA, Peabody Museum).

MacAndrew, C. and Edgerton, R. B. (1969) *Drunken Comportment: A Social Explanation* (Chicago, Aldine).

Mäkelä, K., Room, R., Single, E., Sulkunen, P. & Walsh, B. (1981) *Alcohol, Society, and the State: 1, A Comparative Study of Alcohol Control* (Toronto, Addiction Research Foundation).

Mandelbaum, D. G. (1965) Alcohol and culture [with comments by 6 colleagues], *Current Anthropology, 6*, pp. 281–294.

Métraux, A. (1959) Revolution of the axe, *Diogenes, 25*, pp. 28–40.

Sharp, L. (1952) Steel axes for stone-age Australians, in Spicer, E. H. (Ed.), *Human Problems in Technological Change: A Casebook*, pp. 69–92 (New York, Russell Sage Foundation).

Stearman, A. (1984) The Yuqui connection: Another look at Sirionó deculturation, *American Anthropologist, 86*, pp. 630–650.

Stearman, A. (1985) *Camba and Kolla: Migration and Development in Santa Cruz Bolivia* (Gainesville, FL, University Presses of Florida).

Stearman, A. (1987) *No Longer Nomads: The Sirionó Revisited* (Lanham, NY, Hamilton Press).

Allyn MacLean Stearman is a professor of anthropology and dean of the honors college at University of Central Florida. Among her books are Camba and Kolla; San Rafael, Camba Town; No Longer Nomads; and Yuquí: Forest Nomads in a Changing World.

Whereas Messer writes about human rights in general terms (chapter 3), and Stavenhagen (chapter 13) shows how native peoples are increasingly organizing to secure them throughout various parts of Latin America, Stearman here shows how, in very practical ways, a dedicated anthropologist was able to muster the diverse resources that would make such a development a reality in a relatively isolated community that "outsiders" thought was on the verge of extinction. Academic and applied (or practicing) anthropology are by no means separate endeavors; each can complement and illuminate the other, as also in Bernard (chapter 10), Doughty (chapter 22), and others.

Ethnodevelopment and the Yuquí of Lowland Bolivia

Allyn MacLean Stearman

Lowland Bolivia is one of many areas in the world where indigenous people continue to struggle for the legal recognition of traditional territories and the right to have a determination over their resources. At the same time, safeguarding significant areas of the Bolivian Amazon and its natural resources has become a priority for Bolivian and international conservation and development organizations. Policy makers are now coming to recognize that many of these lands at risk are part of traditional indigenous homelands, and that their continued integrity may depend on supporting native peoples in their fight to secure territorial rights and then assisting them in developing strategies for sustainable resource use. This paper describes a project that attempted to combine conservation interests with efforts to assist the Yuquí, a recently contacted indigenous society, in finding ways to participate in national society without sacrificing their cultural identity and integrity in the process. This project came into being as the result of two unrelated but concurrent recent events in Bolivia: the Yuquí Indians were identified by the Bolivian government as possible recipients of an indigenous territory, and they were also targeted by the Interamerican Development Bank (IDB) as likely to be affected by the completion of a major highway, which made them eligible for significant funding for "ethnic protection."

Facing intense political pressure as the result of a massive march to La Paz carried out in 1990 by native peoples of the Bolivian Amazon who were demanding recognition of their traditional homelands, then-President Jaime Paz Zamora agreed to begin the process of establishing indigenous territories by Executive Order. During this period, negotiations for a highway construction loan were also underway between the IDB and the Bolivian Government. By law, a portion of the funds had to be earmarked to mitigate the possible negative impacts of the bank-funded road project on the environment and on indigenous peoples who fell within the area of influence of the proposed highway. The Yuquí were identified as being at risk from the effects of the new highway. Few in number, unrepresented among indigenous organizations, and therefore virtually invisible in national politics, the Yuquí had been unlikely to have received any notice by the Paz government when land allocations were being deter-

---

Written expressly for *Contemporary Cultures and Societies of Latin America*, Third Edition.

mined. However, their sudden appearance in a major IDB loan document brought their case to national attention at precisely the moment when such decisions were being made.

Thus, as the result of having carried out anthropological fieldwork for more than a decade among the Yuquí, I was contacted by the Bank and the Bolivian Government to help prepare the documentation necessary for both territorial recognition and the ethnic protection component of the loan. Part of my prior research had involved the tracking of resource-use by the Yuquí, and with those data in hand, I was able to convince the Bolivian government to increase the original territorial allocation of less than 50,000 hectares (about 125,000 acres) to more than 100,000. This larger land allotment would assure that the Yuquí would be able to continue their traditional hunting and gathering way of life for at least another two generations, and it would also provide a resource base that, through proper planning, could provide sustainable economic activities into the future. On April 9, 1992, the Yuquí received a grant of 115,000 hectares of land from the President of Bolivia, designated as the Yuquí Indigenous Territory. In May of that same year, I was contracted by the IDB and the Bolivian Government to direct what would become known as the Yuquí Ethnodevelopment Project.

Prior to contact by missionaries in the mid-1960s, the Yuquí Indians of the Bolivian Amazon were one of the few remaining nomadic hunting-and-gathering peoples in the world. They were true foragers, depending only on the resources of the forest they inhabited for their livelihood. They moved almost constantly in their pursuit of game, fish, honey, fruit, and other foods necessary for subsistence. At the time of contact, the first of three bands, all of which were eventually settled at a mission station on the Chimoré River, numbered only 43 people. With natural increase and the addition of two more groups subsequently contacted by the mission, the Yuquí population had reached almost 150 by 1995.

At present, the Yuquí are sedentary and practice some agriculture, but they continue to depend on foraging for much of their dietary intake. Unfortunately, they are located in a region of Bolivia that is being settled by homesteaders from the densely populated highlands who are seeking new lands to farm. The completion of the proposed highway will only increase the rate and density of settlement. With colonists encroaching on their foraging territory and competing for many of the same resources, the Yuquí find it increasingly difficult to feed themselves. Unlike many larger indigenous groups with a defined ancestral homeland and a strong sense of cultural identity, the few remaining Yuquí had become geographically dispersed and the fabric of their traditional culture was being slowly unraveled by the dependency relationship with the mission that had evolved over the course of what was now almost a generation.

The challenge of working with the Yuquí on the ethnodevelopment project was to help rebuild their fading sense of identity while at the same time providing them with the skills necessary to sustain themselves in a world that is aggressively encroaching on their traditional way of life. To this end, I organized a team of individuals skilled in working with tribal peoples and who were committed to the goal of creating greater self-sufficiency among the mission-dependent Yuquí.

Because of the need to develop sound leadership skills among the largely acephalous Yuquí in order to help them deal more effectively with the outside world, we moved quickly to establish a Yuquí Council. Each of the three contact groups selected a representative. One of our team members, José Bailaba, a Chiquitano representative from the major lowland Bolivian indigenous organization, *Central de Pueblos Indígenas del Oriente Boliviano* (CIDOB), was assigned to work with the Council members. Over the course of the 14-month project, José guided the Council members in more clearly understanding appropriate roles in community governance and in taking on wider responsibilities with regard to articulation with state society. One of these tasks was dealing with the increasingly complex problems that surrounded the establishment of the Yuquí Indigenous Territory.

It was one thing to receive government recognition of a Yuquí Territory, but entirely another to demarcate and defend it. Although the Executive Order was a legal and binding document, it was not followed by legislation that would provide funding to map and protect the territory. We decided to undertake this as part of our overall integrated development strategy. A graduate student at the University of Florida volunteered to undertake the mapping project as his master's thesis topic. Using a Global Positioning System (GPS), over a period of three months Keith Jarvis and members of the Yuquí Council mapped the entire territory. Fortunately, in establishing the boundaries, we had had the foresight to follow major rivers where possible, meaning that most of the mapping could be done quickly from a boat running at full speed as data points were automatically taken and stored from the satellite fixes received by the GPS unit. Back in the United States, Keith integrated the GPS data with the Geographic Information System to generate a full color, computerized map of the territory and its landforms. We made numerous copies of this map and circulated them to local residents and government officials. Within a very short time, we had established the credibility of the Yuquí Territory through the dissemination of a very powerful political tool, the map.

Our next task was to select and train three Yuquí forest guards and then convince the government to provide them with proper credentials. Recent legislation that gave greater recognition to indigenous rights facilitated this process, and the Yuquí guards were given written permission to expel illegal colonists and loggers from their territory. More importantly, they could also confiscate wood and equipment from the loggers. We began a schedule of monitoring the territory, at first taking along armed members of the national government's forestry unit to back up the Yuquí. Later, the Yuquí took over the patrols themselves. Within only a few months, word had spread among the illegal loggers that the Territory was now "off limits." A gratifying side effect of this activity was the growing awareness by the Yuquí that they were a "people" and had an identity that was linked to their territory.

With the expertise of Kent Redford, a conservation biologist currently working with the Nature Conservancy, a plan was developed to manage game resources. This plan included the creation of satellite hunting camps to lower pressure on local wildlife, which the Yuquí depend on heavily for subsistence. These camps also served to deter encroachment by colonists into those areas of the Yuquí territory most susceptible to invasion.

We completed a new clinic building, equipped it, and with the assistance of Judy Gill, another team member and a registered nurse, we trained a Yuquí couple to be health-care workers. Judy's efforts also resulted in securing government recognition of the Yuquí health post. This entitled the health-care workers to a salary and access to expertise and medicines provided through the national public health-care system.

We expanded the existing school by increasing the number of classrooms to provide adequate space for the growing student population. Included in the new building was a kitchen and cafeteria to provide daily breakfast, which Yuquí women took turns preparing from surplus food available through the Catholic Relief Service (CARITAS). We also initiated a program of teacher training so that the Yuquí would have their own teachers and introduced bilingual materials into the existing curriculum as well as courses in carpentry and sewing.

Once the new clinic was completed and a new store building erected, the old building that had served as the mission store and clinic was renovated to became a new community center where the Council could meet. The mission also relinquished its involvement in the operation of the store, enabling us to train another Yuquí couple to take over its day-to-day management.

Housing had also become a critical problem, since many Yuquí had abandoned many of the small, single-family dwellings built by the missionaries, in order to reside alongside their extended kin in others. These tiny houses had been hastily constructed and were on the verge of collapse. Eventually, working with groups of extended families, we replaced all of the Yuquí structures with a new design which we called "long-houses" that incorporated several nuclear families in a single structure. This new design better reflected traditional communal living patterns, created a more efficient use of limited space in the settlement in that more dry area was available for house gardens, and the new configuration allowed for the consolidation of latrines, which previously had been largely lacking in the community.

Other projects included building and stocking a carpentry workshop so that young Yuquí could learn to make furniture such as benches and tables for their new homes, something else that was now a felt need. Later, these skills could provide them with an additional source of income. With the carpentry functioning, woodworking was added to the school curriculum as noted above. There were many failures as well. We started a tree nursery to encourage the Yuquí to plant more fruit trees, especially native varieties, but we were unsuccessful in our efforts to discourage them from harvesting mature trees by cutting them down. A crop of any kind that year also proved impossible. The rainy season was protracted and intense, making clearing futile because we could not burn the underbrush. Our efforts to encourage the Yuquí to make modest improvements in agriculture for subsistence were largely unsuccessful.

After 14 months with the Yuquí, we concluded our contract and prepared for the gradual withdrawal of project personnel. It was difficult, knowing that we needed, but did not have, a great deal more time to nurture many of the complex processes that had been initiated. We left behind many tangible results of our work, including a well-equipped clinic with Yuquí health workers, a new store now run by Yuquí, an enlarged and improved school, Yuquí teachers-in-training, a carpentry shop, and new housing. Infrastructure such as this provided capability for many kinds of innovative activities, and for the first time since they had become a sedentary people, the Yuquí felt that their indigenous community had achieved stature among others in the region.

Receiving legal recognition of a homeland, demarcating and mapping this territory, and actively protecting it from encroachment placed the Yuquí in an unusually strong position as an indigenous people. The intangibles, however, are what ultimately will determine their ability to cope with an uncertain future. The Yuquí Council continues to function, but it will be many years before it becomes a stable governmental body. Yuquí leaders are learning the skills necessary to ensure their people's rightful place in Bolivian society, but this process as well will take time. There is a new pride in being Yuquí, particularly among the youth, but there are also powerfully seductive external forces that may lure them away from their people and traditions. For their part, the missionaries are coming to better understand that the Yuquí are capable of taking charge of their own lives and of making choices to determine the course of their future, and that they need support in these efforts and not discouragement. Still, the Yuquí are few in number, and history has shown that the odds are against the cultural survival of such small remnant populations. The Yuquí have some extremely difficult challenges ahead, but if they succeed, those of us who have shared in their struggle will certainly rejoice in their triumph.

Author's Note

The Yuquí are a small group, only recently contacted, in a region of the Amazon Basin that remains relatively unknown even today. Interestingly, one of the earliest comprehensive ethnographic studies carried out in the region was written by the editor of this book: Dwight Heath's 1959 doctoral dissertation, "Camba: A Study of Land and Society in Eastern Bolivia" (Yale). Only two anthropologists have studied the Yuquí in any depth. The other is Erwin Melgar, a Bolivian student of mine. He continues to carry out research among the Yuquí as well as assisting them in ethnodevelopment activities. There have also been brief visits by a few other anthropologists, missionaries, and journalists who are concerned primarily with issues of dependency and religion.

Of my writings, the best overview of Yuquí culture is the ethnography published by Holt, Rinehart and Winston, *Yuquí: Forest Nomads in a Changing World* (1989). Other shorter works of mine that are accessible to readers of English include an article in *Natural History*, "Losing Game" (1994); and several professional publications among which are: "The Yuquí Connection" in the *American Anthropologist* (1984); "Yuquí Foragers in the Bolivian Amazon" in the *Journal of Anthropological Research* (1990); "The Effects of Settler Incursion on the Fish and Game Resources of the Yuquí in *Human Organization* (1990); "Making a Living in the Tropical Forest" in *Human Ecology* and "Only Slaves Climb Trees" in *Human Nature* (1994).

Melgar's senior thesis and other unpublished papers are in Spanish, presumably not available in this country. Articles about the missionaries working with the Yuquí appear in *Time* (December 27, 1982), the *New York Times Magazine* (February 23, 1992), and the *Chicago Tribune Magazine* (December 12, 1993).

Karin Elain Tice is an anthropologist at Formative Evaluation Research Associates. Her best-known book is Kuna Crafts, Gender, and the Global Economy.

Often there is a division of labor between the sexes that results in women's work being depreciated as less gainful that that of men. In some other situations, traditionally "female" crafts provide solid sources of income that women often control for their own purposes.

The distinctive and colorfully ornamented blouses of the Kuna of Panama have rapidly become tourist souvenirs, even sometimes regarded as art objects. In addition to briefly sketching the history of this evolution, Tice shows linkages among social organization, ethnicity, gender, and economics.

Locally appreciated needlework has taken very different directions elsewhere (Femenías, chapter 25), as has female entrepreneurship (Buechler, chapter 18).

Kuna *Molas* and the Global Economy

Karin E. Tice

Although it is clear that the Kuna had at least sporadic access to cloth as far back as the 1600s, there is no known written record of cloth *molas* until the 1800s. In 1868, another explorer described *molas* as "short sleeved chemises extending to the knees" (De Puydt 1868:97). In 1887, yet another traveler wrote: "on the bottom part [of the chemises worn by Kuna women] there is a band of about 10 centimeters with red and yellow designs" (Restrepo Tirado 1887).

Stout provides us with a more detailed description of cloth *molas*. He wrote (1947:67): "Sixty years ago [in the late 1880s] this *mola* was of plain, usually dark blue material with a simple band of red cloth around the bottom. It reached to the knees and was worn with a knee-length underskirt painted with geometric designs. A little later (1890–1900) women began to use brighter colored cloth when it became accessible through the traders and to decorate the blouse along the hem with a simple appliqué of contrasting colors."

Decoration of *mola* blouses steadily increased until by the 1920s Kuna women covered all but the yoke and sleeves of their blouses with designs. In the 1920s, *molas* were again described as almost knee-length chemises. They consisted of two decorated panels (two layers thick), sleeves, and a yoke. The same cotton cloth was used for the sleeves, yoke, and bottom panel. This cloth was printed with tiny dots, flowers, or some other pattern, in two contrasting colors. The second, top layer of the panel was one solid color of cloth. Patterns were cut out of this top layer, partially revealing the patterned cloth below. Raw cloth edges were painstakingly folded under and whipstitched into place. Designs were still basically geometric, though *molas* with flowers and animals were also sewn (Brown 1925).

Wearing *molas* has come to symbolize Kuna ethnic pride tied to a "traditional" way of life (Swain 1982:114). *Molas* are "THE Cuna ethnic boundary marker par excellence in that for both Cuna and non-Cuna it is a constantly visual, striking sign of *Cunaité*" (Sherzer and Sherzer 1976:27). After the Revolution, the majority of Kuna women living in the communities where the colonial police had been stationed proudly and defiantly dressed in *mola* and their *asuolos* (nose rings). Most women living on Nargana, however, the island most heavily influenced by missionaries, continued to wear Western clothing. Since the revolt, wearing *mola* has been seen by conservative and moderate Kuna (both male and female) as an important symbol of the Kuna people's right to self-determination.

Kuna women began to use designs in their *molas* that reflected the socioeconomic changes that were occurring as a result of the increased movement of people, cash, and consumer goods between San Blas, Colón, and Panama City. *Mola* designs became increasingly varied and complex. Pictures of fishnet twine labels, matchbox covers, and shotgun shell boxes, among other things, were copied and embellished (Parker and Parker 1977).

Mola commercialization and the shift from production for personal use to production for exchange did not occur all at once; rather, it has been a process that started in the 1950s and has continued ever since. While few changes related to *mola* production occurred in the 1940s and the 1950s, shifts in the region's articulation with the international market in the 1960s profoundly affected *mola* production and sales. The history of this process, closely tied to the development of the national tourist industry and intertwined with changes in agricultural production, coconut cash cropping, and labor migration, will be the focus of the rest of this chapter.

MOLA COMMERCIALIZATION AND AGRICULTURAL PRODUCTION

Coconuts provided the Kuna with their major source of cash income throughout the first half of the twentieth century. During the 1950s and the 1960s, however, coconut palms were affected by a severe blight, so that coconut production sharply decreased. Initially, the blight affected only the eastern side of San Blas, but it moved quickly westward until the entire region was affected. An anthropologist working on Tupile during the time of the blight wrote (Holloman 1969:122): "the combined effect of decline in the total number of trees and of decreased production from blighted trees accounted for a decline in coconut income among Tupile residents of nearly 80 percent over the decade 1957–67, and even greater decline in total production." Thus, the primary income-generating activity was decreasing at the same time that the market for *molas* was beginning to expand. This decrease in overall income, combined with increased migration of Kuna men in search of wage labor and the subsequent decrease in subsistence farming and fishing, had an enormous impact on households in San Blas. In many households, women began to purchase items such as rice, sugar, and fish, which men had previously provided.

Women began to trade their *molas* for needed goods such as sugar, salt, kerosene, and cloth in local Kuna stores and with Kuna petty traders. The store owners and itinerant traders were all Kuna men. Foreign intermediaries and tourists, both male and female, provided an additional but infrequent option for selling *molas*. Both tourists and foreign intermediaries paid higher prices for *molas* than did the local Kuna store owners and traders, but this alternative was available only to Kuna women living in the area where tourism is concentrated.

It is difficult to pinpoint an exact date for the broader commercialization of *molas* because the Kuna tend not to remember dates, integration into the international market occurred at different times on various islands, and it was a process that took place over a number of years. It is clear, however, that a major shift in the organization of production and marketing relations occurred during the 1960s, when *mola* commercialization became articulated with the international market in a major way. In this decade we find a shift from production for use, with a few incidental sales, to production for exchange on the international market. Intermediaries began purchasing *molas* by the hundreds at very low prices: $2.00 to $2.50 each. Many Kuna women became desperate to sell or trade their *molas*. Households came to rely increasingly on the sale or trade of *molas* to meet their daily needs.

In the 1960s, the sale of *molas* took place through already-existing patterns of exchange. With the decrease in coconut production and new availability of places to sell *molas* in Panama City, San Blas store owners and itinerant traders began to accept both *molas* and coconuts in exchange for merchandise. These Kuna men served as the principal intermediaries between producers of *molas* in San Blas and the non-Kuna store owners in Panama City. Unlike those Kuna men who sold small quantities of *mola* blouses directly to consumers in the Canal Zone as favors to their female relatives, these intermediaries began to purchase *molas* by the hundreds from women on their own and surrounding islands. Store owners in Panama City wanted individual *mola* panels and not whole blouses, so women ripped apart their beautiful blouses before trading or selling them.

Original artists were soon forgotten, and only very recently cut designs could be traced back to their creators. A woman's design might come to her in a dream, or she might use her imagination to create one. Women draw their inspiration from a wide range of visual images, life events, and abstract concepts. In the 1970s, Sherzer and Sherzer 1976:32) noted: "*molas* do not represent Cuna ancestors, mythical beings or scenes, or good or bad spirits of a supernatural nature. Nor do they contain designs or motifs that have a magical value." Women have sewn *molas* drawing design elements from electric fans, televisions, underwear, designs on matchbox covers. As new commercial goods entered the region, *mola* producers incorporated these items into their *molas*. In the 1940s, *mola* makers began to incorporate advertisement, trademark, and package label designs into their *molas*. *Mola* makers have also drawn inspiration from sporting events, Canal Zone and U.S. military themes, Christian religious imagery, illustrations from books and magazines, flight images, Western clothing and common objects, and games and entertainment (Parker and Parker 1977). In the 1960s, when the Kuna were drawn increasingly into national-level politics and the role of the Panamanian national government expanded in San Blas, *mola* blouses began to be used as one way women could express their opinions on political and economic issues. For example, women sewed their favorite presidential candidate on their blouses (Parker and Parker 1977). Sometimes *mola* designs mix reality and abstraction.

In the 1980s, highly skilled *mola* makers and designers had gained prestige within their own communities. Some had become known throughout the region for their special abilities; a few were known by *mola* buyers abroad. Kuna women use intricacy of design, use of color, and fineness of stitching to judge their own and each other's *molas*. Producers talked among themselves about *molas* in process. They shared ideas and pieces of cloth, and critiqued one another's designs and color combinations.

INTERNATIONAL CONTEXT

Interest in ethnic arts in general, and *molas* in particular, increased during the 1960s and the 1970s in the United States and Europe. *Molas* became increasingly sought after by museums, galleries, fashion designers, and home decorators in the United States. They were exhibited in various places, including the Field Museum of Natural History in Chicago, the Pan American Union in Washington, D.C., and several university art departments. Art galleries in several cities, notably Miami and New York, also featured *molas*. Newspaper articles appeared acclaiming *molas* as genuine works of art and urging people to buy quality *molas* while they still could.

Molas also became visible in the realm of fashion, design, and home decoration. For example, in 1970, a *mola* skirt was featured on the cover of the Nieman Marcus

Christmas catalogue. From 1966 to 1978, no fewer than four popular books about *molas* were published in English. These ranged from "how-to" books to those destined for display on coffee tables. During this period, numerous articles appeared in home decorating and craft magazines describing how *molas* could be used as pillows and wall hangings to beautify homes. Promotion of interest in *molas*, whether as part of a commercial endeavor or a cultural event, resulted in increased demand.

With their commercialization, *mola* makers started producing *molas* intended specifically for sale. Appadurai (1986:16) has defined these as "commodities by destination, that is, objects intended by their producers principally for exchange." Throughout the 1980s, different sizes and shapes of *molas* were produced for sale, though women still sold their used blouses. Women sewed *mola* panels (approximately fourteen inches by seventeen inches), *molitas* (little *molas* roughly six inches by seven inches), and round *mola* patches about three inches in diameter. While the panels used in *mola* blouses might vary by several inches, the size of *mola* panels, *molitas*, and patches produced for sale varied little, and these were recognized throughout the San Blas region as distinct size categories. During the 1980s, in Mandinga Bay, the area of San Blas frequented by tourists, women started sewing parrots and the words "San Blas" onto T-shirts to sell to the tourists.

NEW SOCIAL CONTEXTS FOR *MOLA* USE

Whether people buy *molas* as examples of Kuna art, as souvenirs, or for personal use influences the type of *molas* that are produced as well as the producers' relationship to the productive process. *Molas* may be viewed as fine art to be viewed in galleries and museums, as financial investments, as designs removed from their social context to be used for interior decorating, as ethnic handicrafts made by the Kuna people, or as "souvenirs" from an "exotic" place. *Molas* may also decorate other usable items. For example, in 1985 there were a number of non-Kuna Panamanian women who created handbags, skirts, vests, change-purses, and other such items with *molas*. Some bought *mola* panels already made and incorporated them into their designs; others contracted for piecework to provide them with particular shapes and patterns. Out of five of these women I interviewed, four had other women working for them sewing handbags and other items. One woman purchased mass-produced bags and other items and decorated them with *mola* patches.

Within a newly organized *mola* cooperative, personal savings were deposited in an interest-drawing bank account in Panama City. Members might withdraw their savings at any time for personal use. Overhead income was used to pay the administrator and the other women who worked in the cooperative store. It was also used to pay for office supplies and gasoline for the cooperative's boat, which transported members to and from cooperative educational seminars. Leftover funds were used for outreach or helping new local chapters get started, or they went into the revolving fund for cloth or became part of the cooperative's general pool of capital. They also occasionally bought food and other supplies cooperatively, thereby enjoying economies of scale.

In addition to their appeal to tourists, by 1985 *molas* had become a well-recognized symbol of Panama. *Molas* were hung in prominent public places throughout Panama City. Large murals made from numerous *mola* panels sewn together covered entire walls in one of Panama's major hotels and in the lobbies of two banks. In 1985, it was not uncommon to find framed *mola* panels hanging in hotel lobbies, government offices, and banks. The Panamanian flag was a popular theme for these *molas*. In addition to cloth, materials such as paint and tile might be used to create these designs. One gas station had *mola* designs painted in bright yellow and orange on the columns next to the gas pumps. Another had a full wall painted with *mola* designs. Decorative ceramic tiles painted with *mola* designs were prominent on at least two public buildings in the city.

Molas produced specifically as public art might or might not be made by Kuna women. Sometimes designs would be copied from already-existing *molas*, and Kuna women were not involved in either the creation or the production of the items. At other times, Kuna women were asked to sew the *molas* needed for a particular project.

REFLECTIONS

Class, gender, and ethnicity form an intricate tapestry defining who sells what to whom, where, and for how much. The division of labor by gender determines who can sell where and accounts, in part, for unequal access to income from *mola* sales. It is important to note, however, that, although gender clearly defines access to certain markets, socioeconomic differentiation among the Kuna cuts across gender lines. Furthermore, Kuna men and women both earn less than non-Kuna retail store owners and intermediaries who sell to stores in the United States, Europe, and Japan. Selling *molas* has not allowed Kuna merchants to purchase land or labor, or to acquire power locally or nationally.

Although new social contexts for using *molas* have affected Kuna *mola* makers' relationship to their craft, this cannot be viewed as unidirectional. Producer and consumer knowledge about the production, exchange, and consumption of *molas* within specific historical and cultural contexts is a dynamic area within which conflicting and sometimes converging interests are defined and negotiated. *Mola* designs, colors, and shapes have all changed as a result of their commercialization. Graburn (1976:31) points out that the "impetus for innovations may come from inside or outside the Fourth World—as a result of artistic excitement, ethnic revitalization, or simply as an economic response to the *perceived* desires of the consumer."

Kuna *mola* makers not only have responded to the perceived desires of the consumer but also have carefully observed consumer behavior and have attempted to shape that behavior. In some cases, the Kuna have used their knowledge about consumers to their advantage. They have taught tourists and merchants about the social context and value of designs and in the process have developed products with increased value on the market. Creating new designs and products is not always a creative process, however. Some "innovations" have been externally imposed on impoverished *mola* makers who are forced to sew almost anything that provides them with a source of income.

Appadurai (1986:13) has argued that things have a social life and "can move in and out of the commodity state, that such movements can be slow or fast, reversible or terminal, normative or deviant." *Molas* are clearly simultaneously both in and out of the commodity state. Most Kuna women sew *molas* for their own use as well as to sell without ever wearing. The extent to which individual Kuna women commoditize their *molas* depends on a series of interrelated factors related to household subsistence production and migration. One group of Kuna women has attempted to equalize access to the market by organizing a *mola* cooperative.

Active cooperative members were assured of a steady source of income. Also, the cooperative-sponsored savings plan provided women with a reserve of cash to use in case of emergency, illness, or death in their household. This was important during the tourist season as well as at other times. Apart from sewing *molas*, their principal activity as active members was bulk buying of plantains and kerosene both to consume and to resell.

References

Appadurai, Arjun (ed.). 1986. *The Social Life of Things: Commodities in Cultural Perspectives.* Cambridge: Cambridge University Press.

Brown, Lady Richmond. 1925. *Unknown Tribes: Uncharted Seas.* New York: D. Appleton.

De Puydt, Lucien. 1868. *Account of Scientific Explorations in the Isthmus of Darién in the Years 1861 and 1865.* London: Journal of the Royal Geographical Society *(vol. 38).*

Graburn, Nelson. 1976. *Ethnic and Tourist Arts: Cultural Expressions from the Fourth World.* Berkeley & Los Angeles: University of California Press.

Holloman, Regina. 1969. "Developmental Change in San Blas." PhD dissertation. Northwestern University.

Parker, Ann, and Neal Parker. 1977. *Molas: Folk Art of the Cuna Indians.* New York: Clarkson N. Potter.

Restrepo Tirado, Ernesto. 1887. "Un viaje al Darién: apuntes de carretera." Bogotá.

Sherzer, Dina, and Joel Sherzer. 1976. "Mormaknamaloe: The Cuna Mola." In *Ritual and Symbol in Native Central America*, pp. 21–42. Edited by Philip Young and James Howe. University of Oregon Anthropological Papers, no. 9, Eugene: University of Oregon, Dept. of Anthropology.

Stout, David. 1947. *San Blas Cuna Acculturation: An Introduction.* New York: Viking Fund.

Swain, Margaret. 1982. "Being Cuna and Female: Ethnicity Mediating Change in Sex Roles," In *Sex Roles and Social Change*, pp. 102–123. Edited by Christine Loveland and Franklin Loveland. Urbana: University of Illinois Press.

Paul L. Doughty is Distinguished Service Professor Emeritus, having long taught anthropology at University of Florida. He played a variety of important roles throughout much of the history of the Cornell-Vicos Project, as well as having conducted other research in Peru. His best-known books are Huaylas: An Andean District in Search of Progress, *and* Peasants, Power, and Applied Social Change *(with H. F. Dobyns and H. D. Lasswell).*

Imagine, if you can, a U.S. university as landlord of a feudal estate. Imagine a succession of North American academics working hard at trying to understand a community of Indians who dress, farm, and speak much as did the Inca in colonial times. Then imagine those same people trying to introduce democratic principles and appropriate bits of modern know-how, while simultaneously "looking over their shoulders" (figuratively) in an effort to understand the complex processes of cultural change and the equally complex phenomenon of selective resistance to change, or continuity.

It all really happened, and the Vicos project was famous as an enlightened initial experiment in "participant intervention." Controversial, in Peru and elsewhere, it remains unique in terms of local impact combined with anthropological research, as explained here by Doughty, who played a number of different roles at different times.

The self-consciously developmental concern of this project contrasts markedly with the more academically oriented Harvard-Chiapas project (Vogt, chapter 5). The degree of sustained political and administrative involvement was unusual and contrasts markedly with the more consultative approach used by Stearman (chapter 20), or the more revolutionary approach described by Collier (chapter 17).

Ending Serfdom in Peru
The Struggle for Land and Freedom in Vicos
Paul L. Doughty

In 1948 Peru and the other Andean nations were only beginning to confront the negative legacies of three centuries of colonial rule. The Spanish adventurer, Francisco Pizarro, encountered and conquered the Inca Empire, converting its diverse peoples into reluctant subjects of a distant monarchy dedicated to the extraction of all the wealth that could be mined, produced, captured and subsequently exported.[1] A critical element in that colonial process was the unremitting exploitation of the native population.

As this cataclysm unfolded, Andean peoples were subordinated to a colonial system that made them permanent servants of the conquerors, with diminishing ability to control their lives. It was a regime Andean peoples little understood but a domination they had to survive from 1532–1821. By the end of that regime, the Incas had been reduced to a denigrated ethnic class called Indians—*indios*. Ironically, those trends only deepened after the Andean nations won independence from Spain in the 1820s. The creole elites who took over envisioned themselves as the heirs of the colonial regime with rights to the wealth and power that had been the preserve of the Spanish Crown and its agents, including the right to utilize and control the labor and productivity of the Andean peoples. This pattern of sociocultural, economic and political relationships continued with few if any significant changes favoring the native peoples.

THE "INDIAN PROBLEM"

From the earliest colonial years, the survivors of the conquest posed difficulties for the conquerors: they spoke non-European languages; their beliefs and behaviors were

---

Written expressly for *Contemporary Cultures and Societies of Latin America*, Third Edition.

puzzling, and they seemed unresponsive to, or incapable of, any progress or improvement. As decades passed their situation became classified as "the Indian problem" in government and social circles. Thus, the presumed inferiority of Indians served to validate the power and status of elites who claimed to "protect" them from their inadequacies and ignorance.

Although numerous uprisings of peasants and serfs occurred throughout the Andean highlands where the Indian peoples were concentrated, such efforts to lighten the onerous weight of exploitation had only very limited regional and temporal impacts. The onset of the twentieth century saw this former heartland of the Incas struggling to modernize itself through newly established public education, road building, and the re-establishment, in 1919–20, of Indian Communities as corporate landholders (if they could prove they had been awarded a community title under Spanish rule). By the early 1960s, about 1,500 Peruvian indigenous communities succeeded in being reinstated after onerous bureaucratic procedures but an estimated 3,000 communities had not been so recognized. Thus, most of the Indian peoples benefited little from even those ostensibly "liberal" laws and policies.

From early colonial times, a majority of Andean Indians had found refuge in the obscurity of remote hamlets where they were at the fringes of governmental control, or, they lived within the boundaries of large private estates, isolated from participation in national or even regional affairs as landlords "protected" their agricultural labor force from outside contact, sustaining their control of it. Those estates, called *haciendas,* were owned by families belonging to the regional or national upper classes, and, in the 1900s, by corporations such as mining companies or agribusiness operations. Acquired and aggregated through inheritance, purchase, or fraud, such properties included not only former Indian lands but the people who had always lived there. At mid-twentieth century there were some such estates as large as 150,000 hectares, on which lived and worked almost five percent of all Peruvians.[2] The *hacienda* system with its tradition of control and subordination through peonage was a hallmark of Peruvian and South American society in general.

HACIENDA VICOS

A good example of such an estate was one called Vicos, located in the high Andes about 200 miles north of Peru's capital, Lima. Situated in the middle of the 125 mile-long intermontane valley called the Callejón de Huaylas, Vicos occupied hilly lands which rise upward from the valley floor at 9,500 feet, into the spectacular Cordillera Blanca,[3] reaching over 22,000 feet above sea level. With the snow and glaciers of the Cordillera looming overhead, Vicos in 1949 was home to 1,702 serfs (called *colonos*) who were permitted to live on the 43,750 acre estate serving the landlord as farm workers and as unpaid servants for three days a week in "exchange" for tiny plots used as homesites and for planting subsistence crops. As a reward or *temple* for fulfilling these obligations, the landlord provided workers with a daily tip of twenty *centavos* (worth about 6 U.S. cents), a shot of alcohol, and a handful of coca leaf to chew while working. The *colonos* did not own the houses they built, nor were they free to sell their labor or the products thereof outside the *hacienda* without permission of the landlord or his agent.

This form of manor, often likened to Europe's feudal system of the Middle Ages, was the norm for such estates, with the owners usually living elsewhere, visiting the property only at planting or harvest times, if they came at all. In the case of Vicos, the owner was not an individual but ironically, a government welfare agency, The Public Beneficent Society of Huaraz, an institution established in early colonial times when Vicos became one of its properties (in 1594).[4] As one of 55 such estates owned by the

Beneficent Society, Vicos was leased to a bidder on 5–10 year contracts. Hacienda Vicos thus not only had an absentee institutional owner, but a temporary landlord as well who managed the estate through an administrative employee. In a final contradiction, the Beneficent Society used the rents generated from the thousands of impoverished *colonos* like those at Vicos to maintain a hospital for the poor in Huaraz, a place where Vicosinos rarely if ever were allowed to go.

The administrator of the manor held absolute control over the peons, giving or denying permission for them to travel to market or elsewhere in search of paid employment, to seek education, or even to get married. In the name of the landlord, he could incarcerate malcontents in the private *hacienda* jail, administer whippings and alter the distribution of subsistence land without any protection being available to the *colonos* and their families. If asked, the people of Vicos described themselves as "slaves," owned by the landlords. For people living in the industrialized world at midtwentieth century, it was a shocking revelation that such conditions could not only exist in "modern" times, but be a common characteristic of many countries in the Americas.[5]

THE CONTEXTS OF CHANGE

The enormous impact of a colonial system through which Spain ruled its worldwide empire from 1500 to 1820 and its cultural, economic and political legacy provided the guidelines for the people who subsequently governed the independent nations. In 1948 Peru was a nation not only with great socioeconomic disparities, but one which was deeply segregated by region, culture and class. Eighty-seven percent of the country could only be reached on horseback or on foot, and people living on the eastern Andean slopes and Amazon basin were largely untouched by national affairs. In the Andean highlands, where a majority of Peruvians then lived, most Quechua and Aymara Indians as well as many *cholos* and *mestizos*[6] worked as peons or were enmeshed in *hacienda* systems like the one at Vicos.

Consequently in 1950, it was commonly thought that one could not "do much" with the Indians, or expect them to be capable of self-help. Nevertheless, with the end of World War II, a watershed moment arrived; worldwide currents of change began to have their impact in Peru. Demands for resources created new economic conditions for the country; the population was increasing rapidly; and numerous international programs sought to educate, develop, and stimulate societies such as that of Peru. Just as the world was increasingly caught up in vast political, economic and cultural changes (then referred to as "Westernization" or "modernization"), Peru sought to engage itself in this movement. Having signed on to the new United Nations' initiatives, issues of national development, dormant since the 1920s, again became an important concern for Peru.

The government embarked on various programs of agricultural and industrial development seeking investments to improve the productive infrastructure. One of these was the construction of a major hydroelectric plant in the Callejón de Huaylas. At the northern end of the valley, electricity was to be generated by the Santa River as it plunged towards the Pacific coast. The power was destined to drive a French-designed steel mill that was to be built in the small Pacific port of Chimbote, which was already being transformed from a proverbially sleepy fishing town into a sprawling city of squatter settlements by the explosive growth of the fishing industry that made Peru at that time the world's leading fishing nation. In Peru, these developments were considered a harbinger of the industrialization and progress which would elevate the nation to economic leadership in Latin America.[7]

Attracted by these events in 1948, San Marcos University's[8] newly organized Institute of Ethnology, led by two of its professors, Jorge Muelle and Allan R. Holmberg of the Smithsonian Institution, initiated a series of studies designed to examine the changes which would take place in forthcoming years in traditional Andean societies. Undertaking field surveys with their students, they visited the Callejón de Huaylas, studying several of the small provincial towns and villages, including Hacienda Vicos, touted by many as the "most typical" of Andean estates.

Located six kilometers uphill from the small district capital of Marcará, Vicos was rarely visited by any outsiders and seemed isolated from contemporary events in almost every way. The anthropologists thought that the *hacienda* should be included in any larger study of social change as representative of the least modernized and poorest population in the Callejón. Mario C. Vazquez, a Peruvian graduate student, undertook a study of the Vicosinos (people of Vicos) under Holmberg's tutelage, living on the *hacienda* for many months in 1949–50.[9] By this time, Holmberg had joined the Anthropology faculty at Cornell University and incorporated Vazquez's study as part of a bold proposal to assist the Vicosinos as part of Cornell's far-flung studies of sociocultural change.[10] They thought that Vicos would be an excellent place to demonstrate a strategy for improving the lives of people, contrary to the prevailing opinions of many Peruvians, who considered Indians unworthy of such attention and incapable of "advancement."

Enlisting the support of Dr. Carlos Monge Medrano, a prestigious research physician and president of the Instituto Indigenista Peruano,[11] they developed a plan to "attend to the improvement of living standards of the inhabitants of Hacienda Vicos, until the moment that they can take a progressive role in the modern world."[12] They outlined several broad theoretical goals dealing with social change and research methodology in applied contexts and included a plan to train students to deal with Peru's rural development issue. In addition, there was a multifaceted program of activities in the fields of agricultural production and animal husbandry, social organization and cooperatives, marketing, nutrition, health, and education.

THE PROJECT BEGINS

To do this, the Peruvian government signed a unique agreement with Cornell University establishing the basis for project operations and responsibilities. In late 1951, the Cornell-Peru Project (CPP)[13] took over the lease on the estate from a bankrupt agribusiness company at the going rate of about 600 U.S. dollars a year, to be paid the Beneficent Society for a five-year period. This gave the university usufruct of not only the 43,750 acres[14] of the estate for any productive purpose, but also the use of the "free" labor of the resident *colonos* according to custom: as field hands, household servants, shepherds or any other task to be assigned. It was a unique experiment for a university.

Based on Vazquez's initial research and that done by Holmberg and his collaborators in 1951–53, the situation at Vicos was clearly defined with respect to levels of living and estate operations. The initial strategy announced was only a starting point; subsequent actions evolved as all parties to the project gained experience. The anthropologists approached the task with the elementary theoretical and methodological tools that were at their disposal at the time, developed from community studies and ethnographic styles of the era. Holmberg himself had done research in Peru, as well as pioneering studies in the Bolivian Amazon for several years where concerns about the fate of native peoples and his interests in directed cultural change were launched.[15]

The immediate project tasks were clear. The agribusiness concern that had rented the *hacienda* was unsuccessfully raising flax and paid no attention to food crops, a fact which contributed to substantial caloric deficits among the people because, under the *hacienda*, they had customarily lived by stealing a portion of the landlord's crop when they gleaned the fields.[16] The situation therefore was critical for Vicosinos, who, as research revealed, were suffering from endemic malnutrition on about 76% of the minimum daily requirements as determined by the Ministry of Health survey in 1952.[17] Depending upon a largely vegetarian diet, the production of their staple crop, potatoes, had also declined severely as had other important food crops such as corn. This, with all the restraints imposed by peonage, made their situation acute with respect to general health and well-being. They suffered universally from a plethora of gastrointestinal, respiratory and other common diseases to a degree not found in neighboring non-Indian, mestizo towns such as Marcará.

The other indicators which characterized this typical Andean population of Quechua-speaking *colonos*, are summarized by Vazquez:[18]

> In 1952 Vicos was a typical case of Andean socio-economic backwardness: 100% of the population was rural and (96%) illiterate, only 4% were bilingual (Spanish and Quechua), and people lived not knowing about the world outside and shrinking from national institutions: for example they knew nothing of the national government, had no active participation in the modern economy of the country, they did not vote in national elections, they avoided the (obligatory) military service and had no interest in the education of their children.

The most significant fact of life for the Vicosinos however was their subordination to the *hacienda* system of peonage and the absolute control of their lives by the landlord, of which these other characteristics were symptomatic. As one elderly Vicosino explained to me in 1960, "back then, we were just slaves of the *patrón,* worth nothing." The distribution of power in Vicos was controlled by the *patrón* and his agent, who appointed the field bosses and foremen, determined the distribution, size and location of *chacras*[19] to the *colonos,* denied or gave permission for people to work outside the estate, assigned people to work various service tasks at no pay, and administered corporal punishment or incarceration in the *hacienda* jail.

No Vicosinos voted and the only organization that was permitted them on the estate was that of the religious hierarchy, the *varayoc* (staff carriers) who organized the annual calendar of fiestas at the behest of the parish priest in the district capital of Marcará. The priest, however, while using the *varayoc* as his errand boys, rarely put in a appearance at Vicos because Vicosinos usually had no money with which to pay his fees. Hence most Vicosinos, although counted as Catholics, were unbaptized, unconfirmed, and went to their final resting places in the rustic *hacienda* cemetery without clerical attendance.

To alter this situation, the project aimed primarily at encouraging such changes as would enhance the community and average Vicosino's levels of living and ability to function successfully in Peruvian society instead of being largely exploited by it without other recourse. The native Quechua culture of Vicos, although strongly linked to its pre-conquest past, had been heavily modified by almost four centuries of unrelieved serfdom. In a very real sense, the *hacienda* molded the people to its interests, systematically denying them any options to change and thus preserving a particular kind of native culture and society that was introverted, riven with fear and deprivation, and ignorant of alternatives.[20] In this restricted context, a zero-sum game was played out, resulting in feuds, fights, theft and poor social relationships, a situation even more acute than the Mexican case described by Foster, which handicapped constructive growth and change in the community.[21] Unfortunately, in their capacity as dependent *hacienda* serfs, Vicosinos enjoyed no respect from their mestizo neighbors as erstwhile "heirs of the Incas," but rather were denigrated because of it. Indeed, the townspeople in Marcará often referred to them as the "animals closest to man."[22]

In the face of these challenges, the CPP laid out an "integrated plan of action" which eventually covered a wide range of activities carried out with the community by various experts, either hired by the project or working as part of government programs operating in the region. One of the first tasks was to resurrect the decrepit infrastructure of the *hacienda* and build places for outsiders to live. As this proceeded, more detailed studies of the *hacienda* were undertaken, which continued operating with the same administrator but now working for the project. A number of changes were introduced in agricultural operations, and the work and social relations of the *colonos* with the estate were gradually modified to become increasingly less onerous.[23] Over the next five years, the program developed and normal national institutions were brought into Vicos for the first time. Among the numerous events and changes that were manifested in the community were the following:

- Initial nutritional studies carried out by the Ministry of Health led to the introduction of a school lunch program and more research on diet that aided in dramatically improving the nutritional status of the community;

- With technical assistance from the agricultural extension service, a better grade of potatoes was flourishing on both *hacienda* and Vicosino *chacras*; and more food became available to families;

- A primary school was built to replace the small one-room school house and a staff of qualified teachers lived at Vicos during the week;

- The *colonos* began working on *hacienda* lands only as needed, leaving people free to find outside work as they wished;

- The role of the administrator and landlord was gradually altered, as the Vicosino foremen (*mayorales*) were encouraged and trained to assume ever larger roles in the management of the *hacienda*; by 1956, when the community began to operate the estate directly for itself, serfdom had been abolished and the *hacienda* lands became community lands, with work done under the emerging elected community council;

- With profits of increasing potato sales to Lima, people were paid for their work on the *hacienda* and common lands; money was available for various other activities and construction; and a community savings account was started, to be used eventually in buying the estate.

As the project continued, the Vicosinos who had long desired their freedom from patronal power took an increasing role as decision makers as they gained experience, working towards the day when they would be able to assume control of the *hacienda* for themselves. Previously, they had protested against landlords and petitioned the government for relief from peonage in 1912, 1928 and 1946.[24] By 1956–7, when Cornell's lease on the property was over, the government had agreed to permit the community to gain title of the land through an expropriation process, with the community itself paying the value of the estate over the next five to six years, as well as the year-to-year lease, until the sale was completed. The regional elites who controlled the Beneficent Society were strongly opposed to this plan to sell Vicos to the people and repeatedly thwarted attempts to proceed. In their delaying tactics they had the behind-the-scenes support of President Manuel Prado y Ugarteche and his prime minister, Pedro Beltran Espantoso, both of whom were large landowners and feared the precedent it would set if the sale proceeded, as there were over a hundred such requests pending around the country. As adherents of the conservative National Agrarian Society's stand against any serious land reform, they were a formidable barrier to the successful conclusion of the project. Obviously the challenge was to oblige the government to fulfill its agreement.

FEELING PROGRAM IMPACT

In the meantime, inspired by the success of the Vicos project, the Ministry of Labor and Indian Affairs, cooperating with the Health, Agriculture and Education ministries, established in 1957 a widespread program to begin work in the strongly Indian regions in the central and southern highlands to promote development as well as to continue work at Vicos with the CPP.[25] It was the first time a Peruvian government had attempted such a program. Word of the project had spread widely by this time; the Peruvian press ran articles such as "The Peru-Cornell Project is the first firm and sure step for a peaceful agrarian revolution," and a *Readers' Digest* piece entitled "Miracle at Vicos" in both Spanish and English.[26] In addition, the Ministry of Labor's Indigenist Institute distributed circulars and "wall newspapers" about the CPP to all 1500 recognized Indigenous Communities, creating vast interest around the nation among peasants and serfs engaged in struggles against *hacienda* domination. As a result, the project was besieged by community delegations to its Lima office, and multi-page letters written in elementary Spanish arrived recounting abuses and requesting project assistance to "do what you did at Vicos." The CPP conducted a nationwide survey of Indigenous Community conditions in 1961–2, resulting in the first collection of such data[27] and significantly furthering peasant interest in Vicos.

Peru's agrarian problems were beginning to crystallize as national political campaigns in 1962–3 provoked much discussion. In the wake of Fernando Belaunde's election in 1963, there was an immediate reaction throughout the nation. Andean communities, thinking that the new government would support land reform, invaded hundreds of *haciendas* throughout the highlands, precipitating a national crisis. Forced to withdraw, the Indigenous Communities and *hacienda* serfs had to await future policies that would aid them. Understanding the volatile nature of those tensions that were building, it is easy to understand why the Prado government was stonewalling the Vicos agreement. It was, in effect, the worst nightmare for the large-scale landlords.

Critical to project success was the development of a sustaining agricultural base that could provide both sustenance and income to families and operating funds for the community. The management of the farm enterprise also became central to the emergence of an effective community system of governance. The pioneering agricultural credit program built upon the project's successful introduction of new farming methods on *hacienda* lands after 1952. Sharp increases in production were convincing evidence for cautious Vicosinos and led them to accept innovations in their own farming strategies, including the use of credit for new seed and fertilizer. At first utilizing CPP funds, the program was subsequently taken over by a newly organized national program of supervised credit which the CPP had helped to pioneer.[28] Later, the community itself was able to offer crop loans to its members on a limited basis. As the major potato producer in the region, Vicos was visited by peasant delegations from the surrounding area seeking assistance; the community eventually underwrote loans to two other communities in the valley and lent some of its new equipment to one of them.

The Vicos potato crop was shipped directly to the Lima wholesale market, where in 1957–8 they sold 182.9 metric tons—about two percent of the reported yearly total there. In addition, family profits from their own produce sales increased dramatically, with people turning their earnings to their many domestic needs, as family possessions increased as much as four hundred percent for some. They also turned their new wealth to improving their housing, adding rooms, better roofs, doors and windows to their small two-room stone and adobe homes, and by building new houses altogether. The CPP did little directly to guide these family-level investments on the principle that people would need little special pleading to live in more comfortable domestic settings once their own preferences for making such improvements could be based upon their growing outside experience and knowledge of options open to them.

Throughout the CPP's tenure at Vicos, 93 students and senior researchers had lived, worked and researched in the community, producing theses, dissertations, and almost 200 books, articles and monographs. Although much of this work was academic and not directed at immediate project needs, the diversity and flow of research gave constant feedback to the staff. It was an essential "pulse-taking" of program effectiveness and problems, which served to broaden the perspectives of Vicosinos as well as CPP personnel as they came to know each other. At the busiest times, therefore, there might be as many as twenty-five outsiders living at Vicos. These would include from 7–10 primary school teachers, 3–6 PNIPA staff, 1–2 Cornell staff, and up to 8 students. This body of outsiders from other parts of Peru and the United States, not to mention occasional other international visitors, provided Vicos with a cosmopolitan dimension not found elsewhere in the region.

Once the program became known through its publications or articles in the press, there was a constant flow of "intellectual" tourists arriving to "see" the project for a few minutes or hours.[29] Some of these tourists were disappointed to discover that the CPP was not about infrastructure or monumental buildings, although the school buildings, teachers' and project "apartments" and the two-story reconstructed adobe *hacienda* house complemented the old chapel on the grassy plaza and lent a modest village air to the otherwise bucolic scene.[30] Many persons of course, confuse construction with development, and in this case the important changes were occurring in the sociocultural, political and economic areas of life that over the long run would produce the more obvious symptoms of change to the casual visitor.

An illustration of this point came in 1961 when a hostile delegation of members of the Peruvian parliament arrived to "inspect" the project. One of them harangued the community chairman, asking rhetorically where the great buildings and physical signs of the *"gringo"* development investments were. Their absence to him was convincing evidence of failure, coupled with his observation that many Vicosinos continued to chew coca leaf[31]—proof to him and members of Peru's middle and upper classes of the uneducable nature of Indians. The Vicosino leader, Celso León, responded by asking him why he continued to smoke cigarettes when studies showed that it was bad for one's health. Stunned, the parliamentarian did not know what to make of this upstart Indian peon. The changes were there, although not always visible at first!

The Vicosino perception of their community and of themselves changed, becoming less fearful of the surrounding world and more confident to deal with it, even though their anxieties over newly confronted choices increased as the "security" of the *hacienda's* paternalism diminished. Under the *hacienda* the *patrón,* however repressive, had made life predictable by being protective and making all the decisions. While it seems an easy step to move from the certainty and simplicity of dependency to freedom and autonomy, accepting the new complexity of life is not quickly accomplished. For some, especially older Vicosinos, the changes were unsettling.[32]

Another significant factor in these changes came from the school, which for the first time introduced Vicosinos to formal learning and vastly opened their horizons. The first group of teachers was selected with an eye towards finding instructors who would be sympathetic to the goals of the project and effective in working with impoverished, often fearful children who came to school in rags. The impact of the school was quickly seen and felt: literacy is a major tool in development and the ability to speak the national language, Spanish, critical for all work outside the community. With "learned" children, families could deal more confidently in the stores and marketplace in Marcará and not be cheated. Schooling therefore had a payoff in very practical terms as well as serving to raise both self-esteem and levels of social respect accorded Vicosinos by outsiders. By 1960, the first Vicosino was beginning secondary school in the provincial capital of Carhuaz where his presence caused considerable comment among mestizo townspeople. He was soon followed by other Vicos boys, all of whom were much admired by the community and under great pressure to perform well, which they did.

The impact of so many simultaneous modifications and innovations in *hacienda* life was not without problems or dilemmas, however. By deliberately exposing the community to national and international influences, their social isolation was stripped away by school and adult education classes, trips to the Lima potato market, close contact with the project staff, young men being drafted into the army for the first time, and vastly increased commercial activity and interaction with Peruvian and foreign visitors. The Vicos worldview was vastly expanded. They acquired the ability to compare their lives with the different experiences of others, to evaluate them and have a broader basis for their decisions and choices to make which had never been available to them.

Peruvian society in the 1950s was strongly biased in favor of boys and men[33] and thus female attendance in schools was much less than that of boys, especially in all rural and Indian areas of the country, as revealed by census data. On one hand, Vicos families were reticent and fearful about sending their daughters to classrooms with male mestizo teachers, and on the other, the androcentric values of Vicosinos themselves led them to place little importance on educating girls. One of the factors in these attitudes stemmed from the nature of Vicos' patrilineal kinship system, in which everyone was classified as members of only the male line of descent. The patrilineages in Vicos are called *castas*, and were important in the establishment of personal identity and place in the community.[34] These factors combined with the fact that, as in farming communities worldwide, children form an essential part of the workforce and may be held back from regular school attendance. Thus, the young men were the ones who benefited first from educational opportunities, despite project attempts to increase female enrollment, which remained very low until the mid-1960s, and only now is approaching parity with males. A side effect of the school system, particularly, has been the increasing use of Peru's Hispanic kinship terminology with its recognition of the maternal as well as the paternal line of descent in personal names.[35]

Women gradually increased their participation in CPP programs and in other ways enlarged their roles in the society. They were the most active in petty commerce, notably in the weekend market in Marcará. The PNIPA program began a popular "Women's Club" which featured classes in new domestic skills, entertainment and, most attractive to all, learning how to use the project's treadle sewing machines. As elementary or even anachronistic in today's terms as such activities may appear, they were nothing less than revolutionary as far as women were concerned at the time; to be accorded such attention and offered the opportunity to learn within the context of their own organization was truly innovative in light of Vicos' historical experience. An almost immediate effect was to enhance women's status by elevating and increasing their technological skills in areas that were widely appealing to them and so increase their self-respect and recognition by others. Since one's personal appearance is important in all cultures and closely related to concepts of respect, status, and role, Vicosinos' appearance and the "presentation of self," both within their own community and outside it, are useful measures of sociocultural change.

A consequence of the acquisition of sewing skills by Vicos women, therefore, had considerable impact in the community: there was an "explosion" of Vicos dress styles and elaboration of the traditional clothing, which was almost entirely made in the community or neighboring villages. Heavy woolen homespun was, and to a large extent still is, the basis of all traditional dress in Vicos. Normal Vicos men's attire was a woven suit consisting of black pants with ankle slits, held in place by a woven sash of wool with geometric designs; a muslin or wool baize shirt; and a black waist-length wool vest or jacket with pockets.[36] All men had black woolen ponchos. Frequently, as part of their attire, stiff braided leather ropes used for carrying heavy loads on their backs were looped around their shoulders at the ready. In *hacienda* times, most men walked barefoot and a minority used the rubber-tire sandals.

Both sexes wore stiff white felt hats, the women's often having small woolen baubles dangling on the brim. Women's attire featured two to four ankle-length, heavy woolen, red or black skirts and petticoats embroidered at the hem, a muslin blouse with crocheted collars and wristlets, several brass finger rings, and often multiple woven woolen sashes. They also used an embroidered, hood-like shawl which covered the back of their hats and shoulders, sometimes obscuring their braided hair in which red ribbons were frequently interwoven as protection from "evil eye" disease.[37] Augmenting this striking attire, women universally used a red wool baize carrying-cloth which covered their backs and was used to transport babies or anything else. Completing this traditional picture, women's hands were constantly occupied with the spinning of wool as they trudged barefoot along the trails, pastured the family animals or conversed.

This distinctive and striking dress was one of but two areas in which artistic interest could be expressed in *hacienda* times, the other being in decorating the impoverished saints housed in the chapel. The ability to utilize a sewing machine, coupled with greatly increased incomes, created the opportunity for sartorial splendor, Vicos style: more color, more embroidery, and additional sets of clothing where none previously existed. As family incomes rose, both men and women purchased sandals as soon as they were able. In the poverty of *hacienda* times, most children of both sexes were rarely given their "own" clothes until they had survived to 6 or 7 years of age, but instead were wrapped in old pieces of discarded skirts or ponchos. In view of the high infant and child mortality, families could not afford to invest resources in them. As project impacts increased, so did the availability of clothing for children.

CRISIS AND OPPORTUNITY

By 1960, the community was prepared to purchase the estate according to the agreement with the government four years earlier. The sticking point, however, was that a price could not be agreed upon. Through the assessment process the Beneficent Society and its supporters elevated the asking price by nine hundred percent, which greatly exceeded the community accounts. Loans were sought but no lenders could be found who would charge interest that was not confiscatory. As the community became more frustrated, the Beneficent Society hinted of again renting the estate to a new landlord.

In the summer of 1960, as two students watched with horror, a detachment of police passed through Vicos to enter the adjacent *hacienda* of Huapra, where the *colonos* of that estate were trying to build a school like that of Vicos over the objections of the landlord. The police confronted the serfs in a wheat field and shot the defenseless *colonos*, leaving three dead and five wounded as they fled back through Vicos and left. The students had taken photographs of the event and Mario Vazquez immediately took the film to Lima where, the next day, with CPP coordinator Henry Dobyns, he placed an illustrated account of the event on the desks of government officials. This forestalled an anti-project reaction by the Prado government, which, it was feared, would use the event as an excuse to end the program and void the obligation to permit the sale of Vicos to its people.[38]

The situation remained in uncomfortable limbo until the following year when, by happenstance, Vicos received a visitor sent by the then U.S. *chargé d'affaires,* (an old friend of Holmberg's from his Bolivia work) to "learn about Peru" from the CPP. Young Edward Kennedy was preparing to run for the Senate for the first time and visited the Callejón, accompanied by Harvard professor John Plank and others, making stops arranged by this writer and others connected with the CPP. While at Vicos, he was moved by the firsthand accounts of the massacre by Huaprinos, and by the Vicosinos' description of their stalemate with the government. Upon returning to Lima he spoke with the Peruvian president, Manual Prado y Ugarteche, and suggested that the something must be done about the situation if the Alliance for Progress was to be successful. At first dissembling, Prado agreed to "look into" the matter. Over the next year, Monge and Vazquez insistently lobbied the government for a solution and finally succeeded: the community was to pay the Beneficent Society two million *soles* for the estate. On June 13, 1962, the Vicosinos purchased the land with their own money and took possession where they and their ancestors had labored in peonage for 368 years.

UNDERSTANDING HOW THE PROJECT WORKED

To conceptualize the project in terms of its impact on all areas of Vicos life, Holmberg adapted the "policy science" approach developed by Harold Lasswell and Myres McDougal at Yale University to analyze and assess the work. Along with his own theory of "dynamic functionalism"[39] Holmberg viewed social institutions and the cultural values and behaviors which drive them as flexible, inter-related elements of sociocultural systems in which a change in one part precipitates reactions and adjustments throughout them. The character and nature of linkages in all sociocultural systems can be viewed comparatively and through time by using the Lasswellian concepts of institutional cultural values and studying the extent and character of people's participation in each sphere. The basic value-domains with which all societies must be concerned—power, wealth, skill, affection, well-being, enlightenment, rectitude and respect—are orchestrated through the cultural institutions that have been created and have evolved in all communities and nations. Because the access to, organization of, and distribution of these values varies widely both within and among societies, those patterns can be studied and compared in both space and time. In some places, their allocation among group members may be relatively fair and equal, while, in others, be extremely inequitable to the point of deprivation, as was the case in Vicos.[40]

In the case of Vicos, the identification of such inequities indicated the critical conditions which the CPP should attempt to change in order to induce and optimize subsequent alterations in other areas as well. Using these value-constructs in the chart on pp. 242–3 to view what happened, we see the course of changes initiated by the project in one value area and how these impacted among the other value-domains.

For example, by the increasing empowerment of the Vicos community through the reduction (and eventual disappearance) of the traditional roles of *hacienda patrón* and administrator, the way opened for broader and freer sociopolitical participation in Vicos community life and was accompanied by linked, advantageous changes in economic activity, skill, education and well-being which, in turn, earned Vicosinos greater respect and sense of moral worth. The changes were self-reinforcing and have continued to be so. This was the kind of holistic impact across the breadth of community life that was sought and achieved by the strategies employed.

The instrumental method used by the Project was one of "participant intervention" in which the researchers and staff living at Vicos took an active part in studying, analyzing, and creating the conditions for change in various direct and indirect ways.[41] Even though the CPP employed some of the old *hacienda* mannerisms as *patrón* in the first years, important structural adjustments were promoted which were desired by the people but beyond their power to achieve. These included the abolishment of servitude and the conspicuous and unnecessary monopolization of peon labor. This gave Vicosinos the freedom to work as they wished and enjoy a greater sense of self-respect. By constantly obliging Vicosinos to take on managerial responsibilities and to make decisions regarding the operations of the farm enterprise over a period of five years, the Project systematically and increasingly devolved control and governance onto Vicosinos until they took these tasks over completely. This was not easily accomplished since Vicosinos throughout the history of the *hacienda* would have been severely punished for usurping the rights of the *patrón* in such regards. Such power and status was, by definition, not the province of Indians, and the mestizo landlords in the region, seeing what was happening at Vicos, were extremely hostile to such changes for fear of the precedent they would set.

Significantly, the project also served as a shield against those traditional elite interests which opposed such changes, and it was able to harness critical outside support occasionally when required, as evidenced by the role of the Ministry of Labor and Indian Affairs and Carlos Monge Medrano on one hand, and the critical use of Kennedy's brief but adventitious appearance on the scene. Peruvian sociopolitical affairs closely follow the linkages of kinship, background, and economic interest. The power networks available to the project were well-utilized and essential throughout its history. In similar fashion, the CPP was able to engage the services of existing Peruvian agencies to work at Vicos in a coordinated fashion, something which rarely happened then or even now, but which represents one of the project's singular achievements and a model for any development effort. Because of this capacity, it was possible to carry out an integrated, holistic program touching the broad spectrum of Vicos life and needs, and build the "social capital" necessary to carry developments forward. With the continuous involvement of the people, the "hands-on" research-and-development strategy that coordinated the efforts of various agencies and experts already assigned to such tasks, the final costs of the project (an estimated $711,000 or about $35.00 per capita per year) were modest when compared to large-scale "trickle-down" development schemes so much in favor, with per capita expenditures many times that amount.[42]

AFTERMATH

After the community purchased its lands in 1962, numerous changes occurred in its area and with outside institutions. A U.S. Peace Corps contingent arrived to work there under the erstwhile direction of the PNIPA program, which continued to coordinate government agencies in the area.[43] Although the work of some of the volunteers at Vicos was successful in broadening educational opportunities and providing some management skills to community leaders, there were problems. Hostilities developed over misunderstandings regarding the community purchase of the adjacent estate and hot spring "resort" of Chancos[44] in which the volunteers had taken the lead. Ultimately, this brought about a protest resulting in the expulsion of the Peace Corps in 1964, the first such occurrence in the world. Nevertheless, as things settled down, two volunteers were invited back to continue their teaching in new outlying primary schools. Meanwhile, the community welcomed the 63 Chancos *colonos* as Vicos community members and began farming its newly acquired farmland, the only things at that time which interested the Vicosinos.

The small Chancos resort was tentatively operated by the Peace Corps on behalf of its owners, the Beneficent Society. After the Peace Corps finally retired from the scene, Chancos was rented to two Vicosinos, in a paradoxical twist. Since then, the resort has been privately operated by some Vicosinos and their partners.

Several years later, Marcará leaders attempted to take the resort through a bogus legal maneuver but were thwarted at the critical moment by a large group of Vicosinos headed by the senior community leaders. Since that time, the community has operated the rustic Chancos hot springs and restaurant, although its legal status still remains in doubt. After all these years, the popular local spa, despite its decrepit condition, remains the focus of Vicos-Marcará discord.

In retrospect, despite the confusion of the moment and the various actors involved, the expulsion of the Peace Corps was a definitive validation of community authority and the act put various local mestizo interests and government agencies on notice to that effect. Vicosinos, yes; *patrones,* no! In subsequent years, Vicosinos expelled teachers who were behaving badly, and they said "no" to high-handed land reform bureaucrats who attempted to force the reorganization of the community in 1971 with prior consultation, justifying their actions on the grounds that the CPP was an "imperialist scheme" and that the community had been deceived. The public meeting exploded in anger, forcing the bureaucrats to leave. Although the reorganization eventually went forward because of changes in laws governing Peasant Communities,[45] the Vicosinos were prepared to manage the process. Later they expelled agricultural extension representatives who swindled the community in a dairy and ranching scam.[46] In the late 1980s they captured and sent to jail some members of the *Sendero Luminoso* guerrilla group who entered Vicos and Huapra to infiltrate the region. As a result of all these and other similar actions, Vicos has earned a reputation in the region for its "attitude" and independent manner vis-à-vis the mestizo authorities.

In the decades since the end of the project, the community has experienced numerous successes as well as failures as an independent community. Its attempts to diversify the economic base were often thwarted and the farming enterprise was affected by plant diseases, bad market prices, and the like, which harmed the entire region. For several years from 1974–80, self-serving government agency manipulations left the people in the community confused, corrupted their leadership, and eroded their confidence.

In part, Vicos experienced some of those things because the community was famous, having been precursor of the national agrarian reform, which finally got underway in 1969. For a long time after the project was finished, successive government programs (beginning with the first Belaunde presidential administration) attempted to remake the community, to "capture" its aura, so to speak, and use it politically. For good or ill, this is not an uncommon event in the aftermath of programs that gain public attention and hold political interest. Fortunately for Vicos, none of these ill-planned efforts lasted long or were systematically pursued, although they produced mischievous and negative effects by misleading community leaders or by recommending poor development investments.

Forty-Five Years Later . . .

In July of 1997, I returned again to Vicos to visit old friends and reacquaint myself with the community and its current circumstances. Political signs urging the support of various local and regional candidates are painted on the houses in the budding urban area, where the population reportedly is 598 persons. Electricity is carried over the landscape on concrete poles sporting street lights, and wires snake down from them into the adobe homes to power lights, televisions, radios, blenders, tools, stoves and other instruments of contemporary life. Just off the old and still grassy plaza, tall eucalyptus poles rise behind adjacent houses and sport the antennae of Vicos' two competing radio stations, located in the *colcas*[47] of their respective houses.

Today, as the Vicos population approaches an estimated 5,500 persons, the community supports a high school, one large and 9 small primary schools, and a kindergarten, eclipsing its own district capital, Marcará, in all of these respects. In view of the fact that Vicosinos have held the highest elective offices in the province, the politically experienced community now seeks to become a separate municipality, to take its evolution further along the road of empowerment. This is a far cry from the place I first visited in 1960, and Vicos today is the antithesis of what it was in 1952.

The biggest change in Vicos life since the onset of the CPP, however, took place in 1996 when the community decided (as have many other communities in Peru) to parcel out its communal farmlands to its members, following the national and international predilection and policies to "privatize" public holdings and minimize the role of cooperatives. Was this a wise choice? In Vicos, given its dense rural population, the decision has resulted in the formation of an instant "minifundia" system of property ownership, with the average family plot being about one hectare. The only remaining community enterprises are the sale of timber from the project-era reforestation project and, ironically, the Chancos hot springs resort in which the community is building a two-story brick hotel. These changes portend dramatic alterations in Vicos's social organization and class structure in the next few years.

Intending to offer a public slide show illustrating the past 45 years of Vicos life and the role of the Cornell-Peru Project, I paid fifty cents to interrupt a radio broadcast of popular music for the youthful owner *cum* disk-jockey to make an announcement in Quechua and Spanish to that effect over his radio station. An hour later, a crowd of about 50 was jammed into the old community building with more outside. For the older people, it was a chance to "prove" to youthful skeptics how they had lived in the old days; for everyone under 50 it was the first time they had actually seen what the *hacienda* had been like, and how much Vicos had changed. The excitement in the room was palpable as people pointed, identified relatives, and exclaimed their surprise. From their reactions of delight and curiosity, it seemed clear enough that this community, like so many others, needs to treat the past as a living experience which might inform contemporary decisions.

As a new century begins, we see that Vicos is very much a part of its political, economic and cultural environment as it continues to evidence many of the trends initiated by the Cornell-Peru project so long ago. Although these long-enduring impacts in the wider sharing of values that people enjoy are visible to the long-time outside observer, they may not be so apparent to others, even the people who have benefited the most. Vicosinos are now entering an era that is much different from that of just a generation ago. With its people's needs now surpassing the traditional agricultural resources of its lands, and with the full impact of modern wants felt in nearly every family as conveyed through television, radio, migration and education, contemporary changes are inspired by forces which have only indirect ties to past priorities as such.

The Cornell Peru Project is obviously not the source of all that happened during its tenure nor certainly what happened afterwards, but it did set in motion many changes and trends by introducing key innovations and interventions that opened the pathways to power, wealth, enlightenment and the other values which had been almost completely closed to Vicosinos in 1952. Then, the issues had to do with the people gaining equitable shares of those value-domains through a well planned and executed program that would demonstrate the capacity of the Indian peasantry to take control of their lives and improve their conditions, contrary to prevailing national policy and opinion. Secondly, the project provided confirmation as to the effectiveness of applied research, employing a holistic approach that successfully addressed fundamental problems. As a result, Vicosinos altered their society from one of denigrated serfdom and subordination to an autonomous community of Quechua highlanders fending for themselves on a par with others in Peru's complex and uncertain milieu in the new millennium.

Notes

[1] There are many excellent works dealing with this period, including John Hemming, 1970, *The Conquest of the Incas,* Harcourt, Brace and Jovanovich, New York, and Steve J. Stern, 1993, *Peru's Indian People and the Challenge of Spanish Conquest,* University of Wisconsin Press, Madison. The pre-conquest past is capably described and illustrated by Michael Moseley, 1992, *The Incas and Their Ancestors,* Thames and Hudson, New York.

[2] One hectare equals 2.47 acres. *Haciendas* with resident serf populations in Peru constituted over 80 percent of all agricultural land in 1961. The largest single landholding comprised an estimated 557,000 hectares (2,151 square miles) of land, 10 percent larger than the state of Delaware, with almost the same population, i.e., about 200,000 persons. Interesting to note, however, is the fact that while studies of land holdings in Peru often count the numbers of cattle and sheep on them, the number of people living there is not recorded! In contrast, 96 percent of rural Peruvians lived and worked on farmland averaging less than 10 hectares in size and constituted only 10 percent of all agricultural land. See CIDA, 1966, *Perú: Tenencia de la Tierra y Desarrollo Socio-Económico del Sector Agrícola*, Organization of American States, Washington, DC, pp. 31–49; Carlos Malpica, 1968, *Los Dueños del Perú*, 3ra. Edición, Ediciones Ensayos Sociales, Lima. A brief, classic description of the *hacienda* regimen is found in M. C. Vazquez, 1961, *Hacienda, Peonaje y Servidumbre en los Andes Peruanos,* Editorial Estudios Andinos, Monografías Andinas, No. 1, p. 8–10.

[3] Called "Yuraq Janka" in Quechua—"White Range"—second highest of Andean ranges. See John F. Ricker, 1977, *Yuraq Janka: Guide to the Peruvian Andes, Part I, Cordilleras Blanca and Rosko,* The American Alpine Club of New York, Pacific Press of Seattle; or the beautiful description by Hans Kinzl and Erwin Schneider, 1950, *Cordillera Blanca, Perú,* Universitats-Verlag, Wagner, Innsbruck, Austria.

[4] *La Beneficencia Pública* is located in the departmental (state) capital of Huaraz, 30 kilometers south of Vicos. See Henry F. Dobyns, 1966, "The Struggle for Land in Peru: The Hacienda Vicos Case," *Ethnohistory,* Vol. 13, Nos. 3–4, pp. 97–122.

[5] At that time, Colombia, Venezuela, Ecuador, Peru, Chile, Paraguay, Argentina, Uruguay and Brazil had various forms of the *hacienda* system. The Bolivian Revolution in 1952 destroyed the system there, as had the Mexican revolution in 1910–20 and the Cuban Revolution in 1959 in those nations. Such remnants of these systems continue to endure in obscure corners of the world, however, even within the perimeters of advanced industrial nations such as the United Kingdom. On the isle of Eigg off the Scottish coast, tenant farmers just purchased their freedom from the absentee landlord of the island estate on April 4, 1997. See Warren Hoge, June 6, 1997, "Isle of Eigg Journal: Island Tenants Triumph: They're Lairds Now," *The New York Times International*, p. 3.

[6] In the Peruvian Andes, the term "mestizo," which derives from colonial usages, refers to individuals of mixed European and Indian heritage, in both biological and/or cultural terms. The common term of similar origins, "cholo," generally identifies a person of such a background, but who is perhaps poorer and "more Indian" in behavior, dress, language, or phenotype. The word "cholo" is commonly used in daily discourse as a term of address or reference. Andean peoples in either of these very loosely defined statuses are, in varying degrees, bilingual in Spanish and Quechua or Aymara.

[7] In 1951 an avalanche severely damaged the still incomplete hydroelectric plant, postponing its completion for eight years. A description of this project and analysis of its impact is in P. L. Doughty, 1987, "Engineers and Energy in the Andes," and "Update," in H. R. Bernard & P. Pelto, Editors, *Technology and Social Change,* Waveland Press (second edition), pp. 11–36 & 369–73.

[8] Considered to be the oldest university in the New World, founded in 1551 in Lima.

[9] Vazquez was from the same general region in Ancash department and was a native speaker of Quechua. His first research in Vicos is reported in Mario C. Vazquez, 1952, "La Antropología Cultural y Nuestro Problema del Indio: Vicos, Un Caso de Antropología Aplicada," *Perú Indígena*, Vol. 11: 5–6, pp. 7–157.

[10] Cornell University's new Anthropology Department embarked on a worldwide study of the impacts of modern technology in the post WW2 era in its ambitious "Program of Studies in Culture and Applied Science." Research over many years was conducted in Thailand, India, Burma, Canada, the southwestern U.S., and Peru.

[11] The Peruvian Indigenist Institute was a dependency of the Ministry of Labor and Indian Affairs. Monge was the leading Peruvian scientist of his day and a pioneer in the field of research in high-altitude biology and altitude stress on humans. See Carlos Monge, 1948, *Acclimatization in the Andes*, Johns Hopkins University Press, Baltimore.

[12] Allan R. Holmberg and Mario C. Vazquez, 1951, "Un proyecto de antropología aplicada en el Perú," *Revista del Museo Nacional,* Tomos XIX–XX, p. 312 (author's translation).

[13] In Spanish the name is reversed, *Proyecto Perú-Cornell.* There are several summaries of the project, including that by Allan R. Holmberg, 1960, "Changing Community Attitudes and Values in Peru," in *Social Change in Latin America Today*, Council on Foreign Relations, Harper, New York; H. F. Dobyns, P. L. Doughty, and H. D. Lasswell, Editors, 1971, *Peasants, Power and Applied Social Change: Vicos as a Model*, Sage Publications, Berkeley; and P. L. Doughty, 1986, "Vicos: Success, Rejection and Rediscovery of a Classic Program," in E. M. Eddy and W. Partridge, Editors, *Applied Anthropology in America*, Second Edition, Colombia University Press, New York, pp. 145–169.

[14] The actual area of *hacienda* Vicos had never been measured until undertaken by the project, and was unknown to the Beneficent Society.

[15] His first work turned out to be one of the classics of Amazonian ethnography: Allan R. Holmberg, 1950, *Nomads of the Longbow: The Siriono of Eastern Bolivia,* Institute of Social Anthropology, Smithsonian Institution, Washington, DC; and "Adventures in Cultural Change," in R. Spencer, Editor, *Method and Perspective in Anthropology,* University of Minnesota Press, Minneapolis. For a follow-up of these works see the excellent restudy by Allyn Maclean Stearman, 1987, *No Longer Nomads: The Sirionó Revisited,* Hamilton Press, New York.

[16] Strictly organized by the field foremen, the *colonos* harvested the fields by hand in an almost military way, row by row, piling the potatoes behind them. Vazquez filmed the harvest procedure and, on studying the film, noticed that the workers were surreptitiously hiding many potatoes in the furrows. When the field was finished, their families were permitted to glean the field, finding what they could. Because their own plots were inadequate, the gleaning process contributed much to the Vicos diet.

[17] Nutritional data are reviewed by J. Oscar Alers, 1971, "Well-Being," in H. F. Dobyns, P. L. Doughty, and H. D. Lasswell, Editors, *Peasants, Power and Applied Social Change: Vicos as a Model*, Sage Publications, Berkeley.

[18] Mario C. Vazquez, 1965, *Educación Rural en el Callejón de Huaylas: Vicos,* Editorial Estudios Andinos, Lima, p. 12.

[19] The word *chacra* is the generic Andean word for cultivated field.

[20] Allan R. Holmberg, 1967, "Algunas Relaciones entre la Privación Psico-biológico y el Cambio Cultural en los Andes, *América Indígena*, Vol. 27, No. 1, pp. 3–24.

[21] George Foster, 1965, "Peasant Society and the Image of a Limited Good," *American Anthropologist,* Vol. 67, pp. 293–315.

[22] There are numerous analyses about the status of native Andean peoples which demonstrate this denigration as a widespread phenomenon. The project's study of Marcará by Humberto Ghersi, 1959–61, "El Indio y el Mestizo en la Comunidad de Marcará," *Revista del Museo Nacional,* Vols. XXVIII, XXIX, and XXX illustrates this relationship between the two populations.

[23] The *hacienda* administrator, Enrique Luna, was a powerful local personage in Marcará, known for his stern treatment of Indians. Nevertheless he became a friend of Holmberg, Vazquez and other project participants and, as he says, "they changed me to a man who saw the need to change things and be of assistance to the Vicosinos rather than one who used to whip them" (personal communication). In his new role, Luna played an important role in the early period of the CPP, and later with his long friendship with the community.

[24] Mario C. Vazquez, 1952, pp. 36–7. An old photograph shows a Vicos delegation in 1912, standing with Peruvian President Guillermo Billingshurst in his office.

[25] Known as the *Plan Nacional de Integración de la Población Aborigen*, or PNIPA, this bureaucratic agency provided funding for the work of 3–4 specialists in Vicos: a community development trainer and assistant and a social worker. The nuclear school operated from Vicos, reaching out to small hamlets in the vicinity and provided a rural education specialist, agronomist, and, intermittently, a medical doctor. One of its projects in Kuyo Chico, Cuzco, resembled the Vicos effort and met with hard-fought success. Oscar Nuñez del Prado (with W. F. Whyte), 1973, *Kuyo Chico, Applied Anthropology in an Indian Community*, University of Chicago Press, Chicago.

[26] See Henry F. Dobyns and Mario C. Vazquez, 1963, *The Cornell Peru Project Bibliography and Personnel,* Cornell Peru Project Pamphlet No. 2, Department of Anthropology, Cornell University, Ithaca.

[27] Henry F. Dobyns, 1964, *The Social Matrix of Peruvian Indigenous Communities*, Cornell Peru Project Monographs, Department of Anthropology, Cornell University, Ithaca.

[28] Allan R. Holmberg and Henry F. Dobyns, 1969, "Case Study: The Cornell Program in Vicos, Peru," in Clifford R. Wharton, Jr., Editor, *Subsistence Agriculture and Economic Development,* Aldine Publishing Company, Chicago, pp. 392–414.

[29] One tourist guidebook recommended Vicos as a morning stop-over.

[30] Originally in 1952, the 363 Vicos households were scattered over the mountainous slopes, in association with their small *chacras*. As things progressed, however, three families built new houses adjacent to the plaza in 1960–1 and a trend was established that would increasingly lead to a denser settlement pattern.

[31] In the manner of chewing tobacco, the mastication of coca leaves lightly mixed with slaked lime is a 5,000-year-old custom in the Andes. It is often done at rest-periods during the working day and after meals and also is associated with healing and divination practices. For modern Peruvians, traditional coca use is a definitive trait of backward Indians and thought to induce stupidity and maliciousness. Coca-chewing, however, does neither: it is not addictive, nor does it produce the "rush" associated with its chemical derivative, cocaine. Original research done at Vicos was instrumental in leading the way to scientific examination of the effects of coca-chewing. Norman Fine, 1960, "Coca chewing: A Social Versus Nutritional Interpretation" (Cornell, Columbia, Harvard Undergraduate Summer Studies Program), Colombia University, New York, and Cornell Peru Project Papers. Some of the modern studies of traditional coca leaf use are found in D. Pacini and C. Franquemont, Editors, 1986, *Coca and Cocaine: Effects on People and Policy in Latin America*, Report No. 23, Cultural Survival, Cambridge; Roderick Burchard, 1992, "Coca Chewing and Diet," *Current Anthropology*, Vol. 33, No. 1, pp. 1–24; and Catherine J. Allen, 1988, *The Hold Life Has: Coca and Cultural Identity in an Andean Community,* Smithsonian Institution Press, Washington, DC.

[32] See Alers, 1971, pp. 128–9.

[33] Women's suffrage in Peru was only granted in 1956, and became a reality in that year's presidential elections. However, Vicosinos, as illiterate, Quechua-speaking Indians, were not permitted to vote in number by Marcará district officials until the presidential elections of 1962–3.

[34] Mario C. Vazquez and Allan R. Holmberg, 1966, "The Castas: Unilineal Kin Groups in Vicos, Peru," *Ethnology*, Vol. 5, pp. 283–303.

[35] Traditionally, in Vicos a person's name would consist of a given name and the father's last (castal) name alone; in the Spanish system, the given name is always followed in order by the paternal last name and the maternal last name. Thus, Maria Tafur in the Vicos school would now be called Maria Tafur Gonzalez.

[36] This style, worn by all men, is a replica of sixteenth-century peasant dress from Extremadura, Spain and was introduced in early colonial times by Spanish landlords. Ironically, therefore, one of the most distinguishing "Indian" traits today is Spanish and a legacy of colonial serfdom.

[37] Women and children are thought to be particularly vulnerable to *mal de ojo* before "powerful" strangers, whose gaze is believed to cause illness, even inadvertently. Thus, eye contact with strangers is often avoided and mothers may cover a child's face from even the affectionate looks of well-intentioned persons.

[38] For accounts of this episode see Paul L. Doughty, 1986, "Directed Change and the Hope for Peace," in Mary LeCron Foster and Robert A. Rubinstein, Editors, *Peace and War, Cross Cultural Perspectives*, Transaction Books, New Brunswick, pp. 105–118; and William P. Mangin, 1979, "Thoughts on Twenty-Four Years of Work in Peru: The Vicos Project and Me," in George M. Foster et al., Editors, *Long-Term Field Research in Social Anthropology,* Academic Press, New York, pp. 65–84.

[39] Allan R. Holmberg, 1958, "The Research and Development Approach to Change," *Human Organization,* Vol. 17, pp. 12–16; A. R. Holmberg, 1969, "Dynamic Functionalism," in A. S. Rogow, Editor, *Politics, Personality, and Social Science in the Twentieth Century,* University of Chicago Press, Chicago; Harold D. Lasswell and Allan R. Holmberg, 1969, "Toward a General Theory of Directed Value Accumulation and International Development," in R. Braibanti, Editor, *Political and Administrative Development,* Duke University Press, Durham. See also Myres S. McDougal, Harold D. Lasswell, and Lung-chu Chen, *Human Rights and World Public Order*, Yale University Press, 1980.

[40] With relatively few exceptions in the long record of human experience can it be said that balanced and "true" equality of access to values is a relative rarity. Indeed, one may consider all modern state societies as instruments through which values are not only regulated but always unequally distributed among members despite the theoretical entitlements of citizenship. The onus of human rights concern and action rests in correcting the misery and deprivation resulting from the most oppressive, inequitable, and inhumane distributions of values.

[41] See Allan R. Holmberg, 1955, "Participant Intervention in the Field," *Human Organization*, Vol. 14, pp. 23–6.

[42] The costs of the project were met in several ways: on the Cornell side, through two grants from The Carnegie Corporation, which met the "academic" expenses and paid the salaries of the field director and coordinator; earnings from the community produce sales, which financed construction and general operations of the hacienda/community; and the ongoing regular Peruvian ministerial programs in Agriculture, Education and Labor and Indian Affairs. Paul L. Doughty, 1987, "Against the Odds: Collaboration and Development at Vicos," in Donald D. Stull and Jean J. Schensul, Editors, *Collaborative Research and Social Change: Applied Anthropology in Action*, Westview Press, Boulder, pp. 152–3.

[43] See Paul L. Doughty, 1966, "Pitfalls and Progress in the Peruvian Sierra," in Robert B. Textor, Editor, *The Cultural Frontiers of the Peace Corps*, The M.I.T. Press, pp. 221–240.

[44] Also a property of the Beneficence Society.

[45] After the military government announced a sweeping land reform in 1969, they changed the official name of corporate native communities from Indigenous Community (*Comunidad Indígena*) to Peasant Community (*Comunidad Campesina*) on the grounds that the word "peasant" is less negative than "indigenous," the polite term for "Indian"!

[46] This was a severe blow to the community in 1973–4, creating financial difficulties, undermining Vicosino confidence in their leaders and cooperative, and producing a strong distrust of government agencies and programs for several years. See Hector Martinez, 1989, "Vicos: Continuidad y Cambio," *Socialismo y Participación*, No. 48, Centro de Estudios para el Desarrollo y la Participación, Lima, p. 54.

[47] A *colca* is a loft where grain and produce are stored in rural houses.

A Summary of Value Sector Changes and Development in Vicos

1952 Baseline Conditions	Project Decade 1952–1962	Post-Project Changes to 1997
Power		
Exclusive power & control of landlord limits access to all value domains in Vicos; patrilineal male dominance focused within family and religious institutions; exploitation and abuse by mestizos unchecked; no access to citizen or legal rights; no freedom of travel; fear of outsiders prevalent	Elected community council comes to control all decisions by 1962; strong public participation in governance and cooperative management; power within family opening to women & educated children freedom to gain outside employment and movement; sharp decline of fear & organized ability to defend interests increases	Elected community council continues to run affairs; outside, Vicosinos have held highest elective offices in both district and province; one man has held office in a national peasant/farm organization; access to legal and citizen rights equal to that of others in region; Vicos seeking autonomous status as a new district
Enlightenment		
Literacy limited to less than 1% of male population; less than 25% have been more than 30 km from Vicos; most do not recognize their citizenship in Peru; little if any knowledge of wider world; 2% could speak Spanish	Complete primary school is full; female attendance about 8%; 4 Vicos boys attend high school; most Vicosinos travel to regional markets; about half the men & many women have been to Lima; 17% adults could speak Spanish & 35% of children could; battery radios common	Vicos has constructed its own high school & kindergarten; female attendance over 40% of pupils; many university graduates; travel and migration common, including 30 Vicosinos in the US; TV widespread, community satellite dish in use; frequent daily bus service; two Vicos radio stations broadcast to the community and surrounding villages in Quechua and Spanish
Wealth		
No cash savings and little available; daily wage 10¢ if paid; few allowed to leave estate for employment; food resources controlled by landlord on a "share-cropping" basis; local market participation limited; heavy exploitation of women and men by mestizo townspeople; equipment limited to hoes, axes, plow, loom, knives and few other hand tools; the richest 8% of people in Vicos serve landlord interests & pay bribes to maintain their status	Wage labor paid at legal competitive rates; use of money normal; household possessions increase by 200%; Vicos is a major supplier to Lima potato market; widespread regional market & economic participation; farm cooperative buys the hacienda & pays for community mortgage & member wages; community runs crop loan program; work equipment increases substantially; class status no longer depends upon landlord favoritism; class structure greatly broadens with sharp increases in incomes	Community cooperative ended in 1996 and land distributed to member families; potato production variable; other crops good; reforested timber producing income; remittances from migrants spur household improvements & development in community and family projects; personal possessions extensive with widespread electric service and appliances; some ownership of trucks and cars; many new houses in budding "urban" area reflect growth of new social class indicators; the 1996 privatization of community land foretells class restructuring once again

A Summary of Value Sector Changes and Development in Vicos (cont'd)

1952 Baseline Conditions	Project Decade 1952–1962	Post-Project Changes to 1997
Skill		
Basic survival skills in manual farm & domestic activities; spinning and weaving cloth; manufacture of homespun clothing; musical skill limited to three instruments; no carpentry, masonry or mechanical knowledge; strong work ethic valued; physical strength and endurance considered the principal skills for both men and women	Skill increases of up to 400% opening a variety of employment opportunities; positions forestry, trade, construction; farming, domestic and market skills widened; strong work ethic prevails; strength and endurance values augmented by mental skills stemming from education and literacy	Marked rise in skill levels and variety; Vicosinos now hold teaching, clerical, managerial and technical positions in regional private and government agencies; many Vicosinos work as professional musicians; others work as mechanics and chauffeurs; many women and men engaged in petty business and commerce yet more than two-thirds are full-time farmers
Well-being		
Population: 1702; 363 households; nutrition levels 76% of recommended daily level; parasites and infectious diseases rampant; no modern medical services; high fear of landlord; housing of poor quality; clothing scarce and limited to local manufacture; theft and feuding common; alcohol use high; birth and death rates high; high vulnerability to epidemic diseases	Population: 2102; 461 households; food & nutrition near 100% of recommended level; some medical service, but inadequate and unreliable; some anxieties over changes; fighting declines; alcohol use remains high; ample clothing; housing improvements widespread; birth and death rates actually increase; continued vulnerability to disease	Population (est.): 5500; 977 households; nutrition levels high; community-built and staffed clinic being replaced by a small government hospital with a full medical staff; alcohol use remains high; levels of household sanitation conforms to regional patterns; nucleated settlement brings street lights; alcohol abuse continues; many new, large houses; lower morbidity; in 1996 family planning program was underway
Affection		
Patterns of affection limited to family and fictive kin; quarrels and fights frequent; inter-family feuding; abuse by mestizo townspeople; relations with Marcará marked by hostility and avoidance; witchcraft and rumor mongering serve as methods of defense and aggression	Wider circles of friendship develop through school and community participation; reduction in interpersonal conflict aided by development of community council which mediates some disputes; children receive better care and clothing; social universe expands; relationships with Marcará remain antagonistic	Continuation of changing patterns of affect; general reduction of abusive relations; broader social universe and confidence in dealing legal means of resolving disputes; relations with mestizo townspeople remain problematic
Respect		
Little respect shown Vicosinos; their culture and their humanity often ridiculed by mestizos who regard them only as servants; in Vicos, children are often considered a burden until they can work; hard workers respected but little rewarded; limited community recognition of achievement except in religious activity	CPP awards achievement and honors participation in community affairs; personal recognition for success becomes prized; educational prowess is rewarded; Vicosinos gain self-respect at being able to earn money; the purchase of Vicos lands gains recognition and respect in region and nationally; strong work ethic admired	Vicos remains the object of interest and study and thus derives respect outside of area; locally, Vicos enjoys political respect for its strong role in provincial politics, equaled by no other similar community; educational performance a source of prestige
Rectitude		
Vicosinos denied any moral status by society; the church rarely serves them; national culture does not recognize the validity of their culture or language; Indians are classified and treated as incompetent children before the law	Authorities of both church and state recognize the status of Vicosinos as citizens vested with and entitled to rights under the law as moral persons; a sign, emblazoned on the Vicos-owned truck proclaims the rightness of their situation: "Vicos Community Property" and "Shout of Reform"	Patterns continue; Vicosinos remain comfortable with the correctness of their role; the community retains a strong regional identity and autonomy

PART IV

Identity and Ethnicity

The readings in this section were selected to illustrate important aspects of both self and society as they relate to a variety of settings. One of the principal concerns of social scientists, wherever they work, is with the ways in which people relate to each other, as individuals or as groups. It is clear that social relations sometimes are based on judgments about social categories or on networks of interpersonal bonds, neither of which reflect any sort of integral group.

THE SOCIAL AND THE CULTURAL

Some authors make much of the distinction between *social* anthropology (emphasizing society, or social structure) and *cultural* anthropology (emphasizing culture, or patterns of thought and action). Among contributors to this book, such a distinction likely would seem superfluous. Identity and ethnicity are important components of cultural life throughout much of Latin America and have been, in dramatic but constantly changing ways, for centuries. Heterogeneity of the population has been a striking characteristic throughout the region, with important implications attributed to or deriving from such variations, with respect to both individuals and communities.

Unlike many other disciplines, anthropology does not deal with cultures as if they were coterminous with nation-states; often a single country contains many different cultures, but there are also important instances in which single cultures spill over national boundaries (as with the Yanomamö in Venezuela and Brazil; the Quechua in Peru, Bolivia, Ecuador, and Colombia; the Kickapoo in the United States and Mexico, and others).

The Latin American nations are, with a few exceptions, states with highly differentiated plural societies. Many anthropologists and sociologists have been limited in their analyses of such societies because of their tendency to focus on material cultural differences as the bases for distinguishing among components, rather than on social relations. An understanding of the real complexity of plural systems is often ham-

245

pered by the inappropriate use of terms derived from other kinds of systems, such as "race" and "caste." There is a tendency to speak of ethnic groups as if they were biologically significant, although the socially designated categories of "race" generally bear little or no relationship to gene pools and inbreeding populations. Terminology and stereotypes are often confusing in this regard.

A cardinal strength of many recent studies of class, ethnicity, and mobility in Latin America is the recognition that social categories are neither static nor unitary. In complex or plural societies, ethnic identification is largely a matter of subjective perceptions that include conceptions of the self, of one's own reference group, and of socially significant others. As such, ethnic identification is clearly relational and refers less to uniformities within groups than it does to differential participation between groups. In this sense, we have questioned the dual view of Latin American society: it is not that each of the plural components of a complex society has its own institutions; rather, they participate in different ways in many institutions that they share with others.

Although identity is sometimes used with reference to social groups or populations, at least as often it refers to individuals. Religion, race, ethnicity, language, nationality, region, or some other criterion can be used, and identity may be multiple just as it may be situational. A Oaxacan may become a southerner as he moves toward the northern border of Mexico, a *pollito* or an illegal as he crosses into the United States, and then choose to be a Mixtec while settling among other Mexican emigrants near San Diego.

TRULY A NEW WORLD

Just 50 years ago, well within living memory, a majority of the people in most Latin American countries lived in rural areas and worked the land. Now there remain few nations in the area that do not have most of their people living in mushrooming cities, and agriculture has lost its dominance in most economies. In a sheer economic sense, we are seeing something new under the sun—regions and sometimes entire nations in which tourism or remittances from migrant laborers are major economic forces, and traditional ties to the land have loosened or dissolved in ways that no one predicted just a generation ago.

Every Latin American country has at least a small stratum of people who pride themselves on being "white" or "pureblooded" and who claim to trace their ancestry to the conquistadors or other Europeans, without recognizing that the population of Iberia was already strikingly hybridized five centuries ago. Although none are now nobility and they rarely call themselves an aristocracy as in Mexico (Nutini, chapter 38), they long constituted an oligarchy that dominated in terms of wealth and power.

Within a year of the arrival of soldiers from Europe—rarely accompanied by wives or other women—members of what was to become a new social category were born, intermediate between those who were legally recognized as whites or Indians in what was at first designed to be a strictly dual society. The emergence of mestizos (or ladinos, caboclos, cholos, criollos, and so forth) as a culturally disinherited segment of colonial society has been well described. These groups now predominate—numerically, politically, and economically—in most of Latin America; and their assertive dissatisfaction with the distribution of wealth and power fostered political instability far more than any action by Indians, who until recently remained little involved in national or international affairs.

ETHNIC MARKERS

The superficially simple question, "What is an Indian?" has been answered in a bewildering variety of ways, by tax collectors, census takers, and administrators, long before anthropologists began to wrestle with it. The bases for designation as ladino or mestizo have been even more confused and confusing over the years, as is documented in the research of a few scholars who are beginning to shed light on the question in historical and ethnographic terms.

Following the prevailing biological analogy, many authors have identified a third major "racial" component in the population of Latin America, usually labeled "negro," "African," "Afro-American" or "African American." Studies of the cultures of black populations in Middle and South America were pioneered by M. Herskovits, R. Bastide, and others; in recent years, a number of others have contributed significantly, and the emphasis has shifted from the content of culture to definitions of ethnic boundaries and the nature of group relations.

Blacks or people of African descent were a significant portion of the population in those areas of mainland Latin America that relied heavily on slave labor during the colonial period, and the concept of social race is just as pertinent with reference to Afro-Latin Americans as it is with respect to Indians, mestizos, or whites. An enormous literature exists on Brazil, largely because Brazilians enjoy worldwide renown for their egalitarian ethos. A number of local studies demonstrate that practice often differs from the ideal, and it has long been recognized within the country that there was little behavioral conformity with values that were already popularly expressed.

Afro-Latin American populations in other areas of Latin America have received less attention (Dzidzienyo, chapter 24) but have not been totally ignored: the Garífuna, "Bush Negroes" or "Black Caribs" of Guatemala and the Guianas have been studied, as have black populations in Ecuador, enclaves in the Andes, scattered populations on the Caribbean coast of Central America, and a community in Mexico.

Other components of the populations of mainland Latin America have only rarely been subjects of research, and their relatively small numbers are often ignored in general discussions of the area. Among such groups are descendants of Chinese in Peru and Central America; recent Japanese and Ryukyuan immigrants in Bolivia and Brazil; East Indians in Surinam and Guyana; and Europeans, North Americans, and Levantines throughout the area.

Religion is occasionally used as an ethnic marker, with Jews often distinguished as such, regardless of the region from which their ancestors came (Elkin, chapter 23), and Protestants sometimes labeled as such, especially when they comprise a large portion of a local community (Arcand, chapter 36).

There are other important demographic factors that have major implications for the ways in which people relate to each other and for the ways in which a country operates; rural-to-urban migration is one. Contrary to dire sociological predictions, such migration does not inevitably result in breakdown of social relationships, patterns of beliefs, or value orientations. However, the notoriously weak and underdeveloped infrastructure of most Latin American cities has been taxed by the influx; job opportunities have not kept up with hopes or expectations; and shantytowns (known by whatever name in different places) are growing rather than diminishing, yet people there keep ties to kin and community, and many aspects of culture remain vital.

Shifting our focus from the group to the individual, we see that ethnicity often plays a key role in personal identity, both in self-concept and in terms of life-chances. For that reason, considerable attention has been paid to social mobility or "passing," ways in which an individual can move up in the hierarchy that are generally recognized although not formally spelled out in explicit terms. Donning Western clothes is often a first stage, especially for males. Mastering the national language (including nuances of accent that can be giveaways), changing one's surname, or trading sandals for shoes may be among the more obvious ethnic markers. Moving from the country to the city allows a few to dissociate themselves from friends and neighbors, just the opposite of other migrants who cling to such ties as important aspects of their lives. In fact, for a few self-confident groups and individuals, retaining—or even returning to—patterns distinctive of their ancestral ethnic group may serve valuable functions (cf. Conklin, chapter 30).

There is often striking continuity in the face of dramatic changes. Ethnic markers (such as speech or clothing) sometimes lose their significance. In other contexts, they are being given new value as marks of distinction or as remnants of tradition (cf. Femenías, chapter 25, or Tice, chapter 21).

Gender itself is another basic element in personal identity, although the old stereotypes of *machismo* (aggressive masculinity) and *Marianismo* (female deference) have been severely challenged for a generation or two. It had long been ironic that so many professors, senators, physicians, and other professionals were women while the popular culture idealized the image of cloistered virgins or mothers. Just as *macho* now means male but not necessarily aggressive, as in Gutmann (chapter 28), *machismo* often refers to excellence, whether in sports, poetry, rhetoric, or otherwise. There is still some confusion and prejudice with respect to those who do not fit traditional sexual roles (Murray, chapter 27), and gay liberation lags behind the times with the exception of a few widely scattered enclaves.

Age grades differ from one community to another, although there tends to be respect for seniority and the experience and knowledge that it implies. Where there is a civil-religious hierarchy or system of rotating cargos, progression through the ranks brings prestige and, for some, admission to the honored rank of elder. It is fascinating that ethnographers have been able to reveal such dynamics, also frequently showing crucial roles played by members of the extended family, who pool resources and bask in the reflected glory of a few individuals who could not in reality have borne the costs of climbing the social ladder alone.

The fact that ethnic stereotypes are sometimes so negative as to result in a bogey-man effect should not be surprising, and Adams (chapter 26) gives us an example of U.S. *gringas* as viewed by native Guatemalans. Her role as an outsider was crucial in shaping the data that were volunteered to her, and current events at the national and international level do much to illuminate this case study.

If we shift our focus from individuals and local populations to the nation as a whole, the reading by Brandes (chapter 29) is revealing; a rite that is part of the global Roman Catholic liturgy has been adapted and transmogrified into a local holiday and even a symbol of nationhood, with special foods, toys, and other institutions rapidly evolving.

With specific reference to the Kayapó, Wari', and Nambiquara peoples of the Amazon, Conklin (chapter 30) vividly shows the obverse of what many presume to be inevitable pressures toward assimilation in this increasingly globalized world system. Here traditional or native ethnicity and identity are clearly being used, self-consciously and quite cunningly, to communicate their message (about human rights, ecology, and other themes) to outsiders wherever they may be.

Those who are commonly referred to as tribal peoples often do not live in tribes at all, and we sometimes find that the names that have been used for such populations have nothing to do with what they call themselves. Linguistic terms or epithets applied by hostile neighboring groups have sometimes become ossified in the anthropological literature, although sometimes a group can force a change (as when the people known in many articles and monographs as Tarahumara declared themselves to be Rarámuri—see Mares (chapter 14).) Brazil was long more active than any other Latin American country in dealing with indigenous populations, although occasional isolated atrocities continued throughout the twentieth century. The huge Xingu National Reserve was set aside as a sort of halfway house in what was imagined to be the inevitable progression toward assimilation. Perhaps this century will see more serious efforts to come up with feasible alternatives like ethnodevelopment (Stearman, chapter 20) and interethnic organizations, some of which even have hemispheric scope nowadays (Stavenhagen, chapter 13)

The importance of identity and ethnicity, whether to an individual or to a community, may change through time and may even depend on the situational context. But that does not in any great measure lessen its significance, which can only be discerned through an insider's view. Having created many types and stereotypes with respect to Latin American populations, anthropologists are now actively engaged in dismantling or shattering many of those same images that were based on outsiders' views.

FOR FURTHER READING ON IDENTITY AND ETHNICITY

Although there was lively debate about the scope and relative merits of social and cultural anthropology in anthropological journals during much of the 1940s and 1950s, the issue excites few now, as any introductory textbook will explain.

The plurality and hybridization of Latin American cultures is now generally recognized, although the stereotype a generation ago focused on an imaginary duality of modern (generally urban, industrialized and oriented toward Western ways) and backward or traditional (generally rural, agrarian, pastoral or hunting, and distinctly non-Western in at least some important ways). Ethnicity is a concept that has often been used synonymously with religion, nationality, or language. All of those may be components, but rarely does any one of them equate with the kind of affectively charged affiliation and relationships that one tends to find in ethnic groups. F. Barth early recognized the difficulty of distinguishing among *Ethnic Groups and their Boundaries* (Little Brown, 1969); R. Stavenhagen chronicled *Ethnic Conflict and the Nation-State* (St. Martin's, 1996), and G. H. Cornwell and E. W. Stoddard (eds.) offer several case studies of *Global Multiculturalism: Comparative Perspectives on Ethnicity, Race, and Nation* (Rowman & Littlefield, 2000). It seems ironic that some countries, where until recently members of various ethnic groups were not allowed to vote and were scorned as "brute Indians," have rewritten their constitutions to emphasize multiethnicity and cultural pluralism while recognizing various languages as equally valid for legal, educational, and other purposes.

Spanish colonial society explicitly distinguished between white and Indian people in terms of dress, residence, taxation, legal status, and so on, as aptly described by M. Mörner, *Race and Class in Latin America* (Columbia University Press, 1969) and *Race Mixture in the History of Latin America* (Little Brown, 1967). The inevitable intermediates came to predominate in numbers in most areas, as outlined by C. Esteva F., *Mestizaje in Ibero-America* (University of Arizona Press, 1995). Although he treats it as a worldwide issue, Latin American examples dominate in N. Garcia C., *Hybrid Cultures* (University of Minnesota Press, 1995).

Early studies of Afro-Latin Americans tended to focus on surviving "Africanisms," specific traits that could be traced across the Atlantic; see M. J. Herskovits, *The Myth of the Negro Past* (Harper & Row, 1941) and R. Bastide, *African Civilizations in the New World* (Harper & Row, 1972). The Brazilian myth of racial equality was disseminated widely by G. Freye, *The Master and the Slaves*; and *The Mansions and the Shanties* (both trans., A.A. Knopf, 1956 and 1966). One of the most effective unmaskings of that myth was by F. Fernandes, *The Negro in Brazilian Society* (2 vols. trans., Columbia University Press, 1965). A good anthology on *Blackness in Latin America and the Caribbean* was recently compiled by N. E. Whitten and A. Torres (2 vols., Indiana University Press, 1998).

The Garífuna were studied by N. L. S. Gonzalez in *Sojourners of the Caribbean* (University of Illinois Press, 1988). There are many books (some out of print) that cover blacks in Ecuador by N. E. Whitten, in Central America by M. Olien and N. Helms, and in Mexico by G. Aguirre B.

Although they still constitute a small portion of the overall population, Chinese and Japanese immigrants and their descendants tend to monopolize certain small niches in the economic systems of countries where they live; East Indians, by contrast, often remain laborers.

A combined history and sociology of Jews can be found in J. L. Elkin, *Jews of the Latin American Republics* (2nd ed., Holmes & Meir, 2000); see also her *The Jewish Presence in Latin America*. I. Klich and J. Lesser (eds.) deal with both *Arab and Jewish Immigrants in Latin America* (F. Cass, 1998). Italians in Argentina, Spaniards in Mexico, and a few other immigrant groups (including retired expatriates from the United States in Costa Rica) are numerically significant enough to merit being studied.

Whether they are more important or simply more interesting to anthropologists is not clear, but there is much more written about Protestants (both native and immigrant) than about modern Catholics in many Latin American countries. Certainly missionaries set out to change a culture, and converts can make for some social dislocation in traditionally Catholic communities. Illustrative of recent writings on the subject are D. R. Miller (ed.), *Coming of Age: Protestantism in Latin America* (University Press of America, 1994); V. Garrard and D. Stoll (eds.), *Rethinking Protestantism in Latin America* (Temple University Press, 1993); D. Martin, *Tongues of Fire* (B. Blackwell, 1990); and E. Willems, *Followers of the New Faith* (Vanderbilt University Press, 1967).

The relation between dress, self, and craft production is examined in great detail in a highland Guatemalan community by C. Hendrickson, *Weaving Identities* (University of Texas Press, 1995).

Exemplary of a new genre that goes beyond vague generalizations about *machismo* as contrasting ideals for the genders is M. Gutmann, *The Meaning of Macho* (University of California Press, 1996), which deals with workaday behavior. Compare E. E. Brusco, *The Reformation of Machismo* (University of Texas Press, 1995) or S. C. Bourque and K. B. Warren, *Women of the Andes* (University of Michigan Press, 1981).

The difficult roles of gays in Latin America are only recently gaining attention as a subject of ethnographic research; see, e.g., S.O. Murray, *Male Homosexuality in Central and South America* (Instituto Obregon, 1992); and *Latin American Male Homosexualities* (University of New Mexico Press, 1995).

The system of cargos, often called a civil-religious hierarchy, is a series of ranked offices that include costly service to both the church and community, and that bring commensurate prestige to those who spend time and money in elaborate ritual performances. An unusually detailed explication of one such is F. Cancian, *Economics and Prestige in a Maya Community* (Stanford University Press, 1965).

The Day of the Dead has long been noteworthy in art, folklore, and as a symbol of Mexico. Other anthropological studies include E. Carmichael, *The Skeleton at the Feast* (University of Texas Press, 1992); H. G. Nutini, *Todos Santos in Rural Tlaxcala* (Princeton University Press, 1989); and J. Garcia G., *Digging the Days of the Dead* (University Press of Colorado, 1998).

The idea that native peoples (who sometimes prefer to be called First Nations, indigenes, or something else, but rarely Indians) have taken to the world stage to air past grievances and current demands is novel in much of Latin America and is unsettling to some who saw themselves as the natural heirs to wealth and power. Several examples of this have been mentioned in the introductory sections of other parts in this book; one of the most complete and informative treatments of the subject, with special reference to Latin America, is A. Brysk, *From Tribal Village to Global Village* (Stanford University Press, 2000).

Judith Laikin Elkin is an historian, political scientist, and Foreign Service officer. Her books include Imaging Idolatry, Krishna Smiled, The Jewish Presence in Latin America *(with G. W. Merkx),* Latin American Jewish Studies *(with A. Sater), and* Jews of the Latin American Republics.

Long forbidden in areas of Spanish jurisdiction throughout the world, Jews often went to remarkable lengths to conceal their religious beliefs and practices. The situation of Afro-Latin Americans as relatively "invisible" is comparable in many respects (Dzidzienyo, chapter 24), although markedly different in detail. Even since independence, most countries in Latin America have very few Jews. Elkin here briefly introduces the history of their participation—from Jewish gauchos, to refugees, to hunters of Nazi gauleiters—*a fascinating saga that remains in large part untold. Issues of religion, ethnicity, and language in this connection deserve far more scholarly attention that they have received.*

Jews in Latin America
Judith Laikin Elkin

Jews do not figure largely in the postindependence history of Latin America as currently written. Overlooked generally by Latin Americanists as too few and too marginal to affect the area's development, they have likewise been regarded by Jewish scholars as outside the course of Jewish history. So we find that Latin American historians omit mention of a Jewish presence within the independent republics once the fires of the Inquisition have been banked. Historians and sociologists of the Jewish people, for their part, tend to overlook Latin America, grouping its Jewish communities under "Others" after more salient groups have been investigated.

Is there in fact any such entity as Latin American Jewry? The life of Jews moves within the lives of nations among whom they live, is shaped and altered by them. In the case of Latin America, without underestimating the differences that characterize the various republics, we may agree that there are also broad similarities. Cultural congruence, rooted in the phylogeny of their peoples, is the base upon which studies of such continent-wide phenomena as race, the military, the church, and the system of latifundia have all been founded. Immigration, too, is subject to continental analysis. Generally speaking, immigrants have had to integrate into societal molds that were Iberian and Catholic, that demanded of them not only conformity but complicity in a hierarchical social order that consigned them to a specialized and subordinate category. In accommodating to such social orders, Jews all over Latin America faced similar constraints and opportunities. Molded by their own cultural heritage, they made similar adaptations. The result was the emergence of an identifiable Latin American Jewry, sharing certain economic, cultural, and social characteristics that distinguish them both from their matrix populations and from the Jewries of other continents. These shared characteristics include their origin as immigrants, a distinctive demographic profile, characteristic lifestyle, and mode of acculturation. Despite differences of nuance, Latin American Jews constitute an identifiable group, the study of which enlarges our understanding of Latin America and expands the universe of the Jewish diaspora.

The reasons for Jewish invisibility have partly to do with the small number of people involved. There are probably just half a million Jews scattered through the Latin

American continent and adjacent islands. In all countries Jews comprise less than 1 percent of the population, so that recognition of their presence may strike some as an academic nicety. But Jews have been numerically insignificant in all countries where they have dwelt.

Despite the elusive nature of the history of Jews and Jewish converts in the Spanish and Portuguese New World, it is appropriate to open a narrative of modern times with a glimpse into the earlier period. Only in this way can we understand the mentality of the Jews who settled in Latin America following the attainment of independence and discover the preconceptions that greeted them on their arrival.

It is a truism of Latin American history that events and ideologies of the colonial period imposed lasting patterns on the independent republics. In the case of Jews, the pattern was defined long before the imposition of Spanish and Portuguese rule in the Americas. At home, both kingdoms pursued policies that were intended to exclude Jews and the descendants of Jews from society, their purpose being to create a populace united in both political and religious allegiance. Subsequently, Jews and converted Jews were prohibited by law from entering the colonial dependencies of Spain, though, as we shall see, many of them did. Portugal tolerated the emigration of *conversos* to Brazil, but these eventually found themselves fearful for their physical survival. Because society dealt with Jews by proscribing them, Jews and their descendants figure in the history of the colonial period only as objects of legal or ecclesiastical procedures designed to reduce them to conformity, as penitents and impenitents exhibited to the people as examples of the horrors of deviance. This encounter between Jews and conversos, on the one hand, and a church-state system bent on their physical and spiritual eradication, on the other, provides the psychological backdrop to the presence of Jews in the Latin American republics in modern times.

Jews lived in the Iberian Peninsula when Spain was a remote province of the Roman Empire. Before 1492, they functioned as a separate caste under Visigoths, Christians, and Moors, alternately integrated into general society and marginalized from it, subjected to periodic pogroms, but also serving as an incubator for talented individuals who then were tapped for high public office. Characteristically, special legislation ordained and circumscribed the Jews' participation in public life, protected them from excessive religious violence, and kept intact their communities in ghettos that were important sources of revenue for contending princes and princelings.

In 1391, the inflammatory preaching of religious zealots, unrestrained by the church, aroused popular zeal for the extermination of Judaism and the total Christianization of society. Pogroms erupted in Seville and, proceeding northward, forced the conversion of thousands of Jews. In 1412–15, laws requiring Jews to leave their houses and quit their professions forced a wave of "voluntary" conversions, bringing into existence a new class of person: the converso, or New Christian. Mass conversion created its own momentum, leading to voluntary conversions of a considerable number of Jews, probably because conversos were able to integrate themselves into Spanish life, whereas Jews suffered heavy legal disabilities. For the rich and well educated, conversion was an open sesame into lives of influence and public service. At a time when rationalism was challenging the religious beliefs of intellectuals, it may have seemed less important to retain one's allegiance to "the dead law of Moses," as the church called Judaism, than to collaborate with the dominant society in the creation of tolerable living conditions. Intermarriage with the best families of the land became common, and by the sixteenth century there was scarcely a noble family in Spain without its converso connection.

Thousands of Spanish Jews, however, continued to adhere to their ancestral faith, and so the original body of Jewry divided into two groups living side by side: conversos and Jews. Related to each other by blood and marriage ties, the two groups found themselves cast into very different roles by society; yet their fates remained intertwined, for the church alleged that the Jews presented a threat to the adoptive faith of the conversos. In 1480, the Inquisition was formally installed in the peninsula for the purpose of inquiring into the faith of the recently converted. Riding the crest of authority accrued through their defeat of the Moors and the unification of Christian Spain, the Catholic Kings, Isabella of Castile and Ferdinand of Aragon wrested authority over the Inquisition, turning it into an instrument of the crown, not, as it was elsewhere, an instrument of the pope.

As the eight-hundred-year civil war of the Reconquest drew to its close, a thirst for religious as well as national unification gripped the victorious Catholics. Within weeks of the fall of Granada, last Moorish bastion on the peninsula, the process of sieving Jews out of Spanish life culminated in the Edict of Expulsion. The Edict, issued on March 30, 1492, forced Spain's remaining Jews to choose between conversion to Catholicism and exile from Spain. Thousands of professing Jews fled Spain for North Africa, Portugal, Italy, and the Ottoman Empire.

Scattered as they had been by the hazards of expulsion, inquisition, and toleration, Sephardim grasped the opportunities for trade that were presented to them in the sixteenth century by the hostility between Christian Europe and the Ottoman Empire, and in the seventeenth century by the Dutch challenge to the Spanish/Portuguese hegemony in the New World. The family linkages among Sephardim (of all religions or none) enabled them to navigate treacherous political currents to emerge as successful merchants at a time when international trade was still trammeled by the mercantilist policies of the great powers.

The contemporary Jewish communities of Latin America were formed between 1889 and World War I, largely by East European Ashkenazim. The extremely high migration figures for this period reflect the intense pressures that were being exerted upon Jews within their countries of origin, at a time when international travel was relatively cheap and most countries of the Western Hemisphere followed unrestricted immigration policies.

Most migrants of this period originated in the Russian Empire, Poland, and Romania, where a dual policy toward Jews was being exercised by governments of the late nineteenth century. Toleration for the Jewish commercial and industrial bourgeoisie that was engaged in modernization of the economy was accompanied by ruthless oppression and deprivation of the majority, a policy aimed at driving impoverished Jews to emigrate. The pressure was particularly severe in Russia, where the czarist government sought to divert attention from economic upheaval and social and political struggle by encouraging a brutal wave of pogroms.

POST–WORLD WAR I

Global Jewish migration was part of the great immigrant stream that coursed from east to west throughout the nineteenth century. Halted by World War I, the migrants resumed their westward flow once the guns grew silent—but in diminished numbers because barriers were now placed in their way. On the eve of World War II, these barriers became almost insuperable. The communities that are in place today are the product of interwar settlement patterns, as molded and reshaped by events since 1945.

Following the breakup of the Austrian and Ottoman empires and the fulfillment of the pledge of self-determination for small nations, national majorities gained access to the levers of power for the first time and were in a position to shape economic and political policies. Many of these were calculated to make life difficult for Jews long before the rise of Hitler. Sephardim had been abandoning their homes in Turkey and the Balkans ever since the Young Turk rebellion of 1908 and the Balkan War of 1912–13.

German-speaking Jews began appearing in numbers in Latin America in 1933, the year of Hitler's accession to power. But the rise of fascism in Europe coincided with the adoption of exclusionist immigration policies elsewhere. Draconian visa restrictions, initiated by the United States, rippled through the Western Hemisphere in the thirties, narrowing the options of the refugees. Jews who sought to escape the Nazi onslaught found it increasingly difficult to enter their preferred lands of destination and had to go wherever governments would let them in. The result was to increase the celebrated dispersion of the Jews to a greater degree than ever before in their history.

Latin America never absorbed more than a tiny fraction of Jewish emigrants. Over the course of a century, the region absorbed 5 percent of the total European Jewish migration, ranking a distant third after the United States (71.5 percent) and Palestine/Israel (9.7 percent).

Exclusionist immigration policies were adopted almost universally in the years prior to the outbreak of World War II. Worldwide depression and commercial competition in dwindling markets prompted waves of anti-Jewish feeling in many sectors of the continent. In the face of a possible fascist victory in Europe, there was a desire to land on the winning side. As a result, the anti-Semitic broadcasts and publications of professional Nazi propagandists found resonance among classes of people who believed they were losing ground to the more aggressive economic style of the immigrants. Gradually an ambience developed that was less favorable to immigrants generally, and to Jews specifically. Anti-Semitic attitudes were in no instance as strong or as violent as those which swept Europe in the same period, but Jews experienced a general feeling of threat from the right: from nativists, from fascists, from German and Spanish immigrant colonies among whom Nazi-Fascist ideology took root, and from sectors of the unreconstructed church hierarchy. It was in this ambience that the present-day Jewish communities evolved.

From 1935 to 1938 there was a narrow window of opportunity when it would have been possible to resettle Jews in Latin America—not in the modernizing countries that Jews preferred and that had set their faces against their entry, but in smaller countries that had not previously been deemed suitable areas for their settlement. But in such countries resettlement was limited by multiple factors: underdeveloped economies, unbridged racial divisions, policies that favored agricultural laborers, the lack of funds to finance resettlement projects, the rising prestige of fascism, and—not a minor factor—the inability of German Jews to grasp the enormity of the danger they confronted and the corresponding need to seize any chance to escape.

The phenomenon of institutionalized fragmentation, well known throughout Jewish history, has been well explained by Rafael Patai (1971:160):

> A certain degree of acculturation to the non-Jewish environment has taken place in every Jewish Diaspora. In view of these acculturative processes which have been very considerable, especially since the Jewish Enlightenment and emancipation, it is quite clear that the Jewish people as a whole cannot be termed an ethnic group. There are marked cultural differences among the Diasporas, and everywhere the traits in which one Diaspora differs from the others are the traits in respect of which it is similar to its non-Jewish environment. On the other hand, no Jewish Diaspora is culturally identical with its non-Jewish host people; or, to put it positively, every Diaspora differs from its gentile environment in several respects, of which Jewish religion and tradition and Jewish group identification are the most important. In relation to the gentile majority, the Jewish Diaspora of every country thus constitutes a different ethnic group, but the Jews as a whole constitute not one but several ethnic groups.

Jews seeking new homelands exercised their options in ways not too different from non-Jewish immigrants. In societies to which entry was circumscribed by the ambit of Catholicism, landownership, and *abolengo* (good birth), industry and commerce offered entrée to the immigrant, whether as worker, entrepreneur, or lowly vendor of manufactured goods. Arriving as they did from modernized countries, the Ashkenazim in particular found opportunity for those with skills, education, capital, luck, or a combination of all these.

For much of the immigration period, Latin American immigration policies were selective rather than open, largely because so much of the land had already been pre-empted before the age of immigration dawned. Reverence for the immigrant experience and the pioneering thrust westward, so prominent a feature of United States history, is largely absent, even (or most especially) in countries such as Argentina that were populated primarily by immigrants. Among the ambivalently received intruders, Jews were perceived as triple strangers: by religion, by ethnic origin, and by historical experience. Their arrival on the continent was almost in its entirety a product of modern forces: the advance of industrial capitalism from western, to central, to eastern Europe, and its impact upon populations living there. They had not passed through the Spanish crucible, and the autochthonous cultures were even more alien to them. The lives of the first and second generations were anchored, not in the historical or mythical past of their respective countries, but in the more recent past of their own countries of origin and in their collective consciousness of the Nazi holocaust and formation of the State of Israel. This incongruence between the mental frameworks of Jews and the Latin American societies into which they attempted to fit cannot be overstressed.

In their effort to "make America," immigrants were able to make substantial gains, in part because they were untrammeled by local tradition and desperate to find means of subsistence. They rose economically with startling rapidity, a mobility that was shared unevenly by Jews. The latter's late arrival, small numbers, and concentration in a narrow occupational range led to the apparent capture of some sectors of the economy at certain times and certain places, calling down upon their heads ancestral antipathies that had remained embedded in Hispanic Catholicism. What in fact had happened was that Jewish immigrants occupied niches in national economies for which they were suited by experience. Adjusting themselves to local conditions, they became peddlers or artisans, then, adjusting once more, moved into fixed commerce and manufacturing, especially in new branches of industry that were just developing under the impact of new technology. They thus became a part of that much larger immigrant force that was beginning the modernization of Latin America.

Economic advancement was not matched by social integration. Jews had never developed linkages with non-Jewish *campesinos*; under the circumstances outlined here, contact with the proletariat was broken. This is a startling fact, considering that so large and so vocal a portion of Jewish immigrants arrived with leftist and universalist deals, determined to relieve workers of the world of their chains. But the Jewish labor activists who so alarmed conservative elites in the early decade of the century were ahead of their time. They met little positive response from the masses, and severe political repression from the elite, both as activists and as Jews. Meanwhile, economic and political forces converted the majority of the Jewish proletariat into a bourgeoisie. The combination of forces produced a community that, in statistical terms, is almost totally middle class. By the 1960s, when revolutionary ideologies ignited masses of dispossessed people from Cuba to Bolivia, from Chile to El Salvador, the advantaged position of the Jewish majority was no longer conducive to alignment with populist forces; for the most part, Bundism, communism, and the whole panoply of radical ideologies that arrived in the immigrants' baggage had been confined to the shadow-play of communal elections.

Jewish links to the elite classes in Spanish-speaking countries were conspicuously weak from the start. Their exclusion originated in religious shibboleths reaching back hundreds of years. It also derived in part from identification with commerce. Depreciation of entrepreneurial pursuits has been remarked on for all Latin American societies, and entrepreneurial talent was from the start drawn from the foreign-born or the sons and daughters of immigrants. Immigrant entrepreneurs were at the root of modernization, but they lacked social prestige commensurate with their wealth. Within this depreciated group, Jews and Arabs found themselves on the bottom rungs of the social ladder, with a longer and harder climb to the top. The obstacles those "turcos" faced were more numerous and more intractable than those which confronted other parvenus.

Low birth rate, aging population, rising mortality rate, small family size, increasing rates of intermarriage, and fluctuating but continuous emigration characterize the Jewish populations of Latin America, causing them to diminish in size and to shrink to minuscule minorities. Urbanization intensifies all these trends. City life typically reinforces the desire to limit the size of one's family. Higher education paves the way for economic and social mobility, which in turn brings Jewish youth into contact with attractive non-Jewish mates, as well as with the potential for improved quality of life through emigration. Jews at both ends of the spectrum—those who intermarry and ignore their Jewish heritage and those who emigrate in order to lead fuller lives as Jews—contribute to the cultural homogeneity of the Latin American peoples, who are as yet undecided whether to accept cultural pluralism as a valid ideal.

Reference

Patai, Raphael. 1971. *Tents of Jacob.* Englewood Cliffs, NJ: Prentice-Hall.

Anani Dzidzienyo teaches Afro-American Studies and Portuguese and Brazilian Studies at Brown University.

Until recent years, it was a popular truism—debated by only a few scholars—that "racial democracy" could be found in Brazil and a few small Latin American countries (in contrast with harshly repressive racism in Anglo-America). Whatever the truth may have been in the latter part of the twentieth century, most observers agree that the images—and associated practices and attitudes—are diverging from that stereotype.

Dzidzienyo here briefly discredits the simplistic old view and hints at a variety of new influences that are affecting the ways in which people of African descent fit into the diverse local societies of Latin America, no matter what portion of the population they represent. Although markedly different in detail, the situation of Jews as relatively "invisible" is comparable in many respects (Elkin, chapter 23).

No Longer Invisible
Afro-Latin Americans Today
Anani Dzidzienyo

It is self-evident that specific historical, cultural, socioeconomic and political conjunctions result in the emergence of different race relations patterns in the Americas. Brazil and the Caribbean countries, for example, differ significantly from Peru, where people of African descent are in a distinct minority and their position can be properly understood only in relation to a numerically dominant "minority" of indigenous peoples. In the discussion of race relations, however, neither Latin America nor the United States occupies a position of privilege; fluidity, we now understand, requires some rethinking and re-evaluation in light of what we have come to learn about race relations orders and how they interface with orders of power and privilege. If fluidity or ambiguity resulted in the creation of greater maneuverability for individuals, it is by no means clear that such an option was maximally beneficial to groups seeking political action and organization.

The much admired non-contentiousness of race relations patterns in Latin America is beginning to seem rather less benign than it did, if only because of the relative silence of voices from "below." This is not, of course, to deny the presence of contrarian voices; over time and in various ways, and contrary to hegemonic ideologies that assign overriding significance to nationality (*not* race). Many have defined themselves as black and chosen actively to protest disadvantages directly attributable to their race and to propose remedial measures.

Wade's insightful discussion of Colombian race relations posits that they can be understood only in the context of the power relations involved. Indeed, it is precisely the dimension of power and its unequal distribution that frame race relations throughout the Americas.[1] That Afro-Latin Americans have consistently developed cultural initiatives in response to their predicament is testimony to their unwillingness to embrace victimhood. Yet those initiatives in no way address issues of political and economic power and representation, nor do they resolve the tension between actual power and symbolic power.

The most intractable problem for both the state and society in the matter of Afro-Latin Americans is how, for the first time in their collective history, to incorporate demands of non-dominant groups into the system of governance. What lessons or inferences they may draw from the experiences of the United States—which has known continually evolving public articulations of the presence of racial discrimination and the role of state and society in enforcing, modulating and abolishing that discrimination—are not easily predicted. But charges of Americanization and, implicitly, denationalization suggest that individual societies, eager to protect themselves against corrupting influences from extraneous sources, may well justify establishing a *cordon sanitaire*. Latin America's borders are permeable; thus the notion of the hermetic society, when applied specifically to Afro-Latin Americans, means, among other things, forcing a racial group to accept a narrowly conceived identity—that of nationality—while assiduously rejecting all external influences.

Given the dynamics of the real world, however, the predicament of Afro-Latin Americans may be defined as an issue of human rights. This reformulation of the issue effectively expands the conceptual and discursive parameters of the continuing discussion about race, allows for specific responses to specific situations and situates it in the context of debates and struggles that no state, and no society, will easily ignore. Yet if, as so often happens, the official response is mere lip-service, then little is to be gained; the issue of Afro-Latin America will simply languish under the rubric of a broader, more intractable problem.

The importance of this book is that it raises the "visibility" of Afro-Latin Americans from likely, and unlikely, parts of the region. The several countries covered there offer examples of the socioeconomic and political deprivation of their black populations—a deprivation that suggests absence from national and regional power structures. What makes the problems of Afro-Latin Americans particularly tricky is that in the post-colonial period there has been no explicit legal exclusion of blacks from participation at various levels of society. A closer look, however, points to pervasive areas of exclusion, some intended, others not.

Complicating the issue is the very role of the law in defining and managing race relations in the region. A fundamental fact about Latin American polities has to be confronted and "deconstructed." This is that, in the absence of post-abolition legislation specifically targeting former slaves and their descendants, and in the absence of a tradition of compliance—either because such legal provisions do not exist or because the law has an ambiguous role in assuring equality of rights to all citizens—it is highly problematic to plunge headlong into recommending possible roles for the law when there has been no history of the law's functioning in such a manner.

ISSUES OF INCLUSION AND EXCLUSION

In any analysis of Latin American race relations, it is crucial to distinguish between dominant ideas articulated about national unity and race relations and oppositional ideas emerging from Afro-Latin American groups in a way that reflects their political heterogeneity. The role of historical memory cannot be overstated, especially in view of the fact that present-day activists are not necessarily concerned with political genealogies.

The issue of "group" versus "individual" rights is another problematic area. In the case of Brazil, for example, the thrust of post-abolition race relations and social mobility has been predicated upon "individual mobility," as was the case during slavery. This emphasis on individual strategy resulted in the emergence of individuals of stellar quality whose removal from the group did not in any way reflect the general predicament of the group. The dominant society, with no small pride, often cites these "honourable exceptions" as examples of the successful working of the model, though the group from which these individuals emerged might interpret their "exceptionality" rather differently.

At what point in time does the paradigm shift its focus from individual to group? And what are the hurdles that advocates of group identity and group activism have to confront?

To explore such difficult questions, various researchers have sought to investigate the historical formation of Latin American race relations patterns, and so to unravel the gap between professed ideals of unity and one-peopleness, on one hand, and deeply rooted patterns of exclusion of Afros from the political, socioeconomic and educational centers of the polity, on the other. Here lies a fascinating contradiction: between the incorporation into the legitimate national arena of erstwhile African-derived religious, cultural and social traditions once considered societally or politically subversive because of their "primitive" provenance, *and* the absence of a corresponding insertion of Afro-Latin Americans into areas and structures of power and privilege from which they have traditionally been excluded.

To put the issue provocatively: what have been the real rewards for Afro-Brazilians, for example, now that the dominant society, including exclusive hotels, serves *feijoada* (a Creole stew) and the whitest-looking Brazilians are practitioners of Candomblé? Has this legitimating of Afro-Brazilian traditions fundamentally altered the imbalance in power relations between Afro-Brazilians as a group and the dominant society? Is the dominant society thinking "nationally, collectively" but continuing to act racially, exclusively?

BALANCING HISTORICAL, CULTURAL AND POLITICAL REALITIES

Is slavery still relevant? Yes and no. To argue that one cannot continue to talk back to slavery and its socio-racial economic structures to account for the conditions of Afro-Latin Americans does not mean that it *ipso facto* ceases to be relevant, especially in view of images and roles that are linked to slavery. The archaism of slave relations and their supplanting by "modernizing" economic and social relations have not resulted in the emergence of new societies in which status linked to slave origin has totally disappeared. The earlier optimistic expectations about the potential of class relations to undermine archaic socio-racial structures have not entirely materialized.

What is intriguing in this connection is the continuing hold that structures of power and prestige have on Latin American societies, irrespective of the relative size of the "white" population. Whether or not the societal push is to negate, or maintain distance from, blackness or to confine expressions of connection to blackness to the merely symbolic—particularly among those who are not identifiably black—the open articulation of pride in blackness is nowhere acceptable. Specific national permutations on "relations to blackness" (positive or negative) can provide important insights.

If Dominicans, for example, cannot contemplate blackness without the historical "specter" of Haiti and its present-day consequences, collectively and individually, how, specifically, are black Dominicans affected? Does the designation *indio* resolve the problem for them? Do Dominicans of a darker hue constantly face the problem of being mistaken for closet Haitians? The interesting and even insightful notion that Dominican national identity makes sense only in relation to Haiti—to be Dominican is to be not Haitian—does not sufficiently explain the long-range consequences for individual Dominicans.

HISTORY, NATIONALITY AND AFRO-IDENTITY

The impressive presence of historical Africa in the cultural, religious, folkloric and culinary spheres attests to the strength of both the original bearers of these forms and their descendants; it demonstrates, too, the ability of nations to absorb these legacies. To imagine or attempt to establish that from the time of their inception the incorporation of these traditions occurred in a linear fashion is to engage in selective historical evaluation. It is arguably the case that the very process of incorporation reveals certain basic contradictions in the relationship of the dominant society and its black population. Take, as examples, two definitive institutions in the cultural life of Brazil—Carnival and Candomblé. To survey either merely from the perspective of the past ten years is to ignore a complex history of repression of traditions that were of African provenance. That these institutions moved from the clandestine to the marginal to their present status as national institutions is indeed remarkable.

The real problem for Afro-Latin Americans is how successfully to juggle common nationality and the struggle to attain public legitimacy for Afro-identity. Legislation as a regulator of race relations in the post-colonial period can be only part of the solution, as blacks have not been excluded by law from full participation in the society. What is required is not a compilation of constitutional provisions as evidence of the role of law in guaranteeing rights. Given the interplay between (a) laws, customs, etiquette and publicly articulated views about the ideals of interracial harmony and (b) the reality of racial segmentation, not much would be gained by this. Afro-Latin Americans are already, indeed, full members of the "nation." How, therefore, can they structure their questions and demands in strictly legalistic terms? Can they challenge, or change through the mediation of the law, something that has been neither legal nor illegal? Does there exist anywhere in Latin America the modern-day equivalent of the system of customary law established in British colonial Africa—a body of traditional precepts and practices that, though unwritten, came to acquire the force of law?

Entry into government service, particularly the foreign service, as it affects Afro-Latin Americans offers an interesting challenge to the researcher. In Brazil one faces the sheer impossibility of finding anyone who will even acknowledge that race is a not insignificant factor in explaining the absence of blacks from the diplomatic service. Indeed, one even marvels at the sheer ingenuity of the rationalizations offered: to wit, nationality—Brazilianness—binds a multiracial society that enjoys exceptionally smooth relations among its many racial groups, which include a large number of people of mixed blood, and an absence of overt racial tensions. Nationality singularly and effectively eliminates the need for other identities, particularly those whose inherent volatility poses a threat to national unity. Here, too, one can look for comparisons with the exceptional cases of the United States and South Africa.

One commonly hears from non-Afro-Latin Americans perhaps overconfident denials that blacks—be they servants, soccer players, musicians—have any abiding interest in black issues or movements. They speak, too, of their access to Afro-derived religious and cultural institutions, remarkable for its ease when one considers the uneasy divisions of, say, North American society. But what of the Afros themselves—can one imagine a space in which they at times think and act independently of the overarching race-free, classless national identity? Given the power of that identity, all-inclusive yet respectful of implicitly racial privileges, it is not surprising that a certain caution prevails among blacks who in other systems or circumstances might choose to mobilize around race or Africanity.

It is encouraging to learn that Afro-Dominicans, for example, exhibit a reasonable degree of self-esteem in a negrophobic society. But we perhaps risk over-sentimentalization when we note that extensive racial mixing produces offspring who though visibly of different shades—one black, the other white—identify themselves as biological siblings.

COMPARATIVE PERSPECTIVES

There is no evidence to suggest that significant numbers of people of African ancestry anywhere in the Americas actively contemplate voting with their feet. However unsatisfactory existing conditions for those of their kind, they tend not to abandon their home countries to seek other national identities. How to explain this? Afros undoubtedly derive some benefit from the flexible system of racial designations. In post-colonial Latin America blacks have not been the targets of physical lynchings and other racially motivated acts of violence. The *de facto* segregation of Panama's Canal Zone was never the norm in the rest of Latin America. Nor did exclusionary practices—in schools, in clubs, in residential areas—enjoy the kind of legal sanction associated with racial segregation in the United States. Yet, as Abdias do Nascimento has consistently argued, "lynching" has far deeper meaning than the actual physical act. There is a special case to be made for (re)conceptualizing the role of violence as a determinant of "good" or "bad" race relations. A recurrent refrain in his writings since the mid-1940s is that racial violence is multifaceted and extremely subtle. To deny access to structures of education, health and political participation, he observes, constitutes violent actions for those on the receiving end. Such a conceptualization of violence and its role in race relations has the potential of liberating our understanding of the Latin American situation.

The point speaks directly to comparisons between the United States and Latin America. Meaningful comparisons cannot be selectively applied to only the most conspicuous aspects of race relations, especially those regulated by the force of law. Nor can comparisons be magically terminated at some point in the 1950s when the world was left to wonder at images of National Guard troops escorting a little black girl to school in the U.S. South to the taunts and jeers of whites. What happened after such shocking events is central to the comparison. Why, it needs to be asked, do institutions of higher learning in Latin America have so few black students, a paucity made even more astonishing when one compares their numbers with their counterparts in the United States? No amount of "flexibility," "smoothness" or "lack of tension" in racial matters can adequately explain away what is clearly a problem.

In a widely discussed case the daughter of the governor of the state of Espirito Santo, an Afro-Brazilian, was denied entry to an elevator designated for use by residents of a high-rise apartment building and, presumably, their guests. The story, a characteristic example of what one observer has very aptly termed "vertical apartheid," rings a familiar note to the many blacks who have themselves been assumed to be service personnel irrespective of their dress or demeanour. The governor's legal counsel chose not to argue the case on the basis of existing anti-racist legislation as they well understood the difficulties of successful prosecution in a legal climate where precedents are few and, perhaps even more important, the plaintiff bears the burden of proof. Lack of precedent here is linked to the conspicuous absence of multiracial civil rights organizations. The struggle for racial justice presupposes some notion of racial injustice; and as Latin American self-conceptions do not include that crucial notion, prominent multiracial organizations dedicated to racial justice are seen to be fundamentally oxymoronic and crass in their attempt to apply inappropriate North American racial paradigms to their societies.

Future examinations of present-day Afro-Latin Americans need to seek actively to extend the framework of the process to one that permits global comparison. That framework will have no *a priori* victors or successes contrasted with worst-possible cases; it will, one hopes, open the way for Afro-Latin Americans themselves to establish links with other peoples of African ancestry in transnational encounters. The salient feature of these meetings is not the search for ready-made, all-purpose solutions; rather, it is the airing of reflections and histories that transcend individual cases.

A possible future research area would be, for example, inter- and intra-Dominican relations in communities outside the national territory. Do Dominicans in the United

States hold steadfastly to the single commonality of Dominicanness, irrespective of race or colour? What happens when they come into contact with other Latin Americans whose socio-racial mix may not be so directly linked to a Haitian factor but whose societies nonetheless confer privilege, status and power on those who are of lighter hues? What happens when in the United States Dominicans and other Latin Americans confront the rigidly binary division of racial lines? But even this binarism is more complicated than it would appear.

Even more productive would be an exploration of both overt and covert differences, posing the question, Are there in fact certain *constants* in race relations throughout the Americas, constants implicit in oft-repeated phrases: "money whitens"; "in the other Americas an individual has a greater possibility to be whatever he or she chooses or desires"; "there is certainly greater racial mixture in Latin America"; "after all, we are all at least symbolically hybridized or mesticized"? What the literature lacks is an in-depth comparative inquiry, across cultures, that does not give disproportionate credence to colonial nomenclatures, idealized expressions of nationhood or peoplehood that extol race mixture while ignoring the clearly colour-based rank order of preference.

No amount of verbal elegance—or money—can "whiten" a Pelé, a Benedita da Silva or a Peña Gómez and still qualify as an accurate description of reality outside specific national contexts. Emphasizing the particularity of national etiquettes matters precisely because national histories and cultural practices are never to be ignored. However, as soon as individuals or groups cross national boundaries, those etiquettes and practices, be they concrete or symbolic, cannot be maintained in their innocence or originality. Does the *indio* Dominican or the Brazilian *moreno* who insists on being so identified find that North Americans, say, or Europeans, or continental Africans accept these categorizations? Indeed, it would be highly instructive to record African responses to the application of these labels to large numbers of their own, not simply a minority of honorable exceptions.

In 1989 a popular women's program on Venezuelan television discussed the question "Is it punishment to be a black woman in Venezuela?" The participants—a well-known politician, a physician, a model and sibling athletes—offered a range of perspectives. In its modest way the program sheds light on the discussion of race and gender in present-day Latin America. How interesting it would be to compare the program with advocacy initiatives undertaken by, say, Afro-Brazilian women's organizations, together with examples drawn from other national groups.

Visibility, or non-invisibility, is a multifaceted and variable phenomenon. In Peru, where the salient divide is between the indigenous and the mesticized components of the population, any disadvantages associated with blackness pale in comparison to the individual and collective weight of those disadvantages endured by the majority indigenous population. What Peru does share with other Latin American countries is the privileging of whiteness. In this particular race relations universe a study of indigenous-Afro relations in specific situations, over the centuries, could well contribute to our understanding of comparative race relations. Similar work could be done on Ecuador.

On matters of race and colour the novice observer does well to tread lightly when approaching societies and systems such as those in Latin America. Non-whiteness and blackness, one quickly learns, are not interchangeable concepts; never assume blackness—determine, with delicacy, the individual's personal identification, which may not be consistent with that assigned him or her by others. For the Latin American, a similar challenge waits in North America, say, or even continental Africa, where what is perceived as "white" may very well be, to the person concerned, "black."

LOOKING TO THE FUTURE

"Revealing" the true number of blacks in specific societies, in an effort to establish their numerical majority, does not *ipso facto* translate into power holding or even power sharing. Yet Afro-Latin Americans can bring to the study of comparative race relations their unique ability to interrogate Latin American paradigms both in theory and in practice. Those who in varying ways, and often in hostile conditions, struggle to be both true nationals and clear-eyed critics risk accusations of sullying the national image with imported ideas. Unlike their fellow nationals, they are oddly expected to limit their sociopolitical and even cultural thoughts and actions to approved ideals. The success of their struggle ultimately hinges on the legitimacy of a black perspective in national public discourse.

By focusing on the Afro-Latin American experience, we hope to provide a real service, to reopen the historical debate on comparative race relations in the Americas and to transcend the reductionism characteristic of earlier works that imposes a simple binarism—be it religion, history or culture—on what we now understand to be a complex reality. As we are confronted with the ever-increasing Latin Americanization of migrations to North America, the complexities and contradictions of each side's race relations become more fully exposed, making it possible to frame new questions and thus to avoid hackneyed explanations based on ideally constructed images rather than realities in which Latin Americans of African ancestry make themselves heard.

The battle to insert a politically active Afro-identity into the public discourse continues, and we hope to have made a useful contribution to this struggle. In this context, "no longer invisible" should be seen more in a political sense than in merely demographic, cultural or religious terms. It is not that politics and political participation are the sole definers; but without them the battle is only half won, and the fundamental role of power is not sufficiently accounted for or taken into consideration.

Country studies point to the rich heritage of Afro-Latin America and to enduring similarities in the position of Afro-Latin Americans in their societies, particular national conditions and background notwithstanding. The Cuban example both fascinates and frustrates. The only Latin American country to confront racism publicly, Cuba has undertaken concrete measures to integrate Afro-Cubans into institutions and areas of Cuban life from which they were traditionally excluded. It cannot, however, be assumed that race or racial factors have become non-issues. In a period of worsening economic conditions the society is coping with extraordinary pressures that impact negatively on the kinds of initiatives from which Afro-Cubans have derived considerable benefit. The discussion of recent events in Colombia, especially the struggles of Afro-Colombians to attain fuller inclusion in the national polity and its institutions, points to prospects for renewed political participation. Belize, Honduras and Nicaragua reveal complexities related to their histories, and to specific permutations of language, culture and identity tied to the non-Hispanic Caribbean. And the inclusion of the story of Afro-Bolivians, Afro-Mexicans and Afro-Uruguayans is in itself a noteworthy achievement; discussions of the Afro presence in Latin America will now have information, long missing from the literature, on countries that have, to date, been given little or no prominence or thought.

Of particular interest are the multiple meanings of Africa for Afro-Latin Americans. Nowhere in the Americas has there ever existed a unidimensionally positive image of Africa. It is to be hoped that our efforts will generate interest in researching the general and specific consequences of African descent for Afro-Latin Americans.

RECOMMENDATIONS

The book in which this is the concluding chapter could well be the foundation for the development of a data bank that stores information on the history, culture, politics and education of Afro-Latin Americans. For emerging grassroots non-governmental organizations the information provided would be invaluable in their struggle for legitimacy.

Each chapter provides much useful information that could also serve as the scholarly base for film documentaries and other projects examining the history, culture and politics of the societies discussed here. By raising common issues, it lays the groundwork for comparable transnational programs and areas of cooperation.

Might one hope for a program—sponsored, say, by UNESCO or the Organization of American States—that seeks not just to catalogue distinct historical events but, first and foremost, to identify and monitor (currency being of primary importance here) the intersections of history, economics, politics and culture among nations with populations of African descent? The African Diaspora Research Project based at Michigan State University serves as a useful model. That project has, *inter alia,* brought together scholars and graduate students who jointly explore interdisciplinary issues pertaining to the African diaspora. A good point of departure might be Whitten's proposal for reactivating studies of Afro-Ecuadorian communities.

For scholars and non-specialists alike, a perennial problem in their search for information on Afro-Latin Americans is locating materials. At the minimum, we provide a source of recent provenance that is widely available, and one that will contribute mightily to what one hopes will be a move closer to center-stage for a much neglected group.

Africa and Afro-Latin America: reconnecting the two through mutual exchanges of learning and information would surely count as one of the more fruitful outcomes of any effort to shed light on Afro-Latin Americans. A cooperative research undertaking—involving perhaps UNESCO, the Organization of American States and the Organization of African Unity—would seek to collect oral histories, published texts, films, and the like, organize them thematically and disseminate them in both Africa and Latin America. Individual countries, working cooperatively could initiate film and video projects. The challenge would be to reach a broad audience nationally and transnationally.

Fundamental to any understanding of Afro-Latin Americans is, I believe, the question of Africa. Deeply embedded in centuries-old shame, the idea of this continent has a central, though rarely considered, role in the complex relations among its descendants in the diaspora and the larger societies in which they live. The real and imagined meanings of Africa in all its richness and contradictoriness beg to be contemplated, not as aspects of a single phenomenon, but as factors in the dynamic of Afro-Latin American life today.

Note

[1] Wade, P., *Blackness and Race Mixture: The Dynamics of Racial Identity in Colombia,* Baltimore, MD, Johns Hopkins University Press, 1993, p. 3.

References

Barbalet, J. M. 1988. *Citizenship—Concepts in Social Thought: Rights, Struggle and Class Inequality,* Minneapolis, MN, University of Minnesota Press.

Castro, N. A. 1994. "Inequalities in a racial paradise: Labor opportunities among blacks and whites in Bahia, Brazil," SPURS, pp. 6–8. Massachusetts Institute of Technology.

Dzidzienyo, A. 1993. "Brazilian race relations studies: old problems, new ideas?" *Humboldt Journal of Social Relations,* vol. 19, no. 2, pp. 109–29.

Edwards, J. 1995. *Where Race Counts: The Morality of Racial Preference in Britain and America,* London and New York, Routledge.

Fiske, J. 1994. *Media Matters: Everyday Culture and Political Change,* Minneapolis, MN, and London, University of Minnesota Press.

Guimarães, A. S. 1994. "Race, racism and groups of color in Brazil," unpublished paper, March, Atlanta, GA, Latin American Studies Association.

Hall, J. A., and Ikenberry, G. J. 1989. *The State: Concepts in Social Thought,* Minneapolis, MN, University of Minnesota Press.

Hanchard, M. 1994. *Orpheus and Power: The Movimento Negro of Rio de Janeiro and São Paulo, Brazil, 1945–88,* Princeton, NJ, Princeton University Press.

Hellwig, D. (ed.). 1992. *African-American Reflections on Brazil's Racial Paradise,* Philadelphia, PA, Temple University Press.

Higginbotham, A. L. Jr. 1993. "Seeking pluralism in judicial systems: The American experience and the South African challenge," *Duke Law Journal,* vol. 42, no. 5, pp. 1023–68.

Horne, G. 1992. *Reversing Discrimination: The Case for Affirmative Action,* New York, International Publishers.

Merelman, R. M. 1995. *Representing Black Culture: Racial Conflict and Cultural Politics in the United States,* New York and London, Routledge.

Nascimento, A. do and Larkin, E. 1992. *Africans in Brazil: A Pan-African Perspective,* Trenton, NJ, Africa World Press.

Oboler, S. 1995. *Ethnic Labels, Latino Lives: Politics of (Re)Presentation in the United States,* Minneapolis, MN, University of Minnesota Press.

Portocarrero, G. 1993. *Racismo y mestizaje,* Lima, Edición Maruja Martinez/Eduardo Cáceres.

Reichmann, R. 1995. "Brazil's denial of race," *Report on the Americas: Brazil*, North American Congress on Latin America, vol. 27, no. 6, May/June.

Winant, H. 1992. "Rethinking race in Brazil," *Journal of Latin American Studies*, no. 24, pp. 173–92.

Xavier, A., and Pestana, M. 1993. "Survival guide for blacks in Brazil," contribution to the Discussion of Racism in the Constitutional Revision supported by Geledés Black Women's Institute, São Paulo, Brazil.

Blenda Femenías is an independent anthropologist; when she wrote this paper, she was an assistant professor at Brown University, and currently she is teaching at Simmons College.

Clothing carries many levels of meaning, and we might expect that to be especially the case in an area where a few communities are known for distinctive and elaborate styles of dress. By befriending and listening to those whose handiwork becomes such symbolically laden commodities, Femenías lets us in on the readiness of traditional craftspersons to adopt convenient novelties, some of the ways in which esthetic judgments are weighed against economic expediency, and even some of her own changing attitudes toward her subject matter.

A careful reader may never again feel so nonchalant about a garment that reflects the unique input of an individual, or lament the passing of a fashion that the wearers themselves seem eager enough to forego. For very different kinds of ethnic markers, see, for example, Conklin (chapter 30), or for handicrafts oriented to a broader market, Tice (chapter 21).

Ethnic Artists and the Appropriation of Fashion
Embroidery and Identity in Caylloma, Peru
Blenda Femenías

When I'm in Arequipa and I see a lady in embroidered clothes, I always greet her; she's from my land, she's my compatriot . . . [When I teach embroidery], no matter how much one teaches, the motifs don't come out the same. If there are twenty embroiderers, twenty different motifs come out although they have the same name. It's like, even if you're my brother, we're not the same.

Comments by embroidery artist Leonardo Mejía neatly express the character of Caylloma's ethnic clothes: simultaneously shared and individual. Similar appearance is important in recognizing a compatriot, but an artist's style of executing the complex embroidered designs distinguishes his/her work.

Contemporary textile production in Caylloma Province, centered in the Colca Valley, a highland region of southern Peru, occurs mostly in small workshops. Men and women embroider and tailor ornate clothes on treadle sewing machines. About 150 artisans provide garments for about 8,000 female consumers (total province population is about 35,000). This article draws on surveys that I conducted with 110 artisans and vendors, during two years of fieldwork.[1]

Textiles are important emblems of ethnic identity, as is commonly observed. However, I want to move beyond seeing "emblems" as superficial symbols, and to analyze ethnicity as a concept: as a relation of power among social groups with profoundly different resources. The rural, Quechua-speaking Colca Valley peoples are often considered "Indians" by outsiders, but they do not identify themselves as such. *Indio* in Peru is a powerful epithet that accentuates class difference and disguises it in racial terms. The social and economic roles that Colca Valley men and women play in Peruvian society have changed considerably in this century, and increasingly so in this generation. Ethnic artists have been crucial in mediating change, as they continue to produce ethnic clothes.

Written expressly for *Contemporary Cultures and Societies of Latin America*, Third Edition. An earlier version of this article was published in *Contact, Crossover, Continuity* (proceedings of the Fourth Biennial Symposium, Textile Society of America, Washington, 1995).

Through observing everyday and festival garments and discussing aesthetics with women who wear those garments I came to realize how important color and materials had become. In these domains, ethnic artists appropriate national and international tastes according to local cultural preferences, which in turn help to develop and maintain discrete ethnic identities.

Synthetic materials and bright colors are relatively new elements in embroidered clothes. In the Colca Valley, lime green yarn is more of a fashion concern than are changing hemlines. By focusing on "foreign" elements, I aim to disaggregate them as a category and address how and why they became firmly established in the Colca clothing repertoire. The very brightness that is exalted as "lively" by those who use it is often derided as "gaudy" by outsiders, even by textile scholars. This attitude unfortunately inheres in our concepts of "authenticity" and "identity," interfering with our acceptance of change in textiles, although we recognize its importance in other aspects of culture.

My approach challenges an older tendency in Andean textile studies that for many decades privileged an "authentic" indigenous textile: woven, of natural fibers, in a domestic setting, using techniques traced to pre-Columbian antecedents.[2] Numerous embroidered garments are worn in Caylloma—skirt, blouse, jacket, shawl, belt, hat. All have some technical and design elements in common, but few actually resemble pre-Columbian models. In this paper, I do not provide much technical detail about the embroidery and construction process, nor do I focus on the evolution of a single garment or on design motifs (topics that are developed further in Femenías 1997). Here, I focus on the garments as embodiments of artisans' ideas about design and aesthetics. An artist's style emerges as he or she incorporates specific colors, materials and techniques into these handmade objects, combining his/her understanding of contemporary fashions as well as established conventional patterns.

When I tell non-Peruvians that I work in the Andes, they usually ask, "Are the people there Indians?" The answer is both yes and no. There is no easy, straightforward way to answer this question. In fact, I am convinced that "Are they Indians?" is ultimately the wrong question. We need to ask, "When are they Indians?", "Why are they Indians?" and, essentially, "What is an Indian?" The valley's residents claim for themselves a unique identity that is not simply Indian, white, or mestizo; rather, this localized identity is based in specific cultural and material reality. In fact, understanding what *kind* of identity is Peruvian Indian identity today involves unraveling a whole series of complex and sensitive racial and political issues that combine race, class, and gender. This reading is one small effort in that direction.

The Colca Valley: A Place within a Region

The Colca Valley is a rural area near Arequipa, the second largest city in Peru.[3] Wedged between massive snowcapped peaks, terraced fields support the agricultural and pastoral lifeways in fourteen small villages. Most of the embroidery workshops are located in one larger town, Chivay (population about 5,000), the capital of Caylloma province. In and around the other villages, people live primarily by growing maize and other crops and by herding alpacas and selling their wool. The thick and lustrous alpaca fiber has been a major source of commercial wealth for the past century.

The ethnic heritage of the peoples is Inka and pre-Inka, including Collaguas and Cabanas groups, and Spanish. Almost everyone is bilingual in Quechua and Spanish. Archaeological and historical documentation show that outside intervention rather than isolation has characterized the valley's political economy for nearly two thousand years.

In the 1990s, low prices for crops and alpaca, severe droughts which almost paralyzed agriculture, an earthquake, and numerous political and economic factors eroded the resource base of the mountain communities. These problems accelerated migration to the cities. Since the 1950s, for example, the city of Arequipa has quintupled in population, from 200,000 to a million inhabitants.

In Arequipa and in Lima, the national capital, young men and women work mostly in the informal sector: as street vendors, domestic servants, taxi drivers, and/or petty smugglers. Migrants living in Arequipa can return to the valley quickly, in a four-hour bus trip. Young people in particular bring back their tastes and their hard-earned money, some of which the women spend on the fabulous embroidered clothes that make the area famous.

POWER AND APPROPRIATION

One phrase in this article's title, "the appropriation of fashion," may be misleading. Perhaps "appropriation *in* fashion," "*as* fashion," or even "fashion as appropriation" would convey my meaning better. The appropriation *of* fashion sounds as if fashion were an alien concept that ethnic artists must appropriate, having no fashion of their own. Nothing could be further from the truth. Changes in appearance and representation occur constantly among indigenous peoples as much as in so-called modern societies. These changes occur in ways that are structured in part by the power imbalances among groups. Colca Valley ethnic clothes are not survivals from ancient groups in isolated enclaves. In fact, they derive their ethnic meaning in part from the very act of appropriation.

This appropriation has occurred in part through incorporating materials produced outside the valley. Lightweight polyester blouse fabric, acrylic yarn, crushed velvet, and silvery lace are now elements of "traditional" embroidered Colca Valley clothes. While some of these materials are used exclusively for Caylloma clothes, most are appropriated from the non-indigenous domain of white, national Peruvian society, where they are featured in an office worker's blouse, housewife's sweater, or wedding gown. Really, traditional materials are no longer as readily available as in the past. Alpaca wool, in particular, is rarely used because almost all is sold on the international market.

Whatever the new owner takes to herself and makes her own (i.e., appropriates) originates outside the person or group, so we must ask by what right she claims it. I argue that such a right must inhere in a shared understanding of what is acceptable and what is not, based in concepts of power and its limits. Closeness, not distance, is the crucial factor: the closer two groups are, the more important a small detail of distinction becomes. In this case, as the importance of racial basis of Indian identity decreases, that of clothes as markers increases. Clothes mark the border between dominant and subordinate groups.

For a border to be meaningful, it must be shared. Borders are challenged when subordinate groups will not agree to the same meanings, appropriate items from the dominant group, and so refuse to acknowledge that item as the dominator's "own." I believe this has occurred in the Colca Valley through a two-way process of appropriation of materials.

Discussions of appropriation usually focus on the dominant taking from the subordinate groups. By actively appropriating their material and symbolic resources, the dominant enforce the subordination of those below them. Resistance then becomes the defiance of such appropriation. In a major study of everyday resistance, it is defined as the subordinate enacting strategies to *minimize* appropriation or to *reverse* it (Scott 1990:197, emphasis added). Thus, small, daily "rituals of subordination," which include wearing items of clothing, making gestures of deference, etc., become "rituals of reversal" (ibid.:187–88).[4]

Appropriation in reverse, or from below, is as important as that from above, and it is not adequately treated in terms of resistance alone. Emulation and appropriation are important strategies to establish different claims to power, not only to resist the existing power structure, as has been noted recently by Abu-Lughod (1990) and Radner and Lanser

(1993). The interrelationships between domination and subordination are intimate antagonisms that are never completely separate but always contain elements of each other.[5]

PRETTY CLOTHES, LOCAL CUSTOM AND CHANGING MATERIALS: RESULTS FROM THE ARTISAN SURVEYS

To dance in fiestas, and to understand the production and exchange process, I obtained my own set of embroidered clothes. I commissioned my friend Susana to embroider two skirts (*polleras*) for me. When I showed the finished skirts to other people, many of them praised their quality and beauty. However, one older female artisan, Rosalía, heaped scorn on Susana's choice of designs and materials. "That's already old-fashioned. Why did she use that outmoded design?" she complained, pointing to two rows of lime green yarn. I was stunned. I had looked forward so to dressing in the valley style, wearing the latest in *pollera* fashion, flawlessly executed by my talented friend. Yet Rosalía put them down; my skirts weren't fashionable enough!

Many North Americans have a phobia about bright colors. For a long time, I was among them. Only gradually did I come to appreciate the bright colors after a long period of rejecting them. I didn't always like lime green. In conversations with artisans about tourist sales, I never hesitated to point out to them that *gringos* abhor this color. An internal struggle preceded my decision to let Susana embroider my skirt exactly as she saw fit; I chose only the background fabric from the options she offered. After all, she was the expert. I couldn't bring myself to tell her, "I don't want any lime green, it reminds me of neon, acid, Gatorade." Indeed, lime green ended up in my skirt. Eventually I got used to it; I even got to like it, and I began to understand that it *is* an established element of authentic Colca clothes.

Let us consider why such colors claim an important place in Colca textiles—and have done so for so long that, just as I begin to warm to them, they're already beginning to be considered passé! In addition, Rosalía's comments showed me that artists' opinions about embroidery aesthetics and fashions vary widely, and their critical assessments of each other's work are often sharp indeed.

Leonardo Mejía, whom I quoted earlier, says that embroidery is not just a business; it is "an art that should be highly esteemed. I think this way, but others think only about their business. It is an artistic question and not an economic one."

Leonardo is the most adamant among those who claim embroidery as an art form, but he is not alone in recognizing the artists' role in shaping the ethnic and aesthetic consciousness of valley residents. My analysis of color and materials is based on artists' answers to qualitative questions about preferences, tastes, reasons women wear embroidered clothes, and changes.

In the words of Fermín Huaypuna, embroidered clothing "is part of the imagination and it's tradition, custom, and it reproduces the ancestors' creation." In fact, "custom" (*costumbre*) was the term most commonly used in explaining why women wear embroidered clothes. References to "ancestors" (*antepasados*) and various relatives (*abuelos*, "grandparents," *mamá*, "mother") were also frequent, as was "tradition" (*tradición*).

Artists often state that women wear the garments "because they are pretty" (*porque son bonitos*). "Pretty" (*bonito*) was cited by over a third of respondents, making it the next most common term after custom. A related usage, *porque es bonito*, connotes "suitable, nice." But why, I press, in what way are they pretty?

When artists discussed prettiness, they did so in terms of aesthetic or technical features. These features include questions of ethnic differentiation, amount and quality of materials, and innovation. To summarize briefly, the first distinction is one of overall quality. *Polleras* come in different grades: the one that I commissioned was of second quality, gauged by the type of materials used for ground fabric and trim, number of rows of embroidery, amount of color in that embroidery, amount of other trim, and kind of yarn applied. If we compare it to a first-quality *pollera* from Cabanaconde, we see that the latter has more expensive ground fabric, polychrome embroidered bands, and more detailed yarn designs. The ethnic differences are manifested in materials as well as designs: Only in Cabanaconde is rickrack used, and the monkey motif is more common there. The designs and materials are continually changing, leading to a situation in which traditional clothes are equated with the modern.

Livia Sullca, for example, maintains that "the embroidery is more modern, we apply more materials, we put on plenty of decorations." Leandrina Ramos says more is better: "Before it was simpler, now they're more adorned. The skirts are more embroidered every year." Not only are fabrics and trims more numerous than those available in the past, artisans maintain, but superior. They mention specific yarns and trims: *merino* yarn, *brillas* (metallic lace), *grecas* (braids, often metallic), as well as fabrics—including velvet, chiffon, *poliseda* ("*polysilk*")—a daunting array too lengthy to dwell on here. I collected 100 samples (including multiple colorways of the same fabric) from four artisan workshops; this by no means exhausts all the materials. In addition to knowing techniques and designs, artists must command a huge vocabulary of materials.

When I compared the actual decorations on the garments to samples I collected and terms used for them, I could not find any sheep's wool, so I was puzzled about "merino"; later I realized that it is not sheep's wool but a synthetic equally useful for weaving. It is available in many vivid colors as well as white. The typical bright colors (*colores vivos*)—pink, orange, and lime green—are used in background fabrics as well as trims. More recently pastel shades (*colores aguas*) of the same colors are making inroads, but the lively colors still dominate.

One day I asked about the lime green, calling it "light green" (in Spanish, *verde claro*). The artisan corrected me, "No, it's called *q'achu verde*." I learned that *q'achu* in Quechua means "light" only in certain contexts. One cannot say "light blue," *q'achu azul*. *Q'achu* also means new crops, forage, and by extension, freshness. A Quechua-Spanish dictionary defines *q'achu* as *forraje, pasto verde; q'achu q'omer, verde claro; . . . q'achu ch'uñu, chuño fresco, recién helado* (forage, green pasture; light green . . . fresh freeze-dried potatoes, recently frozen) (Cusihuamán 1976:117) (on *q'achu* as forage, see Treacy 1994a:191). The emergence of young crops in the naturally dry environment of the Colca Valley is precious and precarious. Contrasting with the gray and brown landscape, new plants vibrate very greenly indeed. The use of *q'achu verde* accents the importance of these green, growing things that feed people and animals (see Seibold 1995).

However, this cannot explain the apparent preference for synthetic materials. I believe this aspect of appropriation inheres more in the valley's position in the world economy. Cash crops such as barley, the sale of alpaca fiber, and urban migration have all increasingly enmeshed the Colca Valley peoples in a capitalist system. Local alpaca fiber is rarely available; it is almost always sold to the Arequipa textile factories. Likewise, the scarcity of fine sheep wool like merino reflects long-standing, extractive economic policies and lack of incentives for herd improvement.

Many artisans, both male and female, as well as their customers, are returned migrants. Their urban work experience changed both their tastes and their buying power. Their understanding of fashion trends undergirds their roles as "ethnicity brokers" in their own communities. Once they return, they continue to travel. To obtain materials, artisans often venture as far as the Bolivian or Chilean border, or even to the United States.

CONCLUSION

Caylloma's embroidered clothes represent both the revitalization and contestation of traditional values by all those who seek to legitimize their claims to community resources, either by participating in [...] [communiti]es in their home communities or even in [...] ciety, opportunities to display pride in lo[...] uch opportunity.

To the national soci[ety ...] means a rural dweller, poor and powe[...] [be]ing a "natural" economy of kin-based e[...] re, cannot be an Indian. The kind of etl[...] Indianness. Yet, they appropriate what [...] into ethnic symbols. Increasingly, Colc[a ...] st their subordinate position. For exa[mple ...] even national, politics, wearing elabo[rate ...] enías 1997).

To move beyond st[...] we must attend to the opinions and va[lues ...] to dismiss new traditions by relegatin[g ...] g them "authentic" status. Textile studies grounded in the analysis of power relations can explain the continued viability of clothes as ethnic symbols. Ethnicity itself cannot be understood simply by cataloguing cultural traits distinctive of different groups. We must also examine how, and why, some groups choose objects or processes from others who are usually considered dominant over them in order to create different objects that then embody cultural and ethnic identities.

In doing so, it becomes clear how closely bound up fashion is with questions of choice, of people's right to self-representation. Issues of taste, color, and materials are far from trivial; they all figure into the politics of authenticity. The artists whom I interviewed eloquently expressed their pride in their work, and their hope that it would continue to grow and change. In the words of Fermín Huaypuna, "Since it now has regional, national, and—why not say so—worldwide prestige, I believe that [our] embroidery will endure forever."

***

My gratitude goes first and foremost to all the artists of Caylloma, whose vision, creativity, and diligence produce some of the finest machine-embroidery in the world. I am grateful to Elayne Zorn, co-organizer of the panel "Fashioning Identity: Appropriation and Creativity in Pre-Columbian and Contemporary Andean Cloth" at the symposium, and participants Amy Oakland and Nikki Clark, like-minded proponents of the study, Ann Peters, and Katharine Seibold. A student travel award from the Textile Society [of America ...] [par]ticipation. Dissertation fieldwork was funded [...] [Pe]ru Institute on International Education) an[d ...] [R]esearch.

Notes

1 Elsewhere, I have [...] regional phenomenon (Femenías 1996 [199[...] [a]mbiguities of clothing and representation ([...]

2 For one important a[...] [199]7); for an overview of related scholarship, s[...]

3 Many recent publicati[...] 1988), Flores Galindo (1977), Manrique (198[...] [i]rrigation, and social organization, see Gelle[...] y (1994a, 1994b); on pastoralism, see Mark[...] [an]d Escalante (1988).

4 My use of appropriati[on ...] [M]arxist traditions, in which appropriation re[...] alienation. That is, the appropriation of a [...] [est]ablishing capitalist relations of production [...] [...] own product.

5 Other authors who discuss related topics for the Andes are Rasnake (1988) and Smith (1989). Rasnake's exploration of culture as a domain of resistance veers toward a more traditional Andeanism, but he provides evidence of the resilience of cultural institutions in Bolivia. On landlord-peasant relations in central Peru, Smith notes that cultural expressions are not resistance of a completely different sort than class conflict, but that both are political.

References

Abu-Lughod, Lila. 1990. "The Romance of Resistance." In *Beyond the Second Sex,* Peggy Sanday and Ruth Goodenough, eds. Philadelphia. University of Pennsylvania Press.

Benavides, María A. 1988. "Grupos del Poder en el Valle de Colca, Siglos XVI–XX." In *Sociedad Andina Pasado y Presente.* Ramiro Matos M., ed.: 151–178.

Cusihuamán G., Antonio. 1976. *Diccionario Quechua: Cuzco-Collao.* Lima. Ministerio de Educación.

Femenías, Blenda. 1987. "Introduction." In *Andean Aesthetics: Textiles of Peru and Bolivia*, pp. 1–8. Blenda Femenías, ed. Madison. Helen Allen Textile Collection and Elvehjem Museum of Art.

———. 1995. "Ethnic Artists and the Appropriation of Fashion: Embroidery and Identity in the Colca Valley, Peru." In *Contact, Crossover, Continuity: Proceedings of the Fourth Biennial Symposium of the Textile Society of America*, pp. 331–342. Los Angeles. Textile Society of America.

———. 1996 [1991]. "Regional Dress of the Colca Valley: A Dynamic Tradition." In *Textile Traditions of Mesoamerica and the Andes: An Anthology*, pp. 179–294. Margot B. Schevill, Janet C. Berlo, and Edward Dwyer, eds. Austin. University of Texas Press.

———. 1997. *Ambiguous Emblems: Gender, Clothing, and Representation in Contemporary Peru.* Ph.D. dissertation, Anthropology, University of Wisconsin-Madison.

Flores Galindo, Alberto. 1977. *Arequipa y el Sur Andino: Ensayo de Historia Regional, Siglos XVII–XX.* Lima. Editorial Horizonte.

Gelles, Paul. 1994. "Channels of Power, Fields of Contention: The Politics of Irrigation and Land Recovery in an Andean Peasant Community." In Mitchell and Guillet, eds.: 233–274.

Guillet, David. 1992. *Covering Ground: Communal Water Management and the State in the Peruvian Highlands.* Ann Arbor. University of Michigan Press.

Manrique, Nelson. 1985. *Colonialismo y Pobreza Campesina: Caylloma y el Valle del Colca, Siglos XVI–XX.* Lima. DESCO.

Markowitz, Lisa. 1992. *Pastoral Production and its Discontents: Alpaca and Sheep Herding in Caylloma, Peru.* Ph.D. dissertation, Anthropology, University of Massachusetts.

Mitchell, William P. and David Guillet. 1994. *Irrigation at High Altitudes: The Social Organization of Water Control Systems in the Andes.* Society for Latin American Anthropology Publication Series, Vol. 12.

Paeeregaard, Karsten. 1994. "Why Fight Over Water? Power, Conflict, and Irrigation in an Andean Village." In Mitchell and Guillet, eds.: 189–202.

Pease, Franklin, ed. 1977. *Collaguas I.* Lima. Pontificia Universidad Católica.

Radner, Joan N. and Susan S. Lanser. 1993. "Strategies of Coding in Women's Cultures." In *Feminist Messages: Coding in Women's Folk Culture,* Joan Newlon Radner, ed., pp. 1–30. Urbana. University of Illinois Press.

Rasnake, Roger. 1988. *Domination and Cultural Resistance: Authority and Power among an Andean People.* Durham. Duke University Press.

Rowe, Ann. 1977. *Warp-Patterned Weaves of the Andes.* Washington. The Textile Museum.

Scott, James. 1990. *Domination and the Arts of Resistance: Hidden Transcripts.* New Haven. Yale University Press.

Seibold, Katharine. 1995. "Dressing the Part: Indigenous Costume as Political and Cultural Discourse in Peru." In *Contact, Crossover, Continuity: Proceedings of the Fourth Biennial Symposium of the Textile Society of America*, pp. 319–330. Los Angeles. Textile Society of America.

Smith, Gavin. 1989. *Livelihood and Resistance: Peasants and the Politics of Land in Peru.* Berkeley. University of California Press.

Treacy, John. 1994a. "Las Chacras de Coporaque." In *Andenes y Riego en el Valle del Colca, Peru*, María A. Benavides, Blenda Femenías, and William M. Denevan, eds. Lima. Instituto de Estudios Peruanos.

———. 1994b. "Teaching Water: Hydraulic Management and Terracing in Coporaque, the Colca Valley, Peru." In Mitchell and Guillet, eds.: 99–113.

Valderrama, Ricardo and Carmen Escalante. 1988. *Del Tata Mallku a la Mama Pacha: Riego, Sociedad y Ritos en los Andes Peruanos.* Lima. DESCO.

Dr. Adams teaches anthropology at Central Connecticut State University in New Britain, CT, U.S.A.

Modern folklore sometimes includes strange stereotypes, some of which can be downright dangerous. Adams's account of popular images of North American women in Guatemala shows how class, nationality, gender, and garbled accounts of scientific advances are interwoven, with influences from both politics and mass media, in a novel imagery that hurts some people, threatens more, and accommodates the insecurities of still others, gringas (female gringos) have often been bothered by being mistakenly identified in Latin America as "loose and easy"; this peculiar shift adds a new burden.

Gringas, Ghouls and Guatemala
Fear of North American Women and Body-Organ Trafficking

Abigail E. Adams

In 1994, rumors spread through Guatemala that *"gringos* are snatching babies and ripping out their vital organs for sale abroad. Eight babies, the whispers assured, were found with their stomachs slashed open. One had a $100 bill stuck in its abdomen, plus a note that said in English, 'Thanks for your cooperation'" (*Time*, 1994). The rumors sparked a series of attacks on foreigners. Many Americans witnessed one U.S. woman's ordeal on the nightly news. A townsperson had videotaped the riot and attack on Alaskan environmentalist June Weinstock during a highland Maya Holy Week festival.

The 1994 rumor cycle was unique, although the organ harvester legend is not. I have tracked stories since 1986 that accuse the United States of baby trafficking in Central America and elsewhere. The 1994 attacks, however, were the most violent responses in my records. The rumor-cycle was further distinguished by the fact that the victims/suspects of the worst attacks were not *gringos:* they were *gringas,* the term used often in the Guatemalan media for U.S. women.

In this article, I describe the central figure of the *gringa* that provoked the anxieties of so many Guatemalans. I contrast the supposed organ harvesters with other *gringas* who dominated the pages of the Guatemalan press: Marilyn McAfee, the U.S. Ambassador to Guatemala, and Jennifer Harbury, whose disrupted marriage to Efraín Bamaca Velásquez, "Comandante Everardo" of the Guatemalan National Revolutionary Union (URNG), caught the attention of both Guatemalans and *gringos.* Harbury, a Harvard-educated lawyer, was searching for her husband who had disappeared in a March 1992 battle with the Guatemalan military. She and the U.S. Ambassador both earned the sobriquet *gringa* from the Guatemalan media. The rumor-cycle occurred at a powerful moment of transition for Guatemalans, as they put a close to thirty-plus years of civil war. Guatemalans and U.S. observers developed many theories for the origin of the rumors and violence. Many concluded that the Guatemalan military was promoting the attacks. June Weinstock was attacked on the same day, March 29, that the Guatemalan civilian government signed the first of three major accords with the guerrillas, the URNG. That was a major challenge to the military, which had dominated Guatemala during the civil war and whose members had enjoyed nearly complete impunity for their leadership role in the war's massive death toll.[1]

Abridged, with permission of the author and publisher, from the author's article "Gringas, Ghouls and Guatemala: The 1994 Attacks on North American Women Accused of Body Organ Trafficking," *Journal of Latin American Anthropology*, 4 (1):112–131, 1998.

Others described the rumors as social metaphors of trauma resulting from civil war, unstable democracy, economic hardships, and even the U.S.'s role in the 1954 coup and its subsequent military aid (*60 Minutes*; *Washington Post*, May 17, 1994). The rumors were "perhaps a ghastly mirror image of the Central American social reality, of elites dominating a powerless subject population and capable of perpetrating the very crimes now attributed to the United States" (*This Week*, April 11, 1994).

I think these interpretations have weight,[2] but they ignore the fact that the imagery is so marked by sexuality. Furthermore, these explanations do not address what the 1994 rumor-cycle made remarkably clear: that at all levels of Guatemalan society—elite, poor, city, countryside, Mayan and *ladino* (Mestizo or Hispanic-identified)—people believe that organ trafficking exists and that *gringas* play a big part in it. Many U.S. reporters attributed the rumor-cycle to Guatemala's "oral culture" and levels of illiteracy. Reuters described the atmosphere as "magic realism on acid. . . . In a country with 60 percent illiteracy and deep-held beliefs in the mystical and magical, outlandish rumors are taken for fact with amazing ease" (1994). But in fact, as other journalists pointed out, to their credit, the rumor-cycle was largely perpetrated by Guatemala's most literate: the authorities who filled Guatemala's columns and airwaves with the organ-harvesting narratives centered around the *gringa*.

In brief, the *gringa* is a figure found throughout Latin America, whose dark powers derive from the unstable intersection of the North/South hierarchy with the power relationship of male/female hierarchies. The *gringa* embodies exclusive boundaries, and, at the same time, the tantalizing possibilities of border-crossing alliances. Yet in Guatemala, these hierarchies, opportunities, and the flexible *gringa* herself are differently constituted by a *ladino* newspaper columnist or military officer, a Mayan woman missing her child in a crowd, or a U.S. woman working and living in Guatemala—or searching for her missing husband. All *gringa* narratives interweave in today's competition for fatherhood between the military and the civil government—and implicate well-intentioned anthropologists, ambassadors, and activists.

THE ORGAN-HARVESTING RUMORS AND THE ATTACKS

Early in 1994, several Guatemalan papers reported the "discovery" of child-trafficking and organ-harvesting networks run by former government officials and foreigners (*Siglo 21*, February 7, 1994; *Crónica*, March 1994). Then, on March 7, in the lowland town of Santa Lucía Cotzumalguapa, a New Mexican tourist was detained by local police. Rumors spread through the town that she was an organ-harvester, and a crowd gathered around the police station. They demanded the *gringa*, so that they could lynch her. When the police told the crowd they had moved her, the crowd set fire to the station and patrol vehicles. Several policemen were severely injured. No child's dismembered body ever appeared in Santa Lucía, but the New Mexican woman spent nearly two weeks in a Guatemalan city prison. She was freed only after strong pressure from the U.S. Embassy.

The Santa Lucía riot was front page news for days. The country's largest newspaper, *Prensa Libre*, printed a March 13 article, "The market in human organs flourishes," complete with an organ price chart.

> The violence in Santa Lucía uncovered what the authorities could not hide any longer . . . the shameful business in Guatemala of organ trafficking. . . . Here tens of foreigners, Europeans, North Americans, Canadians, who are registered as tourists, . . . act with incredible impunity, with the obvious consent of the Guatemalan authorities.

Throughout 1994, articles appeared denouncing child trafficking, urging parents and teachers to "organize and confront this situation because security forces aren't organized," and posting missing-children bulletins. Graffiti scrawling "*gringo* child-stealers" (*gringos robaniños*) appeared on the capital's streets, including the avenue to the international airport *(Siglo 21*, March 18, 1994). Among other attacks and incidents, U.S. women adopting Guatemalan babies found themselves confronted by hostile crowds.[2]

Meanwhile, June Weinstock decided to experience Guatemala's Holy Week off the tourist trail. She greeted some small children in the San Cristóbal Verapaz marketplace and reportedly took some photos, when two men began following her. A local woman with a Mayan last name was missing her eight-year-old son, and an ice-cream vendor joked that the child was in the *gringa's* suitcase. Rumors spread that she was hiding a stolen boy under her skirts. Someone videotaped while Weinstock tried to board a bus but was pulled off by a crowd. The videotape rolled while the crowd marched her to a judge and picked up a U.S. missionary to translate. People in the crowd explained they were after "a man." "No, it's a woman." "No, it's a man who has turned into a woman." For four hours local police called the U.S. Embassy, which could not fly anyone into the rain-locked region. The police called the governor; neither he nor the bishop could change the crowd's intention. The police called the local army base, but the army arrived only hours later. Officers claimed they feared being framed by human rights workers. The police tried tear gas as people threw stones, broke the windows, hacked with an ax, tried to set the building on fire, and finally, battered the door open. Weinstock was beaten into a coma and left with her skirt pulled up over her broken head, bleeding from her vagina where sticks had been thrust. A U.S. military helicopter flew her to the capital, where U.S. Marines guarded her hospital room. The missing boy reappeared during the riot.

After the attack on Weinstock, another *gringa* ran afoul of the press: U.S. Ambassador Marilyn McAfee. The U.S. Embassy posted a travel warning for U.S. citizens and temporarily pulled Peace Corps volunteers from the field. Fury over the travel warning filled the Guatemalan opinion columns. Ambassador McAfee, along with several Guatemalan doctors, publicly confronted the rumors by asserting that organ trafficking was medically impossible (*Siglo 21*, April 8, 1994). Their statement was duly printed, but against a backdrop of editorials questioning the Ambassador's veracity. Some columnists suggested that she and the doctors were in cahoots with the organ-traffick network *(Prensa Libre*, April 11, 1994). Another columnist accused Ambassador McAfee of imposing a travel warning so that embassy personnel would earn what he called in English a supplementary "danger payment" *(Prensa Libre*, April 28, 1994). Several described the travel warning as a plot to undercut Guatemala's economic independence *(Prensa Libre*, April 28, 1994).

The Guatemalan Chamber of Tourism began a campaign to "correct the erroneous impression" of Guatemala (*This Week*, April 18, 1994) in the midst of a continued stream of threats against foreigners and articles reporting child trafficking *(Prensa Libre*, April 19,1994). President de León considered suspending constitutional guarantees (*Washington Post*, March 31, 1994).

"*YA VIENEN LAS GRINGAS!*"

The *gringas* have become the latest culprits in perennially revitalized accounts about ghoulish foreigners who steal and dismember babies.[3] In 1987, the Nicaraguan Sandinista paper, *Barricada,* and Guatemala's *Prensa Libre* (Harris 1988) reported similar "cases" in which people were arrested for running "fattening houses" where children were prepared for sale to "private North American laboratories which would extract various organs from them."

> In several countries of Central America, where the hegemony of the United States guarantees that all types of trafficking are done with impunity, the police have just discovered networks that export children to sell their eyes, kidneys or

hearts. . . . These scandals seem to open a new chapter of horror that uncovers the exploitation of the Third World, in particular that of Latin America by the United States . . . . (*Barricada*, 1987)

In Guatemala, novelists, ethnographers and journalists have reported such rumors in Mayan communities for decades (See Goldman 1992). During doctoral research with a Mayan evangelical congregation, I learned the early evangelical missionaries were similarly suspected of kidnapping, cannibalism, and dismemberment (Garrard-Burnett 1990:30). International workers in mother-child clinics during the 1950s discovered rumors that older foreign women ate babies, ground up the bones, and then returned these to Guatemala as milk powder (Gonzalez, p.c.; see also Scheper-Hughes 1992:322).

Today, *gringas* are the chief suspects. What, then, is behind this figure *"gringa,"* applied to the alleged organ stealers, Harbury, the U.S. ambassador? The male form, *gringo*, is used to label U.S. Americans when they live in Latin America. The term varies in connotation around the continent; in Mexico, it is an insult for a U.S. citizen; in Costa Rica, it is more neutral, referring to any North American including Canadians, who tend to resent the label. Guatemalans use the term to describe foreigners with a northern European appearance (see Santamaría 1959:564 and 1942:33).

Some folk etymologies state that the term derives from the U.S. Marines' marching through Mexico to the song, "Green grow the rushes ho . . . "; that it was the brave nationalists—but in English!—cry of the Mexican citizenry to the uniformed U.S. soldiers, "Green, go!" A recent version holds that the term refers to U.S. Border Patrolmen—who are said either to wear green and order Mexicans to go, or to be spotted by illegal immigrants who see the green and go. The following entry appears in Volume 1 of *A Dictionary of Americanisms on Historical Principles* (Matthews 1951):

> A term used contemptuously by Spanish Americans for a person from the U.S. (1849 *Audobon Western Journal*) . . . We were hooted and shouted at as we passed through, and called *"Gringoes"* (1948 *Chi. D. News*). Us native Peruvians never cease to marvel at the ingenuity of the *gringo*; (1871 *Republican*) Three Mexicans from Socorro . . . calling her a *gringo* bitch, finally threw her on the body of her husband (1897 Outing).

Gringo is both linguistically and figuratively masculine. In the Latin model, masculinity is dynamic *and* dependent on other men (Lancaster 1992; Pitt-Rivers 1961). Many have noted that the cult of *machismo* has a higher profile in Latin America than in Iberia, perhaps intensifying in the process of the colonial transfer (Burton 1992:36; Stoler 1991). Similarly, these shared ideals of masculinity explain how the organ-harvesting rumors would appear in such divergent national settings as conservative Guatemala and Sandinista Nicaragua. The common theme is that state power is threatened by outsiders, a power that is gendered as male. Central America's masculinity, and therefore national authority, is emasculated by the *gringo* West.

When applied to U.S. women, the term *gringo* changes to *gringa*. It also changes in connotation. The term *gringa* elicits a complicated stereotype. Like all stereotypes, it has many reinforcements. As Pratt found in European colonial travel writings, "women protagonists tend to produce ironic reversals when they show up in the contact zone" (1992:102; Weiss 1993). The *gringa* shows up in Guatemalan homes and communities frequently, in image and in person: Peace Corps volunteers, tourists, *mochileras* (back packers), activists, and anthropologists. The *gringa* appears in U.S. television programs, Mexican soap operas, Guatemalan advertisements, and imported Grade-B movies.

Guatemalan advertisers use the *gringa* to promote their products, such as weight-loss measures which declare ¡*Ya vienen las gringas!* (The *gringas* are coming soon!)—

pills or drops from the U.S. that make one svelte without exercise or dieting (*Prensa Libre*, October 29, 1992). *Gringas*, such as any object with a "United States" label, tease with the limitless possibilities that market consumption holds for self-fashioning.

North American women experience a reprieve from *machista* catcalls when in the Mayan countryside. But even country people's encounters with *gringas* can reinforce the duplicitous, flexible character of the *gringa*. Their behavior contrasts with local gender expectations, such as *gringas*' dress, unchaperoned travel, promotion of birth control, in addition to the practice of some women tourists who collect sexual experiences as vacation souvenirs. The women who appear in the countryside, plaza and market in their wrinkled pants, hiking boots, and unmade-up faces provide a stark contrast to the *gringa* of the billboard and imported goods packaging. The themes of the "man-woman" resonate in people's accounts to me. For example, many people in Alta Verapaz recounted stories of the "pills" that *gringa* Peace Corps volunteers, missionaries and anthropologists took to be so "strong"—stronger than men. Here is a transformation of the diet advertisements that feature *gringas* who consume "exclusive" pills.

Closer encounters with *gringas* contribute to another source of dissonance. Rural Guatemala is precisely where U.S. women postpone child-rearing for altruistic "social motherhood": service as teachers, missionaries, development workers, nurses, nuns. For many of my Q'eqchi' women friends, however, postponing biological motherhood far from one's home does not bring social worth. Becoming a mother means increased social mobility and value. A childless woman is said to feel destructive, often uncontrollable, envy. North Americans, in fact, are suspected of worse: callous indifference towards children. A pastor friend once preached a sermon about how "advanced countries" promote abortion because there is no more room left, and so babies are disposed of, just as used tires are dumped in the Third World, and "wetbacks" are deported.

At one level, the *gringa* is the sexually loose, desirable yet elusive woman. These attractive traits can flip to the negative: the *gringa* elicits catcalls or hisses from doorways. But she is also the target of a gender-inflected xenophobia expressed in the figure of the rapaciously sexual yet sterile woman. The *gringa* can even be said to be "not . . . a woman, but a disguised man" (*Crónica*'s description of Weinstock, April 8, 1994). Such *gringas* are the unsavory "men-women" (*machihembra* in Spanish; *winqiixq* in Q'eqchi') who repel both ladinos and Q'eqchi' Mayans.

The flexible organ-harvesting gringa meshes well with the child-stealing, gynomorphic ghouls of Guatemalan folktales, such as the Siguana horse-faced siren who lures men over cliffs to their death (Lara Figueroa 1984:28). The *Miami Herald* cited the story of Miculax, the ghoul "who turns children into soap" (1994). The *Village Voice* invoked *La Llorona*, the conqueror's concubine who drowns her child, mourns forever and snatches children (Kadetsky 1994). Other anthropologists reminded me of the Chamulans who describe *gringos* as beings who bite and consume each other when they are back in their amoral world (Gossen 1979). The *gringa* is one apparition of the greedy Mayan mountain spirits (Goldin and Rosenbaum 1993).

The *gringa*, however, is not just a fantasy generated from some Maya "cosmovision," nor a superstitious "survival." This other-worldly, supernatural being is reproduced daily, when the North/South hierarchy intersects with and confuses male/female hierarchies. The *gringa* is created both by borders, and by a relationship that allows the *gringa* to transgress that same border. Just as the *gringo* passes the border and takes productive resources, the *gringa* "takes babies" or reproduction. But the *gringo* is recognizably acting like a man, in fact like a *macho*. The *gringa*, however, is not acting like a woman. Instead of taking care of babies, she takes and kills them.

Gringas, then, join the various "shape shifters" that populate the reconstructing Guatemalan countryside (Warren 1993). Like the contradictions of the "betwixt and between" of Douglas (1966) and Turner (1964), the *gringa* may fascinate or horrify. She resembles humans, but dissembles, and disassembles real humans.

A BROAD DEFAMING A(BROAD): JENNIFER HARBURY

The other *gringa* on Guatemala's 1994 scene was Jennifer Harbury. Harbury became interested in Guatemala and the guerrilla movement after helping refugees apply for political asylum (Harbury 1994). She and Efraín Bamaca were married September 1991 in Texas. They were expecting a baby that she later lost. Bamaca returned to Guatemala and disappeared in March 1992. One year later, Harbury learned that he had been captured alive. She filed criminal charges against army officials and the Defense Minister, working through the Guatemalan judiciary and challenging the civil government to use its authority. "We are all chained together by the neck. Everardo is chained to you. I am chained to Everardo. And your pocketbook is chained to me," she told Guatemala's Minister of Defense, referring to U.S. economic sanctions against Guatemala (GHRC/USA, November 8, 1994).

In a December 1994 letter Harbury wrote, "I am still receiving much love and support everywhere I go. . . . Flowers still come in regularly, everyone tells me I am speaking for all of them. . . . Others bring their kids to see me. It's the best country there is. . . . I love them. I just don't love their army" (GHRC/USA 1994). Three years and three hunger strikes after Bamaca's disappearance, Harbury learned through Congressman Robert Torricelli and a State Department official that a Guatemalan colonel on the CIA payroll had ordered the deaths of both a U.S. expatriate innkeeper and Bamaca (*Washington Post*, April 17, 1995; *New York Times*, March 11, March 29, April 23, 1995).

Harbury's case is profiled by human rights groups as a test case. She describes herself as similar to many Guatemalan women, who have no knowledge of their husbands' fate. The difference, she says, is that she has U.S. citizenship and a Harvard law degree. The daily debate in the Guatemalan media demonstrated, however, how radically unlike Guatemalan women she is. One writer, for example, praised "the *gringa*" for donning "the pants that many lack and the skirts that many feminists will not wear" (*Siglo 21*, November 10, 1994).

While some of the articles were friendly or neutral in tone, many Guatemalan editorialists "poured their venom over her," because "Mrs. Jennifer Harbury's hunger strike has provoked the stare of the international community's eyes on Guatemala" (*Siglo 21*, November 10, 1994). Much of the press about Harbury, as with the uproar over the ambassador's travel warning, concerned her call for economic sanctions. There was also talk of the money Harbury allegedly would make defaming Guatemala internationally (*Prensa Libre*, November 14, 1994; January 18, 1995).[7] But the theme of Harbury as an imposter wife was the most popular. One columnist found it "weird" that U.S. journalists would believe the story of a woman who had no photo of herself and her husband together (*Prensa Libre*, January 18, 1995). Another columnist received much approval for describing Harbury's "romance" as a charade that caused Guatemala enormous damage. He was dumbfounded that the *gringa* press believed that there had been a "love affair" between

> . . . one [who] studied to act within the law while the other grew up practically in the law of the jungle. . . . [someone] must be mentally affected to have graduated from one of the most expensive universities of the world to then decide to marry a Third World illiterate terrorist. Does this mean that Jenny—as her friends call her—after having eaten caviar and rubbed elbows with the jet set [English in the original] of Boston preferred to tie her destiny with someone who killed soldiers, civilians, cows, who blew up bombs, abused his countrymen, and owed many lives? Is this normal? (*Prensa Libre*, November 26, 1994).

I believe this columnist was truly dumbfounded by the idea of the marriage. Ladino marriages are often described in Mediterranean terms of honor and shame, but within the context of racial improvement. The social standing of a family is rooted in the mother/wife's *vergüenza*. The term translates as "shame," in the sense of a person's innate moral capacity and potential for education (i.e., to "be civilized"). An educated, cultivated woman has improved her family's genetic potential and can transmit it to the next generation through a good marriage. The acquisition of English can also "whiten" succeeding generations (Smith 1995).[4] The media commentary was peppered with untranslated English terms, often appearing opposite advertisements for English lessons. The Guatemalan elite consider themselves "white" and reinforce their status through association with "whiter" parts of the world—namely Europe and the United States. Darkness is a stain, a mark of the Conquest.

This same racism lies behind Guatemalans' disbelief that North Americans would adopt Guatemalan babies as family members rather than as organ sources. Guatemala has more transnational adoptions than any other Central American country,[5] a situation that leaves "middle-class ladinos smirking when they see adoptive American or Canadian mothers bestowing loving care on their new dark-skinned babies" (*This Week*, March 28, 1994). Several Guatemalan writers mentioned Harbury's miscarriage as emblematic of the couple's unworkability.

Harvard-educated Harbury's marriage and the support it received from U.S. media and leaders profoundly challenged Guatemalan elite eugenic strategies through education. At the same time that the *gringa* lawyer has invoked the elites' complicity with the stain of blood left by the war's violence, she has elicited their anxiety about stained blood and an historical illegitimacy.

GRINGO, GRINGA AND PATRIA POTESTAS

Harbury has revealed certain contemporary tensions in another Guatemalan family line, the state. Whereas the organ-harvesting rumors accused *gringas* of "impunity," Harbury succeeded in challenging the impunity and the father-right of the Guatemalan military. The power of the Guatemalan state is expressed in the *patronato*, which, broadly defined, is the state's parental role as protector of its people. The *patronato* derives from the *patria potestas*, or paternal powers, of the patriarchal Spanish king (Boyer 1989:254). The *patronato* is not modeled after just any parent, but after the father. Mothers, in the words of a Guatemalan editorialist, are "called to lift the family to civil society" (Arriaga 1995). In Guatemala, modern *patria potestas* means that women are treated as minors who need men to secure their rights from the state. A single mother often must recruit male kin to serve as guardians for her children if they are to matriculate in school, if she wants to obtain public health care, or if she wants to leave the country with her child.

Women—indigenous, *ladina*, or *gringa*—who challenge the Guatemalan state provoke attacks on both their femininity and person (Nelson 1995). The *gringa*, however, is a woman not subject to *patria potestas*. The malleable qualities of her body are not available for the *patria*. Such is not the case with Karen Odet Cabrera, a 1992 contestant for the title of Miss Guatemala. Beneath her photo in swimsuit and heels, she states that she hopes to "reflect the best of our country and its people to the world, and so put an end to the bad impression that many, especially foreigners, have accumulated over the past years" (*Prensa Libre*, February 27, 1992).

During the civil war, the Guatemalan military appropriated national fatherhood and encompassed civil authority. These roles were evident in the coverage of the Santa Lucía riot, when the military established order in contrast to the corrupt and incompetent civil police (*Crónica*, March 18, 1994; *Siglo 21*, March 9, 1994). In 1992, the military pushed aside the National Police and occupied the capital's streets in fatigues and with full weaponry (*El Gráfico*, March 8, 1992).

THE *GRINGA* AS "HONORARY MAN," KIN, ANTI-KIN AND *COMPAÑERA*

Guatemalans, however, have challenged the army's assumption of Fatherhood and control of civil society, and *gringos* and *gringas* have supported their challenge. Human rights, solidarity and support groups for relatives of the disappeared, such as the Mutual Support Group and the widows' group CONAVIGUA, took courageous stands against the military's impunity. Forensic teams trained by *gringo* anthropologist Clyde Snow are exhuming the secret mass graves created by the army's policies. Other *gringas* and *gringos* have offered their phenotypic privilege to activist Guatemalans through the strategy of accompaniment, which is the act of physically escorting the activists.[6]

As activists or anthropologists, *gringas* in Guatemala must still work out roles within the contradictions of gender-inflected North-South relations, contradictions we experience every day. These were made monstrously explicit by the scale of June Weinstock's ordeal. She told a potential traveling partner that she wanted to fight poverty and human rights abuses (Kadetsky 1994). Instead, she became a ghoul. The organ-harvesting rumors, whether instigated by the military or not, demonized even those foreigners working in solidarity and human rights work—and conveniently for the military, a demon cannot be a martyr.

The *gringa* is a creature reproduced not from contact with alien cultures, but between increasingly "familiar" peoples. In fact, hundreds of U.S. travelers, anthropologists, missionaries, church members, exchange students, entrepreneurs and volunteers are incorporated into Guatemalan families as *compadres* (Catholic ritual godparents) or *hermanos* (brothers in Christ). But these fictive statuses can shift. Jarocz has shown how in Madagascar, heart-thieving vampires appear as European colonists, administrators, doctors, missionaries and other *vazaha* (foreigners, including herself). They extract hearts and blood without physically touching their victims. The Malagasy consider these beings "non-kin," in contrast to kin and fictive kin. "Non-kin" include the post-colonial *vazaha* who oversee the decimation of Malagasy natural resources (1994). In Guatemala, foreigners are also suspected of mutilating bodies without apparent physical contact. However, the organ-harvesting stories indicate a fourth category of "anti-kin," ghouls who insinuate themselves into society by appearing as potential kin, or by manipulating fictive kin status.

Gringas do some shape-shifting of our own. Many anthropologists have written about the advantages of manipulating gender in the field. As "women," we allegedly have greater access to native women's and people's confidences; as privileged people, we can be "honorary men" (Ehlers 1990:21; Slater 1986:15–16; but see Eber 1991). I wrote home about the benefits of being considered the "honorary male," such as being able to accompany men in settings that Guatemalan women could not. I do not know how closely related the "honorary male" is to the "man-woman" people feared June Weinstock to be. People often commented on my long skirts and encouraged me to wear pants because these looked more "feminine." I wonder now what people thought I, like Weinstock, had under my skirts.

North Americans and Guatemalans negotiate different gender expectations. Expectations are further confused when what is inescapably required of certain "women" becomes a choice for others. Narayan points out that Western feminists, despite our critique of our own culture, are often more a part of it than we realize

(Narayan 1990:261–267). *Gringas* exercise privilege in migrating from one category to another and so appear like the Malagasy vampires and Guatemalan shape-shifters, who insinuate themselves into society in one apparition and then shift to another. Without critical uncoverings of our enculturation in the privileges of patriarchy, the *gringa* is a theoretical transvestite; others would do well to wonder what we have under our skirts. Weiss, working in Latin America, notes that these shifts can take a different form. In her case, they take a linguistic turn. Their perspectives, and prejudices about cultural and gender differences, were reframed through the application of the diminutive. In the process, the diminutive, in its female form, "minimized any pretense at power" conferred on a *gringo*. It "domesticated and pulled [her] close." At the same time, she clarifies, that "it was not simply that I was the stranger for whom many felt affection. Diminutives are often deployed in Spanish to suggest more than endearment; they are ripe for plays with irony" (Weiss 1993:194).

I was not feeling ironic when I watched the footage of June Weinstock's ordeal for the first time. I found the video excruciating to watch, bringing back a rush of memories of the contradictions of being a *gringa*. In April 1994, I called the community where I did research, twenty minutes away from the scene of the attack on Weinstock. Several women friends were waiting to talk, to share news of their families and to hear news of mine. Addressing me as *hermaan* (Q'eqchi' for sister or sister in Christ), all talked about the *gringa* attacks.

But then the conversations took a non-ironic turn. They reported that after the attack on June Weinstock, their townspeople had developed an escort service for Peace Corps volunteers, missionaries and other residents. They were accompanying the *gringas*. Their act of solidarity was one of the more unusual forms of the social webs of support emerging across transnational borders (Alvarez, Dagnino and Escobar 1998). It was an act that quickly put to rest what so much of the international media concluded about the rumor cycle: that indigenous peoples cannot organize and think clearly about the conditions of their oppression; that where folktales circulate, people are driven by groupthink, not individual reason.

I conclude by re-casting the term *gringa*, not as a label for a North American (mis)placed in Latin America, but as a person shaped by her relation to Latin America, a relationship that shifts. Guatemalan-U.S. relations flip between positive and negative poles, with a central axis of transnational kinships formed across a force field of different views of family, gender, and procreation. But to date, U.S.-Latin American relations has meant that one party has borne the burden of any relation's potential violence, its pain and costs. Today, U.S. Americans will form relations of business, of solidarity, maybe of friendship, in ways that reveal our differences, but erase a border that places costs on one side and benefits on the other, that separates pain and anesthesia.

***

Many thanks to Sandra Bamford, Quetzil Castañeda, Fred Damon, Christine Eber, Antonella Fabri, Gillian Feeley-Harnick, Hilary Kahn, Meena Khanderwal, Kimberly King, Chris Lutz, Susan McKinnon, George Mentore, Diane M. Nelson, Rebecca Popenoe, Dan Rothenberg, Carol A. Smith, David Stoll, Kay Warren, John Watanabe, and Wendy Weiss, as well as Hollins College's Faculty Writing Workshop. I am responsible, of course, for the final shape and ideas of the paper.

***

Notes

[1] The civil war and military's counterinsurgency campaigns, paramilitary and clandestine death squads destroyed 440 villages, left some 145,000 people dead or "disappeared," one million people internally displaced, and over 45,000 in exile; those who lived in Guatemala's rural Maya communities suffered most (Human Rights Watch 1994).

[2] Foreign reporters, anthropologists and volunteers encountered the fear, with poor and elite Guatemalans. Many have told me about people in local markets whispering, "Those are the robbers of children." A taxi driver reportedly mistook a U.S. reporter for a Guatemalan and confided, "We ought to kill these *gringos*."

[3] Dismembering ghouls populate the post-colonial globe. Throughout Central Africa, "entrepreneurs" apparently gather at borders to traffick heads of abducted children, which South Africans use as bait to attract fish that have swallowed gemstones (*Washington Post*, October 1995). In Peru, the *pixtacos* are said to appear as *gringos*, who steal human kidney fat to lubricate machinery (Wachtel 1994).

[4] And hopefully fade the tell-tale "Mongolian spot," a darker pigmentation on a newborn's lower back that is said to be evidence of Amerindian genes but fades in a few months.

[5] Guatemala is the fifth source of U.S. adoptions. The U.S. embassy told journalists that it keeps a list of lawyers suspected of unscrupulous procedures. It also requests genetic testing, tests that some "mothers" apparently failed and others never returned for. Goldman's book research brought him in contact with an underground adoption network (Now 1994). The Guatemalan Archbishop's human rights office reports that five unregistered nurseries were found in 1994 (U.S. Embassy 1994; *Miami Herald* 1994).

[6] A joke about the most famous of these Guatemalans opens: "Why is Rigoberta Menchú like a *chile relleno* (typical Guatemalan dish)?" "Because she always appears between two *franceses* (French men/pieces of French bread)." The ways in which Nobel winner Menchú has been defamed through sexual innuendo and misogynist jokes is fascinating (Nelson 1995); the secondary but implicated actors in the joke are the *gringos*.

References

Alvarez, Sonia E., Evelina Dagnino, and Arturo Escobar (eds.). 1998. *Cultures of Politics, Politics of Cultures: Re-visioning Latin American Social Movements*. Boulder, CO: Westview Press.

Arriaga, Oscar. 1995. *Siglo 21*: May 27.

Barrucada. 1987. Trafficking of children. April 21.

Boyer, Richard. 1989. Women, La Mala Vida, and the Politics of Marriage. In *Sexuality and Marriage in Colonial Latin America*, Asunción Lavrín, ed. Lincoln: University of Nebraska Press.

Burton, Julianne. 1992. Don (Juanito) Duck and the Imperial-Patriarchal Unconscious. In *Nationalisms and Sexualities*, Andrew Parker et al., eds. New York: Routledge.

Crónica. 1994. Tráfico de órganos. April 8, 15–20.

——. Infantes a la carta. March 4, 22–23.

——. Contacto con la mafia. March 8, 23–24.

——. La batalla de Santa Lucía. March 18, 23–24.

Douglas, Mary. 1966. *Purity and Danger*. London: Routledge & Kegan Paul.

Eber, Christine. 1991. *Before God's Flowering Face*. Ph.D. dissertation, Anthropology Department, State University of New York at Buffalo.

Ehlers, Tracy. 1990. *Silent Looms: Women and Production in a Guatemalan Town*. Boulder, CO: Westview Press.

Garrard-Burnett, Virginia. 1990. Positivismo, liberalismo e impulso misionero: misiones protestantes en Guatemala, 1880–1920. *Mesoamerica*, 19, 13–31.

Goldin, Liliana and Brenda Rosenbaum. 1993. *Culture and History: Subregional Variation among the Maya*. Comparative Studies in Society and History.

Goldman, Francisco. 1992. *The Long Night of White Chickens*. New York: Atlantic Monthly Press.

Gonzalez, Nancie. p.c. Personal Communication.

Gossen, Gary. 1979. *Chamulas in the World of the Sun*. Cambridge: Harvard University Press.

El Gráfico. 1992. El ejército toma las riendas, March 8.

Guatemalan Human Rights Commission/USA. 1994. Urgent Action and Update: Harbury Harassed, Intimidated by Guatemalan Government. *Summary of Facts*, November 8.

——. *Letter to Supporters*, December 5.

Harbury, Jennifer. 1994. *Bridge of Courage*. Monroe, ME: Common Courage Press.

Harris, Margaret. 1988. *Guatemala Health Rights Support Project*, February 23.

Human Rights Watch. 1994. *Human Rights Watch World Report 1994*. New York: Human Rights Watch.

Jarosz, Lucy. 1994. Agents of Power, Landscapes of Fear. *Environment and Planning D: Society and Space*, 12:421–436.

Kadetsky, Elizabeth. 1994. Guatemala Inflamed. *The Village Voice*. May 31.

Lancaster, Roger. 1992. *Life is Hard*. Berkeley: University of California Press.

Lara Figueroa, Celso. 1984. Leyendas y Casos de la Tradición Oral de la Ciudad de Guatemala. Guatemala: Editorial Universitaria de Guatemala.

Mathews, Mitford. 1951. *A Dictionary of Americanisms on Historical Principles*. Chicago: University of Chicago Press.

Miami Herald. 1994. Rumors, rage, xenophobia in Guatemala, March 28.

Narayan, Uma. 1990. The Project of Feminist Epistemology. In *Gender / Body / Knowledge*, Alison M. Jaggar and Susan R. Bordo, eds. New Brunswick. NJ: Routledge.

Nelson, Diane. 1995. Gendering the Ethnic-National Question: Rigoberta Jokes and the Out-Skirts of Fashioning Identity. *Anthropology Today*.

New York Times. 1995. U.S. Suspends Military Aid to Guatemala, March 11; Congressman Seeks Records on Americans' Death in Guatemala, March 29.

———. More is Told About CIA in Guatemala, April 23.

Now Newsmagazine. 1994. Attacks on North American Women, August 17.

Paz, Octavio. 1961. *The Labyrinth of Solitude*. New York: Grove Press.

Pitt-Rivers, Julian. 1961. *People of the Sierra*. Chicago, IL: University of Chicago Press.

Pratt, Mary Louise. 1992. *Imperial Eyes*. New York: Routledge.

Prensa Libre. 1992. Señorita Cabrera, February 27.

———. Gotas Gringas (advertisement). October 29.

———. 1993. Biomédica (advertisement), July 19.

———. 1994. Floresce el mercado negro en órganos humanos. March 13.

———. Del tráfico de niños para el trasplante de órganos. Cacto. April.

———. Opiniones, Alfred Kaltschmitt, Jose Eduardo Zarco. Apri128.

———. Robo y comercio de niños. Marco Tutio Trejo Paiz. April 19.

———. *Revista Domingo*. October 30.

———. Harbury litiga en Washington. Editorial. November 14.

———. La estafa de Jennifer Harbury y el papel de la prensa gringa. November 26.

———. 1995. Harbury, futura millonaria. Mario Antonio Sandoval. January 18.

Reuters. 1994. Wild Baby-Stealing Fears Take Root in Guatemala. May 24.

Santamaría, Francisco J. 1959. *Diccionario de mejicanismos*. Mexico City: Editorial Porrua.

———. 1942. *Diccionario general de americanismos*, Volume 2. Mexico City: Editorial P. Robredo.

Scheper-Hughes, Nancy. 1992. *Death Without Weeping*. Berkeley: University of California Press.

Siglo 21. 1994. Infierno infantil al desnudo. February 7.

———. El ejército ocupa Santa Lucía Cotzumalguapa. March 9.

———. Crece preocupación por robo de niños. March 18.

———. Falta de información provoca rumores de transplantes de órganos. April 8.

———. Esa gringa que está en el parque. November 10.

60 Minutes. 1994. Transcript. November 6.

Slater, Candace. 1986. *Trail of Miracles*. Berkeley: University of California Press.

Smith, Carol. 1995. Race/Class/Gender Ideologies in Guatemala. *Comparative Studies in Society and History*, 37, 723–749.

Stoler, Ann. 1991. Carnal knowledge and imperial power. In *Gender at the Crossroads of Knowledge*, Micaela di Leonardo, ed. Berkeley: University of California Press.

This Week. 1994. Organ Traffic Rumors. March 14.

———. Security Alert. March 28.

———. New Warning. April 11.

Time. 1994. Dangerous Rumors. April 18.

Turner, Victor. 1964. *Betwixt and Between*. Proceedings of the American Ethnological Society. *Symposium on New Approaches to the Study of Religion*, 4–20.

U.S. Embassy, Guatemala. 1994. Cable. May 9.

Wachtel, Nathan. 1994. *Gods and Vampires*. Chicago, IL: University of Chicago Press.

Warren, Kay. 1993. Interpreting "la violencia" in Guatemala. In *The Violence Within*, Kay Warren, ed. Boulder, CO: Westview Press.

Washington Post. 1994. Guatemalans Attack American Woman. March 31.

———. A Witch Hunt in Guatemala. May 17.

———. 1995. Child abductor arrested. October.

Weiss, Wendy. 1993. Gringo . . . Gringita. *Anthropological Quarterly*, 66(4), 187–196.

Stephen O. Murray—both an anthropologist and a sociologist who has done field research in Guatemala, Mexico, Taiwan, and Thailand—is founder and director of Instituto Obregon, a think-tank of gay studies in San Francisco. Among his best-known books are Group Formation in Social Science, Social Theory, Homosexual Realities, American Gay, Homosexualities, and Cultural Diversity and Homosexualities.

A great many anthropologists have written about the family as a crucial unit in the structure and function of societies around the world, usually emphasizing the positive support that it provides, whether in terms of food, shelter, enculturation, economic and psychological reinforcement, or otherwise. Murray's account of the family as obstacle is, therefore, unusual, as is his choice of a subpopulation who are locally considered "deviant." His sympathetic treatment of the subject rings true, however, providing brief but telling insights into the forms, functions, and tensions of gay life in Mesoamerica, which could well be generalized to much of the rest of Latin America.

For a more traditional view of social structure and extended kinship, see Buechler (chapter 18); for family as a nexus of affect, compare Feijoo and Gogna (chapter 34) and Nutini (chapter 38).

Family, Social Insecurity, and the "Underdevelopment" of Gay Institutions in Latin America

Stephen O. Murray

One major difference between North American and Latin American men engaged in recurrent homosexual relations is that Latin Americans generally live with their family of origin until they marry. Whatever their sexual orientation may be, and regardless of class, Latin American men who do not marry continue to live at home indefinitely. In Carrier's sample of fifty-three homosexually involved men in Guadalajara in 1970–1, 85 percent still lived in their childhood home.[1] And

> of the ten homosexual couples I knew, or heard about, that were living together in Guadalajara, only two had families living in the city... A partner in one of these pairs—in his early thirties—still had to return each evening to his family home to sleep. It was the consensus of my informants that leaving the city or marrying were the only ways open to leave the family and establish a separate household. (Carrier 1972:121)

In my 1980 sample of homosexually active men in Guatemala City, the only men who did not live with their parents lived with wives of their own. In Argentina, aside from the economic impossibility of finding and buying an available apartment, Rafael Freda told Miller (1992:201), "if an unmarried child left home, the implication was that the family was not getting along. There would be no other conceivable reason one would leave." In Cuba, state allocations reinforce this pattern: "Housing is in short supply and top priority is given to couples, especially those with children, so that stable relationships between homosexuals are inhibited" (Salas 1979:171). Residence with families scattered throughout cities precludes the development of gay neighborhoods and is a considerable obstacle to the formation of gay consciousness, culture and community as these have developed in Anglo North America. This chapter will explore some of the not-necessarily-conscious motivations for this residential pattern and its consequence of inhibiting the development of separate gay institutions.

Temporal constraints on homosexual activities supplement spatial ones: "Three quarters of the families require their sons, even in their twenties, to return home at a 'reasonable' hour. During weekdays, a reasonable hour is defined as around 10:00 to 11:00 P.M.; on weekends this might be relaxed to before the sun comes up, but the son is definitely expected to return home" (Carrier 1972:100–1). Ninety-three percent of *pasivos'* parents said that their parents required them to return home to sleep every night (p. 213). Buslines in Guadalajara (and elsewhere) cease running at midnight, which imposes a de facto curfew on any place that is farther than walking distance from the family home.

BASES FOR CONTINUING TO RESIDE WITH ONE'S NATAL FAMILY

Familial Orientation

Of those Carrier (1972:212) interviewed in Guadalajara living with their families, "64% said they were living at home because they wanted to; 18% said it was because parents insisted; 6% said it was for financial reasons; and 11% said it was a combination of parents insisting and finances." In their own view, Latin Americans are more devoted to their families than are other people: "that's just how we are." Idealist[2] social scientists offer the same non-explanation in fancier garb as "familial orientation." In either guise, the "explanation" itself requires explanation. The explanation is that the contemporary Latin American family has more "functions" than does the contemporary family in Anglo-America or in Northern Europe (see Ogburn 1928). Much less socialization of children in Latin America stems from school and peer group than in fully industrialized societies (McGin 1966; Peñasola 1968; Kinger 1973).

Besides greater centrality in socialization, the Latin American family also retains economic functions. The family as a production unit[3] exists to a considerable extent in Latin America, and not just in traditional Indian cultures. In countries far from being welfare states, even urban families that are not production units provide social security. In societies experienced by most as capricious and heartless, the family provides more than merely psychological shelter. If one is struck down by illness or injury and has no family to provide support, s/he will be reduced to begging in the streets. Examples of this horrific danger are readily visible (Fabrega 1971). Thus, the fear that if one is alone in the world—which is to say, without relatives nearby—such a fate might befall one is not irrational. Although no one ever told me he lived with his family because of fear of being reduced to beggary, the fear was obviously salient in the combination of shock and concern expressed in questions about how I dared venture so far from my family and who would take care of me if I fell ill or had an accident (see Muñoz 1989:82). Such concerns express more than fear of a hostile outside world. Latin Americans cannot and had better not take for granted minimum security being supplied against disability, as citizens of welfare states can.

The insurance against disability offered by the family is an economic system, not any perverse, pathological passivity deriving from an obsession with fertility on the part of individuals, the culture, or the Roman Catholic Church.[4] Familial orientation" as well as high Latin American fertility can better be explained by examining the family as an economic unit than by looking to individual-level values.

Mother Identification

Though homosexually active Latin Americans who do not build their own families live at home longer than those who start families of their own and also show somewhat greater concern about maintaining the support of relatives, these relations often involve no intimacy. The popular psychoanalytic obsession with mothers, projected onto the etiology of homosexuality, is useless in explaining homosexuality in Latin America, because the veneration of martyr (Madonna/saintly) mothers is ubiquitous, while homosexuality is not. Regardless of sexual orientation, everyone continues to live at home, not just "mother-fixated" homosexual men.

Premiums Homosexuals Pay for Such Insurance

Because revelation of homosexuality is a basis for expulsion from the home (Carrier 1976a; see Arboleda 1987; examples were also given by my informants in the capitals of México and Guatemala), and because of the economic as well as psychological security provided by the family, homosexually active Latin Americans cultivate family relations to a greater extent than do those who can take them for granted. Many exercise the right of males who have reached sexual maturity to come and go from home at will less than do their brothers.

"Impersonal social relations" (Tax 1941:33) are characteristic, especially of the Mesoamerican highlands. In Guatemala City, a Cuban-born informant observed, "People in the highlands are very private. They don't talk about personal affairs, even if they do have real friends outside the family [which they often do not have], and they can't talk about sex within the family either." A general reserve is further exaggerated when it comes to stigmatizing information. "One's behavior must be especially circumspect in the presence of one's siblings," Peñalosa (1968:687) observed, "There must be no looseness of act or word, particularly in the sexual area." As Argentine-American psychologist Alex Carballo-Diéguez (1989:28) noted: "It is not unusual for relatives of young gay Hispanic men to haunt them with questions and commentaries about girlfriends or marriage plans. A gay Hispanic man may feel it is a lack of respect toward a family member not to answer such questions, and he may resort to evasive answers that, in the end, make him feel badly about himself." Similarly, Parker's (1988:296) primary informant, João told him. "The *casa* [home] is where the name of the family has to be respected. . . . It's the place of good conduct and exemplary morality. The preservation of the traditional family environment is the duty of everyone." Miller (1992:205) tells of an Argentine who lived with a lover, but obeyed "an unstated rule that he was not to talk to or otherwise interact with his nephews, nieces, or cousins." Not only could he not mention same-sex love, he was not even permitted to talk to younger kin who are presumed to be impressionable.[5]

Many people live in a small space. However, they endeavor to live *juntos pero no revueltos* (together, but not scrambled). The lack of intra-familial intimacy is exemplified by one of my México City friends who was unaware that his brother, who slept in the same room he did, was also much involved in homosexual behavior. It is easy to elicit that young men have never discussed their homosexual behavior with family members. It is more difficult to elicit an estimate of whether family members know of it. Some would say, "I think so-and-so knows, but we never talk about it." Many others refused even to speculate about this potentially anxiety-producing topic.

As Lacey (1983:7) noted, there is a "universal tendency of Latin American writers to use euphemistic language in the description of sexual organs and activities, even when these activities are described with disarmingly complete frankness and when the themes are bold, modern and sophisticated: generations of practice in linguistic hypocrisy, in 'saying what one does not say,' are evidently not effaced overnight"—even by the avant garde in print, and still less in family circles in daily life!

A direct relationship between the gay institutional elaboration and security about healthcare within Latin America is demonstrated in Table One. The number of gay facilities in a country is a function of the population size ($r = .95$). Controlling for population, there is a significant correlation between the provision of social security (percentage covered) and the number of gay facilities per capita. The threshold of an effect seems to be around coverage of one-fifth of the population. There is an even stronger correlation between life expectancy and profusion of gay facilities. Life expectancy is positively correlated to the provision of social security and strongly negatively correlated to the percentage of the national population categorized as "Indian." Affluence and security are not easily distinguished, but there does seem to be a relationship between greater security about health and the development of gay bars and clubs that is not a function merely of urban growth. Neither the size of the nation's largest city nor the concentration of that nation's population in its largest city has a significant effect on the number of gay facilities per capita. Values for these values for each country are summarized in Table Two.

Table One

Correlations Between Per Capita Gay Listings and Demographic Variables

	Gay Places Listed	Male Life Expectancy	Percent Covered by Social Insurance	Percent Indian	Percent in Largest City
Life Expectancy	.66**				
Insurance Covered	.43*	.49*			
Indian %	-.35	-.61**	-.32		
Urban-Concentrated	-.19	.10	.58**	-.16	.09

*p<.10**
**p<.05

Table Two

Number of Gay Listings and Healthcare Indicators by Country

Country	Per Capita Health Expenditures	Percent Insured	Per Capita Gay Places	Male Life Expectancy	Percent Indian	Percent Living in Largest City
Costa Rica	51	82	7.14	68.7	0.6	20
Panama	74	47	6.84	68.5	6.8	20
Venezuela	59	30	2.38	65.1	1.5	18
Colombia	49	10	2.34	61.4	2.2	11
Argentina	46	80	2.30	66.7	1.5	34
Dom Republic	73	4	2.00	60.7	0.0	14
Uruguay	14	50	1.43	67.1	1.8	40
Mexico	49	56	1.24	63.9	12.4	20
El Salvador	52	5	1.14	59.7	2.3	7
Brazil	23	83	1.04	61.6	0.2	4
Peru	36	12	.98	57.6	36.8	26
Honduras	48	7	.91	58.2	3.2	12
Ecuador	89	5	.86	60.6	33.9	14
Guatemala	25	14	.78	51.2	59.7	10
Chile	36	50	.75	62.6	5.7	37
Paraguay	20	13	.65	62.8	2.3	15
Bolivia	52	26	0.00	48.6	59.2	15

Sources: Palmero et al. (1981), Stamford (1982), Wilkie et al. (1988), Zschock (1986)

Poverty and Lack of Housing

Lack of economic resources to maintain a place of one's own and the general lack of available housing should not be ignored. The crowding of dwelling units results more from economic necessity than from family feeling.[6] While many would have liked to have more space, none of my friends who had been born in Latin America wished to live apart from his family. "I would be lonely!" each protested at the prospect. That this is not exclusively rationalization of necessity is demonstrated by the extension of the pattern of living with the family while single to the very top of the stratification system. Upper-class informants may maintain *puteria* (more politely called *leonera*) apartments for assignations and parties,[7] while continuing to dwell with their families. Carrier (1976a: 359) also noted that "even in the upper-income strata of the society, a majority continue to live with their family while single."

CONSEQUENCES

Sex and Ignorance about HIV Transmission

Taking prospective sexual partners to where one lives is rarely possible in Latin America. For the affluent, there are visits to resorts, hotels in their own city, automobiles, and trysting apartments (*puterías*). For those who are not affluent, there is the dark. There are also public baths, varying in how predominantly they are patronized by those in search of homosexual encounters (Carrier 1972; Taylor 1978). These are not "gay baths" in the Northern European and American sense. With no acknowledgment that sex is occurring, they also are not venues for AIDS education.

In Mérida, which one alien (Ness 1992) claims is "Mexico's gayest city," a native man with AIDS related the lack of public gay life to his ignorance about how to avoid HIV transmission:

> There is no public, organized gay community there. Underground, informal communities revolve around the one bar and private friendship networks, especially among men old enough and well off enough to have their own homes or apartments. Like nearly all younger men who aren't married, I lived at home. . . . My awareness of SIDA or AIDS was very vague, based only on word-of-mouth rumors. I did not see any pamphlets, posters, or flyers about AIDS and HIV until Walt sent me some from the United States in early 1989. ("J" in Likosky 1992:368–9)

Relationships

As elsewhere in the world, secure privacy for lovemaking is a luxury. The pattern of residence pushes pre- and extra-marital intercourse (heterosexual as well as homosexual) into the streets. This does not prevent quick sexual encounters (*fichas*), but it is a major obstacle to ongoing relationships. Those who wish "to walk in the plan of love" (*amblar en el plan del amor*) do not have the easy path—moving in together— open to *norteamericanos*. Even families that accept a relationship within the family circle (treating the *amante* as another son) do not want outsiders to know that they have produced and are harboring *un raro* (a queer one). In gratitude for this (far-from-certain) minimum of acceptance, few couples are willing to demand more, such as the chance to be alone together sometimes. Some couples do manage to carry on long-term relationships without any place in which they can be together in private, but this is quite a difficult achievement.[8]

The arrangements portrayed in the Mexican film *Doña Herlinda y Su Hijo* are more wish-fulfillment (a fairy tale?) than representative, even of the upper class.[9]

What does seem to me typical is that nothing is said about the homosexual relationship, even by the mother who arranges to co-opt it within her plans to ensure the manufacture of grandchildren. That is, even when homosexuality is known, it is not discussed. "No one wants you to explain [a relationship]. . . . No one wants to know what is going on" (Hugo to Miller 1992:209–10). Monteagudo (1991:16) wrote of what he considers "a system of repression and hypocrisy."

> Little Havana, like big Havana, is a family-oriented society that expects its sons and daughters to reside with their parents until they get, heterosexually, a means of escape. . . . *La familia* comes first . . . In the Cuban community a façade of heterosexuality must be maintained while living at home. If one's sexual orientation is known it is treated as, at best, an unfortunate vice that should only be indulged elsewhere.

Similarly, Muñoz's (1989:61) Cuban-American protagonist's Colombian-American girlfriend knew he was also having sexual relations with a man: "She'd give me this look of disapproval. But we never talked about it. It was as if we had mutually agreed not to discuss the issue. If we spoke about it, everything would end, my relationship with her, with him. Everything."

In such cases, silence is certainly not consent. Rather, silence is the upper limit of "tolerance" for individual desires (Muñoz 1989:147). What Khan (1990:12) wrote about the impossibility of gay life in Pakistan applies directly, suggesting that the same familial incompatibility with gay life occurs in other cultures so long as the structural basis of a welfare society "safety net" is lacking:

> Families are like organisms that extend themselves by absorbing their young, and grow stronger or weaker based on the contributions of the new entrants. This is not just one model of life in Pakistan; it is not a choice; it is the only way of life. . . If a husband takes care of his family's security needs and produces many children, what he does for personal sexual satisfaction is quite irrelevant—and so long as it is kept a private matter—tolerated.... The most successful gay relationships in Karachi are quiet and heavily compromised. They are almost never the most important relationship for either partner; the family occupies that position. (Also see Murray 1992 on Thailand.)

The ongoing liaison between the head of the family and a servant in Mario Vargas Llosa's (1969) novel *Conversación en la Catedral* certainly fits with this characterization.[10]

For less easily hidden gender deviation, exhaustion rather than acceptance is probably more common, as for the small-town families that (mysteriously to itself) spawned a pair of dancer/hustlers in Zapata (1983:100):

> We had real bad times with our families, specially when they found out about what they called our "unnatural behavior." We fought with them, they tried to punish us, they slapped us around sometimes. Other times they almost seemed to give up and realize there wasn't anything they could do about it.

Many families indefinitely manage to deny that they could have produced a homosexual son or daughter.[11]

Collective Consciousness

Gay consciousness is no more an automatic product of homosexual behavior than class consciousness is of "objective class position" or ethnic consciousness of genealogy. In a population of persons with such a characteristic, some will not consider themselves defined in any way by it, and others will deny the characteristic altogether. The existence and importance of a characteristic must be realized if there is to be a consciousness of kind: characteristics are only potential bases (Murray 1979).

In Anglo America such a realization was facilitated by the congregation into neighborhoods with concentrations of gay men after World War II. Recreational facilities concentrated in already gay neighborhoods, drawing non-residents to these areas for socializing (including, but not confined to cruising). In time a full range of separate facilities and services sprang up in these areas (Lee 1978, 1979; Levine 1979; Murray 1979, 1984).

Such residential concentration of homosexually inclined men is precluded where the unmarried indefinitely continue to live at home. The specific pattern of historical development of gay communities in Anglo-America need not be assumed to constitute the only possible route to the rejection of pariah status.

On the other hand, sex does not automatically produce a sense of peoplehood. Cruising areas and social networks of homosexually inclined men partying together exist and have existed with varying degrees of visibility in cities everywhere,[12] while a sense of belonging to a community of those whose identity is based on shared sexual preferences has not. Something more than sexual acts in "the city of night" is needed to provide a conception of a shared fate. Where individual sexual acts are ignored and discretion is the rule of social life, homosexuality may not be conceived as constituting a shared fate.[13]

A Latin American cannot learn about the common experiences of those with homosexual desires from print media,[14] any more than s/he can discuss them with those with whom s/he lives. Material on homosexuality available in Latin America is mostly caricature, with gruesome murders of transvestites especially prominent (Carrier 1972, 1976b; Taylor 1978). There is de facto censorship of anything remotely interpretable as legitimating homosexuality. Police have considerable discretion in making their own judgments of what is contrary to public interest, and judges have similar discretion in labeling printed material dealing with homosexuality as "apologies for vice" or "offending public morality" (e.g., see Green 1994:44–6). What Fuskóva-Komreich (1993:84) wrote of Argentina applies to gay men and to all of Spanish America: "We appeared either in the gutter press or nowhere at all. Any photo [or text] showing women happy and proud to be lesbians was intolerable to the system."

Sociation with like others is also limited. For fear of having their reputation "burned" (*quemada*) and their security thereby endangered, many persons involved in homosexual behavior avoid being seen with or being acknowledged by males who might be judged effeminate, and also avoid places where homosexuals are known to congregate (also see Carrier 1976a: 365; Arboleda 1987). The same pattern existed among homosexual Anglo-Americans in the mid-1960s, although then and there it was fear of losing jobs more than Latin Americans' fear of the family learning of stigmatizing association. The lack of positive literature and the fear of guilt by association were obstacles overcome by gay liberation movements in Anglo America, so there is evidence that such obstacles are surmountable. Indeed, the demonstration that change is possible is an advantage gay movements in their early development today have. In post-war North America, without any known historical precedent, the possibility of change was difficult to conceive.[15] On the other hand, living in a(n emerging) welfare state in which there is not the economic necessity of staying with one's family, a critical mass developed in a visible territory. The growth and metamorphosis of recreational facilities within an area of increasing residential concentration of homosexuals facilitated the sense of shared experience that led gay North Americans to reject stereotypes of homosexuality and to demand full acceptance.

Whether there are functional alternatives to residential concentration is at this point open to question. Even though Latin American homophile organizations seem to be repeating the struggles over tactics and goals characteristic of the era of homophile organizations in the United States (see Marotta 1981; D'Emilio 1983), we need not assume history will repeat itself elsewhere in all its details or that there is only a single possible path of development.[16] A sense of community is easier to instill if there is a visible territory, but this historical correlation is far from being established as a necessary prerequisite. Distinct gay facilities and services might develop without a residential concentration. Continued residence with families scattered throughout cities is a considerable obstacle to the formation of gay consciousness, culture and community as these have developed in Anglo North America. Only time will tell if there are other routes to similar—or other—developments.[17]

Notes

[1] Four percent (all *activos,* that is, insertors) lived with wives. Fifty-three percent of *pasivos* (i.e., recipients) planned to live with their natal family indefinitely, with another 27 percent uncertain (Carrier 1972:211).

[2] Although the penchant for proclaiming ideas and value explanations of social patterns is characteristic of functionalists, particularly Parsonian ones, not all functionalist explanation is necessarily idealist.

[3] "Cottage industry" is the traditional Anglocentric gloss.

[4] Latin American men "tend to wear their Catholicism lightly... [and] simply do not tend to take priests or church doctrine terribly seriously," as Lacey (1983:13) observed, mostly leaving piety to women. The Catholic Church continues to have the power to curb publication of "immoral" literature (Lacey 1983:9), and, concomitant with the inroads of fundamentalist Protestant mission in the countryside, is increasingly intolerant of even covert homosexuality.

[5] Ana Castillo, who is a native of Chicago, challenged as

> a misconception of people who have not really lived among "traditional Mexicans" to think that they are so sexually repressed that they do not ever discuss sexuality, and that they forbid women to do so in mixed company. Men and women do talk and there is even sexual talk, at times, in the presence of your children. I believe it is at the very moment when an adolescent's sexual consciousness emerges, however, that the "censorship" begins. (1991:26)}

Since she shows that it is intense, I don't know why Castillo places *censorship* between quotation marks. The editor of the volume in which Castillo's essay appeared, (New Mexico-born) Carla Trujillo (1991:186), wrote, "As Chicanas, we are commonly led to believe that even talking about our participation and satisfaction in sex is taboo. Moreover we (as well as most women in the United States) learn to hate our bodies and usually possess little knowledge of them." In that Trujillo is writing about post-pubesence, she is not contradicting Castillo. I think that Castillo underestimates the tact (if that is the word for not bringing up personal concerns) of highland southern Mexico and Guatemala, though sex(uality) is not always entirely a tabooed topic even in a heterosocial family setting.

[6] See Arenas (1993:37). After moving to Havana, Arenas stayed with an aunt. Even migration often does not end living under some extent of family supervision.

[7] A group of friends all of whom live with their families sometimes acquire one (Taylor 1978; see Novo 1979; Carrier 1972:122–3). The more affluent can also afford to rent hotel rooms for assignations.

[8] Miller (1992:201) suggested that younger Argentine "gays and lesbians tended to become involved in relationships with someone older and more established who might have his or own place to live." Adam (1993:175) noted that "there are some male couples who have succeeded in living together in [Sandinista-era] Managua, even though they may present themselves as cousins to their neighbors." In a horrific representation of small-town homophobia, "The Siege," the Nicaraguan writer (and later Sandinista vice-president) Sergio Ramirez (1986 [1967]) imagined the attacks (including a rape) of a couple of men who set up house together, countenanced by a police captain who would not tolerate any "indecency" in his town.

[9] The mother trying to shoot her son when she finds him with another boy in Arenas' *Old Rosa* may be extreme, but paternal rejection of sons interested in art and books (long before they engage in homosexuality) is fairly typical among the Mexicans, Mexican-Americans, and Guatemaltecos I know, also in such fictional representations as Muñoz (1989:23, 1991:35, 67, 134–5) and Islas (1984:94).

[10] While accepting this representation of Latino homosexuality viewed from outside, I find Vargas Llosa's attempt to write a gay character from the inside, specifically the title character in *La Historia de Mayta* (1984), completely implausible. It provides more data on the cultural model of homosexuality, but I have never met anyone who experienced his homosexuality as the character Alejandro Mayta does. Vargas Llosa (1991) wrote elsewhere of not being able to write from inside characters alien to his experience, although he did not mention Mayta as an example. (He also did not discuss *Conversación* in this regard.)

[11] See Mujica (1962), Islas (1990), Muñoz (1991), Ruiz (1994) for representations. Fathers' attempts to toughen up sons "to save them from a fate they believed to be worse than death" are recalled bitterly by Monteagudo (1991:15) and Nava (1990:77). Monteagudo recalled that "many a Cuban boy of uncertain sexuality was subjected to hormone shots, a practice that led to a crop of hirsute, deep-voiced gay men who walk the streets of Miami today." Nito in Muñoz (1989:23–4) received hormone shots.

[12] See Murray and Gerard (1983).

[13] Those shaken down by police or fag-bashed still may not conceive of a shared situation. Similarly, many *norteamericano* casualties did not (and, in some cases and places, do not).

[14] On the importance of group-affirming (indeed, group-defining) literature in combating stigma, see Humphreys (1972:130–4) and Goffman (1963:25). On the seriousness with which Latin American regimes take publications, see Lacey (1979:24; 1983:8).

[15] "Latin American gays are in many ways in approximately the same social and psychological situation from which Anglo-Saxon gays, especially in North America, began to emerge 25 years ago" (Lacey 1979:31; 1983:8–12), including the trade/queen (*activo/pasivo, mayate/loca*) distinction. Humphreys (1972), following Toch (1965), emphasized that the "feeling that the status quo is not inevitable and that change is conceivable" is a precondition of social change movements.

[16] Only time will tell if there are other routes to similar—or to other—developments. The "four little dragons" (Hong Kong, Singapore, South Korea, Taiwan) have shown that economic modernization (i.e., industrial production that is competitive in the world market) may occur without modernization theory's vaunted values, so sociologists recently have been quieter than before about proclaiming a singular, universal path to any sort of development. ("Globalization" sometimes seems a new label for the unilinear evolutionary sense in which "modernization" was once used.)

[17] It is difficult to forecast the effect of AIDS on the development of "gay" homosexuality in Latin America. Some officials advocate repressing increasingly public homosexuality because of the specter of AIDS, although to date it has, if anything, provided a basis for increased and increasingly visible gay organizations combating AIDS, as in Anglo North America (Lumsden 1991). Moreover, globalization of "safe sex" campaigns (which often carry many American assumptions) may further disseminate "modern" homosexuality.

References

Adam, Barry D. (1993) "In Nicaragua: homosexuality without a gay world." *Journal of Homosexuality* 24:171–181.

Arboleda G., Manuel A. (1987). "La vida entendida en Lima." In Murray (1987:101–117). Revised version.

Arenas, Reinaldo (1989) *Old Rosa*. New York: Grove Press.

———. (1993) *Before Night Falls*. New York: Viking.

Carballo-Diéguez, Alex (1989) "Hispanic culture, gay male culture, and AIDS: counseling implications," *Journal of Counseling & Development* 68:26–30.

Carrier, Joseph M. (1972) *Urban Mexican Male Homosexual Encounters*. Ph.D. dissertation, University of California, Irvine.

———. (1976a) "Family attitudes and Mexican male homosexuality." *Urban Life* 5:359–375.

———. (1976b) "Cultural factors affecting urban Mexican male homosexual behavior." *Archives of Sexual Behavior* 5:103–124.

Castillo, Ana (1991) "La macha: toward a beautiful whole self." In Trujillo (1991:24–48).

D'Emilio, John (1983) *Sexual Politics/Sexual Communities*. Chicago: University of Chicago Press.

Fabrega, Horacio (1971) "Begging in a Southeastern Mexican city." *Human Organization* 20:277–287.

Fusková-Komreich, Ilse (1993) "Lesbian activism in Argentina: a recent but very powerful phenomenon." In *The Third Pink Book*, ed. by A. Hendriks, R. Tielman, & E. van der Veen, pp. 82–85. Buffalo, NY: Prometheus Books.

Green, James N. (1994) "The emergence of the Brazilian Gay Liberation Movement, 1977–1981." *Latin American Perspectives* 21:38–55.

Humphreys, Laud (1972) *Out of the Closets*. Toronto: Prentice-Hall.

Islas, Arturo (1984) *The Rain God*. Palo Alto, CA: Alexandrian Press. Reprinted, New York: Avon, 1991.

———. (1990) *Migrant Souls*. New York: Morrow. Reprinted, New York: Avon, 1991 (the edition quoted herein).

Khan, Badruddin (1990) "Not-so-gay life in Karachi," *Society of Lesbian and Gay Anthropologists' Newsletter* 12,1:10–19.

Kinger, Nora S. (1973) "Priests, machos and babies." *Journal of Marriage & the Family* 35:300–311.

Lacey, E. A. (1979) "Latin America." *Gay Sunshine* 40:22–31.

———. (1983) Introduction to *My Deep Dark Pain is Love,* pp. 7-13. San Francisco: Gay Sunshine Press.

Lee, John Alan (1978) *Getting Sex*. Toronto: General.

———. (1979) "The gay connection." *Urban Life* 8:175–198.

Levine, Martin P. (1979) *Gay Men*. New York: Harper & Row.

Likosky, Stephan (1992) *Coming Out: An Anthology of International Gay and Lesbian Writing*. New York: Pantheon.

Lumsden, Ian (1991) *Homosexuality, Society and the State in Mexico*. Toronto: Canadian Gay Archives.

McGin, Noel F. (1966) "Marriage and the family in middle-class Mexico." *Journal of Marriage and the Family* 28:305–313.

Marotta, Toby (1981) *The Politics of Homosexuality*. Boston: Houghton-Mifflin.

Miller, Neil (1992) *Out in the World*. New York: Random House.

Mujia Laniez, Manuel (1962) *Bomarzo*. Buenos Aires: Editorial Sudamericana.

Muñoz, Elías Miguel (1989) *Crazy Love*. Houston: Arte Publico Press.

———. (1991) *The Greatest Performance*. Houston: Arte Publico Press.

Monteagudo, Jesse G. (1991) "Miami, Florida." In *Hometowns*, ed. by John Preston, pp. 11–20. New York: Dutton.

Murray, Stephen O. (1979) "The institutional elaboration of a quasi-ethnic community." *International Review of Modern Sociology* 9:165–178.

———. (1984) *Social Theory, Homosexual Realities. Gai Saber Monograph* 3.

———. (1987) *Male Homosexuality in Central and South America. Gai Saber Monograph* 5.

———. (1992) "The 'underdevelopment' of 'gay' homosexuality in Mesoamerica, Peru, and Thailand." Pp. 29–38 in *Modern Homosexualities*, ed. by Ken Plummer. London: Routledge.

Murray, Stephen O., and Kent Gerard (1983) "Renaissance sodomite subcultures?" *Onder Vrouwen, Onder Mannen* 1:182–196.

Nava, Michael (1990) *How Town*. New York: Harper & Row.

Ness, Kristian (1992) "Merida: Mexico's gayest city is still a well-kept secret." *Christopher Street* 186 (31 Aug.): 17–18.

Novo, Salvador (1979 [1973]) "Memoir." Pp. 11–47 in W. Leyland, *Now the Volcano*. San Francisco: Gay Sunshine Press.

Ogburn, William F. (1928) *Family Life Today*. Boston: Houghton-Mifflin.

Palmero, Olga, Manuel Millor, and Margarita Elizondo (1981) *Financiamiento y extension de la seguridad social en America Latina*. México: Instituto Mexicano del Seguro Social.

Parker, Richard G. (1988) *"Within Four Walls": The Cultural Construction of Sexual Meaning in Contemporary Brazil*. Ph.D. dissertation, University of California, Berkeley.

Peñalosa, Fernando (1968) "Mexican family roles." *Journal of Marriage and the Family* 30:680–689.

Ramirez, Sergio (1986) "The Siege." Pp. 27–35 in *Stories*. London: Readers International.

Ruiz Guinazú, Magdalena (1994) *Huesped de un verano*. Buenos Aires: Planeta.

Salas, Luis (1979) *Social Control and Deviance in Cuba*. New York: Praeger.

Stamford, John (1982) *Spartacus Gay Guide*. Amsterdam: Spartacus.

Tax, Sol (1941) "World view and social relations in Guatemala." *American Anthropologist* 39:423–444.

Taylor, Clark L. (1978) *El Ambiente*. Ph.D. dissertation, University of California, Berkeley.

Toch, Hans (1965) *The Social Psychology of Social Movements*. Indianapolis: Bobbs-Merrill.

Trujillo, Carla (1991) *Chicana Lesbians*. Berkeley: Third Woman Press.

Vargas Llosa, Mario (1969) *Conversación en la Catedral*. Barcelona: Editorial Siex Barral (translated by Gregory Rabassa as *Conversation in the Cathedral*). San Francisco: Harper & Row, 1975).

———. (1984) *La Historia de Mayta*. Barcelona: Editorial Siex Barral (translated by Alfred MacAdam as *The Real Life of Alejandro Mayta*). New York: Farrar, Straus and Giroux, 1986.

———. (1991) *A Writer's Reality*. New York: Houghton-Mifflin.

Wilkie, J. W., B. E. Lorey, and E. Ochoa (1988) *Statistical Abstract of Latin America, Volume 26*. Los Angeles: UCLA Latin America Center.

Zapata, Luis (1983) "The red dancing shoes." Pp. 98–102 in W. Leyland & E. A. Lacey, *My Deep Dark Pain is Love*. San Francisco: Gay Sunshine Press.

Zschock, Dieter (1986) "Medical care under social insurance." *Latin American Research Review* 21:99–122.

Matthew C. Guttman teaches anthropology and ethnic relations at Brown University. Having long served as a community organizer, he is also author of The Meanings of Macho: Being a Man in Mexico City, Mainstreaming Men into Gender and Development (with S. Chat), and The Romance of Democracy: Compliance and Defiance in Contemporary Mexico.

28

In the course of addressing gender roles in the world's largest metropolis, Gutmann vividly demonstrates how a series of vignettes from everyday life challenge even the most popular of stereotypes. In one sense, "everybody knows" that Mexican males are heavy drinkers, if only to prove their masculinity (machismo). Similarly, "everybody knows" that Mexican women, in their self-abnegating and decorous (Marianista) way, avoid alcohol lest they be branded as loose or scandalous. However, as is so often the case with stereotypes, what "everybody knows" really doesn't hold up when you begin to observe closely, count instances, and delve below the surface of glib generalizations. By using alcohol as a convenient window upon the rest of culture, not only do we learn about the various roles of drinking in an urban Mexican neighborhood, but we also find that folk beliefs about medicine, religious faith, and even a little competition between communities can be better understood in context.

Abstinence, Antibiotics, and *Estar Jurado*
The Manners of Drinking in Working-Class Mexico City
Matthew C. Gutmann

I regret to state, however, that today there are a great many women quite as tipsy as the men.

—Frances Calderón de Barca, *Life in Mexico*, 1840[1]

LAS COPAS

A friend arrived at our apartment in Colonia Santo Domingo in Mexico City on 12 December 1992. This was the day celebrating the appearance of the Virgin of Guadalupe in 1531, and one of the most important annual holidays in Mexico. After walking several blocks through the *colonia* from the Copilco metro stop, she reported, *"Todos los hombres están en la calle tomados* [All the men are in the streets drunk]."

On a basic level, this was the offhand pronouncement of someone who had just had to weave her way over and around several congregations of male merrymakers still toasting Juan Diego's fortuitous encounter with the Virgin. My friend had intended not a statement of pure fact, but rather hyperbole with a purpose. Every day and even more on holidays, men are found sipping *las copas*[2] in the streets of Colonia Santo Domingo. On another level, however, the comment hints at (mis)conceptions which are revealed in the way scholars and others sometimes refer to men and women, and in the categories we frequently employ to discuss them: "men (typically) do this"; "women (typically) are like that."

Although anthropologically influenced concepts of multiculturalism have served to improve the situation in the past two decades—many now will qualify such statements by stating that "Latin American men do this," "Asian women are like that," and so on—these summary statements still reveal their origins in haphazard and archaic notions of national character and personality studies. Thus they too can blur deeper analysis of how specific group and individual histories impinge on gender identities, as well as the significant extent to which gender relations themselves come to constitute history.

In the social science literature on Mexico, arbitrary reference to "men" and "women" is abundant in discussions regarding the relation between men and alcohol. According to most anthropological studies of other locations and times in Mexico, for instance, it is common to equate *ser hombre* [being a man] with at least periodic public inebriation.

But is this the best way to analyze the mixture of liquor and men in Santo Domingo on 12 December 1992? What of those men who were home and sober throughout that day? Were these men, at least implicitly, less manly than those who were drunk in the streets? In a sense, the answer must be that they were. That is, in the eyes of many commentators, the intoxicated men in the streets were the true and "typical" Mexican *hombres de verdad* [real men].

This is not a quibble over semantics. We should subject to greater scrutiny the celebrated image of the Mexican proletarian male with a bottle of tequila in his hand and a silly, satisfied grin on his lips precisely by examining categories such as "Mexican men" and "*hombres de verdad*," and the benefits and liabilities accruing to scholars and others who utilize such generalizations. In connection with such typologizing, too often we get into trouble by using the quantitative techniques of contemporary social science.

The construction of categories of alcoholic personality types, for example, is based on the premise that alcoholism reflects the problems of individual psychologies. Or, more specifically, the thesis that alcoholism reveals the lack of social integration of particular individuals, and thus that alcoholics should be viewed as a problem *for* society. Such an analysis is very different from one which views alcoholism as socially created and defined, and therefore a product *of* society.[3]

This chapter is based on research done in Santo Domingo, a *colonia popular* on the south side of Mexico City where I lived with my family and carried out ethnographic fieldwork in 1992–93 on changing gender identities and practices in the area.[4] This was two decades after the 1971 invasion by thousands of "parachutist" [squatter] families into the area of volcanic lava flows and caves known as the Pedregales. Among the residents of this self-built neighborhood of Santo Domingo who now number over 100,000, women as well as men have been active as community organizers and leaders, first to build roads and then to bring in electricity, schools, and other social necessities. Because of a conjuncture of special circumstances, also present in other Mexican and Latin American communities in the last twenty years, popular social movements marked by varying degrees of independence from state control have played a prominent role in the cultural politics of Colonia Santo Domingo since the invasion. It seemed like a fine location to study cultural change and resilience, including with respect to alcohol use and abuse, among women and men.

On Huehuetzin Street where we lived, there stood what some neighbors referred to as *la casa de los borrachos* [the house of the drunks], with three generations of heavy drinkers crowded together in a series of shacks. One of the younger members of the household, ten years old, told me that she had spent less than one year in school in her life; instead she occupied her days selling candies on the curb and running to the corner store, a three-year-old sister in tow, for more *caguamas* [quarts] of beer for her elders. While not often this extreme in form, alcohol is part of most people's lives in one way or another in the *colonia*, from young girls who must fetch beer for their mothers and grandmothers, to fathers, uncles, brothers, and cousins who miss work when they go on a *borrachera* [drinking binge], to friends who have to be taken to the emergency room when their kidneys will not tolerate another drop of rum. The fatal effects of alcoholism—direct ones like cirrhosis of the liver and alcoholic psychosis, and indirect ones like accidents and homicides—are leading causes of death among men in the so-called productive ages in Mexico (see Menéndez 1990:9).[5]

THE TEMPLE OF MEXICAN VIRILITY: *LA CANTINA*

Having already lived and conducted ethnographic research in Mexico City over a period of several years, upon arriving in Santo Domingo in 1992 I went looking for that "culturally typical" site of Mexican male bonding, the *cantina*. No one needed to tell me that *cantinas* were the characteristic meeting places of Mexican men, who were the subjects of my study. To my great initial disappointment, however, I was informed by neighbors that while there were a few *pulquerías*[6] in the community, there were no *cantinas* whatsoever in Colonia Santo Domingo.

Not only are there no *cantinas* in Santo Domingo, but few residents travel outside the neighborhood to go to *cantinas* in other *colonias*, because, as my neighbor Juan says, "It's a lot more pleasant to drink at home," not to mention less expensive. Another neighbor, a periodically employed long-haul truck driver, told me that he used to go to the *cantinas* when he lived in the central-city *colonia* of Guerrero, but that was about thirty years ago, when he was young and newly arrived in the capital from his ranch in the state of Guanajuato. "Who's got that kind of money today?" he asked me. He offered the following figures: "Suppose you make a minimum salary of fifteen pesos [then about five U.S. dollars] a day. Who can afford beer in a *cantina*? Say you pay one or two pesos a beer, how long's that going to last you? Even buying a case isn't as cheap as it used to be." *Cantinas*, as far as he was concerned, were for those with significantly more money than he had seen recently.

When men do leave the *colonia* to drink, often it is to find good *pulque*. Luciano, a welder, and his friend Ricardo, a taxi driver, stumbled toward me on their way down the street one afternoon. They told me they had gotten away to the hills in the area known as Contreras in southwestern Mexico City, and that they had spent several hours there drinking *pulque*.[7] I asked why they traveled so far when there were *pulquerías* in Santo Domingo, though I knew these were widely regarded as the haunts of the most pitiful drunks. It turned out there was a reason other than the reputation of the clientele of these establishments. "That shit?" responded Luciano in giggles. He explained that *pulque* is allowed to ferment "naturally" without additives for up to two weeks in Contreras. In Santo Domingo, on the other hand, the beverage is fermented the quick way, by adding human excrement to the brew.

Three times during 1992–93 I was invited to go to *cantinas*, not by friends in the neighborhood as it turned out, but rather each time by one or another Mexican anthropologist. The first time, on our way to the *cantina*, my companion told me that given my interest in male identities, it was imperative I witness firsthand *lo que hacen los hombres* [what men do] and experience this manly environment, which until a few short years ago was by law an exclusively male refuge. ("There's still only a men's bathroom," he pointed out to me.) The second time, I was lectured, "You know nothing of the Mexican man if you don't know the *cantina*."

The *cantina* is an important gathering place for many men in Mexico. The working-class neighborhood of Colonia Obrera, in the heart of Mexico City, for instance, is reputed to have more *cantinas* than taco stands. For this and other reasons, with full justification it might be said that Colonia Santo Domingo is not "representative" of *colonias populares* in Mexico City. But then no neighborhood is or could be, in a metropolitan area of nearly 20 million people. Undoubtedly more drinking by men occurs in *cantinas* in many other parts of the city and country than in Colonia Santo Domingo. Still, according to ethnographic studies from widely scattered areas over the past twenty-five years, if there is any pattern in male drinking behavior in the country, it is more one of diversity than of homogeneity.

All of which has a number of interesting implications for gender relations in Santo Domingo, implications that may not be present to the same degree in all other locations.[8]

For many adult men in Colonia Santo Domingo in the early 1990s, drinking with your *cuates* [buddies] and *compas* [*compadres*, symbolic co-parents] often similarly embodied and extended bonds of friendship, trust, and male-male intimacy. And as Lomnitz shows (1977:175f), *cuates* are first and foremost drinking buddies. Yet even while drinking in the home was often a markedly male activity in Santo Domingo, the very presence of women and children, among other elements, placed constraints on the men.[9] As we will see, the degendering of alcohol consumption indicates that "typical" male behavior varies.

In Colonia Santo Domingo, some men drink in the street in front of their own or friends' houses after work and on weekends. More men drink in their homes during these times, with friends or family. A few admit to occasionally drinking alone. As part of the antipollution efforts of recent years in Mexico City, each vehicle is prohibited from driving one weekday each week. For some friends whose jobs are dependent upon the use of cars or trucks, their day not to "circulate" is also considered as a weekend day and they may drink more heavily then.

Men and women drink together at birthday parties, holiday celebrations, and when visiting friends, more often than not consuming the same beverages, sometimes in the same quantities, though most often with men drinking more than women, and with more women than men abstaining from alcohol altogether. Older teenagers are often allowed to drink during family events. Younger children are frequently offered sips of beer or *cubas*[10] on these occasions. At large and lengthy events—baptism celebrations, *quinceañera* fiestas [celebrations of girls' fifteenth birthdays], and weddings, for instance—some men and less often a few women will drink to the point of intoxication. Depending on the individuals involved, this may lead to violent outbursts revealing long-simmering feuds or tender confessional moments; in either case the parties involved are capitalizing on the belief that drunks should be held less responsible for their words and actions. My friends Juan and Tomás both seemed comfortable when they mentioned that they had reputations for being very temperate when drunk. Angela, Juan's wife, notes that while he is *impulsivo* [impulsive] in everyday life, he's the nicest man in the world after he's had a few *copas*.

Social drinking in moderation on a regular basis has been reported in some ethnographies of Mesoamerica (see, for example, Lewis 1951 and DeWalt 1979). Even where alcohol is more often consumed by men in periods of bingeing on holidays and weekends, its common role in the mediation of everyday social relations is noteworthy (see Brandes 1988). In Colonia Santo Domingo, consuming one or two beers daily is common practice for many men, whereas bingeing, though not uncommon in the 1990s, was according to most accounts more common in the past. Further, nearly all women and men with whom I have spoken on the subject in Santo Domingo maintain that far more women today drink alcoholic beverages in far greater quantities than they did in the past.[11]

THE MANNERS OF DRINKING: GETTING DRUNK

The Mexican who does not drink and get drunk is the dead Mexican.

—J. R. Flippin, *Sketches from the Mountains of Mexico*, 1889[12]

On another occasion in late February, Toño and I spent several hours at the corner *tienda* [shop] with Gabriel, Marcos, the Yucatecan carpenter Marcial, and Marcelo, once again drinking licorice-flavored *anís* cordial. Following a year's abstention, Toño was, two months after the New Year, still celebrating being able to drink again. Other men and a few women who stopped by to purchase something at the store were invited to share our *anís*. Some men would stay a while, either drinking with us or buying themselves a soda instead. While there was little pressure to drink liquor with us, only those drinking alcohol remained very long. As Marcelo commented to me at another time, it is a lot easier to enjoy the company of others if you are either all drunk or all sober.

We drank far more that day than we normally did. After we finished off the first pint of *anís*, someone went to the nearby liquor store for another, and then another, until we had consumed a half-dozen of them. Finally we switched to the liter bottles, ultimately polishing off two or three of the big containers. All this time, Gabriel was repairing one or another VW bus, Marcos was working on the fenders of his 1964 VW bug, and Marcelo, though enjoying his two-hour break from behind the *tienda* counter, was helping out from time to time when customers proved too much for his wife.

After several hours, Marcos's wife Delia brought out tacos, which she had prepared for us to eat in their house next to the *tienda*. While she was there she scolded me in particular: "You shouldn't drink!" Though apparently resigned to my participation with the others, she was not kidding. I may have been singled out as a newcomer, and as someone who should "know better" because of being a *gringo* and a *profesionista* [professional]. But Delia may have also felt that Marcos and the others were to a certain extent putting on a performance for me, and so I was partly responsible for her husband's growing inebriation that day.

This last idea became apparent the next week. Two days after our *borrachera* I saw Don Timoteo at his spot in the grassy median on Cerro de la Estrella. He was waiting for customers to bring him their wicker chairs for repair. "We saw you drinking the other day," he said simply, raising his eyes to stare seriously into mine. He knew that I knew that he had been an alcoholic for many years and that he spoke with authority on the subject.

The next day I bumped into Luciano. He said he had not been around the past Saturday, but that he had heard that the others and I had been *bien pedos* (literally, "well-farted"; i.e., really loaded). "Pretty soon you're going to be like them," he said laughing, pointing to la *casa de los borrachos*. In Luciano's case, unlike with Don Timoteo, this did not seem to bother him in the least. During the rest of my fieldwork in Santo Domingo, several of my friends, and even a few men I hardly knew, would ask me, "Hey, Mateo, want some *anís*?" It became a running gag.

To some extent it is true that such binges are common occurrences for some men in Colonia Santo Domingo, and therefore I chose as part of my research to suffer the indignities of later ridicule and the queasiness of hangover following our merriment. But my case was also in retrospect similar to one highlighted by Brandes when he "tried to be more Andalusian than the Andalusians." In his paper regarding the ill-fated pursuit of anthropological preconceptions, Brandes (1987:362–63) recounts how he found himself in southern Spain drinking in a bar in January, asking himself where all the men had gone. It turned out that although in the fall the men did spend time drinking in bars, in the winter they stayed at home in the evenings. A friend who had kindly continued drinking with Brandes into the winter despite the custom pointed out that his wife was beginning to feel neglected and suggested they repair to his house for a change.

If I did not cause all excess drinking at the *tienda* that afternoon in January, my presence probably did inspire some to show off. And as others demonstrated in the days following that well-oiled occasion, public tolerance for drinking is decidedly a mixture of resignation toward some and persuasive chiding and mockery toward others.

Abstinence, Antibiotics, and *Estar Jurado*[13]

Coercion to drink among men is a standard element of drinking habits throughout Mexico, according to most ethnographic studies to date. "*No se puede escapar a las copas*" [You cannot escape liquor] was a popular saying in one village of Oaxaca (see Kearney 1972:99).[14]

Yet the extent of obligation to drink with other men may hinge on regional patterns, possibly in conjunction with particular cultural changes in specific areas in the recent past.

When I spoke with Esteban and Felipe on the street one day, Esteban wanted me to understand that "there are more drunks in the *campo* [rural area]. There's nothing to do there except drink. When you go visit someone, the first thing they do *en provincia* [in the provinces] is invite you to a *pulque* or a beer."

"Here I can say that I don't want one," I offered.

"There if you don't drink, it's an insult. Here you can say, 'I don't want one,' and you leave. But there you have to wait, you have to drink," Felipe insisted.

"Suppose you don't drink," interjected Esteban. "It's not that they're going to force you to do it, but that the next time you come by, they're not going to invite you because you were insulting about it that time."

"It's really that different in the city?" I asked.

"Yes, it's different here," said Esteban. "'Come on over and have a soda.' 'You know what, maybe in a while. I'll see you later.'"

The interpretations of different drinking styles in the country and city reflect more than personal experiences in both places. Among other things, in the national cinema of Mexico, the social and even physical penalties for refusing to drink when invited by a Mexican are of legendary status. Thus, again, representations of "typical" Mexican male behavior, in this case in the movies, may contribute to creating such comportment.

Of course, some men in Santo Domingo may be more persuasive than others. On the fourth night of the *posadas* (the pre-Christmas nightly reenactments of Mary and Joseph's search for a place to sleep), which were followed on Huehuetzin Street by *piñata* breaking, I found myself watching the celebrations with Alberto. Alberto was taking large gulps of *anís* from a bottle in his hand. After each one he held it out to me, offering a taste. I had no wish to drink *anís* that night, and besides, Alberto looked sickly; I most definitely did not want to share a bottle with him. But as I continued to decline his repeated offers, he grew more insistent. He began calling me *camarón* [shrimp (the shellfish)], a nickname for whites because when they "heat up" they turn red on the outside. Concerned about my ignorance and seeking to avoid a potential confrontation, Martín deftly intervened.

"Say," Martín asked me, "did you know that Alberto is a member of the famous *Púpuras* [the Purples, a street gang]?" I did not. "Isn't it too bad," sympathized Martín out loud, "that Mateo is still taking antibiotics for that nasty infection of his?" I slinked away while Alberto was considering my poor health.

It turned out that I had not completely escaped my drinking obligations. In the days following, I twice bumped into Don Timoteo. Both times he said to me forcefully, "*(Me debe!*" [You owe me!] It turned out that, from the other side of the street in front of his house, Don Timo had seen me standing with Alberto and Martín, though he could not have heard our discussion through the din. At one point Don Timoteo had gone into his house in order to get a *Presidente cuba* for me, he told me. In my flight from Alberto I had missed Don Timoteo's return and my drink. He expected me to collect.

Although he no longer drinks, there is nothing Don Timo likes better than to offer his friends some home-brewed mescal or to buy them a beer. Gabriel talked me into a rather large glass of the mescal three days before my encounter with Alberto, and I was sent reeling. Now, at Don Timo's Gabriel insisted I try another one—"It will help to alleviate the effects of the first . . . ," he lied to me. I demurred. Gabi kept on insisting. Finally I blurted out that I was a co-sponsor of that evening's *posadas*, where I would be expected to help hand out candy to the children and supervise the *piñata*-breaking. This left Gabriel unmoved, but it impressed Don Timoteo enough so that throughout the remainder of the year he praised me for my good sense that day.

It may be that because of his having grown up in a rural area, Don Timo had more of a sense of propriety when it came to community and religious responsibilities, known as *cargos* in other parts of Mexico, where excessive drinking is especially proscribed when it conflicts with fulfilling *cargo* obligations.[15] But I discovered over the course of a year several ways in which abstention from drinking in Santo Domingo was culturally sanctioned, respected, and encouraged, at least one of which has not been previously mentioned in the anthropological literature as far as I can determine.

The next time we saw each other Martín, having helped me to extricate myself from Alberto's insistent offers to drink *anís* with him, offered me some advice: "When people offer you a drink and you don't want one but they are really persistent, you can say either that you're taking antibiotics, or you can tell them, "*Estoy jurado*'."

"*Estoy jurado*" means "I'm pledged," as in "I've pledged not to drink" (for a period of time). Don Timoteo told me that he was drunk every day for fifteen years, but that (as of March 1993) he had been *jurado* for five years and eight months; he always knows precisely how long. He says that he had to quit for his health—"For me, I just can't help myself. It's all or nothing"—and that since then he has taken medications for the damage previously done by alcohol to his body.

When I first met him in November, Toño had been *jurado* for about eleven months and would end his abstinence on December 31, 1992. Indeed, he spent most of the first week of 1993 making up for lost time. But he said he would never go back to the way he was. Unlike Don Timo who had to quit to save his life, Toño had pledged to stay sober for a year just to prove to his family that he could stop. He said that most people are *jurado* to the Virgen de Guadalupe, but that he had made his pledge to the lesser-known Virgen de Carmen. Toño shrugged his shoulders when I asked him why he had chosen the Virgen de Carmen. A neighbor of Don Timo told me that each of the several times during his long life when he had been *jurado* it had always been to God. Marcos emphasized that only religious people become *jurados*. Though on other occasions Marcos described himself to me as deeply religious, while explaining this issue he simply stated that when he wants to quit drinking for a while he just does it, without invoking any saints.

The state of being *jurado* is a clearly and widely recognized cultural category among men in Colonia Santo Domingo that exempts them from drinking, and indeed often brings the respect of others. (I am unaware of the practice among women.) And although one might expect to encounter teasing with respect to a man's being *jurado*—such as what might go on among friends when one of them is trying to cut back on sweets, for instance—I never heard anyone try to tempt a man with a drink if it was known that he was *jurado*. The option of being *jurado* reflects a general concern for the perils of excessive drinking, and men's choices regarding *estar jurado* reflect the differentiated experiences and beliefs of adults in Santo Domingo with regard to alcohol.

YOUTHFUL INTEMPERANCE AND THE DEGENDERING OF ALCOHOL

My friends Miguel and Noé both had periods in their late teens (Miguel of one and a half years, Noé of three years) in which each spent the better part of at least every weekend drunk. Noé had escaped from these years of inebriation when he was sent to live and work with his uncle Héctor in Santo Domingo. In Miguel's case, *fútbol* [soccer] was his out. He excelled at the sport, reaching the lower levels of the professional leagues, and abusive drinking proved incompatible with the discipline required in training for and playing *fútbol*. Heavy drinking is a period through which many pass, Miguel insisted. It seems plausible that heavy drinking, although not conceptualized by him in terms of gender categories, at least until recently has been largely a male stage through which many have crossed. Teenagers often emphasized to me, however, that in the 1990s both young men and young women are drinking in a serious fashion, although young women do so less in the streets than their brothers and boyfriends.

It appears that a stage of alcohol experimentation and abuse may well be—or become—a rite of passage for many young women nearly as much as it is for young men, a complex of culturally salient experiences regarded to a degree as reasonable if not inevitable. Although some youth do not exit this stage, most of them do (as in the United States) and drink much less late in life. Thus, Miguel and Noé emphasized to me, it is important to tolerate heavy drinking by youth. The most important thing, they said, was not to make young people think that others had given up on them.

Notes

[1] Calderón de la Barca 1843:272.

[2] *Las copas*—literally, "the glasses"—refers generically to alcoholic beverages of any kind.

[3] Studies of alcohol consumption must pay attention not only to variation across regions and in different historical periods, but, as DeWalt (1979) points out, they should also document intracultural variability within regions. Further, the issues of power and control are still underdeveloped in alcohol studies in Mexico. For classic studies on alcohol in Mexico see, for example, de la Fuente 1954 and Pozas 1962.

[4] My thanks to Stanley Brandes, Michael Herzfeld, Louise Lamphere, Pedro Lewin, Nelson Minnelo, Carlos Monsiváis, Eduardo Nivón, and Nancy Scheper-Hughes for their comments on earlier drafts and/or many of the ideas which have developed into this essay, and Dwight Heath for inviting me to contribute to the third edition of this volume. Fieldwork was conducted 1992–93, with grants from Fulbright-Hays DDRA, Wenner-Gren, National Science Foundation, Institute for Intercultural Studies, UC MEXUS, and the Center for Latin American Studies and Department of Anthropology at UC Berkeley, and 1993–95, under a grant from the National Institute of Mental Health. My gratitude as well to the Centro de Estudios Sociológicos and the Programa Interdisciplinario de Estudios de la Mujer, both at El Colegio de México, and to the Departamento de Antropología, Universidad Autónoma Metropolitana-Iztapalapa, for providing institutional support during fieldwork in Mexico City. Final revisions on this chapter were made while I was a Postdoctoral Fellow at the Prevention Research Center and the School of Public Health, University of California, Berkeley.

[5] For further discussion of moral and health issues related to alcohol and alcohol consumption, see Menéndez 1987, 1991, 1992; Room 1984; and Heath 1987.

[6] *Pulquerías* sell *pulque*, the alcoholic beverage made from the sap of the maguey (agave, century plant) that has been made in Mesoamerica for centuries. It has roughly the alcoholic content of beer. Without additives it is frothy and white. A small restaurant-*cantina* opened in late 1992 on Papalotl Avenue, one of the main thoroughfares in Colonia Santo Domingo, but it was too early to predict its future success or whether other such ventures would soon follow. Men were the nearly exclusive customers in this new establishment each time I was there.

[7] Vélez-Ibañez (1983:220) reports that in the early 1970s, many families from Netzahualcóyotl—a teeming settlement in the state of México just outside the Federal District—traveled to San Juan Chimalhuacàn to drink *pulque* on Sunday picnics and "get away from it all."

[8] On male social gatherings, see also Limón's (1994) discussion of all male *carnes asadas* [roasts] and the "ritualistic" consumption of barbecued meat and beer in south Texas.

[9] Not that these constraints are totally missing in the *cantina*. A linguist friend, Victor Franco (personal communication), says that in many villages with which he is familiar in the state of Guerrero, children are routinely sent into *cantinas* to retrieve their fathers. The rationale is that in these areas *cantinas* are still culturally (even though no longer legally) off limits to women of good repute. Then, too, the hope is that fathers will respond more favorably to the sad faces of their children begging them to stop drinking and return home.

[10] *Cuba* here means a drink made with Coca Cola and either rum or brandy.

[11] Yet what are we to make of the following conclusion drawn by a psychologist who studied children in a *colonia* near Santo Domingo? "[T]he men of Santa Ursula drink until they lose their memory" (Bar Din 1991:65). All the men? All the time? Such generalizations may tell us more about researchers' preconceptions than about the ostensible subjects of study. And whereas alcohol consumption may go up in some areas in periods of increasing poverty, there are contradictory pressures in other areas that may reduce drinking. Selby (1990:175) and his colleagues found that, following the crisis of 1982, reduced incomes in the sprawling settler area of Netzahualcóyotl had meant *less* drunkenness although drunkenness had not entirely disappeared. It is difficult to draw a causal link between economic immiseration and the rise or fall of alcohol consumption, since it has been shown to go either way.

[12] Flippin 1889:266 (cited in Beezley 1982:81).

[13] To be sworn, "on the wagon."

[14] See Kearney 1972 and Greenberg 1989. A more exceptional case, in the ethnographic literature if not necessarily in the cultures of Mexico, is reported in DeWalt 1979.

[15] See Cancian 1965:118 and Nash 1970:192.

References

Bar Din, Anne. 1991. *Los niños de Santa Ursula: Un estudio psicosocial de la infancia.* Mexico City: Universidad Nacional Autónoma de México.

Beezley, William. 1987. *Judas at the Jockey Club and Other Episodes of Porfirian Mexico.* Lincoln: University of Nebraska Press.

Brandes, Stanley. 1987. "Sex Roles and Anthropological Research in Rural Andalusia." *Women's Studies,* 13:357–372.

———. 1988. *Power and Persuasion: Fiestas and Social Control in Rural Mexico.* Philadelphia: University of Pennsylvania Press.

Calderón de la Barca, Frances. 1843 (1982). *Life In Mexico.* Berkeley: University of California Press.

Cancian, Frank. 1965. *Economics and Prestige in a Maya Community: The Religious Cargo System in Zinacantan.* Stanford: Stanford University Press.

de la Fuente, Julio. 1954 (1991). "Alcoholismo y sociedad," in Eduardo L. Menéndez, ed., *Antropología del alcoholismo en México: Los limites culturales de la economía política, 1930–1979.* Pp. 175–187. Mexico City: Centro de Investigaciones y Estudios Superiores en Antropología Social.

DeWalt, Billie. 1979. "Drinking Behavior, Economic Status, and Adaptive Strategies of Modernization in a Highland Mexican Community." *American Ethnologist,* 6(3):510–530.

Flippin, J. R. 1889. *Sketches from the Mountains of Mexico.* Cincinnati: Standard.

Greenberg, James. 1989. *Blood Ties: Life and Violence in Rural Mexico.* Tucson: University of Arizona Press.

Heath, Dwight B. 1987. "Anthropology and Alcohol Studies: Current Issues." *Annual Review of Anthropology,* 16:99–120.

Kearney, Michael. 1972. The *Winds of Ixtepeji: World View and Society in a Zapotec Town.* New York: Holt, Rinehart and Winston.

Lewis, Oscar. 1951 (1963). *Life in a Mexican Village: Tepoztlán Restudied.* Urbana: University of Illinois Press.

Limón, José. 1994. *Dancing with the Devil: Society and Cultural Poetics in Mexican-American South Texas.* Madison: University of Wisconsin Press.

Lomnitz, Larissa A. 1977. *Networks and Marginality: Life in a Mexican Shantytown.* Cinna Lomnitz, trans. New York: Academic Press.

Menéndez, Eduardo L. 1987. *Alcoholismo II: La alcoholización, un proceso olvidado . . . patología, integración funcional o representación cultural.* Mexico City: Centro de Investigaciones y Estudios Superiores en Antropología Social.

———. 1990. *Morir de alcohol: Saber y hegemonía médica.* Mexico City: Grijalbo.

———. 1991. "Alcoholismo y proceso de alcoholización: La construcción de una propuesta antropológica." In Eduardo L. Menéndez, ed., *Antropología del alcoholismo en México: Los límites culturales de la economia política 1930–1979.* Pp. 13–32. Mexico City: Centro de Investigaciones y Estudios Superiores en Antropología Social.

Menéndez, Eduardo L., ed. 1992. *Práctica e ideologías "científicas" y "populares" respecto del "alcoholismo" en México.* Mexico City: Centro de Investigaciones y Estudios Superiores, en Antropología Social.

Nash, June. 1970 (1985). *In the Eyes of the Ancestors: Belief and Behavior in a Mayan Community.* Prospect Heights, IL: Waveland Press.

Pozas, Ricardo. 1962. *Juan the Chamula: An Ethnological Re-creation of the Life of a Mexican Indian.* Lysander Kemp, trans. Berkeley: University of California Press.

Room, Robin. 1984. "Alcohol and Ethnography: A Case of Problem Deflation?" *Current Anthropology,* 25(2):169–191.

Selby, Henry, Arthur Murphy, and Stephen Lorenzen. 1990. *The Mexican Urban Household: Organizing for Self-Defense.* Austin: University of Texas Press.

Vélez-Ibañez, Carlos. 1983. *Rituals of Marginality: Politics, Process, and Culture Change in Urban Central Mexico.* Berkeley: University of California Press.

Stanley H. Brandes is a professor of anthropology at the University of California, Berkeley. Having worked in both Spain and Mexico, his books reflect diverse interests: Forty: The Age and the Symbol; Metaphors of Masculinity: Sex and Status in Andalusian Folklore; Migration, Kinship, and Community; Power and Persuasion: Fiestas and Social Control in Rural Mexico; and Symbol as Sense (with M. L. Foster).

By closely examining a holiday that is at once colorful and exotic, yet vaguely familiar, this author manages to help us understand some customs that might at first seem odd (like picnicking with the dead), some links between Christian and traditional pagan beliefs and practices (like community charity and dances), global commercialization (with tourism, jack-o-lanterns, and costumes), and Mexican pride in a national symbol. Delving far beyond simplistic analogies, he shows how insights from and about religion, history, ethnography, economics, and politics are all indispensable to appreciating what many would wrongly dismiss as a mere "children's pastime."

For other insights into folk Catholicism, see Canin (chapter 41), Foster (chapter 31), and Greenfield (chapter 44).

The Day of the Dead as Mexican National Symbol

Stanley H. Brandes

THE DAY OF THE DEAD IN MEXICO'S QUEST FOR IDENTITY

As Kertzer (1988) has demonstrated, ritual, religious or otherwise, is "an important means for structuring our political perceptions and leading us to interpret our experiences in certain ways" (p. 85). "The symbols employed" in ritual, he says, "suggest a particular interpretation of what is being viewed" (ibid.). In Mexico the Day of the Dead, celebrated uninterruptedly from colonial times to the present, is on the surface a conspicuously apolitical event, a communal occasion on which families honor their deceased relatives. Yet, this holiday in recent years has assumed an increasingly political cast, linking the celebration specifically to Mexico and Mexican national identity. The Day of the Dead helps to create an interpretation of the world in which Mexico is unique, culturally discrete, and above all different from the two powers that have dominated that country throughout its long existence: Spain and the United States.

Of special significance in this regard is the Mexican reaction to Halloween. Halloween and the Day of the Dead, with obvious common historical origins, have come to symbolize nationally discrete observances. The recent rapid penetration of Halloween symbols into Mexico increasingly evokes Mexican nationalistic sentiments, embodied in a campaign to preserve the country from American cultural imperialism. This chapter explores the Day of the Dead as a political event which expresses, among other things, the complexities of Mexican-U.S. relations.

Before proceeding, it is necessary to define just what the Day of the Dead is. It is a specifically Mexican term referring to the Mexican version of a pan-Roman Catholic Holiday: All Saints' and All Souls' Days, observed on November 1 and November 2, respectively. Strictly speaking, the Day of the Dead—known in Spanish as *El Día de Animas* [Souls' Day], *El Día de los Finados* [The Day of the Deceased], or *El Día de los Fieles*

Written expressly for *Contemporary Cultures and Societies of Latin America*, Third Edition. A preliminary version appeared as "The Day of the Dead, Halloween, and the Quest for Mexican National Identity," in *Journal of American Folklore*, vol. 111, pp. 359–380, 1998.

Difuntos [The Day of the Faithful Departed]—refers to All Souls' Day, which normally falls on November 2. Only when November 2 falls on a Sunday is All Souls' Day celebrated on November 3. The Day of the Dead includes such a range of interlocking activities that in colloquial speech it has come to denote not only November 2 but also, and more usually, the entire period from October 31 through November 2. The Day of the Dead (*El Día de los Muertos*) is actually a sequence of Days of the Dead. Hence, we occasionally also encounter the term *Los Días de los Muertos*—Days of the Dead, in the plural.

Note that, despite the elaborate manner in which the Day of the Dead is celebrated, the Roman Catholic Church requires only the observance of special masses on November 1 in honor of all the saints and on November 2 in honor of the souls in Purgatory. These masses, which originated as early as the eleventh century (Cornides 1967:319, Smith 1967:318) assumed a permanent place of importance in the liturgical calendar (nearly equivalent in significance to Christmas and Easter) by the fourteenth century (Gaillard 1950:927–32). Currently, the Church obliges parish priests to recite one special mass on November 1 and another on November 2, although three masses on November 2 are more common: one in honor of the departed souls, a second in honor of a cause designated annually by the Pope, and a third in recognition of a cause selected by the parish priest himself. These special masses constitute the only official part of All Saints' and All Souls' Days celebrations throughout the Roman Catholic world, including Mexico.

Most observers would agree, ironically, that mass is the least salient part of the holiday in Mexico (e.g., Brandes 1981). Around the end of October, a multitude of foreign visitors descends upon Mexico to witness colorful—some would say carnivalesque—ritual performances and artistic displays. Decorated breads, paper cutouts, and plastic toys, most of them playing humorously on the death theme, are evident everywhere. Sculpted sugar candies in the form of skulls, skeletons, and caskets suggest an almost irreverent, macabre confrontation with mortality. From October 31 through November 2, Mexicans clear, decorate, and maintain watch over relatives' graves. All, from expensive tombstones to simple earthen-mound burial sites, are adorned with flowers, candles and food, aesthetically arranged in honor of the deceased. In Mexico, most of the activities and artistic displays connected with this holiday—including special food offerings, cemetery vigils, altar exhibitions, and the like—are a popular elaboration entirely separate from liturgical requirements. The origin of these folk practices is a source of scholarly and popular debate. What is clear is that, for Mexicans, foreigners, and peoples of Mexican descent, the holiday has come to symbolize Mexico and Mexicanness. It is a key symbol of national identity.

Mexican national identity is no easy subject for discussion. It has long been the object of lengthy deliberation and passionate debate—philosophical, historical and otherwise. Scholarly and literary reflections on Mexican national character include penetrating and influential portraits by Ramos (1962), Paz (1961), and Bartra (1987), among others. The whole topic has recently received sensitive treatment in the writings of Gutmann (1993), who demonstrates that ideas about alleged Mexican distinctiveness undergo transformation from generation to generation in the face of the country's enormous cultural diversity:

> Analysts of a would-be uniform "national character" (or culture) of Mexico often resort to origin myths, downplaying class, gender and ethnic divisions within the geographic boundaries of the nation state, and also discount the fact that new and significant cultural features have emerged since the Revolution and Independence (1993:56).

The Mexican state has been confronted not only by a need faced by many other states, that is, the need to forge a national consciousness and unity among a multitude of diverse regions and peoples. It has also had to—or at least seen fit to—create a sense of national distinctiveness by contrasting itself with the two great powers to which it has been subject over the course of centuries: Spain and the United States. With respect to Spain, Mexico suffers particular difficulty in creating a sense of discreteness. Most analysts would agree, after all, that two of the most salient features uniting any people are language and religion. Mexicans, who overwhelmingly speak Spanish and practice Roman Catholicism, can claim neither of these features as a source of difference from the imperial conqueror. Insofar as Mexican relations with the United States are concerned, language and religion are indeed a potential cultural resource for forging a sense of national identity. More important in U.S.-Mexican relations, however, is Mexican suffering at the hands of the economically and militarily powerful neighbor to the north. From the 1840s (when newly independent Mexico lost approximately half its territory to the United States) to present times, characterized by overwhelming disparities in national wealth and the increasing presence of U.S. financial and manufacturing institutions in Mexico, Mexicans have had to struggle to maintain a sense of autonomy and equality. From one vantage point, Mexican dependency upon and domination by Spain and the United States have impeded the emergence of a fully autonomous nation. From another, however, Mexicans have been able to use these countries as ideological foils against which to emphasize their own undeniable uniqueness.

In its quest for a unique identity, Mexico has enjoyed one enormous resource: the Indian past and present. Gutmann is correct to state that Mexican intellectuals tend to date Mexico today from the times of the Spanish Conquest, "whether for the triumph of the Spanish in the case of Ramos, or for the defeat of the Aztecs in the case of Paz" (Gutmann 1993:53). Nonetheless, it is Mexico's Indian heritage, as demonstrated through archaeological and ethnographic evidence, that clearly separates this country from both Spain and the United States; and it is the Indian heritage which the Mexican state has chosen to elevate symbolically. One effective way to further a sense of discrete national identity is through art and museum displays (Karp and Lavine 1991). In this respect, the National Museum of Anthropology in Mexico City may be considered a glorious monument erected in honor of Mexican uniqueness and authenticity. Its two floors are distributed to show the archaeological record, as displayed chronologically on the lower level, and contemporary indigenous presence, as displayed through rooms devoted to key Indian communities, on the upper. Taken as a whole, the National Museum of Anthropology was designed to exhibit, to nationals and foreigners alike, an official view of an authentic Mexico, unaffected by contaminating outside influences.

Folklore in Mexico, as elsewhere (e.g., Hague 1981, Herzfeld 1982, Wilson 1976), has been important in the quest for national identity. Folklore often reflects popular ideas about the origins of a people. It also is believed to penetrate beneath the superficial and culturally confounding layers of modern life to some authentic core, thereby representing the essence of a people, its principal style and values. Folklore, further, is often shared by a given group in contradistinction to other groups. In all these respects, folklore can serve nationalistic goals.

Ritual and festival in general are among the most prominent forms of folklore in this regard. A people, be they national minority or state-defined nation, can reinforce their separate identity through reference to presumably unique ceremonials. Such ceremonials come to be perceived as part of what makes a group unique and reflect the group's defining norms and values. It is within this ideological context that we must understand Mexico's Day of the Dead.

THE PERCEIVED UNIQUENESS OF THE DAY OF THE DEAD

The Day of the Dead is now and long has been a symbol of Mexico; but the nationalistic dimension dates from relatively recent times, probably no further back than the present century. Almost certainly, from the time of the Spanish conquest in 1521, Mexicans observed All Saints' and All Souls' Days, feasts which then as now were required of all Roman Catholics. Special masses, as part of the obligatory liturgy, were then as now intrinsic to the celebration. There is good evidence (Brandes 1997), too, that at the time of the conquest, All Saints' and All Souls' Days were occasions in Spain and elsewhere in Europe for visiting cemeteries; presenting offerings of flowers, candles, and food to deceased relatives; and soliciting or begging in ritualized form.

With regard to All Saints' and All Souls' Days in New Spain, however, so little written documentation exists that it is impossible to determine the precise ways in which early Mexicans celebrated these holidays. We may assume that, whether through formal Church decree or informal processes of culture transmission (Foster 1960), All Saints' and All Souls' Days in colonial Mexico more or less followed European practices. However, the precise regional distribution of ritual activities and their relative acceptance among diverse linguistic communities and social classes are matters for speculation alone. We do know that in the 1740s, in the Valley of Mexico, All Saints' and All Souls' Days began to assume the flavor of the contemporary event. It is from that time that we first hear from a Capuchin friar (Ajofrín 1958:87) of the commercial production and sale of whimsical figurines made of the sugar paste known in Mexico as *alfeñique*. That pivotal account also incorporates the first known use in Mexico of the term Day of the Dead. Both the existence of sugar-paste figurines and the reference to All Saints' and All Souls' Days as "The Day of the Dead" are characteristic of the Mexican celebration (Brandes 1997).

The degree to which the overall celebration of the Day of the Dead is in reality unique to Mexico is a source of an ongoing debate which cannot be resolved here. It is necessary to repeat, however, that key elements of the contemporary popular celebration of All Saints' and All Souls' Days in Mexico—including family cemetery vigils; the erection of home altars; and preparation of special sweets; the presentation to the deceased of flowers, candles, and food; and the performance of ritualized begging or solicitation—can be found throughout much of the Roman Catholic world, including Latin America and southern Europe. Ritualized begging is even common on All Souls' Day among Indian pueblos in the southwestern United States, pueblos conquered and influenced by Spain (Espinosa 1918, Parsons 1917). What seems to me unique to Mexico are three features of the celebration: first, the name Day of the Dead; second, the abundance and variety of whimsical sweet breads and candies; and three, the humor and gaiety that pervade the holiday.

Much of the reason for uncertainty about the origins of the Day of the Dead is an absence of adequate source material. The Day of the Dead, like Carnival, always presented a threat to the official political and religious establishment. Hence, during the colonial era, the Spanish rulers attempted to tone down, if not entirely eradicate, the popular celebration of All Saints' and All Souls' Days. One historian notes:

> The nocturnal visit which village men, women, and children made to the cemeteries, the festivities and drunkenness that took place there, could only scandalize and above all horrify the illustrious elites, who looked to expel death from social life. This fiesta, which drew boundaries between the living and the dead and partially inverted their roles, showed up the presence of death in the midst of life in an era in which the elite of New Spain . . . tried to forget its existence. (Viqueira 1984:13)

It is not surprising, he says, that in October 1766 the Royal Criminal chamber (*Real Sala del Crimen*) prohibited attendance at cemeteries and also imposed a prohibition on the sale of alcoholic beverages after nine in the evening (ibid.).

Nearly a hundred years later, following Mexico's independence from Spain, the Day of the Dead still seemed to pose a threat to public order and stability. In 1847, liquor stores were closed for all but two or three hours on November 1 and 2, as a security measure. The *North American Star*, a newspaper serving the U.S. community in Mexico City, declared on November 2 that "Yesterday, the first day of the festival, went off with perfect quietness, with no disturbance of any kind, that we could hear, and we presume we shall be able to say the same to-day and to-morrow." Despite the observed calm, the holiday apparently caused some anticipation of social unrest. It is precisely this unrest, whether justifiably feared or not, that undoubtedly produced some degree of press censorship. Throughout the colonial era and nineteenth century, Mexican newspapers and other popular sources provide only the most limited, sanitized coverage of Day of the Dead activities. From these sources we obtain the elite view of the event, which consists primarily of accounts of formal religious activity. Textured ethnographic detail—which might allow an assessment of which aspects of the holiday derive from Spain, which from ancient Mexico, and which from the colonial encounter—is virtually absent.

What is of main interest here is not, however, the actual historical derivation of the Day of the Dead but rather its *attributed* derivation and connection to Mexico. Consider, for example, the second chapter of Octavio Paz's (1961) *Labyrinth of Solitude* entitled "The Day of the Dead." For him, this ritual occasion reflects that the Mexican "is familiar with death, jokes about it, caresses it, sleeps with it, celebrates it; it is one of his favorite toys and his most steadfast love" (p. 57). Paz believes that the Mexican looks at death "face to face, with impatience, disdain or irony" (ibid.). In this respect the Mexican view of death is very different from either the North American or European views:

> The word death is not pronounced in New York, in Paris, in London, because it burns the lips. . . . The Mexican's indifference toward death is fostered by his indifference toward life. He views not only death but also life as nontranscendent. . . . It is natural, even desirable to die, and the sooner the better. . . . Our contempt for death is not at odds with the cult we have made of it (ibid.).

Paz, one of the most widely read and penetrating Mexican men of letters, clearly uses the Day of the Dead as a lens through which to discern a peculiarly Mexican view of death. It is a perspective shared by numerous other Mexican intellectuals, including Caso (1953:122), Covarrubias (1947:390), Díaz Guerrero (1961:15), Fernández Kelley (1974:533), and Lope Blanch (1963:8). Foreigners, too, have long identified what is for them a specifically Mexican attitude toward death. For Soviet filmmaker Sergei Mikhailovich Eisenstein, this attitude is nowhere better displayed than during the Day of the Dead:

> At every step [in Mexico] life and death fuse constantly; so too do appearance and disappearance, death and birth. On the "Day of the Dead" even small children stuff themselves with crystallized sugar skulls and chocolate coffins, and amuse themselves with toys in the form of skeletons. The Mexican despises death. . . . Most important of all, the Mexican laughs at death. November 2nd, "Death Day," is given over to irresistible mockery of death (quoted in Sayer 1993:45).

To Mexicans and the world at large, the Day of the Dead represents Mexico and things Mexican. Gutiérrez and Gutiérrez (1971:75) sum up this attitude perfectly by stating that the only thing that the Day of the Dead has in common with All Souls' Day is that "both are cases of a day sanctified to honor the memory of deceased relatives." There are, of course, many other features shared by the European and Mexican celebrations, but these and many other authors hail Mexico's Day of the Dead as a unique phenomenon. The Day of the Dead, and the attitude toward death that it represents, have come to symbolize Mexico itself.

The Day of the Dead and the Mexican Indian

Mexico's indigenous past and present are, ironically, what distinguish this country undeniably from both Europe and the United States. It is not surprising, then, that in the quest for national identity the Indian should be closely associated with the Day of the Dead. This association appears explicitly throughout the literature. Perhaps more than any other Mexican ritual, Day of the Dead has acquired the reputation of being either a basically pre-conquest Indian survival with a European Catholic veneer or a near-seamless fusion of pre-conquest and Roman Catholic ceremonial practices. Consider the statement of Haberstein and Lamers (1963:592) that "In Mexico everywhere the Day of the Dead celebrations combine a curious admixture of ancient Indian and Catholic beliefs and practices." Similarly, Childs and Altman (1982) claim that

> the beliefs and practices associated with contemporary observances of Los Días de los Muertos, although not a direct and simple survival of pre-Hispanic ritual, have their roots in the ancient religions of Mesoamerica. . . . However successful the Spanish church may have been in the destruction of state cults, it is apparent on close scrutiny that much "Catholicism" of contemporary Indian communities is pre-Hispanic in origin, especially the beliefs and customs related to death and the dead (pp. 6–7).

Yet another expression of this viewpoint comes from Sandstrom and Sandstrom (1986:254), who claim that, at least for three indigenous linguistic groups in the central Mexican highlands (the Nahua, Otomí, and Pepehua), "Even observances that clearly have a pre-Hispanic base, such as All Souls and Carnival, are syncretized with the Christian celebration of similar character."

The alleged pre-Hispanic base of All Souls is indeed "clear" in the minds of many scholars. Unfortunately, this relationship never receives systematic demonstration. Rather, there is a presumption of pre-Hispanic survival, manifested in a casual association of the Day of the Dead with Aztec ritual on the one hand and contemporary Indian funerary ritual on the other. Carmichael and Sayer (1991) compiled an enormous amount of documentary and ethnographic information regarding the Day of the Dead, with a full chapter devoted to pre-Hispanic beliefs and practices regarding death and mourning. Even so, they did not establish an explicit connection between past and contemporary events. Although they state that "to what extent these pre-Hispanic festivals and their associated rituals were transmuted into the Christian festivals remains a matter of keen debate" (p. 33), they never actually discuss the content of this debate. Their chapter on the pre-Hispanic background remains an implicit endorsement of the idea that the Day of the Dead can in fact be traced to pre-Hispanic ritual.

It is true that Mexican Indians have demonstrated, through both archeological and ethnographic evidence, that they possess complex and subtle ideas about death and the dead. They also have always celebrated the dead through the performance of specific rituals. But the possession of elaborate ideas about death as well as the ritualized commemoration of the deceased are human facts, characteristic of all known societies past and present (see Metcalf and Huntington 1991). The celebration of death cannot itself be presented reasonably as evidence for an indigenous origin to the Day of the Dead. Nonetheless, Day of the Dead ceremonies are presented throughout Mexico as if they were unambiguously Indian. The alleged indigenous character of this fiesta means that it is automatically associated with Mexico and correspondingly dissociated from Europe and North America.

There are various mechanisms through which the Day of the Dead as an "Indian" holiday becomes publicly acknowledged and asserted. Among the most prominent is the popular belief that there exists a limited number of communities—all Indian communities—where the Day of the Dead is celebrated in its fully elaborate and authentic state. These towns include the Purépecha island of Janitzio in the state of Michoacán; the Nahua village of Mixquic in the State of México; and the Zapotec village of Xococotlán in the state of Oaxaca. All of these communities, and some others like them, share one major characteristic: they are famous nationally and internationally for their Day of the Dead celebrations and draw enormous numbers of tourists from both Mexican cities and abroad. Yet anyone who visits cemeteries in Mexico City during the Day of the Dead also can attest to the elaborate observance of this holiday also in the country's immense, highly industrialized and commercialized metropolitan capital. The decoration of tombstones, flower and food offerings, presence of relatives respectfully holding vigil over their deceased relatives, and the like are as elaborate in Mexico City's Panteón Jardín, Panteón Municipal, and Panteón Francés as can be found anywhere in the country. In city cemeteries such as these, however, the touristic presence is minimal. Middle-class Mexicans from Mexico City, Guadalajara, and elsewhere, searching for cultural roots, prefer to travel to the handful of Indian towns and villages which have become famous for the "authenticity" of their Day of the Dead celebrations. Often these Mexicans form part of international tour groups.

Another Mexican scholar who has carried out extensive research on the Day of the Dead (Garciagodoy 1994:33–34) decided for purposes of investigation to join two such groups, which visited Day of the Dead ceremonies in Xococotlán in the state of Oaxaca. She reports as follows:

> We were each given a bouquet of flowers, two *veladoras* (votive candles), and torches which consisted of a candle set into a split bamboo shaft and protected by orange cellophane paper. Before the tour departed from the meeting point, we were given a short lecture (once in Spanish, once in English, the latter much more brief and simple) about the importance of *Los Días de los Muertos*. We were reminded that we would be guests at a spiritually important event and [were] counseled to behave appropriately. And we were instructed to place our flowers and candles on graves that were unadorned and untended; we would gain spiritual merit this way and be rewarded in the hereafter. A majority of the people on the tour was from the United States; there were a few from Canada, Europe, and Mexico. The male and female bilingual guides were Mexican [parentheses in the original].

I myself visited Xococotlán during the Day of the Dead in 1996, at which time I was lecturing to a group of Americans on a University of California Extension School study tour. Even without making a firm head-count, it was clear to us all that there were many times more foreigners wandering around the cemetery of Xococotlán on the night of November 1–2 than there were inhabitants of the town itself. With its multiple food vendors and throngs of visitors crowding its narrow streets, Xococotlán had taken on a carnival atmosphere.

The same occurs during the Day of the Dead in Tzintzuntzán, with the difference that most outside visitors are Mexicans rather than foreigners. Tzintzuntzán, a community of about three thousand artisans, farmers, and merchants, is located several hundred miles northwest of Mexico City on the shores of Lake Pátzcuaro in the state of Michoacán. Tzintzuntzán is famous for having been the capital of the ancient Purépecha Empire, a political entity which successfully resisted Aztec domination. No doubt because of its illustrious past, Tzintzuntzán is perceived as a Purépecha settlement. Tzintzuntzán's reputation as a center of Purépecha culture, both ancient and contemporary, has been codified and propagated through an ethnological display occupying a full exhibition hall of the National Museum of Anthropology in Mexico City. This exhibit, a permanent installation, portrays Tzintzuntzán as the epitome of enduring Purépecha culture. The reality is that Tzintzuntzán is and long has been an overwhelmingly mestizo community, with only about 7 percent of villagers able to speak Purépecha throughout the 1980s and 1990s (Kemper n.d.). Even in 1960, the start of the decade which saw construction and design of the National Museum of Anthropology, only 11.4 percent of the population could be identified as indigenous (Foster 1988:35). Yet, the community's fame as a center of Purépecha culture has increased since that time rather than abated.

One reason for this persistent misidentification is the governmental promotion of Tzintzuntzán's Day of the Dead ceremonies as an authentic indigenous religious ritual (Brandes 1988:88–109). Tzintzuntzán long celebrated the Day of the Dead exactly as did countless other rural communities throughout Michoacán and Mexico as a whole, that is, in relatively muted fashion. There were always special masses, of course. Families erected home altars in honor of the departed and visited the graves of recently deceased relatives, in whose honor they decorated the burial sites with flowers and candles. Foster and Ospina (1948) describe activities on November 2, 1945, as follows:

> About four o'clock in the morning family groups begin to wend their way to the cemetery, carrying *arcos* [decorated latticework displays] and other offerings of food, to take up their vigil by the graves of departed relatives. Again yellow marigolds are scattered over all graves and candles are lighted. Toward dawn perhaps 40 tombs are thus arranged, and the twinkling of several hundred candles in the dark suggests will-o-the-wisps run riot. . . . After daylight other persons come, to talk with friends keeping vigil, to eat a little, and to see what is happening. By 11 o'clock most people have gone home and the graveyard is again deserted (p. 220).

In 1971, governmental agencies intervened in such a way as to transform the event entirely. It was in that year that the Ministry of Tourism of the State of Michoacán, together with two state agencies—the Casa de la Cultura and the Casa de Artesanías—began a campaign to attract tourists to Michoacán. They selected eleven towns, among them Tzintzuntzán, as targets of tourism. Widely disseminated posters and radio commercials, directed at an urban, middle-class public, announced the traditional celebration of the Day of the Dead in Tzintzuntzán and elsewhere. Images on the posters show an indigenous woman, flanked by tall candles, kneeling at a gravesite. In Tzintzuntzán itself tourists receive a brochure with a cover bearing the title *Noche de los Muertos en Michoacán* [Night of the Dead in Michoacán], with the prominent Purépecha translation, *Animecha Kejtzitakua*. In the period since the intervention of state agencies, Day of the Dead as a denomination for this holiday became known as Night of the Dead, in recognition of the fact that villagers *en masse* began to spend the entire nights of November 1 and 2 at the cemeteries. The agencies had encouraged this transformation and, in any event, tourists had come to expect it. Tourists, who began to arrive by the thousands in large busses and long automobile caravans, had been led by publicity to anticipate the presence of certain ritual activities, which now began to be practiced in conformity to their expectations.

Gradually, over the course of the 1970s and 1980s, massive tourism increasingly defined the contour of Tzintzuntzán's Night of the Dead. There was the all-night vigil, of course, although its potential picturesqueness was often marred by the presence of television cameras recording the scene live for a national audience. Enormous, noisy electric generators were strategically situated in the cemetery to provide illumination for the cameras. High above the town, on an esplanade spread out at the foot of five imposing pre-Columbian pyramids, the Ministry of Tourism established a "Festival of Dances and *Pirekuas*" (Purépecha songs). Using an eighteenth-century open-air chapel as stage, state agencies also mounted a production of José Zorrilla's nineteenth-century Spanish classic drama, "Don Juan Tenorio." Drama and dance performers alike were brought in from outside and, since a substantial fee was charged for the entertainment, it was tourists and tourists alone who attended. Along the highway leading through Tzintzuntzán, tourists could buy food and drink from any of the numerous temporary stands set up to accommodate their needs. They could seek medical assistance by visiting the temporary Red Cross station set up near the town plaza.

By the end of the 1980s and beginning of the 1990s, the event began to change names yet again. It was now commonly referred to as *La Féria*, the Fair. One middle-aged villager reported her opinion of the changes that had taken place: "The event has become shameful. People hardly talk about the Night of the Dead anymore. They say *Féria*, or *"Vamos a la Féria de los Muertos!"* [Let's go to the Fair of the Deceased!]. It's practically scandalous!" This reading of the event probably reflected a minority opinion among townspeople themselves, many of whom earn substantial income from the tremendous influx of tourists. In fact, young unmarried men, who used to toll church bells all evening and solicit contributions of food and drink from village households, now no longer play this time-honored role; they are too busy helping their families run food stands for the tourists. "The event used to be so sad," reminisced one elderly man, as if this emotion were somehow inappropriate to the occasion.

Despite radical transformations, the event since 1971 has been billed by the government of the state of Michoacán as both traditional and indigenous. It has thus become famous nationally as a survival of ancient practices and hence a cultural treasure for the Mexican people as a whole. A similar process has occurred in other communities—be they allegedly indigenous, as in the case of Tzintzuntzán, or actually so, as in the case of Xocotepec—all over Mexico.

THE DAY OF THE DEAD VERSUS HALLOWEEN

Any observer of the Day of the Dead ceremonies in the 1990s would be impressed by the presence of Halloween symbolism. Prefabricated children's costumes (mainly witches, devils and ghosts) are displayed for sale in markets all over the country. There are a plethora of plastic and rubber masks, everything from comical likenesses of Mexican and American political leaders to red-faced satanic figures, apes and myriad unidentifiable beasts. One can also find plastic jack-o-lanterns in every imaginable size. These items are mixed indiscriminately among the more usual Day of the Dead ware, including special seasonal sweet breads, colorfully decorated sugar and chocolate skulls and caskets, wooden and papier-mâché skeletons with moveable joints, as well as long-stemmed, bright orange marigolds and tall white candles destined to be used as offerings at burial sites and home altars.

On the face of it, the presence of Halloween symbolism should cause no surprise. For one thing, Halloween, which occurs on All Saints' Eve, has for centuries shared a close resemblance in some aspects with the Day of the Dead. Santino traces Halloween back to the pre-Christian Celtic (Irish, Scottish, Welsh) festival of Samhain, the New Year's Day of the Celts, celebrated on November 1, which

> was also a day of the dead, a time when it was believed that the souls of those who had died during the year were allowed access to the land of the living. It was a time when spirits were believed to be wandering (Santino 1994:xv).

Many of the beliefs and practices characteristic of Samhain survived to the Christian era. These include the belief that October 31 was a time of the wandering dead and the practice of providing food and drink to masked and costumed revelers on this night, known to Christians as the Eve of All Saints or Hallows Even, a term yielding the familiar contraction *Hallowe'en*. Symbols of the dead, including skeletons, ghosts, and malevolent creatures such as witches and the devil, were the transmuted pre-Christian gods and goddesses, incorporated into All Saints' Eve by the early Christians as a syncretic means to spread their new religion.

Santino calls the Day of the Dead a "cognate" (ibid:xviii) or, we might say, a functional equivalent of Halloween. Indeed, the historical origins of these two holidays, if not identical, are nonetheless closely intermeshed. For centuries, too, they have displayed an array of shared symbols of death—a kind of playing with death—including humorous replicas of skulls, skeletons, and souls. During Halloween the latter take the form of ghosts; during the Day of the Dead, inanimate but ever-present spirits. Special sweets are an important part of both Halloween, with its characteristic black and orange candies, and the Day of the Dead, with its *pan de muertos* (bread of the dead) and sugar skulls and skeletons. Ritualized begging is significant in the two holidays as well. During All Saints' and All Souls' Days in Mexico as much as in Europe, bands of young men wander from house to house asking for food and drink. I myself have observed this custom in Tzintzuntzán, Mexico (Brandes 1988:94-95) and in Becedas, Spain (Brandes 1975:135), although institutionalized begging and charity-giving have been traditional everywhere in the Catholic world on this day (e.g., Aguirre Soronda 1989, Brandes 1997, Espinosa 1918, Llabrés Quintana 1925, Parsons 1917). Halloween, of course, incorporates an especially aggressive form of begging known as "trick or treat" (Tuleja 1994).

These common origins and shared symbols by no means erase major differences between Halloween on the one hand and All Saints' and All Souls' Days on the other. One major difference, of course, is that All Saints' and All Souls' Days remain a part of the sacred Roman Catholic calendar, while Halloween has long assumed a completely secular cast. Despite possible readings to the contrary, we might also say that the occasion of All Saints' and All Souls' Days is fundamentally one of adult ritual performance while Halloween, at least as celebrated in the contemporary United States, is largely a children's holiday. Over and above this differentiation, a major symbolic cleavage has appeared in the representation of the Day of the Dead and Halloween: in Mexico the Day of the Dead has come to symbolize Mexican identity and autonomy, while Halloween has become a symbol of the United States and its cultural imperialistic designs. The actual origins and meaning of ritual beliefs and practices during Halloween and the Day of the Dead have ironically become irrelevant to the growing significance of these holidays with reference to national identity.

A Mexican anthropologist said, "I cannot count how many informants have answered my questions as to the meaning of *Los Días de los Muertos* for them, their reasons for performing this or that aspect of it, their reason(s), for that matter, to celebrate it at all by saying, '*Es muy mexicano*' [It's very Mexican], or '*Porque somos mexicanos*' [Because we're Mexican] (Garciagodoy 1994:28). Then, speaking as a Mexican herself, the author continued,

> Many of us feel more patriotic during this celebration and because of it. This is partly because we think our way of relating to death and the dead—and by implication, to life—is unique in the world, setting us apart from (and at least a little above) everyone else [parenthetical expression in original text]. We are *más machos*, braver, and we have *más corazón*, more heart, than other cultures (ibid.).

As an international scholar, Garciagodoy well understands how the Day of the Dead contributes to Mexican national identity, but as a Mexican she cannot help but experience the nationalistic sentiments increasingly associated with this holiday. In fact, at one point in her discussion she actually includes herself among a group of "nationalistic Mexican scholars" who not only reaffirm the Day of the Dead as a symbol of Mexican national identity but correspondingly reject Halloween as a threat to national tradition and identity. On a recent trip to Mexico City, Gonzales-Crussi (1993:36) found it "disquieting" that

> the stores are stocked with objects intended for use at Halloween, many imported from the United States. In shop windows, hollowed-out pumpkins, most made out of plastic, with cutout holes that figure eyes, nose, and mouth, beam their ghostly smiles, abetted by the flickering light within. Groups of children come out of schools or private homes disguised as monsters, werewolves, vampires, and extraterrestrial beings. Have we come this far to see an imitation, in third-world gear, of the North American Halloween?

Exactly how has Halloween entered into the celebration of the Day of the Dead? Garciagodoy (1994) correctly identifies two groups of Mexicans which now celebrate the Day of the Dead by drawing on symbols and customs more usually associated with Halloween. First are urban middle-class Mexicans, many of whom dress their children in store-bought, Halloween-style costumes. Judging from the costumes on sale at middle-class malls, as well as from what the children wear, this author would say that almost all the costumes play on one of five themes: witches, ghosts, skeletons, vampires, and devils. Unlike in the United States, I have never seen a Mexican adult wear a costume—or even a portion of a costume—him- or herself. For example, in 1996 in the city of Oaxaca I observed a parade of hundreds of costumed schoolchildren, accompanied by dozens of teachers and other adults. None of the grown men and women donned so much as a witch's cap.

The urban middle-class Halloween manifests itself, too, in disco dances, with advertisements and disco decorations based on icons like witches, carved pumpkins, ghosts, and the like, usually colored in black and orange. Newspapers all over Mexico display commercial advertisements aimed at a middle-class audience and incorporating Halloween symbols. Consider a computer store advertisement that appeared on October 31, 1997, in the national daily, *Reforma*. The advertisement appears with black background, white lettering, an orange jack-o-lantern, and the silhouette of a cloaked death figure wielding a scythe. "Do our competitor's prices scare you?" reads the ad. A Goodyear tire advertisement that appeared on October 30, 1996 in *Reforma* is drawn in white against a black, nighttime scene. Bats fly high above, scraggly cats arch their backs, and jack-o-lanterns grin at the readers. "Macabre nighttime sale on tires," the advertisement states. Expensive clubs all over Mexico City—Snob and The Men's Club, for example— use the press to announce Halloween parties and dances at this time of year.

For the working class, the Halloween appeal is somewhat different. For one thing, although some children might put on an inexpensive mask, for the most part they go uncostumed. Halloween for these children—and the participants seem uniformly to be boys rather than girls—means a money-making opportunity. Carrying any sort of small receptacle they can find, everything from a battered cardboard box to a miniature plastic jack-o-lantern with handle (the kind that U.S. children sometimes use to collect candy), the boys beg through the streets and among the graves, asking for their "Halloween." The word Halloween is even entering the Mexican Spanish lexicon spelled phonetically, *Jaloüín*. Children might also beg for *"mi calabaza"* (my pumpkin). Other than this form of simple solicitation, the working-class Halloween seems limited to the purchase of orange, white and black colored candy in the shape of witches, ghosts, and jack-o-lanterns. Too, the occasional carved pumpkin or plastic jack-o-lantern rests on gravesites, along with usual offerings, during the Day of the Dead.

Most middle-class Mexicans are well aware that Halloween symbols are part of U.S. culture and probably use them consciously as a means of elevating their status. It is unclear that this can be said of the working classes, for whom Halloween seems to have become seamlessly interwoven with the fabric of Day of the Dead proceedings. I asked a Mixtec Indian fruit vendor and his mestiza wife, who run a small store in Mexico City, why they were selling Halloween candies and whether their customers complain about the recent introduction of Halloween. The wife just laughed. "We Mexicans are *muy fiesteros* [great merrymakers]. We like everything that adds to festivities!" While watching schoolchildren carry out their Halloween march in 1996 in the city of Oaxaca, I asked a couple of teenage passersby to tell me when the march was initiated. They answered, "Maybe ten years ago, or fifteen . . . or five." They did not know. They did say, however, that if I really wanted to learn about "these customs," I should go to the surrounding villages where they have been practiced as long as anyone can remember. Rural schoolchildren in Oaxaca do not participate in Halloween marches, nor do they dress as witches, ghosts, devils and the like. These two teenaged boys simply confused Halloween with the Day of the Dead. For them, as for most Mexicans in central and southern Mexico, there is one major holiday at the end of October and beginning of November. The distinction between Day of the Dead elements and Halloween elements does not occur to them.

In fact, there are parts of Mexico where celebration of the traditional Day of the Dead is relatively recent. The northern states of Chihuahua, Coahuila, and Sonora, for example, are places in which Halloween has long enjoyed a visible presence. A middle-class, middle-aged friend of mine from the state of Coahuila remembers celebrating Halloween and Halloween alone as a child. He claims that there was no Day of the Dead in the 1940s and 1950s in Coahuila. Occasionally around the end of October his family would take him to Mexico City to visit relatives. He remembers being horrified at the elaborate displays of skulls and skeletons he found there and attributed to the people of Mexico City a kind of morbidity lacking in his home state. In 1996, however, key clerics in the northern Mexican states actually prohibited the celebration of Halloween on the grounds that this holiday, which they declared secular and commercial, represented a threat to the sanctity and very existence of the Day of the Dead.

Numerically there are probably few Mexicans who perceive Halloween as posing a threat to their national culture. But those who do are articulate and visible Mexicans, the intellectuals, representatives of the Church, the State, and outspoken members of major cultural institutions. Currently, all over Mexico there appears evidence of formal and informal resistance to the Halloween invasion from the north. A large mural painted along a wall in Tepoztlán, in the state of Morelos, shows a soccer player kicking and knocking down an individual whose head is in the form of a jack-o-lantern. The accompanying text reads, "No to Halloween. Preserve your cultural traditions." All over Mexico, town governments are beginning to mount competitions with prizes for best Day of the Dead altar. Among the contest guidelines for the city of Oaxaca competition is that "Altars which present elements foreign to our tradition [*elementos ajenos a nuestra tradición*] will be automatically disqualified." On October 29, 1996, the national daily *La Jornada*, famous for its photographic displays, showed a picture of a man out on a busy street dressed and masked in skeleton costume. The caption reads, "*Costumbre foránea*" [foreign custom]. Ironically, this costume is not all that foreign to traditional Mexico. Death figures don very similar garb in traditional village dances, where they play the role of clown figures (Brandes 1979).

El Imparcial, an Oaxaca city newspaper, published a feature article on October 31, 1996 entitled, "Halloween or No Halloween? A Fearful Dilemma." The term fearful was rendered in Spanish, "*de miedo*," a clear reference to the scariness theme of Halloween, such that the article itself, which questions the validity of Halloween, actually underscores the influence of this holiday. The article describes a unified campaign by both Catholic and Protestant churches in Oaxaca to stamp out Halloween. A seven-year-old boy is quoted as saying, "I don't know what to do. In church they told me that it's not good to participate in Halloween because it has to do with evil spirits, and that's why the stores choose witch and vampire costumes to wear in the streets. The bad thing is that my friends already have their costumes and I do want to accompany them, but I don't want to do anything sinful." The article also tells about a third grader who heard at mass that he should not participate in Halloween. In school, he was told that it was all right to do so, "as long as he first familiarizes himself with the Mexican traditions of the Day of the Dead."

For many Mexican intellectuals, Halloween represents the worst of the United States. It is reputed to be excessively commercial. Garciagodoy (1994:131) declares that

> while *Los Días de los Muertos* is undoubtedly an occasion for extravagant spending, it does not enter the style of consumerism that characterizes U.S. celebrants of Hallowe'en all year round. . . . As far as the inculcation of beliefs is concerned, I would speculate that the most important belief the exporters of Hallowe'en wish to inculcate is one on the acceptability of seasonal, disposable merchandise.

For her, as for other Mexican intellectuals, Halloween serves political interests as well:

> I do not want to fuel the fires of xenophobia or cultural paranoia, but I would not want to trivialize the cultural impact of the exportation of holiday traditions which, surely inadvertently, serve American interests not only economically, but also by cultivating a strong pro-U.S. element that will continue to insure political and diplomatic harmony between two countries with an extraordinarily long and porous border. It is not impossible that such an effect is consciously desired by a few powerful people on one or both sides of the *Río Bravo* [Rio Grande]. Still, to me it seems more likely that the cultural impact is a side-effect of the principal objective of economic gain (ibid:129).

Economic gain is in fact close to the heart of the traditional Day of the Dead proceedings as well. Since at least the eighteenth century, there has been a brisk market in sugar-candy figurines. Consider the words of Ajofrín (1958), dating from the 1760s and mentioned earlier in this chapter:

> Before the Day of the Dead they sell a thousand figures of little sheep, lambs, etc. of sugar paste [*alfeñique*], which they call *ofrenda*, and it is a gift which must be given obligatorily to boys and girls of the houses where one has acquaintance. They also sell coffins, tombs and a thousand figures of the dead, clerics, monks, nuns and all denominations, bishops, horsemen, for which there is a great market and a colorful fair in the portals of the merchants, where it is incredible [to see] the crowd of men and women from Mexico City on the evening before and on the day of All Saints. (ibid:87)

He goes on to explain that sugar figurines and other "cute little things" (*monerías*) are made in rapid succession by "clever" artisans who sell them cheaply. However, he warns the innocent consumer against advance payment which often results in receipt of tardy delivery or defective goods.

Clearly, even in colonial times, the Day of the Dead had a commercial cast. In cities all over Mexico stores now decorate their windows with humorous Day of the Dead icons. Newspapers are filled with advertisements playing on Day of the Dead themes, mostly skulls, skeletons, and the satiric verses which are themselves known as *calaveras*, or "skulls." Some traditional artisans throughout Mexico have for generations supported their families mainly through the production of sugar skulls and figurines. Judging from contemporary testimony, they do not object to the introduction of Halloween symbols, so long as their handiwork sells. Witness the testimony of one such artisan, Wenceslao Rivas Contreras (quoted in Carmichael and Sayer 1991:115) from Toluca, the capital of the state of Mexico and a famous center of *alfeñique* production:

I've often been told to stick to what's Mexican, yet I enjoy trying my hand at different things. Ten years ago I added skulls in pumpkins to my range. Pumpkins are a feature of Halloween in North America, but I'll make them if I can sell them, and witches as well! I want my displays to have variety, and my customers to have choice. In truth, although these various styles sell, skulls sell best—they belong to us, to Mexico!

The Day of the Dead apparently has always incorporated a degree of commercialism. Even the most sacred portion of the fiesta, the special observance of mass in honor of the departed souls, originally had an economic component. In colonial Mexico, for example, it was customary to give part of the food-offering to the priest in return for the recital of these special masses (Carmichael and Sayer 1991:45).

Yet, this aspect of the festivities, which has grown through time and persists in a major way to the present day, remains relatively unacknowledged in the collective mind of Mexican cultural nationalists. For them, Halloween is by comparison the grossly commercialized and profane holiday. Halloween to these nationalists also contaminates the Day of the Dead by introducing foreign elements into otherwise ancient, sacred proceedings. In other words, Halloween and the Day of the Dead, holidays which stem largely from a common source and which still exhibit many similar features, have become metaphors for relations between the United States and Mexico, respectively. Halloween has become a symbol of gringo imperialism.

Given the long-term presence of American communities within Mexico, as well as the lengthy border shared between the two countries, it is not surprising that Halloween symbols have been evident in Mexico over the past several generations. It is only recently, however, that the markers of Halloween—particularly costumes and jack-o-lanterns—have become an obvious part of the end-of-October celebrations throughout central and southern Mexico. Only at the end of the twentieth century have there emerged vociferous reactions from Mexico's religious and intellectual elite and the beginnings of organized opposition to the incursion of Halloween symbols into Day of the Dead activities.

Currently, the destinies of Mexico and the United States are closer than ever. The North American Free Trade Agreement (NAFTA), ratified in 1993, has increased the presence of U.S. citizens in Mexico enormously. Sanborn's, a gigantic department store chain located throughout Mexico and catering to the ever more prosperous middle and upper-middle classes, has begun large-scale marketing of Halloween costumes and candies. As far as the working classes are concerned, the ever increasing migrant stream means growing numbers of Mexican returnees, who bring to Mexico an exposure and predilection for certain aspects of North American popular culture, including Halloween, which many of them learned about in a United States classroom. This trend is fomented, too, through the omnipresence of U.S. programming on Mexican television, programming which familiarizes the Mexican public with typically U.S. holidays, like Halloween.

As a result of all these developments, Halloween has indeed become a palpable part of Day of the Dead proceedings. Mexicans who resent the growing U.S. influence over the Mexican economy and cultural scene respond effectively by focusing on a concrete, discretely defined event like Halloween. Halloween's success, to these Mexicans, represents Mexico's failure. In truth, the Day of the Dead correspondingly has become an important part of Halloween celebrations in the United States as well. The increasing presence of the Day of the Dead within the United States causes little commentary within our borders, however, because the balance of power in the relations between the two countries clearly is in our favor. But this story, yet another in the centuries-old saga of All Saints' and All Souls' Days, still remains to be told.

***

An earlier version of this paper was presented on March 3, 1997 at the Watson Center for International Studies of Brown University. I wish to thank those who attended the presentation for their commentaries, which were useful in formulating the published article. I am also grateful to John Carter Brown Library and the John Simon Guggenheim Foundation for the financial support necessary to carry out some of the research on which this chapter is based.

***

References

Aguirre Soronda, Antxon. 1989. El fuego en el rito funerario vasco. In *La Religiosidad Popular, vol. 2: Vida y muerte: la imaginación religiosa* (Carlos Alvaraz Santaló, María Jesús Buxó y Rey, and Salvador Rodríguez Becerra, eds), pp. 344–584. Barcelona: Anthropos.

Ajofrín, Francisco de. 1958. *Diario del viaje que por orden de la sagrada congregación de propaganda fide hizo a la América septentrional en el siglo XVIII.* (Dir., Vicente Castañeda y Alcover). Madrid: Real Academia de la Historia.

Bartra, Roger. 1987. *La jaula de la melancolía: identidad y metamórfosis del mexicano.* Mexico City: Grijalbo.

Brandes, Stanley. 1975. *Migration, Kinship, and Community: Tradition and Transition in a Spanish Village.* New York: Academic Press.

———. 1979. Dance as Metaphor: A Case from Tzintzuntzán. *Journal of Latin American Lore* 5(1): 25–43.

———. 1981. Gender Distinctions in Monteros Mortuary Ritual. *Ethnology* 20(3): 177–190.

———. 1988. *Power and Persuasion: Fiestas and Social Control in Rural Mexico.* Philadelphia: University of Pennsylvania Press.

———. 1997. Sugar, Colonialism, and Death: On the Origins of Mexico's Day of the Dead. *Comparative Studies in Society and History* 39.

Carmichael, Elizabeth, and Chloë Sayer. 1991. *The Skeleton at the Feast: The Day of the Dead in Mexico.* Austin: University of Texas Press.

Caso, Alfonso. 1953. *El pueblo del sol.* México, D.F.: Fondo de Cultura Económica.

Childs, Robert V., and Patricia B. Altman. 1982. *Vive Tu Recuerdo: Living Traditions in the Mexican Days of the Dead.* Los Angeles: Museum of Cultural History, University of California at Los Angeles.

Cornides, A. 1967. All Souls' Day. *New Catholic Encyclopedia.* New York: McGraw-Hill.

Covarrubias, Miguel. 1947. *Mexico South: The Isthmus of Tehuantepec.* New York: Knopf.

Díaz Guerrero, Rogelio. 1968. *Estudios de psicología del mexicano.* México, D.F.: F. Trillas.

Espinosa, Aurelio M. 1918. All Souls' Day at Zuñi, Acoma, and Laguna. *Journal of American Folklore* 31:550–552.

Fernández Kelley, Patricia. 1974. Death in Mexican Folk Culture. *American Quarterly* 25(5): 516–535.

Foster, George M. 1960. *Culture and Conquest: America's Spanish Heritage.* Viking Fund Publications in Anthropology, Number 27. New York: Wenner-Gren Foundation.

———. 1988. *Tzintzuntzán: Mexican Peasants in a Changing World.* Prospect Heights, IL: Waveland.

Foster, George M., and Gabriel Ospina. 1948. *Empire's Children: The People of Tzintzuntzán.* Smithsonian Institution, Institute of Social Anthropology, Publication 6. Washington: Smithsonian Institution.

Gaillard, Jacques. 1950. *Catholicisme.* Paris, Press Catholique.

Garciagodoy, Juanita. 1994. *Romancing the Bone: A Semiotics of Mexico's Day of the Dead.* Ph.D. dissertation, University of Minnesota.

Gonzalez-Crussi, Frank. 1993. *The Day of the Dead and Other Mortal Reflections.* New York: Harcourt Brace.

Gutiérrez, Elektra, and Tonatiúh Gutiérrez. 1971. La muerte en el arte popular mexicano. *Artes de México* 1(45): 75–86.

Gutmann, Matthew. 1993. *Primordial Cultures and Creativity in the Origins of "Lo Mexicano."* Kroeber Anthropological Society Papers 75–76: 48–61.

Haberstein, Robert W., and William M. Lamers. 1963. *Funeral Customs the World Over.* Milwaukee: Bultin.

Hague, Abu Saeed Zahurul. 1981. *Folklore and Nationalism in Rabindranath Tagore.* Dacca: Bangla Academy.

Herzfeld, Michael. 1982. *Ours No More: Folklore, Ideology, and the Making of Modern Greece.* Austin: University of Texas Press.

Karp, Ivan, and Steven D. Lavine (eds.). 1991. *The Poetics and Politics of Museum Display.* Washington, DC: Smithsonian Institution Press.

Kemper, Robert V. n.d. *Tarascan Speakers in Tzintzuntzán, 1945–1990*. Unpublished paper presented at the Annual Meeting of the American Anthropological Association, November 1996.

Kertzer, David I. 1988. *Ritual Politics and Power.* New Haven: Yale University Press.

Llabrés Quintana, Gabriel. 1925. Los panetets de mort. *Correo de Mallorca*, October 1925.

Lope Blanch, Juan M. 1963. *Vocabulario mexicano relativo a la muerte*. México, D.F.: Universidad Nacional Autónoma de México, Centro de Estudios Literarios.

Metcalf, Peter, and Richard Huntington. 1991. *Celebrations of Death: The Anthropology of Mortuary Ritual*. Cambridge and New York: Cambridge University Press.

Parsons, Elsie Clews. 1917. All Souls' Day at Zuñi, Acoma, and Laguna. *Journal of American Folklore* 30:495–496.

Paz, Octavio. 1961. *The Labyrinth of Solitude: Life and Thought in Mexico*. Lysender Kemp, trans. New York: Grove.

Ramos, Samuel. 1962. *Profile of Man and Culture in Mexico*. Peter G. Earle, trans. Austin: University of Texas Press.

Sandstrom, Alan R., and Pamela Effrein Sandstrom. 1986. *Traditional Papermaking and Paper Cult Figures of Mexico*. Norman: University of Oklahoma Press.

Santino, Jack, ed. 1994. *Halloween and Other Festivals of Life and Death*. Knoxville: University of Tennessee Press.

Sayer, Chloë (ed.). 1993. *Mexico: The Day of the Dead*. Boston: Shambhala Redstone.

Smith, C. 1967. Feast of All Saints. *New Catholic Encyclopedia*. New York: McGraw-Hill.

Tuleja, Tad. 1994. Trick or Treat: Pre-Texts and Contexts. In *Halloween and Other Festivals of Life and Death* (Jack Santino, ed.), 82–102. Knoxville: University of Tennessee Press.

Viqueira, Juan-Pedro. 1984. La ilustración y las fiestas religiosas populares en la Ciudad de México (1731–1821). *Cuicuilco* (Revista de la Escuela Nacional de Antropología e Historia) 14–15: 7–14.

Wilson, William A. 1976. *Folklore and Nationalism in Modern Finland*. Bloomington: Indiana University Press.

Newspapers Cited: *Correo de Mallorca* (Spain), *La Jornada* (Mexico), *The North American Star* (Mexico), *Reforma* (Mexico).

Beth Conklin teaches anthropology at Vanderbilt University. Her best-known books include Consuming Grief: Compassionate Cannibalism in an Amazonian Society; Images of Health, Illness and Death among the Wari' (Pakaas Novos) of Rondonia, Brazil; *and* Development in the Brazilian Amazon: Health Consequences for Native Peoples.

30

Rarely do we think of the body image that a people prize among themselves as potentially valuable in their relations with other populations. Ironically, the exotic accoutrements of some Indians in the Amazon Basin have helped to further their cause of cultural and political activism on a global stage as well as in the nations that had virtually ignored them for generations. Questions of imagery, "authenticity," appropriate technology, ethnicity, and social boundaries are all intimately interwoven in Conklin's sensitive explication of representations and cultural brokerage in Brazil and in front of the world.

The Yuquí in Bolivia chose a more low-key approach to preserving ethnicity and their environment (Stearman, chapter 20), and the Mixtec have asserted their ethnicity only after mingling with their new neighbors on both sides of the Mexico-United States border (Kearney, chapter 7). The highly variable meanings of dress (Femenías, chapter 25), language (Bernard, chapter 10), and religion (Elkin, chapter 23) are all linked, in different ways, with the self-identification of both individuals and groups (Wolf, chapter 39).

Body Paint, Feathers, and VCRs
Aesthetics and Authenticity in Amazonian Activism

Beth A. Conklin

Every connoisseur of anthropology department bulletin boards knows this *Far Side* cartoon (Larson 1984): A grass-skirted native man in a tall headdress stands at the window of a thatched hut. He has just spotted a couple of pith-helmeted, camera-toting creatures coming ashore and sounds the alarm: "Anthropologists! Anthropologists!" His two companions, similarly attired with bones through their noses, rush to unplug their television, VCR, lamp, and telephone and stash them out of sight. The cartoon captures a persistent stereotype about native peoples and cultural authenticity. The first, obvious idea is that outsiders (anthropologists included) tend to see complex Western technology as a corrupting force that undermines traditional cultures. "Real" natives don't use VCRs.

A second, more subtle message in Gary Larson's sketch concerns the importance of exotic body images in defining cultural integrity. Hide the television, but keep the grass skirt, and the "authenticity" of the natives goes unquestioned.

Authenticity has its rewards. In Larson's modernist model of colonial encounters, grass-skirted natives may claim the attention of visiting anthropologists and any concomitant benefits of prestige or payment. In contemporary indigenous identity politics, exotic body images carry a similar strategic weight in asserting symbolic claims to authenticity.

In this article I explore relations among the trilogy of elements highlighted above: indigenous body images, high technology, and Western notions of cultural authenticity. My purpose is to offer a reflection on the centrality of body images in defining indigenous authenticity for Western audiences, and to raise questions about the political implications of replicating these symbolic constructs in pro-indigenous activism and

Abridged from the author's article of the same title, in *American Ethnologist* 24(4):711–737. Copyright © 1993 American Anthropological Association. Reprinted with permission. (Notes have been renumbered.)

advocacy. I focus on interethnic politics in Brazil, where native costume took on new meanings in the 1980s as the rise of environmentalism and the spread of new modes of communication created transnational audiences and support networks engaged with Amazonian Indian causes.

The recent transformation of native Amazonian activism is a case study in how local-global interactions and encounters with the social conditions of postmodernity—especially accelerated flows of information, images, technologies, and people across social and geographic boundaries—shape cultural imaginations and cultural politics (see Appadurai 1990; Knauft 1994:120). In the past decade, the surge of public concern about threats to the tropical rainforest catapulted Brazilian Indians into the limelight of global media attention. Certain individuals from remote Amazonian communities found themselves deluged with invitations to travel abroad, speak at ecology conferences, meet world leaders, accompany rock stars on concert tours, and testify before policy makers at the World Bank, the United Nations, the United States Congress, and the European Union headquarters. As Indian activists journeyed into these arenas of intercultural dialogue, they encountered Western value systems and technologies of representation that offered new perspectives on their own cultures and new channels for communicating their concerns to influential outsiders. Responding to these possibilities, Indian activists transfigured the ways in which they presented themselves and their cultures to the world.

Native Amazonians who once took pains to hide external signs of indigenous identity behind mass-produced Western clothing now proclaim their cultural distinctiveness with headdresses, body paint, beads, and feathers. Many anthropologists have interpreted this revival of native costume as an expression of political assertiveness and renewed pride in being Indian (Turner 1992b:299). It certainly is. It is equally clear that this shift responds not only to indigenous values and internal societal dynamics, but also to foreign ideas, aesthetics, and expectations about Indians. As some native South Americans have learned to speak the language of Western environmentalism and reframe their cosmological and ecological systems in terms of Western concepts like "respect for Mother Earth," "being close to nature," and "protecting biosphere diversity," so some also have learned to use Western visual codes to position themselves politically.[1]

In assessing the role of symbols of Indian identity in Amazonian eco-politics, I develop two major points. First, I show how ideological, technological, and political developments of the 1980s and 1990s influenced the construction of the public (body) images of native activists. Second, I argue that, along with the political and cultural benefits, there are potential contradictions and problems, for Indians, with using these strategic representations (and the kind of identity politics with which they are associated) to pursue indigenous goals of self-determination.

Indigenous body images constitute a form of "representing culture" (Myers 1991) that is both a dimension of the self-production of Amazonian activists and a channel through which they communicate with non-Indian audiences. In this article, my intent is not to focus on the meanings that native activists themselves attach to these images. Rather, I am concerned with exploring the political consequences for Indians of relying on political strategies whose efficacy depends on representing indigenous actors and their causes in terms that conform to outsiders' stereotypes of Indianness. Western images of Indians are the product of Western discourses. These images often say more about Westerners than about Indians and tend toward simplistic notions that do not encompass the complex realities of most native peoples' lives. As an ethnographer who works with a relatively "unpoliticized" Brazilian Indian population that remains largely outside the discourses of eco-activism, national party politics, and pan-Indian organizing, I am especially concerned with how the objectification of culture in ethnic representations affects those native peoples who neither produce nor conform to them.

Visual symbols are at the heart of this story because the politics of the Indian alliance is primarily a symbolic politics. Images and ideas, not common identity or mutual economic interests, mobilize political cooperation among people separated by wide distances and differences of language, culture, and historical experience. Symbols are important in all politics, but they are central in native Amazonian activism; in the absence of electoral clout or (in most cases) economic influence, the "symbolic capital" (Bourdieu 1977) of cultural identity is one of Brazilian Indians' most important political resources.

As native Brazilian activists entered the global public arena, *visual* images—especially body images—emerged as a privileged sphere for negotiating representations of Indian identity. Visual imagery is especially critical because language barriers impede communication with foreign journalists, most of whom do not speak Portuguese. Pictures, however, speak volumes in the competition for media attention. Those activists—both Indians and non-Indians—who wield positive symbols of indigenous identity achieve a "profit of distinction" (Bourdieu 1984), which offers strategic advantages in media-sensitive transnational politics.

As cultural productions, indigenous body representations, while created from Amazonian cultural elements, have constructed—to borrow a phrase from Myers (1991:35)—a *permissible* image that identifies native elements with Western concepts and thereby wins the approval of outsiders. In Amazonian eco-politics, both Indian and non-Indian spokespersons have come to promote an idealized image that Redford (1990) dubbed the "Ecologically Noble Savage." Amazonian Indians are represented as guardians of the forest, natural conservationists whose cultural traditions and spiritual values predispose them to live in harmony with the earth. Graham and I have discussed problems with assuming that native Amazonian attitudes toward nature and priorities for managing ecological resources can be equated directly with Western environmentalist principles (Conklin and Graham 1995).[2] Here, the point I wish to emphasize is that generic stereotypes of Indians, no matter how sympathetic, can become liabilities. The current popular appreciation for the ecological wisdom of native peoples has an undeniable basis in Amazonian cultural ecology and ethnobiology.[3] But in moving into the realm of popular culture and environmental politics, ideas about native ecology merged with two long-standing currents in Western thought: exoticism (which emphasizes the attraction of cultural difference) and primitivism (which celebrates non-Western societies' antithetical relation to Western civilization and its corruptions). These intellectual traditions have a long history of distorting Westerners' relations with non-Western peoples (see Berkhofer 1978, 1988; Hemming 1978:1–23; Thomas 1994:173). Their recent recycling into a "green" guise deserves critical consideration.

For anthropologists, the trajectory of Amazonian eco-politics calls attention to the ironic divergence between the academic politics of postcolonial ethnography and the pragmatic politics of postcolonial ethnographic "subjects." Over the past two decades, myriad critiques of ethnographic representation have denounced tendencies to depict non-Western peoples in terms of essentialist images of cultural isolation, stasis, ahistoricity, and internal homogeneity (see, for example, Clifford 1988; Clifford and Marcus 1986; Said 1978; Wolf 1982). Contemporary ethnographers are enjoined to treat cultures as dynamic processes, not as bounded objects frozen in time, and to recognize intracultural diversity and non-Western societies' engagement with global political, economic, and cultural processes.[4]

Simultaneously with this reorientation of ethnographic perspectives, political activism among indigenous peoples grew enormously around the world, adding weight to the pressures to recognize native involvement in global systems. Ironically, however, much of the most vociferous and effective indigenous activism (in Brazil and elsewhere) has been channeled into ethnic identity politics based on projecting generic essentialisms of the sort that anthropologists have come to regard as pernicious (see Thomas 1994:170–195).[5]

Indigenous self-representations present a paradox. On one hand, identity politics—especially in its ecological variants—has brought unprecedented visibility and transnational support to native peoples' struggles for land and legal rights critical to their survival. In many ways the participation of Amazonian Indians in transnational eco-politics represents a radical departure from dependency relations of the past. The Indian-environmentalist alliance articulates a model of partnership, not paternalism, and champions indigenous self-determination—the right of native peoples to make choices about their own destinies. On the other hand, even in this self-consciously anticolonial, postmodern politics, limiting stereotypes persist. Reductionist constructions of Indian identity ignore inter- and intracultural diversity and distort the complexity of native Amazonian goals and relations to natural environments and national economies. More troubling than the intellectual contradictions are the problematic political implications. Probing the ambiguities of translating authenticity through native body images highlights some of the tensions and contradictions in indigenous peoples' participation in end-of-the-millennium symbolic politics predicated on Western notions of cultural authenticity.

INDEXING AUTHENTICITY

The equation of visual exoticism (nudity, body paint, colorful ornaments) with genuine Indianness has persisted since the earliest European voyagers' accounts of their encounters with Brazil's native peoples (see Berkhofer 1978; Hemming 1978:1–23; Polhemus 1988:72–76). A classic example of the contemporary salience of the idea that cultural integrity can be read on the body surface was *People* magazine's 1988 article about the British rock singer, Sting, and his visit to a Kayapó village in central Brazil. The headline proclaimed: "On a Three-Day Tour Break, Sting Goes Native— Very Native—To Meet a Chief Amazon Indian." What is meant by going "native—very native" was elucidated by Sting himself, who exulted, "it didn't take long for the varnish of civilization to leave us. After 48 hours, we were naked, covered with paint, and fighting snakes" (*People* 1988:116). The two accompanying photographs attested to the seeming genuineness of the rock star's transcultural experience by emphasizing body transformations: one showed Kayapó designs painted on Sting's bare chest; the other focused on Chief Raoni's huge wooden lip disk.

For outsiders, native costumes tend to carry a heavy semiotic load. A study of *National Geographic* magazine by Lutz and Collins found that readers perceived clothing to be the single most important marker of cultural identity: "Exotic dress alone often stands for an entire alien life-style, locale, or mind-set . . . Local costume suggests something about the social stability and timelessness of the people depicted" (1993:92). The loss of traditional costume indexed the loss of cultural traditions: "Clothes identified as Western seemed often . . . to be a sign of cultural degradation, while non-Western clothing was taken as a sign of authenticity" (Lutz and Collins 1993:247).

This equation of non-Western cultural authenticity with visual exoticism and primitivism resonates with long-standing notions of "primitive" art. The Western art world defines primitive art as exotic (markedly different from the West) and ahistorical or unchanging.[6] Primitive artworks tend to be viewed as undifferentiated products of "age-old tradition governed by communal custom" rooted in religious and mythical conceptions (S. Price 1989:64). The primitive is significant "above all because of an originary, socially simple and natural character" (Thomas 1994:173). This emphasis on cultural continuity as the essence of authenticity reflects a Western commonsense notion of tradition that "presumes that an unchanging core of ideas and customs is always handed down to us from the past" (Handler and Linnekin 1984:273; see also Dominguez 1986:549; Linnekin 1991:447). Authenticity implies integration and wholeness—continuity between past and present, and between societal values and individual agency, and between sign and meaning (see Clifford 1988:215). This leaves little room for intercultural exchange or creative innovation, and locates "authentic" indigenous actors outside global cultural trends and changing ideas and technologies.

By the early 1990s, the *Far Side*'s modernist stereotype opposing Western technology to native culture had been stood on its head. Striking counterimages came from Sting's hosts, the Kayapó, who became famous for their skill at turning video to indigenous purposes. Kayapó now film, produce, and edit videos that document their own dances and rituals, political events, and meetings with Brazilian politicians and corporate officials (Turner 1992a). Since 1989 global media have disseminated numerous pictures of Kayapó cameramen—resplendent in headdresses, body paint, feathered armbands, and earrings—photographed in the act of filming.

The appropriation of complex Western technologies by indigenous people challenges views that equate authenticity with purity from foreign influences. The contested nature of this issue was evident in an incident described by Payakan, a Kayapó activist who was active in the Kayapó struggle to win legal rights to their land in the 1980s. A Brazilian judge questioned whether Payakan, an articulate, Western-educated individual, could legitimately represent the interests of less acculturated Kayapó:

> Judge: "I understand that you know how to operate a VCR. Is this true?"
>
> Payakan: "Yes, Your Honor."
>
> Judge: "How can you call yourself an Indian if you work with these machines? Even *I* don't know how to use a VCR. How can you be a real Indian?"
>
> Payakan: "Your Honor, the only reason that *I* know how to operate a VCR and your Honor doesn't is because *I* took the time to learn."[7]

The use of complex First World technology by Fourth World peoples is a trend that resonates worldwide. Solar panels, optic fiber technology, telephones, personal computers, modems, fax machines, camcorders, and VCRs have spread to some of the more remote corners of the global village (see Annis 1991, 1992; Zimmer 1990). Contemporary media revel in images of "primitive" folk with modern technology, the unexpected juxtaposition of "high-tech" Western elements next to "low-tech" indigenous elements such as feathers, body paint, lip plugs, and war clubs (Hess 1995:230–231). Primitive/modern visual contrasts have been a long-running theme in *National Geographic* magazine photography (Lutz and Collins 1993:110–112, 247–253) and are an increasingly prominent motif in advertising and fashion photography. Rather than marking the "natives" as active participants in the modern world system, such images tend to represent them as passive (and often confused or amazed) receptors of Western artifacts and the ironic gaze of Western viewers.

In anthropology, shifts in ethnographic representation echo the trend to acknowledge the spread of Western technologies to native peoples. Anthropologists celebrate the recent explosion of indigenous film and video production from Australia to the Americas (see, for example, Ginsburg 1991, 1993; Spitulnik 1993; Turner 1992a) and appreciate the possibilities implicit in turning Western technology to locally empower-

ing, grassroots purposes (Annis 1991, 1992). The emphasis is on indigenous compe-
tency and control. No longer must we hide the VCR; instead, it has become
fashionable to highlight Third and Fourth World peoples' creative appropriation of
"high-tech" foreign communications equipment.

Old stereotypes about how Western technology corrupts traditional cultures may
be passé, but visual exoticism retains its enduring role in defining indigenous authenticity. Today, with the shift away from essentializing notions of culture, few anthropologists would subscribe openly to a simplistic equation between exotic costume and
authenticity. Nonetheless, there still is a general tendency "to see the retention of
indigenous dress as a positive sign of cultural maintenance and strength" (Ehrenreich
in press) and to consider the adoption of Western dress to be a sign of diminished cultural integrity. The imprint of this cultural coding is familiar to any ethnographers who
have caught themselves sorting through fieldwork slides, selecting the more "interesting," "authentic" pictures with the fewest "foreign" or commercial "intrusions."[8]

CLOTHING AS STRATEGIC DISSEMBLING

The appreciation for exotic native bodies expressed in contemporary Western popular culture is light-years away from the attitudes that most Amazonian Indians confront in dealing with non-Indians at the local level. In Brazil, Indians historically
have had a number of motivations (pragmatic, social, and political) to reduce or abandon nudity and the use of native body styles. Every native group sustaining contact
with outsiders has adopted Western clothing to some extent.

I work with the Wari' (Pakaa Nova), a population of about 1,500 people who live in
the western Brazilian state of Rondônia.[9] The Wari' entered peaceful relations with the
national society in the late 1950s and 1960s. Prior to the contact, they had no clothing;
personal modesty (which Wari' value highly) was expressed in discreet body postures.
Soon after the first contact, Wari' were inundated with unwanted attention because of
their nudity. It became fashionable for army officers and their wives from the military
base at Guajará-Mirim to take Sunday excursions upriver to the Tanajura contact site
to stare at the naked savages. Wari' quickly understood the value of clothing in relations
with outsiders. They now wear Western clothing at all times, including ritual occasions.

Many other aspects of Wari' life also changed after the contact, but they maintain
a high degree of social cohesion and cultural integrity. The native language is the only
language spoken in the vast majority of Wari' homes and there is little marriage with
outsiders. In the past two decades, only a few Wari' have moved away and nearly
everyone continues to depend on farming, hunting, fishing, and foraging to make a living. Visitors to Wari' villages are now frequently disappointed because "they don't look
like real Indians," but Wari' themselves suffer no confusion about their own identity.

Most Brazilian Indians must interact with non-Indians (such as government
agents, rubber-tappers, farmers, ranchers, shopkeepers, missionaries, nurses, and
teachers) who view nudity as a sign of subhumanity, barbarism, and poverty, and who
see body painting as a manifestation of negatively valued exoticism opposed to Brazilian social norms. In local interethnic encounters, using Western clothing may be a
strategy to gain greater respect and equality in face-to-face interactions. Turner
reports that this motivated Kayapó to adopt clothing some three decades ago:

> The Kayapó had learned from their earliest contacts with Brazilians that nudity, lip
> plugs, body paint, and penis sheaths were inconsistent with minimal Brazilian stan-
> dards of social intercourse. Recognizing that some social intercourse with Brazilians
> had become essential to their survival, they needed little urging from SPI [Indian
> Protection Service] agents and missionaries to adopt minimal clothing and discard

other flagrantly "savage" aspects of their traditional appearance. By the time of our arrival in 1962, most men had removed their lip plugs, had their hair cut short Brazilian style, and had taken to wearing shorts and occasionally T-shirts in the village. . . . The chiefs and most of the older men possessed complete Brazilian-style outfits (shoes, sometimes even socks, long pants, and long-sleeved shirts) for wear on trips to Brazilian towns, visits to the village by Brazilian officials, or attendance at the missionaries' Sunday services; with such fancy-dress outfits no body paint or Kayapó ornaments were worn. [1992b:289]

As Ehrenreich (in press) observes, "the adoption of non-indigenous clothing, and the cultivation of an appearance which mirrors that of outsiders, serves to promote the cultural survival of the group at large." Instead of speeding the destruction of indigenous cultural autonomy, nonnative dress may help to preserve it.

NEW AMAZONIAN MIRRORS

In the past decade and a half interethnic dress codes have undergone a revision: in some Brazilian Indian groups, male leaders and activists have resumed the use of native body decorations when meeting with outsiders.[10] In this and following sections, I explore how this change responded to the development of a communications infrastructure and technologies of representation that simultaneously broadened indigenous peoples' political consciousness and expanded the arena for indigenous activism.

In the 1970s the Brazilian government launched a series of huge development projects aimed at creating an infrastructure to integrate the Amazonian interior with the rest of the country. The new roads and airstrips that cut through the rainforest sparked massive invasions of Indian lands and unleashed waves of violence and epidemics that devastated scores of native communities. This explosion of interethnic conflict catalyzed Indian activism and the development of pan-Indian organizing in opposition to government policies.

For Indians living away from native communities, questions of identity and authenticity come to the fore along with the issue of body images. "(We) spend most of our lives trying to reaffirm that we are Indians," says Potiguara (1992:46), an urban-born Indian activist, "and then we encounter statements like, 'But you wear jeans, a watch, sneakers, and speak Portuguese!' . . . Society either understands Indians all made-up and naked inside the forest or consigns them to the border of big cities." Combining native decorations with Western clothing offers a way to mark a distinctly indigenous identity. For migrants from rural Indian communities, this has the advantage of differentiating them from the non-Indian rural Amazonians (*caboclos*) and the urban poor who occupy the lower-class categories into which such Indians generally have been assimilated. It also has aesthetic appeal for the urban intellectuals who have been the major source of domestic political support for Indian causes.[11]

For Indians in native villages the 1970s and '80s brought the spread of communications technologies that reflected new self-images and offered new channels for self-representation. In particular, the development of compact, portable, battery-operated electronics enabled native Amazonians to participate for the first time in producing the images and information about themselves that circulate outside their communities. The cassette tape deck—much less cumbersome than reel-to-reel models—was a transformative innovation. In the late 1970s, Mario Juruna, a Xavante leader, captured Brazilian public attention by pioneering a visually oriented media politics that made extensive use of exotic body images, often juxtaposed with images of Western communications technology in indigenous hands (Conklin and Graham 1995; Hohlfeldt and Hoffmann 1982). Juruna was famous for using a cassette tape deck to record government officials' promises to Xavante seeking land titles; when promises were broken, he would call a press conference and play back the recordings. Flanked by dozens of boldly painted Xavante warriors armed with war clubs, bows, and arrows, Juruna staged dramatic confrontations with government officials that were broadcast nationwide on the television news. By the early 1980s, Juruna was a national symbol of opposition to the dictatorship.[12] He became a protégé of Darcy Ribeiro, an anthropologist-turned-politician, and in 1982, Juruna was elected (by urban voters in Rio de Janeiro) to the national Congress of Deputies. Juruna positioned himself as both insider and outsider to national party politics, a stance signified in his dress. As Congressman, he usually wore a well-tailored business suit but always kept his distinctive Xavante coiffure and earplugs.

Where Juruna's position required the trappings of elite business attire, later Indian activists positioned themselves as pure outsiders to mainstream politics and projected correspondingly different images. The Kayapó are a prime example. Turner reports, "Today, however, the same chiefs and other men are again wearing their hair long . . . when chiefs go to a Brazilian city, they make a point of wearing shorts (or sometimes long pants) and shoes, but no shirt or jacket. Their faces, arms, and upper bodies are painted, and they wear traditional shell necklaces and bead earrings. The whole ensemble is often topped off with a feather headdress . . . " (1992b:299). In the case of the Kayapó, the revival of indigenous costume reflects a shift in the balance of power between them and Brazilian national society. Since the mid-1980s Kayapó communities have had an annual income of several million dollars in profits from a gold mine and contracts with commercial timber companies (Turner 1993:535–536). This money, combined with their exceptional skill at garnering media attention and support from celebrities like Sting, gives Kayapó considerable clout in dealing with outsiders. Even in some other native groups without such exceptional resources, however, a renewed pride in native body styles is evident. Again, technology has played a role.

Like the invention of the cassette tape deck, the development of portable, easy-to-operate video equipment put a powerful technology for self-representation into indigenous hands. Asad (1991:323) observes that, just as modern modes of transportation altered time and space, so new modes of representation are helping to reconstitute colonized subjectivities.[13] Among the Wari', I saw the introduction of a simple cassette tape recorder spark renewed interest in Wari' music, which snowballed into a full-scale revival of major festivals that had not been held in more than 20 years.

Amazonian natives have long been the subject of outsiders' films, but video differs from film, not only in being cheaper and easier to use, but also in the fact that videotapes can be played back on the spot for those who were filmed. The potential for this to transform native peoples' view of themselves was vividly illustrated in an incident recounted by Brazilian filmmaker Vincent Carelli, who directs a "Video in the Villages" project aimed at introducing video to Indian communities (see Carelli 1989). Carelli reports that when his team videotaped a Nambiquara female initiation rite, the Nambiquara participants were clad in their usual garb of dresses, shorts, and T-shirts:

> When we finished filming, we all went into a hut and watched the ceremony, and people started complaining. . . . they didn't like it—they said they were wearing too much clothing and not enough paint on their faces. So we recorded it again. The young girl was taken out of the hut again, and the whole ceremony was re-enacted. The men wore smaller shorts and the women wore pieces of cloth tied around their waists as skirts. They were much happier with the result—they felt the film was more authentic. [Carelli as quoted in Smith 1989:30–31]

In this Nambiquara community, the self-reflective encounter with the "mirror" of video images evoked not just a one-time dressing up (or down) in native style but also more profound reassessments of how body images relate to cultural identity:

> The tribe's young men, who hadn't pierced their upper lips or nose for 10 years because the passage-to-adulthood custom had died out as a result of their contact with the outside world, decided to stage a piercing ceremony for the camera. One adolescent, tears streaming down his cheeks as he stoically had his lip skewered by a bamboo stick [*sic*], was comforted by a tribal elder who said: "If you don't do this, how will you prove you are an Indian?" [Carelli as quoted in Smith 1989:30–31]

Turner describes how Kayapó political consciousness was transformed by similar encounters with anthropologists, photographers, journalists, and others:

> The cumulative effect of these contacts was to catalyze the development of an awareness on the part of the Kayapó of the potential political value of their "culture" in their relations with the alien society. . . . [F]or many native peoples, the fact that anthropologists and other relatively prestigious outsiders, who plainly disposed of impressive resources . . . were prepared to spend these resources, not to mention much of their lives, on the study of native "cultures," may have done more than anything else to convey to these peoples the awareness that their traditional way of life and ideas were phenomena of great value and interest in the eyes of at least some sectors of the alien enveloping society. [Turner 1992b:301]

These Kayapó and Nambiquara experiences attest to the transformative power of new modes of self-reflection. As Amazonian Indians have seen themselves reflected in new ways—in the eyes of sympathetic outsiders, as well as on video screens—some have begun to envision and project new self-images.

If technology is changing how native Brazilians see themselves, it also has altered radically the dynamics of Amazonian interethnic politics by facilitating cooperation between native peoples and distant supporters. The same new roads and airstrips that carried hordes of invaders into Indian territories also made it easier for sympathetic outsiders and journalists to visit remote native villages and for Indians to travel to conferences, protest demonstrations, and political gatherings. Telephones, satellite communications systems, fax machines, computers, and VCRs offer native communities and organizations unprecedented abilities to communicate rapidly with allies and journalists in urban Brazil and foreign countries, as well as with other native groups.[14] The synergistic effects of linking electronic communications to attention-getting identity politics have been evident in a number of recent indigenous rights victories.

THIS *IS* OUR SUIT AND TIE

Of all Brazilian Indians, the Kayapó most fully realized the political possibilities of using indigenous dress and undress to play off Western symbolic constructs and gain media attention. This came to the fore in 1988 when two Kayapó leaders faced legal prosecution in a court in Belém, Pará. Payakan and Kube-i were accused of sedition (under a law applying to *foreigners*) for "betraying the national interest" by speaking with U.S. Congressmen and World Bank officials about funding for a hydroelectric dam project that would have flooded Kayapó villages (see CEDI 1991:326–28; Turner 1993:537). When Kube-i arrived at the courthouse to give his deposition, he appeared shirtless, wearing body paint and feathers—for which he promptly was charged with contempt of court and refused admittance to the public building (CEDI 1991:326). In response to the judge's order to show respect by "dressing appropriately" in suit and tie, Kube-i replied, "Your Honor, this *is* how we Kayapó show respect. This is the Indian's suit and tie." Besides, he pointed out, "When we invite you to our village, we don't ask you to take off your clothes and paint up like a Kayapó."

The most important indigenous rights victory—one that affected all Brazilian Indians—occurred in 1988, when the nation adopted a new constitution. For months while it was being written, hundreds of native leaders and representatives from several dozen Indian groups traveled to Brasília to lobby the Constituent Assembly delegates. Native costumes and attention-getting images attracted extensive television and press coverage. Ultimately the campaign paid off: the constitutional provisions that were ratified represented significant advances for the legal status and land rights of Indians and officially recognized their right to distinct languages, cultural traditions, and forms of social organization.

Brazilian Indian activists were able to turn exotic body images into effective political tools largely because new openings for indigenous activism developed at the national and international levels in the late 1980s (see Van Cott 1994). Democratization opened Brazilian political discourse to Indian voices, while the rise of international environmentalism created a global public receptive to Amazonian Indian causes.

The ideological basis for the Indian-environmental alliance was, of course, the growth of Western views of rainforest natives as "natural conservationists" whose traditional resource management practices embody Western environmentalist values of ecosystem preservation, sustainability, and appropriate technology (see Howard n.d.). The ecological rationales for promoting Amazonian Indians' land rights and cultural survival that emerged in the late 1980s were premised on the idea of cultural continuity—the assumption that *past* traditions will orient *future* Indians to use natural resources in ways that are ecologically nondestructive. The eco-Indian alliance, in other words, hinges on a particular construction of indigenous authenticity.

With cultural survival reframed as a global environmental issue, Amazonian Indians gained influential new allies.[15] Before the 1980s, Brazilian Indian rights advocacy was grounded mostly in human rights arguments (Wright 1988); Indians had only a narrow base of domestic political support (primarily among intellectuals and leftist clerics) and limited foreign support. Connecting native issues to global ecology linked Fourth World (native) causes to much larger, better-funded First World environmentalist networks (Brysk 1996).[16] International support freed some native Amazonian groups from their former dependence on local patronage and government officials, enabling them to take their causes directly to foreign supporters and media (Brown 1993:321)[17] International pressure became a critical factor. The "greening" of native struggles vastly expanded the audience receptive to indigenous messages, so that local conflicts over land and legal rights increasingly have been played out on an international stage where "the whole world is watching."

ADVOCACY AND AUTHENTICITY

The importance of symbolic markers of indigenous identity in Amazonian politics is intensified by the fact that most funding for Indian causes now comes from international agencies. Nongovernmental organizations (NGOs) such as Cultural Survival, Environmental Defense Fund, Friends of the Earth, National Wildlife Federation, Nature Conservancy, Rainforest Action Network, and World Wildlife Fund tend to be ideologically oriented to support grassroots communities and concerned that funds should not be consumed by bureaucratic intermediaries. The authenticity of Indian representatives is thus a matter of concern.

In Colombia, pro-Indian organizations in Amazonia and in the Andean highlands articulate different political concerns and different symbolic constructions of Indianness (Jackson 1991). Contestations over authentic forms of Indianness have generated an implicit symbolic hierarchy of cultural purity in which lowland (Amazonian) Indians are seen as more authentic than Andean Indians, and Makú hunter-gatherers are seen as purer ("almost hyper-real Indians") in comparison to their horticulturalist neighbors, the Tukanoans (Jackson 1995:7, 20).[18]

The ways in which indigenous authenticity is communicated to the supporters of advocacy organizations constitute another concern. NGOs rely heavily on motivating donors to make voluntary contributions, and photographs, slides, and video are important fund-raising tools. Advocates who hope to evoke interest and sympathy for indigenous peoples often consciously recognize the potency of exotic visual images as symbolic communicators of authenticity. An extreme example of this was an incident that occurred some years ago in a Wari' community administered by the regional Catholic diocese and partially supported by European donations. When one of the priests was about to embark on a fund-raising campaign, the community overseer paid a group of young Wari' men to remove their clothes and pose naked for pictures to be shown at slideshows in France and Germany (Von Graeve 1989:125).

Uses of Amazonian Indian images by NGOs clearly do not rest on such blatant exploitation. Nonetheless, visual appearances can influence decisions about where to direct publicity and resources. Exotic-looking peoples like the Yanomami and Kayapó offer exceptionally "good visuals" for public relations. In Brysk's interviews with North American activists, "[a]n Indian rights supporter who has held several policy positions in the U.S. government" described how eco-activists viewed the Kayapó leader, Payakan, as an ideal "image-bearer to represent the complex issues of sustainable development and indigenous self-determination in the Amazon." Recalled the activist: "We needed someone to represent the human side. . . . Paiakan had a genuine appearance and of course the regalia made good media. He really seemed to represent the forest" (Brysk 1994:36). These symbolic associations are part of a Western aesthetic vocabulary out of which Amazonian activists constructed public images that turned notions of primitivism, authenticity, and environmentalism to the advantage of indigenous advocacy.

When native Amazonian activists appear at media events and transnational gatherings, what types of body decorations do they use? A review of photographs of Brazilian Indian representatives in a variety of magazines, newspapers, videos, films, and NGO publications reveals considerable selectivity.[19] Traditional elements that are emphasized include: semi-nudity (men often do not wear shirts); colorful ornaments, especially feathered headdresses and earrings; and body paints, principally red annatto (*Bixa orellana*) and black charcoal, applied in rather limited quantities, principally to the face, arms, and torso. A notable feature of these body decorations is their impermanence: feathers, annatto, and charcoal can be easily put on and taken off.

It also is worth noting what types of body decorations are *not* emphasized. The semipermanent black dye genipap (*Genipa americana),* which is widely used in native Amazonian communities, appears infrequently in media contexts. The monkey-tooth bracelets and jaguar-tooth necklaces commonly worn by both Indians and non-Indians throughout the Amazon are also seldom seen on the environmental lecture circuit.

The traditional aesthetics of many native Amazonian peoples like the Wari' and Kayapó place a strong value on obtaining a smooth, sleek, heavily oiled body surface. In many groups, eyebrows are plucked, portions of the scalp are shaved, or sections of hair are cut in uneven lengths. Odors are also important; strong-smelling paints and ointments are often essential accessories for the well-dressed presentation of self. These aspects of native Amazonian body aesthetics, however, fail to survive the cross-cultural journey.

The body images that Indian activists have constructed resonate with the ideology and aesthetic sensibilities of their environmentalist allies. The rejection of Western costume obviously marks Indians' difference, separation, and opposition to Western traditions that, in environmentalist ideologies, are seen as destructive and corrupt.[20] Feathers are an evocative visual correlate to the oft-repeated idea of Indians as "close to nature."[21] Monkey and jaguar teeth might also evoke the idea of closeness to nature; they appear to be unacceptable, however, perhaps because they too graphically indicate acts of killing that offend Western sensibilities. (Feathers, in contrast, may or may not be obtained without killing the birds from which they originate.)

A related concept is the "naturalness" of Indians, who are represented as part of nature, born into a way of life that effortlessly embodies principles of Western conservationism. The downplaying of certain indigenous aesthetic elements—such as extreme haircuts, the removal of facial hair, and the heavy use of body oils—may reflect the fact that such radical modifications of the body contradict Western concepts of "natural" body aesthetics. In addition, such practices may edge toward communicating an undesirable degree of cultural difference. Indians are, after all, represented as essentially "like us," the responsible stewards of important resources, with views of nature that are presumed to be fundamentally similar to those of their non-Indian supporters. There is a fine line between the exotic and the alien—between differences that attract and differences that offend, unnerve, or threaten.

A final dimension of neo-indigenous body decorations is that, taken together, they evoke a dimension of mystery. The indigenous cultural meanings of body decorations always require translation for a Western audience. This translation may be as simple as *People* (1988:116) magazine's photo caption stating (erroneously) that a Kayapó chief "wears a lip disk to frighten enemies." Or it may be expressed with a more sophisticated reference to a headdress's mythological meanings. In any event, the *need for a translation of meaning* in itself evokes the existence of a level of ineffable experience and significance beyond the ken of Westerners. Just as nearly any sympathetic media discussion of native peoples inevitably alludes to their deep spirituality and harmony with nature, so the use of exotic decorations may have become a kind of symbolic shorthand signaling an authentic, embodied experience of being that is presumed to be of an order entirely different from that of non-Indians (cf. Fry and Willis 1989:114).

In native Amazonian societies, corporeal ornamentation communicates complex, culture-specific messages that indicate "the relationship of the individual to his society" (Gregor 1977:176). The human body surface serves as a "social skin"—a sort of canvas where personal identity is expressed and an individual's social identity and status are inscribed (Turner 1980; see, for example, Turner 1992c, and Vidal and Verswijver 1992 on cultural meanings of Kayapó body decorations). In interactions with non-Indians, however, these internal significances get lost. Meaning rests with the culture of secondary interpretation, which conflates all native decorations into a sign of generic Indianness. As Torgovnick (1990:82) observes, the elevation of the Other into the mainstream is often seen as decolonization; but it is still a process largely controlled by the West.

NATURAL SYMBOLS AND POLITICAL ARTIFICE

To acknowledge that the body images of native activists are produced in relation to Western discourses and media dynamics is not to say that Amazonian Indians have sold out. Nor are they passive victims of a Western "gaze," cultural "others" put on display for outsiders' ideological purposes. All politics are conducted by adjusting one's discourse to the language and goals of others, selectively deploying ideas and symbolic resources to create bases for alliance. Reformulated representations of ethnic identity are strategic adaptations to specific political and social environments (Barth 1969). In their "rebellion against political invisibility," their struggle to be seen and heard, Brazilian Indians must "appeal to the efficacy of certain symbols they know will strike home among whites. In this," comments Ramos, "they are no different from the powers-that-be when the latter invoke, for instance, the image of the flag, the sound of the national anthem, the idea of Union, of *brasilidade* [Brazilianness], in an attempt to amass popular support and build legitimacy" (Ramos 1988:232). By identifying certain Amazonian cultural elements with Western values, Brazilian Indian activists developed visual images that proved spectacularly effective at getting their causes onto the world's front pages and airwaves.

In costuming themselves to meet their audiences' expectations, native activists partially accept the role assigned to them as representatives of exoticism; at the same time, however, they have tried to expand outsiders' conceptions of who Indians are. Brazilian Indian activists traveling abroad have tended to mark their autonomy and distinctive agency by presenting themselves as mediating among multiple discourses and cultural systems, so that this display of complexity in itself undermines simplistic notions of a restrictive primitivism. The Kayapó, for example, did this by foregrounding their mastery of Western technologies. Turner (1992a:7) emphasizes that Kayapó see the dissemination of media images of their indigenous cameramen as essential to their self-definition in relation to the larger world. Their ostentatious affirmation that real natives *do* use VCRs aims to subvert limiting constructions of Indian identity and notions of fixed cultural boundaries and authentic types. Yet, as I noted at the beginning of this article, this can go only so far. The transnational audiences to whom eco-Indian activism must appeal retain relatively rigid ideas about cultural integrity and the importance of body images as signs of authenticity. Recognizing this, Kayapó cameramen dress the part for media events.

To dress to impress one's allies and intimidate one's opponents is nothing new for native Amazonians. What is new in media politics is the extent to which effective presentations of self must be tailored to fit outsiders' ideas about how "authentic" Indians should appear. How this affects native peoples' sense of themselves and their feelings of self-worth is a complex question with which South American ethnographers are just beginning to grapple.

Anthropologists who work with the Xavante and the Kayapó—the two groups with the most experience in mobilizing large numbers of native people for media events—emphasize the enhanced sense of self-worth and pride in cultural traditions that have come with their successes in confronting the outside world (Fisher 1994; Turner 1992b, 1993). Graham (1995 and personal communication) observes that when Xavante dress in native garb to confront their opponents they experience a dual sense of empowerment. First, they mark themselves as distinct from outsiders and as self-confident in their identity. Second, body decorations identify the individual with the larger Xavante collectivity, past and present. The act of applying body paint and putting on feathered ornaments connects the wearer with other Xavante and with the Xavante tradition of mythic discourses that celebrate the triumphs of heroic individuals who overcome great odds. That their distinctive body images have proved so effective as political theater further reinforces Xavante confidence in the supremacy of their traditions.

There may also be a political price for cultural politics that are heavily constrained by Western ideas about Indians. In the short run, exotic native images have served the shared interests of NGOs and Indians like the Kayapó who engage in symbolic politics aimed at an international public. Their effects in Brazilian domestic politics, however, have been more ambivalent.

An Amazonian leader's feathered headdress is no more (or less) artificial than a U.S. President's tuxedo. I suggest, however, that there is a difference in how the two costumes are perceived. Indigenous body decorations tend to be seen by outsiders, and represented by the activists who wear them, not merely as conventional attire or as costuming, but as integral expressions of the self—of spiritual and cultural roots. The salient message in the body styles discussed above is an affirmation of Indians as "natural" actors whose behavior flows from enduring traditions and primordial identity (see Howard n.d.). In part, it is these notions of naturalness and cultural continuity that distinguish indigenous claims from those of other ethnic minorities.

Brazilian journalists were quick to pick up on the possibility of "posing" in a vituperative press campaign aimed at undermining the legitimacy of the Indian rights movement (see Neves 1994). Over the past five years the Kayapó have borne the brunt of these attacks, which focused on accusing them of hypocrisy and corruption for their involvement in lucrative commercial ventures while presenting themselves as ecologists and victims.[22]

Most indigenous people and anthropologists would agree that native political claims should not be judged by conformity to stereotypes of cultural purity. Yet pro-Indian rhetoric that invokes the content of "traditional culture" as an argument for native rights relies on similar distancing dichotomies and oppositional representations of Indian and non-Indian cultures. This approach can backfire when the gap between necessarily simplified representations and the complexities of Amazonian Indian communities' own objectives becomes evident to outsiders. This is what has happened to the Kayapó, whose leaders forged alliances with environmentalists as a way to further their quest for self-determination and control over their land. Social scientists, journalists, and Kayapó activists have attributed Kayapó eco-activism to specific features of Kayapó culture and "the resiliency of their cultural traditions which flourish only in harmony with the tropical forest" (Fisher 1994:221). Fisher argues that by focusing on traditional cultural content, we miss the point that, for Kayapó, environmentalism is above all a strategic tool for communication and political mobilization.

While some aspects of the Kayapó story are specific to their situation, their experiences illustrate a broader problem in indigenous identity politics. There is a risk for Indians in relying on the symbolic capital of representations structured according to outsiders' notions of what Indians are like. Indigenous actors who fail to conform to these images are categorized as corrupt and inauthentic, undermining the symbolic values on which their participation in transnational politics is based. Native activists face a quandary: they can forge alliances with outsiders only by framing their cause in terms that appeal to Western values and ideas about Indians, but this foreign framework does not necessarily coincide with indigenous peoples' own visions of themselves and their futures.[23]

ARTFUL COMPETITION

The images that Indian activists constructed as actors on the global political stage have also become a force in relations among native groups within Brazil. Wari' from the communities where I work confronted this for the first time when some men attended a 1991 regional meeting of Rondônia's "forest peoples," where they were lectured by a Suruí Indian who exhorted them to take off their shirts during the meeting. The Wari' representatives found this idea utterly foreign; as one man told it, "I said to the Suruí: 'I don't like that; I'm wearing my shirt.'"

Particular constructions of Indian identity privilege those who correspond best to the idealized image (Thomas 1994:189).[24] The feathered headdresses that formerly were part of Kayapó sacred rituals have become secular political props and the sine qua non of activist apparel. Not all Brazilian Indians have such headdresses. Wari', for example, use feathers as head ornaments in two ways: they either stick bits of white down onto oiled hair or insert a single scarlet macaw feather behind the crown. Neither style would translate well in the context of external political encounters, and neither has the visual impact and media appeal of Kayapó-type headdresses.

In an era when it often pays to be a "real" Indian, the renewed emphasis on body images as an index of authenticity may work against the interests of people like the Wari', Awá, and Pataxó who do not fit outsiders' visual stereotype of authentic Indianness. The Wari' and Awá strategy of dissimulation, of trying to look as "normal" as possible, has, until now, been adaptive in dealing with outsiders at the local level. Ironically, it may prove to be a liability in a new situation in which alliances with distant supporters have become critical political resources, media attention goes first and foremost to those who offer exotic visual images, and obtaining funding from governments and NGOs can depend on meeting criteria of authenticity (see Jackson 1995; Ramos 1994b). Even more ironic is the fact that, at the same time that indigenist rhetoric champions Indian self-determination, this media-oriented reification of exotic body images devalues the choices of people like the Wari' and Awá, who have strategically chosen to downplay their visual exoticism in order to preserve some degree of cultural autonomy.

CONCLUSION

Two contrasting images of native costumes juxtaposed with Western technology have framed this essay, reflecting divergent models of cultural identity. The first—our glimpse of the *Far Side*'s grass-skirted natives hastening to hide their television and VCR—expresses a long-standing view of cultural identity as an impermeable boundary to be maintained. In this modernist aesthetic, the primitive and the civilized must be kept separate, the taboo enforced against mixing bodies, beliefs, or technologies.

The second image—the picture of a Kayapó video cameraman in body paint and feathers—reflects a contemporary rethinking of these categories. This is a vision in which cultural identity is not defined by fidelity to traditions but instead is seen as "mixed, relational, and inventive" (Clifford 1988:10). The video camcorder, postmodern icon par excellence, marks the impetus of globalization, the blurring and shifting of boundaries between peoples and technological systems, and the corresponding transformations of individuals' sense of self and place in the world. In indigenous hands, the camcorder also stands as a sign of the refusal of native peoples to fit into other people's stale categories—of their capacity to define, and insistence on defining, cultural futures on their own terms.

Around the margins of this discussion, perhaps there lurks a third, more easily forgotten image: of Wari' men in their store-bought shirts and polyester pants, not fitting much of anybody's idea (but their own) of what Indians ought to look like.

As different as our readings of these three images are, they share a common theme: the role of exotic appearances as markers of indigenous authenticity. In this article, I have explored why this equation persists, and is even reinforced, in the postcolonial politics of eco-Indian activism. Transnational symbolic politics propel native activists to present themselves and their causes in terms of essentialisms that fit into the narrow imaginative space allowed for Indians in Western popular imaginations. Doing so has served many Indian interests well, as evidenced by the concrete gains of the past decade. Throughout the Americas, indigenous issues are now on the agendas of governments and NGOs to an unprecedented extent, and bureaucrats in offices ranging from the World Bank to remote outposts of Brazil's Indian agency are aware that they will have to answer questions about how their policies affect Indians. The heightened visibility of native causes has influenced environmentalism as well. A decade or so ago, environmentalists mostly talked about the need to preserve flora and fauna; today they are more likely to speak of "sustainable development" that recognizes forest peoples' right to make a living using natural resources. These changes came about largely because native activists and their NGO allies made indigenous identity politics a force to be reckoned with.

Brazilian Indians' experiences, however, also call attention to limitations and tensions that are inherent in symbolic politics. However positive their content, essentialist constructions of Indian identity constitute a "legislation of authenticity" (Thomas 1994:179) that can work against Indian interests, undermining the legitimacy of both native people who promote them and those who do not. People like the Wari', who do not conform to idealized images, tend to be seen by outsiders as not Indian enough, or not the "right" kind of Indians. People like the Kayapó, who capitalize on symbolic identifications with Western values, are perceived as corrupt poseurs when their actions diverge from the messages that outsiders read in their public images. Given the complex economic and political pressures that confront Amazonian Indian communities today, it is inevitable that native peoples' self-determined choices often will diverge from the expectations held by outsiders who locate authenticity in static cultural traditions. As Turner comments,

> One of the most disconcerting things about free-ranging "Others" to some current Western champions of cultural "difference" is how little concerned they tend to be with the "authenticity" of their life-styles, as defined from the base-line of nostalgic . . . notions of "traditional culture." [1992a:12]

The paradox of contemporary indigenous eco-identity politics is that many of its most powerful arguments for indigenous rights rely on invoking just such notions about "traditional culture." Reification of cultural difference is hardly unique to indigenous activism; with the rise of multiculturalism, ethnic politics of all sorts emphasize oppositional representations that reduce intragroup diversity to idealized, homogenized images. In this respect, the essentializing of Indian images may be an inevitable component of any effective symbolic politics.

What distinguishes Amazonian eco-politics from other kinds of identity politics— and what makes symbolic reductionism especially problematic—is the degree to which cultural identity (packaged to appeal to Western aesthetics) constitutes the major source of Brazilian Indians' power to create a broad base of public support. There is an inherent asymmetry at the core of the eco-Indian alliance: the symbolic value of Indian cultural identity is bestowed on terms defined primarily by non-Indians. Transnational symbolic politics accommodate native peoples' definitions of themselves and their goals only to the extent that these self-definitions resonate with Western ideological and symbolic constructs. The irony of this pro-Indian politics is that, by insisting that native Amazonian activists must embody "authenticity," it may force them to act "inauthentically."

***

I would like to thank Deborah Gewertz, Laura Graham, Thomas Gregor, Jean Jackson, Stuart Kirsch, Larry McKee, Donald Pollock, David Price, and William Fisher for helpful comments during the paper's evolution. I am especially grateful to Catherine Howard for her careful reading of the text and generous insights. Fieldwork among the Wari' was supported by the Inter-American Foundation, the Fulbright Commission, and the Wenner-Gren Foundation.

***

Notes

[1] In a critique of essentialisms, it is disconcerting to fall back on the reifying terminology of *Western, non-Western, First World, Fourth World*, and so on. I do so reluctantly, in the absence of convenient alternatives. The reader should keep in mind that these are fuzzy, contextually determined categories.

[2] On the question of how Native American ecological orientations differ from Western environmentalism, see *Cultural Survival Quarterly* 1991, Redford 1990, Simard 1990, and White and Cronon 1988. A growing ethnographic literature addresses the question of whether indigenous peoples' views of nature are consistent with Western environmentalist principles and whether such views contribute to the regulation of ecological processes. See, for example, Ellen 1993, Hames 1987, Sillitoe 1993, and Stocks 1987. López (1994) presents a critique of Redford's (1990) interpretation of the "Ecologically Noble Savage" image.

[3] For reviews of recent literature on native Amazonian environmental knowledge and resource management practices, see Berlin 1992, Clay 1988, Hames and Vickers 1983, Posey and Balée 1989, Redford and Padoch 1992, and Sponsel 1995.

[4] Along with changing views of culture has come a revision in anthropological views of tradition. Where earlier generations held an organic model of "culture" as an entity that endures over time and equated the "invention of tradition" (Hobsbawm and Ranger 1983) with inauthenticity and insincerity, contemporary scholars, following Wagner 1975, have "naturalized the artifice of invention" (Thomas 1992:213). Anthropologists increasingly recognize that "all traditions—Western and indigenous—are invented, in that they are symbolically constructed in the present and reflect contemporary concerns and purposes rather than a passively inherited legacy" (Linnekin 1991:447). From this perspective, the reformulation of ethnic identity is seen not as ersatz repackaging but as a creative, negotiated enterprise.

This academic view, however, is at odds with much discourse in contemporary ethnic politics. A case in point is the controversy that erupted in New Zealand in response to Hanson's 1989 article, which showed that key aspects of Maori oral tradition were authored by Europeans. As Linnekin (1991:447) observes, "[w]hat many anthropologists view as an advance in cultural theory can be read popularly as 'destructive' of native claims to cultural distinctiveness." Warren (1992) presents a provocative example from Guatemala, where Mayan intellectuals responded negatively to her presentation of a cultural constructionist interpretation of ethnicity as fluid and contextual; instead, the Maya asserted that Indian identity should be located in the continuity of cultural traits. Warren notes the irony that "North American anthropology is exploring social constructionist perspectives on ethnicity at the very moment Mayas have rediscovered essentialism. . . . For Mayas—who are, in actuality, creating all sorts of novel ethnicities and levels of identity—essentialism is a powerful rejection of the Ladino definition of Mayas as the negative or weaker other" (1992:209). See Campbell 1996:93 for a penetrating critique of anthropologists' positions in clashes with Mayan intellectuals over constructivist interpretations of identity. On the clash between anthropological representations and ethnic self-representations in identity politics, see Friedman 1992; Jackson 1989, 1995; and Linnekin 1991. Handler (1985) discusses problems in anthropological writings that take "the native's point of view" (and thereby employ the native's reified categories) in nationalist movements that construct ethnicity and culture as bounded objects.

[5] The issues raised here resonate far beyond the Amazon. On parallels in Australian cultural politics and Aboriginal imagery, for example, see Hamilton 1990; Myers 1991, 1994; and Thomas (1994:170–195).

[6] Received notions about primitive art have come in for a great deal of criticism recently. In particular, the equation of authenticity with cultural stasis has been thoroughly discredited in academic art criticism (Errington 1994:202; and see Clifford 1988; Fabian 1983; Price 1989; Torgovnick 1990). My concern here is with the considerable influence this notion retains in Western popular culture.

[7] I am grateful to Catherine Howard for this account, which Payakan presented in a speech in Toronto, Canada, in December 1988, for which Howard translated.

[8] Keesing 1994 suggests that reification and essentialism are inherent in anthropological conceptions of culture and anthropologists' vested interests in emphasizing the exotic otherness of those they study. Founded on an emphasis on cultural differences, anthropology is pervaded by hierarchies of exoticism and cultural purity; the discipline has long accorded greater prestige to those who study remote, "purer" cultures (Herzfeld 1987; and see Carrier 1992, Jackson 1995:19). Keesing argues that this tendency persists even among postmodernist American cultural anthropologists with roots in the interpretive/cultural constructionist tradition, despite their avowed concern with transcending old preoccupations with authenticity and closed boundaries. "Critically examin-

ing the takens-for-granted of Western thought, post-structuralism has undermined the old dualisms—civilized vs. primitive, rational vs. irrational, Occident vs. Orient. . . .Yet at the same time, poststructuralist thought, too, urgently needs radical alterity, to show that our takens-for-granted represent European cultural constructions" (Keesing 1994:302).

[9] On Wari' (Pakaa Nova) society and interethnic relations, see Conklin 1989, 1995; Mason 1977; Meireles 1986; Vilaça 1992; and Von Graeve 1989.

[10] This discussion focuses on male costume because few Brazilian Indian women have been prominent in national and transnational activism. One exception was Tui'ra, a Kayapó woman who became famous at the Altamira protest when she brandished a machete in the face of the utility company spokesman. Tui'ra later traveled to the United States on a speaking tour. It is worth considering whether Western preferences for certain native body images favor male activists, who can display their bodies in ways that women cannot.

[11] Visual exoticism evokes romantic images of Indians that have a long-standing place in Brazilian intellectual history. Generations of writers and artists have looked to the nation's Indian roots in attempts to construct a distinct nationalist identity "with a unique, non-European flavor" (Ramos 1994b:78). A central idea is the image of the Indian as "natural man"—courageous, sensual, and free from repressive societal conventions: distanced from the status quo, yet quintessentially Brazilian (Pereira 1990).

[12] Ramos (1994b) notes that, under the dictatorship, "a common procedure [for non-Indian opponents of the government] . . . was to use the Indian issue as a channel to air criticisms against the military regime. . . . The 'Indian' theme was then one of the very few political issues one dared raise without being caught by censorship." On the changing politics surrounding "the Indian question" in Brazil, see Maybury-Lewis 1991.

[13] On indigenous cinematography and issues of how film and video interact with indigenous self-reflection and self-representation, see Arhem 1993; Carelli 1989; Elsass 1991 ; Ginsburg 1991, 1993; and Turner 1992a.

[14] The potential of "informational empowerment" (Annis 1992) for geographically and politically marginalized groups was dramatized in January 1994, when Zapatista guerrillas in the rainforest of Chiapas, Mexico, sent their communiqués and war dispatches directly to a global public via e-mail and the Internet. The Internet, suggests Halleck (1994:32), is a powerful tool for generating solidarity:

> The Chiapas computer conferences [with Zapatista guerrillas online] . . . have allowed many people to feel closer to a revolutionary process. . . . Perhaps the most effective outcome of Chiapas online has been the boosting of psychological morale of Latin American activists, anti-GATT cadre and human rights workers worldwide. . . . There was a sense of direct connection, of an authentic "interactive" movement, as groups and individuals forwarded messages, excerpted passages, pinned up tear sheets and posted their own comments online.

[15] Opposition to ecologically destructive development schemes also offered a rallying point for cooperation among Indians groups who formerly had little common ground. Pan-Indian organizations proliferated in Brazil in the 1980s and found a stronger voice and broader political support by appealing to environmental concerns (Brysk 1996); and see Rich 1994.

[16] On the history of linkages between environmental NGOs and native rights organizations in Brazil, see Arnt and Schwartzman 1992; Brysk 1994, 1996; Schwartzman 1991; and Van Cott 1994.

[17] Transnational NGOs have been especially well-positioned to influence Brazilian policy during the past decade because the nation's huge debt to multinational lending agencies made the government and national business elites sensitive to foreign criticism (Fisher 1994:220; Viveiros de Castro 1992:14).

[18] Ramos, an anthropologist who works with the Yanomami, takes a more critical view. She suggests that in Brazil, some indigenist advocacy organizations have a hard time dealing with flesh-and-blood Indians whose goals and behavior do not match the idealized images on which NGO support for Indians is premised. Following Baudrillard's notion of the simulacrum, in which "signs of the real [substitute] for the real itself" (Baudrillard 1983:4), Ramos argues that NGO bureaucracies tend to create "a simulacrum of the Indian: dependent, suffering, a victim of the system, innocent of bourgeois evils, honourable in his actions and intentions, and preferably exotic. . . . That," she caustically remarks, "is why the Yanomami are so popular among NGOs" (Ramos 1994b: 163).

[19] CEDI 1991 is an excellent source of photographs of Brazilian Indian representatives in a variety of domestic and foreign contexts,

[20] The emphasis on Indians as outsiders to Western civilization reflects the oppositional stance adopted by many indigenous rights movements in Latin America. Hale 1994 observes that in contrast to leftist attempts to subvert the dominant system from within, *indígena* resistance "attacks

Mestizo society from the outside; rather than attempting to shift the balance of power by subverting particular symbols from within, they reject the Mestizo culture wholesale." *Indígena* identity politics emphasize "radical difference: their spiritual grounding, their disdain of the materialism and quest for political power inherent in Western culture, their adherence to a distinct world view, all of which imbues *indígena* identity with a content of radical political opposition" (Hale 1994:28).

[21] Ramos (1994a) traces historical transformations of the edenic discourse of Brazilian Indians as inhabitants of Paradise on Earth from the sixteenth century to contemporary environmentalism.

[22] Accusations of hypocrisy, of "posing" for foreigners, resonate with the Brazilian concept of *para inglês ver*, "for English to see"—an ironic reference to historical tendencies for Brazilian elites selectively to present images that satisfy foreigners (see Fry 1982). A classic example of *para inglês ver* occurred during the 1992 Earth Summit, when the government cleaned up Rio de Janeiro in anticipation of the international visitors' arrival. In a city where millions of people lack the most basic housing and sanitation, huge amounts of money were poured into constructing nature walks and jogging trails, refurbishing parks, and financing police sweeps that removed street children and beggars from the vicinity of the conference.

[23] The Kayapó are unusual in terms of the amount of income that they have earned from timber and gold mining concessions. They are, however, far from unique in being willing to consider proposals to exploit forest resources for short-term profits at the expense of long-term productivity. (See Colchester 1989 on the difficulties that Amazonian Indians face in finding ways to participate in the cash economy.) In Brazil, Indian leaders have consistently defined self-determination to include control over their lands' natural resources and the right to use them as they see fit. In several cases in which native communities have asserted control over commercially valuable resources, they have chosen environmentally destructive options, such as clear-cutting or intensive logging (see Redford 1990, Turner 1993). Recently, however, some Kayapó leaders and factions have rebelled against the large-scale commercialization of tribal resources and are promoting environmentally sustainable alternatives (see Turner 1995).

[24] Feest (1990) examines Europeans' long history of lionizing American Indian visitors, which has spawned numerous instances of non-Indians passing themselves off as Indians by dressing the part. He observes, "Some of these fake visitors look like they came straight out of the ever-popular Indian novels . . . those whose appearance closely matched the imagery stood and stand a better chance of being taken for real" (Feest 1990:322–23).

References

Annis, Sheldon. 1991. Giving Voice to the Poor. Foreign Policy 84:93–106.

———. 1992. Evolving Connectedness among Environmental Groups and Grassroots Organizations in Protected Areas of Central America. World Development 20:587–595.

Appadurai, Arjun. 1990. Disjuncture and Difference in the Global Cultural Economy. Public Culture 2(2):1–24.

Arhem, Kaj. 1993. *Millennium* among the Makuna. Anthropology Today 9(3):3–8.

Arnt, Ricardo Azambuja, and Stephan Schwartzman. 1992. Um Artifício Orgânico: Transição na Amazônia e Ambientalismo (1985–1990). (An organic artifice: Transition in Amazônia and environmentalism [1985–1990].) Rio de Janeiro: Rocco.

Asad, Talal. 1991. From the History of Colonial Anthropology to the Anthropology of Western Hegemony. *In* Colonial Situations. George Stocking, ed. Pp. 314–324. Madison: University of Wisconsin Press.

Barth, Fredrik. 1969. Introduction. *In* Ethnic Groups and Boundaries. Fredrik Barth (ed.). Pp. 9–38. Boston: Little, Brown.

Baudrillard, Jean. 1983. Simulations. New York: Semiotext(e).

Berkhofer, Robert E., Jr. 1978. The White Man's Indian. New York: Random House.

———. 1988. White Conceptions of Indians. Handbook of North American Indians, 4: History of Indian-White Relations. Wilcomb E. Washington, ed. Washington, DC: Smithsonian Institution Press.

Berlin, Brent. 1992. Ethnobiological Classification. Princeton, NJ: Princeton University Press.

Black, Jan Knippers. 1992. Brazil's Limited Redemocratization. Current History (February): 85–89.

Bourdieu, Pierre. 1977. Outline of a Theory of Practice. Richard Nice, trans. Cambridge: Cambridge University Press.

———. 1984. Distinction: A Social Critique of Judgement and Taste. Richard Nice, trans. Cambridge, MA: Harvard University Press.

Brown, Michael F. 1993. Facing the State, Facing the World: Amazonia's Native Leaders and the New Politics of Identity. L'Homme 33(2–4):307–326.

Brysk, Alison. 1994. Acting Globally. *In* Indigenous Peoples and Democracy in Latin America. Donna Lee Van Cott, ed. Pp. 29–51. New York: St. Martin's Press.

———. 1996. Turning Weakness into Strength: The Internationalization of Indian Rights. Latin American Perspectives 23, No. 2 (89):38–57.

Campbell, Howard. 1996. Isthmus Zapotec Intellectuals: Cultural Production and Politics in Juchitán, Oaxaca. *In* The Politics of Ethnicity in Southern Mexico. Howard Campbell, ed. Pp. 77–98. Nashville: Vanderbilt University Publications in Anthropology.

Carelli, Vincent. 1989. Video in the Villages: Utilization of Video Tapes as an Instrument of Ethnic Affirmation among Brazilian Indian Groups. CVA Review, Fall.

Carrier, James G. 1992. Occidentalism: The World Turned Upside Down. American Ethnologist 19:195–212.

CEDI (Centro Ecumênico de Documentação e Informação) [Ecumenical Documentation and Information Center]. 1984. Povos Indígenas no Brasil/1984. (Indigenous peoples in Brazil/1984.) Aconteceu Especial 15. São Paulo.

———. 1991. Povos Indígenas no Brasil: 1987, 1988, 1989, 1990. (Indigenous peoples in Brazil: 1987, 1988, 1989, 1990.) Aconteceu Especial 18. São Paulo.

Clay, Jason W. 1988. Indigenous Peoples and Tropical Forests. Cambridge, MA: Cultural Survival.

Clifford, James. 1988. The Predicament of Culture: Twentieth-Century Ethnography, Literature, and Art. Cambridge, MA: Harvard University Press.

Clifford, James, and George E. Marcus (eds.). 1986. Writing Culture: The Poetics and Politics of Ethnography. Berkeley: University of California Press.

Colchester, Marcus. 1989. Indian Development in Amazonia: Risks and Strategies. The Ecologist 19(6):249–254.

Conklin, Beth A. 1989. Images of Health, Illness and Death among the Wari' (Pakaas Novos) of Rondônia, Brazil. Ph.D. dissertation, University of California, San Francisco and Berkeley.

———. 1995. "Thus Are Our Bodies, Thus Was Our Custom": Mortuary Cannibalism in an Amazonian Society. American Ethnologist 22:75–101.

Conklin, Beth A., and Laura Graham. 1995. The Shifting Middle Ground: Amazonian Indians and Eco-Politics. American Anthropologist 97:695–710.

Cultural Survival Quarterly. 1991. Just What Is Conservation? Cultural Survival Quarterly 15:20–29.

Cummings, Barbara J. 1990. Dam the Rivers, Damn the People: Development and Resistance in Amazonian Brazil. London: Earthscan Publications.

Dening, Greg. 1993. The Theatricality of History Making and the Paradoxes of Acting. Cultural Anthropology 8:73–95.

Dominguez, Virginia R. 1986. The Marketing of Heritage. American Ethnologist 13:546–555.

Economist. 1993. The Savage Can Also Be Ignoble. The Economist 327(7815):54.

Ehrenreich, Jeffrey David. In press. The Awá Body Transformed: Identity, Dissembling, and Resistance among an Indigenous People of the "True" Rainforest. *In* Native South Americans. 2nd ed. Patricia Lyon, ed. Prospects Heights, IL: Waveland Press.

Ellen, Roy. 1993. Rhetoric, Practice and Incentive in the Face of the Changing Times: A Case Study in Nuaulu Attitudes to Conservation and Deforestation. *In* Environmentalism: The View from Anthropology. Kay Milton, ed. Pp. 126–143. New York: Routledge.

Elsass, Peter. 1991. Self-Reflection or Self-Presentation: A Study of the Advocacy Effect. Visual Anthropology 4:161–173.

Errington, Shelly. 1994. What Became Authentic Primitive Art? Cultural Anthropology 9:201–226.

Fabian, Johannes. 1983. Time and the Other: How Anthropology Makes Its Object. New York: Columbia University Press.

Feest, Christian F. 1990. Europe's Indians. *In* The Invented Indian: Cultural Fictions and Government Policies. James A. Clifton, ed. Pp. 313–332. New Brunswick, NJ: Transaction.

Fisher, William H. 1994. Megadevelopment, Environmentalism, and Resistance: The Institutional Context of Kayapó Indigenous Politics in Central Brazil. Human Organization 53:220–232.

Friedman, Jonathan. 1992. The Past in the Future: History and the Politics of Identity. American Anthropologist 94:837–859.

Fry, Peter. 1982. Para Inglês Ver: Identidade e Política na Cultura Brasileira. (For English to see: Identity and politics in Brazilian culture.) Rio de Janeiro: Zahar Editores.

Fry, Tony, and Anne-Marie Willis. 1989. Aboriginal Art: Symptom or Success? Art in America, July:109–116, 159–160, 163.

Ginsburg, Faye. 1991. Indigenous Media: Faustian Contract or Global Village? Cultural Anthropology 6:92–112.

———. 1993. Aboriginal Media and the Australian Imaginary. Public Culture 5:557–578.

Gomes, Laurentino, and Paulo Silber. 1992. A Explosão do Instinto Selvagem. (The explosion of the savage instinct.) Veja (São Paulo, Brazil) 25(24):68–84, June 10.

Graham, Laura R. 1995. Performing Dreams: Discourses of Immortality among the Xavante of Central Brazil. Austin: University of Texas Press.

Gregor, Thomas. 1977. Mehinaku: The Drama of Daily Life in a Brazilian Indian Village. Chicago: University of Chicago Press.

Hale, Charles R. 1994. Between Che Guevara and the Pachamama: Mestizos, Indians and Identity Politics in the Anti-Quincentenary Campaign. Critique of Anthropology 14:9–39.

Halleck, Deedee. 1994. Zapatistas On-Line. NACLA Report on the Americas 28(2):30–32.

Hames, Raymond. 1987. Game Conservation or Efficient Hunting? In The Question of the Commons: The Culture and Ecology of Communal Resources. Bonnie J. McCay and James M. Acheson, eds. Pp. 92–107. Tucson: University of Arizona Press.

Hames, Raymond, and William Vickers (eds.). 1983. Adaptive Responses of Native Amazonians. New York: Academic Press.

Hamilton, Annette. 1990. Fear and Desire: Aborigines, Asians, and the National Imaginary. Australian Cultural History 9:14–35.

Handler, Richard. 1985. On Dialogue and Destructive Analysis: Problems in Narrating Nationalism and Ethnicity. Journal of Anthropological Research 41:171–182.

Handler, Richard, and Jocelyn Linnekin. 1984. Tradition, Genuine or Spurious. Journal of American Folklore 97(385):273–290.

Hanson, Allan. 1989. The Making of the Maori: Culture Invention and Its Logic. American Anthropologist 91:890–902.

Hecht, Susanna, and Alexander Cockburn. 1989. The Fate of the Forest: Developers, Destroyers and Defenders of the Amazon. New York: Verso.

Hemming, John. 1978. Red Gold: The Conquest of the Brazilian Indians, 1500–1760. Cambridge, MA: Harvard University Press.

Herzfeld, Michael. 1987. Anthropology through the Looking-Glass: Critical Ethnography in the Margins of Europe. Cambridge: Cambridge University Press.

Hess, David. 1995. Science and Technology in a Multicultural World: The Cultural Politics of Facts and Artifacts. New York: Columbia University Press.

Hobsbawm, Eric, and Terence Ranger (eds.). 1983. The Invention of Tradition. Cambridge: Cambridge University Press.

Hohlfeldt, Antônio and Assis Hoffmann. 1982. O Gravador do Juruna. (Juruna's tape-recorder.) Porto Alegre, Brazil: Mercado Aberto.

Howard, Catherine. n.d. Conservation and Conversion: Religion in the Rainforest. Department of Anthropology, University of Chicago, unpublished manuscript.

Ireland, Emilienne. 1991. Neither Warriors Nor Victims, The Wauja Peacefully Organize to Defend Their Land. Cultural Survival Quarterly 15:54–60.

Jackson, Jean. 1989. Is There a Way to Talk about Making Culture without Making Enemies? Dialectical Anthropology 14:127–143.

———. 1991. Being and Becoming an Indian in the Vaupés. In Nation States and Indians in Latin America. Greg Urban and Joel Sherzer, eds. Pp. 131–135. Austin: University of Texas Press.

———. 1995. Culture, Genuine and Spurious: The Politics of Indianness in the Vaupés, Colombia. American Ethnologist 22:3–27.

Keesing, Roger M. 1994. Theories of Culture Revisited. In Assessing Cultural Anthropology. Robert Borofsky, ed. Pp. 301–312. New York: McGraw-Hill.

Knauft, Bruce. 1994. Pushing Anthropology Past the Posts: Critique of Anthropology 14:117–152.

Larson, Gary. 1984. Far Side Cartoon. July 10. San Francisco: Chronicle Features.

Linnekin, Jocelyn. 1991. Cultural Invention and the Dilemma of Authenticity. American Anthropologist 93:446–448.

López, Kevin Lee. 1994. Returning to the Fields. Cultural Survival Quarterly 18:29–32.

Lutz, Catherine A., and Jane L. Collins. 1993. Reading National Geographic. Chicago: University of Chicago Press.

MacCannell, Dean. 1976. The Tourist: A New View of the Leisure Class. New York: Schocken Books.

Mason, Alan. 1977. Oronao Social Structure. Ph.D. dissertation, University of California, Davis.

Maybury-Lewis, David. 1991. Becoming Indian in Lowland South America. *In* Nation States and Indians in Latin America. Greg Urban and Joel Sherzer, eds. Pp. 207–235. Austin: University of Texas Press.

McCallum, Cecilia. 1995. The Veja Payakan: The Media, Modernism, and the Image of the Indian in Brazil. CVA Newsletter 2/94:2–8.

Meireles, Denise Maldi. 1986. O's Pakaas-Novos. M.A. dissertation, Universidade de Brasília.

Myers, Fred. 1991. Representing Culture: The Production of Discourse(s) on Aboriginal Acrylic Paintings. Cultural Anthropology 5:26–62.

————. 1994. Culture-Making: Performing Aboriginality at the Asia Society Gallery. American Ethnologist 21:679–699.

Nelson, Diane M. 1994. Rigoberta Menchu Jokes: Fashioning Identity on the Outskirts. Anthropology Today 10(6):3–6.

Neves, Zanoni. 1994. Os índios na mídia. (Indians in the media.) Boletim da Associação de Antropologia (Brazil) 22:16.

People Weekly. 1988. On a Three-Day Tour Break, Sting Goes Native—Very Native—To Meet a Chief Amazon Indian. People Weekly 29 (March 28):115–117.

Pereira, Renato. 1989. Poder Kayapó. (Kayapó power.) Ciência Hoje 9:78–79.

————. 1990. Como os Indios se Travestam de Indios Para . . . (How Indians Dress Up Like Indians for . . .). Paper presented at International Conference on Nature and Communications, Milan, February 15–16.

Polhemus, Ted. 1988. Body Styles. Luton, UK: Lennard Books.

Posey, Darrell, and William Balée (eds.). 1989. Resource Management in Amazonia: Indigenous and Folk Strategies. New York: New York Botanical Garden.

Potiguara, Eliane. 1992. Harvesting What We Plant. Cultural Survival Quarterly 16:46–48.

Price, David. 1989. Before the Bulldozer: The Nambiquara Indians and the World Bank. Washington, DC: Seven Locks Press.

Price, Sally. 1989. Primitive Art in Civilized Places. Chicago: University of Chicago Press.

Ramos, Alcida Rita. 1988. Indian Voices: Contact Experienced and Expressed. *In* Rethinking History and Myth: Indigenous South American Perspectives on the Past. Jonathan D. Hill, ed. Pp. 214–234. Urbana: University of Illinois Press.

————. 1994a. From Eden to Limbo: The Construction of Indigenism in Brazil. *In* Social Construction of the Past: Representation as Power. George Clement Bond and Angela Gilliam, eds. Pp. 74–88. New York: Routledge.

————. 1994b. The Hyperreal Indian. Critique of Anthropology 14:153–171.

Redford, Kent H.

————. 1990. The Ecologically Noble Savage. Orion Nature Quarterly 9(3):25–29.

Redford, Kent H., and Christine Padoch, eds.

————. 1992. Conservation of Neotropical Forests: Working from Traditional Resource Use. New York: Columbia University Press.

Rich, Bruce. 1994. Mortgaging the Earth: The World Bank, Environmental Impoverishment, and the Crisis of Development. Boston: Beacon Press.

Said, Edward. 1978. Orientalism. New York: Pantheon.

Schwartzman, Stephan. 1991. Deforestation and Popular Resistance in Acre: From Local Social Movement to Global Network. The Centennial Review (Spring):397–422.

Sillitoe, Paul. 1993. Local Awareness of the Soil Environment in the Papua New Guinea Highlands. *In* Environmentalism: The View From Anthropology. Kay Milton, ed. Pp. 160–173. New York: Routledge.

Simard, Jean-Jacques. 1990. White Ghosts, Red Shadows: The Reduction of North-American Natives. *In* The Invented Indian: Cultural Fictions and Government Policies. James A. Clifton, ed. Pp. 333–369. New Brunswick, NJ: Transaction.

Smith, Geri. 1989. Space Age Shamans: The Videotape. Americas 41(2):28–31.

Sponsel, Leslie E. (ed.). 1995. Indigenous Peoples and the Future of Amazonia. Tucscon: University of Arizona Press.

Spitulnik, Debra. 1993. Anthropology and Mass Media. Annual Review of Anthropology 22:293–315.

Stocks, Anthony. 1987. Resource Management in an Amazon Varzea Lake Ecosystem: The Cocamilla Case. *In* The Question of the Commons: The Culture and Ecology of Communal Resources. Bonnie J. McCay and James M. Acheson, eds. Pp. 108–120. Tucson: University of Arizona Press.

Thomas, Nicolas. 1992. The Inversion of Tradition. American Ethnologist 19:213–232.

————. 1994. Colonialism's Culture: Anthropology, Travel and Government. Cambridge: Polity Press.

Torgovnick, Marianna. 1990. Gone Primitive: Savage Intellects, Modern Lives. Chicago: University of Chicago Press.

Turner, Terence S. 1980. The Social Skin. *In* Not Work Alone. Jeremy Cherfas and Roger Lewin, eds. Pp. 113–140. Beverly Hills, CA: Sage Publications.

——. 1992a. Defiant Images: The Kayapó Appropriation of Video. Anthropology Today 8(6):5–16.

——. 1992b. Representing, Resisting, Rethinking: Historical Transformations of Kayapó and Anthropological Consciousness. *In* Colonial Situations. George Stocking, ed. Pp. 285–313. Madison, WI: University of Wisconsin Press.

——. 1992c. Symbolic Language of Bodily Adornment. *In* Kaiapó Amazonia: The Art of Body Decoration. Gustaf Verswijver, ed. Pp. 27–35. Royal Museum for Central Africa (Tervuren, Belgium). Ghent, Belgium: Snoeck-Ducaju and Zoon.

——. 1993. The Role of Indigenous Peoples in the Environmental Crisis: The Example of the Kayapó of the Brazilian Amazon. Perspectives in Biology and Medicine 36:526–545.

——. 1995. An Indigenous People's Struggle for Socially Equitable and Ecologically Sustainable Production: The Kayapó Revolt against Extractivism. Journal of Latin American Anthropology 1:98–121.

Urban, Greg, and Joel Sherzer (eds.). 1991. Nation States and Indians in Latin America. Austin: University of Texas Press.

Van Cott, Donna Lee (ed.). 1994. Indigenous Peoples and Democracy in Latin America. New York: St. Martin's Press.

Veber, Hanne. 1992. Why Indians Wear Clothes . . . : Managing Identity across Ethnic Boundaries. Ethnos 57(1–2):51–60.

——. 1996. External Inducement and Non-Westernization in the Uses of the Ashéninka Cushma. Journal of Material Culture 1:155–182.

Veja. 1993. O fim do romantismo. (The End of Romanticism.) Veja, April 28:74–75.

Viana, Francisco. 1992. Indio gente fina: Os caciques brasileiros que enriqueceram explorando como bons capitalistas as riquezas de suas reservas. (High-class Indians: Brazilian chiefs who got rich exploiting the riches of their reserves like good capitalists.) IstoÉ, July 1:38–41.

Vidal, Lux, and Gustaf Verswijver. 1992. Body Painting among the Kayapó. *In* Kaiapó Amazonia: The Art of Body Decoration. Gustaf Verswijver, ed. Pp. 37–47. Royal Museum for Central Africa (Tervuren, Belgium). Ghent, Belgium: Snoeck-Ducaju and Zoon.

Vilaça, Aparecida. 1992. Comendo Como Gente: Formas do Canibalismo Wari'. (Eating like people: Forms of Wari' cannibalism.) Rio de Janeiro: Editora Universidade Federal do Rio de Janeiro (UFRJ).

Viveiros de Castro, Eduardo. 1992. Prefácio. (Preface.) *In* Um Artifício Orgânico: Transição na Amazônia e Ambientalismo (1985–1990). (An organic artifice: Transition in Amazônia and environmentalism [1985–1990].) Ricardo Azambuja Arnt and Stephan Schwartzman, eds. Pp. 13–23. Rio de Janeiro: Rocco.

Von Graeve, Bernard. 1989. The Pacaa Nova: Clash of Cultures on the Brazilian Frontier. Peterborough, Canada: Broadview Press.

Wagner, Roy. 1975. The Invention of Culture. Englewood Cliffs, NJ: Prentice-Hall.

Warren, Kay B. 1992. Transforming Memories and Histories: The Meanings of Ethnic Resurgence for Mayan Indians. *In* Americas: New Interpretive Essays. Alfred Stepan, ed. Pp. 189–219. New York: Oxford University Press.

White, Richard, and Willian Cronon. 1988. Ecological Change and Indian-White Relations. *In* Handbook of North American Indians, 4: History of Indian-White Relations. Wilcomb E. Washington, ed. Pp. 417–429. Washington, DC: Smithsonian Institution.

Whittemore, Hank. 1992. A Man Who Would Save the World. Parade, April 12:4–7.

Wolf, Eric R.. 1982. Europe and the People without History. Berkeley: University of California Press.

Wright, Robin. 1988. Anthropological Presuppositions of Indigenous Advocacy. Annual Review of Anthropology 17:365–390.

Zimmer, Carl. 1990. Tech in the Jungle. Discover, August 1990:42–45.

PART V

Relations of Power

In any society or segment of society, relations of power play important roles in shaping how people act in relation to each other. Power is not a vague abstraction as it refers to social relationships, nor is it measured in terms of tanks, ballistic missiles, or firepower. In simplest terms, it is the ability to limit or make the choices of another, and, whether phrased in hierarchical terms or not, such an ability is unevenly distributed among every population. It is a relevant variable, whether one is considering one-on-one relations or the balance or imbalance between masses of people, machines, or organizations. As such, power has to do with access to all of what sociologists refer to as life-chances, the goods (both tangible and intangible) that can make the difference between satisfaction and frustration in the life of any individual or group of people.

DEFENDING ONESELF

The interpersonal networks of social relationships that each individual develops are unique, though overlapping and intertwined. In some populations, ties of kinship have large and lasting importance, whether reckoned along lines of descent (lineal) or extended outward by marriage (collateral). It is also common in Latin America that similar bonds, implying reciprocal rights and responsibilities that last throughout one's lifetime, can be founded on what some anthropologists call fictive kin ties, *compadrazgo* or ritual co-parenthood. In various contexts, ranging from birth to baptism, first haircut to first menstruation, marriage to house building, a *compadre* (or feminine *comadre*) is honored to be selected, provides gifts, and continues to have a special quasi-kin relationship with the principal.

Individuals strive to defend themselves and those who are dear to them before they strive to dominate others. In fact, the underdog can often be seen to be subtly guiding the choices of another who ostensibly has power over him or her. Negotiating a dyadic contract (Foster, chapter 31) can be a clever, often implicit way in which a seemingly powerless individual influences someone else with the vague offer to defer (thereby granting power to the other) in the long run. When the dyadic contract is extended to the supernatural realm, the cult of the saints as a long-maligned aspect of folk-Catholicism is revealed to be quite logical and practical rather than the ignorant worship of idols, as it had long been characterized by outsiders.

The idea of patronage and clientage so aptly introduced by Foster (chapter 31) is one of those that lends itself to use as a template for better understanding a broad range of relationships in cultures far removed from Latin America. Such linkages between human and supernatural beings are neatly illustrated by Canin (chapter 41) and by Greenfield (chapter 44); those between human beings are revealed especially in Doughty (chapter 22) and Buechler (chapter 18).

The relationships of patronage and clientage should not be construed as peculiar to Latin or peasant communities. Many students find it a revealing exercise to think in those terms, perhaps preferring the term "reciprocity," on the local level—about the school they are attending, an academic department or fraternity, or the dorm in which they live; state and national government decisions often make more sense in terms of patronage and clientage at other levels.

MANAGING NUMBERS

Even within the relatively egalitarian context of a single household and nuclear family, power differentials between individuals can be important in certain realms of activity. Children are often obliged to do things when they'd rather not; females often feel subordinated to males in many respects; and the young often defer to their elders. (Interestingly, the vast panoply of cross-cultural variation is such that some exception can be found to almost any such generalization—the infamous "ethnographic veto" that has made the quest for human universals such a slippery venture.) Power is even more irregularly distributed beyond the household, which can be both an integrative factor that allows groups to operate more effectively and a source of friction and dissatisfaction that interferes with smooth interaction. Part of that difference lies in ideas about the justification of such differences in power, and also in ideas about the relevance of its application in a given situation. Authority is often mentioned as appropriate or generally accepted power, without which restriction of choice is viewed as wrong. The justification for one individual's having power over another may have wholly different grounds—formal schooling, certification, initiation and apprenticeship, possession by a spirit, or other signs can be construed as culturally appropriate reasons.

Throughout much of Latin America, the dominant stereotype held by outsiders, that of a dual society, appeared to have considerable basis in reality with wealth, prestige, and power concentrated in the hands of a few and the great majority of the population presumed to be "living lives of quiet desperation," devoted to little more than hard work and subservience. To those who lived in such a system, however, that dreary picture was grossly distorted in that it ignored the frequent joys of living simply in a supportive family, sharing with kin and neighbors, and occasionally basking in some celebration that breaks the routine and gives special recognition to someone within the local community.

The term *caste* was once freely used by social scientists as well as laypeople in describing nations and communities in which self-styled "whites" generally dominated and derided "Indians" or blacks, with intermarriage discouraged and access (to education, good jobs, and other things) sharply limited along the lines of social categories that were often erroneously characterized in terms of biological race. The reality of social mobility and the growing influence of other groups (mestizo, ladino, or criollo, depending on the region), usually referred to as intermediate but treated more as a residual category, have discredited that uncritical use of the Asiatic caste model.

In fact, some degree of social differentiation was found within every group, and differences in wealth and power—no matter how small in absolute terms—often were important at the local level. Beyond that, fine-grained descriptions of workaday life that ethnographers added to the toolkit of social science revealed that "passing" from one category to another was not only possible but commonplace. The social system was neither so dual nor so ossified as was generally assumed. The great sociological theorist Max Weber made a lasting impact by spelling out how bureaucracy became established as one of the most efficient and effective modes of administration on a large scale. He cited the imperatives of ignoring relationships and treating all comers as impersonally interchangeable, following clear and explicit rules within an explicitly delineated table of organization, with regularized channels of communication, and so forth. A feature of Latin American government (and other institutions) that long attracted invidious comparisons with institutions in other parts of the world was that ostensibly bureaucratic organizations did not really function according to the rules as Weber had decoded them.

Elaborate tables of organization could easily be bypassed by anyone who had personal relations that gave quick or easy access to individuals at a higher level; rules could easily be bent at the discretion of a bureaucrat to favor (or to punish) anyone they chose. Bribes, anathema to Weber's ideal type of bureaucracy, might well be expected by a real Latin bureaucrat as the fee or honorarium appropriate for whatever service was requested or offered. All of this may sound anarchic or chaotic but it need not be, as Aron-Schaar (chapter 32) illustrates in some detail.

Although some gross abuses can be committed in the name of a government, the people do not always accept them all with quiet resignation. Few groups in a totalitarian context might seem more powerless than the mothers of young people who have been killed or "disappeared" by the authorities (Feijoo and Gogna, chapter 34) or homemakers protesting that economic dislocations make it difficult for them to put food on the table (Boyle, chapter 33), yet both of these voices were unexpectedly heard around the world.

One might also presume that high-ranking military officers in a repressive regime would be callous and arrogant in their positions of nearly absolute power. Some people did (and still do) in fact act that way, and some can be disarmingly meek and mild once they have lost such power. In dealing with such shifting circumstances, Robben (chapter 35) gives us a sensitive portrait of an alleged abuser of power and of his own moral and ethical misgivings in maintaining the close and sustained relationship that is required for ethnographic research on such a subject.

Although most would hesitate to characterize themselves as powerful, or as tools of power, Arcand (chapter 36) shows that at least some missionaries in Latin America are both. The title of his article should also prompt some thought about the meanings and implications of power in international relations.

SOCIAL CATEGORIES

The culture of poverty (see Lewis, chapter 37) is one of the ideas originally set forth by an anthropologist that has gained currency, rightly or wrongly, with people in many other fields of study and with laypersons as well. Its brief but important role in discussions of public policy sometimes turned anthropology's vaunted cultural relativism back on its believers; politicians eager to cut back on welfare asked, "If that's their culture, we shouldn't intervene to make them better off, now, should we?" The article is included in this section of readings not because it reflects what the editor considers the best of current anthropological thinking, but because of its historical importance and because it serves as an excellent springboard for critical evaluation and discussion on the part of interested students.

It would be a mistake to concentrate only on power as it is embodied in formal institutions, however. What is spoken of as social stratification usually has a strong, if implicit, connotation of power differentials. Age grading is a simple example; differences in schooling, occupation, or income are not, as they are labeled by survey researchers, "basic demographic variables" but rather links to a system of classification that has more to do with power than with much of anything else.

Much of the sociological literature in the mid-1900s dealt with either elites or "the masses." Political scientists often wrote about the church and the military as powerful institutions that loomed large, in different ways and at different times, in the governance of almost every country in Latin America. While Uruguay was being quietly praised for having developed its own style of beneficent socialism, other countries were caricatured as irresponsible "banana republics" (dependent on a single crop and governed by a small clique of greedy and irresponsible cousins who took turns at wearing the presidential sash). The earlier Mexican revolution had been interpreted as an aberration until Bolivia and Cuba, in fairly quick succession, showed that real social revolution was a possibility.

Within living memory there have been situations in which tribal Indians were hunted for sport, a union leader gunned down at home in front of his family, or peasants and tenant farmers treated as virtual serfs by landlords who acted as lords of the manor, above the law and dominant over all who served them. Similarly, mayors, sheriffs, and state governors, appointed rather than elected, could exploit the people and resources of their jurisdictions with virtual impunity in many areas. Even at the national level, coups and caudillos were more common in Latin America than in other parts of the world, sometimes imposing reigns of terror in which real or imagined opponents were tortured, killed, or "disappeared" in numbers that shocked the world. The latter half of the twentieth century saw widespread erosion of those kinds of raw power, combined with an upswelling of popular movements that gave to "the masses" new measures of self-determination. For peasants, this often came in the shape of agrarian reform, not simply reallocating land but simultaneously breaking the back of the old oligarchic order. For indigenous peoples, this often started with local protests against abuses of human rights and progressed with the establishment and spread of native organizations (see Stavenhagen, chapter 13) and is culminating with hemispheric organizations of self-designated "First Nations" as well as the revision of national constitutions to recognize their multiethnic and pluricultural citizenry, frequently incorporating non-Western languages in education and law, setting aside various kinds of reserves (see Stearman, chapter 20), and approaching the egalitarian ideal that has been so broadly diffused on the global scene during that same period.

The situation of the urban poor sharply contrasts with that of the aristocracy (see Nutini, chapter 38). Although they are not necessarily wealthy, their participation in relations of power is dramatically different across almost the entire range of encounters, as has rarely been described in detail by a social scientist. Even so, as the culture in which they live has changed, so have their situation and the prerogatives that used to be associated with it, requiring adaptations and adjustments unthinkable in earlier generations.

In talking about power and its impact on behavior, it has long been insufficient to deal with nothing larger than the nation-state, as far removed as that may be from some isolated rural communities. In the modern world-system, foreign companies or conglomerates are often powerful in many nations, extracting precious minerals and leaving pollutants in one area, practicing monocrop large-scale agriculture in another, thereby depriving local people of their traditional homes and livelihood and making them dependent on a market with which they are unfamiliar. At the level of a single vendor in a local market, mass-produced flavors and textures combined with TV advertising may render redundant the industriousness, imagination, and considerable skills of a cook who deals in "street food" (see Chiñas, chapter 16).

Private, profit-oriented actors are not the only ones to flex their muscles on the international scene. The power of another country can much too often be evident on almost any sovereign nation in Latin America. To cite just a few examples, consider the many roles of the United States. Misguided U.S. intervention was very much in the news in the 1950s, but it was not a new phenomenon. Earlier instances ranged from underwriting Panama's secession from Colombia to wresting the great Southwest from Mexico, intervening in the "banana republics" that had been created as vast plantations for bananas, and fighting the Spanish-American war in Cuba. More recently, large-scale involvement, ostensibly to build economic infrastructure to help everyone, was often a pretext for supporting dictators who promised to deliver cheap raw materials or preventing Communism from taking hold in the hemisphere. Long before the fruitless war on drugs provided another alleged justification, U.S. officials sent large-scale foreign aid to virtually all Latin American countries, underwriting a wide range of projects from agricultural expansion to the building of roads and dams, all couched in terms of helping to liberate people from grinding poverty and ignorance while in actuality often shoring up regimes that were repressive of their own people.

How Systems Relate

In writing or talking about institutions, groups of people, countries, or other collective entities there is a common danger to treat them as if they were sentient and active beings. We must always keep in mind that *groups* don't meet—they never trade, or lend, or steal, or borrow. It is always *individuals* who do those things, no matter how misleading the description of any trans-societal, cross-cultural, or intergroup relationship may be.

Until the 1950s, although anthropologists were certainly aware of those distinctions, few bothered to wrestle with the nicety of trying to analyze them when it was inconvenient—and, in that era of early description and conceptualization, such relatively coarse-grained reports were welcomed and informative. Only after some fairly sophisticated theorizing, new questions from subdisciplines, and serious attempts to deal with process as well as content did it become imperative to deal with social systems in terms of how they truly operate and how the business of group living gets accomplished.

As simple and unprepossessing as it may at first appear, Wolf's wedding of historical and ethnographic perspectives on the Mexican case study (chapter 39) was a milestone in the anthropological description and analysis of power, not only identifying the interface between groups as the locus of key actions but also singling out a few brokers as the individuals who operate in those interstices, deftly combining the norms, values, and modalities of each group to build the invisible bridges that link them. This elementary insight, once pointed out, became the cornerstone of a fresh approach to intergroup relations that brought new vitality to the flagging field of social organization studies, allowing us to understand better how systems actually change (or resist change) and how social institutions can be comprehended as something other than just vaguely superorganic.

For Further Reading on
Relations of Power

Anthropologists have long included in their studies discussion of differential distribution of rights, goods, obligations, and other factors in the societies in which they worked, but few have tried in a systematic way to come to grips with issues of power in such stark terms. Often overlooked are the perceptive volumes by R. N. Adams that examined the concept and related realities in Latin America in detail but did not signal the fact: *Energy and Structure* (University of Texas Press, 1975) and *The Second Sowing* (Chandler, 1967). E. R. Wolf's reading in this book (chapter 39) served as a cornerstone for much that followed. We are fortunate that he finished *Envisioning Power* (University of California Press, 1999) just before he died, and several of his papers were edited (with S. Silverman) as *Pathways of Power: Building and Anthropology of the Modern World* (University of California Press, 2001).

The ego-centered method of network analysis provided some fresh insights but did not long remain vital in anthropology. Good examples include J. Johnson, *Selecting Ethnographic Informants* (Sage, 1990); S. T. Kimball and W. L. Partridge, *The Craft of Community Studies* (University Presses of Florida, 1979); and S. Wasserman and J. Galaskiwicz (eds.), *Advances in Social Network Analysis* (Sage, 1994).

The dyadic contract, patronage/clientage, and *compadrazgo* loom large in most ethnographic reports on Latin America, even when they are not accorded special status. One anthology that re-examined familiar data in these terms is A. Strickon and S. M. Greenfield (eds.), *Structure and Process in Latin America: Patronage, Clientage, and Power Systems* (University of New Mexico Press, 1972); based fully on data from Mexico is H. G. Nutini, *Ritual Kinship* (Princeton University Press, 1980). The long-term implications of vows to Christian saints can be appreciated in F. Cancian, *Economics and Prestige in a Maya Community: The Religious Cargo System in Zinacantán* (Stanford University Press, 1965); R. Reina, *The Law of the Saints* (Bobbs-Merrill, 1969); or J. M. Watanabe, *Maya Saints and Souls in a Changing World* (University of Texas Press, 1992).

Max Weber's work is probably most accessible to readers of English in H. H. Gerth and C. W. Mills (eds.), *From Max Weber: Essays in Sociology* (Oxford University Press, 1946). A special value of the anthropological perspective lies in the fact that the observer does not take organizations at face value and expect the logical impersonal relations that bureaucracies supposedly foster; by paying close attention over time to what actually occurs it can often be discerned that informal channels are used far more frequently and are more effective than formal ones.

Argentina's Mothers of the Plaza de Mayo and the protesting housewives in Chile are dramatic examples of a broader and more important movement, chronicled in many manifestations by E. Jelin (ed.), *Women and Social Change in Latin America* (Zed, 1990); and S. A. Radcliffe and S. Westwood (eds.), *"Viva!": Women and Popular Protest in Latin America* (Routledge, 1993).

The psychological and ethical difficulty of dealing at close hand with violence is addressed further in C. Nordstrom and A. C. G. M. Robben (eds.), *Fieldwork under Fire: Contemporary Studies of Violence and Survival* (University of California Press, 1995); or A. C. G. M. Robben and M. D. Suarez-Orozco (eds.), *Culture under Siege: Collective Violence and Trauma* (Cambridge University Press, 2000).

O. Lewis developed the concept of a culture of poverty in a series of books beginning with *Five Families: Mexican Case Studies in the Culture of Poverty* (Basic, 1959) and extending to *La Vida: A Puerto Rican Family in the Culture of Poverty* (Random House, 1966). His most sustained critic was C. A. Valentine, *Culture and Poverty: Critique and Counter-Proposals* (University of Chicago Press, 1968). A colleague who had worked with Lewis in Cuba reflected on his long-term contributions in S. M. Rigdon, *The Culture Facade: Art, Science, and Politics in the Works of Oscar Lewis* (University of Illinois Press, 1988).

Anthropologists rarely used the terms *elites* and *masses*, but it was not out of order at the time for S. Lipset and A. Solari to edit a volume on *Elites in Latin Amer-*

ica (Oxford University Press, 1967) or for I. L. Horowitz to edit a companion volume on *Masses in Latin America* (Oxford University Press, 1970).

Agrarian reform as a promising means of redressing the gross imbalance of power that affected much of Latin America in the mid-twentieth century was reflected in works such as C. Senior, *Land Reform and Democracy* (University of Florida Press, 1959); H. A. Landsberger (ed.), *Latin American Peasant Movements* (Cornell University Press, 1969); and R. Stavenhagen (ed.), *Agrarian Problems and Peasant Movements in Latin America* (Doubleday, 1970).

The emergence of native groups and organizations as meaningful symbols of ethnicity and potential power is an important, if recent, development throughout much of Latin America. A good summary is A. Brysk, *From Tribal Village to Global Village* (Stanford University Press, 2000); other good sources include S. E. Alvarez and A. Escobar (eds.), *The Making of New Social Movements in Latin America* (Westview, 1992); J. Beauclerk, J. Narby, and J. Townsend, *Indigenous Peoples* (Oxfam, 1988); J. E. Kicza, *The Indian in Latin American History* (Jaguar, 1993); and P. Wearne, *Return of the Indian* (Temple University Press, 1996).

The germ of the idea had been around for some time when I. Wallerstein galvanized scholarly attention by analyzing economic, cultural, and historical relations in terms of *The Modern World System* (3 vols., Academic, 1974–76). Similar in concept was E. R. Wolf's treatment of *Europe and the People without History* (University of California Press, 1983). Developments and applications of that global concept can be found in T. K. Hopkins and I. Wallerstein (eds.), *Processes of the World System* (Sage, 1980) and their *The Age of Transition: Trajectory of the World System, 1945–2025* (Zed, 1996).

George M. Foster is a professor of anthropology (emeritus) at University of California, Berkeley. An early proponent and practitioner of applied anthropology, he also contributed significantly to conceptualization and teaching on both Latin America and anthropology. Among his best-known books are Applied Anthropology, Anthropologists in Cities *(with R. V. Kemper),* Culture and Conquest: America's Spanish Heritage, Hippocrates' Latin Legacy: Humoral Medicine in the New World, Long-Term Field Research in Social Anthropology, Medical Anthropology *(with B. G. Anderson),* Peasant Society *(with J. M. Potter and M. N. Diaz),* Traditional Cultures and the Impact of Technological Change *(two editions), and* Tzintzuntzan: Mexican Peasants in a Changing World *(various editions).*

31

One of the best things that one can say of a social scientist's interpretation is that it not only "rings true" but also "makes sense" out of some things that the reader had not previously been able to understand; such a reaction is commonplace with respect to George Foster's writings. One of the most influential—as evidenced by references to it throughout this volume—is this article focusing on the scarcity of corporate ties in a traditional peasant community and showing how dyadic relationships predominate, whether between peers or hierarchically. The continuing quest of some for patrons (to buttress one's security), and of others for clients (to extend one's range of influence) fits with the ethic of personalismo *that pervades much of Latin culture—and that can increasingly be discerned in many aspects of Anglo life. This paper is one of the cornerstones of Durston's (chapter 9) and Greenfield's (chapter 44) work; for other perspectives on patronage and clientage among individuals, see Aron-Schaar (chapter 32); and on power relationships among groups, see Wolf (chapter 39).*

The Dyadic Contract in a Mexican Village

George M. Foster

RECIPROCITY: THE BASIS OF SOCIAL RELATIONSHIPS

It is common that, in such major institutions as religion, health, conflict-resolving mechanisms, and in views about wealth, cultural forms and behavior combine to maintain a basic equilibrium state in Mexican culture. A satisfactory condition is one in which there is an even balance between opposing forces and people, in which Good is evenly distributed, and in which no one takes unjustly from another. The same view of equilibrium helps us to understand the basic principle that underlies social relationships. This principle is one of reciprocity between partners, of an even exchange whereby an individual acquires the support he needs in ordinary and special times, without running the risk of being accused of taking something from others.

Before explaining the system of reciprocity that underlies social relationships in Tzintzuntzan, it may be helpful to remind the reader that the villagers, like other peasants, feel they have no real knowledge of, and consequently no significant control over, natural and supernatural forces, and over the wider social and economic systems—including those of cities and the national government—in which they live. These are areas in which direct intervention is felt to be useless. Yet Tzintzuntzeños, like all other men, believe that to live they must have mastery over some significant part of their environment. Since only the local village world, and the people and

---

Abridged, with permission of the author and publisher, from "The Dyadic Contract" (chapter 11) in his 1988 book *Tzintzuntzan: Mexican Peasants in a Changing World*, Waveland Press, Prospect Heights, IL. [That, in turn, evolved out of his 1961 paper "The Dyadic Contract: A Model for the Social Structure of a Mexican Peasant Village," *American Anthropologist 68*: 1173–1192 (1961), which was widely reprinted and had enormous impact in anthropology. At my request, expressly for this volume, Foster has added a brief "Afterword" to update his view of the subject.]

beings with whom they have continuing contact, are seen as really knowable, *in Tzint-zuntzan concern with social relationships and manipulation of the social environment takes precedence over concern with manipulation of nature and of extra-village systems in general.* Tzintzuntzeños are enormously preoccupied with their relationships with each other, within the formal structures of family and *compadrazgo* (ritual co-parent-hood), and within the formal structures of friendship and "neighborhoodship." They are also interested in their ties with outsiders with whom they have or may have sig-nificant contact, and—at another level—with Christ, the Virgin Mary, and the saints. Some personal security in a generally unpredictable world can be achieved, it is felt, only through the ability to exploit all these relationships to best advantage.

Every Tzintzuntzeño's primary concern is to be able to "defend" himself in the *lucha,* the struggle he conceives life to be. In this struggle he knows he is basically on his own and that it is up to him, with his scant resources, to defend himself and his family against the dangers of the world. On a formal and institutional level, an indi-vidual expects to receive a good deal of help from members of his family and from favorite *compadres.* These are legitimate forms of support, appropriate to an honor-able man because their reciprocal quality is recognized. Beyond these obvious ties, the ideal of successful defense in life is to be able to live *sin compromisos,* without obliga-tions, without entangling alliances, to be strong, masculine, independent, and able to meet life's continuing challenges with a minimum of help from others.

The Importance of Obligations

Yet, paradoxically, strength and relative independence can be achieved only by saddling oneself with a wide variety of *compromisos.* One's ability to defend himself stems from the number and quality of the obligations he recognizes toward others for, of course, each obligation is coupled with an expectation of a particular kind of sup-port at the appropriate time. Hence, no one loses sight of the necessity for continually manipulating and exploiting the institutional and other ties that exist or can be cre-ated which will minimize life's dangers and maximize its opportunities.

Yet the most important thing of all in the social structure of Tzintzuntzan is an informal, unnamed principle of reciprocity that underlies all formal ties, cross-cutting them at every point, serving as the glue that holds society together and the grease that smoothes its running. This principle of reciprocity, which I call the "dyadic con-tract," can be thought of as a sociological model that reconciles the institutional roles already described with the real behavior that can be observed. Its particular utility as a model lies in the fact that it explains the behavior of people in all the situations in which they find themselves: between those of the same socioeconomic status, between people of different statuses, between fellow villagers, between villagers and outsiders, and between man and the beings of the supernatural world.

The Dyadic Contract Model

The dyadic contract model postulates an informal structure in which most of the really significant ties within all institutions are achieved (hence selective) rather than ascribed (hence nonselective). The formal social institutions of Tzintzuntzan present each individual with a near-infinite number of people with whom he has culturally defined bonds implying mutual obligations and expectations. But no individual could possibly ful-fill all the roles imposed upon him by the statuses he occupies in his village's institutions; he is forced to pick and choose, to concentrate on relatively few. In other words, the formal institutions of society provide everyone with a panel of candidates with whom to interact;

the individual, by means of the dyadic contract mechanism, selects (and is selected by) relatively few with whom significant working relationships are developed.

In Tzintzuntzan everyone, from an early age, begins to organize his societal contacts outside the nuclear family, and even to some extent within it, by means of a special form of contractual relationships, and as he approaches and reaches adulthood, these relationships grow in importance until they dominate all other types of ties. These contracts are informal, or implicit, since they lack ritual or legal validation. They are based on no idea of law, and they are unenforceable through any type of authority, even one as diffuse as public opinion. They exist only at the pleasure of the participants. They are noncorporate, since social units such as extended families, barrios, or villages are never bound. Even nuclear families cannot truly be said to enter into contractual relationships of this type with other families.

These contracts are essentially dyadic: they bind *pairs* of contractants rather than groups. That this distinction is important becomes clear when we remember that in Tzintzuntzan there are no vigorous voluntary associations or institutions in which an individual recognizes identical or comparable obligations to two or more people (always excepting the basketball team). Each person is the center of his private and unique network of contractual ties, a network whose overlap with other networks has little or no functional significance. That is, *A*'s tie to *B* in no way binds him to *B*'s partner, *C*. *A* may also have a contractual relationship with *C* as well, but the fact that all three recognize comparable bonds gives rise to no feeling of group association. An individual conceptualizes his relationships with others as a focal point at which he stands, from which radiate a multiplicity of two-way streets, at the end of each of which is a single partner, completely separate from all the others.

The kinds of people (or beings) with whom a villager forms these ties include persons of comparable socioeconomic position both within and without the community, people of superior power and influence, and supernatural beings such as Christ, the Virgin Mary, and the saints. Contracts develop between members of a family as close as siblings; they bind *compadres* beyond the formally defined limits of the institution; and they unite friends and neighbors in close union.

TYPES OF DYADIC TIES

Two basic types of contractual ties may be recognized, depending on the relative statuses of the partners. "Colleague" contracts—the expression is mine, and not the villagers'—tie people of equal or approximately equal socioeconomic position who exchange the same kinds of goods and services. These contracts are phrased horizontally, and they can be thought of as symmetrical since each partner, in position and obligations, mirrors the other. Colleague contracts operate primarily within Tzintzuntzan, but they also tie villagers to individuals in adjacent peasant communities.

"Patron-client" contracts—again the expression is mine—tie people (or people to beings) of significantly different socioeconomic statuses (or orders of power) who exchange different kinds of goods and services. Patron-client contracts are thus phrased vertically, and they can be thought of as asymmetrical, since each partner is quite different from the other in position and obligations. Patron-client contracts operate almost exclusively between villagers and non-villagers (including supernatural beings), since socioeconomic differences in Tzintzuntzán are seen as so slight as to preclude the role of patron.

In addition to these informal, implicit contracts, villagers of course also recognize formal and explicit contracts, represented by such acts as marriage, establishing *compadrazgo* ties, and buying and selling property. These contracts rest on governmental and religious law, are legally or ritually validated through specific acts, are usually registered in writing, and most are enforceable through the authority of the particular system that brings them into being. They often are dyadic, but they may also bind several people, as when the baptism of an infant brings two parents, two godparents, and a godchild together. These formal contracts may be but are not necessarily congruent with the informal dyadic contracts, since the latter cut across all formal institutional boundaries and permeate all aspects of society. For example, two *compadres* are bound by formal ties validated in a ritual ceremony. This tie may be reinforced and made more functional by an implicit dyadic contract, making the two relationships congruent. Or two people may sign a paper authorizing one to sharecrop a field of the other; this formal relationship may be underlain as well by the general exchange pattern that spells a dyadic contract between the two signers.

COLLEAGUE TIES

With these preliminary remarks in mind we can turn to examine in more detail how this contractual system functions, first considering ties between colleagues and second those between patrons and clients. Between colleagues, reciprocity is expressed in *continuing* exchanges of goods and services. The goods and services are tangibles; incorporeal values play little part in the system. For example, a partner whose special knowledge about a glazing process is a trade secret is not likely to instruct a dyadic partner, just because they exchange many other things. Over the long term the reciprocity is complementary, because each partner owes the other the same kinds and quantities of things. Over the short term the exchanges are not necessarily complementary, because a material item or service offered to partner A by partner B does not require subsequent return of the same thing to cancel the obligation (and it may in fact require something different, as pointed out in the following paragraph). Rather, it is a question of long-range equivalence of value, not formally calculated yet somehow weighed so that in the end both partners balance contributions and receipts. In the usual situation each member of the dyad simultaneously counts a number of credits and debits that are kept in approximate balance.

Within the long-term complementary pattern, there are short-term exchanges, often noncomplementary, in which a particular act elicits a particular return. For example, a friend fixes a bride's hair for the wedding; the friend must be invited to the wedding feast, or if for any reason she cannot come, food must be sent to her from the scene of the dining. One *compadre* organizes a saint's day *mañanitas* pre-dawn serenade for another compadre, providing guitar players, a chorus, and a tray, or "crown" of fruit and flowers. The honored *compadre* reciprocates by inviting the serenaders in for drinks and the hominy-like pork *pozole* expected at many ceremonial meals. But these specific, non-complementary exchanges are merely minor oscillations within the long-term, major dyadic patterns which bind partners over years and decades. The non-complementary saint's day exchange probably will be made complementary later in the year, when the second *compadre* returns the favor.

A very important functional requirement of the system is that *an exactly even balance between two partners never be struck.* This would jeopardize the whole relationship since, if all credits and debits somehow could be balanced off at one time, the contract would cease to exist. At the very least a new contract would have to be gotten underway, and this would involve uncertainty and possibly distress if one partner seemed reluctant to continue. The dyadic contract is effective precisely because partners are never quite sure of their relative positions at a given moment. As long as they know that goods and services are flowing both ways in essentially equal amounts as time passes, they know their relationship is solidly based.

TYPES OF EXCHANGES

The forms of exchanges can be examined in terms of services and goods offered and reciprocated in ritual and non-ritual settings. These lines are not hard and fast in the minds of Tzintzuntzeños, however, and a material return in a nonritual setting may help counterbalance a service previously offered in a ritual setting, and so on around the circle of logical possibilities.

Services lent in a ritual context usually are associated with life crises such as baptism, confirmation, marriage, and death. They include a *compadre's* go-between services to make peace after an elopement, making funeral arrangements for a godchild who dies a "little angel," help and comfort extended on the occasion of a death, such as sitting up all night at the wake with a bereaved husband or wife, and the like. Goods offered in a ritual context include the financial responsibilities of marriage godparents, the expenses incurred by a baptismal godfather when his godchild dies young, aid to a father with the costs of his son's marriage, and particularly the help given partners when they are faced with major fiesta expenses. When a man is a *carguero* he visits the homes of relatives, *compadres*, and friends with whom dyadic contracts are recognized, asking them to "accompany" him—that is, to contribute foodstuffs and money. Emphasizing the ritual character of this transaction is the fact that raw foodstuffs equal to about half that given are returned following the fiesta.

At ceremonial meals, such as a saint's day fiesta, a wedding, a baptism, or a funeral, guests bring pots into which they pour surplus food from the heaping dishes served them. This is taken home to be eaten the following day. At any festive meal some people invited are unable to come, and others not specifically invited must be remembered. After the guests have been served, children are sent with plates of hot food to the homes of those who have not come, so they, too, can share in the festivities.

Services in a nonritual context take an unlimited number of forms. One helps nurse a sick friend or relative, gives a hypodermic injection without the usual small charge, purchases something on request in Pátzcuaro, loans a stud boar without asking the *maquila* fee, sews a dress or makes a picture frame free of charge. San Judas Tadeo and San Anacasio are very helpful in the return of lost or stolen objects. People who have pictures of these saints on their family altars sometimes will loan them to others to help recover a lost item. The picture of San Anacasio of the late Tiburcio Peréz and his wife María Morales is considered "miraculous," since it has helped in recovering so many things. As a part of their exchange obligations Tiburcio and María permitted neighbors and friends to burn vigil lights on their altar, beneath San Anacasio's picture, as they implored him to lend them help. Any one of a thousand helpful acts is considered, and remembered, as a service incurring some form of reciprocal obligation.

In a nonritual context goods are exchanged when neighbors drop in to borrow an egg, a few chiles, or some other food or household item immediately needed. When men went to the United States as *braceros* they always borrowed money from friends and relatives, returning the money upon completing their contracts and adding as well some item such as a pair of nylon stockings or a sports shirt that served to keep alive the exchange relationship. A person with heavy medical expenses expects to receive money as an outright gift and as a loan, thus simultaneously being repaid for earlier transactions and incurring new obligations.

THE ROLE OF FOOD AND DRINK

The continuing informal exchange of food and drink is particularly important in maintaining the dyadic contract. Except on ceremonial occasions invitations to meals almost never occur. But when someone—a relative, a neighbor, a *compadre*, or a friend—with whom the exchange pattern is fully developed drops in, he or she usually is not allowed to leave without being offered whatever food is available: a tortilla, perhaps with a fried egg or beans, a bit of candied sweet potato, a glass of milk, a cup of coffee, or fresh fruit. The nature of the food or drink is not important, but if they are offered they *must* be accepted. Failure to accept proffered food or drink seriously jeopardizes an exchange relationship, since it appears to represent a denial of mutual understanding, and friendly feelings, which are basic to the dyadic contract.

Since men do not cook, they are denied the opportunity to express affection and friendship to partners by offering them food. But they *can* offer drinks, which represent the same symbolic values. This is certainly a major reason why men drinking in a store feel compelled to invite any friend who enters to drink with them, and why they become so angry and belligerent on the rare occasions when their invitation is refused; symbolically, their proffered friendship is being rejected. Undoubtedly many Tzintzuntzan men drink more than they really want to simply because they are caught in a trap in which only through offering and accepting liquor can they maintain important social relations.

Temporary hostility between people normally on good terms is sometimes expressed by refusing to accept food and should someone, simply because of lack of appetite, not eat, the cook begins to speculate as to the cause of what she interprets to be anger directed toward her. Children, irritated with their mothers, will often suffer hunger pains rather than make the gesture that will heal the breach, and few filial acts are more distressing to mothers than a child's refusal to eat. Micaela recalls how her first husband, Pedro, when angry with her, would punish her "by not eating for three days," and she would not eat either "from mortification." No one should refuse food (or drink) by saying he is not hungry (or thirsty), since he knows his motives are immediately suspect. Only by appealing to an upset stomach, or better yet medical treatment that forbids certain items, can proffered food or drink be gracefully refused.

The food and drink exchange, important in all institutions, seems especially so between friends and neighbors. Because the ties to these people are unstructured, in a formal sense, in contrast to those of the family and the compadrazgo, even greater attention to constantly reaffirming the relationship is deemed desirable. The offering of food and drink is the quintessence of this reaffirmation, and if someone professes friendship but fails in this informal exchange, he is said to be a "friend with his lips on the outside," that is, not a genuine friend.

Food exchanges tell us something else about dyadic contracts: they are not all of equal intensity. The situation is similar to that of American friendship patterns in which we see, visit, and interact more with some friends than with others, but the friends we see less often are still qualitatively different from mere acquaintances or professional associates, since we do recognize social and other obligations toward them. High-intensity contracts can be distinguished from low-intensity contracts by the way in which food is handled. If we see some people almost always being offered food when they come to a house, we may be sure that a high-intensity dyadic contract is operating. If continuing exchanges of various types with other people are noted, but less thought is given to informal offerings of food, then we know the contract is of lesser intensity.

LINGUISTIC EXPRESSIONS OF RELATIONSHIPS

In colleague contracts, as has been pointed out, a functional imperative of the system is that an even balance in exchanges never be struck, since only when partners simultaneously recognize both obligations and expectations as being outstanding do they feel a relationship is in good order. Conceptually, a precise balancing of debits with credits is tantamount to terminating a contract. Consequently, behavior that suggests the striking of an even balance, or the desire to strike an even balance, is interpreted as unfriendly, and normally to be avoided—unless, of course, an individual does in fact wish to terminate a relationship. To put the matter in a slightly different way, behavior forms between partners that confirm or reaffirm recognition of a contract are highly valued, whereas behavior forms which do not reaffirm recognition of a contract, or which may suggest the speaker or actor feels the contract is no longer very important, are seen as threatening and hostile. Once the importance of this point is grasped, certain aspects of behavior in Tzintzuntzan which at first seem puzzling and incomprehensible fall nicely into place.

When I first began to take presents to people in Tzintzuntzan I was much disturbed when they were accepted with what seemed to me a distressing lack of enthusiasm, bordering on ungraciousness. At most a perfunctory *gracias* would be mumbled, and often nothing at all would be said. I feared I was not pleasing, or that more had been expected of me. Then I realized that this was standard behavior between the villagers themselves. When a tray of uncooked food, covered by a cloth, would be sent as a contribution to a *carguero's* fiesta expenses, his wife would accept it unceremoniously at the door, carry it without looking under the cloth to the kitchen, unload the tray, and return it and the cloth to the donor with no more comment than normal passing of the time of day.

This "lack of courtesy" among a normally courteous and ceremony-minded people puzzled me until I realized that the objects offered were viewed not as gifts, but rather as one among many items forming the exchange system existing between partners, an item for which repayment would be made in another way at a later date. Tzintzuntzeños recognize—realistically, I think—that in their society there can be such a thing as a "gift" given apart from an existing or a potential exchange pattern between people only in a very special sense. Any favor, whatever its form, is part of a quid pro quo negotiation, the terms of which are recognized and accepted by the participants.

Both linguistic and other behavior forms show why the word "gift" is inappropriate to describe the goods and services that are exchanged in Tzintzuntzan. In American society a gift is thought of as something transferred from one person to another without measurable compensation. That it may, in fact, be part of a continuing exchange pattern is beside the point. A gift is accepted with enthusiasm and with thanks, verbally expressed, which symbolize something more than the courtesy thanks that accompany commercial transactions, since the words are recognized, subconsciously at least, as striking a conceptual balance with the donor's thoughtfulness.

In Spanish thanks are expressed in two distinct linguistic forms: *gracias* (literally the plural form of "grace"), usually translated into English as "thank you," and *Diós se lo pague*, meaning "May God (re)pay you for it." The first form serves for casual, informal interchanges of no moment between persons of equal status, or equal status at least as far as the occasion that calls forth the word is concerned. But *Diós se lo pague* is used in an entirely different sense, in which the thanker acknowledges the great difference in position and the fact that the object or service can never be reciprocated. Beggars, for example, acknowledge alms with this expression. Only by asking God's favor for the donor can the beggar in any way repay the giver; neither expects any other balance. An item acknowledged with *Diós se lo pague*, then, can properly be considered a gift in the American sense. An item or act acknowledged by *gracias* is something else, for the form is a courtesy and nothing more.

In Tzintzuntzan both forms are used. I hear *Diós se lo pague* when I give something considered by the recipient to be far outside the normal patterns of friendship exchange, such as a substantial monetary contribution to help with unusual medical expenses. When I give lesser items, such as a cut of cloth for a skirt or dress—something within the normal range of exchanges—I may hear *gracias,* or perhaps nothing at all. The recipient and I know the item given will be reciprocated with pottery, a tule-reed figure, fish, or something else commanded by the recipient; the cut of cloth is not a gift, nor are the pottery, the figure, or the fish.

The usual absence of verbal thanks and visible enthusiasm accompanying exchanges does not mean, of course, that the transactions are cold, calculated, and emotionless. People enjoy these transactions enormously; it is gratifying to know one is living up to his obligations, and that one's partners continue to value the association. Some of the fundamental values of the culture are expressed in the "change acts" themselves, and people sense and appreciate this fact, even though they would have trouble verbalizing it.

PATRON-CLIENT TIES

With patron-client contracts, in contrast to colleague contracts, one of the two partners is always of significantly higher position, from which stems the power which permits him to be a "patron" to the other. The Spanish word *patrón* has several related meanings: an employer of workers, a ceremonial sponsor, a skipper of a small boat, the protecting saint of a village or parish, the protecting saint to all people who bear his (or her) name. All these definitions are correct for Tzintzuntzan. A patron, it is clear, is someone who combines status, power, influence, authority—attributes useful to anyone—in "defending" himself or in helping someone else to defend himself. But a person, however powerful and influential, is a patron only in relation to someone of lesser position—a client whom, under specific circumstances, he is willing to help. Tzintzuntzeños all look up to a number of patrons. Each recognizes the saint whose name he bears as *mi santo patrón,* and everyone knows San Francisco is patron of the village. All accept the Virgin of Guadalupe as patron of America and Mexico, and consequently as their patron as well. In addition, a few adults refer to people in Pátzcuaro, Morelia, and other towns as *mi patrón,* because of relationships in which they assume the position of subordinate partner. Tzintzuntzeños have no corresponding word for themselves as clients. Since they represent near-bottom in the Mexican socioeconomic hierarchy, they do not look down upon others from the lofty position of patron, and they do not think of the relationship as one in which a person may be either patron or client, depending on relative position and power.

Analytically, two basic types of patrons may be distinguished in Tzintzuntzan: (1) human beings, and (2) supernatural beings. The former include politicians, government employees, town and city friends, godparents or *compadres* of superior status, influence, or special abilities, and church personnel, especially the local priest. The latter—the supernatural patrons—are God, Christ, the Virgin Mary, and the saints, the last three in any of their geographical or advocational manifestations. Even the devil is a potential patron since he can bring one great wealth. All human patrons, except the local priest, are from outside Tzintzuntzan, since the status differences that are essential for a patron-client relationship are lacking within the community. Supernatural patrons are those associated with the local churches or with family altars, as well as those found in more distant communities.

As is true of colleague contracts, the partners' recognition of mutual obligations underlies and validates the patron-client system. There are, however, two important differences in exchange patterns. First, the patron and client exchange different kinds of goods and services, and second, *whereas all colleague contracts are continuing, a sig-*

nificant part of patron-client exchanges are non-continuing, or short-term. That is, a particular good or service offered by a prospective client requires an immediate and specific return from the potential patron. If the offer is reciprocated, the patron-client contract is established, but the act of reciprocation either simultaneously terminates the contract or establishes conditions for termination in the near future. To be more specific, patron-client relationships involving human beings are like colleague contracts, in that goods and services are exchanged as time passes, with no attempt to strike a balance, since this would cancel the contract. In some instances in which the patron is supernatural, the relationship continues for a long period, with no attempt to strike an exact balance. But in many other instances, and particularly those in which a supplicant asks for help in time of sickness or other crisis, it is expected that the granting of the request is cancelled out, or balanced off, by the supplicant's compliance with his vow. Hence, no contract exists until the request is granted, and no contract exists after the supplicant complies. This type of patron-client contract is terminated by striking what is recognized as an even bargain between the contractants, the very act that is zealously avoided by colleague contractants so that their relationship will not be terminated.

Tzintzuntzeños, recognizing their humble position and lack of power and influence, are continually alert to the possibility of obligating a person of superior wealth, position, or influence, thereby initiating a patron-client relationship which, if matters go well, will buttress the villagers' security in a variety of life crises that are only too certain: illness, the sudden need for cash, help in legal disputes, protection against various forms of possible exploitation, and advice on the wisdom of contemplated moves.

Exploiting the *compadrazgo* system is one of the most obvious ways of gaining a patron, and wealthy city relatives, local ranchers (of whom there are only a few), and storekeepers in nearby Pátzcuaro with whom one may have commercial relations are common targets. When Pánfilo Castellanos' son Lucio was married, his wife's nephew, who had become a successful Pátzcuaro doctor, agreed to be marriage godfather. A pre-existing family tie was thereby strengthened, and the new godfather was under strong obligation to help with free medical attention, possible loans, and advice that the greater experience of a town dweller makes possible. Pánfilo and his wife, in return, expect to take presents from time to time to their nephew, to invite him to family fiestas and meals in Tzintzuntzan, and perhaps to drum up trade among ill villagers. Macaria Gómez persuaded a distant bachelor cousin, Isaac Martín, whose mother controls one of the few remaining haciendas in the Pátzcuaro area, to be baptismal godfather to her eldest daughter, Laura. Isaac, in addition to the general prestige he sheds on Macaria, has loaned her money to help with her chicken ranching, and he gave her a fairly large sum when she underwent a major operation. His return is less clear. When be visits Tzintzuntzan, on rare occasions, he is fawned on and made over in extravagant fashion, and perhaps in a land where large landowners are not popular, it is good to have villagers who speak well of one.

Patron-client *compadrazgo* relationships, although formally identical to those binding socioeconomic equals, are in fact recognized as quite distinct by all participants. This is especially apparent in linguistic usage. *Compadres* of the same status, as has been pointed out, usually are extremely formal with each other, in theory at least dropping the familiar second person singular personal pronoun *tú* in favor of the formal *usted*. Client *compadres*, of course, are extremely formal with their patron *compadres*, as with all other human patrons, but patron *compadres*, almost without exception, address their village *compadres* with the familiar "*tú*" so that the relative status of the two partners is never in doubt. Isaac Martín, for example, is considerably younger than Macaria Gómez; yet, because of his superior status, it is taken for granted by both that he will address her as *tú* and she will address him as *usted*.

Although the *compadrazgo* institution is an excellent way to establish a patron-client contract, less formal acts also work well. One day while I sat with Silverio Caro in his roadside pottery stand, a small car drove up with three people. Silverio greeted the driver, *Buenos días, doctor*, in such a way that it was clear that they had had previous contact. After buying several pieces of pottery the doctor and his friends left. Silverio then explained that this was a relatively new doctor in Pátzcuaro whom he had consulted professionally, and it became clear to me that he was carefully building a relationship with him. The regular price of the merchandise selected was $16.50, but Silverio had charged only $13.00. If, on future visits to Pátzcuaro, the doctor were to show a bit more consideration than usual, or go out of his way to show friendship in some other way, Silverio would take presents of pottery and feel that his relationship with the doctor was good health insurance.

Within Tzintzuntzan, although there are wealth differences, there are no social distinctions sufficiently great to justify using the patron-client concept to describe personal relationships, the priest being the single exception. The three priests who have served in recent years have been reluctant to accept *compadrazgo* ties, although they have done so on rare occasions, thereby establishing patron-client bonds. But other less specific ties exist. The priests need helpers to maintain church ritual, to arrange flowers and candles on altars, to clean the buildings, and as sources for some of their food. They, in turn, can confer extra spiritual blessings on their supporters, and they can, because of their education and knowledge of the world, give temporal advice as well. So, it seems to me, it is proper to think of the priests as participating in exchange relationships with the villagers, in which they are patrons and the villagers are clients.

In these patron-client relationships between human beings, one sees both similarities to and differences from the colleague contracts. As with the latter, the relationships are continuing, and neither patron nor client attempts to strike an immediate balance, which both recognize would terminate the contract. But unlike the colleague contracts, the partners are not equals and make no real pretense to equality. It is, in fact, this asymmetry, and particularly the ability to offer one's partner something distinct from that which he offers, and to receive something one's fellows do not have at their disposal, which makes the system worthwhile. Within the village, local colleague ties provide a man with all he needs, at peak periods of demand, of the kinds of goods and services to which he himself also has access. The patron's utility lies in the fact that he can provide things not normally available in the village, things that at times are badly needed.

At first glance the patron-client *compadrazgo*, which is formally as well as informally contractual, appears to contradict the dyadic principle: in its important forms it binds a minimum of five and a maximum of eight people (e.g., for baptism, the child, parents, and godparents; for marriage, the godparents, the couple, and the parents of both bride and groom). The contradiction, however, is more apparent than real, since the *meaningful exchange-based* ties which underlie the system's formalities seem normally to involve dyads only. Above all, the patron is always an individual. For example, Isaac Martín, godfather to Laura Prieto, is patron both to her and her mother, by means of two distinct ties. The basic, implicit, informal contracts bind two people, and though they may appear to "blanket in" others, there are no doubts in the participants' minds as to the nature of the relationship.

SUPERNATURAL BEINGS AS PATRONS

Just as individuals cast about among human beings for patrons, so do they turn to the saints, and to the various manifestations of Christ and the Virgin, testing their willingness to enter contractual relationships with them (i.e., by helping, by responding to overtures). Some of the resulting dyadic contracts are, like all those previously described, continuing, in that an even balance is never struck. Other contracts are rather different, in that they are called into being for a specific crisis, in response to the supplications of a human being. If the contract is made, i.e., if the supernatural being grants the request of the supplicant, the latter is obligated, at his earliest convenience, to fulfill his part of the bargain, to strike the balance by complying with his offer. This terminates the contract. An individual may try to renew the contract at a later time for a new crisis but, as will be seen, he often will attempt a contract with a different patron on each new occasion.

Continuing patron-client contracts with supernatural beings are best seen in the daily prayers and lighting of candles practiced by most villagers. Every home has one or more simple altars, usually a shelf with a few wilted or artificial flowers and guttered candles beneath several pictures of Christ, the Virgin, and an assortment of saints. This low-pitched daily homage is believed to gain the protection of the beings invoked, not for specific crises, but against the thousand and one unthought-of dangers that lie in wait for the unwary. In the room in which Laura Prieto sleeps and sews, the wall altar holds pictures of the Virgin of Guadalupe, as well as several other virgins and saints. When she sits down to sew, or at other times when she "just feels like it," she lights a vigil light "to all of them." She is paying her respects, asking them to continue to watch over her in return for this attention. Her mother pays little attention to this altar, but she prays to the Virgin of Guadalupe before arising in the morning, and Divine Providence is the object of a credo before she goes to sleep. In return, the mother hopes to receive her "daily necessities." Laura's stepfather is addicted to Souls in Purgatory and Our Lady of Perpetual Help, to both of whom he prays daily. In other homes the pattern is similar.

A noteworthy point in this pattern is that altars are not really centers of family rites, even though several members may light candles. Each member of the family has his special responsibility toward the patrons he has selected, whom he feels favor him. No one, except upon special request, is responsible for acts of deference and respect for other family members. If Laura is away for a day or two on a pilgrimage, her mother feels no compulsion to light candles to Laura's patrons, although she will certainly ask her own patrons to care for her daughter. In the continuing type of relationship with supernatural patrons, the dyadic pattern that characterizes other village relationships is the rule.

Apart from what may be called "obligatory" patrons—Christ and the Virgin, shared by all villagers—how does one select continuing patrons? There is no rule; one simply follows hunches or whims, as in the case of Laura, who decided to add San Martín de Porres to her altar after hearing about him in a radio *novela*. Manuel Herrera, with impeccable logic, says he supposes the Virgin is really the most powerful. After all, *Ella tiene más parentesco con el Mero Jefe*, "She's the most closely related to the Big Boss."

Other patrons who logically fall in the "continuing" category are relatively unimportant. San Francisco, patron of Tzintzuntzan, is, as we have seen, not highly regarded for his miraculous qualities, and his fiesta is perfunctory. A person's name saint likewise receives little attention, although his day itself is often marked by the equivalent of an American birthday party. Occupational patrons—San Isidro for farmers, for example—also receive short shrift in Tzintzuntzan. The devil as patron is more theoretical than real; no one, of course, admits to this relationship. Yet stories are told, usually about people in nearby villages, in which a petitioner becomes wealthy by selling his soul to the devil, thereby establishing a relationship that endures not only through life but through all eternity.

THE VOW

Noncontinuing or short-term contracts with supernatural patrons are best seen in the practice of votive offerings. When an individual faces a crisis, such as illness, accident, or an unusual need for money, he (or she) makes a *manda* or *promesa,* a vow or solemn promise to a saint or one or another of the many images or manifestations of Christ or the Virgin, to do some pious act known to be pleasing to the patron. In the simplest pious acts, for rather minor crises, the petitioner lights a candle and prays, or hangs a silver *milagro,* at the altar of the patron invoked. The silver (sometimes base metal) votive offerings are small representations of parts of the body such as an arm, a leg, eyes, breasts, or even an entire body in kneeling posture, or of pigs, goats, sheep, horses, or cattle. The one selected depends, of course, on the nature of the supplication: a pig for a lost or sick sow, and an arm for a sore arm.

In more serious crises the client promises the patron to wear a *hábito, a* plain religious garment, for a number of months, and to refrain from all kinds of public entertainment and amusements if the request is granted. Women who suffer from headaches or who are otherwise sickly, and who may believe their long hair is an excessive drain on their systems, occasionally cut off their braids and hang them at the altar of the Virgin, pleading for relief. Guadalupe Huipe recently offered her braids to the *Imaculada* image of the Virgin, and to comply with her promise painstakingly glued each hair to a skullcap to be worn by the Virgin. Ofelia Zamora did the same thing 20 years ago, but with the passage of the years the hairs fell out and the Virgin became a bit bald, so Guadalupe had the opportunity to do something she felt would be particularly welcome to the Virgin.

When a person finds himself in sudden, grave peril, he commends himself to one of the avocations of Christ or the Virgin, and if he is saved, he orders a *retablo,* in classic form a painted metal sheet which graphically portrays the danger, shows the patron floating in the sky, and at the bottom has a line or two describing the miracle. For other grave crises, or in the hope of very special favors, a supplicant promises the Santo Entierro advocacy of Christ to assume the role of penitent during one or more Good Fridays, either hobbling about with leg shackles or carrying a wooden cross along a prescribed route through the village. In other cases—usually illness—one appeals to a "miraculous" saint or image of Christ or the Virgin in another town, promising to go on a religious pilgrimage to fulfill the vow if the request is granted.

Do two or more people jointly petition a single patron? For example, might two daughters say to the Virgin of Health in Pátzcuaro, "We promise to wear your habit if our mother is restored to health?" All the evidence I have indicates that this is not done. No informant ever used a plural personal pronoun in describing a petition; no informant ever suggested that his responsibility was shared with another; and no informant ever said that anyone else was equally implicated with him. The petitioner who fulfills his vow is a single person. Several people may take action in the face of a single calamity threatening a family, but each action is dyadic, independent of the others, involving a single petitioner and a single patron. Patron-client relationships are enormously personal, and the benefits that accrue from a successful contract are not willingly shared by a client. It rather seems as if the bounty of a supernatural patron, like all other good things in life, is looked upon as a Limited Good, and to the extent one shares it with others, so in that degree is one's portion reduced. Two petitions to a single patron will not produce twice the bounty; they will simply dilute and divide a finite quantity. Where this point of view prevails, it is clear that several people individually appealing to several patrons is a more logical policy, offering greater potential help, than the same people appealing collectively to a single patron.

Afterword

This is a significantly revised version of "The Dyadic Contract in Tzintzuntzan: Patron-Client Relationship," the second of a pair of articles (the first is Foster 1961) that together suggest a model for the social structure of Tzintzuntzan, Michoacán, Mexico (and by extension for similar Latin American peasant communities). They were based on two periods of field research; the first was my initial experience in Michoacán in 1945–1946 (described in *Empire's Children: The People of Tzintzuntzan* (Foster and Ospina 1948). The second period began in 1958 after a hiatus of a dozen years and represents the first five years of research trips that have continued virtually annually until the present.

Today the idea of repeat visits to research sites over a period of years is largely taken for granted by anthropologists. They assume that major changes will occur in the communities they study, and that they should monitor and report on these changes. This view of the research enterprise is relatively new; the first monograph-length treatment of the topic dates only from 1979 (Foster et al. 1979). Longitudinal studies afford anthropologists the luxury of taking a second look at their early work, both to evaluate it in hindsight and to note the extent to which changing conditions may have outdated their conclusions.

As Dwight Heath points out, the dyadic contract articles were generally well received by Latin Americanist anthropologists because they seemed to "ring true," to "make sense" of a variety of data the relationships of which were not immediately apparent. I continue to feel my interpretation is basically sound, both for Tzintzuntzan and other similar Latin American communities, *as of the mid-twentieth century.* So, when asked to comment on the dyadic contract model 35 years after publication, rather than discuss ways in which the articles might have been improved, I propose (1) to place the articles in the context of the development of anthropological peasant studies, and (2) to consider the extent to which the model, after nearly half a century of social change—change so rapid in Mexico that the concept of "peasant" itself is almost meaningless—still fits the village.

The Development of Peasant Studies

Anthropologists, and other observers of rural life, were writing about peasant communities well before the term itself came into general use, in the early 1960s. Prior to that time, most studies of Indian and Mestizo communities in Latin America were cast in the context of Robert Redfield's "folk society." Redfield, who pioneered the study of peasant communities in Latin America, first called his subjects "folk" in the subtitle of his classic study, *Tepoztlán: A Study of Folk Life* (1930). Only subsequently did he appreciate the greater utility of the peasant concept. Because of professional cultural lag, and the influence of Redfield's writing, a long line of anthropologists continued to talk about "folk culture" when, in fact, they were discussing peasant societies. Stimulating as it was, the "folk society" model was notoriously deficient insofar as providing integrative principles that could explain social structure and community cohesion. This lack of an adequate model to deal with problems of social structure stood in glaring contrast to British social anthropology, the practitioners of which, working largely in Africa and Oceania, had developed a formidable analytical tool—the concept of "structural-functional" studies of non-Western, often tribal, societies. Their approach stressed the importance of analyzing the functions of, or integrative roles played by, unilinear descent groups such as clans and lineages, and other "corporate" entities based largely on kinship, in structuring social life.

What applied to African and Oceanian societies obviously did not apply to most Latin American peasant communities, where kinship is bilateral rather than unilinear, the primary social unit (the village) is based on locality rather than tribal affiliation, and a great many legal and administrative functions are fulfilled by extra-community national agencies. The dyadic contract articles represented an attempt to bring something of the rigor of the British structural-functional analysis into our explanations of how peasant communities, in the absence of the more formal mechanisms found in African societies, hang together and function as going concerns. I felt that the model accounted for the nature of the interaction between people of the same socioeconomic status, between people of different statuses, between fellow villagers, between villagers and outsiders, and between human beings and the supernatural.

Briefly, the model hypothesizes that in Tzintzuntzan every adult organizes his societal contacts beyond the nuclear family by means of informal contractual relationships. These contracts are implicit, since they lack legal or ritual basis, and hence they are unenforceable, existing only at the pleasure of the contractants. The contracts are dyadic, since they are formed between pairs of people, and they are noncorporate, since units such as villages, barrios or extended families never are bound by them. Were I writing the articles today I would dwell more on the concept of *friendship*, since this is the basis on which horizontal contracts rest. The friendship concept does not, however, apply to contracts with supernatural patrons. I have never heard a village say, "My friend, San Antonio," in identifying a supernatural patron!

The Status of the Dyadic Contract Today

The question can be asked thusly: would an anthropologists beginning research in Tzintzuntzan today be apt to formulate the dyadic contract model? When in the village I continue to note many examples of the contract in action: Neighbors borrow chairs and benches for weddings and saints' day fiestas; the *compadrazgo* still plays a major role in family and friendship context; food is offered to some people who visit a home but not to others; and owners of trucks will bring purchases to a friend who does not have a vehicle, or whose truck is temporarily out of commission. At the same time, the totality of contractual ties appears to be significantly less than when I first wrote about the dyadic contract. This is due, I believe, to the fact that the functional demands placed on the system are fewer and less intense than formerly.

The dyadic model is particularly appropriate to communities where, as in the Tzintzuntzan of the mid-twentieth century, people felt they had few resources with which to "defend themselves" against life's threats, yet wished to avoid the *compromisos* which in fact were essential to the limited security they could achieve. In societies such as these, almost all interpersonal contacts are calculated, at least to some degree, in terms of their potential for strengthening defenses. Logically, then, as people acquire more means to "defend" themselves (e.g., through education and a higher standard of living), contractual obligations become less essential to the achievement and maintenance of individual and family security.

Tzintzuntzeños as a group are now far better equipped to defend themselves, to meet the challenges of life, than they were earlier. The village now has its own secondary school (junior high school), and senior high schools are readily available in Quiroga (five miles distant) and Pátzcuaro (10 miles). Increasing numbers of young people now enroll in the university in Morelia (35 miles), and considerable numbers attend institutions of higher learning in Mexico City. In these and other cities they acquire degrees in law, medicine, dentistry, veterinary medicine, engineering, computer sciences, agronomy, and other fields. Well over two hundred young people have become schoolteachers.

Economically, too, Tzintzuntzan is far better off than in 1960. Although the community is far from wealthy, most people have greater resources than even a few years ago. While monetary incomes are notoriously difficult for anthropologists to determine, rising standards of living can be measured in material possessions. Here the contrast is evident from census data for the years 1960 and 1990. In 1960 no homes in the village had television sets, sewers, refrigerators, flush toilets, telephones, or washing machines. By 1990, 78% of the homes had television, 66% sewers, 30% refrigerators, 25% flush toilets, 15% telephones, and 12% washing machines. In addition, the two propane gas stoves appearing in the 1960 census had swollen to 79% of all homes in 1990, the single hot shower to 19%, and the one truck to 17% of homes with motor vehicles.

A good deal of the material prosperity found in Tzintzuntzan comes from legal and illegal migrants in *el norte* (the United States), where men (and often wives and older children) work at a variety of tasks. Half a dozen young men spend six months a year on fishing boats out of Alaskan ports, earning in that time up to $20,000 U.S.! Obviously the demands placed on a contractual system of the type described in my two old papers are less stringent in a community of relatively well-educated and knowledgeable people who are not living, economically speaking, on the razor's edge, than they were in the Tzintzuntzan of 1960. Dyadic ties continue today, in the form of friendship, and they will continue into the distant future. But as a distinct, recognizable social institution, they will be harder and harder to recognize. I doubt that an anthropologist beginning research in Tzintzuntzan now would be struck, as I was many years ago, by the way in which seemingly odd bits of behavior conformed to a pattern of mutual obligations enabling people better to "defend" themselves.

References

Foster, George M. 1961. The dyadic contract: A model for the social structure of a Mexican peasant village. *American Anthropologist* 63, 1173–1192.

Foster, George M., assisted by Garbiel Ospina. 1948. *Empire's children: The people of Tzintzuntzan*. Mexico City: Smithsonian Institution, Institute of Social Anthropology, Publ. no. 6.

Foster, George M., Thayer Scudder, Elizabeth Colson, & Robert V. Kember (eds.). 1979. *Long-term field research in social anthropology*. New York: Academic Press.

Redfield, Robert. 1930. *Tepoztlán: A Mexican village. A study in folk life*. Chicago: University of Chicago Press.

Adrianne Aron-Schaar was an independent social scientist who sometimes taught at the University of California Extension, Santa Cruz, when she wrote this chapter. The editor has been unable to contact her lately, but has no reason to doubt that she is still a free-lance researcher.

Graft, inefficiency, and favoritism (personalismo) have long loomed large in the stereotypical view of Latin American public administration. In some instances the stereotype is justified, and this analysis of one provincial capital goes far toward explaining why. What looked like bureaucratic institutions did not always function in impersonal bureaucratic ways, although recent nationwide reforms have aimed at changing this situation.

This study is of special interest in terms of anthropological methods; it was written by someone who had never been to Bolivia but was able to derive fresh insights from detailed fieldnotes collected by me and others in the course of research on other topics, sponsored by Research Institute for the Study of Man.

Local Government in Bolivia
Public Administration and Popular Participation

Adrianne Aron-Schaar

It is difficult to describe Bolivian local government as an ordered system, for its most striking feature is a seeming lack of systemization. A day at city hall in any of the communities might easily be mistaken for a carnival of random behavior.

The men who planned the government structure appear to have had something fairly precise in mind, for there are numerous laws providing for the establishment of public offices at the local level. There are even vague statements of purpose for these offices, and people with desks and typewriters carrying out duties. Local government in Bolivia is a fact; only the principles which order it are a mystery. It is to this mystery that my paper is addressed.[1]

Taking the community of Coroico as an example, we may explore the nuances of local administration. A provincial capital of about 2,000 people, Coroico is the largest and most important town in its province. Heading the *Alcaldía,* or town administration, is the *Alcalde,* whose position is roughly equivalent to that of the North American mayor. The Alcalde is provided with a salary and is required to relinquish his former occupation and sources of income when he takes office in order to devote himself solely to his administrative duties. As the highest-ranking public official in the community, he receives the largest salary of any civil servant—420,000 Bolivianos per month, exchangeable for $33.60 in United States currency.

In Bolivia $33.60 might support a frugal bachelor for a month, but it will not maintain a family of five, even at bare subsistence, for that length of time. Eating modestly, a family of five would exhaust this amount in three weeks on food expenditures alone. The mayor is expected to abandon his previous means of making a living, and yet he is not provided with sufficient funds to avoid starvation. As Max Weber points out, either politics can be conducted honorifically, by independently wealthy men, or political leadership can be made accessible to propertyless men, who must then be rewarded.[2]

We must logically conclude that, owing to the meagerness of the reward, no *poor* man could accept the post of mayor. In an order where wealth is traditionally associ-

---

Written expressly for *Contemporary Cultures and Societies of Latin America.*

ated with large landholdings, one might expect that, by default, the position must fall to a member of the landed aristocracy. Considering that the Agrarian Reform Act of 1953 altogether abolished the landed aristocracy of Coroico, we are faced with a logical impossibility. The only eligible candidate for public office is the *nouveau riche* (rarely popular or civic minded) or the fool.

Realizing that the law has created a hopeless situation, custom has intervened to permit the authorities to supplement their meager salaries. Precisely how this should be done, however, has never been defined; therefore, it is usually the officials themselves who decide by what means and by what amounts their income should be increased. What begins as a liberalization of law for the sake of establishing a government to protect the people often ends as an established government which exists to exploit the people. The impossibility of surviving on a government salary becomes the *carte blanche* for a wide variety of spectacles. It explains, for example, why a judge and his wife and three children are living rent-free on the second floor of the town hall in a suite of rooms designed as public offices. It explains why the postmaster removes the stamps from incoming letters, erases the cancellation mark, and sells the restored stamps as new. It explains why the town library has disappeared book by book, and why the money sent by the government for the construction of a local hospital was spent by the state doctor.

What is remarkable is that such deeds not only are openly tolerated by the citizens, but are looked upon with sympathy. When the doctor walked around town complaining, "What could I do? They sent it to me in small bills, Bs. 5,000 ($0.40) here, 5,000 there, and pretty soon it was all gone," the people agreed, saying, "You're right; how can the government expect you to watch small bills? They never should have sent small bills."

More typical than these individual solutions to the problem of making a living are two basic patterns, followed with such frequency and regularity that they can be considered institutions. These are the maintenance of private enterprises by public officials and the custom of graft. While the one undermines the notion of professional authorities who make politics a vocation, the other undermines the whole theory of responsible and democratic government. Taken together, these two institutions, better than any constitution or code of laws, capture the essence of local government in Bolivia.

POLITICS AND BUSINESS

It is not the maintenance by public officials of private business per se which is inimical to honest government; the danger lies in the powerful and continuing temptation to use one's office for private gain. Obviously, some businesses and professions offer more alluring temptations than others. The pharmacist who became deputy mayor[3] turned his drugstore over to a manager during his tenure and both his public office and private drugstore were able to run smoothly, without interference from each other. The lawyer who became a judge, however, presents us with a very different set of circumstances. Not only does he continue to practice law, but it is not unusual for him to appear as both counsel and judge of a defendant brought before the court. Even the tolerant people of Coroico regard this court as an outrage. But once it has been granted that a public authority must eat, and that he may practice his profession while in office in order to secure a reasonable income, one has already forfeited one's right to recourse and must resign himself to the risks that ensue. Outrage, in effect, becomes institutionalized.

This is not to say that the union of private profit and public office is necessarily catastrophic. The argument has been made, after all, that what is good for General

Motors is good for the country. When the mayor, who is by trade a coffee merchant, discovered that the community was suffering a flour shortage, he promptly made a trip to La Paz to deliver coffee and returned with 1,700 pounds of flour. Using the town hall as a warehouse, he began selling flour at bargain prices "as a public service." Thus while gaining favor among housewives, he was able simultaneously to make a small profit and to eliminate the flour shortage.[4] The difficulty, of course, is that the public finds itself subject to the whims of the authorities, without any assurance that what benefits the authorities will in any way coincide with the public welfare. If the authorities would rather be feared than loved, the people are in trouble.

THE CUSTOM OF GRAFT

Unlike the maintenance of private sources of income, which may have neutral or even beneficent effects on a community, the practice of graft inevitably produces discrimination and inequality before the law. The man who does not know that payment is expected, or the man who hasn't enough money to offer an attractive sum—in short, "the little man"—is inescapably a victim of the system.

It should be pointed out that there are two meanings for what I have chosen to call graft.[5] Because their general consequences are identical I have grouped them together, but actually they differ substantially in their methods. The one kind of graft is virtually synonymous with bribery and is used to induce an official to forgo his legal responsibilities. Typically the transaction is carried out surreptitiously, and when it is completed the official has tacitly agreed to protect his benefactor from inconvenience, punishment, and discomfort. The other kind of graft is paid quite openly to the official in return for a service rendered in the line of duty. It is paid not as a favor, but on demand, as a commission or a fee.

Why then should something as ordinary as a fee be placed in the same category as an outright bribe? There are three good answers to this question. One is that the Bolivian Constitution expressly forbids salaried functionaries to exact fees for their services, so that the practice is manifestly unconstitutional.[6] Second, being illegal, the fees cannot be fixed—given price for a given service—and consequently they are completely arbitrary and set by the officials themselves capriciously. Third, it is utterly impossible to receive the services of the authorities unless one is prepared to pay for them. The public servants are in fact neither public nor servants. They are men who receive a small stipend from the government for occupying an office and remaining on call in the event that a private citizen wishes to hire their services. The system is quite literally that of "rent-a-cop."

The police chief explains his role in the following way:

> Let's say that your brother is murdered. You come to Coroico for justice. I'm interested and sympathetic, but I have no transportation and no allowance for travel. So, if you want me to go investigate, you have to pay my way, with meals, and pay for [the travel and meals of] another policeman [who comes] as my helper. And you have to provide lodging for us as long as we're investigating. Well then, suppose we're lucky and find the guilty party within a few days. We still have to bring him back to Coroico. So you, as the interested party, have to pay his transportation as well as ours. Then when he's in jail here, you have to . . . arrange to have his food brought in. Then you have to pay for his trip to La Paz and for [the trip of] his escort, a *carabinero* who has to eat and have lodging for a few days in La Paz [before you pay his expenses back] to Coroico, where he's stationed. All this the interested party alone has to pay; we have no funds. So justice is expensive, and many people let things go because they can't afford such costs. It's a shame, but there's no remedy.

If the service orientation of public office is a myth, the law enforcement orientation, at least where profit is to be had, is a vital reality. And, as might be expected, the same citizens who are barred by reasons of inadequate funds and influence from enjoying government services are the ones most familiar with the law enforcement procedures of the government officials. If there is a fine to be imposed, a tax to be levied, a crime to be punished, it is again the little man who is the natural victim.

One might find it curious that the poor man should be sought for revenue purposes when there is plainly more money to be gained by taxing the rich man. It is not curious at all though, if one looks beyond man's economic motivations to his social relations, where common sense dictates that a peer is to be treated with greater consideration than a stranger. This fellow I have called the little man is best described abstractly as a stranger, an outsider, a person who is not a part of the reference group of the men who hold power. He is the likely one to be taxed or fined or punished because it is doubtful that any social repercussions will occur if he is exploited; he is a safe victim. Moreover, if an outsider can be found, an insider can often be spared discomfort.

Typically, the outsider, or little man, is the *campesino*, who is at once the poorest, the least educated, the least assimilated member of the community. The *campesino* is further handicapped by an imperfect command of the Spanish language and by a history of servitude which he has not yet overcome. Thus he is more than a marginal man who is pushed around by those who wield power; he is a member of a social class which is pushed around by members of a superior class.

There is but one protective measure available to the *campesino*: He may join a *campesino* syndicate and benefit from the influence which these syndicates possess both in La Paz and locally. Whereas the upper classes are united only emotionally and doctrinally, sharing a fierce contempt for the Revolution of 1952, the *campesinos* are actually organized. Knowing that the *campesinos* could, by exerting pressure on the capital, unseat them, it behooves the local mestizo authorities to handle the *campesinos* with some delicacy. Hence in a town like Coroico, where the *campesinos* of nearby Cruz Loma are well organized, instances of overt discrimination against *campesinos* are uncommon. Instead, discrimination is practiced with the utmost subtlety.

What was to me the most ingenious case of oblique discrimination occurred in Coroico when the public lavatories were opened. These lavatories were built for the ostensible purpose of serving the *campesinos,* who come into town from the countryside and have no access to private facilities. The municipal intendant, whose job it is to look after public sanitation, took it upon himself to inspect the lavatories after each use, to guarantee that they were being used properly. As a person left the room, the intendant would rush in to inspect, and every time he found the condition of the room less than satisfactory be would impose a fine of Bs. 40,000 ($3.20) on his mortified victim. Since the *campesinos* are the only members of the community who are not accustomed to modern sanitation facilities, they were the only ones fined for improper use of the toilets. Yet it would be quite impossible to prove that these inspections were designed to exploit a single segment of the population. The inspections continued until the word was spread sufficiently and no more *campesinos* came to the public lavatories.

Since proof is more difficult to establish, discrimination against *campesinos* as a class is more easily carried out than discrimination against a particular individual, but the latter form is not necessarily less effective. It has its own special virtues.

The lone *campesino* who has been treated unfairly, either by another citizen or by one of the officials, usually cannot enlist the support of his syndicate for his personal cause. Nor, as we have seen, can he usually afford to buy protection from the authorities. But there is still one avenue open to him. He can seek a sponsor from the upper class, either a *compadre* or a former *patrón,* and with the help of his sponsor pursue his cause.

Earlier I called the syndicate the only protective agency available to the *campesino*. It must be emphasized that that statement still pertains, for while the *campesino* may turn to the *patrón* for assistance, it is not in his interest to do so.

The former *patrón* may provide the *campesino* with the necessary money for use as graft and intervene on his behalf before the authorities, but his motives are not as altruistic as they might seem. It is altogether in his interest to befriend the *campesino,* for it rekindles the spirit of vassalage that prevailed before the Revolution. It is a reminder to the *campesino* of his helplessness in the face of adverse conditions, of his need for the personal protection of the patrón. Every step taken by a *campesino* toward the former *patrón* is a step away from the class independence which the syndicates are striving to inspire. And every loss suffered by the syndicates is a gain for the upper classes.

The *campesino,* then, is everywhere faced with untenable situations. Having no friends among the public officials, he can expect no favors. Lacking sufficient funds for bribery, he is denied protection of the law. Lacking protection, he is the likely target for abuse. Once abused, he must either accept his plight with stoical resignation or turn to his former master for help. If he turns to his former master he reestablishes his feudal ties and abandons hope for emancipation.

The structure of local government in Bolivia, far from advancing the egalitarian ideals of the Revolution, systematically obstructs them. What appears, even after careful study, to be utterly devoid of systematization turns out on still closer analysis to be a quite elaborate system geared to keeping alive the class distinctions which the Revolution pronounced dead in 1952.

To anyone familiar with the work of Max Weber, it should be clear that the existing structure of local government in Bolivia can be understood by enumerating Weber's criteria of responsible government and simply bearing in mind that in Bolivia precisely the *opposite* conditions prevail. The criteria are essentially these: fixed hierarchy, jurisdiction, and tenure in public office; division of labor; strict adherence to rules; impersonality; technical qualifications for holding offices; and specified salaries for the office holders.[7]

To get a purchase on the problem I have dealt selectively with these concepts and have confined my discussion to a single community. The data strongly suggest that if the same task were undertaken in any of the other towns studied in this project, the results would be virtually identical. This is not to say that it is always the *campesino* who is victimized by the system, or that in all places the degree of discrimination is constant. It is the *spirit* of government that remains unchanged—the idea that government exists to grant privilege to some and deny rights to others. In Sorata, for example, where revolutionary upheaval placed *campesinos* in control of the government, exclusion and privilege are as prevalent as in Coroico and even more rigidly enforced; only the roles are reversed. Here the *blanco* is denied equal protection of the law, while the *campesino* plunders the community wealth.

Who is on top is not a significant issue. What matters is that built into the very foundations of Bolivian government are the provisions for sustaining inequality.[8] My argument began by identifying the insufficiency of government salaries as the catalyst for unscrupulous and arbitrary administration. That it is a catalyst and not a cause must be stressed, for if the salaries of all government officials were tripled, the laws of the land strictly observed, and professional qualifications demanded of all personnel, the spirit of personalism and privilege would linger. Merely altering the government structure could not erase the historical, psychological, and social factors which have combined since the Conquest to define a people's way of life and way of thinking about the world. The present form of government is not responsible for, but is rather responsive to, the Bolivian way of life.

Notes

[1] An earlier version of this paper was presented at a meeting of the American Anthropological Association, held at Pittsburgh, Pa., November 1966. It is based on ethnographic and survey data collected in Coroico as part of the Bolivia project of the Research Institute for the Study of Man, supported by Peace Corps Grant No. PC(W)-397. Coroico is one of six small communities in the study; for more details, see William J. McEwen, et al., *Changing Rural Bolivia* ([New York] Research Institute for the Study of Man, 1969,) esp. pp. 105–163.

[2] Max Weber, "Politics as a Vocation," in Hans Gerth and C. Wright Mills (eds.), *From Max Weber: Essays in Sociology* (London: Routledge and Kegan Paul, Ltd., 1952), p. 86.

[3] This official's title is *official mayor;* I use the term "deputy mayor" as the nearest counterpart in the North American system.

[4] The Mayor has even articulated his defense of plutocracy: "Why should I want graft? I have enough income from my private business." But another citizen has expressed worry about wealthy men in public office: "Chances are that the rich man has made his money illegally and will continue with his illegal activities in office."

[5] The local term for graft is *coima,* although many Bolivians would also recognize the term *mordida,* by which such practices are known throughout much of Latin America.

[6] The Constitution of Bolivia, Section 17, Article 118, in N. Andrew N. Cleven, *The Political Organization of Bolivia* (Washington, DC: The Carnegie Institution, 1940), p. 225. [Editor's note: Although Bolivia has had nearly half a dozen constitutions since the one cited, it is noteworthy that this specification has been reiterated in each.]

[7] Max Weber, "Bureaucracy," op. cit., passim.

[8] [Editor's note: Because some of the facts described here could be construed as negative, it may be in order to emphasize that the present-tense verbs relate to the time of the study; some or all of the conditions described may well have changed in ensuing years.]

Catherine M. Boyle teaches Spanish and Spanish American Studies at King's College, University of London. She is a co-founder and co-editor of Journal of Latin American Cultural Studies *(formerly* Travesía*) and writes widely on theater and cultural studies throughout Latin America.*

By briefly describing how and why middle-class women in Chile took to the streets to demonstrate in protest against governmental restrictions and austerity, Boyle turns a spotlight on the seldom-described process of politicization. The mobilization of formerly voiceless constituencies has been a rare but powerful force throughout history, increasing in Latin America in recent decades and toppling old stereotypes about the distribution of wealth and power, and the social order in general. Feijoo and Gogna (chapter 34) describe an analogous dynamic in Argentina; Robben (chapter 35) sensitively sheds some light on "the dark side" of such protests.

Touching the Air
The Cultural Force of Women in Chile
Catherine M. Boyle

THE CREATION OF THE CULTURAL

Culture is how people express their daily lives and how people express themselves in their daily lives. Cultural expression is the *material* expression of the interaction between an internal self and experience with an external reality. Culture cannot be seen as an immutable solid apart from or pinned onto society, for it is integral to society, it grows from it and feeds it, it elucidates its day-to-day workings, and provides ways of talking about ourselves within our different contexts. Without cultural expression a society is void of forms and means of reference. It is void of concrete evidence of the meeting points between the inner self and external realities.[1]

When the upper-class women of Santiago's *barrio alto* took to the streets with their empty pots their motivation was anger: the welfare of their domain had been seriously compromised, the comfort of their domestic setup destroyed. The government had failed them on the most basic of levels, the level of nutrition. In this instance, the pot was not a kitchen utensil, it was a symbol, a representation of basic human provision; the empty pot was the representation of the failure of the state to satisfy a basic need. This failure on the part of the government resulted in the inability of the mother to carry out a key role, that of caring for her family. The empty pot did not only mean physical need, it meant a role threatened, it meant crisis in the household. The demonstrations, orchestrated, as Mattelart (1976) shows, with almost military precision by Poder Femenino, meant that this perception of reality and its penetration of the area of political action heralded definitive trouble for President Allende: women on the march augured badly. As Kirkwood pointed out, the demonstrations prompted renewed worried questioning in the left about women's so-called conservatism, about the direction their political participation had taken (Kirkwood 1990: 49–50). These demonstrations were a shock. Women who had been regarded as apolitical stepped beyond the bounds of decorum of the middle-class housewife and occupied the streets. The kitchen, the home, became political. This invasion of the public by the private had a lasting impact on the collective memory and imagination, providing images that, as we have seen, were evoked in 1988 in the public declarations of the women against Pinochet, and in newspaper articles. The empty pot had become embedded in the collective memory as a political symbol.

This was clearly seen in the movement for democracy, and the plebiscite campaigns. In the early 1980s, the space for political expression began to open; people began, they said, to lose fear and to take up political action to rid themselves of President Pinochet, who, naturally, fought back. In 1985 he imposed a state of siege, and Chile experienced one of the worst periods of repression since the mid-1970s. Protest was, once again, sent underground. Yet, throughout this period, people subverted Pinochet's imposition of silence and civic invisibility in order to make a voice heard. This voice found representation in the noise of the pots.

At a given hour on days of protest, people would go outside, into backyards or gardens, and bang pots. In the *poblaciones*[2] the din would be unbearable; in some areas of the centre of Santiago, the same would be the case, but the noise died out to the timid sound of the occasional solitary pot towards the middle- and upper-class districts. A past symbol of right-wing opposition, a symbol of the downfall of Allende, was consciously and successfully subverted. And behind the use of this symbol lay the same reasons, albeit of a very different magnitude. The long-term economic policies of the regime, which had benefited large numbers of the middle and upper sectors, had caused huge unemployment that had hit the *poblaciones* hardest. Empty pots did not mean, in this case, not being able to serve the dish of your choice. Empty pots meant no food, eating tea and bread, buying *calugas de aceite* (caramel-sized quantities of cooking oil). In simple terms, an empty pot meant not being able to *parar la olla* (fill the family pot). Pinochet, who had trusted that women and their domestic trappings—such as pots—would, after the coup, return indoors to a designated docility, had, in these sectors, achieved exactly the opposite. Repression, disappearances, high levels of malnutrition, infant mortality, family breakdown, growing prostitution including unprecedented levels of teenage prostitution, had all meant that the private sphere of the domestic was constantly invaded and undermined by the consequences of the socioeconomic policies. Women for whom the family was the core of their lives, for whom the family was the central and uniting element in their community, fought to defend it. And again, out of a reality of daily existence, came its physical expression in an expression of protest. The pot had been used as a vehicle of protest by the right, but the very fact that the pot is part of every single household means that it is a potential symbol for all. Like all symbols, it belongs exclusively to nobody, yet to everyone; it can be and is consciously used to store up memories and, like all symbols, it is open to subversion or appropriation by other groups. In the 1970s a network of signs was created that was linked primarily with testimonial forms, and women were at the centre of this process.

LO QUE ESTÁ EN EL AIRE: WHAT IS IN THE AIR

In 1989, at the time of the plebiscite, there was a demonstration by 2,000 women in Santiago.[3] The women walked in silence along the main avenues of the centre of Santiago, carrying cardboard cut-outs of disappeared people, each one with a name. No words were spoken; only the image was seen, uncontaminated by slogans, for by that time the word was not to be trusted in Chile. The function of the march was to save "the disappeared" from a further disappearance: elimination from the collective imagination at a time of public euphoria. The women knew it was fundamental that, with the return to democracy, human rights issues, the fights of the groups for the detained and disappeared, should not be pulled into the euphoria of the plebiscite and forgotten or abandoned as a threat to stability. The women knew that elimination from the collective imagination was the first step to elimination from the collective memory. They were no longer the "well-behaved feminists" of before, they were aware of the continued workings of authoritarianism. And if words like "democracy," "stability," "tranquility" and "peace" were now in the mouths of the centre and the left, that did not mean that their meaning was strong and honest. It meant, rather, that these words had to be reinvested with pure meanings, meanings that would remember the past and make way for the future.

The women who organized these demonstrations were poets and writers. They were in tune with what was in the air in terms of the collective preoccupations in society in the process towards democracy, whether explicitly stated or relatively unarticulated. They knew the key symbols of cultural expression under authoritarianism, and more than that, they had been part of the building of a system of elaborating and diffusing these symbols, of speaking and saying, keeping alive the languages of memory and the telling of experience. Women had transcended the private level to be an integral part of the naming and expressing of the present, and of a dynamic impetus for the future.

There has been a palpable change in the presence of women in Chile. On many levels, the same questions as before remain ingrained in society; deep fears still exist about the strength of apparently safe social structures. But, on other levels, the experience of the Pinochet years, throughout which women were at the heart of the struggle against authoritarian rule, is not, as in other situations, a short hiatus in the invisibility of women in Chilean society. This is not a case of women stepping in to fill places left vacant by men. This is a case of positive transgression, a transgression made slowly into worlds of men's power, slowly and with solidarity for men's struggles, a solidarity built on the knowledge that equality and respect between men and women was and is the only progressive way forward. This transgression is built on creation, the creation of bonds, of links, and, most of all, a multiplicity of languages that articulate not only female experience, but a history. Women in Chile have become part of the community who feel the air and give memory and experience their words, images and symbols, which, like all words, images and symbols, can belong to everyone.

Notes

[1] For a concise discussion of popular culture, see Rowe and Schelling 1991.

[2] I have used the word *población* in the original Spanish because I feel that the usual translation of shantytown in inadequate. Here I borrow the definition of Carolyn Lehmann in an as yet unpublished article, "Bread and Roses: Women Who Live Poverty": "A *población* is one of the urban, marginated densely populated areas peripheral to the center of the capital city, Santiago. Each *población* has its own character, its own name, its history, its pride. The word cannot satisfactorily be translated as 'shantytown' or 'urban slum'" (pp. 1–2). Some *poblaciones* have well-developed social and cultural organizations.

[3] For information on the demonstrations by women throughout the Pinochet regime, see Molina 1990.

References

Kirkwood, J. 1990. *Ser Política en Chile: Los Nudos de la Sabiduría Feminista*. Santiago: Editorial Cuarto Propio.

Mattelart, M. 1976. "Chile: the feminine version of the coup d'état," in J. Nash and H. I. Safa (eds.), *Sex and Class in Latin America*. New York: Bergin Publishers, 279–301.

Molina, N. 1990. "El estado y las mujeres: una relación difícil," in *Transiciones: Mujeres en los Procesos Democráticos*. Santiago: Isis Internacional. Ediciones de las mujeres 13, 83–97.

Rowe, W. and Schelling, V. 1991. *Memory and Modernity: Popular Culture in Latin America*. London: Verso.

María del Carmen Feijoo is coordinator of the Working Group on the Situation of Women, in the Consejo Latinoamericano de Ciencias Sociales. Mónica Gogna is an anthropologist with the Centro de Estudios de Estado y Sociedad, in Buenos Aires, Argentina.

As "the land of the tango," Argentina rarely comes to mind as the home of an important and widely respected women's movement. Feijoo and Gogna show how the nonviolent demonstrations of the Mothers of Plaza de Mayo have persistently reminded political leaders and others of their demands for information about "disappeared" relatives (presumably killed in a time of ruthless domestic suppression of protests), and by so doing are seen as quiet heroes by many. Different in immediate motivation and format, but similar in demonstrating the strong will and potential power of traditionally inconspicuous urban women, are the pot-rattling marches in Chile (Boyle, chapter 33).

Women in the Transition to Democracy
Argentina's Mothers of the Plaza de Mayo
María del Carmen Feijoo and Mónica Gogna

HISTORY, MEMORY, AWARENESS

From a historical perspective, feminist, feminine and/or women's struggles date back—with differing character, composition and objective—to the end of the nineteenth century and beginning of the twentieth century (Feijoo, 1982a). Their objectives included a complex bundle of demands, centering alternately on problems related to civil, political and labor rights, though not necessarily in this historical order. These struggles were fragmented, dispersed and conjunctural, and they left a more or less permanent and diverse impression on women's memory. We know little about them in terms of scientific knowledge, but more from personal experience and self-examination. This relative permanence within the subjects themselves combines with the "public" absence of these struggles when it comes to research, analysis and retrieval, as feminist historiography has so often shown (Feijoo 1982b, Rowbotham 1976). They are struggles that have been forgotten, but somehow remain present and operative in women's memory, in determining the basis of their identity, and in the collective imagination. Not everyone remembers the same milestones. For some women, the memory is of Evita Perón proclaiming the passing of the law for female suffrage in 1947 (Navarro 1981); for others, it is Cecilia Grierson entering the Faculty of Medicine dressed as a man to begin her studies at the end of the nineteenth century. Finally, for others it is that of anonymous working women, sexually harassed by their supervisors in the industries set up in the capital city at the beginning of the twentieth century. These varied contents, fixed in our memory, surely form the fragile thread of identity that makes us Argentine women, taking our different places in society, especially in terms of class.

The reappearance of the women's movement on the political scene from 1981 to the present must by necessity refer back to these issues. The idea of reappearance, however, by no means suggests an automatic return to developments of the past or the simple retrieval of known political behavior. In reality, it is a "new" phenomenon, although this assertion should be made with care. In order to understand it, the analysis should go back to at least 1975, to the birth of the situation used by the 1976 military coup to legitimize the intervention. It is also necessary to make some reference to the policies adopted by the Peronist government in relation to its position regarding women and to measures principally affecting women, in order to understand the characteristics of the movement's re-emergence and its capacity to play a relevant role in the process of overthrowing the dictatorship.

THE CRISIS OF THE LAST PERONIST GOVERNMENT, THE COUP AND WOMEN

There appears to be no general agreement among the various authors regarding the severity of the crisis suffered by Argentina in 1975 (Landi 1978). This crisis affected the whole of society, and each sector under attack responded to it according to its capacity. In this context, the situation of women was not viewed as especially critical. Women had participated vigorously in the pre-election campaign of 1973 and had succeeded in gaining a significant parliamentary representation compared with the number of women participating in the previous parliament: 17 elected legislators in 1973 against one deputy in 1963 (Casas 1982). The majority were Peronists. Since the death of President Perón in 1974, his widow and vice-president, Maria Estela Martinez—popularly known as Isabel—had taken over the presidency of the country. There is little need to point out that having a woman in this office did not guarantee per se implementation of policies to improve women's situation. Furthermore, the Peronist movement, in spite of all it had achieved for women in previous periods (1946–55), took what, to say the least, can only be called an ambiguous stance on women's issues during the 1973–76 period. Some of the measures taken did reflect their concern for the situation of women in the popular sectors. The law on neighborhood nurseries was passed in 1973 for women's benefit but it was never ratified and therefore never implemented. There were also measures changing the basis for access to social services and social security, such as extending those rights available to legitimate wives of affiliates to the scheme to cover common-law wives, whom we prefer to call *de facto* partners. This meant they were recognized as wives with full rights, at least for the purposes of social security. These measures were consistent with a certain tradition within Peronist governments that led to substantive progress in the situation of women. The law on women's suffrage, passed in 1947, the law giving equal rights to children born in and out of wedlock, and the brief period (from 1954 up to the military coup in September 1955) during which the divorce law was in force, were measures aimed at improving the subordinate position of women in society. The figure of Evita completed the image of a combative woman committed to popular struggles.

As mentioned above, in spite of this tradition in the 1973–76 period, other measures caused astonishment among women and in some cases gave rise to veiled resistance, although this was never organized on any significant scale. We refer, among other measures, to population policies that included prohibiting sales of female contraceptives—a measure stemming from the need to increase the country's demographic potential. Another, and one which certainly caused greater concern, was the veto from the Executive—the President herself—(paradoxically by a woman, as has often been pointed out) of the law concerning the right of both parents to exercise *patria potestad*.[1] Both Chambers had approved this draft law that constituted an important claim by women in a society in which mothers were in a frankly subordinate position within the family.

Despite the unease caused by these measures, however, women's capacity for response was limited. The feminist movement was only beginning (Cano, 1982) and in only a few cases had women's sections in political organizations been consolidated. When these groups did exist—such as in all of the popular mass organizations—they discussed the general political crisis affecting the country. Seen in retrospect, even the political organizations that attempted to develop women's sections, such as the Evita Group of the Peronist Youth, found it difficult to deal with specifically women's issues, becoming instead additional arenas for the discussion of the same issues. Though the behavior of the Female Branch of the National (Peronist) Movement for Justice does merit more detailed examination, the summons to women within this group nevertheless did not succeed in going beyond traditional appeals.

Thus, 1975 culminated in a state of generalized crisis. Armed organizations carried out some spectacular actions—even at the very gates of the city of Buenos Aires—and indiscriminate repression, especially at the hands of para-police groups, reached unimaginable limits, such as a shooting at the base of the Obelisk itself—a monument that symbolizes the physical center of the city. The government, under attack and with no room for maneuver, became weaker every day, while some of the mass media and other sectors began to work openly in favor of the military coup, which was to put an end to the disorder. The economic crisis and soaring inflation during February and March 1976 were presented as evidence of Mrs. Perón's inability to govern (Landi, 1978). Obviously, in this context of generalized crisis, there was little room for the discussion of women's problems.

The unease affecting all social sectors before the coup rapidly turned into a nightmare when the military junta's government adopted its first economic measures and put the state firmly behind the continuation of policies of terror, which until then had been carried out principally by para-police groups. The naive dreams of those who believed in military "order" rapidly disappeared. Almost without exception, the whole of the population came under scrutiny and women were threatened, like so many other groups. The need to reinstate order was used to justify repression (Quevedo 1984).

The main victims of the military junta's socioeconomic policies were the popular sectors. The brunt of the neo-liberal economic policy adopted—together with the consequent reordering of the social structure—hit the popular sectors in particular. The policies implemented in this process included: a drastic cut in real wages, cuts in state provision of social services for workers, the introduction of charges on health services, a reduction in state education provisions and the indexation of loans for housing and small-scale real estate (Frenkel 1980; Llovet 1984; Feijoo 1983). Altogether these measures translated into a considerable deterioration in the living standards of the popular sectors. As has been shown (Jelin and Feijoo, 1980), in Argentina the decrease in working-class purchasing power for goods and services in times of crisis was compensated for in two ways. On the one hand, there was an increase in the number of goods repaired or replaced by home production, thereby increasing the number of hours women spent mending and making clothing and tending to vegetable plots, even in suburban neighborhoods. The domestic unit, thus converted into the only possible palliative to the economic crisis, implied a restructuring of women's role within the unit by multiplying the number of tasks necessary to guarantee the family's daily upkeep. On the other hand, with regard to the increasing cost or lack of some basic services, it was women who had to spend more time waiting for treatment in health centers or who had to travel away from their neighborhoods in search of hospitals that did not charge, or which offered free milk or medicines with the medical care. In either case, it was women, especially those of the popular sectors, who were doubly victimized by these policies, because as women they were responsible for reproduction and, in terms of class, they belonged to the least favored sector of society.

In this context women, therefore, suffered the general oppression experienced by the population as a whole but aggravated by a specific oppression, which stemmed from the old process of subsuming the needs and problems of women in the needs and problems of the "family"—an easy transposition that affected the condition of women as "subjects." A "normal" woman should never entertain desires or aspirations different from those of her family. Paradoxically, the government's attempts to privatize what was public and strengthen the family as a mechanism of social control could not prevent the family itself—now the only safe nucleus in a violent society—from becoming a refuge where opinions on the horrific situation could be exchanged and where an alternative socialization with a different discourse (both political and in opposition to the government) could flourish (Entel 1983). The privatization of public life thus turned out to be a boomerang.

THE MOTHERS OF THE PLAZA DE MAYO

Brief history: The movement of the Mothers of the Plaza de Mayo was formed in April 1977, as a response to the policy of forced disappearance of individuals implemented by the military dictatorship in March 1976. The original group comprised 14 women, aged between 40 and 60 years of age. They got to know each other while going to and fro in the endless search for their children, and decided to bring their pain out into the open by demonstrating in front of the government palace and demanding that their children "reappear alive." Walking around the Mayo pyramid, they established links, shared their suffering and began a solitary resistance to brute power. They grew in experience and number and by July that year there were already more than 150. In October, they reached public opinion for the first time with a demand published in the daily newspaper *La Prensa* entitled "All we want is the truth," in which 237 mothers demanded a reply from the government regarding the whereabouts of their children (Bousquet, 1983). A few days later, they handed in a petition to the authorities with 24,000 signatures, demanding an investigation into the disappearances, freedom for those illegally detained, freedom for those detained without trial and the immediate transfer to civil courts of those already on trial. The police dispersed the mothers who delivered the petition, with tear gas and shots fired into the air, and about 300 were detained for several hours while their records were checked. In December, the organization of relatives of the disappeared received a harsh blow: several people who had been preparing the text of a demand to be published at Christmas were kidnapped as they came out of the Church of the Holy Cross. A few days later, Mrs. De Vicenti, one of the founders of the Mothers, was also kidnapped. Many of the mothers were overcome with fear but they maintained their fighting spirit and renewed their struggle.[2] The football World Cup in June 1978 was another difficult time: the Mothers felt bewilderment and pain at the population's jubilation, and many no longer dared to demonstrate. But they were also aware of the possibility that foreign reporters might take photographs of their walk around the Mayo pyramid and record their testimony of pain and hope. At the end of that same year, during one of their now customary walks around the square, the Mothers broke through the police cordon and installed themselves in front of the *Casa Rosada* (the government house); some of them refused to go away and were taken to the police station for identity checks. The following Thursday the police prevented them from entering the square— the same thing happened the next week. They then decided to abandon the square—to which, save sporadic appearances, they would return only in January 1980—and become officially constituted as an association. In August 1979, 20 women, before a public notary, signed the founding document of the Mothers of the Plaza de Mayo Movement.

Anticipating the problems for social movements in the process of transition to democracy, this document established that the founders—from among whom an executive committee was elected—could not join any political party. That same year, 1979, saw the visit of the Inter-American Human Rights Commission of the Organization of American States (OAS). During this period the Mothers contacted those relatives of the disappeared living in the provinces, arranged lodgings for those coming to Buenos Aires to make their accusations, and stood in queues for many hours to give their testimonies to the Commission. These contacts gradually gave a more complete picture of the scale and magnitude of the horror, if it needed to be corroborated at all. The visit, which had raised the Mothers' hopes, left them with a bitter taste (Bousquet, 1983). In December, a few days before Christmas, they resumed their Thursday walk around the square: they demanded a Christmas without disappearances and political prisoners, objectives they had been seeking for over three years. In 1980 a "dialogue" between the Ministry of Internal Affairs and leaders of representative sectors got underway. This period also saw a change of direction in the Mothers' strategy: they tried to persuade their compatriots to join in the protests being raised abroad. The Mothers and Relatives of the Disappeared and People Detained for Political Reasons, a human rights organization created in October 1976, which "assumes disappearances and imprisonment as a political fact,"[3] launched a campaign for national mobilization aimed at getting the list of detained-disappeared people published. They also turned to the politicians, hoping to receive support for their cause. In August that year they succeeded in publishing a public request in the newspaper *Clarín*, in which certain prominent public figures supported the demands of the relatives of the disappeared. The year 1981 saw the human rights movement shifting from a purely defensive position to one of greater initiative. The Mothers' unnegotiable rallying cry was gradually taken up by other human rights groups. In December of that year, 150 mothers staged the first "Resistance March." A year later they were joined on the second march by the Grandmothers[4] and Relatives, making a total of over 5,000 demonstrators.

Defeat in the Malvinas/Falklands war, an adventure that the Mothers had been the first to denounce, had accelerated the regime's deterioration. In this context, the tenacious struggle of the Mothers and the whole of the human rights movement (MDH) effectively narrowed the margin for negotiations upon which the retreating dictatorship wished to embark (González Bombal, 1984a). The Mothers then led the March against the Law of National Peace (April 1983) and toured Europe in an attempt to gain support in the form of pressure from several governments (Palermo and García Delgado, 1983). With politics back in play, they attended every political meeting; they asked the Multiparty Commission not to inherit the problem of the disappeared; and during the election campaign they demanded that leaders adopt the issue and demand the return of the disappeared. A month before the elections they organized the third Resistance March, with a turnout of around 15,000, during which the streets in the center of Buenos Aires were covered with silhouettes to symbolize those who had disappeared. Another reason for the march was to announce that "come what may, whoever wins [the elections], their children must appear alive and those guilty of crimes against the people should be punished."[5] Days before the constitutional government took office, the Mothers publicly declared their position in face of the new circumstances:

> In order to achieve the democracy we have longed for, we will exercise participation and criticism; we will petition and dissent and we will mobilize to obtain the legitimate rights of the people; we therefore request the newly-elected government to bring back alive those who were detained-disappeared; we request freedom for all political and trade union prisoners and that those responsible be put on trial.[6]

The strategy they proposed in order to achieve their objective was the creation of a bicameral parliamentary commission with full powers, in which the Mothers and other representatives of human rights organizations would have a voice; and the ratification by the Congress of the Law to Introduce Trial by Jury to determine the sentences for crimes committed according to the common penal code.[7] The Radical government's reply was to repeal the amnesty and order a summary trial before the Supreme Court of the armed forces of the three military juntas. In addition, the national executive gave instructions through Decree No. 187 for the creation of a National Commission on the Disappearance of Persons, made up of six legislators and ten figures from the civilian sphere, whose basic task was to receive accusations and hear evidence on human rights violations and pass them on immediately to the courts. Finally, following a heated parliamentary debate,[8] the government brought into force Law No. 23.049. The Military Code of Justice was thus reformed and it became possible for sentences passed by military tribunals (who had jurisdiction for cases of military persons tried for excesses committed in the struggle against terrorism between 24 March 1976 and 26 September 1983) to be subject to appeal before the Federal Courts. This new policy obviously did not satisfy the Mothers' expectations and on weighing up the constitutional government's first year in office they repudiated what had been done in the following terms:

> We asked him for a bicameral Commission and he [Alfonsín] gave us a national commission [CONADEP] which we did not elect. We said no to military justice and he gave us military justice. We said no to the dictatorship's judges and he confirmed 90% of them in their posts . . . [9]

The different reactions to the government's response gave rise to splits in the human rights movement (MDH). Some of these had been noticeable during the election campaign and became more evident when the CONADEP report was presented (September 1984) and at the time of the Resistance March and the march organized by the Permanent Assembly for Human Rights, in December 1984.

Questions and reflections on the women's movement: Collective action can be seen as a sign open to many interpretations (Melucci, 1980). On the basis of this premise, we now present some reflections on women's unreported, unwavering presence in the political and social arena that flows from their concern for the situation of women. This does not mean we reject the idea that the human rights movement is an appropriate framework for an analysis of the history and driving force of the Mothers of the Plaza de Mayo. Rather, it corresponds to our view that movements basically made up of women who organize and mobilize themselves from the standpoint of their role as "mothers" also throw light on issues such as "women's place" in Argentine society, the relationship between women and politics and the possibility of finding links between the varying demands of social protagonists who, as women, share the same gender.

Why only women? If, as social anthropologists maintain, rituals reflect the practices and ideas of the society in which they take place, then the Mothers' walks around the pyramid in the Plaza de Mayo every Thursday, wearing their white scarves, convey something more than just the tenacity of a struggle or the bravery of a handful of women.

The most basic question to be asked within our chosen analytical perspective is why was it the mothers and not other members of the family who first challenged the dictatorship by demonstrating their pain and their demands before the seat of government? When confronted with this question, once the mass media began to take notice of them, members of the movement themselves gave the answer—one that refers back to the dominant sexual division of labor in our society:

> At the beginning we all went together, spontaneously. But the men had to carry on working for the upkeep of the home. The majority of us were housewives and those who were working, resigned or retired from their jobs.[10]

It also refers back to ideological and cultural factors that reveal a society in which the role of mother (as a fundamental element of women's identity) offered relatively greater security compared with other roles when faced with possible repression:

I remember we used to tell the men not to go to the square for fear that the repression would be greater against them . . . a mother always seems more untouchable.[11]

"We'd better go," the women said. "If there are only women they might not dare to intervene . . ."[12]

Those who received the relatives of the detained-disappeared as they visited the different state offices in search of information also unwittingly contributed to making the mothers the driving force behind the resistance. Thus, one of the mothers explains another factor involved in the question "why women?":

> . . . especially when at the beginning we went to the military commandos with our husbands. They used to come out and say: "Come on, you the mother, you can come in." I don't know, perhaps they thought that because we were women we'd be more easily deceived . . . . That's when we began to see our own strength.[13]

Let us link this thought to another: "we know perfectly well that they look down on us: they think of us as those mad old women." They are treated with respect and contempt. The actions of the Mothers of the Plaza de Mayo Movement left their adversaries little room for hypocrisy, and confronted society with a sad truth: the glorification of mothers as part of our "national tradition" has more to do with folklore than reality.

The case of the Mothers of the Plaza de Mayo must surely resemble other women's movements which, without being concerned about changing the ideology of femininity, in fact caused a transformation in women's consciousness and the female role (Kaplan, 1982; Swerdlow, 1982).

It could be said that the Mothers, while emphasizing global issues (justice, freedom, solidarity), challenged privatization and isolation and also put an end to the myth that women are incapable of uniting, or providing mutual solidarity. Basically, the women destroyed their image of resignation and weakness.

The members of the movement have themselves reflected on this unsought effect of their actions:

> I think one of the prejudices that exists regarding women is their supposed capacity for resignation. That is to say, the traditional "feminine" woman is passive, resigned, with a tendency to only resort to words. I think that in this case it was shown that they can fight in a very combative way. Submission is another thing women are accused of and atavistically so because of a series of biological and historical circumstances. But in this case it was shown how they can set aside their submissiveness when they become really aware.[14]

How the experience of the Mothers has affected the image of women and their political participation at the level of Argentine society as a whole, and specifically as women, is a question we are not in a position to answer here. The obligatory references to the Mothers of the Plaza de Mayo Movement by different sectors of the community (the ruling party, left-wing parties, artists, women's groups) speak of the existence of "some impact." This irruption in the public world, which was both symbolic and effective, transformed all that is "public" by drawing the ethical principle of the defense of life into its space, and radically changed the traditional parameters of political discussion.

Even though the Mothers do not explicitly redefine what is private, and are not interested in doing so, they are in fact redefining the "traditional female role." Moreover, they offer the image of a mother as a woman who does not sit down and cry when her child disappears but goes out on to the street and fights "like a lion" against the dictatorship,[15] who maintains that the defense of others' lives and freedom is the best way of defending one's own life and one's own freedom, and who advises other mothers to teach their children about freedom and solidarity and basically, "that they learn from them."[16] This is clearly a long way from the mother stereotype that stresses only the role of passive transmitter of dominant values.

Peace as a weapon: Historical research into women's movements has shown that there is a common pattern: a focus on the issues of consumption and peace. Women's capacity to conceive and give life and, therefore, their greater predisposition to defend it, has been offered as an explanation for this recurrence,[17] a recurrence which, as we have seen, can be illustrated with several examples in recent Argentine history.

The Mothers of the Plaza de Mayo explicitly defined themselves as defenders of life, as a movement that was not "passive but pacifist."[18] From the beginning of its first public actions, in its first statements, the movement declared itself "against all violence, whoever the perpetrators might be."[19] The symbol that identified them—the white headscarf—has the following connotation for them: "We began using that color because it is the symbol of peace, something which unites all mothers."[20]

Interviews with the movement's members show that their "no to violence" stance had both a strategic and a tactical value:

> We tried not to be aggressive with words, thinking of our children as hostages.
> The no to violence was also a way of defending ourselves: we knew that if we were to generate violence, it could cause the opposite reaction to what we wanted.[21]

This dual characteristic defined an option that the Mothers adopted as their own distinctive trait, distinguishing them from their opponents: "We had gained the respect of the community. Precisely because we have different moral principles including the no to violence."[22]

The Mothers' permanent mobilization shows that their identification with peace does not imply passivity, nor does it imply naivety: their steadfast demand for "judgement and punishment of the guilty" made Argentine society aware that justice is a fundamental requisite for the construction of a real and lasting peace.

Notes

[1] *Patria Potestad* is the parents' (or guardians') legal jurisdiction over children. Traditionally this has been the prerogative only of the father or male head of family (Translators).

[2] Testimony of Hebe Bonafini, in *La Voz*, 28 April 1983, p. 12.

[3] *El Periodista,* Year 1, No. 2, p. 41.

[4] The movement of Argentine grandmothers of disappeared grandchildren was created in 1977 with the specific aim of looking for disappeared children—babies born in captivity or children taken by the forces of repression when only months old—and reuniting them with their legitimate families. In 1980 it changed its name to the Grandmothers of the Plaza de Mayo.

[5] *Madres de Plaza de Mayo*, December 1984, p. 2.

[6] "The Mothers' [of the Plaza de Mayo] Page," in *El Porteño*, November, 1983.

[7] Ibid.

[8] The project was supported by the provincial blocs in the Senate and by the UCD in the Chamber of Deputies; it was opposed by the PJ (Justicialist Party), the PI (Intransigent Party) and the DC (Christian Democrats); *El Bimestre*, Year 3, No. 13, p. 108.

[9] Ibid.

[10] *Mujer*, Year 2, No. 100.

[11] *Alfonsina*, May 1984, p. 10.

[12] Bousquet, Jean Pierre. *Las Locas de Plaza de Mayo* (El Cid Editor) 1983, p. 47.

[13] *Mujeres*, Year 2, No. 100.

[14] *Alfonsina*, May 1984, p. 10.

[15] Hebe de Bonafini, *Humor* magazine, October 1982, p. 49.

[16] *La Voz*, 16 October 1983 and 24 November 1983.

[17] Some feminist theorists suggest the existence of a "female consciousness"—a product of the sexual division of labor—that implicitly contains a language of social rights and the actual possibility of rethinking politics. (Kaplan, 1982; Elshtain, 1982; Swedlow, 1982).

[18] *Alfonsina*, May 1984, p. 9.
[19] *El Porteño*, October 1983, p. 16.
[20] *Humor*, October 1982, p. 45.
[21] *Alfonsina*, May 1984, p. 10
[22] Ibid.

References

Bousquet, Jeanne Pierre. 1983. *Las locas de Plaza de Mayo.* El Cid Editor, Buenos Aires.

Cano, Inés. 1982. "El movimiento feminista argentino en la década del 70," August, in *Todo es Historia.* Buenos Aires.

Casas, Nelly. 1982. "Qué pasó con las mujeres políticas a partir del 51," in *Formación política para la democracia,* Redacción, Buenos Aires.

Elshtain, Jean. 1982. "Antigone's daughters," April, *Democracy* 2 (2).

Entel, Alicia. 1983. "Los nuevos refugiados," October 28 in *Clarín,* Buenos Aires.

Feijoo, María del Carmen. 1982a. *Las feministas, la vida de nuestro pueblo.* CEAL, Buenos Aires.

———. 1982b. "La mujer en la historia argentina," in *Todo es Historia,* Buenos Aires.

———. 1983. "Mujer y política en América Latina: viejos y nuevos estilos," mimeo.

Frenkel, Roberto. 1980. *Las recientes políticas de estabilización en la Argentina: de la vieja a la nueva ortodoxia.* Institute of International Relations, Pontificia Universidad Católica, Argentina.

González Bombal, Inés. 1984a. "El movimiento de derechos humanos en la Argentina," mimeo.

Jelin, Elizabeth and Feijoo, María del Carmen. 1980. "Trabajo y familia en el ciclo de vida femenino: el caso de los sectores populares de Buenos Aires," in *Estudios CEDES*, Buenos Aires.

Kaplan, Temma. 1982. "Female consciousness and collective action: the case of Barcelona, 1910–1918," in *Signs* 7 (3).

Landi, Oscar. 1978. *La tercera presidencia de Perón: gobierno de emergencia y crisis política.* CEDES, Documento de Trabajo 10, Buenos Aires.

Llovet, Juan José. 1984. *Servicios de salud y sectores populares. Los años del Proceso.* Estudios CEDES, Buenos Aires.

Melucci, Alberto. 1980. "The new social movements: a theoretical approach," in *Social Science Information* 19 (2): 199–226.

Navarro, Maryssa, 1981. *Evita.* Corregidor, Buenos Aires.

Palermo, Vicente and García Delgado, Daniel. 1983. "El movimiento de derechos humanos en la transición a la democracia," mimeo.

Quevedo, Luis Alberto. 1984. "Discurso político y orden social," unpublished thesis (Licenciatura), University of El Salvador.

Rowbotham, Sheila. 1976. *Hidden from History.* Vintage Press, London.

Swerdlow, Amy. 1982. "Ladies Day at Capitol: Women Strike for Peace vs HUAC," in *Feminist Studies* 8 (3).

Newspapers, Magazines and Journals:
Alfonsina
Aquí Nosotras
Boletín de Dima
Clarín
Diario Popular
El Bimestre
El Periodista
El Porteño
Humor
La Nación
La Voz
Madres de Plaza de Mayo
Mate Amargo
Mujer
Paz y Justicia

35

Antonius C. G. M. Robben teaches anthropology at Utrecht University in Netherlands. His best-known books are Sons of the Sea Goddess: Economic Practise and Discursive Conflict in Brazil, Fieldwork under Fire *(with C. Nordstrom), and* Cultures under Siege *(with M. Suarez-Orozco).*

The subjects of our research are fellow human beings, so anthropologists expect to find a broad range of feelings and reactions wherever they work. Just as in one's home country or institution, some individuals are spontaneously friendly and helpful, others cordial enough but a little reserved until they develop confidence, and some persist in being suspicious or aloof if not downright hostile. In an area that had recently been poisoned by internal warfare, whole groups may be similarly different in their reactions, not only to an outsider but to others among them. Robben sensitively describes some of the misgivings and dilemmas that he encountered in dealing both with victims of atrocities and with the alleged perpetrators, even in a setting where civility and reason seemed to have been restored.

Studying Violence
Victims, Perpetrators, and the Ethnographer
Antonius C. G. M. Robben

"Let me help you," he said, as he held up my coat. "Thank you very much," I said. My arms slipped effortlessly into the sleeves as he gently lifted the coat onto my shoulders. Before I could return the gesture, he had already put on his overcoat.

We passed through the dark corridors of the old palace, walked down the marble stairway, and left the Officers' Club through the main entrance, "You know, Dr. Robben," he began, I am a very religious man. And I know deep down in my heart that my conscience before God is clear." We turned the corner at the Café Petit Paris and continued along Santa Fé Avenue. I looked at him and tried to speak above the noise of the traffic: "Well, general, but there are many Argentines who . . . " "Look out!" he yelled and stretched his right arm in front of me. A taxi nearly hit me as I was about to step on the pavement. How was I to reconcile his demeanor with the characterization of him as an "unfeeling butcher" that I had been consistently given by other, apparently equally credible respondents?

A few months later, the general was released from criminal prosecution by a presidential decree (*indulto*). He had been indicted for ordering the "disappearance" of Argentine citizens, and for responsibility for their rape and torture, by men under his command. The decree did not acquit him of the charges or exonerate his military honor but merely dismissed his court case and those of dozens of other high-ranking officers. The Argentine president, Carlos Menem, hoped that this decree would "close the wounds of the past" among a people sharply divided by the violence and repression of the 1970s.

I had arrived in Buenos Aires to study whether these wounds were closing and how the Argentine people were coping with the tens of thousands of dead and disappeared in what the military had called the "dirty war" against the leftist insurgency.[1] If Argentine society was to be pacified, then the people had to reconcile themselves with each other and their past. History cannot be undone by decree. Crucial to

---

Abridged, with permission of the author and publisher, from the author's chapter "The Politics of Truth and Emotion among Victims and Perpetrators of Violence," in Carolyn Nordstrom and Antonius C. G. M. Robben (Eds.), *Fieldwork under Fire: Contemporary Studies of Violence and Survival*, pp. 81–103 (Berkeley: University of California Press). Reprinted with permission. All rights reserved.

national reconciliation was how the Argentine people made sense of the years of intense political repression and violence during the 1976–1983 military dictatorship. Many welcomed the coup d'état of March 1976 as necessary to end the country's political and economic chaos. Constitutional rights were suspended, the Congress was sent home, and the unions were placed under military guardianship. People were aware of censorship of the mass media, the pervasive intelligence network of security forces, and the many arrests that were made, often under the cover of darkness. They also heard about worldwide denunciation of human rights violations in Argentina, but the military government was quite successful in convincing the many Argentines who had not been affected personally that those accusations were being orchestrated by the revolutionary Left at home and abroad. It was only after the 1982 defeat of the Argentine armed forces at the Falkland/Malvinas Islands that the public learned of the extent and brutality of the political persecution during the dictatorship. The Argentine people wanted to know and understand what had happened. At the fall of the military regime in 1983, retired generals, former cabinet ministers, human rights activists, union leaders, bishops, and politicians were flooding the news media with their conflicting accounts and analyses.

The historical reconstruction of the 1970s became intensely contested during the decade following the return to democracy, not only through conflicting discourse but also through controversial political actions, including one guerrilla attack on an army base, three amnesties, and five military mutinies. The conflicting interpretations came principally from the armed forces, former guerrilla organizations, human rights groups, and the Roman Catholic Church. The public discourse of the leaders of these former groups became the centerpiece of my research on the contested historical reconstruction of the political violence of the 1970s. I was not interested in writing a history of the so-called dirty war. Instead, I focused on how that history was being remembered, contested, negotiated, and reconstructed in public by its protagonists. I was not in Argentina to establish truth or guilt; that was the prerogative of Argentine society. I made it clear at the start of every interview that I wanted to talk to the principal political actors and understand their explanations of the recent past in a time when opinions and interpretations were still being formed and reformulated. I wanted them to explain their positions, just as they had done previously in television and radio programs, newspaper articles, public speeches, and their numerous meetings with local reporters, foreign correspondents, diplomats, and international fact-finding delegations.

It was in my interviews with the Argentine military that I first realized the importance of seduction as a dimension of fieldwork. My military interlocutors must have known that the image I had received abroad—and which they reckoned was being confirmed in my talks with their political opponents—was one of officers torturing babies and ordering the disappearance of tens of thousands of innocent Argentine civilians. I had, of course, anticipated their denial of these serious accusations, but I did not expect to be meeting military men who exuded such great civility and displayed a considerable knowledge of literature, art, and classical music. The affability and chivalry of the officers clashed with the trial records I had read, affected my critical sensibility, and in the beginning distracted me from my research focus. It was only later that I realized that I had been a victim of ethnographic seduction. This process of seduction and subsequent awareness repeated itself in my meetings with bishops, human rights activists, and former guerilla leaders. Each group was seductive in its own way, and it was only after months of interviewing that I succeeded in recognizing their defenses and strategies and learned to distinguish seduction from good rapport.

I have chosen the word *seduction* to describe those personal defenses and social strategies because it means literally "to be led astray from an intended course."[2]

Seduction is used here exclusively in its neutral meaning of being led astray unawares, not in its popular meaning of allurement and entrapment. I prefer seduction to other terms, such as concealment, manipulation, or deception, all of which carry negative overtones and suggest dishonesty or bad intent. Seduction can be intentional but also unconscious and can be compared to the ways in which filmmakers, stage directors, artists, or writers succeed in totally absorbing the attention of their audiences.

I am aware of the risks of using the word *seduction* in the context of violence. The association of the words *victim* and *seduction* makes me vulnerable to the charge that I am implying that somehow the victim brought on himself or herself the pain that was inflicted, while the mere suggestion that victims of violence might mold what they tell us runs the danger that I will be accused of contributing to their victimization. Ultimately, it might make people question my moral standards. How can I place doubt on the horror stories I have been told and distrust their narrators? It is much easier to acknowledge manipulation by victimizers than by victims. We generally prefer unmasking abusers of power to doubting the words of their victims. I have the same sympathies. However, I also realize that in the end the victims may be harmed and their testimonies discredited if we report their views naively and uncritically. We need to analyze their accounts and be attentive to our own inhibitions, weaknesses, and biases, all to the benefit of a better understanding of both victim and victimizer. The ethnographic seduction by victims and perpetrators of violence will in this way become a font of instead of an obstruction to insight.[3]

This article focuses on the ethnographic encounter because the most common transmission of cultural knowledge in fieldwork takes place through open interviews with key informants. I will argue that seduction is a dimension of fieldwork that is especially prominent in research on violent political conflict because the interlocutors have great personal and political stakes in making the ethnographer adopt their interpretations. The importance of seduction is enhanced by the special circumstances of conflict in studying higher-status individuals. An anthropologist who wishes to understand a major armed conflict from the perspective of its principal protagonists cannot resort to participant observation in the traditional sense but is restricted to interviews. These interviews may range from a unique half-hour meeting to a series of long conversations. It is during these face-to-face encounters that ethnographic understanding and inquiry are most vulnerable to seduction.

Most of my Argentine informants were public figures with great conversational experience and finesse. I could therefore safely assume that they had become sensitized to the effectiveness of various rhetorical devices. Invariably there was an exchange of social courtesies to create a friendly atmosphere for what we perceived could become a weighty and possibly painful conversation. These courtesies failed to seduce because of their blatant transparency. Seduction does not work through openness but through secrecy and mystification. Hence the common ground that became established at the start of a conversation depended to a great extent on an acquaintance with each other's cultural identity. Many of my interviewees had visited Europe, expressed their love of seventeenth-century Dutch painting, their admiration of the canals, or recalled with glee the title-match victory of Argentina over the Dutch team at the 1978 World Championship soccer tournament in Buenos Aires, during the heyday of the military regime. They also interpreted my presentation of self, assessed my class background, and tried to detect my political ideology. My being Dutch yet living in the United States, my status as a university professor, and above all my access to their political adversaries were of great importance. I, in turn, would praise the friendliness of the Argentine people, the beauty of the countryside, and the architecture of the main avenues of Buenos Aires.

Aside from this obvious impression management, there was a seductive dimension to discourse that was much harder to isolate but that first became clear to me in my conversations with former guerillas. Many of them had been college students. They had perfected a sophisticated political discourse through innumerable discussions in cafés, prisons, hideouts, and foreign hotels. They would speak in the intellectual's tongue. Well versed in the jargon of sociology and political science, their historical interpretations had a truthful ring. It was difficult to distinguish their vocabulary and semantic constructions from my own.

It was tempting to become absorbed in this discourse. It had an emotional pull. It seduced me by an indescribable familiarity, by its allure of going to the heart of historical events together with their architects; all this set in the special atmosphere of the grand cafés of Buenos Aires with their dense cigarette smoke, the buzzing of voices, and the waiters swiftly maneuvering through the maze of wooden tables while carrying trays of small coffee cups. I felt that I could take my guard down in this environment and become absorbed in a close discussion in which I could share intellectual doubts and queries with people of my own generation. I felt that I could not afford such openness with the military, the clergy, or with human rights activists who might become offended by too-penetrating questions and deny me another interview. What I did not realize was that by this openness I had also abandoned my critical detachment.

EMPATHY AND DEHUMANIZATION

Ethnographic understanding through empathy and detachment has been generally accepted as a common dialectic in fieldwork. We must establish a good rapport with our subjects in order to grasp the world from their perspective, while a simultaneous reflective detachment as observers must objectify our perceptions and enhance our analytical insight.[4] "One of the most persistent problems we confront is how to so subject ourselves and yet maintain the degree of 'detachment' necessary for us to analyze our observations: in other words, to be anthropologists as well as participants" (Ellen 1984:227). Malinowski conceived of anthropological research in these terms, and it was to remain a canon of our profession until the 1960s when Geertz began to problematize fieldwork and ethnography with his notion of "thick description."

Geertz calls attention to the many-layered subjective construction of culture and argues for reproducing this complexity in the ethnographic text.[5] He notes that the relation between informant and field-worker is distorted by mutual misunderstandings, clientelistic interests, power games, and cultural proselytizing. These problems of cultural interpretation are of central concern to the ethnographer. Geertz (1973:15) proposes, therefore, the "thick description" of culture "cast in terms of the constructions we imagine" our subjects "to place upon what they live through, the formulae they use to define what happens to them." A question that arises immediately is whether people's constructions and formulas—not just their content—change under social tension and to what extent violent conflict will therefore affect the thick description of culture. I aim to show that an examination in the field of the principal methodological and epistemological problems of conducting ethnographic research under violent conflict can yield significant insights about people's interpretation and construction of the conflict under study.

The problem of ethnographic seduction deserves attention because it subverts the conversation that precedes its description in ethnographic texts. We may become engulfed in seductive strategies or defenses that convince us of the thinness of social discourse. We believe to be seeing the world through our subject's eyes. Yet these eyes are looking away from that which we think they are seeing.

This manipulation of appearances touches on the heart of seduction, so Baudrillard (1990) tells us.[6] Appearance rests on a deep faith in the immediacy of our senses and emotions. Sight, sound, and feeling are intimately tied to our subjective experience of authenticity. However, what is revealed to us is nothing more than a *trompe l'oeil* (illusion), and a surreal one at that. The ethnographic seduction trades our critical stance as observers for an illusion of congeniality with cultural insiders.[7] We no longer seek to grasp the native's point of view, but we believe, at least for the duration of the meeting, that we have become natives ourselves. We have become so involved in the ethnographic encounter that we are led astray from our research objectives, irrespective of the theoretical paradigm we are using and the anthropological understanding we are pursuing.

Problems of representation, intersubjectivity, complexity, and the historicity of truth—all of which have already been discussed at length in anthropology—are only a few of the epistemological pitfalls of ethnographic seduction. Ethnographic seduction subverts our understanding of social and cultural phenomena by dissuading an inquiry beyond their appearance. The difficulty with ethnographic seduction is that we are seldom aware it is taking place. Unlike ethnographic anxiety, which according to Devereux (1967:42–45) is produced by our repression of cultural experiences in the field that correspond to unconscious desires and wishes, ethnographic seduction often puts the ethnographer at ease. Repression makes the ethnographer "protect himself against anxiety by the omission, soft-pedaling, non-exploitation, misunderstanding, ambiguous description, over-exploitation or rearrangement of certain parts of his material" (ibid., 44). Seduction, instead, makes us feel that we have accomplished something profound in the encounter, that we have reached a deeper understanding and have somehow penetrated reality. We are in a state of well-being, and have an empathy with our informants that we mistakenly interpret as good rapport. It is only when we look back at our meeting and review the information gathered that we realize that we displayed a personal inhibition against breaking our rapport with critical questions. We realize that we have mistaken seduction for shared feelings.

If, on the one hand, seduction disarms our critical detachment and thus debilitates the gathering of cultural knowledge, then, on the other, our empathy in research on violent conflict may be hindered by our awareness of the protagonism of our interlocutors. Going one morning from an interview with a mother who had lost two sons during the first year of the dictatorship to a meeting with a general who might well have ordered their disappearance, it became hard not to dehumanize them both. How can we engage in constructing an intersubjective understanding with a person who either has violated or transcended the humanity we are trying to understand?

At the early stages of my research I was confounded both by the veil of authenticity that shrouded the personal accounts of my subjects and by the public discourse that depicted military officers as beasts or saviors and human rights activists as subversives or saints. We can become so overwhelmed by the presence of political actors who have been dehumanized in society that we may also begin to see them only as saints and sinners or heroes and cowards. As I became more conscious of these public characterizations in Argentine society, I realized that this same process of dehumanization had contributed to the escalation of political violence in the 1970s, when political opponents became enemies and, as enemies, were less than human, only fit for elimination.

Ethnographic seduction sidesteps empathy and detachment. The Socratic dialectic that brings us ever closer to the truth, the positivist model of an oscillation between inductive and deductive steps through which falsification becomes possible, and finally the hermeneutic model of a spiraling ascendance between whole and part that deepens understanding all encompass epistemological approaches that become suspended by seduction. Ethnographic seduction reduces communication and knowledge to appearance.

THE MANAGEMENT OF IMPRESSION AND AMBIGUITY

Around the same time that Geertz problematized ethnography, questions were raised about the ethics of covert fieldwork in Latin America and Southeast Asia. In the 1960s, anthropologists began to take a closer look at their research practices. This methodological reflection was greatly influenced by West Coast sociologists such as Herbert Blumer, Harold Garfinkel, Erving Goffman, Aaron V. Cicourel, and Harvey Sacks, who inspired ethnographers to focus on the dramaturgical dimension of the relation between fieldworkers and their informants. Anthropologists should not routinely study the social and cultural conduct of their subjects but have to realize that the actors might deliberately manipulate and obstruct the gathering of ethnographic knowledge. "The impressions that ethnographer and subjects seek to project to one another are . . . those felt to be favorable to the accomplishment of their respective goals: the ethnographer seeks access to back-region information; the subjects seek to protect their secrets since these represent a threat to the public image they wish to maintain. Neither can succeed perfectly" (Berreman 1972:xxxiv).

The work of Goffman (1966; 1969) on impression management remains highly relevant for our understanding of the interactional processes that develop in ethnographic encounters.[8] Nevertheless, impression management encompasses only part of the much more comprehensive and complex dimension of ethnographic seduction. Ethnographer and subject may try both to protect their public image and to gain access to each other's back stage, as Berreman explains, but which boundary should they protect and which region do they wish to enter? The ethnographer's definition of the secret knowledge of the subject may not coincide with the respondent's perception. This misunderstanding provides opportunities not only for dramaturgical impression management but also for unintended and counteractive seduction. For example, victims of repression who assumed that I regarded the torture session as the most personal and therefore most valuable back-region, assumed that this appraisal could enhance their credibility as a reliable source of information about the years of political violence. Even though many informants intended to tell about it, they still veiled their experiences to impel the inquisitive ethnographer to urge them to share their stories. The more persuasion that was needed, the more persuasive their accounts would be. A troubling similarity between interrogation and interview appeared which could not have escaped the attention of these victims of torture. But now, they had control over how and which valuable information they would give. Several interviewees were conscious of the manner in which this knowledge was imparted and therefore delayed its disclosure. Others did not try to withhold their revelations, but the effect was the same: I stopped at the threshold of their back-region. Why did I not eagerly accept the valuable knowledge that was eventually offered?

Baudrillard (1990:83) has written that "to seduce is to appear weak." Certain interviewees did not try to dominate or overpower me but, instead, disarmed me by showing their vulnerabilities. In my interviews with victims of torture, I seldom asked directly about the abuse they had been subjected to but usually concentrated on their interpretation of the political violence of the 1970s. Being accustomed to journalists who invariably asked them to provide graphic descriptions, several expressed their surprise at my reluctance and volunteered to give me detailed accounts. I generally responded that such painful recollection was not necessary because I had already read their declarations to the courts. Maybe I wanted to spare them, but I probably also wanted to protect myself. Whatever my motives, this voluntary offering of very personal experiences enhanced, in my eyes, the credibility of the entire interview, whether justifiably or not. The ethnographic seduction operated through a partial revelation of a dark world that was not further explored but was taken at face value in the belief that such hidden knowledge could always be uncovered.

RHETORIC AND PERSUASION

Persuasion seems to be the counterpole of seduction. Seduction wins us over by appearance, persuasion by argument.[9] It is not appearance and emotion that seem at stake but reason. We are supposed to become persuaded by a clear exposition of hard evidence that moves us to reconsider our poorly informed opinions. But how is the proof presented to us? How is the evidence rhetorically couched? How is the information molded to make its greatest impact on us and divert us from the questions we want to examine in depth? Are the interlocutors always aware of the rhetorical dimension of their conversations?[10]

Plato and Aristotle made a distinction between dialectical reasoning based on logical and rigorous proof, which would lead to truth, and rhetorical reasoning, which tried to persuade people by arousing their emotions. "Rhetoric is that part of any self-consciously calculated piece of communication which fails to meet a philosopher's standards of accuracy, coherence, and consistency, but is still necessary if the communication is to be fully successful" (Cole 1991:13). Our suspicion of rhetoric comes from a distrust of such manipulation of our emotions. We feel somehow robbed of the ability to weigh the pros and cons of an argument. Nevertheless, rhetorical and aesthetic modes of exposition are not only an inextricable part of scientific discourse (see Gilbert and Mulkay 1984; Gross 1990) but also "potentially powerful resources for the advancement of the sciences: promotion of hypotheses by appeal to aesthetic criteria; jocular and satirical critique of standard and entrenched practices" (Jardine 1991:236). Rhetoric stirs us discursively with tropes, allegories, and modes of exposition. Like seduction, rhetoric may become a play of appearance that diverts us from our research objectives.

Unlike the pseudoacademic discourse of the revolutionary Left, which allowed me to retain many of my conceptual tools, my interviews with the other three groups obliged me to adapt my vocabulary. For example, human rights groups use the term "concentration camp" (*campo de concentración*) to describe the secret places where disappeared persons were held. This term conjures up images of the Second World War and, by extension, suggests that the Argentine military are Nazis at heart. The use of the term "concentration camp" in conversations with military officers would immediately brand me as a sympathizer of the human rights groups and thus hinder the exchange. I therefore used their own term, "detention center" (*centro de detención*). This neutral term was part of an objectifying vocabulary that gave a semantic rationality to the violent practices of the dirty war.

The discursive strategy of the military consisted of appealing both to my common sense and to the dispassionate logic of reason that is supposed to be the hallmark of any scientist. This discursive technique consisted of an outright dismissal of any major human rights violations without denying that they could have occurred. If this technique failed to have the intended effect on me, then they began to relativize the Argentine abuses by making a comparison with atrocities committed by the so-called civilized Western world. In one interview, I asked the general mentioned at the beginning of this article about the relevance of licit and illicit rules of engagement, as defined by international law, to the "dirty war strategy" employed by the Argentine military.

> I say that when we go to war—and in a war I have to be willing to kill my enemy because otherwise there would be no war—when I am willing to kill my enemy I can kill him with an arrow, but if the other has a machine gun then the arrow will be of

no use to me. I have to find a cannon. . . . [When] I have a cannon, the other will look for a larger cannon or an aircraft. When the other has an aircraft, I will have to try, try to take a missile, and so on. That is to say, war by itself is a social phenomenon. . . . What is licit and what is illicit, when war presupposes that I am going to kill my enemy? Now, the philosopher of war par excellence is [Carl von] Clausewitz. And he says that war is evidently a human phenomenon in which I try to impose my will on the enemy and I therefore resort to violence. Now, he talks about the tendency to go to extremes. He then says that he who tries to impose violence without any consideration will have an advantage over he who has consideration. Well then, what happens? When they talk to me about restrictions in warfare, these are lucubrations made by jurists. The nations have not respected them. For example, when they. . . [dropped] the nuclear bomb on Hiroshima and Nagasaki, this was forbidden according to the Geneva Convention. But who was to say to Mister Truman, "Mister Truman, this is forbidden. Why did you . . . [drop] it? You come along, we are going to take you to the Nuremberg tribunal." No, because he won the war. Who was going to do it? Now, why did Mister Truman do it? Because he said, "Well, 200,000 persons will die, but if we do not . . . [drop] the bomb then 600,000 North Americans will die, or one million. Well then, between 200,000 Japanese and one million North Americans, let 200,000 Japanese die," and he . . . [dropped] the bomb. Because the distinction between the licit and the illicit in warfare is absurd to me, because war presupposes from the start the use of violence—as Clausewitz says—and the use of violence without restraint until the objective is attained.

Other Argentine officers also referred frequently to the bombings of Hiroshima, Dresden, and Nagasaki and to the double standard of the "human rights prophets," the French, who collaborated with the Nazis during the Vichy government, tortured Algerian partisans, and in 1985 bombed a Greenpeace ship in New Zealand, yet who convicted in absentia the Argentine navy officer Alfredo Astiz for his alleged role in the disappearance of two French nuns who had collaborated with subversive organizations (or so the Argentine military argued). When I objected that two wrongs do not make a right, that the comparisons do not hold, or that many of the offenses by Western nations were backed by written orders, the Argentine military men appealed to the vicissitudes and unpredictabilities of warfare.

Such rational discourse may be highly persuasive from a logical point of view—especially when one has not yet found equally powerful counterarguments or succeeds in listening dispassionately to the rationalizations—but it produces an uncomfortable tension with one's emotional aversion to the consequences of warfare. Just as it is hard to reconcile our instantaneous repudiation of violent death with a military necessity to fire on people, so it becomes very difficult to stand one's moral ground in the face of these techno-rational arguments for human suffering. The barrage of sophisticated rationalizations of violence, together with the argument that the use of force is the constitutional prerogative of the security forces, are very hard to counter. My objections that the violence was disproportional, that more humane counterinsurgency methods could have been used, that the prisoners were not given due process, that these methods violated the very principles of civilization that the military professed to protect, and, finally, that what was justified as mere excesses of war were deliberate and planned violations to paralyze the political expression of the Argentine people were all dismissed as either leftist propaganda or manifestations of my unfamiliarity with the practice of warfare.

Another discursive tactic was to sketch ominous scenarios of what would have happened if the Argentine military had not destroyed the insurgents, root and branch. The grave situation in Peru during the late 1980s, when the Shining Path revolutionaries controlled large areas of the highlands, and had even succeeded in reaching the gates of Lima at the time of my fieldwork, was mentioned as a nightmare that had been prevented in Argentina through the resolute action of the armed forces. Finally, the fall of the Berlin wall and the subsequent disenchantment with communism in Eastern Europe were presented as arguments for the moral righteousness of the repression in Argentina during the 1970s.

The human rights activists and former guerillas could have equally made appeals to common sense, but many preferred to make an emotional plea to a moral sense of humanity and justice. How to respond to an indignant rejection of torture, to the kidnapping of babies for the benefit of childless military families, and to the extraction of money from desperate parents with misleading information about the whereabouts of their disappeared son? Rational arguments, such as those given to me by the military, justifying torture as a conventional practice in counterinsurgency warfare, as was the case in Algeria, South Africa, Vietnam, Indonesia, Northern Ireland, Spain, Peru, El Salvador, and many other countries, are impotent against the tears of the parents of a revolutionary who was abducted, tortured and executed. I became virtually unable to penetrate this emotional shroud with questions that might be easily misperceived as apologetic, uncaring, cold, callous, and hurtful.[11] The more emotional the reaction, the greater my personal inhibition to discuss these issues further.

The following fragment from an interview with the father of a seventeen-year-old member of the outlawed Peronist Youth (*Juventud Peronista*) who disappeared in April 1976 demonstrates this inhibition, despite encouragement by the subject that I continue. After his son failed to arrive at a birthday party where he was expected, the father began a desperate search. He contacted an acquaintance who is a police officer, and they began to make inquiries at the precincts and hospitals of Buenos Aires, all to no avail. After several months, the father came into contact with a colonel on active duty, through the mediation of a befriended retired first lieutenant. The following dialogue took place.

> And he says, "Tell me what happened." So I told him what happened. And with all virulence, . . . I looked at this man, but I tell you as I told you before, that I tried to see from all sides if I could find . . . the thread or the needle in the haystack [*punta del ovillo*], trying to discover anything. After telling him everything, he says, "Good. Look you have to do the following: you have to pretend as if your son has cancer." I was listening and saying to myself, What is he saying? [The colonel continues.] "Pretend that he has cancer and . . . that he is in an operating room and that there is a butcher and a doctor; pray that it will be the doctor who will be operating on him." And then I looked at the one with whom I had made a certain friendship, and he took hold of his head and covered his face. Because he must have said: What is this sonofabitch saying? Because then he realized that all his venom, his virulence came out of him. [He thought,] This man had stuck a dagger in my wound and had twisted it inside me. I say to him, "Pardon me," I say, "Sir, but do you know something?" I said this because of what he was telling me. "No, no, I am weighing the various possibilities and I am making a supposition. I don't know anything of what might have [happened]." And I say, "But how do you have the gall to . . ." and because of my nerves the words couldn't come out, but I had wanted to say "You are a son of a thousand bitches." You see, tell him whichever barbarity. And then the other saw my condition because he thought that I was going to lose it. . . . I wanted to grab him by the throat and strangle him, but then anyone of those who were there would have taken their gun and killed me. There, for the first time in my life, the desire came over me to murder someone. I had been destroyed. . . .
>
> Something [my wife] didn't know. With the passage of time I have told her. These are unfortunate things that happen to you in life. And there, yes, it crossed my mind that yes, that day I could have ended up killing that man. I don't know what stopped me. Because I was desperate. But you cannot imagine how, with what

satisfaction, he said what he was telling me. And you should analyze that, that this man was in active service.

But I was unable to analyze. Exactly as he had tried to detect any sign in the face and words of the colonel that betrayed the tiniest bit of information about his son but became paralyzed by the cruel supposition, so I became unable to stand aside and observe. He had incorporated me into his torment, sometimes discursively placing me in his shoes and at other times highlighting the moments of his greatest anguish. I could have asked him about the place of the meeting, the spatial arrangement of the offices, which army regiment had been involved, whether he ever heard of the colonel again, how he knew that the man was a colonel and not an extortionist who would try to wrest money from him, whether he ever saw the first lieutenant again, and so on. But my mind went blank, and I could only share this man's sorrow in silence.

I intuitively hesitate to present this account as an example of rhetorical seduction because the term "seduction" immediately evokes the association of an intentional manipulation of truth for dishonest ends. This is not the case here. I do not have any reason to doubt that this dialogue—whatever the exact words—took place, and I believe even less that the narrative was consciously constructed. Still, I think that the term "rhetorical seduction" is appropriate here because the repeated telling of the same story has led to a formulation that has proven to be the most moving and therefore most persuasive.[12] The account affected my emotional state to such a degree that I was no longer able to see the discourse behind the conversation. I could not ask further questions but allowed my subject to take me along on the incessant search for his son.

Sometimes, I would end an interview, unable or unwilling to continue. At other times, I would gently relieve the tension by leading the conversation into neutral waters, discussing highly abstract concepts such as war, justice, or political freedom. Only a radical break with my emotions would allow me to regard the conversation once again as analyzable knowledge.

This example has demonstrated the emotional incorporation of the ethnographer in the ethnographic encounter, but this intersubjectivity also has a counterpart in the subject's reactions. An Argentine anthropologist who knew one of my interviewees, a former guerilla, recounted to me one day his rendition of my meetings with him. He had told a friend that during a stirring moment of our conversation in which he was reflecting on the terrible waste of lives in the political struggle of the 1970s, he saw tears in my eyes. This intensified the awareness of his own tragedy and made him break down as well. At these moments of a complete collapse of the critical distance between two speakers, we lose all dimensions of the scientific enterprise. Overwhelmed by emotion, we do not have the need for any explanation because we feel that all questions have already been answered. What else is there to ask? What else is there to tell? What more do we need to know? What more is there to know?

SECRECY AND TRUTH

Any research on political violence runs into too many skeletons to handle, too many closets to inspect. Aside from deliberate lies, half-truths, and unfounded accusations—many of which are impossible to trace or verify—there is a lot of malicious gossip and character assassination. One way in which interlocutors try to add credibility to their charges is by means of a staged confession introduced by statements such as "Let me tell you a secret," or "I have never told this to anyone," or "I will tell you this, but you may not record it or write it down."

Secrecy seduces. The belief that the interlocutor is hiding a darker side is seductive because it teases the ethnographer to surrender. Only a surrender to the subject's conditions of truth will yield the desired information. The remarks about secrecy made by my informants served as a strategy to overpower my interpretive stance as an observer. It was an invitation to complicity. I do not want to exaggerate the political influence of social scientists, but most of my subjects were aware of the potential impact of an authoritative analysis of the last dictatorship. The impartiality of local scholars is called into question by most Argentines. They are accused of writing polemic books, books for waging war. These books are believed to sacrifice scientific accuracy to political ends. Foreign authors are regarded as more neutral than national scholars, and some of them, such as Potash (1969, 1980) and Rouquié (1987a, 1987b) have become household names.

The political weight of my research became most apparent during my last interview with the general who had saved me from being run over by a taxi. Almost two months after the presidential decree that dismissed the court case against him, I met him again at the Officers' Club. After a quarter of an hour I told him that I noticed a change in his demeanor. He was much more relaxed than during our last series of interviews. He laughed and said that four months ago he was in the middle of a political battle. "Now," he said, "everything is history, and eventually the Argentine people will realize that the military acted in a correct way." Comparing this last interview with our previous conversations, he had become almost aloof and seemed uninterested in persuading me of his rightness. His short answers were delivered in a casual and offhand manner. The political battle had ended. Had I been one of its foot soldiers? Had I been used as a sparring partner for a future crossfire examination by the public prosecutor, or had I been used as a gullible courier of the general's political message?

The question of truth does not receive much attention in the many books on fieldwork that have appeared in the last three decades.[13] In contrast, earlier generations of anthropologists were much more concerned about prying the truth out of their informants (see Rosaldo 1986). For instance, Griaule (1957) writes in his book on fieldwork: "The role of the person sniffing out social facts is often comparable to that of a detective or examining magistrate. The fact is the crime, the interlocutor, the guilty party, all the society's members are accomplices" (quoted in Clifford 1983b:138). Nadel, Griaule's contemporary, favored equally inquisitive methods: "In the case of interviews which bear on secret and forbidden topics, I have found it most profitable to stimulate the emotionality of a few chief informants to the extent of arousing almost violent disputes and controversies. The expression of doubt and disbelief on the part of the interviewer, or the arrangement of interviews with several informants, some of whom, owing to their social position, were certain to produce inaccurate information, easily induced the key informant to disregard his usual reluctance to speak openly, if only to confound his opponents and critics: (1939:323). Finally, a classic field guide recommends: "It is sometimes useful to pretend incredulity to induce further information" (RAI 1951:33).

Clifford (1983b:143–144) has remarked, "By the late sixties the romantic mythology of fieldwork rapport has begun publicly to dissolve. . . .Geertz undermines the myth of ethnographic rapport before reinstating it in an ironic mode. Like Griaule, he seems to accept that all parties to the encounter recognize its elements of insincerity, hypocrisy, and self-deception." However, a major difference between the two authors is that Griaule was still hunting for undisputable truth. Geertz, instead, is representative of an entire generation of anthropologists who accompanied the interpretive turn of the 1960s and 1970s. Function and explanation were exchanged for meaning and understanding, and many anthropologists felt more identified with notions such as the definition of the situation and the social construction of reality than with a positivist belief in truth and method.[14]

Even though most anthropologists today feel much closer to Geertz than to Griaule and Nadel, our informants continue to think in terms of truth and falsehood. This issue becomes especially relevant in research on violence because the protagonists of major political conflicts are often accused of undermining the very foundation of society and of being responsible for the ensuing human suffering. The question of historical interpretation is of great political importance to them, and they will do their best to convince us of their rightness and to ignore dissenting views. We can, of course, not expect our interlocutors to incriminate themselves or recount their traumatic experiences with an anesthetized detachment but, instead, we should anticipate that they may consciously or unconsciously try to divert us from our investigative aims by disarming our critical gaze. In response to Geertz: not all Cretans may be liars, but some are, and some of them are seducers as well.

Having become temporarily disillusioned by the subtle strategies of persuasion of my Argentine informants, I turned to the texts they had produced in the 1970s. This led to a search for secret army documents, intelligence reports, human rights pamphlets, and the clandestine publications of the revolutionary Left. I realized, of course, that those written sources were just as much discursive constructions as the spoken word of their authors. Nevertheless, the texts were concurrent with the historical events I was studying, and I could compare the oral accounts I had recorded of those actions, decisions, and events with contemporary clandestine, classified, and official sources. I hoped to puncture the appearances of my interlocutors, disentangle myself from their seduction, and reach back in time to the origin of their talk, the events, ideological articulations, power struggles, and armed confrontations. The anxiety of not being able to rely on oral history made me cling to contemporary inscriptions that at least had an appearance of authenticity.[15] I do not use "authenticity" here in the sense of true or real but rather as genuine to the informant's own sense of truth and reality. "Authenticity relates to the corroborative support given an account . . . by its internal consistency or cross-reference to other sources of information" (Brown and Sime 1981:161; see also Denzin 1970, on triangulation). An analysis of the interviews and a comparison with statements made during the time of repression allowed me to distance myself from the surface account that they tried to make me accept as the only true reality.

Clearly, the ethnographer of violence and political conflict may become encapsulated in the webs of seduction spun by his or her informants and interlocutors. Just as Lenin had inverted von Clausewitz's definition of war by stating that politics is the continuation of war by other means, so seduction became the continuation of Argentine politics after the turn to democracy in 1983.[16] Neither brute force nor coercion but the molding of appearances became the weapon of influential players in the Argentine polity. Ethnographic seduction was my personal experience with a national debate in Argentina among the adversarial protagonists of the decades of political violence.

SHREDDING SHROUDS OF POWER

I went to Argentina to understand the contested historical reconstruction of the violence of the 1970s but soon became entangled in the rhetoric and seduction played upon my by its protagonists. Disillusioned, I sought refuge in the denuded truth of some "hard facts," only to discover that my understanding had run aground in the shallowness of the written word. I had to retrace my steps and stop where seduction, rhetoric, interpretation, and intersubjectivity suffused the ethnographic encounter. I could only subvert seduction by playing along with it and grasp its meaning from the inside. This experience made me sensitive to what many Argentines, especially those who had suffered the disappearance of a relative, had felt during the years of repression. The disappearance was a form of deceit in which all appearances were kept up; the appearance of justice, of innocence, and due process. People became surface manifestations. Lives changed course surreptitiously. And reappearance depended on a gesture, on a nod of the head. It was in this clearing that I realized that ethnographic seduction crosscuts the interplay of empathy and detachment that sound fieldwork ordains. Standing in this clearing, it became finally possible to realize that the many directions I had been sent to were only intended to entice me away from where I was already standing.

Notes

[1] The research in Buenos Aires, Argentina, was made possible by grants from the National Science Foundation and the Harry Frank Guggenheim Foundation. I thank Adam Kuper, James McAllister, Carolyn Nordstrom, Frank Pieke, and Jan de Wolf for their thoughtful comments.

[2] Devereux (1967:44–45) has used the term "seduction" in his discussion of countertransference reactions among anthropologists. However, he defines it not as conscious manipulation but as emotional allurement.

[3] An additional danger of using the term "seduction" is that it might result in an unwelcome association with Freud's seduction theory. For all clarity, my use of the term stands clear from Freud's theory about hysteria and distances itself from the implied notions of the repression of sexual desire.

[4] Rapport is generally regarded as essential to successful fieldwork, "simply because of the assumption that people talk better in a warm, friendly atmosphere, and the additional assumption that attitudes are somehow complex and hidden and a lot of talking is essential before the attitude is elicited" (Hyman 1954:22). The issue of rapport has been discussed with much greater depth in sociology than in anthropology, possibly because the methodological emphasis on participant observation makes anthropologists downplay the actual importance of interview situations for acquiring local knowledge. See, e.g., the discussion of rapport by Hyman (1954:153–170) and Turner and Martin (1984:262–278) and the critique by Cicourel (1964:82–86).

[5] Despite this call for attention to the native tongue, Clifford (1983a, 1988:38–41) has argued that Geertz has always remained the authoritarian voice that arbitrated the interpretational disputes among his informants. Clifford has emphasized the dialogic intersubjectivity of the ethnographic encounter with its polyphonic variations and discursive conflicts, as examplifed by Dwyer (1982) and Crapanzano (1980).

[6] This article has drawn inspiration from Baudrillard's general statements about seduction but should not be taken as an application of his ideas (for a feminist critique, see Hunter 1989).

[7] The opposite of the illusion of the cultural insider is the illusion of the objective investigator. "Methodological objectivism is a denial of the intersubjective or dialogical nature of fieldwork through which ethnographic understanding develops" (Obeyesekere 1990:227).

[8] The open-ended interview is not a context-free exchange of information but in the first place a social relationship with all its concomitant complexities (Brenner 1978, 1981). The impression management during my research in Argentina involved an array of stratagems. The location of the interview was chosen with the aim of exuding authority or familiarity. Some preferred their homes, while others invited me to the stately buildings of the church and the armed forces or the personalized offices of the human rights and former guerilla organizations. Impression management also involved a manipulation of the senses. Dress, physical gestures, facial expressions, and ways of making eye contact and shaking hands are all part of a presentation of self that influences the social interaction between ethnographer and subject (Agar 1980:54–62). For an analysis of the unique problems of female researchers who study the military, see Daniels 1967.

[9] Simons (1976:134–138) distinguishes between co-active, combative, and expressive forms of persuasion. The co-active form attempts to bridge the psychological differences among interlocutors by stimulating the identification between speaker and audience. The combative form tries to persuade through coercion and intimidation. Combative approaches are most effective in situations of social conflict. Finally, there is an expressive approach that deliberately rejects the conscious manipulation of the audience but that hopes to raise people's consciousness through self-criticism and by openly sharing experiences. The co-active form of persuasion is the most versatile strategy because it can incorporate aspects of the other two forms.

[10] Roloff (1980) analyzes aspects of rhetorical persuasion that remain hidden to both speaker and audience.

[11] A scene from *Shoah* comes to mind in which Claude Lanzmann virtually coerces Abraham Bomba, a survivor of Treblinka, to recall his experiences: "AB: A friend of mine worked as a barber—he was a good barber in my hometown—when his wife and his sister came into the gas chamber. . . . I can't. It's too horrible. Please. CL: We have to do it. You know it. AB: I won't be able to do it. CL: You have to do it. I know it's very hard. I know and I apologize. AB: Don't make me go on please. CL: We must go on" (Lanzmann 1985:117).

[12] Part of the dialogue quoted here can be found in almost the exact same words in Cohen Salama (1992:230).

[13] Historians and sociologists have paid more attention to deliberate distortion; see Dean and Whyte, 1970; Ginzburg 1991; Gorden 1975:445–460; Henige 1982:58–59.

[14] During the same period, there was also considerable interest in action research and Marxist and feminist analyses. These three approaches are at the opposite end of seduction because the ethnographer tries to seduce people into accepting his or her interpretation of social reality as the most objective and correct analysis. The language of oppression and exploitation is used as a powerful rhetoric of persuasion.

[15] Devereux (1967:46) explains this "anxious clinging to 'hard' facts" as an expression of the ethnographer's fear that he or she is not properly understanding or communicating with the informants.

[16] War, according to von Clausewitz (1984:87) is "a continuation of political activity by other means."

References

Agar, Michael, II. 1980. *The Professional Stranger: An Informal Introduction to Ethnography*. New York: Academic Press.

Baudrillard, Jean. 1990. *Seduction*. New York: St. Martin's Press.

Berreman, Gerald D. 1972. "Prologue: Behind Many Masks, Ethnography and Impression Management." In *Hindus of the Himalayas: Ethnography and Change*, ed. Gerald Berreman, xvii–lvii. Berkeley, Los Angeles and London: University of California Press.

Brenner, Michael. 1978. "Interviewing: The Social Phenomenology of a Research Instrument." In *The Social Contexts of Method*, ed. Michael Brenner, Peter Marsh, and Marylin Brenner, 122–139. London: Croom Helm.

———. 1981. "Patterns of Social Structure in the Research Interview." In *Social Method and Social Life*, ed. Michael Brenner, 115–158. New York: Academic Press.

Brown, Jennifer, and Jonathan Sime. 1981. "A Methodology for Accounts." In *Social Method and Social Life*, ed. Michael Brenner, 159–188. New York: Academic Press.

Cicourel, Aaron V. 1964. *Method and Measurement in Sociology*. New York: Free Press.

Clausewitz, Carl von. [1832] 1984. *On War*. Princeton: Princeton University Press.

Clifford, James. 1983a. "On Ethnographic Authority." *Representations* 1 (2): 118–146.

———. 1983b. "Power and Dialogue in Ethnography: Marcel Griaule's Initiation." In *Observers Observed: Essays on Ethnographic Fieldwork*, ed. George W. Stocking, 121–156. Madison: University of Wisconsin Press.

———. 1988. *The Predicament of Culture: Twentieth-Century Ethnography, Literature, and Art*. Cambridge: Harvard University Press.

Cohen Salama, Mauricio. 1992. *Tumbas anónimas: Informe sobre la identificación de restos de víctimas de la represión ilegal*. Buenos Aires: Catálogos Editora.

Cole, Thomas. 1991. *The Origins of Rhetoric in Ancient Greece*. Baltimore: Johns Hopkins University Press.

Crapanzano, Vincent. 1980. *Tuhami: Portrait of a Moroccan*. Chicago: University of Chicago Press.

Daniels, Arlene Kaplan. 1967. "The Low-Caste Stranger in Social Research." In *Ethics, Politics, and Social Research*, ed. Gideon Sjoberg, 267–296. Cambridge: Schenkman.

Dean, John P., and William Foote Whyte. 1970. "How Do You Know If the Informant Is Telling the Truth?" In *Elite and Specialized Interviewing*, ed. Lewis Anthony Dexter, 119–131. Evanston: Northwestern University Press.

Denzin, Norman K. (ed.). 1970. *Sociological Methods: A Sourcebook*. Chicago: Aldine.

Devereux, George. 1967. *From Anxiety to Method in the Behavioral Sciences*. The Hague: Mouton.

Dwyer, Kevin. 1982. *Moroccan Dialogues: Anthropology in Question*. Baltimore: Johns Hopkins University Press.

Ellen, R. F. (ed.). 1984. *Ethnographic Research: A Guide to General Conduct*. London: Academic Press.

Geertz, Clifford. 1973. *The Interpretation of Cultures*. New York: Basic Books.

Gilbert, G. Nigel, and Michael Mulkay. 1984. *Opening Pandora's Box: A Sociological Analysis of Scientists' Discourse.* Cambridge: Cambridge University Press.

Ginzburg, Carlo. 1991. "Checking the Evidence: The Judge and the Historian." *Critical Inquiry* 18 (1):79–92.

Goffman, Erving. 1966. *Behavior in Public Places: Notes on the Social Organization of Gatherings.* New York: Free Press.

———. 1969. *The Presentation of Self in Everyday Life.* London: Allen Lane.

Gorden, Raymond L. 1975. *Interviewing: Strategy, Techniques, and Tactics.* Homewood, IL: Dorsey Press.

Griaule, Marcel. 1957. *Méthode de l'Ethnographie.* Paris: Presses Universitaires de France.

Gross, Alan G. 1990. *The Rhetoric of Science.* Cambridge: Harvard University Press.

Henige, David. 1982. *Oral Historiography.* London: Longman.

Hunter, Dianne (ed.). 1989. *Seduction and Theory: Readings of Gender, Representation, and Rhetoric.* Urbana: University of Illinois Press.

Hyman, Herbert H., et al. 1954. *Interviewing in Social Research.* Chicago: University of Chicago Press.

Jardine, Nicholas. 1991. *The Scenes of Inquiry: On the Reality of Questions in the Sciences.* Oxford: Clarendon Press.

Lanzmann, Claude. 1985. *Shoah: An Oral History of the Holocaust.* New York: Pantheon Books.

Nadel, S. F. 1939. "The Interview Technique in Social Anthropology." In *The Study of Society: Methods and Problems*, ed. F. C. Bartlett et al., 317–327. London: Kegan Paul, Trench, Trubner.

Obeyesekere, Gananath. 1990. *The Work of Culture: Symbolic Transformation in Psychoanalysis and Anthropology.* Chicago: University of Chicago Press.

Potash, Robert A. 1969. *The Army and Politics in Argentina, 1928–1945: Yrigoyen to Perón.* Stanford: Stanford University Press.

———. 1980. *The Army and Politics in Argentina, 1945–1962: Perón to Frondizi.* Stanford: Stanford University Press.

RAI (Royal Anthropological Institute). 1951. *Notes and Queries on Anthropology.* 6th ed. London: Routledge and Kegan Paul.

Roloff, Michael E. 1980. "Self-Awareness and the Persuasion Process: Do We Really Know What We're Doing?" In *Persuasion: New Directions in Theory and Research*, ed. Michael E. Roloff and Derald R. Miller, 29–66. Beverly Hills, CA: Sage Publications.

Rosaldo, Renato. 1986. "From the Door of His Tent: The Fieldworker and the Inquisitor." In *Writing Culture: The Poetics and Politics of Ethnography*, ed. James Clifford and George E. Marcus, 77–97. Berkeley, Los Angeles and London: University of California Press.

Rouquié, Alain. 1987a. *Poder Militar y Sociedad Política en la Argentina I—hasta 1943.* Buenos Aires: Emecé Editores.

———. 1987b. *Poder Militar y Sociedad Política en la Argentina II—1943–1973.* Buenos Aires: Emecé Editores.

Simons, Herbert W. 1976. *Persuasion: Understanding, Practice, and Analysis.* Reading, MA: Addison-Wesley.

Turner, Charles F., and Elizabeth Martin (eds.). 1984. *Surveying Subjective Phenomena*, Vol. 1. New York: Russell Sage Foundation.

Dr. Arcand teaches anthropology at Université Laval, in Québec, Canada.

Unless hired to help resolve a specific problem or to achieve some goal(s) set by the local population, most anthropologists have traditionally striven to understand how and why people do things in the way they do, or how local institutions and systems work, without significantly affecting the situation. Most missionaries, by contrast, strive to discredit at least some traditional beliefs and practices, and pride themselves on substituting new and alien customs and cosmologies. An extreme example of this contrast is Arcand's chronicling of the discrepancy between what one group of missionaries claim to be their aim, and their actual impact on a hunting-and-gathering community he was studying in the jungle of eastern Colombia.

A very different approach to native languages is offered in Bernard (chapter 10), and some very different approaches to native adjustment to the rest of the world are described in Conklin (chapter 30), Stearman (chapter 20), and Stavenhagen (chapter 13).

God Is an American

Bernard Arcand

I could never work up much enthusiasm for the idea that some people consider the sun a deity, while others wait for a messiah and my neighbours believe in the greatness of Allah or accept the notion of virgin birth. So, when the Summer Institute of Linguistics (SIL) claims that all the organization does is to offer Christian mythology as an alternative to indigenous mythologies, that statement, in itself, does not strike me as being especially disturbing. What bothers me is the pretence that a mythology is something which can be offered as a simple alternative. Such a suggestion may apply within the context of a university seminar, but to claim that the same end can be achieved through mission work in South America is not only ludicrous but criminal. From what I have witnessed of missionary work among the Cuiva Indians of Colombia, the efforts of the SIL have little to do with religious beliefs or mythology, and an awful lot to do with economics and politics.

The SIL became interested in the Cuiva during the mid-sixties. Following a rapid survey which showed that Cuiva language was significantly different from that of the neighbouring Guahibo (where the SIL already had a team at work), two missionaries were given the customary task of translating into Cuiva some, if not all, of the New Testament with the usual goal of completing their work within a decade. Of course, it wasn't that simple and much of the work remains to be done.

We often hear that the SIL is an organization of "American" missionaries, but they are not just any kind of Americans. They usually come from rural America and often from the Midwest, an area sometimes called "the heartland" of the U.S. They are most often recruited in smaller communities within the rural areas of the country, "the heartland of America," "the silent majority." This normally means that they look healthy, are physically large, tend to vote conservative, and are totally dedicated to the Protestant ethics of hard work and individualism. These people have been brought up with the ideal of the American melting pot, the coming together of all cultures under God and the flag.

Reprinted, with permission of the publisher, from same author's "God Is an American," pages 77–84, in Søren Hvalkof and Peter Aaby (eds.), *Is God an American? An Anthropological Perspective on the Missionary Work of the Summer Institute of Linguistics,* IWGIA, International Work Group for Indigenous Affairs, Copenhagen; and Survival International, London, 1981.

The two missionaries sent to the Cuiva had a difficult task. They began establishing contact with one band around 1965, when the Cuiva were still living as nomadic hunters and gatherers. The two women trying to reach them would set up camp on the bank of the main river within the band's territory and then simply wait for visitors. The Cuiva would come, stay with the missionaries for a few days, accept all presents offered, and leave. With their awkward equipment of outboard motor, tent, cooking tools, clothing, tape recorders, etc., the two women could never hope to follow. The Cuiva, who carry very little, are able to leave any camp within a few minutes and usually change site every few days. Under these circumstances, the best the missionaries could hope for was to establish preliminary contact and become known to the Cuiva, while learning perhaps some of the basic elements of the language.

These short visits and very limited contacts could have gone on for years, but a tragic incident was to change profoundly the direction of Cuiva history. Faced with mounting pressures from Colombian settlers who had been slowly invading their territory, members of the band with which the SIL had established contact decided to build permanent houses and create a small village as a base camp for migrations and where the group would cultivate the soil to supplement hunting and gathering.

> The site chosen for this village was minutes away from the ranch of a settler who had maintained friendly relations with the band and for whom quite a few Cuiva had worked in the past. . . . The village experiment did not last long. As soon as a few houses were completed (others were in construction) and after the soil had been cleared and sown, Mario Gonzales, the neighbouring settler, whom the Cuiva thought friendly, together with five of his friends, came to the Cuiva village at midday on the 20th of July 1966. At the very moment when they were welcomed as friends, these settlers began shooting in all directions. Most of the Cuiva escaped into the forest, but one man (a cripple who could not run as fast as the others) was killed and six others were wounded. The settlers even took pains to cut up the body of the dead man and throw the parts into the river; some parts of the body remained hanging from branches overlooking the river. (Arcand 1972:13)

The creation of the village had been encouraged by newly arrived American missionaries, unrelated to the SIL, whose mission was mostly to work with the local inhabitants of the neighbouring Colombian village of Cravo Norte, but who also occasionally traveled by boat to visit the Cuiva for a few hours. It was they who provided the tools and seeds for cultivation, who made sure all those injured in the massacre received proper medical treatment and who insisted to the local police authorities that charges be pressed against the settlers.

In the days following the attack on their village, the Cuiva regrouped, moved and pitched camp next to the ranch of a Swiss settler who had lived in Colombia for thirty years and who had always seemed to have a marked sympathy for the Indians. The Cuiva felt protected by his presence and, in any case, at that particular moment, anything was better than massacre. Much of their traditional territory was occupied by settlers and agriculture appeared to be the only way to survive. On a small plot of land next to the ranch, they began to build houses, create a village and cultivate the soil. Within a few months, the Cuiva lost an economy based on hunting and gathering for an economy which would soon become dependent on agriculture.

This radical change perfectly suited the aims of the SIL missionaries. They no longer needed to chase the Cuiva over their vast hunting territory. They encouraged the Swiss settler and the other American missionaries in Cravo Norte to supply the needed seeds, tools and advice. They paid some Cuiva to build a thatchroofed house for themselves, five times larger than any Cuiva shelter. They paid for the construction of a short air-strip in the nearby savanna. These constructions meant easy access by air to a field-camp with a population of roughly 200 Cuiva and a relatively comfortable house from which to operate. Nevertheless, the missionaries came only rarely. When I first met the Cuiva in 1968, the missionaries were back in the U.S. on sabbatical leave. They returned to Colombia in 1969 and during all of the following year they visited the Cuiva village only twice, for a total of 11 weeks. When I returned to the same village in 1973, the missionaries were again absent. The main reason for this apparent lack of dedication seems to be that the missionaries prefer to do most of their work at the SIL Colombian headquarters at Lomalinda. There, they can find all the material comfort of North America in a camp inhabited only by SIL missionaries living in complete isolation from Colombian society. Since they must work on learning the language, they bring with them to this base two, three, or four Cuiva, to whom they offer room and board, in return for language instruction and domestic services.

From the missionaries' point of view, the result of this policy of bringing the Cuiva to oneself rather than going to them is reasonable progress in learning the language, with the added advantages of comfort and tranquility. The price they must pay is ignorance of much of Cuiva culture. Not even the wildest theoretician of linguistic determinism, or the strongest proponent of formal analysis of language, would seriously claim that one can understand a culture by simply talking with a native speaker of a language in a closed room totally removed from the language's physical, social and intellectual contexts. What the missionaries learn this way is an elementary command of the syntax and grammar of the language. But their knowledge of semantics is often minimal. They merely strive to acquire the means of transmitting their own message. This message becomes very clear when we look at the tools by which they hope to teach literacy. Teaching the Cuiva to read is part of the SIL contractual engagement with the Colombian government and is the obvious prerequisite to giving them a translation of the New Testament. Besides the missionaries' direct interventions with Cuiva society which we shall consider later, the teaching of reading represents the SIL's strongest effort at influencing and modifying Cuiva culture. Their strategy uses two separate methods, one public and the other quite secret. The latter consists of giving the Cuiva written versions of their own myths which have been transformed to incorporate a Christian content. These texts are prepared on the SIL's private photocopying machine and are almost certainly distributed without the knowledge of the government, since they are proof of a flagrant violation of the SIL contract with Colombia: the spreading of evangelical propaganda. Let me give an example of this method. The Cuiva have a number of myths dealing with the character of "Namoun" (called "Nacom" by the missionaries, no doubt a difference in phonetic hearing), a cultural hero said to be responsible for the creation of people, the growth of trees, and the menstrual cycle, among other things. In the hands of the missionaries, the story printed and distributed to the Cuiva becomes:

> Nacom in the language of the non-Indians is called Dios! He, Nacom, made the earth. He made all the earth and all the savanna. He made the animals and the birds. He made all Indians and all non-Indians. He blew on them. He made the sky, the stars and the moon. He made it all good.

Then, in the following story, the missionaries introduce a mythical character totally alien to Cuiva culture:

> Satan created all bad things, illness, death. He does not like Nacom, nor his son Jesus Christ.

And the stories go on. Having seen these texts and being one of the few outsiders who can understand them, I consider myself in a privileged position to call a liar any SIL missionary claiming to respect indigenous cultures or claiming, as the SIL does to the Colombian government, that the organization is not involved in promoting Christianity.

Far less secretive, the other method for teaching reading is directly supervised by the "Indian Affairs" department of the Colombian government. It involves printing and distributing short stories written in "basic Cuiva" and quite similar to primary school textbook stories anywhere. But even these short stories carry a powerful message and seem aimed at teaching far more than literacy. Here is an example of one such story:

> A man cleans the land surrounding his house with a rake. He decides to leave and go plant corn in his field. Soon he returns home because he has forgotten his hat. That night, he hears a woolly opossum that has come to eat his chickens. He gets up from his hammock and throws a stick at the animal to chase it away. One chicken is dead and the man proposes to eat it in the morning.

This short story seems straightforward enough when it mentions the house, the field, the planting of corn and the ownership of chickens. Yet it is remarkable: every single detail of the story corresponds to the state of affairs which the missionaries are hoping for and which contrasts sharply with traditional Cuiva culture. "Cleaning the land surrounding a house" was rarely done by the Cuiva: only after remaining at the same site for a long period of time will the surroundings become dirty, and then it is much easier to change camping site than clean the surroundings. "Soon he returns home because he has forgotten his hat": in over two years I had never seen a Cuiva forget anything when leaving on a trip; the hat of course is also new, but the very idea of needing a hat is interesting: hunters and gatherers typically leave the cool shade of the forest either early in the morning or late in the afternoon, when a hat is quite unnecessary; only an agriculturalist would be silly enough to cut down the trees for cultivation and to work under the burning sun. ". . . he hears a woolly opossum . . . gets up from his hammock and throws a stick at the animal to chase it away": the woolly opossum is considered a funny animal by the Cuiva, one that stinks badly and has a funny scream, but it is not in any way a dangerous animal and a man would never leave the comfort of his hammock in the middle of the night to chase it away; except, of course, if he had chickens to worry about. Finally, "the man proposes to eat it (the chicken) in the morning": the Cuiva do not eat chicken and this is somewhat of a puzzle for settlers and missionaries; some Cuiva have had chickens for years and eat nothing but their eggs, refusing to kill the animals even in periods of hunger and always preferring to sell them to settlers.

This text is illustrated by rather poor drawings depicting a man wearing a hat and standing next to a woman in Western dress. The two characters are situated in a clearing, not the forest, and in the background hangs a hammock with mosquito-net.

The missionaries would probably find these comments petty and unfair. I have heard them say this is obviously what the future will bring the Cuiva, that agriculture is their only hope for survival, that hats and mosquito-nets can be very practical and are in fact much appreciated by the Cuiva. Perhaps, but the point I am trying to make is that the SIL has no intention of "respecting cultures" as the official propaganda would have the world believe. It is involved in the imposition of a new culture and in the destruction of the traditional Cuiva way of life. The missionaries play an active and essential role in a process which can only be to the advantage of settlers and other foreign invaders. Their intervention is a deliberate effort to limit the Cuiva to a minimum space and get them to accept this as the irreversible outcome of history. Christian missionaries have been performing this task for centuries and the SIL is certainly no different. What are perhaps different are the incredible public statements to the effect that the Cuiva were forced into this unfortunate situation by settlers and that all the missionaries are trying to do is to bring some relief into their lives, before God brings them final relief in heaven.

By transforming myths and imposing new stories, by remaining passive in face of the pressing issue, the missionaries must have an impact on Cuiva culture. But they also interfere directly with society in a number of other domains which would seem to have little to do with religion and be rather remote from their stated goal of learning the language and translating the Bible.

Their very life-style is an influence. The missionaries have always owned the largest, best-built and, whenever they are in camp, cleanest house in the village. Between 1970 and 1973, they paid for the building of a new, larger and even more elaborate house and suggested the Cuiva build their houses in a semi-circle around it. Half the band did and the impression is that of a small medieval kingdom. Furthermore, the material wealth of the missionaries is awesome. They usually reach the village by means of a small plane filled to the brim with petrol tanks, cooking equipment, stove, plates, books, tape recorder, cloth hammocks, mosquito nets, etc. Life in their house is a pale effort to model middle-America, with hair-curlers and Jello pudding. It is not always easy for two women to live in a remote Indian village and they are tough enough to get by on what must seem to them the bare minimum. To anyone else the contrast is shattering: two women, using radio to keep in daily contact with Lomalinda and sometimes even with the U.S., while a few metres away Cuiva houses are little more than simple lean-to shelters, protecting a family of 6 or 7 in a crowded space littered with pieces of old cloth, oil cans and broken knives.

The missionaries hope to influence more than by simple example. They also very much want to encourage private ownership and the private use of gardens. When the Cuiva began cultivation, not everyone participated and even then not all with the same enthusiasm; the result has been that some families now own fairly large gardens, whereas their neighbours may never have bothered to plant anything. Nevertheless, at the same time, the Cuiva have maintained their traditional system of distributing all available food among all those present in camp. This is the customary egalitarian system adopted by most societies with an economy based on hunting and gathering; however, here it means that whether one cultivates or not will not really determine the amount of vegetables one will be able to eat; those who cultivate give to those who have no gardens. This seems to infuriate the missionaries. It conflicts with their beliefs of how society should be organized and with the principle that reward should come only to those who toil. It conflicts with what others would call the Protestant ethic and the spirit of capitalism. From their point of view, the Cuiva system of food distribution is an aberration and I have seen them blame people for scavenging from their neighbours and suggest that if they wanted vegetables they should themselves plant and harvest. The missionaries will be happy only when both production and consumption are fully individualized. Private ownership of the means of production, the possibility of creating surpluses, the birth of capital and profits . . . the rest of the story is well known. This is the way of God, and it seems equally important to impose all this on the Cuiva as it is to translate the Bible.

These economic principles also regulate how the missionaries themselves relate to the Cuiva. Although they bring food as part of their own equipment, they remain partly dependent on hunters for their meat supply and always pay in money or goods whenever they obtain meat from anyone. To them, the anthropologist's habit of accepting food freely and reciprocating, often much later, with gifts was doubly scandalous: on one hand, I was exploiting the generosity of the Cuiva and on the other, I was perpetuating the Cuiva tendency to accept gifts for nothing. My behaviour was seen as unethical, if not clearly immoral. Yet, it followed closely the rules of Cuiva economy.

Gradually, those who worked gardens gave away their vegetables quite freely, but hunted less and gave far less meat than they received. If the missionaries have it their way, the gardeners could experience a rapid decline in the protein content of their diet, while the hunters, now limited to exploiting the relatively small area close to the village, could risk short-term shortages if they can no longer rely on the more constant supply of vegetables produced by the gardeners. The longer-term risk is the complete destruction of the Cuiva economy, with all this implies for the foundation of social relations, and its replacement by a privatized economy based on individualism and very likely leading to exploitation.

For the missionaries, it is the traditional Cuiva economy which is exploitative: some worked and produced more than others, yet in the end all were equal. Hard work was not recognized for its worth and laziness could escape without penalty. This notion of fairness, which in the missionaries' mind turns to stingy accounting, does not seem to be of great concern to the Cuiva: within relatively broad limits, it never seemed to matter much whether individuals produced more or less, according to their inclination, energy and taste, as long as there was plenty for all. This, to the missionaries, is supremely unfair. And behind their position, as well as behind so much of the "American way of life," lies the notion that human action can always be quantified and moneyfied. Everything has a value which translates into material wealth. This materialistic philosophy is surely one of the more blatant paradoxes of an organization claiming that spiritual salvation is the central focus of life on earth.

The missionaries pay for the construction of a house, pay for its repair, pay for food, pay for all menial services and pay their informants. For the Cuiva, this translates into clothes, cooking pots, knives, machetes, and other foreign goods. But since the missionaries cannot supply the needs of the whole community, they also buy Cuiva handicrafts at whatever prices these may fetch with other missionaries at their base camp of Lomalinda. The problem, of course, is that the Cuiva make little more than hammocks and bows and arrows, which can never hope to occupy a competitive place on a handicraft market dominated by the more elaborate artifacts other missionaries bring back from Amazonia or the Choco. So, this new trade is almost irrelevant for the Cuiva: they can produce many of these items in a few hours and the market created by the missionaries is too small to justify additional efforts. It also means that the missionaries help maintain the need for imported goods, and that when a Cuiva wants something from Colombian society the simplest solution is to work for wages at one of the local ranches. In this indirect way, the missionaries press the Cuiva into entering the lowest level of the Colombian economy.

The only time the missionaries have interfered, but without their characteristic sense of mercantilism, is when they helped the sick and provided free medical supplies. Their equipment is adequate, they have received professional training in nursing and on the whole their medical assistance has been efficient and of high quality. But this assistance can only last the length of the missionaries' stay with the community. When they proudly said to me, shortly after a woman died, that this was the first death ever to occur while they were present in camp, the claim was, of course, that they had saved all the others. But if one calculates how long they had actually spent with the Cuiva over the last decade, their claim was reduced to saying there had been no death over a period of about six months. I could make the same claim, without any professional training and with only very inadequate medical supplies. It may be very unfair to try to diminish the missionaries' valuable medical assistance, but so much is made of their role as medical officers that it seems important to place it within its proper context and reduce it to its real proportions. The SIL often stresses the glory of its medical assistance, but it must also be stressed that this is only occasional help at best and that never has an ounce of penicillin cost a people so much.

The missionaries also interfere with many other aspects of daily life besides economic and health matters. They are quite outspoken in their opposition to hallucinogenic drugs. They insist on wearing dresses, even during the mosquito season when they wear them over trousers, simply because this is to them the only proper dress for a woman. Of course, anything approaching nudity would offend their sense of decency and would be met with strong disapproval. The practical problems created by this attitude are well known even to the missionaries. Cuiva traditional clothing had the double advantage of being easily replaceable and of leaving most of the skin exposed so that the frequent rains did not mean one stayed wet for hours risking respiratory diseases. The missionaries insist that clothing is an essential protection against mosquitoes and they want to eliminate the health hazard by providing the Cuiva with more and more clothes and teaching them to change dress more often. Never would they suggest that Western clothing is not really necessary during the dry season, when it never rains and there are no mosquitoes. It is also tempting to add a more subjective, personal note and say that the clothing given to the Cuiva usually consists of old rags which make them look like tramps, which is precisely how they enter Western civilization.

The missionaries also interfere with disputes or quarrels and do not hesitate to walk across camp, in the middle of the night and with flashlight in hand, to stop a marital fight. These disputes can certainly be dangerous and sometimes people do get hurt, but again, this is an example of how the missionaries do not hesitate to pass value judgments on Cuiva society, decide what is wrong, show no concern for Cuiva authority structure, while interfering directly to change the culture. Any behaviour is evaluated on the basis of middle-American Christianity, which always prevails in the end.

On the whole, the Cuivas' reaction to the missionaries has been dominated by their remarkable sense of polite hospitality. Unlike many settlers, the missionaries have behaved in a rather civilized manner and the Cuiva have responded in kind. We must also understand that Cuiva culture and social organization, like that perhaps of many other hunting and gathering societies, are characterized by flexibility and the ability to incorporate foreigners smoothly and, to a large extent, also their ideas. For example, new Western medicine is not seen as a threat to traditional Cuiva curing techniques, but as an added and welcome contribution; in fact, it would be just as impolite to refuse this help as it would be impolite not to give away most of one's personal belongings. So, by helping cure the sick, the missionaries are behaving correctly and this is much appreciated. The same holds true to some extent for the introduction of new ideas, may these be tales of distant lands or new concepts on cosmology or theology. Cuiva adults, during their long hours of leisure, seem to enjoy nothing better than intelligent discussions of abstract concepts. The missionaries' doctrine of a single God, creator of all things and father of us all, does at least provide an interesting topic for discussion.

The Cuivas' sense of politeness often presses them into appearing as if they gladly accept the authority of the missionaries. It is never proper to disagree openly with someone or to appear to be blatantly refusing what has been requested. The customary and polite way to show disagreement is for a person to remain calm, keep smiling, say nothing openly, but go and live in another part of the territory. After a few weeks, the disagreement will most often be forgotten and all can live together again. Since the missionaries never stay in camp very long, the Cuiva relate to them with somewhat of a double standard. Their informants, those individuals most closely associated with the missionaries, know perfectly well how they disapprove of drugs, certain modes of clothing, etc., and will normally refrain from these whenever the missionaries are in camp. As soon as they leave, these informants quickly return to a more normal life style; so muc[...] at times left with the impression they are celebrating the missi[...]

But all politeness[...]ng reason why the Cuiva react the way they do to missionarie[...]ny other friendly outsider is simply that given their tragic hist[...]te society, they are very much aware of needing all the help th[...]future is better than genocide.

The two SIL missi[...]ear strange to them, but probably no more than any other n[...] two adult unmarried women living together connotes lesbia[...]ment among some Cuiva males. Their habit of taking people aw[...]their base camp of Lomalinda causes grief among their close re[...]heard crying for days after their departure), but it is now well-es[...]ed that these informants will on the whole be treated nicely and that there is little to fear for them.

The missionaries' relations to the anthropologist were often far more delicate. During the two months we spent in the same community our relations were of correct avoidance and neither side interfered with the other's work. However, I did get the clear impression I was an intruder on a territory with scarce resources. I was also clearly seen as a very bad influence on the Cuiva. To give only one example, I was told that by being the first non-Indian to take drugs I was encouraging the Cuiva to use them. It had never before crossed anyone's mind that the Cuiva needed a foreigner's approval to take drugs! The more aggressive side of the SIL was never shown by the two missionaries themselves but came from more indirect sources. Friends who at the time were doing fieldwork in the Vaupés area of Colombia reported to me how SIL pilots had told them that I was importing guns from Venezuela in preparation for a Cuiva revolt and that I was sharing my hammock with five or six young Cuiva girls. I immediately wrote a letter to Clarence Church, then head of SIL operations in Colombia, pointing out that nothing was gained by his organization's spreading such rumours. He never bothered to reply.

The missionaries had practically very little to do with Colombians, since they flew almost directly from the U.S. to their base camp at Lomalinda and then to the Cuiva. It seems that only the highest officials of the SIL have relations with Colombia and then only with higher government authorities from whom they must obtain the necessary permits and protection for the whole operation. Individual missionaries are cared for and transported by fellow Americans, often without any Colombian intervention, and some do not even speak much Spanish. The missionaries I knew tried as much as possible to avoid contact with Colombians and appeared definitely ill at ease whenever settlers came to visit them or when they had to travel to a nearby Colombian village. What is worse, they seemed to suffer from some acute form of revolutionary paranoia. When it was reported that a group of Guahibo Indians in the Planas area had begun a guerilla uprising, the two missionaries became extremely nervous and made hasty preparations to return to Lomalinda. The Planas area is at least 300 kilometers from Cuiva territory, but they were convinced the rebels would soon arrive and execute them. This kind of paranoia may be in part the result of the ancient persecution of Protestants in Colombia and of American anti-communist indoctrination, but it also clearly indicates an extraordinary ignorance of Colombian society and politics. It further explains why the SIL, through its missionaries in the Planas area, is said to have been eager to provide scouts and interpreters for the army during its repression of the Guahibo. If true, that incident alone should be enough to undermine forever the myth that the SIL works to protect Indians from massacre at the hands of Colombians.

The distance which they carefully maintain between themselves and Colombian society can only constitute an insult to any nationalist. When we say that the SIL tries to integrate the Cuiva into Western society, we really mean that they force upon them the values of white Anglo-Saxon Protestant Americans and certainly not those of rural Colombia. To the SIL missionaries, most Colombians are little more than backward and ignorant peasants for whom they have very little sympathy. Once their entry into the country is sanctioned by the upper echelon of the government, they are quite wary of any form of intervention by Colombian institutions. They do not trust Colombian planes, Colombian food, and even less Colombian linguists or missionaries. To them, Colombia is a third-world country on its slow path to becoming as advanced as the United States and there is thus no point in living like Colombians or in teaching Colombian society to the Cuiva.

Yet, the very presence of Colombian peasants constitutes an essential part of the SIL ideology. Whatever their efforts to transform Indian society, these are always justified *post facto* by the claim that change is inevitable and, if it were not for the SIL, the Cuiva would be left in the hands of Colombians. And that, by their own definition, would of course be far worse. The argument makes some sense when one looks at the number of settlers in the area who would gladly rid their neighbourhood of all Indians. But the missionaries are much less convincing when they face friendly settlers, local medical authorities, or the new generation of Colombian linguists and anthropologists who have all shown interest in helping the Cuiva. The SIL does not really want to hear of such people since much of the justification for its presence rests on a simplistic view of the most typical Colombian in the area as an armed cowboy fully intent on genocide.

It would be surprising if they do not succeed, through repeated bribery or the sheer weight of their propaganda, to convince and "convert" at least a handful of Cuiva. This would be enough to transform profoundly a society which has always depended on consensus and close cooperation. Although Christianity teaches love and tolerance, it has a long history of generating prejudices and social divisions. The new Cuiva converts will begin producing by themselves, living by themselves, and the proudness of their faith will turn into contempt for those who do not "recognize Jesus-Christ as their personal savior." The goal of the SIL will then be achieved, Indian society will be divided and shaped more along the lines of a Western model, and the Cuiva will begin despising one another. Fractured and divided, Cuiva society will be even more vulnerable, even less capable of resisting or even surviving the foreign invasion of its territory and its life. But, the missionaries would say, a handful of Cuiva could then make it to heaven.

Reference

Arcand, Bernard. 1972. *The Urgent Situation* of *the Cuiva Indians of Colombia,* Copenhagen: IWGIA, Document No. 7.

Oscar Lewis was a professor of anthropology at the University of Illinois at his untimely death in 1970. His early research yielded such varied books as The Effects of White Contact upon the Blackfoot Indians *(1942),* Life in a Mexican Village: Tepoztlán Restudied *(1951), and* Village Life in India *(1958). He achieved widespread recognition of the literary and humanitarian value of ethnography with a series of volumes in which the narration of the informants themselves predominated and the "culture of poverty" provided a controversial thread of continuity:* Five Families: Mexican Case Studies in the Culture of Poverty *(1959),* The Children of Sánchez *(1961),* Pedro Martínez: A Mexican Peasant and his Family *(1964),* La Vida: A Puerto Rican Family in the Culture of Poverty—San Juan and New York *(1966), and* Death in the Sánchez Family *(1969). A number of his influential papers were compiled as* Anthropological Essays *(1970).*

Ever since Lewis first wrote about a "culture of poverty," the concept has been a focus of controversy, championed by some and criticized by others, while the author continued to sharpen his definition. Without either idealizing or deploring poverty of poor people, he specified an increasing number of traits that recur cross-culturally, with reference to the larger society, the local community, the family, and the individual. Critics interpreted the concept as providing justification for policies of benign neglect and progressive curtailment of social welfare. This revised version of this most mature treatment of the subject was written just before his death, after he had done comparative research in Cuba to test his hunches about how the dominant economic system may affect the culture of poverty. Rightly or wrongly, this is one of the few instances in which an anthropologists' ideas have had clear and direct impact on public consciousness and political leaders.

This author's use of the term "Negro" in a context where today's usage would be "Black" or "African American" is only one evidence of the rapidity with which some aspects of language change. The social and cultural connotations remain much as they were described here, attesting to the conceptual value of this paper, in spite of that dated (and politically incorrect) label.

The Culture of Poverty

Oscar Lewis

Although a great deal has been written about poverty and the poor, the concept of a culture of poverty is relatively new. I first suggested it in 1959 in my book *Five Families: Mexican Case Studies in the Culture of Poverty*. The phrase is a catchy one and has become widely used and misused.[1] Michael Harrington used it extensively in his book *The Other America* (1961), which played an important role in sparking the national anti-poverty program in the United States. However, he used it in a somewhat broader and less technical sense than I had intended. I shall try to define it more precisely as a conceptual model, with special emphasis upon the distinction between poverty and the culture of poverty. The absence of intensive anthropological studies of poor families from a wide variety of national and cultural contexts, and especially from the socialist countries, is a serious handicap in formulating valid cross-cultural regularities. The model presented here is therefore provisional and subject to modification as new studies become available.

Throughout recorded history, in literature, in proverbs and in popular sayings, we find two opposite evaluations of the nature of the poor. Some characterize the poor as blessed, virtuous, upright, serene, independent, honest, kind, and happy. Others characterize them as evil, mean, violent, sordid, and criminal. These contradictory and confusing evaluations are also reflected in the infighting that is going on in the current war against poverty. Some stress the great potential of the poor for self-help, leadership, and community organization, while others point to the sometimes irreversible, destructive effect of poverty upon individual character, and therefore emphasize the need for guidance and control to remain in the hands of the middle class, which presumably has better mental health.

These opposing views reflect a political power struggle between competing groups. However, some of the confusion results from the failure to distinguish between poverty per se and the culture of poverty and from the tendency to focus upon the individual personality rather than upon the group—that is, the family and the slum community.

As an anthropologist I have tried to understand poverty and its associated traits as a culture or, more accurately, as a subculture[2] with its own structure and rationale, as a way of life which is passed down from generation to generation along family lines. This view directs attention to the fact that the culture of poverty in modern nations is not only a matter of economic deprivation, of disorganization, or of the absence of something. It is also something positive and provides some rewards without which the poor could hardly carry on.

Elsewhere I have suggested that the culture of poverty transcends regional, rural-urban, and national differences and shows remarkable similarities in family structure, interpersonal relations, time orientation, value systems, and spending patterns. These cross-national similarities are examples of independent invention and convergence. They are common adaptations to common problems.

The culture of poverty can come into being in a variety of historical contexts. However, it tends to grow and flourish in societies with the following set of conditions: (1) a cash economy, wage labor, and production for profit; (2) a persistently high rate of unemployment and underemployment for unskilled labor; (3) low wages; (4) the failure to provide social, political, and economic organization, either on a voluntary basis or by government imposition, for the low-income population; (5) the existence of a bilateral kinship system rather than a unilateral one;[3] and finally, (6) the existence of a set of values in the dominant class which stresses the accumulation of wealth and property, the possibility of upward mobility, and thrift, and explains low economic status as the result of personal inadequacy or inferiority.

The way of life that develops among some of the poor under these conditions is the culture of poverty. It can be best studied in urban or rural slums and can be described in terms of some seventy interrelated social, economic, and psychological traits. However, the number of traits and the relationships between them may vary from society to society and from family to family. For example, in a highly literate society, illiteracy may be more diagnostic of the culture of poverty than in a society where illiteracy is widespread and where even the well-to-do may be illiterate, as in some Mexican peasant villages before the revolution.

The culture of poverty is both an adaptation and a reaction of the poor to their marginal position in a class-stratified, highly individuated, capitalistic society. It represents an effort to cope with feelings of hopelessness and despair that develop from the realization of the improbability of achieving success in terms of the values and goals of the larger society. Indeed, many of the traits of the culture of poverty can be viewed as attempts at local solutions for problems not met by existing institutions and agencies because the people are not eligible for them, cannot afford them, or are ignorant or suspicious of them. For example, unable to obtain credit from banks, they are thrown upon their own resources and organize informal credit devices without interest.

The culture of poverty, however, is not only an adaptation to a set of objective conditions of the larger society. Once it comes into existence it tends to perpetuate itself from generation to generation because of its effect on the children. By the time slum children are age six or seven they have usually absorbed the basic values and attitudes of their subculture and are not psychologically geared to take full advantage of changing conditions or increased opportunities that may occur in their lifetime.

Most frequently the culture of poverty develops when a stratified social and economic system is breaking or is being replaced by another, as in the case of the transition from feudalism to capitalism or during periods of rapid technological change. Often it results from imperial conquest in which the native social and economic structure is smashed and the natives are maintained in a servile colonial status, sometimes for many generations. It can also occur in the process of detribalization, such as that now going on in Africa.

The most likely candidates for the culture of poverty are the people who come from the lower strata of a rapidly changing society and are already partially alienated from it. Thus landless rural workers who migrate to the cities can be expected to develop a culture of poverty much more readily than migrants from stable peasant villages with a well-organized traditional culture. In this connection there is a striking contrast between Latin America, where the rural population long ago made the transition from a tribal to a peasant society, and Africa, which is still close to its tribal heritage. The more corporate nature of many of the African tribal societies, in contrast to Latin American rural communities, and the persistence of village ties tend to inhibit or delay the formation of a full-blown culture of poverty in many of the African towns and cities. The special conditions of apartheid in South Africa, where the migrants are segregated into separate "locations" and do not enjoy freedom of movement, create special problems. Here the institutionalization of repression and discrimination tend to develop a greater sense of identity and group consciousness.

The culture of poverty can be studied from various points of view: the relationship between the subculture and the larger society; the nature of the slum community; the nature of the family; and the attitudes, values, and character structure of the individual.

1. The lack of effective participation and integration of the poor in the major institutions of the larger society is one of the crucial characteristics of the culture of poverty. This is a complex matter and results from a variety of factors that may include lack of economic resources, segregation and discrimination, fear, suspicion or apathy, and the development of local solutions for problems. However, "participation" in some of the institutions of the larger society—for example, in the jails, the army, and the public relief system that barely keeps people alive, both the basic poverty and the sense of hopelessness are perpetuated rather than eliminated.

Low wages, chronic unemployment, and underemployment lead to low income, lack of property ownership, absence of savings, absence of food reserves in the home, and a chronic shortage of cash. These conditions reduce the possibility of effective participation in the larger economic system. And as a response to these conditions we find in the culture of poverty a high incidence of pawning of personal goods, borrowing from local moneylenders at usurious rates of interest, spontaneous informal credit devices organized by neighbors, the use of second-hand clothing and furniture, and the pattern of frequent buying of small quantities of food many times a day as the need arises.

People with a culture of poverty produce very little wealth and receive very little in return. They have a low level of literacy and education, usually do not belong to labor unions, are not members of political parties, generally do not participate in the national welfare agencies, and make very little use of banks, hospitals, department stores, museums, or art galleries. They have a critical attitude toward some of the basic institutions of the dominant classes, hatred of the police, mistrust of government and those in high position, and a cynicism that extends even to the church. This gives the culture of poverty a high potential for protest and for being used in political movements aimed against the existing social order.

People with a culture of poverty are aware of middle-class values, talk about them, and even claim some of them as their own, but on the whole they do not live by them. Thus it is important to distinguish between what they say and what they do. For example, many will tell you that marriage by law, by the church, or by both, is the ideal form of marriage, but few will marry. To men who have no steady jobs or other sources of income, who do not own property and have no wealth to pass on to their children, who are present-time oriented, and who want to avoid the expense and legal difficulties involved in formal marriage and divorce, free unions or consensual marriage makes a lot of sense. Women will often turn down offers of marriage because they feel it ties them down to men who are immature, punishing, and generally unreliable. Women feel that consensual union gives them a better break; it gives them some of the freedom and flexibility that men have. By not giving the fathers of their children legal status as husbands, the women have a stronger claim on their children if they decide to leave their men. It also gives women exclusive rights to a house or any other property they may own.

2. When we look at the culture of poverty on the local community level, we find poor housing conditions, crowding, gregariousness, but above all a minimum of organization beyond the level of the nuclear and extended family. Occasionally there are informal, temporary groupings or voluntary associations within slums. The existence of neighborhood gangs that cut across slum settlements represents a considerable advance beyond the zero point of the continuum that I have in mind. Indeed, it is the low level of organization that gives the culture of poverty its marginal and anachronistic quality in our highly complex, specialized, organized society. Most primitive peoples have achieved a higher level of sociocultural organization than our modern slum dwellers.

In spite of the generally low level of organization, there may be a sense of community and *esprit de corps* in urban slums and in slum neighborhoods. This can vary within a single city, or from region to region or country to country. The major factors influencing this variation are the size of the slum, its location and physical characteristics, length of residence, incidence of home and land ownership (versus squatter rights), rentals, ethnicity, kinship ties, and freedom or lack of freedom of movement. When slums are separated from the surrounding area by enclosing walls or other physical barriers, when rents are low and fixed and stability of residence is great (twenty or thirty years), when the population constitutes a distinct ethnic, racial, or language group, is bound by ties of kinship or *compadrazgo*, and when there are some internal voluntary associations, then the sense of local community approaches that of a village community. In many cases this combination of favorable conditions does not exist. However, even where internal organization and *esprit de corps* are at a bare minimum and people move around a great deal, a sense of territoriality develops which sets off the slum neighborhoods from the rest of the city. In Mexico City and San Juan [Puerto Rico] this sense of territoriality results from the unavailability of low-income housing outside the slum areas. In South Africa the sense of territoriality grows out of the segregation enforced by the government, which confines the rural migrants to specific locations.

3. On the family level the major traits of the culture of poverty are the absence of childhood as a specially prolonged and protected stage in the life cycle, early initiation into sex, free unions or consensual marriages, a relatively high incidence of the aban-

donment of wives and children, a trend toward female- or mother-centered families and consequently a much greater knowledge of maternal relatives, a strong predisposition to authoritarianism, lack of privacy, verbal emphasis upon family solidarity which is only rarely achieved because of sibling rivalry, and competition for limited goods and maternal affection.

4. On the level of the individual the major characteristics are a strong feeling of marginality, of helplessness, of dependence, and of inferiority. I found this to be true of slum dwellers in Mexico City and San Juan among families who do not constitute a distinct ethnic or racial group and who do not suffer from racial discrimination. In the United States, of course, the culture of poverty of the Negroes had the additional disadvantage of racial discrimination, but as I have already suggested, this additional disadvantage contains a great potential for revolutionary protest and organization which seems to be absent in the slums of Mexico City or among the poor whites in the South.

Other traits include a high incidence of maternal deprivation, of orality, of weak ego-structure, confusion of sexual identification, a lack of impulse control, a strong present-time orientation with relatively little ability to defer gratification and to plan for the future, a sense of resignation and fatalism, a widespread belief in male superiority, and a high tolerance for psychological pathology of all sorts.

People with a culture of poverty are provincial and locally oriented and have very little sense of history. They know only their own troubles, their own local conditions, their own neighborhood, their own way of life. Usually they do not have the knowledge, the vision, or the ideology to see the similarities between their problems and those of their counterparts elsewhere in the world. They are not class-conscious, although they are very sensitive indeed to status distinctions.

In considering the traits discussed above, the following propositions must be kept in mind. (1) The traits fall into a number of clusters and are functionally related within each cluster. (2) Many, but not all, of the traits of different clusters are also functionally related. For example, men who have low wages and suffer chronic unemployment develop a poor self-image, become irresponsible, abandon their wives and children, and take up with other women more frequently than do men with high incomes and steady jobs. (3) None of the traits, taken individually, is distinctive per se of the subculture of poverty. It is their conjunction, their function, and their patterning that define the subculture. (4) The subculture of poverty, as defined by these traits, is a statistical profile; that is, the frequency of distribution of the traits both singly and in clusters will be greater than in the rest of the population. In other words, more of the traits will occur in combination in families with a subculture of poverty than in stable working-class, middle-class, or upper-class families. Even within a single slum there will probably be a gradient from culture of poverty families to families without a culture of poverty. (5) The profiles of the subculture of poverty will probably differ in systematic ways with the difference in the national cultural contexts of which they are a part. It is expected that some new traits will become apparent with research in different nations.

I have not yet worked out a system of weighing each of the traits, but this could probably be done and a scale could be set up for many of the traits. Traits that reflect lack of participation in the institutions of the larger society or an outright rejection—in practice, if not in theory—would be crucial traits; for example, illiteracy, provincialism, free unions, abandonment of women and children, lack of membership in voluntary associations beyond the extended family.

When the poor become class-conscious or active members of trade-union organizations, or when they adopt an internationalist outlook on the world, they are no longer part of the culture of poverty, although they may still be desperately poor. Any movement, be it religious, pacifist, or revolutionary, which organizes and gives hope to the poor and effectively promotes solidarity and a sense of identification with larger groups, destroys the psychological and social core of the culture of poverty. In this connection, I suspect that the civil rights movement among the Negroes in the United States has done more to improve their self-image and self-respect than have their economic advances, although, without doubt, the two are mutually reinforcing.

The distinction between poverty and the culture of poverty is basic to the model described here. There are degrees of poverty and many kinds of poor people. The culture of poverty refers to one way of life shared by poor people in given historical and social contexts. The economic traits that I have listed for the culture of poverty are necessary but not sufficient to define the phenomena I have in mind. There are a number of historical examples of very poor segments of the population that do not have a way of life that I would describe as a subculture of poverty. Here I should like to give four examples.

1. Many of the primitive or preliterate peoples studied by anthropologists suffer from dire poverty which is the result of poor technology and/or poor natural resources, or of both, but they do not have the traits of the subculture of poverty. Indeed, they do not constitute a subculture because their societies are not highly stratified. In spite of their poverty they have a relatively integrated, satisfying, and self-sufficient culture. Even the simplest food-gathering and hunting tribes have a considerable amount of organization, bands and band chiefs, tribal councils, and local self-government—traits which are not found in the culture of poverty.

2. In India the lower castes (the Chamars, the leather workers, and the Bhangis, the sweepers) may be desperately poor, both in the villages and in the cities, but most of them are integrated into the larger society and have their own *panchayat*[4] organizations which cut across village lines and give them a considerable amount of power.[5] In addition to the caste system, which gives individuals a sense of identity and belonging, there is still another factor, the clan system. Wherever there are unilateral kinship systems or clans one would not expect to find the culture of poverty, because a clan system gives people a sense of belonging to a corporate body with a history and a life of its own, thereby providing a sense of continuity, a sense of a past and of a future.

3. The Jews of eastern Europe were very poor, but they did not have many of the traits of the culture of poverty because of their tradition of literacy, the great value placed upon learning, the organization of the community around the rabbi, the proliferation of local voluntary associations, and their religion which taught that they were the chosen people.

4. My fourth example is speculative and relates to socialism. On the basis of my limited experience in one socialist country—Cuba—and on the basis of my reading, I am inclined to believe that the culture of poverty does not exist in the socialist countries. I first went to Cuba in 1947 as a visiting professor for the State Department. At that time I began a study of a sugar plantation in Melena del Sur and of a slum in Havana. After the Castro Revolution I made my second trip to Cuba as a correspondent for a major magazine, and I revisited the same slum and some of the same families. The physical aspect of the slum had changed very little, except for a beautiful new nursery school. It was clear that the people were still desperately poor, but I found much less of the despair, apathy, and hopelessness which are so diagnostic of urban slums in the culture of poverty. They expressed great confidence in their leaders and hope for a better life in the future. The slum itself was now highly organized, with block communities, educational committees, party committees. The people had a new sense of power and importance. They were armed and were given a doctrine that

glorified the lower class as the hope of humanity. (I was told by one Cuban official that they had practically eliminated delinquency by giving arms to the delinquents!)

It is my impression that the Castro regime—unlike Marx and Engels—did not write off the so-called *lumpen proletariat* as an inherently reactionary and anti-revolutionary force, but rather saw its revolutionary potential and tried to utilize it. In this connection, Frantz Fanon makes a similar evaluation of the role of the *lumpen proletariat* based upon his experience in the Algerian struggle for independence. In his recently published book he wrote:

> It is within this mass of humanity, this people of the shanty towns, at the core of the lumpen proletariat, that the rebellion will find its urban spearhead. For the lumped proletariat, that horde of starving men, uprooted from their tribe and from their clan, constitutes one of the most spontaneous and most radically revolutionary forces of a colonized people.[6]

My own studies of the urban poor in the slums of San Juan do not support the generalization of Fanon. I have found very little revolutionary spirit or radical ideology among low-income Puerto Ricans. On the contrary, most of the families I studied were quite conservative politically and about half of them were in favor of the Republican Statehood Party. It seems to me that the revolutionary potential of people with a culture of poverty will vary considerably according to the national context and the particular historical circumstances. In a country like Algeria, which was fighting for its independence, the *lumpen proletariat* was drawn into the struggle and became a vital force. However, in countries like Puerto Rico, in which the movement for independence has very little mass support, and in countries like Mexico which achieved their independence a long time ago and are now in their postrevolutionary period, the *lumpen proletariat* is not a leading source of rebellion or of revolutionary spirit. In effect, we find that in primitive societies and in caste societies, the culture of poverty does not develop. In socialist, fascist, and highly developed capitalist societies with a welfare state, the culture of poverty tends to decline. I suspect that the culture of poverty flourishes in, and is generic to, the early free-enterprise stage of capitalism and that it is also endemic in colonialism.

It is important to distinguish between different profiles in the subculture of poverty depending upon the national context in which these subcultures are found. If we think of the culture of poverty primarily in terms of the factor of integration of that society, or with a new emerging revolutionary tradition, then we will not be surprised that some slum dwellers with a lower per capita income may have moved farther away from the core characteristics of the culture of poverty than others with a higher per capita income. For example, Puerto Rico has a much higher per capita income than Mexico, yet Mexicans have a deeper sense of identity.

I have listed fatalism and a low level of aspiration as one of the key traits for the subculture of poverty. Here, too, however, the national context makes a big difference. Certainly the level of aspiration of even the poorest sector of the population in a country like the United States with its traditional ideology of upward mobility and democracy is much higher than in more backward countries like Ecuador and Peru, where both the ideology and the actual possibilities of upward mobility are extremely limited and where authoritarian values still persist in both the urban and rural milieus.

Because of the advanced technology, the high level of literacy, the development of mass media, and the relatively high aspiration level of all sectors of the population, especially when compared with underdeveloped nations, I believe that although there is still a great deal of poverty in the United States (estimates range from thirty to fifty million people), there is relatively little of what I would call the culture of poverty. My rough guess would be that only about 20 percent of the population below the poverty line (between six and ten million people) in the United States have characteristics which would justify classifying their way of life as that of a culture of poverty. Probably the largest sector within this group would consist of very low-income Negroes, Mexicans, Puerto Ricans, American Indians, and Southern poor whites. The relatively small number of people in the United States with a culture of poverty is a positive factor because it is more difficult to eliminate the culture of poverty than to eliminate poverty per se.

Middle-class people, and this would certainly include most social scientists, tend to concentrate on the negative aspects of the culture of poverty. They tend to associate negative valences to such traits as present-time orientation and concrete versus abstract orientation. I do not intend to idealize or romanticize the culture of poverty. As someone has said, "It is easier to praise poverty than to live in it"; yet some of the positive aspects which may flow from these traits must not be overlooked. Living in the present may develop a capacity for spontaneity and adventure, for the enjoyment of the sensual, the indulgence of impulse, which is often blunted in the middle-class, future-oriented man. Perhaps it is this reality of the moment that the existential writers are so desperately trying to recapture but which the culture of poverty experiences as a natural, everyday phenomenon. The frequent use of violence certainly provides a ready outlet for hostility so that people in the culture of poverty suffer less from repression than does the middle class.

In the traditional view, anthropologists have said that culture provides human beings with a design for living, with a ready-made set of solutions for human problems so that individuals don't have to begin all over again each generation. That is, the core of culture is its positive adaptive function. I, too, have called attention to some of the adaptive mechanisms in the culture of poverty—for example, the low aspiration level helps to reduce frustration, the legitimization of short-range hedonism makes possible spontaneity and enjoyment. However, on the whole it seems to me that it is a relatively thin culture. There is a great deal of pathos, suffering, and emptiness among those who live in the culture of poverty. It does not provide much support or long-range satisfaction and its encouragement of mistrust tends to magnify helplessness and isolation. Indeed, the poverty of culture is one of the crucial aspects of the culture of poverty.

The concept of the culture of poverty provides a high level of generalization which, hopefully, will unify and explain a number of phenomena viewed as distinctive characteristics of racial, national, or regional groups. For example, matrifocality, a high incidence of consensual unions, and a high percentage of households headed by women, which have been thought to be distinctive of Caribbean family organization or of Negro family life in the United States, turn out to be traits of the culture of poverty and are found among diverse peoples in many parts of the world and among peoples who have had no history of slavery.

The concept of a cross-societal subculture of poverty enables us to see that many of the problems we think of as distinctively our own or distinctively Negro problems (or problems of any other special racial or ethnic group) also exist in countries where there are no distinct ethnic minority groups. This suggests that the elimination of physical poverty per se may not be enough to eliminate the culture of poverty, which is a whole way of life.

What is the future of the culture of poverty? In considering this question, one must distinguish between those countries in which it represents a relatively small segment of the population and those in which it constitutes a very large one. Obviously the solutions will differ in these two situations. In the United States, the major solution proposed by planners and social workers in dealing with multiple-problem families and the so-called hard core of poverty has been to attempt slowly to raise their level of living and to incorporate them into the middle class. Wherever possible, there has been some reliance upon psychiatric treatment.

In the underdeveloped countries, however, where great masses of people live in the culture of poverty, a social-work solution does not seem feasible. Because of the magnitude of the problem, psychiatrists can hardly begin to cope with it. They have all they can do to care for their own growing middle class. In these countries the people with a culture of poverty may seek a more revolutionary solution. By creating basic structural changes in society, by redistributing wealth, by organizing the poor and giving them a sense of belonging, of power, and of leadership, revolutions frequently succeed in abolishing some of the basic characteristics of the culture of poverty even when they do not succeed in abolishing poverty itself.

Some of my readers have misunderstood the subculture of poverty model and have failed to grasp the importance of the distinction between poverty and the subculture of poverty. In making this distinction I have tried to document a broader generalization; namely, that it is a serious mistake to lump all poor people together, because the causes, the meaning, and the consequences of poverty vary considerably in different sociocultural contexts. There is nothing in the concept that puts the onus of poverty on the character of the poor. Nor does the concept in any way play down the exploitation and neglect suffered by the poor. Indeed, the subculture of poverty is part of the larger culture of capitalism, whose social and economic system channels wealth into the hands of a relatively small group and thereby makes for the growth of sharp class distinctions.

I would agree that the main reasons for the persistence of the subculture are no doubt the pressures that the larger society exerts over its members and the structure of the larger society itself. However, *these are not the only reasons*. The subculture develops mechanisms that tend to perpetuate it, especially because of what happens to the worldview, aspirations, and character of the children who grow up in it. For this reason, improved economic opportunities, though absolutely essential and of the highest priority, are not sufficient to alter basically or eliminate the subculture of poverty. Moreover, elimination is a process that will take more than a single generation, even under the best of circumstances, including a socialist revolution.

Some readers have thought I was saying, "Being poor is terrible, but having a culture of poverty is not so bad." On the contrary, I am saying that it is easier to eliminate poverty than the culture of poverty. I am also suggesting that the poor in a precapitalistic caste-ridden society like India had some advantages over modern urban slum dwellers because the people were organized in castes and *panchayats*, and this organization gave them some sense of identity and some strength and power. Perhaps Gandhi had the urban slums of the West in mind when he wrote that the caste system was one of the greatest inventions of humankind. Similarly, I have argued that the poor Jews of Eastern Europe, with their strong tradition of literacy and community organization, were better off than people with the culture of poverty. On the other hand, I would argue that people with the culture of poverty, with their strong sense of resignation and fatalism, are less driven and less anxious than the striving lower middle class, who are still trying to make it in the face of the greatest odds.

Notes

[1] There has been relatively little discussion of the culture of poverty concept in the professional journals, however. Two articles deal with the problem in some detail: Elizabeth Herzog, "Some Assumptions About the Poor," in *The Social Service Review,* December 1963, pp. 389–402; Lloyd Ohlin, "Inherited Poverty," Organization for Economic Cooperation and Development (no date), Paris.

[2] While the term "subculture of poverty" is technically more accurate, I have used "culture of poverty" as a shorter form.

[3] In a unilineal kinship system, descent is reckoned either through males or through females. When traced exclusively through males it is called patrilineal or agnatic descent; when reckoned exclusively through females it is called matrilineal or uterine descent. In a bilateral or cognatic system, descent is traced through males and females without emphasis on either line.

In a unilateral system, the lineage consists of all the descendants of one ancestor. In a patrilineal system, the lineage is composed of all descendants through males of one male ancestor. A matrilineage consists of all the descendants through females of one female ancestor. The lineage may thus contain a very large number of generations. If bilateral descent is reckoned, however, the number of generations that can be included in a social unit is limited, since the number of ancestors doubles every generation.

Unilateral descent groups ("lineages" or "clans") are corporate groups in the sense that the lineage or clan may act as a collectivity; it can take blood vengeance against another descent group, it can hold property, and so on. However, the bilateral kin group (the "kindred") can rarely act as a collectivity because it is not a "group" except from the point of view of a particular individual and, furthermore, has no continuity over time.

In a unilateral system, an individual is assigned to a group by virtue of his birth. In contrast, a person born into a bilateral system usually has a choice of relatives whom he chooses to recognize as "kin" and with whom he wants to associate. This generally leads to a greater diffuseness and fragmentation of ties with relatives over time.

[4] A formal organization designed to provide caste leadership.

[5] It may be that in the slums of Calcutta and Bombay an incipient culture of poverty is developing. It would be highly desirable to do family studies there as a crucial test of the culture-of-poverty hypothesis.

[6] Frantz Fanon, *The Wretched of the Earth*. New York, Grove Press, 1965, p. 103.

Hugo G. Nutini is a professor of anthropology at University of Pittsburgh. His varied and ambitious research are reflected in his books, including Bloodsucking Witchcraft, Game Theory in the Behavioral Sciences *(with I. R. Buchler),* Ritual Kinship *(with B. Bell),* San Bernardino Contla: Marriage and Family Structure in a Tlaxcalan Municipio, Todos Santos in Rural Tlaxcala, *and* The Wages of Conquest: The Mexican Aristocracy in the Context of Western Aristocracies.

Although most of us think only rarely about the aristocracy (a hereditary nobility, or privileged class) or plutocracy (a class with power and/or influence based on wealth) at the beginning of the twenty-first century, those groups have clearly played important parts in the recent history of Mexico, as chronicled here by Nutini. A summary of their roles during the century after their country won independence from Spain reveals important currents of both continuity and change. It also demonstrates that—contrary to some postmodern critique about our being "colonialists in practice," whether intentionally or not—anthropologists can and do "study up" quite effectively.

The Aristocracy in Modern Mexico
Hugo G. Nutini

THE NEW POLITICAL CLASS AND
SOCIAL AND ECONOMIC CONSEQUENCES

The armed struggle of the Mexican Revolution and the twenty years of unrest and reorganization that followed did not radically transform the political and socioeconomic structure of the nation, for the movement was not a Russian-style revolution, and the socialist elements that it introduced were tempered with capitalist ideas; free enterprise was never explicitly an object of suppression. The fighting was seldom dictated by ideological considerations; rather it was the expression of basic, historically rooted inequalities that major segments of the body politic wanted to redress quickly. Pragmatic economic and political considerations rather than ideological convictions initiated and sustained the Mexican Revolution, and although the latter were present, they were never strong enough to have radically transformed the country politically, economically, and stratificationally. In fact, it is difficult to identify any clear segment that may properly be termed a political class from the fall of Díaz (1910) to the assassination of Carranza (1920). Throughout this period the main revolutionary leaders came from almost the entire spectrum of the stratification system. Most leaders, however, came from local middle–class or peasant stock. They were generally motivated by a genuine desire for political and economic reform, but, also quite generally, by the hope for personal gain as well. One ideological trait shared by virtually all revolutionary leaders was *indigenismo,* which, of course, took different forms but focused essentially on creating a new Mexico for Mexicans, emphasizing native over foreign.[1]

Out of this motley configuration of personages, a political class began to emerge during the Obregón regime (1920–24) that came to fruition with the institution of an official party during the Calles dictatorship (1924). But not until the fateful years of the Cárdenas administration (1934) did a political class coalesce that centered on the official party. From then on, the new rulers of Mexico kept a tight rein on the political affairs of the nation. With the exception of the higher position of revolutionaries in the hierarchy—the president, state governors, and a few other offices—the new ruling class was not staffed exclusively by members of revolutionary extraction, and indeed after the Second World War it was composed mostly of militant party officials with no revolutionary antecedents at all (Garcia Purón 1964). Until the end of the Cárdenas administration (1940), the background of the budding ruling class was uniformly middle class, with a sprinkling of politicians from peasant stock who had risen to important positions. There were, of course, no formal prohibitions against individuals and groups that had been associated with the ruling and political classes of the Porfiriato (1876–1910), but most circles of the new political class rather jealously guarded entrance to political participation (Nutini, Roberts, and Cervantes 1982). In other words, from the start of the revolution, politics became a rather restricted arena available mostly to individuals of kindred orientation and class position.

The revolution did not destroy the old industrial, manufacturing, and banking establishments of Mexico, but it certainly modified them, reconfiguring labor practices, management, and ownership. Much foreign capital remained in place, some plutocratic magnates retained control of their enterprises, but access to capitalist ventures became more fluid. Under revolutionary conditions and the dictatorial ambiance of governments until the Cárdenas administration, one could not speak of a ruling class vested in great plutocratic magnates, owners of the most important means of production. The budding political class was in a sense also the ruling class, for the remaining plutocratic magnates did not influence the functioning of the government.

The aristocracy's influence in conducting governmental actions disappeared quickly after the onset of the revolution. Once uprisings in the countryside became common and largely uncontrolled, aristocrats and their plutocratic allies suffered not only loss of property but physical violence and loss of control as well. Most *hacendados* enfranchised in the country left their landed estates and took refuge in the capital or large provincial cities, while a few temporarily left the country. Many country mansions were sacked and destroyed, and not infrequently peasants occupied land of the *haciendas*. Most *hacendados* nonetheless retained legal possession of the land, as revolutionary leaders, from Carranza to Calles, engaged largely in token land reform. From 1911 to 1920, a certain amount of land was either allotted to landless peasants by the federal and state governments or illegally occupied by Indian and Mestizo villages. The real problem, however, was that most *haciendas* throughout the country were abandoned by their owners, or else that productivity fell dramatically due to revolutionary activity and turmoil caused by intermittent fighting. With some notable exceptions in areas not directly trampled by revolutionary activity, the *hacienda* did not survive well the disastrous years of the armed conflict (Nutini, Roberts, and Cervantes 1984).

The loss of agrarian income dealt a deathblow to the aristocracy as a ruling class during the first phase of the revolution. Meanwhile, deep-seated antagonism, both of an economic and political nature, prevented aristocratic participation at all levels of government and administration. Only at the local level, once revolutionary activity ebbed, did *hacendados* retain a modicum of control. In the cities, aristocrats succeeded in protecting their mansions, but they lost the determinant influence and control that they had enjoyed during the Porfiriato. Significant numbers of aristocrats, both in the country and the city, suffered a modicum of violence and outrage, and perhaps a few were killed, but these acts generally resulted from immediate individual or group resentment and not from a concerted effort on the part of responsible revolutionaries and guerrilla leaders.

The reluctance of Presidents Obregón and Calles to dismantle the great landed estates and the return to a modicum of peaceful prosperity led *hacendados* to hope that further redistribution and illegal appropriation of land by the government would stop and that the *hacienda* system, though modified, would survive. The years from 1920 to 1934 were a period of relative recuperation for the aristocracy, whose expectation of retaining their landed estates fueled a relative improvement as a social class. Upwardly mobile elements of the political and economic sectors sought rapport with the aristocracy as a legitimating mechanism, which many aristocrats welcomed as a survival strategy. Despite Calles' anticlericalism and his openly antagonistic policy toward the church, the aristocracy did not unduly suffer throughout these troubled times, and to a certain extent it even reasserted its former place as a social class. Although a few aristocrats were able to retain a foothold in the new plutocracy by virtue of converting agrarian and urban property into banking and manufacturing operations, the overwhelming majority of aristocrats languished in the expectation that ultimately the land problem would be resolved in their favor.

The *hacienda* system survived in its overall configuration until 1934, and though crippled by violence, it continued to produce a modicum of income. As an instrument of expression and as a focal point of the aristocratic *imago mundi*, however, it had been mortally wounded by 1920.

Those *haciendas* that survived the fury of the revolution or that could be repaired and refurbished continued to play a role in the expressive life of aristocratic families even after the massive land reform, but by then most families did not have enough money to undertake the massive job of reconstruction. In fact, as early as 1930, many aristocratic families began to acquire country residences, if they did not already have them, within relatively short distances of Mexico City and a few other urban centers. After 1940, most manor houses lay in ruins or had been badly damaged, many had been bought by members of the new political and ruling classes and ostentatiously refurbished, and only a few were still occupied by aristocrats.

As a social class, the aristocracy survived, both as a clearly discernible group and as the collective carrier of superordinate expressive behavior. Simply put, as the model of upwardly mobile aspirations, aristocrats provided a unique commodity and this expressive component alone made the aristocracy a viable social group until the late 1970s. Until the beginning of the Cárdenas administration, most of the great aristocratic mansions in Mexico City and important provincial cities were still inhabited by their original owners. Not until after the massive land reform were almost all of these mansions either expropriated or sold by their owners for economic reasons. In the old Colonial mansions and in the new, nearly suburban residential areas established during the Porfiriato, many aristocratic families played leading roles in homogenizing the disparate elements of the evolving political and ruling classes. Some aristocrats played a substantial role in business and industry, and their visibility enhanced the desirability of aristocratic expression for those vying for a place in the superordinate stratification of the country. For the upwardly mobile people of the time, the ineffable aristocratic aura was still strong, and this was perhaps the main expressive attribute that sustained the aristocracy for another fifty years or so.

THE MASSIVE LAND REFORM AND ARISTOCRATIC CONCENTRATION IN MEXICO CITY (1934–50)

These sixteen years were the most critical period for the Mexican aristocracy since the onset of the Revolution of 1910. Stripped of their land and rapidly losing social and economic control of the provincial cities traditionally associated with the *hacienda,* a massive migration to Mexico City took place. The ambiance of the capital had always promised security in violent and uncertain times, and there in the security of numbers the aristocracy experienced one last moment of social saliency and visibility. Though revolution did not directly cause the obliteration of the aristocracy, the massive land reform most certainly launched this social class into a final process of disintegration.

Demise of the *Hacienda* System and Economic Disintegration

The massive land reform initiated by Cárdenas was a shock of cataclysmic proportions for the Mexican aristocracy. In the short period of six years, the *hacienda* system had come to an end. Whatever hopes the *hacendado* aristocracy cherished of retaining its landed estates dissolved and its residual inputs as a ruling class vanished overnight. Expressive constraints conspired against aristocrats becoming successful plutocrats, and most aristocratic families were reduced to relative poverty. A small number, however, made the transition successfully, and between the end of the Cárdenas administration and the late 1960s, they could be counted among the rich and powerful. These exceptions may be explained in two ways. First, throughout the nineteenth century there had always been aristocrats who successfully combined agrarian operations with banking and industry, and when these families lost their landed estates, they were not totally ruined. Second, another small group of aristocratic *hacendados* were realistic enough to realize that the *hacienda* would not survive, given the reluctance of Obregón and Calles to break up the great landed estates. Thus, between 1920 and 1933, this group sold most of their land to small farmers, individual peasants, and even to Indian communities, investing the profit in urban property and the manufacturing industry. By the 1960s, perhaps 10 percent of aristocratic families had survived economically and had established a plutocratic basis in the new haute bourgeoisie. But the great majority of aristocrats were devastated by the Cárdenas land reform and forced into the liberal professions.

During the Cárdenas administration, the great landed estates of Mexico were abolished and the *ejido* system came into being. The *ejido* was land expropriated from private individuals—including the great *haciendas* as well as large farming enterprises and agrarian enterprises owned by foreign companies—by the government and given to groups of landless peasants, not as personal property but with rights of cultivation and transmission to their children (Mendieta y Nuñez 1966). Except in broad outline and intention (the termination of the landed estates), the agrarian reform was not uniform throughout the country. Taking into account density of population and the availability of land—that is, the incidence and size of *haciendas*—the land allotted to individuals directly or as part of collective *ejidos* varied greatly from adequate, plot sizes ranging from ten to twenty hectares, to miserably inadequate, plots ranging from one-half to one hectare. In most parts of the country, particularly in the more densely populated areas, the land reform was a failure, for it did not significantly improve the living standards of peasants. Only in the north and along the gulf coast was reform successful in ameliorating the overall economic situation, and this success may be attributed to lower population density resulting in larger plots of land allotted to individual and collective cultivation, particularly of commercial crops such as sugarcane (Nickel 1988:171–81). By the late 1950s, the agrarian reform had become a political weapon to defuse potentially violent situations, and thus led to the further breakup of medium-sized, efficiently cultivated farms.

The agrarian reform not only distributed land among landless peasants, but also legislated the amount of land that could be owned by individuals. The legislation varied from state to state with respect to the quality of the land and the use to which it could be put, limits which remain in effect. For example, an individual can own no more than 100 hectares of irrigated land, and no more than 200 to 300 hectares of nonirrigated land, though these limits may be stretched depending on the region or state and the cultivation of specialized crops. Animal husbandry, mostly in the north, south, and coastal areas, requires larger plots regulated by the quality of land and livestock (Mendieta y Nuñez 1966). *Hacendados* could own land as allowed by law in addition to the *casco* (house). Many *cascos* had been damaged beyond repair during the armed phase of the revolution, while perhaps many more were in various stages of disrepair in 1934, and, given the economic decline of their owners, were allowed to deteriorate further.

About half of aristocratic *hacendados* sold the land that the law allowed them to retain by 1955. They either sold the land to peasants of nearby communities or to prosperous farmers, who frequently accumulated land in excess of what the law allowed. In these cases, former *hacendados* became almost entirely disconnected from the land, and as they gravitated toward Mexico City their ties with the ancestral *hacienda* loosened, particularly when the *hacienda* was located in such faraway places as the far north and Yucatán. In areas closer to the capital, the *hacienda* connection persisted longer, but by the late 1960s, less than a fourth of former aristocratic *hacendados* derived income from the exploitation of their ancestral estates. In a few cases, aristocrats bought land elsewhere and have continued to farm, sometimes on a scale larger than the law allows.

The land reform had another aspect that, though illegal, may have been a plus for the agrarian productivity of Mexico. Before the Cárdenas land reform, many revolutionary leaders acquired land, and some of them may even be called *hacendados,* given the large tracts that they had managed to accumulate. After 1934, landholdings beyond what the law allowed continued under veiled government protection and by the use of *presta nombres* (name-lenders). Since the onset of massive agrarian reform, it has been a standard practice to register land under the names of several individuals (usually kinsmen or close friends) in order to circumvent the law and consolidate larger parcels of land. The most powerful members of the political class probably do not even bother with this subterfuge, but most politicians and average large-farm operators do, including aristocratic farmers. On the lands of their former *haciendas* or of nearby communities, an appreciable number of aristocrats continue to farm on a moderate scale and derive good incomes from these agrarian operations (Carlos de Ovando, pers. comm.)

The Cárdenas land reform terminated nearly four centuries of aristocratic agrarian dominance and eliminated perhaps the most salient feature of the expressive configuration of the Mexican aristocracy. During the past fifty years the land has had little or no economic value for the aristocracy as a class, but it still looms large in the consciousness of most aristocrats and continues to play an important role in the expressive retreat that has been going on for more than two generations. The city-country axis of expressive realization was not entirely destroyed, as considerable numbers of *hacienda* mansions are still in the hands of aristocrats, and they continue to provide solace and psychic support to their owners. Economically, the agrarian reform transformed the aristocracy into urbanite professionals and small-to-medium businessmen with a foothold in the world of powerful plutocrats. The aristocracy is no longer rich, and it has lost all its once-great power and influence.

Exodus to Mexico City and Professional (Embourgeoisement) Growth

Since its formation in the sixteenth century, the Mexican aristocracy had always gravitated toward Mexico City. By the start of the twentieth century, a degree of decentralization had taken place and more than ever before aristocratic families were enfranchised in important provincial cities; still, perhaps as many as 50 percent kept residences in Mexico City. This traditional pattern began to change with the fall of Porfirio Díaz, and by 1950 more than 80 percent of all aristocratic families resided permanently in the capital. In 1910, and to some extent until 1934, the most important nuclei of aristocratic families were located in cities such as Puebla, Guadalajara, Querétaro, Oaxaca, Mérida, Morelia, Chihuahua, Xalapa, Durango, San Luis Potosí, Zacatecas, and Tampico. The violence and disruption of the early revolutionary years meant the abandonment of *haciendas*. With Obregón, relative peace and order came to the countryside and *hacendados* and their families cautiously resumed the routine of the city-country axis.

Massive migration to Mexico City began in 1936, triggered not only by the total loss of *haciendas* and a serious decrease in income but by a new awareness of middle-class action and revolutionary assertion that made provincial life uncomfortable for aristocrats accustomed to undisputed control. The upwardly mobile element in provincial cities was asserting itself as never before and was no longer willing to accept passively the haughtiness and paternalism of aristocrats. With their *haciendas* gone and their local business interests in shambles, most aristocratic families opted for migration to Mexico City, a process completed by the early 1950s. Within the next two generations, those aristocratic families that remained in provincial cities became downwardly mobile, and most of them lost aristocratic affiliation; they became part of local elites of politicians, new businessmen, and small-scale industrialists that in time developed into local plutocracies. These former aristocratic families are known today as *familias venidas a menos* (dropouts, downwardly mobile families). Bona fide aristocrats regard them as no longer part of the group but still accord them minimum recognition. Only in Guadalajara, Querétaro, and perhaps one or two more cities do there remain small nuclei of aristocratic families that are recognized as an integral part of the Mexican aristocracy.

In Mexico City the provincial arrivals found a much larger, more congenial environment than in the rapidly changing cities that they had once so thoroughly controlled. In the capital, aristocrats found a measure of security in numbers; they presented a fairly united front against the hostile world developing around them. For *hacendado* aristocrats who did not have any other source of income, migration to Mexico City was simply a matter of economic survival. For a considerable number of aristocrats, however, the demise of the *hacienda* system was not a crashing blow, for they possessed a diversified economy in banking, industry, and urban property. Thus, during the two decades following the massive land reform, the Mexican aristocracy concentrated in the capital included rich aristocrats, well-off ones, and those who had to start pretty much at the bottom.

The main economic survival strategy of the majority of aristocrats was to join the liberal professions. Becoming a doctor, a lawyer, or an engineer was nothing new to aristocrats. But, whereas a career was undertaken in the nineteenth century as a hobby or in pursuit of strictly scientific or intellectual interests, it was now done in order to survive. Aristocrats became architects, chemists, business administrators; some became archaeologists, anthropologists, and historians, choosing fields in which members of the aristocracy had excelled in the nineteenth century. In a short generation, the aristocracy had made the transition from a rich landed base to a fairly comfortable economic position by engaging in the professions and a rather wide array of business and industrial enterprises.

Ideologically and expressively, the Mexican aristocracy remained unified and unchanged, supportive of its members, and quite close as a social group until the late

1940s. In pursuing new means of economic survival, once cohesive aristocratic networks grew apart, both in the process of building new nonaristocratic connections and
establishing different patterns of social and economic activities that were not entirely
compatible. From 1950 onward, two types of aristocratic families emerged, types that
have remained distinct. On the one hand, there are those families that, most constrained by the aristocratic *imago mundi,* have totally refrained from social interaction with the haute bourgeoisie, have centered their lives in the household,
interacting exclusively with small selected networks of kinsmen and friends of their
own class. This conservative sector adheres to a traditional view of aristocratic behavior and to a static conception of aristocratic roles. It refuses to make any concessions
to the rich and powerful and has therefore not participated in the expressive process
of aristocratic-plutocratic acculturation since its inception in the early 1940s. True to
their exclusive, endogenous principles, this segment has gone underground, living
mostly in the past. On the other hand, there are those families least constrained by
the aristocratic *imago mundi,* more forward looking, and with the most entrepreneurial skills. This group constitutes the majority of aristocratic families, among whom are
the most affluent, with a firm foothold in plutocratic circles, and with whom the haute
bourgeoisie has interacted rather closely, beginning right after the end of the Second
World War. Since the late 1930s, this sector has provided the model for expressive
aristocratic-plutocratic acculturation of the emerging haute bourgeoisie. Intermarriage between aristocrats and plutocrats began in the late 1940s and became fairly
common in the next generation, when the expressive arrays of these social classes
began to coalesce and a new acculturative entity was born.

Even during the most difficult and insecure times of the 1920s and 1930s, the
Mexican aristocracy was the undisputed social leader in the capital, while in provincial cities this position of superordination was lost. Aristocratic life experienced a
renaissance in Mexico City. Their ranks increased by migration; the aristocracy dominated social and religious events. Despite their loss of wealth, a rather large number
of aristocratic families were sufficiently affluent to be in the limelight, constantly
reported in the press, and still universally recognized by the middle and even lower
classes of a city of nearly three million people. This state of affairs continued until the
late 1940s. Another generation had to pass for the aristocracy to lose this position,
and for the population at large to lose the ability to discriminate between traditional
aristocrats and new plutocrats. The phenomenal demographic growth of the city, the
growth and assertion of the middle classes, and the final formation of a very rich and
powerful plutocracy caused this terminal transformation. While the renaissance
lasted, the aristocracy remained a closed social class, its social life admired, and its
expressive culture envied. What made this last outburst of aristocratic control possible was, above all, the sheer weight of four hundred years of domination and the symbols that went with it.

ASCENDANCE OF A NEW PLUTOCRACY AND ITS INTERACTION WITH THE ARISTOCRACY (1950–70)

By the late 1950s, only a few isolated pockets of aristocrats were still enfranchised in
provincial cities, and from this time onward the Mexican aristocracy must be regarded
as a social class enfranchised in Mexico City. The traditional recognition of aristocratic
membership began to blur; the lower and middle classes were increasingly unable to discriminate between social standing and power and wealth, and only at the highest rungs
of the stratification system were aristocrats recognized as a distinct class or group.

Three rather distinct classes had come into existence: a political class embodied in the ruling party; a ruling class of plutocrats; and a social class still constituted by the aristocracy. This superordinate segment of the Mexican stratification system I have elsewhere called the haute bourgeoisie (Nutini, Roberts, and Cervantes 1984). The aristocracy remained for generations the preeminent social class by virtue of expressive and behavioral attributes that were desirable to political and plutocratic elites in their quest to validate social standing. Slightly different forms and mixtures of the political ruling-social triad have been the basic model of superordinate stratification and upward mobility in Western stratification throughout modern times. As the aristocracy declined, the model paradoxically acquired renewed importance in shaping new political and ruling classes in superordinate positions. The model, with the aristocracy as an essential element, ultimately falters when ruling and political classes begin to create new expressive arrays independent of the acculturative aristocratic model.

Socioeconomic Accommodation and Aristocratic-Plutocratic Preponderance

The presidency of Miguel Alemán (1946–52) was a period of industrial growth and economic advances. In the fifteen years after World War Two, many new fortunes were made and older ones increased. Industry, manufacturing, banking, and service concerns experienced unprecedented growth, and the new plutocracy came to maturity. Disregarding the important minority of former politicians, the composition of the plutocracy was as follows: The majority were self-made men of middle-class origins, a considerable number of whom had a university education. A considerable number were foreigners of U.S., European, and Near Eastern extraction, most of whom had been residents of Mexico for more than a generation. Finally, a sprinkling were aristocrats and old plutocrats of Porfirian extraction who had managed to retain a modicum of wealth and now came into their own.

While this plutocracy spread throughout the country, the richest and most powerful plutocrats, in the traditional centralist fashion of Mexico, were enfranchised in Mexico City. Demonstrating another aspect of centralization, many plutocrats who made fortunes in the provinces or initiated business concerns in provincial cities eventually moved to Mexico City.[2] By the late 1950s, the great majority of plutocratic magnates resided very visibly in Mexico City. Together with some members of the political class, plutocratic magnates began to dominate the social life of the city, and certainly they occupied the limelight. Plutocrats' mansions proliferated in the most fashionable quarters of the city; their doings and activities were prominently reported by the press, and their economic success made them as talked about as prominent politicians. Mexico City already had more than six million people, and in this environment the aristocracy had little or no visibility, except in the upper range of the stratification system, whereas the plutocracy commanded attention second only to that of highly placed political leaders. It is difficult to pinpoint the wealth of plutocratic magnates, for it ranged considerably, but the average fortune was on the order of fifty to sixty million dollars. More difficult still is to calculate the strength of this group, but an educated guess is that it surpassed one thousand families.

Throughout these twenty years, social interaction between aristocrats and plutocrats was generalized, no longer consisting of aristocratic condescension toward upstart plutocrats. Since Colonial times the aristocracy had always had a rather close circle of social "retainers." These were well-to-do, "upper-middle-class" families, or *gentes propias* (proper people) as they were called, with whom the aristocracy interacted on a basis of near equality. By standing tradition, these "proper" people and the aristocracy had enough in common expressively to ensure smooth and fluid social interaction and occasional intermarriage. By plutocrats, by contrast, I mean middle-class individuals who had risen to power and wealth during the previous generation and were socially upwardly mobile, but did not enjoy a standing relationship with the aristocracy. This statement, however, should be qualified. Some, perhaps 15 percent, of the plutocratic families could claim proper genteel extraction, and in the process of upward mobility, these families interacted most successfully with the aristocratic group. The average plutocratic family, meanwhile, though it did not traditionally share with the aristocracy a complex of social and expressive forms, was composed of fast, willing learners.

In the 1940s, plutocratic families established a modicum of social interaction with aristocratic families and learned some of their expressive domains. During the following two decades, the plutocracy came into its own. As its power and wealth vastly surpassed that of the dwindling aristocracy, the plutocracy no longer accepted a passive role in its upwardly mobile aspirations. Aristocrats and plutocrats came into rather continuous and occasionally close contact in a wide array of social, economic, and "cultural" contexts and situations that tended to homogenize the two classes. It cannot be said, however, that the entire aristocracy and plutocracy participated in this process of rapprochement; rather the process was dominated by the interaction of the most forward-looking, liberal segment of the aristocracy and the most upwardly mobile and powerful segment of the plutocracy. As these segments constituted the majority of the two classes, the overall social and expressive rapprochement of a single superordinate group was strengthened. The conservative aristocratic minority retreated and dropped out of the system, and the less rich and powerful plutocratic minority—the segment of the plutocracy of more humble origins—uninterested in upward social mobility also remained outside the system. Economically, aristocrats emulated plutocrats and not infrequently occupied important positions in plutocratic enterprises. Socially, aristocrats and plutocrats interacted in several contexts and occasions: in the household, albeit with a certain degree of reticence on the part of aristocrats; in the more public ambiance of weddings, balls, and kindred events outside the household; in clubs, theaters, and musical affairs; and so on.

What dynamic propelled this increasing interaction? The answer is twofold. First, in the time-honored fashion, aristocratic-plutocratic interaction was configured in terms of needs: the desire of plutocrats to validate social standing in the game of upward mobility after reaching a high level of power and wealth and the necessity of aristocrats to gain or consolidate economic assets or to make new economic allies to preserve their social predominance. The difference between the present situation (the last renewal of elites) and the three earlier situations is social and economic dominance. In the three earlier transformations the aristocracy had total predominance; it was secure in its social and economic position of superordinate nation, and the process of plutocratic acceptance and internalization was imbalanced. Now the situation was reversed: the aristocracy was little more than a social class, no longer in control and insecure of its social predominance, whereas the plutocracy was richer and more powerful and able to assert itself in several domains.

Second, though need configured aristocratic-plutocratic rapprochement in a fairly balanced manner, compromise established the guidelines of the process, and the give and take of aristocrats and plutocrats culminated in a reversal of fortune. For the first time aristocrats were incorporated into a budding social class of plutocrats, while the majority of aristocrats retreated, socially and expressively unable to surrender their traditionally undisputed role. But as long as the acculturative role of aristocrats survived, they remained an active social class, still visible, and grudgingly accepted as a superordinate segment.

Expressive Transmission and Behavioral Acculturation

In the short-range historical perspective, the aristocracy, as the traditional social class of Mexican society, is still largely endogamous, and distinguishable in behavior and expression. A large complex of manners and behavior constitutes the endogenous parameters of the group. Those who do not behave according to the rules are not regarded as aristocrats, and this reality is subtly manifested in social and economic situations. It was under these conditions that plutocrats until 1950 had always striven to acquire aristocratic recognition and were eventually fully incorporated into the group. Throughout the 1950s and 1960s, plutocrats in one fashion or another sought aristocratic recognition, but incorporation did not necessarily follow, primarily because the plutocracy innovated socially and expressively on its own and pursued an independent course and secondarily because the aristocracy no longer exercised political and ruling functions.

Aristocrats regard themselves as the arbiters of social life, specialists in the niceties of ritual and ceremonial behavior, practitioners of complex codes of etiquette and traditional standing, and upholders of good manners and family traditions. Members of the plutocracy most likely internalized the social ambiance to which they had been exposed outside Mexico City, rather than copying directly from the aristocracy. Still, the aristocracy in situ was the validating group of good manners and genteel behavior. The catalysts in the aristocracy-plutocracy interaction are economic necessity and social ambition: the desire of the former to expand its economic horizons and acquire a measure of ruling control, and the ambition of the latter to be regarded not only as economically and politically powerful but as socially acceptable as well. These factors, however, cannot entirely explain the persistence of the aristocracy as a largely endogamous, viable, quite self-contained class. What has ensured this survival are the aristocracy's expressive components, which buttress the group's identity and strengthen the structure of the group.

What are the main components of this large complex of expressive behavior? They belong mainly to the domains of the household and kinship behavior, the life cycle and socialization of children, etiquette and personal behavior, patterns of entertainment and celebrations, the fine arts, interpersonal relations, and patterns of dress and demeanor. In all instances of social mobility, what attracts or compels the aspiring individual or group to acquire and master the behavior of a superordinate stratum is not the notion that such mastery will bring acceptance and make him or the group more similar to the aspired object, but the belief that it will confer the security, sense of superiority, and natural demeanor that distinguishes those superordinately placed. Why else would plutocrats care about the social standing of aristocrats, when they have most of the economic and political power and prestige and could create their own standards?

For aristocrats, the common body of expressive behavior unites them as a self-directed group and at the same time affords them significant security. They regard the various domains of expressive behavior as a legacy of the past, a validation of the exalted place that they once occupied. The refinement of behavior, the protocol of certain ritual and ceremonial occasions, and the circumspection and savoir faire that social interaction requires are always very much in the individual and group consciousness and are regarded as epitomizing civilized living. This kind of behavior and social interaction impose restrictions upon the average aristocrat, who is generally quite willing to restrict his or her social life to the familiarity of an increasingly poorer social milieu.

When plutocrats reach a certain plateau of wealth and economic power, they seem to develop a rather strong desire for social recognition and interaction with the aristocracy. Certainly this desire has characterized the Mexican plutocracy since the early

1940s. The Mexican plutocracy is composed of two generations: those who initiated the enterprises that brought them wealth and their married or unmarried children. The older generation had its beginnings when the aristocracy was significantly more visible than it is today, that is, before World War Two. Curiously, would-be plutocrats either developed a strong desire for social acceptance and actively sought to interact with the aristocracy, or they had been somehow scarred and developed a strong aversion to imitating the ways of their social superiors. The younger generation, however, generally has sought acceptance and increasing social interaction with the different segments of the aristocracy, and they have sought opportunities in this quest. The natural resistance of aristocrats to social rapport with the plutocracy has slowly broken down. By the early 1970s, the average plutocrat had acquired such outward trappings of aristocratic behavior as dress, certain patterns of language and demeanor, expressive travel, forms of entertainment, and so on. But plutocrats know that they cannot manufacture pedigrees or an illustrious past. They realize that these values come only with time, and as time passes and they achieve more wealth, they worry less.

Aristocrats are well aware that by acquiring their expressive behavior, plutocrats are vying for social recognition. Aristocrats regard this recognition as an important commodity, a source of satisfaction and self-validation to be used wisely. They know too that they cannot press their expressive claims too strongly, for wealth and power will eventually bring plutocrats the social recognition they desire anyway. At this juncture, the relationship between aristocrats and plutocrats is a delicate one. The former expect to maximize expressive claims by engaging in social interaction without totally giving in, while the latter try to encourage social interaction without appearing overly obsequious. Both sides of this acculturative equation exhibit a rather wide range of behavior: from aristocrats who adamantly refuse to accept plutocrats as their social equals and have nothing but contempt for them to those who maintain that as a matter of survival it is necessary to achieve an intimate rapport between social status and power and wealth; from plutocrats who regard aristocrats as anachronistic, unproductive drones with whom they would have nothing to do to those who feel drawn strongly to aristocrats and wish to cement strong social and matrimonial alliances. By the mid-1970s, the equation was skewed significantly toward the liberal side of the spectrum, including primarily the richest and the younger on both sides.

The principal context of interaction has always been economic: the world of business, banking, and manufacturing. Rich aristocrats are of course part of that world, and they therefore interact intimately with plutocrats in business clubs and associations and at the attendant social occasions. Most aristocrats, however, interact with plutocrats from a position of economic subordination: as high- or middle-level executives in banks and business enterprises, or as borrowers of money or buyers of products. In all cases, social occasions arise when plutocrats and aristocrats interact: club reunions, dinner parties, cocktail parties, and so on. Quite often executive and middle-level male and female personnel with aristocratic background are drawn into the ranks of banking and business enterprises. Given the international character of many such enterprises, this personnel is regarded as a considerable asset, capable of the social nuances and interpersonal savoir-faire that such business transactions involve.

The other significant contexts of aristocratic-plutocratic interaction are the world of music and fine arts and the domain of certain sports (polo, equitation, sailing). Aristocrats and plutocrats join forces in sponsoring artistic and musical events. For public relations, the main banking institutions often sponsor exhibitions of the best collections of Colonial pottery, family portraits, porcelain, furniture, and so on. These various events are always social occasions, but they invariably occur in the fairly impersonal ambiance of banks and other public buildings. Social gatherings of aristocrats and plutocrats in the context of sports are probably the most intimate and include the homes of the two groups. Thus, the greatest rapport between aristocrats and plutocrats has occurred among this small group, where the highest degree of social homogeneity and recognition can be observed.

One may summarize the interaction of the aristocracy and plutocracy from the early 1950s to the 1970s as displaying a significant degree of asymmetrical expressive transmission complemented by symmetrical behavioral acculturation. Many domains of the aristocratic expressive array were internalized by plutocrats, both as the price of social recognition and as the realization that such an expressive acquisition was intrinsically valuable as an economic tool. Aristocrats and plutocrats reciprocally influenced each other, and their respective worldviews were substantially modified to accommodate disparate behaviors.

THE TERMINAL STAGE: PLUTOCRATIC PREDOMINANCE AND ARISTOCRATIC WITHDRAWAL

This period witnesses the divergent paths of the aristocracy and plutocracy and the near demise of the former as a distinct social class in the Mexican stratification system. The aristocracy by now is little more than a self-defined and self-recognized group, although it continues to be somewhat vaguely recognized by the political and ruling sectors of the haute bourgeoisie and the upper-middle class. The plutocracy, meanwhile, asserts itself overwhelmingly, pursues its own social and expressive course, and insofar as the aristocracy retreats, becomes *the* social class. The situation is more complex than this characterization, for some aristocrats are rather completely plutocratized, while some plutocrats are significantly aristocratized. The essential consideration of this terminal period, however, is that the aristocracy loses its last asset, the expressive component, and no longer plays a determinant role in the emerging superordinate system.

A New Superordinate System Comes into Being

By the mid-1970s, the Mexican plutocracy residing in the capital and two or three provincial cities had reached a plateau of power and wealth unparalleled since the mining boom of the second half of the eighteenth century. More than one thousand millionaire families constituted the ruling class of the country, with an important political class component, and it was on the verge of becoming the social class. The plutocracy had come of age and, during the following decade and a half, dominated most aspects of public life, achieved a high level of recognition, and acquired a wide network of international connections. The plutocracy had been growing in wealth and self-awareness since the late 1940s, and by the late 1970s it had transformed into a self-directed group with a clear vision of its position within the body politic. With close ties to the political class, the plutocracy was second only to the highest holders of political office in directly and indirectly formulating policy, managing its consequences, and supporting the status quo engendered by the ruling party.[3] In this respect, the economic interests of the plutocracy are tied to the political aims of the ruling party, even though at times they diverge on important issues.

The devaluation of the peso in 1976 was a blow to the Mexican economy, and it affected the wealth of the plutocracy. At that point, the absolute wealth of the plutocracy peaked, but comparatively speaking successive devaluations did not diminish the power of the ruling class. Though the average plutocratic fortune decreased in absolute value, and many of the several hundred million, perhaps billion, dollar fortunes were significantly scaled down, this effect was to some extent compensated by the increasing number of foreign capitalists who acquired plutocratic status and reinforced the power of the plutocracy as a class. By now the plutocracy had acquired extensive international networks, and its economy extended beyond the domestic operations of a generation before. This multinational tie not only enriched the Mexican plutocracy economically but socially and expressively as well, giving it a new maturity and confidence. During the last two decades the plutocracy became the overwhelmingly predominant class of the superordinate system. The majority of plutocrats no longer feel the attraction that in the early years of upward mobility had so impelled them to seek alliances with the aristocracy. The plutocracy has become an independent social class, no longer in awe of aristocratic lineage and expression, and to some extent it creates its own expressive domains. For at least the last twelve years, the plutocracy has been interacting with the aristocracy on a basis of social equality and, indeed, the last ten years of aristocratic-plutocratic interaction may even be characterized as a growing apart, a situation of studied indifference.

Aristocrats themselves present a varied interaction with the plutocracy that may be outlined as follows. First, the conservative sector of the aristocracy, a distinct minority, has, so to speak, gone underground: totally centered in the household, entirely endogamous, and under no circumstances willing to interact with anyone but its own. All grown-up members of this group fit this characterization, but their children are another matter. Some of them adhere to the views of their elders, but many are in open revolt and in search of wider social horizons, namely, interaction with the rich and powerful, among whom their names still count in the marriage game. Second, the majority of aristocrats are still open and maintain social relations with the various sectors of the plutocracy in several contexts. While the household is still the endogenous center of social activity, it is now more open to social interaction with plutocrats, and the overall configuration of relationships has become fairly symmetrical. Intermarriage with plutocrats has increased since the late 1970s, and it is now accepted as a matter of course and necessity. Third, 10 percent of aristocrats straddle the aristocratic-plutocratic spectrum; they are the most acculturated to plutocratic ways, and their intermarriage with plutocrats is common.

Terminal Value of the Aristocratic Expressive Commodity

The process of acculturation that has affected the aristocracy and plutocracy of Mexico since 1940 may be summarized in three developmental stages. (1) During the early 1940s, the new plutocracy made its appearance as a group to be reckoned with economically. Its social recognition by the aristocracy came fairly slowly, and it was not until the mid-1950s that its presence was generally established. This period was characterized by tentative, groping advances on the part of the plutocracy and cautious appraisal and grudging acceptance on the part of the aristocracy. Within fifteen years, the majority of the plutocracy shed its outward middle-class trappings and acquired those of the aristocracy. The social interaction of the two sectors occurred mainly in the public context of business and banking, and on the whole it remained quite formal. (2) From the mid-1950s until about the mid-1970s, the plutocracy became well versed in the details of upper-class genteel behavior. It took a more forceful social position, making its wealth and economic power an explicit instrument of assertive mobility. The aristocracy became increasingly willing to extend social recognition, some aristocrats opened themselves completely, as the manners and mores of the plutocracy came to resemble their own. Social interaction was extended to the home, though still somewhat asymmetrically, in that plutocrats extended themselves willingly and lavishly, whereas aristocrats largely retained the home as a last bastion of endogenous expression. (3) Since the mid-1970s the acculturative cycle of expressive transference from the aristocracy to the plutocracy has ended, and a significant homogenization of expressive and behavioral patterns has been achieved, including the transference of plutocratic attitudes to the aristocracy. Most plutocrats have been sufficiently transformed to pass for upper-upper class, while aristocrats have toned down their ancient claims so as to interact as equals with those who have most of the wealth and economic power. The center of social interaction has now significantly shifted to the almost sacred preserve of the aristocratic household, and only the most conservative and recalcitrant aristocrats do not extend full social recognition to the average plutocrat.

Intermarriage between aristocrats and plutocrats has taken place in all three acculturative stages, but only recently has it become common. There is no doubt that intermarriage will soon become generalized. When it does, and the cherished endogamy of the aristocracy comes to an end, it will certainly accelerate the conclusion of the final stage: the last gasp of the aristocracy as a self-defined, highly conscious, and delineated group.

Throughout this chapter, I have used the term *aristocracy* with some hesitation to characterize the descendants of the old ruling class of Mexico. My justification for using the term is essentially taxonomic, in that it discriminates properly the three main sectors of the haute bourgeoisie since the Mexican Revolution. Despite their self-awareness as a class and pride in their illustrious past, most aristocrats acknowledge their anomalous position: they are the holders of social prestige but cannot buttress it with the kind of wealth that had traditionally accompanied it. When asked to define their social class, most aristocrats today respond *"éramos aristócratas pero ahora somos de clase alta"* (we were aristocrats but now we belong to the upper class). Even the few who quixotically maintain that they are still aristocrats by virtue of lineage and tradition qualify their answer by saying *"aunque ahora lo único que vale es el dinero y pronto vamos a pasar a la historia"* (though today money is the only thing that counts and we shall soon pass into oblivion). Eighty years of hardship and dwindling wealth have made aristocrats realize that social status and prestige without adequate wealth can carry them only so far and that they are reaching a stage when they will no longer be able to maintain collective consciousness and self-identity.

In terms of lineage and tradition, who are aristocrats today? (1) Descendants of conquistadors, *encomenderos,* and settlers (quite often founders of cities and towns), the original nucleus of the aristocracy that by 1560 was the budding social and ruling class of New Spain. This group of aristocratic families is very small, numbering less than 10 percent. (2) Descendants of plutocrats of various extractions who achieved aristocratic rank by the end of the first renewal, most of whom had become or would soon become great *hacendados* engaged in mining and commercial operations. Perhaps 25 percent of all aristocratic families can substantiate this claim, and they are among the most prominent families today. (3) Descendants of plutocrats who achieved aristocratic status during the second renewal, that is, the great *hacendado,* mining, and trading plutocracy that dominated New Spain from the middle of the eighteenth century until the end of Colonial times. Slightly over 50 percent of aristocratic families fall into this category. (4) Descendants of plutocrats who achieved aristocratic status during the third renewal, mainly bankers, manufacturers, and assorted businessmen of domestic and foreign extraction who amassed great fortunes during the second half of the nineteenth century. Perhaps 15 percent of families fall into this category. These are recognized segments of the aristocracy today. But within the wider context of the haute bourgeoisie, the aristocracy is perceived as a fairly homogeneous group, as social and expressive relations with the plutocracy have unfolded during the terminal renewal.

The Mexican Revolution is the sufficient but not necessary cause of the aristocracy's political, economic, and social decline over the past eighty years. It would have taken longer, and the aristocracy would have survived with a greater social role, had the revolution not taken place. In short, the aristocracy would not have been able to compete economically with the rising plutocracy: agrarian-generated wealth since the early nineteenth century has never been able to compete with industrial wealth; and, as Pareto (1980:31–93) brilliantly describes, elites come to an end and are superseded by newer elites because they cannot adapt themselves to new constraints and are not able to innovate sufficiently to prevail. The Mexican aristocracy was not able to adapt to an economic world in which land was no longer the main wealth-producing mechanism. Though a few aristocrats became successful businessmen, the great majority were constrained by an *imago mundi* that even dire economic necessity could not totally overcome.

The Mexican aristocracy survived because of the unusual ethnic and colonial conditions that existed in Mexico until the turn of the century. With these conditions gone or greatly altered since 1910, the aristocracy eighty years later is reduced to an almost subterranean social class. Still, even with its expressive commodity largely unmarketable, the aristocracy survives as a marriage market, as an almost atavistic symbol of the past. By contrast, western European aristocracies have survived somewhat better, perhaps because, for the past 130 years at least, revolutions have not accelerated their demise and their symbolic and physical presence—as embodied in titles of nobility, the ritual roles that aristocrats still occasionally play, and the palaces still in their hands—is more historically imprinted in the societal consciousness. In Mexico, lack of awareness of the aristocracy has been a negative factor for its survival as a distinct social class, as its palaces and titles are beyond the perception of the overwhelming majority of the population.

The plutocracy, on the other hand, still ascends socially and as a ruling class, and barring a major upheaval it will have reached maturity within a generation. The continuing democratization of society will undoubtedly preclude the configuration of a social class approaching the position of the aristocracy at the end of the nineteenth century, for it was the de facto estatelike configuration of Mexican society until the 1910 Revolution that allowed the aristocracy to constitute an endogenous, largely endogamous, and quite closed social class. It is in this sense that aristocracies have come to an end in the twentieth century, as the last one hundred years have witnessed a thorough transition to a class system. The last vestiges of estate privilege, and the implicit and explicit constraints that it imposes on the development of society, have been largely eliminated. The Mexican plutocracy today is a fluid social class with none of the characteristics of a possible "aristocracy" of the future.

Notes

[1] *Indigenismo* was a kind of nativistic movement, with which one cannot but sympathize, but it was doomed to failure because of the overwhelming predominance of Western-Spanish cultural components in the institutional and overall configuration of the nation at that time. Nonetheless, *indigenismo* was a salutary reaction to centuries of oppression of the masses of peasants and the dispossessed; it fostered a new pride in being Mexican, and I think it was instrumental in creating a Mexican national mentality.

[2] My observations of superordinate stratification of several elites in central Mexico—primarily Puebla, Jalapa, Orizaba, and Córdoba— indicate the formation of plutocratic nuclei at the top of the system beginning in the late 1930s. This formation coincides with the massive migration of local aristocrats to Mexico City, and the vacuum they left in the cities they formerly controlled was undoubtedly related to the form that local superordinate stratification took throughout the country. Without the benefit of an aristocratic input, provincial plutocracies, as local ruling and social classes, acquired different configurations.

[3] Throughout Colonial times, the ruling class and the political class were distinctly separated and occasionally antagonistic to each other. Since Independence, however, the demarcation between the political class and the ruling class was never clear, and throughout the nineteenth century an uneasy alliance brought them together. During the Porfiriato, their common interests coincided to a high degree, even though the ruling class and the political class embodied different social strata. The 1910 Revolution destroyed this state of affairs, but the new ruling and political classes that replaced the traditional ones retained the unspoken principle that had held together the "ancien régime."

References

García Purón, Manuel. 1964. *México y sus Gobernantes: Biografías.* México, D.F.: M. Porrúa.

Mendieta y Nuñez, Lucio. 1966. *El Problema Agrario de México.* México, D.F.: Porrúa Hermanos.

Nickel, Herbert J. 1988. *Morfología Social de la* Hacienda *Mexicana.* México, D.F.: Fondo de Cultura Económica.

Nutini, Hugo G., John M. Roberts, and María Teresa Cervantes. 1982. "The Historical Development of the Mexican Aristocracy: 1519–1940." *L'Uomo* 6: 3–37.

———. 1984. "The Mexican *Haute Bourgeoisie*: An Outline of Its Ideology, Structure, and Expressive Culture." *L'Uomo* 8: 3–28.

Pareto, Vilfredo. 1980. *Trattato di Sociologia Generale.* Milano: Edizioni di Comunitá.

Eric R. Wolf, who recently died, was Distinguished Professor of Anthropology at Herbert H. Lehman College of the City University of New York. He did fieldwork in Europe as well as Latin America, and many of his writings are broadly comparative as well as conceptually insightful. Among his best-known books are Europe and the People without History, The Human Condition in Latin America (with E. C. Hansen), Peasants, Peasant Wars of the Twentieth Century, Sons of the Shaking Earth, and Envisioning Power: Ideologies of Dominance.

In a sense, this paper represents an intellectual cornerstone of this book, because Wolf here provides a way of dealing with local institutions and small communities in relation to larger systems in complex nation-states. Although he illustrates his approach in terms of a brief analysis of the social history of Mexico, his spotlighting of "brokers" as key individuals or groups who " . . . stand guard over the crucial junctures or synapses of relationships which connect the local system to the larger whole" has set the direction of much of the anthropological work that has been done since this paper was written.

When I invited him to draft a brief "Afterword" reflecting on the unexpected impact that this paper had had, he characteristically declined to "rehash old stuff" but cheerily recommended that I read his next book. Fortunately, it (Envisioning Power: Ideologies of Dominance) was completed shortly before he died.

Foster's chapter (31) extends the idea of brokerage even further, to include dealings with supernaturals. Some anthropologists demonstrate remarkable skills in various kinds of cultural brokerage, such as Stearman (chapter 20), Bernard (chapter 10), Ehrenreich (chapter 11), and Vogt (chapter 5), whereas others tend to downplay it.

Aspects of Group Relations in a Complex Society: Mexico

Eric R. Wolf

I

Starting from simple beginnings in the twenties, anthropologists have grown increasingly sophisticated about the relationship of nation and community. First, they studied the community in its own terms, taking but little account of its larger matrix. Later, they began to describe "outside factors" which affected the life of the local group under study. Recently they have come to recognize that nations or "systems of the higher level do not consist merely of more numerous and diversified parts," and that it is therefore "methodologically incorrect to treat each part as though it were an independent whole in itself" (Steward 1950:107). Communities are "modified and acquire new characteristics because of their functional dependence upon a new and larger system" (ibid. 111). The present article is concerned with a continuation of this anthropological discussion in terms of Mexican material.

The dependence of communities on a larger system has affected them in two ways. On the one hand, whole communities have come to play specialized parts within the larger whole. On the other, special functions pertaining to the whole have become the tasks of special groups within communities. These groups Steward calls horizontal sociocultural segments. I shall simply call them nation-oriented groups. They are usually found in more than one community and follow ways of life different from those of their community-oriented fellow villagers. They are often the agents of the great national institutions which reach down into the community, and form "the bones, nerves and sinews running through the total society, binding it together, and affecting

---

Originally published in *American Anthropologist*, vol. 58 (1956), pp. 1065–1078.

it at every point" (ibid. 115). Communities which form parts of a complex society can thus be viewed no longer as self-contained and integrated systems in their own right. It is more appropriate to view them as the local termini of a web of group relations which extend through intermediate levels from the level of the community to that of the nation. In the community itself, these relationships may be wholly tangential to each other.

Forced to understand the community in terms of forces impinging on it from the outside, we have also found it necessary to gain a better understanding of national-level institutions. Yet to date most anthropologists have hesitated to commit themselves to such a study, even when they have become half convinced that such a step would be desirable. National institutions seem so complex that even a small measure of competence in their operations seems to require full-time specialization. We have therefore left their description and analysis to specialists in other disciplines. Yet the specialists in law, politics, or economics have themselves discovered that anthropologists can be of almost as much use to them as they can be to the anthropologist. For they have become increasingly aware that the legal, political or other systems to which they devote their attention are not closed systems either, but possess social and cultural dimensions which cannot be understood in purely institutional terms. They have discovered that they must pay attention to shifting group relationships and interests if their studies are to reflect this other dimension of institutional "reality." This is hardly surprising if we consider that institutions are ultimately but cultural patterns for group relationships. Their complex forms allow groups to relate themselves to each other in the multiple processes of conflict and accommodation which must characterize any complex society. They furnish the forms through which some nation-oriented groups may manipulate other nation-oriented or community-oriented groups. The complex apparatus of such institutions is indeed a subject for specialists, but anthropologists may properly attempt to assess some of their functions.

If the communities of a complex system such as Mexico represent but the local termini of group relationships which go beyond the community level, we cannot hope to construct a model of how the larger society operates by simply adding more community studies. Mexico—or any complex system—is more than the arithmetic sum of its constituent communities. It is also more than the sum of its national-level institutions, or the sum of all the communities and national-level institutions taken together. From the point of view of this article, it is rather the web of group relationships which connect localities and national-level institutions. The focus of study is not communities or institutions, but groups of people.

In dealing with the group relationships of a complex society, we cannot neglect to underline the fact that the exercise of power by some people over others enters into all of them, on all levels of integration. Certain economic and political relationships are crucial to the functioning of any complex society. No matter what other functions such a society may contain or elaborate, it must both produce surpluses and exercise power to transfer a part of these surpluses from the producing communities to people other than the producers. No matter what combination of cultural forms such a society may utilize, it must also wield power to limit the autonomy of its constituent communities and to interfere in their affairs. This means that all interpersonal and intergroup relationships of such a society must at some point conform to the dictates of economic or political power. Let it be said again, however, that these dictates of power are but aspects of group relationships, mediated in this case through the forms of an economic or political apparatus.

Finally, we must be aware that a web of group relationships implies a historical dimension. Group relationships involve conflict and accommodation, integration and disintegration, processes which take place over time. And just as Mexico in its synchronic aspect is a web of group relationships with termini in both communities and national-level institutions, so it is also more in its diachronic aspect than a sum of the histories of these termini. Local histories are important, as are the histories of national-level institutions, but they are not enough. They are but local or institutional manifestations of group relations in continuous change.

In this article, then, we shall deal with the relations of community-oriented and nation-oriented groups which characterize Mexico as a whole. We shall emphasize the economic and political aspects of these relationships, and we shall stress their historical dimension, their present as a rearrangement of their past, and their past as a determinant of their present.

II

From the beginning of Spanish rule in Mexico, we confront a society riven by group conflicts for economic and political control. The Spanish Crown sought to limit the economic and political autonomy of the military entrepreneurs who had conquered the country in its name. It hoped to convert the conquistadores into town dwellers, not directly involved in the process of production on the community level but dependent rather on carefully graded handouts by the Crown. They were to have no roots in local communities, but to depend directly on a group of officials operating at the level of the nation. The strategic cultural form selected for this purpose was the *encomienda*, in which the recipient received rights to a specified amount of Indian tribute and services, but was not permitted to organize his own labor force nor to settle in Indian towns. Both control of Indian labor and the allocation of tribute payments were to remain in the hands of royal bureaucrats (Simpson 1950: esp. 123, 144; Zavala 1940).

To this end, the Crown encouraged the organization of the Indian population into compact communities with self-rule over their own affairs, subject to supervision and interference at the hands of royal officials (Zavala and Miranda 1954:75–79). Many of the cultural forms of this community organization are pre-Hispanic in origin, but they were generally repatterned and charged with new functions. We must remember that the Indian sector of society underwent a serious reduction in social complexity during the sixteenth and seventeenth centuries. The Indians lost some of their best lands and water supply, as well as the larger part of their population. As a result of this social cataclysm, as well as of government policy, the repatterned Indian community emerged as something qualitatively new: a corporate organization of a local group inhabited by peasants (Wolf 1955a:456–461). Each community was granted a legal charter and communal lands (Zavala and Miranda 1954:70); equipped with a communal treasury (ibid. 87–88; Chávez Orozco 1943:23–24) and administrative center (Zavala and Miranda 1954:80–82); and connected with one of the newly established churches. It was charged with the autonomous enforcement of social control, and with the payment of dues (ibid. 82).

Thus equipped to function in terms of their own resources, these communities became in the centuries after the Conquest veritable redoubts of cultural homeostasis. Communal jurisdiction over land, obligations to expend surplus funds in religious ceremonies, negative attitudes toward personal display of wealth and self-assertion, strong defenses against deviant behavior, all served to emphasize social and cultural homogeneity and to reduce tendencies toward the development of internal class differences and heterogeneity in behavior and interests. The taboo on sales of land to outsiders and the tendency toward endogamy made it difficult for outsiders to gain footholds in these villages (Redfield and Tax 1952; Wolf 1955a:457–461).

At the same time, the Crown failed in its attempt to change the Spanish conquerors into passive dependents of royal favors (Miranda 1947). Supported by large retinues of clients (such as *criados*, *deudos*, *allegados*, *paniaguados*; cf. Chevalier 1952:33–38), the colonists increasingly wrested control of the crucial economic and political relationships from the hands of the royal bureaucracy. Most significantly, they developed their own labor force, in contravention of royal command and independently of the Indian communities. They bought Indian and Negro slaves; they attracted to their embryonic enterprises poor whites who had come off second best in the distribution of conquered riches; and they furnished asylum to Indians who were willing to pay the price of acculturation and personal obligation to a Spanish entrepreneur for freedom from the increasingly narrow life of the encysting Indian communities. By the end of the eighteenth century, the colonist enterprises had achieved substantial independence of the Crown in most economic, political, legal, and even military matters. Power thus passed from the hands of the Crown into the hands of local rulers who interposed themselves effectively between nation and community. Effective power to enforce political and economic decisions contrary to the interest of these power holders was not returned to the national level until the victory of the Mexican Revolution of 1910 (Wolf 1955b:193–195).

Alongside the Indian villages and the entrepreneurial communities located near haciendas, mines, or mills, there developed loosely structured settlements of casual farmers and workers, middlemen and "*lumpen*-proletarians" who had no legal place in the colonial order. Colonial records tended to ignore them except when they came into overt conflict with the law. Their symbol in Mexican literature is *El Periquillo Sarmiento*, the man who lives by his wits (cf. Yañez 1945:60–94). "Conceived in violence and without joy, born into the world in sorrow" (Benítez 1947:47), the very marginality of their origins and social position forced them to develop patterns of behavior adapted to a life unstructured by formal law. They were thus well fitted to take charge of the crucial economic and political relationships of the society at a time when social and cultural change began to break down the barriers between statuses and put a premium on individuals and groups able to rise above their traditional stations through manipulation of social ties and improvisation upon them.

The transfer of power from the national level to the intermediate power holders, and the abolition of laws protecting the Indian communities—both accomplished when Mexico gained its independence from Spain (Chávez Orozco 1943:35–47)—produced a new constellation of relationships among Indian communities, colonist entrepreneurs, and "marginals." The colonists' enterprises, and chief among them the hacienda, began to encroach more and more heavily on the Indian communities. At the same time, the Indian communities increasingly faced the twin threats of internal differentiation and of invasion from the outside by the "marginals" of colonial times.

Despite the transcendent importance of the hacienda in Mexican life, anthropologists have paid little attention to this cultural form. To date we do not have a single anthropological or sociological study of a Mexican hacienda or hacienda community. Recent historical research has shown that the hacienda is not an offspring of the *encomienda* (Zavala 1940; 1944). The *encomienda* always remained a form of royal control. The hacienda, however, proved admirably adapted to the purposes of the colonists who strove for greater autonomy. Unlike the *encomienda*, it granted direct ownership of land to a manager-owner and permitted direct control of a resident labor force. From the beginning, it served commercial ends (Bazant 1950). Its principal function was to convert community-oriented peasants into a disciplined labor force able to produce cash crops for a supra-community market. The social relationships through which this was accomplished involved a series of voluntary or forced transactions in which the worker abdicated much personal autonomy in exchange for heightened social and economic security.

Many observers have stressed the voracity of the hacienda for land and labor. Its appetite for these two factors of production was great indeed, and yet ultimately limited by its very structure. First, the hacienda always lacked capital. It thus tended to farm only the best land (Gruening 1928:134; Tannenbaum 1929:121–122), and relied heavily on the traditional technology of its labor force (Simpson 1937:490). Hacienda owners also curtailed production in order to raise land rent and prices, and to keep down wages (Gama 1931:21). Thus "Mexico has been a land of large estates, but not a nation of large-scale agriculture" (Martínez de Alba, quoted in Simpson 1937:490). Second, the hacienda was always limited by available demand (Chávez Orozco 1950:19), which in a country with a largely self-sufficient population was always small. What the hacienda owner lacked in capital, however, he made up in the exercise of power over people. He tended to "monopolize land that he might monopolize labor" (Gruening 1928:134). But here again the hacienda encountered limits to its expansion. Even with intensive farming of its core lands and lavish use of gardeners and torch bearers, it reached a point where its mechanisms of control could no longer cope with the surplus of population nominally under its domination. At this point the haciendas ceased to grow, allowing Indian communities like Tepoztlán (Lewis 1951:xxv) or the Sierra and Lake Tarascan villages (West 1948:17) to survive on their fringes. Most hacienda workers did not live on the haciendas; they were generally residents of nearby communities who had lost their land, and exchanged their labor for the right to farm a subsistence plot on hacienda lands (Aguirre and Pozas 1954:202–203). Similarly, only in the arid and sparsely populated North did large haciendas predominate. In the heavily populated central region, Mexico's core area, large haciendas were the exception and the "medium-size" hacienda of about 3,000 ha. was the norm (ibid. 201; also Simpson 1937:489).

I should even go so far as to assert that once the haciendas reached the apex of their growth within a given area, they began to add to the defensive capacity of the corporately organized communities of Indian peasantry rather than to detract from it. Their major innovation lay in the field of labor organization and not in the field of technology. Their tenants continued to farm substantial land areas by traditional means (Aguirre and Pozas 1954:201; Whetten 1948:105) and the hacienda did not generally interfere in village affairs except when these came into conflict with its interests. The very threat of a hacienda's presence unified the villagers on its fringes in ways which would have been impossible in its absence. A hacienda owner also resented outside interference with "his" Indians, whether these lived inside or outside his property, and outsiders were allowed to operate in the communities only "by his leave." He thus often acted as a buffer between the Indian communities and nation-oriented groups, a role similar to that played by the hacienda owner in the northern highlands of Peru (Mangin 1955). Periodic work on the haciendas further provided the villagers with opportunities, however small, to maintain aspects of their lives which required small outlays of cash and goods, such as their festive patterns, and thus tended to preserve traditional cultural forms and functions which might otherwise have fallen into disuse (Aguirre and Pozas 1954:221; Wolf 1953:161).

Where corporate peasant communities were ultimately able to establish relations of hostile symbiosis with the haciendas, they confronted other pressures toward dissolution. These pressures came both from within and without the villages, and aimed at the abolition of communal jurisdiction over land. They sought to replace communal jurisdiction with private property in land, that is, to convert village land into a commodity. Like any commodity, land was to become an object to be bought, sold, and used not according to the common understandings of community-oriented groups, but according to the interests of nation-oriented groups outside the community. In some corporate communities outsiders were able to become landowners by buying land or taking land as security on unpaid loans, e.g., in the Tarascan area (Carrasco 1952:17). Typically, these outsiders belonged to the strata of the population which during colonial times had occupied a marginal position, but which exerted increased pressure for wealth, mobility and social recognition during the nineteenth century. Unable to break the monopoly which the haciendas exercised over the best land, they followed the line of least resistance and established beachheads in the Indian communities (Molina Enríquez 1909:53). They were aided in their endeavors by laws designed to break up the holdings of so-called corporations, which included the lands of the Church and the communal holdings of the Indians.

But even where outsiders were barred from acquiring village lands, the best land of the communities tended to pass into private ownership, this time of members of the community itself (Gama 1931:10–11). Important in this change seems to have been the spread of plow culture and oxen which required some capital investment, coupled with the development of wage labor on such holdings and increasing production for a supra-community market. As Oscar Lewis has so well shown for Tepoztlán, once private ownership in land allied to plow culture is established in at least part of the community, the community tends to differentiate into a series of social groups, with different technologies, patterns of work, interests, and thus with different supra-community relationships (Lewis 1951:129–157). This tendency has proceeded at different rates in different parts of Mexico. It has not yet run its course where land constitutes a poor investment risk, or where a favorable man-land ratio makes private property in land nonfunctional, as among the Popoluca of Sayula in Veracruz (Guiteras-Holmes 1952:37–40). Elsewhere it was complete at the end of the nineteenth century.

The Mexican Revolution of 1910 destroyed both the cultural form of the hacienda and the social relationships which were mediated through it. It did so in part because the hacienda was a self-limiting economic system, incapable of further expansion. It did so in part because the hacienda prevented the geographic mobility of a large part of Mexico's population. The end of debt bondage, for example, has permitted or forced large numbers of people to leave their local communities and to seek new opportunities elsewhere. It did so, finally, because the hacienda blocked the channels of social and cultural mobility and communication from nation to community, and tended to atomize the power of the central government. By destroying its power, the Revolution reopened channels of relationship from the communities to the national level, and permitted new circulation of individuals and groups through the various levels (Iturriaga 1951:66).

The new power holders have moved upwards mainly through political channels, and the major means of consolidating and obtaining power in the regional and national level in Mexico today appear to be political. Moreover—and due perhaps in part to the lack of capital in the Mexican economy as a whole—political advantages are necessary to obtain economic advantages. Both economic and political interests must aim at the establishment of monopolistic positions within defined areas of crucial economic and political relationships. Thus political and economic power seekers tend to meet in alliances and cliques on all levels of the society.

The main formal organization through which their interests are mediated is the government party, the Revolutionary Institutional Party or, as someone has said, "the Revolution as an institution" (Lee 1954:300). This party contains not only groups formally defined as political, but also occupational and other special-interest groups. It is a political holding-company representing different group interests (Scott 1955:4). Its major function is to establish channels of communication and mobility from the local community to the central power group at the helm of the government. Individuals who can gain control of the local termini of these channels can now rise to positions of power in the national economy or political machine.[1]

Some of the prerequisites for this new mobility are purely economic. The possession of some wealth, or access to sources of wealth, is important; more important, however, is the ability to adopt the proper patterns of public behavior. These are the patterns of behavior developed by the "marginal" groups of colonial times which have now become the ideal behavior patterns of the nation-oriented person. An individual who seeks power and recognition outside his local community must shape his behavior to fit these new expectations. He must learn to operate in an arena of continuously changing friendships and alliances, which form and dissolve with the appearance or disappearance of new economic or political opportunities. In other words, he must learn to function in terms which characterize any complex stratified society in which individuals can improve their status through the judicious manipulation of social ties. However, this manipulative behavior is always patterned culturally—and patterned differently in Mexico than in the United States or India. He must therefore learn also the cultural forms in which this manipulative behavior is couched. Individuals who are able to operate both in terms of community-oriented and nation-oriented expectations then tend to be selected out for mobility. They become the economic and political "brokers" of nation-community relations, a function which carries its own rewards.

The rise of such politician-entrepreneurs, however, has of necessity produced new problems for the central power. The Spanish Crown had to cope with the ever-growing autonomy of the colonists; the central government of the Republic must similarly check the propensity of political power seekers to free themselves of government control by cornering economic advantages. Once wealthy in their own right, these nation-community "brokers" would soon be independent of government favors and rewards. The Crown placed a check on the colonists by balancing their localized power over bailiwicks with the concentrated power of a corps of royal officials in charge of the corporate Indian communities. Similarly, the government of the Republic must seek to balance the community-derived power of its political "brokers" with the power of other power holders. In modern Mexico, these competing power holders are the leaders of the labor unions—especially of the labor unions in the nationalized industries—and of the *ejidos*, the groups in local communities who have received land grants in accordance with the agrarian laws growing out of the 1910 Revolution.

Leaving aside a discussion of the labor unions due to limitations of time and personal knowledge, I should like to underline the importance of the *ejido* grants as a nationwide institution. They now include more than 30 percent of the people in Mexican localities with a population below 10,000 (Whetten 1948:186). A few of these, located in well-irrigated and highly capitalized areas, have proved an economic as well as a political success (ibid. 215). The remainder, however, must be regarded as political instruments rather than as economic ones. They are political assets because they have brought under government control large numbers of people who depend ultimately on the government for their livelihood. Agrarian reform has, however, produced social and political changes without concomitant changes in the technological order; the redistribution of land alone can neither change the technology nor supply needed credit (Aguirre and Pozas 1954:207–208; Pozas 1952:316).

At the same time, the Revolution has intensified the tendencies toward further internal differentiation of statuses and interests in the communities, and thus served to reduce their capacity to resist outside impact and pressure. It has mobilized the potentially nation-oriented members of the community, the men with enough land or capital to raise cash crops and operate stores, the men whose position and personality allow them to accept the new patterns of nation-oriented behavior. Yet often enough the attendant show of business and busyness tends to obscure the fact that most of the inhabitants of such communities either lack access to new opportunities or are unable to take advantage of such opportunities when offered. Lacking adequate resources in land, water, technical knowledge, and contacts in the market, the majority also lack the instruments which can transform use values into marketable commodities. At the same time, their inability to speak Spanish and their failure to understand the cues for the new patterns of nation-oriented behavior isolate them from the channels of communication between community and nation. Under these circumstances they must cling to the traditional "rejection pattern" of their ancestors, because their narrow economic base sets limits to the introduction of new cultural alternatives. These are all too often nonfunctional for them. The production of sufficient maize for subsistence purposes remains their major goal in life. In their case, the granting of *ejidos* tended to lend support to their accustomed way of life and reinforced their attachment to their traditional heritage.

Confronted by these contrasts between the mobile and the traditional, the nation-oriented and the community-oriented, village life is riven by contradictions and conflicts, conflicts not only between class groups but also between individuals, families, or entire neighborhoods. Such a community will inevitably differentiate into a number of unstable groups with different orientations and interests.

III

This article has dealt with the principal ways in which social groups arranged and rearranged themselves in conflict and accommodation along the major economic and political axes of Mexican society. Each rearrangement produced a changed configuration in the relationship of community-oriented and nation-oriented groups. During the first period of post-Columbian Mexican history, political power was concentrated on the national level in the hands of royal officials. Royal officials and colonist entrepreneurs struggled with each other for control of the labor supply located in the Indian communities. In this struggle, the royal officials helped to organize the Indian peasantry into corporate communities which proved strongly resilient to outside change. During the second period, the colonist entrepreneurs—and especially the owners of haciendas—threw off royal control and established autonomous local enclaves, centered on their enterprises. With the fusion of political and economic power in the hands of these intermediate power holders, the national government was rendered impotent and the Indian peasant groups became satellites of the entrepreneurial complex. At the same time, their corporate communal organization was increasingly weakened by internal differentiation and the inroads of outsiders. During the third period, the entrepreneurial complexes standing between community and nation were swept away by the agrarian revolution and power again returned to a central government. Political means are once more applied to check the transformation of power seekers from the local communities into independent entrepreneurs. Among the groups used in exercising such restraint are the agriculturists, organized in *ejidos* that allow the government direct access to the people of the local communities.

Throughout this analysis, we have been concerned with the bonds which unite different groups on different levels of the larger society, rather than with the internal organization of communities and national-level institutions. Such a shift in emphasis seems increasingly necessary as our traditional models of communities and national institutions become obsolete. Barring such a shift, anthropologists will have to abdicate their newfound interest in complex societies. The social-psychological aspects of life in local groups, as opposed to the cultural aspects, have long been explored by sociologists. The study of formal law, politics, or economics is better carried out by specialists in these fields than by anthropologists doubling as part-time experts. Yet the hallmark of anthropology has always been its holistic approach, an approach which is increasingly needed in an age of ever-increasing specialization. This article constitutes an argument that we can achieve greater synthesis in the study of complex societies by focusing our attention on the relationships between different groups operating on different levels of the society, rather than on any one of its isolated segments.

Such an approach will necessarily lead us to ask some new questions and to reconsider some answers to old questions. We may raise two such questions regarding the material presented here. First, can we make any generalizations about the ways in which groups in Mexico interrelate with each other over time, as compared to those which unite groups in another society, such as Italy or Japan, for example? We hardly possess the necessary information to answer such a question at this point, but one can indicate the direction which a possible answer might take. Let me point to one salient characteristic of Mexican group relationships which appears from the foregoing analysis: the tendency of new group relationships to contribute to the preservation of traditional cultural forms. The Crown reorganized the Indian communities; they became strongholds of the traditional way of life. The haciendas transformed the Indian peasants into part-time laborers; their wages stabilized their traditional prestige economy. The Revolution of 1910 opened the channels of opportunity to the nation-oriented; it reinforced the community orientation of the immobile. It would indeed seem that in Mexico "the old periods never disappear completely and all wounds, even the oldest, continue to bleed to this day" (Paz 1947:11). This "contemporaneity of the noncontemporaneous" is responsible for the "commonsense" view of many superficial observers that in Mexico "no problems are ever solved," and "reforms always produce results opposite to those intended." It has undoubtedly affected Mexican political development (Wolf 1953:160–165). It may be responsible for the violence which has often accompanied even minor ruptures in these symbiotic patterns. And one may well ask the question whether both processes of accommodation or conflict in Mexico have not acquired certain patterned forms as a result of repeated cyclical returns to hostile symbiosis in group relationships.

Such considerations once again raise the thorny problems presented by the national character approach. Much discussion of this concept has turned on the question of whether all nationals conform to a common pattern of behavior and ideals. This view has been subjected to much justified criticism. We should remember, however, that most national character studies have emphasized the study of ideal norms, constructed on the basis of verbal statements by informants, rather than the study of real behavior through participant observation. The result has been, I think, to confuse cultural form and function. It seems possible to define "national character" operationally as those cultural forms or mechanisms which groups involved in the same overall web of relationships can use in their formal and informal dealings with each other. Such a view need not imply that all nationals think or behave alike, nor that the forms used may not serve different functions in different social contexts. Such common forms must exist if communication between the different constituent groups of a complex society are to be established and maintained. I have pointed out that in modern Mexico the behavior patterns of certain groups in the past have become the expected forms of behavior of nation-oriented individuals. These cultural forms of communication as found in Mexico are manifestly different from those found in other societies (see especially Carrión 1952:70–90; Paz 1947:29–45). Their study by linguists and students of kinesics (Birdwhistell 1951) would do much to establish their direct relevance to the study of complex societies.

A second consideration which derives from the analysis presented in this article concerns the groups of people who mediate between community-oriented groups in communities and nation-oriented groups which operate primarily through national institutions. We have encountered several such groups in this article. In post-Columbian Mexico, these mediating functions were first carried out by the leaders of Indian corporate communities and royal officials. Later, these tasks fell into the hands of the local entrepreneurs, such as the owners of haciendas. After the Revolution of 1910, they passed into the hands of nation-oriented individuals from the local communities who have established ties with the national level, and who serve as "brokers" between community-oriented and nation-oriented groups.

The study of these "brokers" will prove increasingly rewarding, as anthropologists shift their attention from the internal organization of communities to the manner of their integration into larger systems. For they stand guard over the crucial junctures or synapses of relationships which connect the local system to the larger whole. Their basic function is to relate community-oriented individuals who want to stabilize or improve their life chances, but who lack economic security and political connections, with nation-oriented individuals who operate primarily in terms of the complex cultural forms standardized as national institutions, but whose success in these operations depends on the size and strength of their personal following. These functions are of course expressed through cultural forms or mechanisms which will differ from culture to culture. Examples of these are Chinese *kan-ch'ing* (Fried 1953), Japanese *oyabun-kobun* (Ishino 1953), Latin American *compadrazgo* (Mintz and Wolf 1950).

Special studies of such "broker" groups can also provide unusual insight into the functions of a complex system through a study of its dysfunctions. The position of these "brokers" is an "exposed" one, since, Janus-like, they face in two directions at once. They must serve some of the interests of groups operating on both the community and the national level, and they must cope with the conflicts raised by the collision of these interests. They cannot settle them, since by doing so they would abolish their own usefulness in others. Thus they often act as buffers between groups, maintaining the tensions which provide the dynamic of their actions. The relation of the hacienda owner to his satellite Indians, the role of the modern politician-broker to his community-oriented followers, may properly be viewed in this light. These would have no raison d'être but for the tensions between community-oriented groups and nation-oriented groups. Yet they must also maintain a grip on these tensions, lest conflict get out of hand and better mediators take their place. Fallers (1955) has demonstrated how much can be learned about the workings of complex systems by studying the "predicament" of one of its "brokers," the Soga chief. We shall learn much from similar studies elsewhere.

Summary

This article has argued that students of complex societies must proceed from a study of communities or national institutions to a study of the ties between social groups operating on all levels of a society. It then attempted to view Mexico in this light. Emphasis on the external ties between groups rather than on the internal organization of each alone led to renewed questions as to whether these ties were mediated through common cultural forms, and to a discussion of "broker" groups which mediate between different levels of integration of the same society.

***

A first draft of this paper was prepared while the author was Research Associate of the Project for Research on Cross-Cultural Regularities, directed by Julian Steward at the University of Illi-

nois, Urbana, Illinois. Parts of it were read before a meeting of the Central States Anthropological Society at Bloomington, Indiana. The author is indebted for helpful criticisms to Julian Steward, to Oscar Lewis of the University of Illinois, and to Sidney Mintz of Yale University.

***

Note

[1] [Editorial note: Although PIR lost the presidency in 2000, it remains strong in the legislature; it is too early to judge whether its dominance in Mexican politics is past.]

References

Aguirre Beltrán, Gonzalo, and Ricardo Pozas Arciniegas. 1954. "Instituciones indígenas en el México actual," in Caso et al., pp.171–272.

Bazant, Jan. 1950. "Feudalismo y capitalismo en la historia económica de México," *Trimestre Económico* 17:81–98.

Benítez, Francisco. 1947. "México, la tela de Penélope," *Cuadernos Americanos* 6:44–60.

Birdwhistell, Ray L. 1951. *Kinesics*, Washington, DC, Foreign Service Institute, U.S. Department of State.

Carrasco, Pedro. 1952. *Tarascan Folk Religion: An Analysis of Economic, Social, and Religious Interactions*, Middle American Research Institute Publication 17:1–64, New Orleans, Tulane University.

Carrión, Jorge. 1952. "Mito y magia del mexicano," *México y lo mexicano* 3, México, D.F., Porrúa y Obregón.

Caso, Alfonso, et al. 1954. *Métodos y resultados de la política indigenista en México*, Memorias del Instituto Nacional Indigenista 6, México, D.F.

Chávez Orozco, Luis. 1943. *Las instituciones democráticas de los indígenas Mexicanos en la época colonial*, México, D.F., Ediciones del Instituto Indigenista Interamericano.

———. 1950. "La irrigación en México: ensayo histórico," *Problemas Agrícolas e Industriales de México* 2:11–31.

Chevalier, François. 1952. *La formation des grands domaines aux Mexique: Terre et société aux XVIe—XVIIe Siècles*, Travaux et Mémoires de l'Institut d'Ethnologie 56, Paris.

Fallers, Lloyd. 1955. "The Predicament of the Modern African Chief: An Instance from Uganda," *American Anthropologist* 57:290–305.

Fried, Morton H. 1953. *Fabric of Chinese Society*, New York, Praeger.

Gama, Valentín. 1931. *La propiedad en México—la reforma agraria*, México, D.F., Empresa Editorial de Ingeniería y Arquitectura.

Gruening, Ernest. 1928. *Mexico and Its Heritage*, New York, Century.

Guiteras-Holmes, Calixta. 1952. *Sayula*, México, D.F., Sociedad Mexicana de Geografía y Estadística.

Ishino, Iwao. 1953. "The *Oyabun-Kobun*: A Japanese Ritual Kinship Institution," *American Anthropologist* 55:695–707.

Iturriaga, José E. 1951. *La estructura social y cultural de México*, México, D.F., Fondo de Cultura Económica.

Lee, Eric. 1954. "Can a One Party System Be Democratic?" *Dissent* 1:299–300.

Lewis, Oscar. 1951. *Life in a Mexican Village: Tepoztlán Restudied*, Urbana, University of Illinois Press.

Mangin, William. 1955. "*Haciendas, Comunidades* and Strategic Acculturation in the Peruvian Sierra," paper read before the American Anthropological Association, Boston, November 18.

Mintz, Sidney W., and Eric R. Wolf. 1950. "An Analysis of Ritual Co-parenthood (*Compadrazgo*)," *Southwestern Journal of Anthropology* 6:341–368.

Miranda, José. 1947. "La función económica del encomendero en los orígenes del régimen colonial de Nueva España, 1525–1531," *Anales del Instituto Nacional de Antropología e Historia* 2:421–462.

Molina Enríquez, Andrés. 1909. *Los grandes problemas nacionales*, México, D.F., Imprenta de A. Carranza e Hijos.

Paz, Octavio. 1947. *El laberinto de la soledad*, México, D.F., Cuadernos Americanos.

Pozas Arciniegas, Ricardo. 1952. "La situation économique et financière de l'Indien Américain," *Civilisations* 2:309–329.

Redfield, Robert, and Sol Tax. 1952. "General Characteristics of Present-Day Mesoamerican Indian Society," in *Heritage of Conquest*, Sol Tax, ed., Glencoe, IL, Free Press, pp. 31–39.

Scott, Robert E. 1955. "The Bases of Political Power in the Caribbean," lecture delivered at the University of Illinois, Urbana, January 14 (Mimeographed).

Simpson, Eyler N. 1937. *The Ejido: Mexico's Way Out*, Chapel Hill, University of North Carolina Press.

Simpson, Lesley Byrd. 1950. *The Encomienda in New Spain: The Beginning of Spanish Mexico*, rev. ed., Berkeley, University of California Press.

Steward, Julian. 1950. *Area Research: Theory and Practice*, Social Science Research Council Bulletin 63, New York.

Tannenbaum, Frank. 1929. *The Mexican Agrarian Revolution*, Washington, D.C., Brookings Institution.

West, Robert C. 1948. *Cultural Geography of the Modern Tarascan Area*, Smithsonian Institution, Institute of Social Anthropology Publication 7, Washington, D.C.

Whetten, Nathan. 1948. *Rural Mexico*, Chicago, University of Chicago Press.

Wolf, Eric R. 1953. "La formación de la nación: Un ensayo de formulación," *Ciencias Sociales* 4:50–62, 98–111, 146–171.

———. 1955a. "Types of Latin American Peasantry: A Preliminary Discussion," *American Anthropologist* 57:452–471.

———. 1955b. *The Mexican Bajío in the Eighteenth Century: An Analysis of Cultural Integration*, Middle American Research Institute Publication 17:177–200, New Orleans, Tulane University.

Yañez, Agustín. 1945. "Fichas Mexicanas," *Jornadas* 39, México, D.F., El Colegio de México.

Zavala, Silvio. 1940. *De encomiendas y propiedad territorial en algunas regiones de la América Española*, México, D.F., Robredo.

———. 1944. "Orígenes coloniales del peonaje en México," *Trimestre Económico* 10:711–748.

Zavala, Silvio, and José Miranda. 1954. "Instituciones indígenas en la colonia," in Caso et al., pp. 29–112

PART VI

Views of the World

Apart from outward appearances, some of the most fundamental differences among people and peoples have to do with views of the world, not just with how they see things but also with how they interpret them and then choose to act in response. The readings in this section are intended to provide an introduction to the broad range of very different views of the world that are to be found in Latin America today, and also to show how different worldviews prompt people to make very different choices in life. Rather than abstruse philosophy, anthropologists are dealing with actual reasons people give—and often those that they sincerely feel are true—as justifications for their actions as well as for beliefs. Once again, we might well affirm Terence's assertion that the broad range of human views should not be alien. Rather than positing that all things are good and right, in essence the doctrine of cultural relativism takes the stance that all cultural norms make some kind of sense when viewed in their context. We may not all agree on matters of value, but that is usually because we base such judgments on different premises.

Relations with the supernatural often come first to mind in connection with worldview, but anthropologists tend to use the term in a much broader sense. They include not only cosmologies and pantheons of supernatural beings but also prosaic ideas about reality, the nature of things and their relationships, what constitutes right or wrong behavior in particular contexts, and a host of other aspects of culture that might be thought of as scientific, moral, or even recreational.

In this realm, as in most of the others previously discussed as organizing principles throughout this volume, the breadth and subtlety of variation from one population to the next is truly impressive—to the degree that an encyclopedic treatment would be out of the question. It would be futile even to try to offer some sort of representative sample, whether the representation were by country, ecological region, linguistic family, or any other grouping that authors have traditionally used when dealing with large topics on a continental basis. The readings presented here are clearly a random sample, not in any statistical sense but in the sense of offering only a set of contrasting examples.

A good illustration of non-cosmological views of the world is Ferreira's explication of mathematical reasoning in some Amazonian tribes (chapter 13). In one sense, it is difficult to imagine so consistently different a way of calculating with the same numerical system that we use, yet there is a compelling logic to the system as they explain it.

For most of the past 500 years, the dominant intellectual institution in Latin America has been the Roman Catholic Church. This is not to imply that it had a monopoly on education, although its impact on that aspect of life was both deep and broad. More importantly, it favored a mindset that was generally accepting of hierarchy, was ideally oriented to blessedness rather than to accumulation and achievement, was dominated by males, and involved a large measure of unquestioning faith. At first a close ally of the Crown, always the frequent beneficiary of largesse from guilt-ridden men and heir to wealthy widows, the church was a rich and powerful institution, little challenged until the mid-twentieth century. It has always been flexible in accommodating native beliefs and practices to produce a syncretic folk-Catholicism that distinguished Latin American patterns from the supposedly universal forms (cf. Brandes, chapter 29). Widespread dissatisfaction with the modernizing of the liturgy combined with an abrupt decline in clergy, promulgation of Liberation Theology (see Canin, chapter 41), and increasing missionization by Protestant groups collectively eroded— but did not displace—the dominance of the church. A number of African-American spiritist and related churches, long popular among the urban poor in Brazil, became more popular at other levels of society (see Greenfield, chapter 44).

It is widely accepted nowadays that the quest for altered states of consciousness is not deviant in itself, because it has deep ethological roots in other animals and is played out in so many different ways among human beings that it has been called "the fourth need" (after food, drink, and sex). For reasons that are not at all clear, more than three-fourths of the biological sources of psychoactive substances are native to the Western Hemisphere, and most of them occur in Latin America. They are used in different ways and for different purposes, sometimes diametrically opposed; a single substance can be a sacrament to one population and sacrilege to another, feared by some as a poison yet cherished by others as a giver of visions. Altered states of consciousness may also have value only to certain individuals and in limited contexts (such as divining, curing, prophesying, and so forth), but such states are also recognized as potentially dangerous—not to be sought too often, nor by everyone, nor for frivolous purposes. Drug use has a long and distinguished history, and it is by no means always linked with abuses. Wilson's reading (chapter 42) provides a brief introduction to this sometimes mysterious and always somewhat tangential way of viewing the world.

One of the many subdisciplines that have recently flourished within anthropology is that of ethnoscience, which attempts to describe and comprehend the understandings other peoples have about the nature of the world and how things operate within it. Increasingly we have found that many of the cures, farming practices, and other customs that had been viewed as traditional instruments of survival do have a firm basis in what Westerners view as science. An effective example of this is found in the work of Orlove and his colleagues (chapter 43). Beginning with an explanation of native beliefs, they proceed to demonstrate, with some of the most advanced techniques of astroscience and meteorology (that no one had foreseen a generation ago and that few Westerners understand even today) how and why those beliefs were accurate and agricultural practices based on them were productive. No amount of liberal mouthing of adherence to cultural relativism could be nearly so dramatic a demonstration that, within different societies, very different views of the world may be equally valid and useful.

In the previous section's introduction and in Foster's reading (chapter 31) on the dyadic contract, we saw how patronage and clientage provide a mutually beneficial linkage between different levels of a social hierarchy, sometimes even when supernatural beings are involved. Obviously, power is not the only good that is brokered in such relationships. Canin (chapter 41) gives us insight into the very special linkages that people feel with a local patron saint, even while some of the basic foundations of traditional Catholicism are being challenged by a more humanistic—and some would say socialistic—view of the world.

Another example of patronage and clientage in the religious sphere is offered by Greenfield (chapter 44), who shows that some people who consider themselves "good Catholics" are quick to embrace Umbanda or related Afro-Brazilian spiritist religions when a practitioner, said to be possessed by a spirit from Africa, offers relief in terms of health or other workaday problems. It would be misleading to think of such behavior as frivolous or anti-Catholic; there is little reason to doubt that some of these people may return to Catholicism. It is not uncommon for a man who has a drinking problem to convert to Protestantism (inasmuch as most of the missionary groups in Latin America are evangelicals who disallow alcohol) and later, if successful in overcoming the problem, to abandon that church in turn, returning to the more populous and popular Catholic religion that has familiar rites, less pressure to be active in religious affairs, and fewer restrictions on the usual local patterns of socializing.

It is often presumed that the mother-child bond is universally and incredibly strong from birth onward. And yet we know that many women lose nearly half of those infants they bear, without suffering depression or debilitating sadness. In an extract from her book that has won many prizes from literary and beneficent as well as anthropological organizations, Scheper-Hughes (chapter 45) reveals both how she came to focus on this problem and how her neighbors in a Brazilian shantytown adapt to the harsh realities of high infant mortality. Again we find that behavior some outsiders might find callous and unfeeling is realistic and appropriate within the cultural context. A worldview that sees young *angelitos* as having been "loaned" to a woman who should never take special pride or invest too much affect in an offspring, and that promises for such a little angel an eternity without the pain and suffering that are so common on earth, renders logical some choices that might otherwise seem harsh.

The difficult life that is the lot of many poor people in Latin America is reflected both in their low expectations and in the harsh realities of hunger, war, and relative powerlessness they experience. Glittenberg's account (chapter 46), set in a Guatemalan rural clinic, vividly shows how the peasant worldview articulates with their social and cultural situation.

A former priest who is now an anthropologist, Bastien (chapter 47) tells how his own worldview has been colored by experience, with love emerging as a value fully as important as the scientific enterprise.

Latin American values and attitudes have long been cited by North Americans as major obstacles to greater efficiency, the imposition of stricter direction on labor, and so forth, whereas lack of domestic capital has been especially lamented by national critics. Although we do not understand the process very well, there are enough examples of abrupt and enthusiastic adoption of commercial-industrial values to question whether the stereotypical cavalier-picaresque outlook severely impedes development; and the regular flight of huge amounts of capital to Europe and the United States is well known. It seems evident that worldview plays at least some part in the sharp differences that are seen between countries and among populations, in Latin America as elsewhere.

The nature, extent, and meaning of social relationships cannot be appreciated without an understanding of a people's view about other people. A basic theme throughout this volume has been the rich diversity of cultures and societies in contemporary Latin America, The reality of difference, however, should not obscure that widespread underlying unity which derives, in large part, from the Iberian heritage. Latin Americans and others generally agree on the importance of *personalismo, dignidad de la persona*, and *suerte* in the life of individuals, and a variety of institutions express these basic ethos-components, even though there is often a marked divergence between ideals and actions. Such easy characterization should not obscure the real complexity of views, which include such apparent oppositions as: easy dependence on paternalism and a high value on self-determination; strong and widespread bonds of familism and ritual kinship coupled with personalized individualism; high value on the dignity of the unique person in a context of fairly strict social hierarchy; a double standard of extremely contrasting morality for the sexes; and strong formal emphasis on centralization of authority together with an emphasis on the adeptness of the individual.

Five centuries of close and sustained contact between and among ethnic groups have not resulted in large-scale assimilation or acculturation. Insofar as the pluralism within complex societies is cultural as well as social, worldview is probably the most variant and pervasive kind of cultural difference.

In one sense, virtually all of the readings in this book deal with the dynamics of change, whether planned or unintended. This fact may seem ironic in terms of worldview: one of the significant differences often cited between Anglo and Latin outlooks is that the former emphasizes change, self-determination by humankind and by individuals, and a time-focus that is predominantly future oriented; whereas Latins, by contrast, are often characterized as emphasizing tradition and continuity, resignation and fatalism (both individual and collective), and concern with living only for the present.

In fact, however, concern for change is a driving force in much of contemporary Latin American society, although there are great conflicts about what goals should be sought and by what means. There are even some grounds for the recent observation that Anglo-America's rapid assimilation of Latin style and worldview is outpacing Latin America's adaptation to the more ascetic norms of the Anglos who claim to dominate the modern world-system.

FOR FURTHER READING ON VIEWS OF THE WORLD

There was a brief moment in which it looked as if the Roman Catholic Church that had so long dominated much of Latin American thought was undergoing drastic renovation, and Liberation Theology returned to some basic principles said to have been taught by Jesus in the Sermon on the Mount. The poor were to be a focus of concern, with social welfare and equity as important values and aims. That view was famously both preached and practiced by Archbishop H. Cámara in Brazil, author and priest G. Gutiérrez in Peru, and revolutionary Colombian priest C. Torres, among many others. Some of those who took part in local "Christian base communities" interpreted the movement simply as a means of providing a realistic and more liberal way to integrate religion with daily life, whereas others saw it as a truly revolutionary doctrine that might well foster class warfare. A few key sources include P. Berryman, *Liberation Theology* (Pantheon, 1987); and D. Levine (ed.), *Religion and Political Conflict in Latin America* (University of North Carolina Press, 1986). For an anthropological view of how it worked at the local level, see R. Lancaster, *Thanks to God and the Revolution: Religion and Class Consciousness in the New Nicaragua* (Columbia University Press, 1988).

Protestant missionaries are increasingly active in many Latin American countries, and converts to evangelical churches are ever more numerous. D. Stoll has written about this often, including *Fishers of Men or Founders of Empire?* (Zed, 1982) and *Rethinking Protestantism in Latin America* (Temple University Press, 1993). Other pertinent sources include D. R. Miller, *Coming of Age* (University Press of America, 1994); and D. Martin, *Tongues of Fire* (B. Blackwell, 1990).

To a remarkable degree, some African deities survived the trans-Atlantic voyage and ensuing slavery to live on in the minds of Brazilians at all levels of society. A variety of Afro-Brazilian religions had long been deprecated as "cults." However, detailed ethnographic studies revealed subtleties and complexities that colorful journalistic accounts about vivid rituals, often including spirit possession, had overlooked. A convenient overview is R. Bastide, *African American Religions* (trans., Columbia University Press, 1978); good case studies include R. E. Harding, *A Refuge of Thunder: Candomble and Alternative Sources of Blackness* (Indiana University Press, 2000) and S. Leacock, *Afro-Brazilian Religion* (Bobbs-Merrill, 1971).

The idea of altered states of consciousness as a "fourth need" is spelled out by A. Weil, *The Natural Mind: A New Way of Looking at Drugs and the Higher Consciousness* (Houghton Mifflin, 1972) and R. Siegel, *Intoxication: Life in Pursuit of Artificial Paradise* (E.P. Dutton, 1989). Multiple roles of hallucinogens in various Latin American cultures are described by M. Dobkin de Rios, *Visionary Vine* (Waveland, 1984) and *Hallucinogens: Cross-Cultural Perspectives* (University of New Mexico Press, 1984); M. J. Harner, *Hallucinogens and Shamanism* (Oxford University Press, 1973); and P. T. Furst, *Hallucinogens and Culture* (Chandler & Sharp, 1976). Most studies of the drug war are sensationalistic; some exceptions by anthropologists include M. Leóns and H. Sanabria (eds.), *Coca, Cocaine, and the Bolivian Reality* (State University of New York Press,1997); H. Sanabria, *The Coca Boom and Rural Social Change in Bolivia* (University of Michigan Press, 1993); and E. Morales, *Cocaine: White Gold Rush in Peru* (University of Arizona Press, 1989).

Successful experiments in the revival of ancient agricultural practices include the intensive farming on *chinampas* (floating manufactured islands) near Mexico City, ridged terraces near Lake Titicaca, and a return to green fertilizer (compost and animal dung) in many areas. Herbal cures continue to be effective, as amply documented by J. Bastien, *Healers of the Andes: Kallawaya Herbalists and their Medicinal Plants* (University of Utah Press, 1987), and pharmaceutical companies are always eager to learn about ethnomedicine.

Many anthropologists make brief mention of the difficulties to which Latin Americans are often subjected in the earliest days and months of their lives, but few have written as eloquently on the topic as N. Scheper-Hughes. Her major contributions include *Death without Weeping* (University of California Press, 1992); *Child Survival: Anthropological Perspectives* (Reidel, 1987); and *Small Wars: The Cultural Politics of Childhood* (University of California Press, 1998).

The idea that values and worldview could serve as obstacles to development was implicit in much of the early writing that focused on Latin American societies as dual, with the traditional component a drag on the modern. L. P. Harrison has developed that idea in a more sophisticated way in *Underdevelopment Is a State of Mind: The Latin American Case* (University Press of America, 1985), and *The Pan-American Dream: Do Latin America's Cultural Values Discourage True Partnership with the United States and Canada?* (Basic Books, 1992).

Mariana Kawall Leal Ferreira teaches anthropology at University of Tennessee (Knoxville). Her best-known book is Historias do Xingu: Colletânea de Depoimentos dos Índios Suyá, Kayabi, Juruna, Trumai, Txucarramâe e Txicâo.

Many readers are appalled by a confrontation with some of the strikingly different views of the world that delight anthropologists. They react to such cultural alternatives as if they were not only "outlandish" but even downright "unnatural." Sometimes they even reject the social scientist's concern for stories, norms, and values, which are thought to be inherently "mushy" or "slippery," in comparison with more "serious" and eternally objective verities that are the stock in trade of what they think of as "hard science." Unfortunately for them, even so allegedly nonrelativistic a field as mathematical calculation is subject to alteration by social construction and understandings, as is vividly represented—and explained—in Ferreira's insightful probing among people whose parents rarely had occasion to count, but who now make elaborate calculations—in their own distinctive but logically consistent ways.

When 1 + 1 ≠ 2:
Making Mathematics in Central Brazil

Mariana Kawall Leal Ferreira

Squatting on the white sand banks of the Xingu River, Chief Carandine Juruna carefully sorts out the bamboo arrows he has just exchanged for pottery with the upriver Kayabi. As he sets aside the different fish, game, and bird-hunting weapons according to specific arrowheads, the 60-year-old man makes sure each household that has contributed animal-shaped clay pots receives its share of goods. Large families are privileged in the quality and number of arrows they get and so are good hunters, hardworking pottery makers, elders, and the Juruna to whom the Kayabi were previously indebted.

The Juruna nod approvingly as their leader distributes the arrows, commenting on the quality of the bamboo, feathers, wax, and tree-bark ties employed by the Kayabi. The transmission of wealth is only one element of a much broader and enduring contract between the Juruna and the Kayabi. It embodies and records the entire credit structure of the community, including symbolic, interpersonal, economic, and emotional associations that reach far beyond the sole exchange of property—a "system of total services" (Mauss 1990[1950]:5). The fairness of the leader's distribution of goods is not questioned, nor is there a concern for immediate material profit in this vast system of services rendered and reciprocated.

Meanwhile, an employee of the National Indian Foundation in Brazil (FUNAI) standing nearby nervously operates his calculator, attempting to stipulate a price for each arrow he intends to buy from the Juruna and resell in Brasília, the country's capital. Antonio's reasoning is based on the monetary profit he customarily earns from the sale of indigenous "art craft." Waving the number of Brazilian cruzeiro[1] bills that represents a "fair" price for the 20 arrows he wants, Antonio is outraged when Tarinu Juruna, Carandine's son, remarks that "only seven arrows are for sale," and that he himself will calculate their monetary value. The reasoning behind the "exorbitant" price at which Tarinu arrives is far beyond Antonio's comprehension.

Unwilling to accept or understand a system that attributes different values to goods, Antonio angrily tosses the piece of paper listing Tarinu's calculations and shouts in indignation:

I came all the way from Brasília to help you guys and you want to cheat me? Where on earth does 7 times 5 equal 125? I've pacified[2] more than 500 Indians in my life, I've caught malaria more than 100 times in 20 years, and you guys want to charge me 125 cruzeiros for 7 arrows! I could get arrows just like those anywhere in Brasília for as cheap as 2.50 apiece! You lazy Indians know nothing about money, about buying and selling. It's true what people say, that Indians are too stupid to learn math. [January 1982]

In this article, I discuss aspects of mathematical activity in the Xingu Indian Park and, more specifically, at the Diauarum Indian Post. It was at this post that the Juruna, Suyá, and Kayabi founded the Diauarum School, where I taught Portuguese and mathematics from 1980 through 1984. Transactions among different Xingu tribes, and between Indians and merchants, loggers, cattle ranchers, and other non-Indians, have increasingly involved arithmetical operations and monetary calculations. Conflicts and tensions arise when the parties engaged in the exchanges privilege different structuring resources when generating and solving arithmetical dilemmas. In other words, values are attributed to goods under forms that are not exclusively material— that is, that can be easily quantified. Symbolic capital (Bourdieu 1991[1972]:171–183) is also accounted in arithmetical operations, and the process of transforming symbolic into material, quantifiable capital magnifies discrepancies found in dilemmas requiring (among other structuring resources) arithmetical operations.

A World of Numbers: The Kayabi, Juruna, and Suyá of the Xingu Indian Park

The Xingu Indian Park was officially demarcated in 1961 by the Brazilian government as a reservation that would conveniently encapsulate both local tribes (such as the Suyá and the Juruna) and other populations (such as the Kayabi) whose territories were sought for their large supplies of gold, timber, and other natural resources. With the transfer of these groups into the park, the emptied land became available for federal development projects of the 1950s and 1960s. Today there are approximately 3,500 individuals from 17 different tribes living in the park (CEDI 1990:57), an administrative territorial unit of the Brazilian state located in Mato Grosso.[3]

Questions the white men ask always start with how many, how much, how long or when. They want to know for how long I've lived near Diauarum, when I was born, how many children I have, how much I earn, and so on. Yours is a world of numbers. (Kuiussi Suyá, November 1981)

New forms of retribution and reciprocity have mediated social relations between the various Xingu tribes. The reciprocal killings and acts of revenge—instances of retributive logic (Trompf 1994)—that often punctuated in initial intertribal transactions have gradually been de-emphasized to the benefit of alliances based on principles of positive reciprocity (Lévi-Strauss 1969[1949]). A common territory and collective concerns regarding the Xingu tribes' position within an organized Brazilian Indian Movement has demanded the articulation of different worldviews and logics.[4] Knowledge of mathematics has become a critical tool to the Juruna, Kayabi, and Suyá who enact these new logics and principles within arenas of exchange that have increasingly involved recourse to numbers.

The Kayabi, Suyá, and Juruna who live near or work at the Diauarum Post are inevitably tied to a world of figures. Guarding the reservation against invaders and claiming the possession of traditional land requires understanding such map features as scale and area. Operating the radiophone twice daily involves buying gasoline to generate energy for its battery, charging the battery a certain number of hours, turning the radio on at the correct time, and filling out details such as the radiogram number, the number of words, and the transmission time. Operating the local pharmacy or understanding how to take prescribed medication for malaria, tuberculosis, or influenza all involve buying medicine, paying health professionals, scheduling patient visits, and prescribing, measuring, and ingesting specific quantities of medicine. Indians employed by FUNAI as nurses, boat pilots, truck drivers, and accountants must handle their paychecks and checkbooks. Money management is also a constant concern for those who sell and buy goods to and from outsiders.

FUNAI officials who occasionally visit the park usually lecture on the Indians' customs to their employees or guests. These speeches are also invariably punctuated by figures: how much money the federal agency has spent to keep the Indians alive and well ("privileged people, when compared to non-Indians"), birth and death rates ("they're not doing so bad, after all"), the park's area ("too much land for so few Indians"), and so on.

> You tell us in school what mathematics is good for and how it works, but I will tell you what it is not good for. Don't try to learn our patterns of weaving using numbers; don't try to ask me exactly how much tree bark ashes you should mix in the clay for pottery. These are things that don't ask for numbers, and that's why you are so confused. (Nunu Juruna, author's weaving and pottery teacher, February 1983)

That we have turned our lives into an "arithmetic problem" (Simmel 1968, 1987) is no news at all. What it means to impose a numerical culture upon peoples who did not orient themselves extensively by means of numerical calculation until recently is a question that has seldom been posed. Making sense out of a numerical world reaches far beyond the exclusive relations among its arithmetical elements: it means more than understanding standard systematizations of quantitative relations. As Lave (1988:120) points out, "in practice, relations among arithmetic elements and other kinds of concerns in the world are often equal to, or more important than, the arithmetic relations among those same elements, and relations of quantity are merged (or submerged) into ongoing activity." Identifying these concerns is critical to understanding how arithmetic unfolds in action within different settings and, in this particular case, in a cross-cultural situation.

> Knowing a little mathematics has made our lives easier. . . . To tell you the truth, numbers don't scare me anymore. What goes on behind numbers, what the white men actually think, is more important than adding or subtracting. (Aturi Kayabi, a former teacher at the Diauarum School, June 1990)

Different worldviews—the socially constituted world and its cosmological foundations—and the everyday experience of active individuals account for the diversity of strategies of mathematical reasoning. In other words, different cultures, and individuals within any given culture, proceed differently in their logical schemes in the way they manage quantities and, consequently, numbers, geometrical shapes and relations, measurements, classifications, and so forth (D'Ambrosio 1990:17). This is exactly what Aturi Kayabi meant by "what goes on behind numbers"; that is, "what the white men actually think" makes all the difference when it comes to managing quantities—how much land and money the Indians are entitled to or "deserve," for example.

CAXIRI: THE OBLIGATION TO GIVE, TO RECEIVE, AND TO RECIPROCATE

The Juruna proceed downriver back to their home village, carrying in dugout canoes the bamboo arrows they have just exchanged for pottery. They are greeted by Suyá and Kayabi guests who have been invited for the *caxiri*[5] ceremony by Chief Carandine

Juruna and his wife. The alcoholic beverage of manioc, sweet potato, and corn has been fermenting for days in specially carved canoes. As the Juruna women lift the straw mats to show their guests how generous their offering is, the sweet and sour odor that emanates from the thick foamy drink arouses passionate emotions among both hosts and guests. While the Juruna women tie their guests' hammocks to wooden poles in the central plaza, I ask them whether the Kayapó who live down river are also coming:

> Not this time. We've already had the Kayapó and the Panara over for a huge *caxiri*. This feast is for the Kayabi and Suyá, who have recently given us arrows, fish, beads, cotton and invited us to their ceremonies. We know the Kayabi harvested lots of peanuts this year, and some of our young men have been courting Suyá girls lately. (Nunu Juruna, January 1982, my translation)

Caxiri, in the Xingu Park, is a gift. As an object of exchange, the *caxiri* (both the ceremony and the beverage itself) carries with it the obligation to give, to receive, and to reciprocate. It is an economic commodity that circulates among the Juruna as well as between the Juruna and other Xingu tribes, receiving its meanings from the responses (or countergifts) it triggers—in this case, peanuts and young girls. *Caxiri* is also, however, a vehicle and instrument "for realities of another order, such as power, influence, sympathy, status, and emotion," embodied in the skillful game of exchange (Lévi-Strauss 1969[1949]:53). These realities are the essence of the *caxiri* as "symbolic capital . . . *the most valuable form of accumulation*" (Bourdieu 1991[1972]:179).

As part of their system of reciprocity—of their gift exchange—the Juruna believe that to refuse to invite, just as to refuse to accept whatever they are offered by other peoples in the area, is to reject highly praised alliance ties in the Xingu Park. The obligation to give food to visitors, like the visitors' obligation to accept it and to reciprocate the offering, is a rule among the Juruna (Lima 1986:46; Oliveira 1969:69–70). The production and circulation of *caxiri* reflect the "basic principles of sociability" of this tribe, to the members of which "social inebriation" is the core of adult life. Being inebriated thus implies "the consumption and retribution of a gift" (Lima 1986:18, my translation). In Mauss's words the *caxiri* is a "total system of giving" through which

> collectivities impose obligations of exchange and contract upon each other. . . . What they exchange is not solely property and wealth, movable and immovable goods, and things economically useful. In particular, such exchanges are acts of politeness: banquets, rituals, military services, women, children, dances, festivals, and fairs, in which the economic transaction is only one element, and in which the passing on of wealth is only one feature of a much more general and enduring contract.[6] (Mauss 1990[1950]:51)

As I pass on the gourd of *caxiri* to a Juruna elder, I ask him if the Juruna have always been so polite and generous toward their neighbors:

> Oh no, no! We used to invite the Kayapó to drink with us, and when they were really drunk we'd kill them! We did that to other Indians, too. Sometimes we wanted their women or children; sometimes we were interested in something else. So we'd ask them over for a *caxiri*. But now that we live all together in this park, we have to get along, to be friends. (Axin xin Juruna, January 1982)

The gift exchange is not "disinterested" or purely "symbolic" (that is, devoid of any material or concrete effect). Although the circulation of *caxiri* cannot be measured by the yardstick of monetary profit, its symbolic interests "never cease to conform to economic calculations even when it gives every appearance of disinterestedness by departing from the logic of interested calculation (in the narrow sense) and playing for stakes that are non-material and not easily quantifiable" (Bourdieu 1991[1972]:177).

The Suyá and Kayabi gift exchanges often involve the circulation of food among neighboring populations. Among the Suyá the circulation of "goods and resources, where the goods may be intangibles and the resources symbolic" (Seeger 1981:181), is usually undertaken by the *meropakande* (a village controller), who is primarily known for a fairness that transcends his kinship ties. Food is never stored or put away; it must circulate. Suyá ceremonies are thus characterized by the frequent public distributions of food in the central village plaza (Seeger 1987:13).

Norms for the circulation of food among Kayabi villages are described by Travassos (1984:45–49) as part of a broader system that involves local Kayabi villages, other Xingu tribes, and outsiders. Every household offers each visitor entering a Kayabi village a gourd full of fermented beverage, "one of the main symbols of hospitality. . . . The beverage is carried in huge pots which are lent to the visitors; the host later uses the return of the pot as an excuse to return the initial visit." Within a newly formed social arena where alliances among the different tribes are more valued than former hostilities, "even the Kayapó-Metuktire" are now included in the ceremonial gift-exchanges of the Kayabi, as are Upper Xingu peoples whose sorcerers are feared and to whom "one cannot deny anything because sorcerers are revengeful and powerful" (Travassos 1984:49).

These intertribal alliances also place Xingu populations within the Brazilian Indian Movement, the latest accomplishments of which include the establishment of constitutional rights to education in both Portuguese and in native languages and the possession of traditional indigenous territories.

BANG-BANG: CAPITALISM, CALCULUS, AND CASTLES OF DREAMS

Antonio returns to the Diauarum Indian Post the following day in his motorboat, boasting about his most recent acquisitions: a blond mistress, a rifle, three head of cattle, and five bottles of whiskey. After rehearsing his speech on "what a waste of time it is for a person with [my] looks and education to spend such precious years of [my] life trying to teach savages how to count," Antonio tells me his plans for the future:

> Unlike you, I make good money here.[7] . . . I bought a farm nearby where I have 65 head of cattle. I am getting rich, rich! That's why I can tolerate these goddamn Indians, the mosquitoes, the filth. . . . I just need a few more years until I retire, and that'll be it. I'll have enough money for yet another farm, more cattle, and I've just heard there are mining lots for sale at the *Castelo dos Sonhos* [Castle of Dreams]. (January 1982)[8]

While the Juruna, Kayabi, and Suyá feasted at the Tuba-Tuba village, Antonio enjoyed himself at a Saturday night *baile* ("ball") in Bang-Bang,[9] a small town located near the eastern border of the Xingu Park. He was joined by gold prospectors, loggers, and cattle ranchers who came from nearby settlements to renew their supplies of industrial goods such as ammunition, alcoholic beverages, canned food, and medication against malaria. At the local nightclub, women were also for sale. They were displayed on stage one by one, their price set according to the number of teeth they still possessed.[10] Slavery, an antiquated mode of production, still prevails in this town that is literally named after the common practice of killing local Indians: "Shoot 'em up."

Bang-Bang's inhabitants are shocked that the natives seem content with producing what is strictly necessary for their own consumption. They constantly invoke images of Indian indolence and incapacity to work hard. As the owner of a local store told me in March 1990:

> The Kayabi don't want to become my partners. . . . They'd raise the cattle [on the reservation] and I'd sell the meat, we could all become millionaires! But they say

there's a lot of game on their land, that hunting and fishing is enough. I know they're just too lazy to do anything else besides sleeping in hammocks and messing around with their women all day.

Systematic exploitation characterizes the relationship between most merchants and Indians in Bang-Bang. Goods (such as sugar, coffee, soap, fishing equipment, clothing items) are always overpriced. No matter how much merchandise the Juruna, Kayabi, and Suyá bring into the stores to be exchanged, a 30 percent monthly inflation rate during the 1980s plus interest sent debts skyrocketing. Here is Ipó Kayabi:

> I had to give almost half the bananas I planted this year to pay my debts at Tonhaä's. That is, to pay for 3 kilos of salt, 2 kilos of sugar, a pair of boots, 10 medium-size fishing hooks and 4 large batteries for my flashlight which I bought 4 months ago, I had to give him 240 dozen bananas. He had originally asked for 30 dozen, but he said the inflation was very high so I had to pay him more. (May 1983)

Exact calculations, that is, mathematics—and a very specific form of mathematics—became an important structuring resource for the rise of the industrial civilization. As several scholars have pointed out,[11] the modern Western form of capitalism is dependent on science, especially on mathematics. This is, however, a dialectical process, since "the development of these sciences and of the technology resting upon them now receives important stimulus from these capitalistic interests in its practical economic applications" (Weber 1983[1904]:28). Modern mathematics has therefore developed a strong tie to the capitalistic enterprise, which positions the discipline as the promoter of a certain model of power through knowledge (D'Ambrosio 1990:24).

The capitalist need for a calculable legal system has equated calculation with "rational" thinking, and the progress of such "rationality," based on the pursuit of forever renewed profit, has shaped mathematical concepts (D'Ambrosio 1990:28; Lave 1988:125; Weber 1983[1904]:28). Thus the social, economic, and political meanings of modern mathematics determine that to buy, borrow, inherit, earn, receive, accept, or even steal implies surplus or gain. On the other hand, to sell, lend, donate, pay, give, or deliver indicates deprivation or loss. Translated into arithmetical operations in problem-solving activities, the concepts of surplus or gain are structuring resources that call for addition or multiplication, whereas deprivation and loss require subtraction or division.

We shall now examine how mathematical concepts were shaped at the Diauarum School during problem-solving activities. I begin with Tarinu Juruna's explanation to his classmates of the dilemma with which he was faced when negotiating the price for the arrows Antonio wanted to buy.

THE DIAUARUM INDIAN SCHOOL: MATH IN PRACTICE

Tarinu Juruna, son of chief Carandine, has just returned to Diauarum after the two-day stay at his home village for the *caxiri* ceremony. He is one of the 13 Juruna living at the Diauarum Indian Post in order to attend the recently founded Diauarum School,[12] the first school to operate in the Lower Xingu. Tarinu stated his main goal as a student at the Diauarum School on the very day the school was inaugurated: "I want to learn mathematics so that the white man cannot deceive us with numbers anymore."[13]

Tarinu starts his presentation with Antonio's unfortunate remark that "Indians are too stupid to learn math." His updated ($7 \times 5 = 0$, rather than $7 \times 5 = 125$) explanation of the arithmetical dilemma exemplifies the articulation of structuring resources in everyday mathematical activities. On the school's blackboard Tarinu demonstrated how he had articulately resorted to school-learned algorithms, principles of reciprocity, and aspects of the capitalist economic action:

7 arrows at 5.00 each = 0

7	6	18.00	35.00	125.00
x 5	x 12		72.00	−125.00
35.00	72.00		+18.00	0
			125.00	

Tarinu then verbally explained the reasoning behind his calculations:

> Antonio wanted to buy 20 arrows, but we would only sell him 7, since we need arrows to hunt and fish with and he doesn't. Antonio wants to make more money, selling arrows to white men in Brasília. We know that he sells arrows for much more than he buys them from us, so instead of selling them for 2 cruzeiros, we wanted to sell them for 5 cruzeiros each. So that would be 7 times 5 equals 35. But Antonio owes us money for the 6 clay pans he bought last month and didn't pay us for. That's 12 for each pan; so 6 times 12 equals 72. He also owes us 18 cruzeiros for the deer we killed for him last week, which he feasted on for days. That is, 35 plus 72 plus 18 equals 125. But Antonio did not accept the price, since he is a greedy and selfish man who only thinks about getting rich on our backs. So he didn't pay us the 125. That is, 125 minus 125 equals 0. (February 1982)

"What did Antonio want to pay?" asked Tarinu's classmates. "He wanted to buy 20 arrows for 40 cruzeiros, that is, 2 cruzeiros per arrow. I told him that only 7 arrows were for sale, so he wanted to give me 14," answered Tarinu. "Why only 2 cruzeiros per arrow?" they inquired. "Well," said Tarinu, "he thinks he could buy them cheap because he's had so many malarias, and because he's pacified lots of Indians in his life, the kind of story whites like to tell.[14] But I know that what he really wants is to make money."

When figuring out how much Antonio should pay for the arrows he had requested, Tarinu was confronted with the transformation of symbolic into material capital. In other words, Tarinu needed to convert the arrows' value into monetary form (Marx 1978[1867]:313). He articulated not only features of the Juruna system of gift exchange, but also aspects of the capitalist mode of exchange. In the total price Tarinu included structuring resources inherent to both systems: Antonio's previous debts to the Juruna (the obligation to reciprocate gifts) and a considerable amount of interest—the goods would be resold (according to the principle of the expansion of value, an objective basis of money circulation, as Marx argued 1978[1867]:324).

Arrows also served as a vehicle for expressing the Juruna's antipathy toward the whites' greediness and selfishness and as a means to reinforce the Indians' power in a decision-making process that involved money. These are symbolic features that transcend the purely economic aspect of the transaction and indicate that different categories of "value" are at stake. People's social relationships also give structure to their mathematical activities, as does their political interaction.

Antonio was infuriated by Tarinu's exorbitant price, basically because it would interfere with his profitable business of selling Indian art craft. It would reduce the surplus value of the arrows—that is, the increment over their original value—that would constitute his profit. Antonio structured the same arithmetical dilemma according to his own interests, which were based on the circulation of money as capital. The process of buying arrows to resell them for a higher price characterizes Antonio as a capitalist, and this "expansion of value" was his subjective aim (Marx 1978[1867]:332–334). In arguing against Tarinu's solution, however, Antonio accused the Indians of being incapable of learning mathematics, a common and useful explanation that reduces the specificity of arithmetical practice to conventionally structured relations among problems.

The specificity of Antonio's and Tarinu's arguments cannot be reduced to the "contingencies" of modern accounting procedures, according to which different methods of accounting depend on chance or uncertain events of some kind while mathematics is believed to be the universal that allows for standard bookkeeping variation. Nor can the complexity of this arithmetical dilemma be explained by Antonio's or Tarinu's alleged arithmetical incapacity or confusion. Antonio probably knew he owed the Juruna money and that this previous debt was somehow being taken into account. Tarinu, on the other hand, was aware that the employee had figured out the arrows' value from the perspective of his desire for profit.

Furthermore, the transformation of the value of commodities (such as arrows) into monetary form does not necessarily transform a reciprocal system of exchange into one geared exclusively toward the accumulation of material wealth. No doubt money as an abstraction is, as Trompf has shown for Papua New Guinea, "capable of being divinized and mythologized, on the one hand, and held up as the supreme symbol of secularity and this-worldly success, on the other" (1994:410). In the Xingu Park, however, it similarly happens that, "in the heat of the newer business transactions of a supra-local and largely urban kind, money becomes quickly detached into a mundane or profane sphere of its own" (1994:410). Exchanges of industrial goods in the Xingu Park have increasingly been monetarized, while ceremonial gift exchanges among different tribes are less likely to entail presentations of money.

It is thus of fundamental importance to distinguish between reciprocity and the circulation of money in capitalist societies. As Crump sees it:

> Reciprocity is the principle upon which the circulation of money is based. Its general meaning is that for every benefit conferred by one person upon another, something must eventually be given in return. In the context of money, either the original or the return benefit must take the form of a payment. . . . This may add up to no more than an established pattern of gift-giving, for as Mauss (1968:194) demonstrated in his classic study, the acceptance—in any traditional society—of any gift, automatically implies the acceptance of any number of well recognized social obligations which go with it. (1992[1990]:96)

Let us look, finally, at another example involving money in which reciprocal and capitalist structuring resources were articulated. In May 1982 Paiê Kayabi, a student at the Diauarum School, published his report of a trip to Bang-Bang in the local Indian newspaper *Memória do Xingu*:

> On [May] 15 I joined Canísio [Kayabi] downriver because he wanted to buy 80 liters of gasoline. He took 108 bunches of bananas to sell in Bang-Bang. He sold each one for 500. He was only able to sell 50 [bunches of bananas]. It came out to 25,000, and the rest he sold for 200 each. He was only able to sell 30 bunches of bananas. He received another 6,000. Total money was 31,000. The rest of the bananas he gave to the white men. (as cited in Ferreira 1994b:31, my translation)

Paiê articulates the dilemma and its solution both simultaneously and dialectically. The data involving the banana sale are worked out mathematically and the answers to each subproblem are presented at particular points during the narrative. The intent to buy gasoline contextualizes the situation in which the bananas were sold, but it is not presented as a dilemma that requires a solution. The gift of the remaining bananas to non-Indians can be interpreted according to the Kayabi system of food distribution. The basic principles of such a generous system oblige people to give food and to embarrass those who ask for it (Travassos 1984:56–62). In this sense there are no "rests"; the Kayabi do not neglect the remains of a transaction as mathematics pejoratively does, because such remains do not represent loss or something that should have been "profitable" but was not. In this case, the notion of what constitutes an arithmetical "problem" is intrinsically tied to the economy of a basically egalitarian society (Ferreira 1994b:31). Nevertheless, Paiê also resorted to notions of capitalist exchange in the processes of generating and solving the (arithmetical) dilemma.

THE DIAUARUM SCHOOL: IS GIVING ALWAYS A MINUS?

As the day breaks, Tarinu Juruna bathes in the Xingu River with other Juruna, Suyá, and Kayabi who study at the Diauarum School. The temperature is still cool, and the water feels warm to those who have spent the night in hammocks slung across the beams of the post's thatched-roof houses. At 7:00 A.M. everyone is already at work, tending gardens, grating manioc roots, sharpening arrowheads, or setting up the school's activity grounds. Not all the didactic programs are held indoors. Some involve trips to nearby villages in order to interview elders for the journal *Memória do Xingu* or to collect information on housebuilding and other activities.

Wenhoron Suyá tells us that a *timbó* fishing expedition[15] is taking place near the Suyá village. He invites Tarinu and several other fellow students to visit the site. The group departs immediately, taking plenty of arrows, spears, baskets, and food for the day in their canoes. The students also carry writing materials with them in order to record whatever aspect of the fishing expedition they later want to share in school.

At the end of the day the people who remained at the post shout with pleasure at the sight of the loaded canoes coming ashore. The trip has been a success. Fish is distributed by the Suyá to all who have come to the port. The circulation of food is a necessary requirement of their gift-exchange system, as we have seen. The fish racks in each house, including my own, are now loaded, and the smell of fish being smoked attracts those who have hitherto been unaware of these events back to their homes.

On the following day Wenhoron Suyá presented figures he collected during the expedition to his classmates. He had counted the fish carefully ("total = 323; 57 big, 98 medium and 168 small"). On the basis of the information that he and his friends had brought to school, several arithmetic dilemmas were created in order to practice sign operations (addition, subtraction, division, and multiplication). The choice of which sign operation to use—plus or minus, multiplication or division—challenged most students, to my initial surprise:

> I know you want me to use the minus sign here instead of the plus sign, but I don't understand why. Does giving away always mean minus for you guys? (Wenhoron Suyá, March 1982)

The first dilemma we dealt with was:

> I caught 10 fish last night and gave 3 of them to my brother. How many fish do I have now?

When we decide which operation to use, the fact of having given the fish away determines, according to our utilitarian and "rational" thinking, that I will be subtracting 3 from 10; the supposedly correct and logical answer is 7. The answer at which Tarinu Juruna arrived, however, was different: "I ended up with 13 fish," he wrote, and explained his reasoning:

> I ended up with 13 fish since, whenever I give my brother anything, he pays me twice as much back. Therefore, 3 + 3 = 6 [what his brother would pay him back]; 10 + 6 = 16; and 16 – 3 = 13 [the total amount of fish minus the 3 that were originally given away].

Robtokti Suyá also came up with "13" as an answer to the same arithmetical dilemma, although he had calculated it in a slightly different way:

> I gave 3 fish to my brother, so that is 10 + 3 = 13.

When I argued that having given the fish away meant that he would have less fish than before, Robtokti replied:

> When the Suyá give something to somebody, it doesn't mean we are going to have less of it. When I give my brother fish, he always pays me back. So if I have 10 and give him 3, he will give me more fish when he goes fishing. So that is 10 + 3, and not 10 − 3.

The explanations provided by the Juruna, Kayabi, and Suyá for such divergent solutions gradually made it clear that it was not a question of "cognitive incapacity," the explanation commonly invoked by mathematics teachers on Indian reservations, but rather that principles of reciprocity were structuring the arithmetical reasoning.

"Giving" fish to one's kin does not mean being deprived of such goods, since the recipient is necessarily obliged to reciprocate. The specified ways through which the gifts will be returned, however, depend on previous debts, kinship relations, personal emotions, and other symbolic, interpersonal, and economic associations between the giver and the recipient. Such associations provide structuring resources for the arithmetical strategies that are performed, and the proportional articulation of such resources accounts for the variety of responses to a single "problem." Let us look at how similar structuring resources were differently articulated by two Juruna teenagers when solving the same dilemma (cited in Ferreira 1994b:35–37):

> I received 10 fishing arrows from the Kayabi. I lost one in the river and gave 3 to my brother-in-law. How many arrows do I have now?

This is how Tarupi Juruna structured his arithmetic strategy:

$$
\begin{array}{cccc}
10 & 13 & 12 & 2 \\
\underline{+\ 3} & \underline{-\ 1} & \underline{-10} & \underline{+7} \\
13 & 12 & 2 & 9
\end{array}
$$

Answer: I have 9 arrows now.

The result would be considered incorrect—a "mistake," which could be tested and shown to be wrong according to a particular set of presuppositions—if we did not interpret it according to the Juruna system of gift exchange and through Tarupi's interpersonal relations with his kin and with the Kayabi:

> My brother-in-law will pay me the 3 arrows back. If the Kayabi gave me 10 arrows, I will then have 13. Then I will subtract the 1 I lost, so 12 remain. But since I will pay the Kayabi 10 arrows back, 2 will remain. These 2 arrows, plus the 7 I already have at home, make 9 arrows.

A different result was reached by Lavuciá Juruna when solving the same dilemma:

$$
\begin{array}{cccc}
10 & 19 & 25 & 24 \\
\underline{+\ 9} & \underline{+\ 6} & \underline{-\ 1} & \underline{-\ 3} \\
19 & 25 & 24 & 21
\end{array}
$$

Now I have 21 arrows because I already had 9, so that is 10 + 9 = 19. My brother-in-law will pay me back the 3 I gave him plus 3 he already owed me. That is 19 + 6 = 25. Since I lost 1 arrow in the river, now I have 24. But my father-in-law had given me 3 arrows, so that is 24 − 3 = 21.

That the specificity of arithmetical practice varies according to particular situations has several implications. Most important, the allegedly eternal verities of mathematics[16] are shown to be socially construed. Gift exchange carries with it connotations that shape mathematical concepts. The reverse, however, can also be true. Standard forms of material capital (such as systems of currency and of measurement) and algorithmic arithmetic "carry meaning and values *as such*, and these too are subjectively experienced" (Lave 1988:124). This reversibility is precisely what characterizes the dialectical movement between symbolic and material capital. According to Bourdieu, "the exchange of gifts, words, challenges, or even women must allow for the fact that each of these inaugural acts may misfire, and that it receives its meaning, in any case, from the response it triggers off, even if the response is a failure to reply that retrospectively removes its intended meaning." (1991[1972]:5)}

GIFTS, CURVES, AND MACAW FEATHERS

To say that "'mathematics' is the product of social work and symbolic fashioning" (Lave 1988:126) means that it stems from human constructions and creates new concepts (Piaget 1952, as cited in Piatelli-Palmarini 1980, as cited in Crump 1992[1990]:28). It also means that "there is not one universal grammar of number" (Chomsky 1980, as cited in Crump 1992[l990]:28). In order to assert what these grammars, understandings, and concepts are, our gaze should be directed to the discrepancies between experience and incorrigible beliefs that can render intelligible what happens when $1 + 1 \neq 2$—the so-called "mistakes" (Pollner 1974, as cited in Lave 1988:126). In other words, looking at discrepancies and discontinuities within arithmetical practices and in situations that require mathematical reasoning would allow us to understand not only why central Brazilian Indians are challenged (and sometimes threatened) by "mathematics," but also why "nearly half of the adults in the U.S. can't handle arithmetic" (Celis 1993). It would thereby also effectively demolish the charge of illiteracy.

Certain forms of credit or gifts, whether material or symbolic, have determined the fate of indigenous populations in Brazil. The Yanomami have been cast aside as "primitive" rather than "modern" individuals because they "do not even know how to count" (*O Estado de São Paulo* 1993). This "lack of numeracy" has been used to impede the Yanomami from participating in decision-making processes regarding the size of their officially demarcated territory, health-care solutions, schooling, and so on (CCPY 1989). Being "primitive" is, according to the common sense of rationalism, tantamount to being less than human and therefore justifiably liable to extermination by numerically "advanced" and "complex" societies.

Such a canonical understanding of mathematics denies individuals the opportunity to engage in and control qualitative decision-making processes that involve arithmetic, reasserting the common belief that numbers "control the wills of those who make use of them" (Crump 1992[1990]:13). By labeling different options or answers as "failures," such an approach reduces individuals to objects, and the variety of ways of constituting and solving arithmetical problems that exist in the world is relegated to a secondary level that is then used to validate genetic or racial determinisms.

Aturi Kayabi, the former teacher of the Diauarum Indian School, evaluates the mathematical knowledge and experience he has accumulated both in his home village in the state of Pará and in the Xingu Indian Park:

> I've learned that there are different ways of making mathematics. When I go to Bang-Bang, Brasília, or São Paulo, I know I have to think the way you guys do. So then when I spend my money, give it to somebody else, I know I am not going to get it back. So I use a minus. When, on the other hand, I am figuring out how many macaw feathers I should give my father-in-law I don't think the same way. Sometimes, however, I think both ways. So I've learned that there are different mathematics, different ways of working with numbers. (June 1990)

***

I dedicate this piece to the memory of my father, Professor Jorge Leal Ferreira, who devoted his life to the study of mathematics and physics. To my colleagues in the Diauarum Indian School—

the Kayabi, Suyá, Juruna, and Panara, and especially to Nunu Juruna, my weaving teacher in the Xingu Park—I owe my first insights into cross-cultural values and symbolic properties of mathematics. I am especially indebted to Adriana Petryna for her critical reading of the manuscript. Ivo Patarra, Carlos Leal Ferreira, João Biehl, and Leba Morimoto also contributed with valuable suggestions. This research was funded by grants provided by the Brazilian agencies CNPq, FAPESP, and FORD-ANPOCS.

***

Notes

[1] The *cruzeiro*, the monetary unit of Brazil at the time, was replaced by the *real* in July 1994.

[2] FUNAI expeditions to contact "isolated" Indians are still called pacification fronts. The image of pacification derives both from the fact that Portuguese colonizers called Indians beasts and pagans (i.e., creatures needing pacification [Perrone-Moisés 1992]) and from the natives' resistance to such "civilizing" attempts. The term *animal taming* was also used by non-Indians to describe pacification well into this century (Nimuendaju 1952:432, as cited in Oliveira 1969:47). In Brazil there are today approximately 75 Indian tribes living in isolation from the broader Brazilian Society (FUNAI n.d.)—that is, as yet not "pacified" or "contacted." "Pacified" Indians are usually hired by FUNAI to serve as potential translators when approaching the group to be contacted and as jungle guides, cargo haulers, and providers of firewood, drinking water, and game. The Juruna, for example, participated in the pacification of the Suyá in 1958 (Ferreira 1994a:38–40), the Kayapó-Metuktire in that of the Panara (Ferreira 1994a:216–217), and the Kayabi in that of the Arara (Ferreira 1994a:111–117).

[3] The documented history of the Xingu populations dates back to the late 1800s, when the German explorer Karl von den Steinen described his exploratory expedition to central Brazil (Steinen 1942). The southernmost area of the park—Upper Xingu—is inhabited by communities (such as the Kuikuru and Yawalapiti) that have occupied the area for at least 400 years (Franchetto 1992:341). The northern section of the park—Lower Xingu—was increasingly populated, from the mid-1800s on, by tribes (Juruna and Suyá, among others) seeking refuge from Portuguese settlers and missionaries, fur traders, gold prospectors, and rubber tappers. Waterfalls and rapids along the Xingu River made the area—later a reservation—inaccessible to the so-called civilizing fronts of northern Brazil. Other groups (Panara, Kayabi, and Tapayuna) were brought in as of the mid-1950s, as mentioned above.

[4] In 1980, for instance, several Xingu peoples joined together to kill 11 *peões* (individuals working off indebtedness, or peons) who were logging inside the park (Ferreira 1994a:202–204). The Xingu War, enacted against FUNAI in 1984, is also a clear example of how hostilities among peoples of the Xingu Park gave way to intertribal alliances that eventually came to cede the indigenous societies' right to self-determination and respect for their constitutional rights (Lea and Ferreira 1984).

[5] *Caxiri is* a word in Portuguese for a variety of fermented alcoholic beverages. It has been adopted by Xingu tribes to refer to most alcoholic beverages. The term in Juruna for the fermented drink is *yacuha*.

[6] The system of gift exchange has also been described in detail by ethnographers such as de Coppet (1968, 1970), Malinowski (1964[1922]), and Trompf (1994) in Melanesian societies; by Evans-Pritchard (1940, 1951) among the Nuer of Sudan; and by Boas (1925) among the North American Kwakiutl.

[7] At the time FUNAI paid teachers on Indian reservations the minimum salary, which was equivalent to U.S.\$60 per month. (In June 1995 the minimum salary—and thus the teacher's wage—was raised to U.S.\$100 per month.) Antonio, on the other hand, was hired by FUNAI as a so-called coordinator of pacification fronts, that is, as a supervisor of expeditions carried out to contact isolated Indians. At the time his salary was approximately 30 times the minimum salary; this is a considerable income in a country where 16 percent of the working population (62 million total) earn less than the minimum salary per month and is especially high for someone who dropped out of school in fourth grade.

[8] *Castelo dos Sonhos* is a well-known prospecting site in northern Mato Grosso, near the western border of the Xingu Park. The site is divided into individually owned lots. Prospectors use the BR-080 road that cuts the Xingu Park from east to west, just north the Diauarum Post, to go to Bang-Bang.

[9] The official name of Bang-Bang is São José do Xingu. It is not called by that name, however, either by its inhabitants or by outsiders.

[10] See Dimenstein 1992 for a detailed account of the traffic of women in northern and central Brazil in the late 1980s. I have witnessed one of these sales in Bang-Bang in March 1990, when a woman with all her teeth was sold to a goldminer for U.S.\$40.

[11] See, for example, D'Ambrosio 1990:28, Lave 1988:125, Tambiah 1991[1990]:18, and Weber 1983[1904]:28–29.

[12] In 1981 the Diauarum Indian School was founded in the Diauarum Indian Post by the Juruna, Kayabi, Suyá, and Panara populations of the Xingu Indian Park. I was invited by leaders Carandine Juruna, Mairawê Kayabi, and Kuiussi Suyá in April 1980 to help establish the Diauarum School, after having worked in 1978–79 as a schoolteacher among the Xavante of the Kuluene Indian Area, also located in central Brazil (Ferreira 1981). This research is thus based on my experience in the Xingu Indian Park from 1980 to 1984 (with a six-month interruption in 1983 to help set up the Xikrin-Kayapó Indian School in northern Brazil) and on two short visits to the park in February-March and June-July 1990.

[13] All new students were asked to state their reasons for attending the Diauarum School. Of the approximately 300 students who attended the school between 1980 and 1984, 84 percent cited mathematics (although they spoke no Portuguese) as the main reason for their studies. Others (15 percent) stated the need to learn Portuguese as the main reason (Ferreira 1992).

[14] The number of malarial attacks one has suffered, and the number of "wild Indians one has pacified" are sometimes used by FUNAI employees to present themselves as "old-timers" in the Indian "business." The killing of Indians, a valued performance during the colonial period, has still persisted well into this century. See, for example, descriptions of the massacre of the Juruna Indians by rubber tappers in 1915 (Oliveira 1969:46–47) and of the recent Yanomami massacres (CCPY 1989).

[15] During the dry season (June-October), when the waters are low, fish get trapped in small lakes and ponds, which form near the river beds. Several Xingu tribes thus engage in fishing sprees in which a natural fish poison (*timbó*) is used to numb fish, making it easy to spear or collect them in baskets.

[16] Gardner (1992) reminds us of the historical changes and developments mathematics has undergone. Babylonians, for instance, saw it as a means of astronomical reckoning, while for the Pythagoreans "it was thought of as an embodiment of the universe's harmonies." During the Renaissance scientists used it to uncover "nature's secrets." For Kant, "it was the perfect science whose propositions were constructed in the deepest layer of our rational faculties," while for Frege and Russell, "it became the paradigm of clarity against which ambiguities of ordinary language could be judged" (1992:165).

References

Adalberto, Príncipe da Prússia. 1977[1847]. *Brasil: Amazonas Xingu*. Belo Horizonte: Ed. Itatiaia.

Boas, Franz. 1925. Contributions to the Ethnology of the Kwakiutl. *Columbia University Contributions to Anthropology*, 3. New York: Columbia University Press.

Bourdieu, Pierre. 1991[1972]. *Outline of a Theory of Practice*. New York: Cambridge University Press.

Carraher, Terezinha, David W. Carraher, and Analucia D. Schliemann. 1991[1988]. *Na Vida Dez, na Escola Zero*. São Paulo: Cortez Editora.

CCPY (Comissão pela Criação do Parque Yanomami). 1989. *Roraima: O Aviso da Morte. Relatório da viagem feita pela Comitiva da "Ação pela Cidadania."* São Paulo: CCPY/CEDI/CNBB.

CEDI (Centro Ecumênico de Documentação e Informação). 1990. *Terras Indígenas no Brasil*. São Paulo: CEDI/PETI.

Celis, William III. 1993. Study Says Half of Adults in U.S. Can't Read or Handle Arithmetic. *New York Times*, September 9:A16.

Cole, Michael, John Gay, Joseph A. Glick, and Donald W. Sharp. 1971. *The Cultural Context of Learning and Thinking: An Exploration of Experimental Anthropology*. New York: Basic Books.

Crump, Thomas. 1992[1990]. *The Anthropology of Numbers*. Cambridge and London: Cambridge University Press.

D'Ambrosio, Ubiratan. 1990. *Etnomatemática*. São Paulo: Editora Ática.

de Coppet, Daniel. 1968. Pour une étude des échanges cérémoniels en Mélanésie. *L'Homme* 8(4):45–57.

———. 1970. Cycles des meurtres en cycles funéraires: esquisse de deux structures d'échange. In *Echanges et communcations. Mélanges offerts à Claude Lévi-Strauss à l'occasion de son 60éme anniversaire*. Jean Pouillon and Pierre Miranda (eds.). Pp. 759–781. The Hague: Mouton.

Dimenstein, Gilberto. 1992. *Meninas da Noite. A Prostituição de Meninas-Escravas no Brasil*. São Paulo: Editora Ática.

Evans-Pritchard, E. E. 1940. *The Nuer: A Description of the Modes of Livelihood and Political Institutions of a Nilotic People*. Oxford: Clarendon Press.

———. 1951. *Kinship and Marriage among the Nuer*. Oxford: Clarendon Press.

Ferreira, Mariana K. Leal. 1981. Uma Experiência de Educação para os Xavante. In *A Questão da Eclução Indígena*. Aracy Lopes da Silva (ed.). Pp. 64–87. São Paulo: Ed. Brasiliense.

———. 1992. Escrita e oralidade no Parque Indígena do Xingu: inserção na vida social e a percepção dos índios. *Revista de Antropologia* 35:91–112 São Paulo: Universidade de São Paulo.

———. 1994a. *Histórias do Xingu. Coletânea de depoimentos dos índios Suyá, Kayabi, Juruna, Trumai, Txucarramãe e Txicão*. São Paulo: Núcleo de História Indígena e do Indigenismo-USP/FAPESP.

———. 1994b. *Com quantos paus se faz uma canoa! A matemática na vida cotidiana e na experiência escolar indígena*. Brasília: Ministério da Educação e do Desporto.

Franchetto, Bruna. 1992. 'O aparecimento dos caraíba': para uma história kuikuro e alto-xinguana. In *História dos Indios no Brasil*. Manuela Carneiro da Cunha (ed.). Pp. 339–356. São Paulo: Companhia das Letras/Secretaria Municipal de Cultura/FAPESP.

FUNAI (National Indian Foundation in Brazil). n.d. Coordenadoria de Indios Isolados. Levantamento Provisório de Indios Isolados em Terrotório Nacional. Brasília: FUNAI. Unpublished manuscript.

Gardner, Howard. 1992. *Frames of Mind*. Princeton, NJ: Educational Testing Service.

King, A. Richard. 1967. *The School at Mopass: A Problem of Identity*. New York: Columbia University Press.

Lave, Jean. 1988. *Cognition in Practice*. Cambridge and London: Cambridge University Press.

Lea, Vanessa, and Mariana K. L. Ferreira. 1985. A guerra no Xingu: Cronologia. In *Povos Indígenas no Brasil/1984*. Carlos A. Ricardo (ed.). Pp. 246–258. São Paulo: CEDI.

Lévi-Strauss, Claude. 1950. *Sociologie et anthropologie: Precede d'un introduction à l'oeuvre de Marcel Mauss*. Paris: PUF.

———. 1969[1949]. The Principle of Reciprocity. In *The Elementary Structures of Kinship*. Rodney Needham (ed.). Pp. 52–68. Boston: Beacon Press.

Lima, Tânia. 1986. A Vida Social entre os Yudjá (Indios Juruna). Elementos de sua Ética Alimentar. M.A. dissertation. São Paulo: Universidade Estadual Paulista/UNESP.

Malinowski, Bronislaw. 1964[1922]. *Argonauts of the Western Pacific*. London: Routledge and Kegan Paul (Reprinted 1984 by Waveland Press, Prospect Heights, IL).

Marx, Karl. 1978[1867]. *The Marx-Engels Reader*, Robert C. Tucker (ed.). New York: W. W. Norton and Company.

Mauss, Marcel. 1990[1950]. *The Gift: The Form and Reason for Exchange in Archaic Societies*. New York and London: Norton.

O Estado de São Paulo. 1993. Índio não Mente. Clipping do Estadão. *Ano* 2:17.

Oliveira, Adélia E. 1969. Os Índios Juruna do Alto-Xingu. Ph.D. dissertation, Rio Claro, S.P.: Faculdade de Filosofia, Ciências e Letras de Rio Claro.

Perrone-Moisés, Beatriz. 1992. Índios livres e índios escravos: Os princípios da legislação indigenista do período colonial (séculos XVI a XVII). In *História dos Indios no Brasil*. Manuela Carneiro da Cunha (ed.). Pp. 115–132. São Paulo: Companhia das Letras/Secretaria Municipal de Cultura/FAPESP.

Piaget, Jean. 1952. *The Child's Conception of Number*. London: Routledge and Kegan Paul.

Seeger, Anthony. 1981. *Nature and Society in Central Brazil: The Suyá Indians of Mato Grosso*. Cambridge, MA: Harvard University Press.

———. 1987. *Why Suyá Sing: A Musical Anthropology of an Amazonian People*. New York: Cambridge University Press.

Simmel, Georg. 1968. *The Conflict in Modern Culture and Other Essays*. K. Peter Etzkorn, trans. New York: Teachers' College Press.

———. 1987. A metrópole e a vida mental. In *O Fenômeno Urbano*. Gilberto Velho (ed.). Rio de Janeiro: Editora Guanabara.

Steinen, Karl von den. 1942. *O Brasil Central*. São Paulo: Nacional.

Tambiah, Stanley J. 1991[1990]. *Magic, Science, Religion, and the Scope of Rationality*. Cambridge and New York: Cambridge University Press.

Travassos, Elizabeth. 1984. Xamanismo e Música entre os Kayabi. M.A. dissertation, Rio de Janeiro: Universidade Federal do Rio de Janeiro/Museu Nacional.

Trompf, Gary W. 1994. *Payback: The Logic of Retribution in Melanesian Religions*. New York: Cambridge University Press.

Weber, Max. 1983[1904]. *Max Weber on Capitalism, Bureaucracy and Religion: A Selection of Texts*. Stanislav Andreski (ed.). London: George Allen and Unwin.

Eric Canin teaches anthropology at California State University, Fullerton, and is studying millenial religious movements in the context of globalization. His first book will probably be Between Religion and Revolution: Grassroots Christian Communities and Social Change in Urban Nicaragua.

Roman Catholicism had long been viewed as a nearly universal and important aspect of the dominant cultures throughout most of Latin America. But Catholicism meant something very different there than it did elsewhere in the world. With Liberation Theology, serious rifts occurred among Catholics during the last quarter of the twentieth century, even before Protestantism began to spread rapidly.

Canin describes some of those changes and what they mean through a case study, contrasting "popular" or "revolutionary" Catholicism with "formal" or "official" Catholicism in post-revolutionary Nicaragua. This is reminiscent of what Redfield called "the great tradition" and "the little tradition."

On the importance of a patron saint and of hierarchy, compare Foster (chapter 31); for other aspects of folk Catholicism, see Brandes (chapter 29). Other popular movements are discussed in Stavenhagen (chapter 13) and Collier (chapter 17); grassroots outcomes of rapid social change are also important in Heath (chapter 19) and Doughty (chapter 22).

Mingüito, Managua's Little Saint
Christian Base Communities and
Popular Religion in Nicaragua
Eric Canin

Myths appear as timeless stories, their mythic power and lessons seeming to apply to the present as they did to the past. Similarly, rituals appear as ever-repetitive actions, reassuring us that stability exists at the core of our changing lives and the external world. But do these appearances point to a central core of meaning at the heart of myth and ritual, or are they managed by a power system in an effort to instill "faith" in that very system; does religion arise from truth or power? I cannot resolve this question but will help you look closely at a ritual, a saint's festival, and the myth of how it originated, in historical context. The Santo Domingo fiesta is a ritual of rebellion against the social order in general, but I intend to show its relation to actual rebellion against the social order of the Sandinista Revolution. In turn, I intend to show how various dominant political and religious actors have attempted to control and use the ritual for their own ends, and how participants in the fiesta have resisted those attempts at appropriation.

From the 1979 revolution that overthrew the dictatorship of Anastacio Somoza to the present, Nicaragua has been undergoing profound change. Such change has not been unidirectional, as the fortunes of the poor have deteriorated after a brief improvement in the wake of the revolutionary triumph, and as political power has shifted from Sandinista socialism to Violeta Chamorro's neo-liberalism to Arnoldo Alemán's return, in tempered form, to strong-armed authoritarianism.

Amid these changes, the inhabitants of the capital city Managua, a vast majority of whom identify themselves as Catholics, look toward their religion as a source of solace, refuge, explanation, or social action. Unlike other revolutionary regimes inspired by Marxism, the Sandinista government during the 1980s did not seek to curtail popular religious expression despite incidents and tensions with the institu-

Written expressly for *Contemporary Cultures and Societies of Latin America*, Third Edition.

tional Catholic Church. Indeed, the Sandinistas not only tolerated religious worship, rituals and celebrations, they even promoted such events as an annual contest of altars dedicated to the Immaculate Conception of the Virgin Mary.

This apparent collaboration between religion and revolution derives partly from the fact that many Sandinistas regarded themselves as Christians, and three ministerial posts were even held by Catholic priests. Many Nicaraguans became revolutionaries through their participation in Christian base communities (*comunidades eclesiales de base,* CEBs). These small groups began in 1966 in response to the historic shift of the Catholic Church from support for the status quo to Liberation Theology's "option for the poor" and concern for social justice. They took up the call to promote social, political and economic development at the local level. During the insurrection that culminated in the 1979 revolution, several CEBs supported the political overthrow of the dictatorship and, during the 1980s, they participated in the reconstruction of Nicaraguan literacy, health, nutrition, and credit programs. CEBs, priests, religious institutes and foreign activists together make up the "Church of the Poor," an active and vocal movement within the Catholic Church. More than merely coordinating development efforts, that movement also has sought to forge participatory democracy within the hierarchical Catholic Church as well as to build a revolution where Christian ideals of community service, brotherhood, and faith would be central.

Christian base communities and the Church of the Poor have had to deal with a dilemma in their treatment of popular religion: to what extent are they an authentic expression of traditional culture, and to what extent are they the product of the old, paternalistic Church's attempt to control the faithful by focusing their attention away from poverty and suffering in this world and toward miracles and salvation in the next world? By focusing on the Santo Domingo fiesta, the attempt by the Church of the Poor to reinterpret the festival and its myth as "popular religion of liberation," and two incidents in which the saint was "stolen" (in 1961 and 1991), I hope to demonstrate that "truth" and "power" follow a popular logic that resists easy appropriation by religious or political structures.

THE FIESTA OF SANTO DOMINGO

Each year on August 1, tens of thousands of people accompany the diminutive statue of Santo Domingo on a procession from the Las Sierras Church on the outskirts of Managua to the Church of Santo Domingo in the capital's center. A core of several hundred people march and dance along the route to fulfill vows they made to the brown saint, affectionately called "Mingüito." They feel they are "paying" the saint for a miraculous cure or protection from illness. Dozens walk on their knees at the end of the journey into the church and up to the altar where the saint rests. These images of slow-moving masses of the faithful invoked for the poet Pablo Antonio Cuadra the dual, mestizo character of Nicaraguan processions in the pilgrimages of the Spanish to saints' shrines and of Indians to volcano gods, prompting him to declare that "Nicaraguan faith is processional" (Cuadra 1971:72).

My own participation in the processions in 1989 and 1991 showed that while faith was indeed processional, it is not necessarily orderly. Apart from those fulfilling vows were tens of thousands of people, a great many drinking clear rum from plastic bags (which they call *agua,* or water) as they sold goods from pushcarts, danced, sang, played music, and sometimes even fought. In a world momentarily turned upside down, the poor owned the streets, especially bands of ragged teenagers rebelliously coating everybody in sight with black grease. Devout Christians dressed as devils or pagan Indians (some wearing the long feathered headdresses stereotypical of North American—but not local—Indians). Gay men, "came out" and displayed open affection, while transvestites swaggered, to whistles and cheers, knowing that on other occasions they would be met with scorn and derision. Frail old men and women dressed in elaborate outfits featuring bull horns danced as if possessed and charged the crowd at unexpected intervals. As Lancaster has noted (1988:44), small signs of reversals and inversions permeate the fiesta: male and female, conqueror and conquered, good and evil.

The Santo Domingo fiesta, like other carnivals and festivals in Europe and Latin America, is a ritual of inversion and rebellion, at the same time expressing dissent and acknowledging social and cultural conventions within a ritual context.[1] Bakhtin (1984:10) notes how European carnival "celebrated temporary liberation from the prevailing truth and from the established order" through such subversive elements as ritual humor. A Nicaraguan anthropologist notes that rural fiestas are like "tranquil revolutions":

> Rural life in Nicaragua is organized by means of the everyday relation with the patron saint. This silent cult is the germ of the large popular demonstrations of the delirious mobs that spring up at all times of the year in paths, villages, barrios, and cities. The carnivalesque processions with dance troops and street theater constitute a species of sacralization of popular identity. These demonstrations are true tranquil revolutions where saints, devils, and imps and other imaginary personages drive traditional values, releasing the brakes in an apparent popular anarchy where we live the sensation of true liberation from the social order. (Palma, 1988, p. 23)

Yet, beyond merely functioning as an "escape valve" for dissent against the status quo, this ritual rebellion has exploded into actual rebellion within the fiesta at specific historical moments that have preserved a historically forged culture of rebellion. More than just providing the passing sensation of liberation, rituals such as the Santo Domingo fiesta have provided the framework, if not the material conditions, for the transformation of the social order.

Between this riotous procession to the Managua church and the return ten days later to the countryside, revelers take advantage of the temporary crowds surrounding the churches to drink, disco dance, gamble, buy and sell sex, watch displays of machismo in the bullfight arena, and partake in all manner of other activities that hardly seem "religious." The scene is only slightly more solemn inside the churches where, amidst the devout approaching the altar on their knees, others push and shove to touch the saint's image or to light candles. At one point in a recent celebration, a fight broke out involving the shattering of glass bottles, reminiscent of a barroom brawl. When the saint entered the church, cries of "*viva* Santo Domingo" were intermingled with the cries of some people that they were being trampled, and scattered shouts of "stop that man, he stole my purse."

Santo Domingo is popularly known in Managua as the patron saint of *alegría*, or joyfulness. Some believe him to have been a doctor who treated the sick regardless of their social class or ability to pay, a healer of the poor who has been transformed into a saint of the poor (Lancaster 1988:44). More to the point (as a reeling celebrant confided to me), some call him the saint of drunks and sinners. He is not, however, the official patron saint of Managua but has usurped that status from the comparatively placid Santo Santiago, whose cult has all but lapsed into obscurity.

Santo Domingo de Guzmán, an austere thirteenth-century missionary, ironically made his mark combating a heretical sect in southern France, earning the epithet "hound of God" (Farmer 1978), which contrasts markedly with the saint of joyousness that the Nicaraguans celebrate today. Either as the miraculous saint who practiced Western medicine or as the saint of vice who persecuted heretics, Santo Domingo's life and legend augment the inversions that permeate his celebration.

The day-long march and fiesta, the saint's return to the city's outskirts on August 10, and a series of traditional events in the interim continued uninterrupted during the popular insurrection in the late 1970s and the 11 years of the Sandinista revolution. Although some in the socialist Sandinista government regarded the celebration of Santo Domingo as a pagan rite, the official and widely accepted policy of the Sandinistas was to respect the cultural traditions of the people.[2]

The Sandinista mayor of Managua helped each year with the preparations and took his place on the float on which the saint was raised during the last few miles of the procession. Though Sandinista police patrolled the route in abundance, they rarely intervened except to curtail frequent drunken fights. They made no effort to stop the consumption of alcohol, although glass bottles were confiscated for safety reasons. Some say that vices, such as gambling and prostitution, have been under control, if not curtailed, since the Revolution (Arnaiz Quintana 1990:143). Not only did the Marxist-inspired Sandinistas tolerate this kind of popular religious practice, they have sought to legitimate their authority among traditional Catholics by participating in some of the ritual acts.

CHRISTIAN BASE COMMUNITIES AND POPULAR RELIGION

Even as the Sandinistas both tolerated and participated in the festivities, their religious allies, the Christian base communities, seemed almost to ignore the Santo Domingo celebration. Hardly a member with whom I spoke admitted to marching in the procession, much less to fulfilling a vow to the saint. Several stated that the bands of drunks and youths performing pranks made the fiesta too dangerous to attend. Traditional Catholics echoed this concern that the celebration had devolved into a drunken revel. At most, members would stand on the sidelines to view the parade as it passed by. Doña Adilia, who ran a CEB at that time, sold soy cakes on the side of the road. She regarded the fiesta as an opportunity to spread the word about the nutritional value of soy, and how it could be incorporated into the Nicaraguan diet if properly prepared, as well as to raise funds for the CEB project for malnourished children. The religious aspect of the event was for her a secondary consideration, and she regarded it largely as a cultural expression.

This image of the CEBs standing on the sidelines in the midst of a wave of popular religious expression presents a problem. It seems to contradict the stated precepts of their theology of liberation and pastoral action, their supposed collaboration with the poor. This contradiction mirrors the ambivalence that the CEBs hold toward traditional popular religion. Although many elements of popular religion possess alienating features, mystifying the actual relations of power in society, other elements are said to contain "seeds of the Word"[3] that express an inherent resistance to domination. In Marx's terminology, religion is at once "an *expression* of real suffering and a *protest* against real suffering" (Marx in Tucker 1978:54, italics in text). For CEB members, this protest remains beyond the conscious level of most believers and within the confines of a sacred space and time prescribed by the dominant religious class. Most of the year, the image of Santo Domingo lies hidden behind the altar of Las Sierritas church on the outskirts of Managua. For a 10-day period, the saint is taken out of the temple away from the control of institutional Church authority and belongs to the people. The rest of the year, the pronouncements and ritual acts of the Church hierarchy carry considerable weight among the population.

The leadership of Managua's Christian base communities slowly began to realize the contradiction between "respect" for cultural tradition and actual participation in these traditions. During meetings of the CEB coordinating body before the Santo Domingo fiesta in August 1991, participants recalled how, in the early years of the revolution, they had wished that some revolutionary edict could get rid of the alienating and mystifying popular religious practices by which, as one participant put it, the Church "maintains a stranglehold on the poor." They came to realize that this attitude of revolutionary "political correctness" had in fact served to alienate them from the mass of the people, and that they had not done enough to accompany them in their religious practices and their faith. Indeed, some institutes in Managua associated with the Church of the Poor have been a primary force in salvaging, preserving and documenting cultural traditions. They have attempted to give these traditions a liberationist spin, emphasizing the strength of Nicaraguan culture (as a nationalist construct of local traditions), showing how it has been able to resist the material and symbolic domination of capitalism, and how it provided the conditions for the Revolution to occur.

SANTO DOMINGO IN MYTH AND HISTORY

At one meeting, Sister Margarita of the CEB animating team read from an illustrated pamphlet which related, in common language, a version of the origin myth of the Santo Domingo fiesta, as well as the actual life of Santo Domingo de Guzmán. In comic book format, it had been produced several years earlier by the Antonio Valdivieso Ecumenical Center and sold at its bookstore. Now this material, characteristic of revolutionary popular education[4] in combining word and image in a popular medium relevant to people's lives, served as the basis for an educational campaign among CEB members.

By intertwining myth with history, an oral history of rebellion in the fiesta as well as the documented history of the saint, the CEBs have appropriated the cultural tradition of a myth in order to show the liberating potential of popular religion. Myths are strongly structured stories that resolve logical contradictions in human social life (Lévi-Strauss 1963:229). However, these structures are more social than innate in humans, and the contradictions that myths resolve change with changes in the social formation. Myths "operate in men's minds without their being aware of the fact" (Lévi-Strauss 1969:12), but the material conditions and historical moment in which they live affect how myths operate. For example, the myth of a healing saint may express the human powerlessness to cure epidemic disease in one period and be a protest against an alienating or inadequate medical system in another. The relation between illness and cure in this myth may point a way toward spiritual as well as physical salvation, or it may indicate a practical alternative to unsuccessful medical procedures.

The relation between myth and historical conditions is dynamic. A myth, such as the origin of a saint's fiesta, gathers around it remembered historical events from specific fiesta celebrations that enhance its significance. In turn, events such as fiestas, and revolutions, are viewed by the participants through the cultural filter of myth, as reenactments of the mythic story (Sahlins 1981).

The significance of history for the Christian base communities lies in their reading of the sacred history encoded in the Bible and in popular tradition as the unfolding struggle and eventual triumph of the poor against oppression *within* history.[5] They believe that Christ died on the cross for his commitment to the poor, so that he could serve as an example of sacrifice in the struggle of the poor for liberation. In addition, the CEBs' analysis of actual social conditions showed the continued oppression of the poor as rooted in their ignorance of their own history of struggle as much as in economic marginalization. Thus, the notion promulgated by Somoza that Augusto Sandino (from whom the Sandinistas took their name) was a cutthroat bandit obscured the fact that in the 1920s and 1930s, he led an army of poor peasants fighting for land and sovereignty. Liberation is achieved through a self-conscious awareness of a people's history and culture, as well as by their owning the means of production and reproduction.

CEB members view themselves as pastoral agents acting as mediators who, through education and by example, endeavor to accompany and teach the poor majority that they are conscious subjects of their own destiny.[6] They serve as catalysts, but the poor themselves must, according to theologian Richard (1985:21), "break the mechanisms of alienation which have invaded their religious consciousness and bring about the advance from a popular religion of resistance to a popular religion of struggle." In contrast with members of millenarian movements, CEBs endeavor to teach the poor to work actively for material and spiritual liberation in this world, rather than to wait for the shadowy promise of salvation in the next. In this context, myth is not a timeless story, revealing part of a universal moral code, or a quaint tale displaying the common people's idiosyncratic traditions, views that the Church hierarchy tends to take, depending on the "official" status of the myth in Catholic dogma. Rather, for the Church of the Poor, myths are exemplary tales which occur at determinate points in the historical past yet still have resonance for the present.

Let me summarize the illustrated pamphlet version of the myth.[7]

> In the mid seventeenth century there lived a poor charcoal maker named Vincente Aburto. One day when he was out chopping wood, he spotted a black tree which was ideal for making charcoal. On the first swing of his ax he struck a hard object in the trunk which turned out to be a sculpted image of a tiny brown saint. He took the saint to the priest of the Vera Cruz church in Managua who identified it as the image of Santo Domingo and placed it on a mantle in the church.
>
> A few days later Vincente returned to the forest to collect firewood, and once again he found the saint's image in the same tree trunk. He then rushed to the priest and inquired, "*padrecito,* why have you brought me the *santito* again?" The shocked priest replied that he had not and then discovered that the saint was missing from the altar of the locked church.
>
> This phenomenon was repeated three times.
>
> The priest told Vincente that this was a sign from the saint to the people that on August 1, the day he was discovered, they should carry the saint from its home in the outskirts of Managua to the capital in a joyous procession accompanied by popular music.

This tale, the origin myth of Managua's Santo Domingo fiesta, reflects the ambivalence of the encounter between the European conquerors and the conquered Americans. The seventeenth century marked the wide diffusion of saints' cults in Latin America, and their fiestas, through the missionary activity of religious orders and their attempt to impose strict Christian religious practices on the native populations (Arnaiz Quintana 1990:51). The story follows a literary form, the returning saint, well known in Europe and widespread in Latin America.[8] In another version of the myth, the saint thwarted the priest's wish to bring the image to the capital by growing heavier at each step of the journey (Palma 1988:92). Although the priest had authority, the saint, comprising both foreign and indigenous elements, was in control.

The seventeenth-century colonial encounter also signaled an increase in mestizo populations and sociocultural forms. The peasant Aburto also possessed a dual mestizo character, the mystified seeker of the guidance of colonial religious authority, and at the same time one of many discoverers of "miracle-yielding saints," an Indian "who is chosen by history to provide the civilized and conquering race with a miraculous icon" (Taussig 1987:189). Even the chop of his ax further sanctified the image by releasing its miraculous power: the statue has a cut in its head that is believed to possess curative powers if touched. In yet another version of the myth, Vincente encountered the saint while trying to find a bark remedy for his sick daughter, and "a brown image appeared in the groove cut in the trunk of the tree announcing that the little girl had been cured" (Palma 1988:91). Subsequently, the saint supposedly cured numerous other people.

After the presentation at the base community coordinator's meeting by Sister Margarita, the participants held a discussion regarding the significance of the Santo Domingo myth in establishing the identity of poor mestizo peasants as "people of God." This discussion evolved in a political context where, after the defeat of the Sandinistas in the 1990 elections, the Church of the Poor shared a credibility gap with the revolutionary party. They now undertook better to understand the needs, interests, traditions and religiosity of the poor.[9] The participants at the meeting arrived at three conclusions concerning what the myth reveals about Nicaraguan popular culture. First, the tiny brown saint is of the people, and wants to be with the people. Second, the saint was discovered by a poor, faithful mestizo peasant, not the white urban priest, and in fact most Managuans are mestizos and trace their cultural roots to the countryside. Third, the people express their devotion to the saint in their *own* manner with their own cultural traditions. If this includes drunken revelry, so be it. But more importantly, "in their own manner" points up the fact that the people are autonomous actors who not only had the potential for defiance and rebellion, but who were also capable of a revolution in 1979.

Still, if identity and rebellion were integral to the myth, the base community members felt that it lacked a sense of what the people stand for. Their solution was to depict the saint as a human being who devoted his life to the poor rather than an otherworldly dispenser of salvation. Thus, after the myth, the pamphlet goes on to depict the life of Santo Domingo de Guzmán, the thirteenth-century founder of the Dominican order of preachers, who left the comfortable life of the noble Spanish clergy to work among the poor. That this work involved complicity in the suppression of the Albigensian heretics of southern France is alluded to but not emphasized. Neither does it mention the role of Dominicans in the Spanish Inquisition. Rather, the last section of the pamphlet highlights the Dominican defenders of the Indians, "Sons of Santo Domingo in Latin America": Fray Bartolomé de las Casas and Fray Antonio Valdivieso, third bishop of Nicaragua, after whom the religious center that produced the pamphlet was named. The saint is associated with some of the most powerful figures in the history of liberation in Nicaragua.

Nevertheless, the pamphlet ends on a note, not of austerity or joy, tragedy, or farce, but of earnest conviction: Santo Domingo "lived his Christian faith preaching among the poor and incarnating the gospels in the new social order that arose in his era. He is an example for us" (Centro Antonio Valdivieso n.d.:15). It characterizes this new order, the collapse of the feudal system and the increasing exploitation of the poor during the thirteenth century, as parallel to the conditions of late capitalism that gave rise to the revolution of 1979 in Nicaragua. Despite the vastly different circumstances of these new orders, the pamphlet depicts a quasi-mythical parallel to the past, as the CEBs have done when comparing the Revolution to the biblical Exodus.

However, the Church of the Poor did not introduce the idea of presenting both the myth and history of Santo Domingo. The priest of the Santo Domingo church wrote a complete account of the Santo Domingo celebrations from 1949 to 1970.[10] Through oral history, he fixed the date of the saint's discovery to 1885, a two-century difference from the pamphlet.

Pinedo represents the conservative view that fiestas such as that of Santo Domingo express the authentic religiosity of the people, a pristine form characterized by religious observance, folklore, and order (1977:114). Opposed to this, in his view, is a "mafia" of thugs and drunks who seek to subvert the fiesta for their own selfish and blasphemous ends, a tendency which the Church and State (the Somoza dictatorship at the time) should control, through force if necessary. By sketching how the fiesta has moved from a romantic "jewel" of the people's religious expression into the "mud" of debauchery,[11] Pinedo inadvertently laid the foundation for a social history of resistance to Church authority during the Santo Domingo fiesta. This written social history, reproduced and sold along the fiesta route in a newspaper "Homage to Santo Domingo,"[12] augments an oral history preserved in the collective memory of Managuans that has become integral to the Santo Domingo myth.

This myth—or history—pits the forces of hierarchical order and orthodoxy, not against an image of chaos and immorality, but against a popular order operating upon different principles. During the 1950s, the Santo Domingo fiesta had developed a reputation as a bacchanal, a religious cover for a roving party featuring drinking, prostitution, fights, and gambling. The Nicaraguan Church hierarchy had tried to temper the fiesta, appealing for order through the pulpit and newspaper editorials. The archbishop of Managua resorted to a ban on the fiesta in 1961 by refusing to let the saint's image out of the Las Sierritas church. This enraged a group of devotees, who carried out an almost legendary "kidnapping" of the saint. They evaded guards by entering Las Sierritas church through a secret back passage and stole the saint from his altar, while others created a diversion at the front of the church. They led the saint on a procession to Managua, picking up hundreds of surprised people along the way, and then they used a tree trunk to force open the doors to the Santo Domingo church. No mere Church edict could deter the saint from being with the people. Many Managuans viewed the edict as yet another oppressive act by authorities in the context of the times, where elite landholders, with the blessing and complicity of the Church, were engaged in massive expropriation of peasant land. The theft was seen as a redress, if largely symbolic, against a Church that had become distant from its constituents.

The Church responded to this challenge by recommending the excommunication of the group who had stolen the saint. However, the edict banning the procession was rescinded, and the fiesta continued in the following years, though the image was taken from Managua to the Sierritas, a reversal of the normal path. This prompted the Chávez group to make another attempt at stealing the image, which resulted in the leader's imprisonment. Finally, by 1965, the fiesta proceeded according to tradition, once the Church authorities had decided that it was better to coopt popular tradition than oppose it. Thus, after the 1972 earthquake that destroyed Managua, including its cathedral, the Nicaraguan Church's curia moved to the Las Sierritas church. The local Cardinal subsequently used that pulpit as the center of Managua's popular religion (albeit far from its geographical center) to exhort the people to respect the sanctity of the fiesta.

Most Nicaraguans, including revolutionary Christians, respect the cardinal as their spiritual leader and are proud that a fellow mestizo Nicaraguan has attained such a high position in the Church. However, although for the most part they follow his lead on such social issues as abortion, there is little evidence to suggest that he has succeeded in directly pacifying the fiesta. For the celebrants, there is no contradiction between sacred and profane: the very presence of the saint among the people bestows sanctity upon them, no matter whether their actions accord with the moral prescriptions of the Church. Yet one element explains the Church's tolerance of the fiesta: the saint, as a divine intermediary bestowing sanctity, serves as a surrogate for the authority structure of the Church hierarchy. Although he occupies a position above temporal authority, he validates a hierarchical order more important to the Church than its system of moral codes.

The Church of the Poor calls into question that very authority structure, and their use of the Santo Domingo myth (or myth/history complex) serves this end. They seek to establish a kind of participatory democracy of the spiritual life, where priests and bishops serve the "people of God" through education and rite, and as exemplary models of good Christians. In appropriating the myth they seek to transform this image of the saint as divine intermediary. In their view, the saint's image is merely an emblem of an all too human figure acting as an example of service to the poor in the cause of social change. The miraculous appearance of the saint's image represents one moment in this historical and teleological process which merges the life of the saint with the concrete actions of the poor in history.

The Nicaraguan Church hierarchy's ties to State-level power had been weakened by their break with the Somoza regime in the 1970s, and further under the socialist Sandinistas. The Church hierarchy was in a position where it had to defend against this challenge to its authority from the "popular Church," and it did so with charges that revolutionary Christians were Communists and heretics.[13] Its authority relied on the traditional hierarchical chain of command, based upon patronage and obedience to one's spiritual betters, as much as it relied on faith in the "Kingdom of God." The appropriation of the saint's "home" in the Las Sierritas church served to legitimate the tie to a saint with a high position on this "chain of being." In this context, the interface of myth and history become privileged arenas for an ideological conflict between the hierarchical and the grassroots sectors of the Catholic Church.

By issuing pamphlets, meeting in study groups, and using the platform of progressive priests, the Church of the Poor has attempted to reconstruct a myth which appropriates both popular story and Church history, in a sense to outflank the Church hierarchy's own attempt at appropriation. This myth interweaves poor people's self-awareness of their own faith, identity, and history with the example of service to one's fellow in the cause of liberation. It promotes rebellion and the subversion of the Church's hierarchical authority structure by offering an example of a saint who left that hierarchy to work directly with the poor.

THE RECURRENCE OF RESISTANCE

In 1991, amidst deteriorating economic conditions, the procession of Santo Domingo into Managua developed a twist that demonstrates its continued efficacy as a vehicle for popular protest. In mid-route, a downpour began which lasted for the rest of the day. Red paint on those masquerading as Indians and black paint on devils began to wash off, and the numerous youths bathing unsuspecting victims with grease did so to little avail. A dozen men stoically carried the platform with the saint's image that seemed to grow heavier as in the myth. A hundred or so men and women carried a rope forming a circle around the saint to seal off the "sacred space" as part of their promise, but even they began to appear fazed by the heavy downpour. The usually boisterous brass and marimba bands sounded disheartened, but the air still somehow cracked with the sound and smoke of rockets and firecrackers fired by boys expert in keeping their powder dry.

Even before the rain, the numerous mobile vendors, many driven to this occupation by the massive layoffs in the public sector after the 1990 Sandinista electoral defeat, had trouble selling their food, drink, trinkets, and votive offerings. The economic situation had been steadily worsening, and nobody had money to spend, especially the poor participants in the procession, many of whom lived in shantytowns which the government had promised to eliminate.

Eleven hours into the procession, the new ultrarightist mayor of Managua took his place as the fiesta's *mayordomo* on the float where the saint had been lifted. The crowd responded with vehement disapproval. It proceeded to pelt him with insults, stones, bottles and watermelon rinds. Ironically, the anti-Sandinista mayor had to take cover protected by the Sandinista police. The float took off at full speed for the last 20 blocks to the church, where the mayor retreated into a nearby school. The saint, protected by a double cordon of police, was whisked into a side door of the church. This caused an uproar: several hundred people forced their way into the church, fighting their way through the police and the mayor's loyalists. Despite sustaining many injuries in this bloody struggle, the usurpers managed to carry the saint out of the church, its flower-covered platform in shreds but the image itself intact. There they and the people waiting outside performed the traditional dance with the saint and afterwards took it back into the church through the main doors. People soon realized that, for a short period, the saint again had been stolen.

That mayor, who had sat out the years of Sandinista rule in Miami and come back to ride the electoral wave that brought the opposition coalition to power, enacted policies which alienated both the poor and traditionalists.[14] He supported an economic development of Managua which involved removing squatters from their land and taxing the pushcarts of small informal sector vendors. In addition, he did not allow the main group of Santo Domingo "traditionalists" to participate in the preparations, since this group was led by the man who had "kidnapped" the saint. He had eventually reconciled with the Church to the point where he had been allowed to oversee the fiesta's preparations. Though he did not identify himself as a Sandinista, he had cooperated with the Sandinistas in arranging the fiesta, and they appreciated his past as a thorn in the side of the Church hierarchy. Thus his removal fit within the mayor's policy of "change," which Sandinistas characterize as a policy of *revanchismo* (revenge). Many suspected that people sympathetic to the kidnapper had planned this new "theft" of the saint. The identity of the perpetrators remained the subject of dispute, but the mayor had become a symbol of arrogant authority, an object of revolt in this ritual of rebellion.[15]

Despite the apparent anarchy of the fiesta, both ritual and real rebellions, these behaviors exist within a broader set of "rules of the game." These rules became dramatized when they were broken: the mayor rejected the "legitimate" traditionalists and some of their pre-procession customs, and the saint was taken through the wrong door without allowing people the traditional dance with him. After the incident, a peasant woman proclaimed before the assembled people and the startled media that "Santo Domingo does not belong to the UNO [government] nor to the Sandinistas; he belongs to the people."

This statement was featured on that evening's television news on both the government and Sandinista stations, and it became the subject of discussion during the following days among Managuans and in the press. According to the political preference of the person or media, the saint did not belong to the neo-liberal government, the Sandinista-controlled mobs and police, or even U.S. imperialism, but always carried an implication that brazen, unsubtle political manipulations of the religious celebration violated the rules of the game. These rules followed a logic defined by class, even after the Revolution. On the actual saint's day, August 4, the saint was taken on a boisterous, zigzag journey through the chaos of Managua's popular central market, Mercado Oriental, punctuated with drummers pronouncing couplets satirizing sexual and political relations. Meanwhile, the elites engaged in brazen political posturing in an expensive, pageantry-filled and orderly horse parade which never crossed the path of the popular procession or the saint.[16]

CEB members were heartened by what they regarded as a spontaneous revolt against injustice which demonstrated the inherent rebelliousness of the people. But some noted that this rebellion did not go beyond challenging political authority within the confines of the religious event. At this juncture, people were not prepared to follow the example of saints or revolutionary martyrs. Others argued that the participation of these people in the revolutionary transformation of society had already begun to transform their class and religious consciousness, allowing them to act independently of authority structures, whether on the political right or left.

In 1991, the government of Violeta Chamorro lacked a substantive social base and, caught between reactionaries in the legislature and Sandinistas in the army and police, lacked the ability to function effectively. The Sandinista Front suffered from a routinization of their charisma caused by its inability to stem the U.S.-sponsored war, an economic crisis, and a tendency toward centralizing (and sometimes abusing) their power. Nevertheless, the Sandinista Revolution itself left a legacy of a people aware of their identity and defiantly disposed against authority, regardless of its ideological color, whether Sandinista red and black or UNO white and blue. By succeeding in overthrowing the Somoza dictatorship, the people of Nicaragua had begun to regain their history, validated in myth, and stand poised to challenge new forms of centralized political or religious authority. As an organized movement, the Church of the Poor may have run up against objective limits: its identification with Sandinista authority. In the pursuit of rapid economic and political changes that favored a centralized, vertical leadership structure, the Sandinistas succeeded in alienating the very poor for whom they had fought. But one might say that the poor majority, at least in Managua, are but a stone's throw away from the real process of cultural creation and historical re-creation that often lies beyond the appropriation or anticipation of leaders. Both the popular uprising initiating the 1979 revolution and the spontaneous rebellion during the fiesta demonstrate this. To paraphrase Marx, the women and men of Nicaragua have made their own history, but not precisely of their own choosing.[17]

Notes

[1] The extensive literature on carnival has made the celebration synonymous with rituals of reversal and inversion, especially amenable to symbolic and semiotic analysis. See for example Turner, 1969; Babcock, 1978; Sebeok, 1984.

[2] In 1980 the FSLN issued an official communiqué stating their position on religion: "The FSLN has a profound respect for all the religious celebrations and traditions of our people and strives to rescue the true sense of these celebrations, attacking the vice and the manifestations of corruption that the past imprinted on them." Frente Sandinista de Liberación Nacional 1980, Position #5.

[3] This phrase comes from the Vatican II "Decree on the Missionary Activity of the Church" (*Lumen Gentium*), which exhorts missionaries to recognize and promote the implicit religiosity of popular practices: "Let [Christians] share in cultural and social life by the various exchanges and enterprises of human living. Let them be familiar with their national and religious traditions, gladly and reverently laying bare the seeds of the Word which lie hidden in them" (Abbott 1966:597–8).

[4] The revolutionary Christian news monthly *El Tayacán* has published in illustrated pamphlet form the 1987 Nicaraguan Constitution (1987a) and the history of the Church of the Poor (1987b), among other material. The Sandinista government regularly published illustrated inserts in the news dailies *Barricada* and *El Nuevo Diario*, including tips on planting crops so as not to cause deforestation and soil erosion, and steps to prevent diarrhea and cholera.

[5] This biblical hermeneutic is another aspect of the *lectura popular de la biblia* (popular bible reading) (cf. Pixley and Santin, in Girardi et al. 1989:209–22).

[6] Cf. Wolf's notion of social groups, instrumental in revolutions, that mediate between peasants (poor urban dwellers in this case) and the larger society because they "stand at the junctures in social, economic, and political relations which connect the village [or the barrio] to wider-ranging elites in markets or political networks" (Wolf 1969:xii). CEBs stand at the juncture between their neighbors and international development aid and religious reforms.

[7] Adapted from CAV, n.d., *Santo Domingo de Guzmán: Patrono de Managua*, Centro Ecuménico Antonio Valdivieso.

[8] This etiological myth of the fiesta's origin, especially the central role of the humble peasant, appears in European folk tradition (see Christian 1989, on Spain) as well as that of the Americas (see Ingham 1990, on Mexico).

[9]"In the language of liberation theology, revolutionary Christians must reaffirm their "option for the poor as historical subject." Many had worked within revolutionary structures and thus "distanced themselves from the Christian community and, at times, from a religious search" and now sought to "reintegrate into their former communities, not as refuges, but as spaces for nurturing, reflection, prayer, friendship and common searching" according to a pamphlet written after the Sandinista electoral defeat entitled "Nicaraguan Revolutionary Christians Face the Crisis of Civilization" (CAV April 1991:13).

[10] He ambitiously titled his book *Popular Religion*, though he rarely treats the topic in general.

[11] Pinedo entitles his chapters "*La Joya*" (the jewel) and "*El Lodo*" (the mud), which invokes the biblical reference "neither cast your pearls before swine."

[12] "*Homenaje a Santo Domingo de Guzmán en el aniversario 106 de su milagroso hallazgo*" (Anonymous, August 1991). No author's names or publication data appears, but it includes salutes to the fiesta from the government of Violeta Chamorro and the mayor of Managua, Arnoldo Alemán. The following account comes from this anonymous source, Pinedo 1977:53–76, and oral sources.

[13] Cardinal Obando y Bravo often refers to the "popular Church" as the ideological arm of the FSLN, warning against their involvement in politics.

[14] Alemán won the presidential elections in 1996, a fact that indicates that neither the poor nor traditionalists hold significant power in the Nicaraguan political arena.

[15] See Lancaster 1988:38–51, for a discussion of Santo Domingo and reversals in the fiesta.

[16] The division between upper- and lower-class celebrations of patron saints is nothing new, but the extreme polarity in Nicaragua is renowned. For example, I witnessed the patron saint of the town of Moyogalpa, Santa Ana, being led in a procession that at one point circumambulated around the bull ring, where most of the elites chose to spend the saint's day.

[17] Marx said in "The Eighteenth Brumaire of Louis Bonaparte": "Men make their own history, but not of their own free will; not under circumstances they themselves have chosen but under the given and inherited circumstances with which they are directly confronted" (1973:146).

References

Abbott, Walter (ed.). 1966. *The Documents of Vatican II*. New York: America Press.

Anonymous. 1991. "Homenaje a Santo Domingo de Guzmán en el aniversario 106 de su milagroso hallazgo." Managua: N.p. August 1991.

Arnaiz Quintana, Angel. 1990. *Historia del pueblo de Diós en Nicaragua*. Managua: Centro Ecuménico Antonio Valdivieso.

Babcock, Barbara (ed.). 1978. *The Reversible World: Symbolic Inversion in Art and Society*. Ithaca: Cornell University Press.

Bakhtin, Mikhail. 1984. *Rabelais and His World*. Bloomington: Indiana University Press.

Centro Antonio Valdivieso. n.d. *Santo Domingo de Guzmán: Patrono de Managua*. Managua: Centro Ecuménico Antonio Valdivieso.

———. 1991. "Nicaraguan Revolutionary Christians Face the Crisis of Civilization." Pamphlet, April 1991. New York: New York Circus Publications.

Christian, William. 1989. *Person and God in a Spanish Valley*. Princeton: Princeton University Press.

Cuadra, Pablo Antonio. 1971. *El Nicaragüense*. Managua: PINSA.

Farmer, David. 1978. *The Oxford Dictionary of Saints*. Oxford: Clarendon Press.

Frente Sandinista de Liberación Nacional. 1980. "Comunicado Oficial de la Dirección Nacional del FSLN Sobre la Religión." *Patria Libre*, Oct.–Nov.

Girardi, Giulio, et al. (eds.). 1989. *Pueblo revolucionario, pueblo de Diós*. Mexico, D.F.: Paradigmas Ediciones.

Ingham, John. 1990. *Mary, Michael, and Lucifer: Folk Catholicism in Central Mexico*. Austin: University of Texas Press.

Lancaster, Roger. 1988. *Thanks to God and the Revolution: Popular Religion and Class Consciousness in the New Nicaragua*. New York: Columbia University Press.

Lévi-Strauss, Claude. 1969. *The Raw and the Cooked: Introduction to a Science of Mythology, Volume One*. Translated by John and Doreen Weightman. Chicago: University of Chicago Press.

Marx, Karl. 1973. "The Eighteenth Brumaire of Louis Bonapart," in *Surveys From Exile: Political Writings*, Vol. II. New York: Vintage Books.

Palma, Milagros. 1988. *Revolución Tranquila de Santos, Diablos y Diablitos*. Bogotá, Colombia: Editorial Nueva América.

Pinedo, Ignacio. 1977. *Religiosidad Popular: Su Problemática y su Anecdota*. Bilbao, Spain: Mensajero.

Sahlins, Marshall. 1981. *Historical Metaphors and Mythical Realities*. Ann Arbor: University of Michigan Press.

Sebeok, Thomas (ed.). 1984. *Carnival!* Berlin: Mouton Publishers.

Taussig, Michael. 1987. *Shamanism, Colonialism, and the Wild Man: A Study in Terror and Healing*. Chicago: University of Chicago Press.

El Tayacán, Periódico Popular. 1987a. "Constitución Política de la República de Nicaragua," Numero Especial, Año 5, No. 223, 31 de enero al 6 de febrero.

———. 1987b. *Historia de la Iglesia de los Pobres en Nicaragua*. Managua: El Tayacán.

Tucker, Robert (ed.). 1978. *The Marx-Engels Reader*. Second Edition. New York: W.W. Norton and Co.

Turner, Victor. 1969. *The Ritual Process*. New York: Aldine Publishing.

Wolf, Eric. 1969. *Peasant Wars of the 20th Century*. New York: Harper and Row.

David J. Wilson teaches anthropology at Southern Methodist University; he is the author of Indigenous South Americans of the Past and Present: An Ecological Perspective.

The use of psychoactive substances to alter human consciousness was widespread for religious, medical, and other socially approved purposes long before it became a recreational activity, enjoyed by some and deplored by others. What is now South America is home to a wide variety of plants that people somehow learned early to use that way, and Wilson here offers a brief introduction to associated customs and to some associated beliefs, practices, and still-unanswered questions. These simple sketches show vividly how human beings transform "nature" in myriad ways, and how similar plants take on very different meanings. Other examples of how the cultural context makes for very different reactions toward a single substance can be seen with respect to alcohol (Heath, chapter 19).

Hallucinogenic Plants in Indigenous South American Cultures

David J. Wilson

In the fascinating book *Plants of the Gods,* Richard Evans Schultes and Albert Hoffman (1992) point out that of all traditional societies in the world the indigenous groups of South America are second only to those of Mexico in the number and diversity of hallucinogenic plants used in magic and ritual. It is therefore relevant to discuss the nature and importance in indigenous adaptive systems of several of the more extensively used hallucinogenic plants of the eastern tropical lowlands and the Andes.

First, it comes as something of a revelation to learn that of the 150 hallucinogenic plants currently known to ethnobotanists, fully 130 of them are from the New World, whereas only 20 are known from the Old World. Given the equally diverse plant communities of both areas, not to mention the far greater time-depth of the human occupation of the Old World, it is surprising that so many plants should be known and used by the indigenous inhabitants of the Americas. Schultes and Hoffman believe that this anomaly comes from the fact that the societies of the Old World for the most part evolved to "highly agricultural levels," whereas those of the New were, or still are, basically hunting societies. Since a hunter's success depends on "medicine power," which is often acquired by carrying out vision quests under the influence of psychoactive plants, these plants are thus far more important in the ritual and religion of indigenous New World societies.

Although this is an interesting hypothesis, this chapter should have already begun to make clear that hunter-gatherer subsistence systems on the South America continent are and have been based at least as much on plant foods and fishing as on animal foods, if not far more so—never mind that where protein is in relatively short supply compared to carbohydrates, drug use and ritual may well focus on the former food resource rather than on the latter.

In any case, many or most of these groups still rely on hallucinogenic plants in carrying out traditional rituals. In contrast, many hunter-gatherer groups of the far south, although based heavily on guanaco hunting for their livelihood, did not take hallucinogenic drugs at all because none was available.

Moreover, horticulturist-hunter groups of the Amazon have other reasons for ingesting hallucinogens besides the enhancement of hunting prowess. In the case of the Jívaro of eastern Ecuador, this includes the acquisition of a "killer" soul—not only to stimulate a man's desire to go out and kill other people but also to make him succeed in the attempt. Finally, the highly developed agriculturists of the Andes employed plants with psychoactive powers in their own religious systems.

Although Schultes and Hoffman's well-taken question of why the use of hallucinogens was so prevalent in the New World is not yet answered, it seems that nearly all indigenous South Americans have used psychoactive plants wherever they are found in the local environment. To make the point another way, expert lay botanists would have rather quickly discovered the properties of all plants in their local environment—whether these properties were nutritional, mind-altering, or even lethal! But even where such plants are unavailable, there are cases where a group has found out about their hallucinogenic powers from its neighbors and has devised a means of acquiring the plants.

Five principal genera of hallucinogenic South American plants are discussed here (with indigenous names given in parentheses). They include *Anadenanthera* sp. (yopo, huilca), *Banisteriopsis* sp. (ayahuasca, yajé, natemä, caapi), *Brugmansia* sp. (yas, huacachaca), *Trichocereus* sp. (San Pedro), and *Virola* sp. (ebene, epená, nyakwana). (The most commonly used name, whether a single indigenous one or the genus name, is employed here in accordance with the terms used in the Schultes and Hoffman book as well as in the anthropological literature.)

YOPO (*ANADENANTHERA* SP.)

Two species of *Anadenanthera* are used by indigenous South Americans to make hallucinogenic snuffs—one of them in the Orinoco and northern Amazon (*Anadenanthera peregrina*) and the other in northern Argentina and the southern Amazon (*Anadenanthera colubrina*). Although the distribution indicates that the present, or recent, use of yopo has been confined to these two areas of the eastern lowlands, it was probably also employed in prehispanic times in indigenous religion and ritual in the northern Colombian Andes, where it was obtained by Chibchan groups (near what is now Bogotá) through trade with people of the forests to the east.

Where still in use, yopo snuff, which is prepared from the seeds of the plant, may be taken daily by shamans to induce trances and visions that permit them to carry out a variety of magico-religious tasks. Among the Guahibo of eastern Colombia, for example, these tasks include communicating with the *hekura* spirits, making prophesies and divinations, helping prevent sickness, improving the men's ability to hunt, and improving the alertness of the dogs in hunting and protecting the village. Quite a bit of variation exists in the preparation of yopo, but generally it involves toasting and grinding the seeds from the plant, after which lime from pulverized snails or the ashes of plants may be added to produce an alkaline admixture. In northern Argentina the Mashco people prepare a snuff from *Anadenanthera* seeds and also smoke them to produce similar hallucinogenic trances and visions.

Taking yopo produces a number of physical reactions, in addition to the hallucinogenic visions, including an initial loss of consciousness followed by a feeling of looseness in the limbs. A late-eighteenth-century report (Gumilla 1791) on its use in the Orinoco observes that the men who took it were thrown into a frenzy, whereupon they would injure themselves and, finally, seized with great rage, go out on raids against their enemies. In the Orinoco area today, many groups inhale powdered yopo from a small wooden tray into the nose through the thin leg bones of birds that have been tied together in the shape of the letter Y so that the powder enters both nostrils with equal force at the same time.

AYAHUASCA (*BANISTERIOPSIS* SP.)

One indication of how widely plants of the second genus, *Banisteriopsis*, are used in indigenous religious systems is the many different names it has in the area of its distribution. Nevertheless, South Americanist scholars most frequently call it *ayahuasca* ("vine of the soul"), the Quechua language term for it. According to Schultes and Hoffman (1992), ayahuasca is generally considered by all who use it to free the soul (or one of them, at least, among groups where multiple souls exist) so that it can wander freely, releasing its owner from the constraints of daily life to discover "true reality." Many groups gather a number of different types of ayahuasca and mix it with various other psychoactive plants to produce an equally great variety of trance and vision experiences.

Ayahuasca is gathered by scraping the bark from a rainforest liana. Then, depending on the area, it is prepared either by boiling the bark for several hours to produce a thick, bitter liquid, which is then ingested in small doses, or by pulverizing it and adding it to cold water to be taken in larger doses (since it is less concentrated in this form). Its physical effects on the body usually include such unpleasant reactions as nausea, dizziness, and vomiting. Its psychotropic effects include euphoria and aggression, and everywhere it is taken, for reasons still unknown to scientists, it produces visions of jaguars and huge snakes, although these animals are certainly present in the environments included in the distribution.

With respect to the jaguar, probably the most dangerous and feared animal of the rainforest, shamans of the Yekuana, or Makiritare, of central Venezuela who take ayahuasca *become* the jaguar and are able to exercise the powers of a cat as they carry out curing or bewitching activities. And snakes seen by shamans in ayahuasca-induced visions among the Conibo-Shipibo of eastern Peru are acquired as powerful allies that defend them in supernatural battles against the hostile shamans of other, nearby groups. Above all, throughout the area of the plant's use it aids shamans in carrying out healing rituals in curing the ill. Once shamans take ayahuasca, they are able to summon healing spirits who respond to the entreaties to cure their patients. Schultes and Hoffman also point out that many who take it experience the sensation of flying and in so doing are able to carry out such feats as flying to the Milky Way to encounter heaven, flying about in the sky as a bird, or traveling in a supernatural canoe to retrieve souls.

BRUGMANSIA SP.

Once thought to belong to the genus *Datura*, recent research has shown plants of the genus *Brugmansia* to be different enough to warrant placing them in a distinct generic category—although both genuses nonetheless are quite similar in appearance. Schultes and Hoffman think that knowledge of the properties of *Datura* probably was brought by the first Paleoindians arriving in the New World, since many species of this genus exist in the Old World. Not only would this have aided them in recognizing related New World species of *Datura*, but also, once in South America, the strong similarity of the *Daturas* to the *Brugmansias* would have made it rather quickly clear that the latter plants had similar hallucinogenic properties.

Many species of *Brugmansia* exist along the western side of South America. For example, three are found at elevations above 1,800 meters in the Colombian Andes, where indigenous groups use the seeds as an additive to *chicha*, or maize beer. Crushed leaves and flowers are added to hot or cold water in preparing *Brugmansia* species as a form of tea. But however the plant is ingested, its effects always bring about a physically convulsive, or violent, phase. Those who take it first fall into a heavy stupor, with eyes vacant and nostrils dilated. This is followed by the violent phase, during which eyes roll, foam comes out of the mouth, and the body goes through a period of severe convulsions. The third phase is more peaceful, as the taker of this powerful hallucinogen falls into a sleep that lasts for several hours. After waking up, he may recount the details of visits made to the ancestors. Lingering longer than these first physical effects and the hallucinations, however, are some very unpleasant aftereffects that include, in more-or-less ascending order of seriousness, pronounced nausea, outbursts of violence, and temporary insanity.

Among the Jívaro a species of *Brugmansia* is added to parched maize and administered to recalcitrant children, who, while intoxicated, are lectured on behalf of the spirits as to how to behave properly. In Peru, where local species are called *huacachaca*, *Brugmansia* is taken to enable the finding of treasures in ancient tombs, or *huacas* (hence the meaning of *huacachaca* in Quechua, "plant of the tomb"). In the Colombian Andes the plants of this genus have just about as many uses as mentioned earlier for yopo—including its being given to patients to relieve rheumatism (its tropane alkaloids make it an effective medicine), to the men to make them better hunters, and to the dogs in helping them search for game.

SAN PEDRO CACTUS (*TRICHOCEREUS* SP.)

Although the use of most of the South American hallucinogenic plants may well go back to the time of the first Paleoindian inhabitants of the continent, San Pedro cactus (*Tikhocereus* sp.) is one of the few for which we have excellent evidence of its antiquity in prehistoric adaptive systems, even if this evidence is confined to more recent millennia. For example, judging from its depiction on various media including pottery, textiles, and stone in the Chavín art of Early Horizon Peru, San Pedro played an important role in the religious activities of this culture beginning as early as 900 B.C.

The stems of this columnar cactus, which grows in desert conditions both on the coast and in the highlands, are sliced into thin cuttings and boiled for some hours until a thick potion is produced. Upon ingesting the liquid, shamans at first experience drowsiness and dizziness, followed by a feeling of tranquility and psychic detachment from the physical world. As the rituals associated with San Pedro proceed, the shamans are able to free themselves from the constraints of material reality to fly freely and ecstatically through the cosmos, communicating with the spirits.

San Pedro is widely sold in traditional markets throughout the coast of Peru, and it is used by *curanderos*, or curing shamans, in treating a variety of illnesses. Occasionally, to increase its potency and effectiveness, dust and powdered human bones from cemeteries are added to it. During a nighttime ritual a shaman sets up a *mesa*, or "table," of power objects placed on a cloth on the ground and ingests San Pedro to carry out a battle with the hostile forces that have brought about the illness. Sometimes the hallucinogenic potion is given to the patients themselves, whose reactions run the gamut from remaining calm and somnolent to engaging in violent dancing and falling writhing upon the ground. San Pedro works other magico-religious wonders as well: For example, it is able to guard houses much as a guard dog does, whistling in ghostly fashion to scare away intruders on the owner's property.

VIROLA SP.

Virola is the fifth of South America's most widely used "sacred inebriants," as Schultes and Hoffman call them. Obtained from the bark of a tree, it is used by village groups throughout the rainforests of the eastern Amazon as well as in most of the Orinoco Basin area. The Tukano of eastern Colombia have a myth that *Virola*, which they call *viho*, was received by humans at the beginning of the cosmos when the Sun's daughter, who had engaged in an incestuous act with him, scratched his penis, whereupon the sacred snuff powder issued forth with his semen. From that time until now it has been used only by the shamans to contact the snuff person, Viho-mahse, who from his home in the Milky Way guides human affairs and controls access by the shamans to all other spirits. *Virola*'s use is also restricted to the shamans among other nearby groups who employ it in rituals of curing, prophecy, and divination.

The methods of preparation vary from place to place. For example, among groups of eastern Colombia the soft, inner layer is scraped away from the bark, which must be collected in the early morning hours. After mixing the shavings with cold water for some minutes, the shaman boils down the resulting brownish liquid to a thick syrup, which is left to dry and finally pulverized into a powder that is combined with ashes from cacao bark. The Makú, a group of band societies of this same area, simply ingest the inner layer of the *Virola* bark directly without any preparation at all.

Elsewhere in the eastern lowlands, for example, in the Orinoco area, its use and the methods of preparation are somewhat distinct. Any male who has gone through the puberty rites that occur at ages thirteen to fourteen may use *Virola*, or *ebene* as it is called here. It is often used on a daily basis for communicating with the spirits, who may be summoned either to cure or to carry out some act of vengeance against a nearby enemy. The Waiká dry the inner bark shavings over a fire so that they may be stored for later use. Then, after a procedure of boiling, drying, and pulverizing very similar to that of groups in the Colombian Amazon, the snuff powder is mixed with the ashes from the bark of a rare, leguminous tree as well as with the aromatic leaves of third, nonhallucinogenic plant cultivated just for this purpose.

Schultes and Hoffman note that among some rainforest groups this hallucinogen is taken in "frighteningly excessive amounts," involving various inhalations in rapid succession and from three to six teaspoons of snuff in each inhalation. Everywhere that *Virola* is dried into a powder, it is snuffed into the nostrils by one or another tubed instruments. For example, the Yanomamö take *ebene* by having another person blow it with substantial force through a long tube into their nostrils and sinuses. This causes the taker of the drug to reel backward with equal violence, whereupon the eyes begin to water and copious amounts of green mucous are discharged from the nostrils. With his eyes rolling from the effects of ebene and a dreamlike expression on his face, the taker enters a period of hyperactivity during which the *hekura* spirits are contacted. The session ends with a protracted period of stupor and inactivity.

Some thirteen thousand years of experience with the natural environment have given indigenous South Americans an exquisitely detailed knowledge of the nutritional and psychoactive properties of their continent's flora.

References

Gumilla, Joseph. 1791. *Historia natural civil y geográfica de las naciones situadas en las riveras del Río Orinoco*. Barcelona: C. Gilbert y Tuto.

Schultes, Richard Evans, and Albert Hofmann. 1992. *Plants of the Gods: Their Sacred, Healing, and Hallucinogenic Powers*. Rochester, VT: Healing Arts Press.

Benjamin S. Orlove teaches environmental sciences and policy at University of California (Davis), and is editor of the major international journal Current Anthropology. *His best-known books include* The Allure of the Foreign: Imported Goods in Postcolonial Latin America; Apacas, Sheep, and Men; In My Father's Study; Land and Power in Latin America *(with G. Custred);* The Social Economy of Consumption *(with H. J. Rutz);* Lines in the Water: Nature and Culture at Lake Titicaca; *and* State, Capital, and Rural Society *(with M. W. Foley and T. F. Love).*

John C. H. Chiang is a postdoctoral fellow in climate and global change, at the University of Washington's Joint Institute for the Study of the Atmosphere and Ocean.

Mark A. Cane teaches earth and climate sciences at the Lamont-Doherty Earth Observatory of Columbia University.

In an imaginative experiment, Orlove and his colleagues have melded qualitative ethnographic reports, based on observations of workaday behavior, with elaborately quantified data, some of which have only recently become available through extraterrestrial imaging. As has often been the case before, Western science can be said to have vindicated traditional local ethnoscience—or, some might suggest, finally to have caught up with it.

The insight and sophistication of native peoples has been repeatedly demonstrated—in metallurgy, medicine, agriculture, construction, and other fields. Anthropologists long ago ceased to characterize populations as "primitive" just because they lacked writing, and a society that has a relatively "simple" technology may have an incredibly complex cosmology or kinship system.

Some of the indigenous empires in various parts of what is now Latin America dazzled the Spaniards when they first arrived. Yet the highly sophisticated knowledge of astronomy and meteorology that is reflected in these patterns of planting was ignored by the self-styled "White" class of landlords, who treated these same people as beasts of burden and virtual serfs in a quasi-feudal system until recent years (compare Doughty, chapter 22).

Forecasting Andean Rainfall and Crop Yield
Western Science and Folk-Wisdom

Benjamin S. Orlove
John C. H. Chiang
Mark A. Cane

Farmers in drought-prone regions of Andean South America have historically made observations of changes in the apparent brightness of stars in the Pleiades around the time of the southern winter solstice in order to forecast interannual variations in summer rainfall and in autumn harvests. They moderate the effect of reduced rainfall by adjusting the planting dates of potatoes, their most important crop.[1] Here we use data on cloud cover and water vapour from satellite imagery, agronomic data from the Andean altiplano and an index of El Niño variability to analyze this forecasting method. We find that poor visibility of the Pleiades in June—caused by an increase in subvisual high cirrus clouds—is indicative of an El Niño year, which is usually linked to reduced rainfall during the growing season several months later. Our results suggest that this centuries-old method[2] of seasonal rainfall forecasting may be based on a simple indicator of El Niño variability.

We reviewed anthropological accounts of indigenous Aymara- and Quechua-speaking farmers of the Peruvian and Bolivian Andes (hereafter central Andes). In 12 villages,[3–16] the inhabitants observe the Pleiades in late June in order to forecast the weather during the growing season (October–May). Observations often begin around

Abridged and reprinted by permission from *Nature*, vol. 403 (6765), pp. 68–71. Copyright © 2000 Macmillan Magazines Ltd.

15 June and culminate on 24 June, the festival of San Juan. They occur an hour or two before dawn, when the Pleiades are located low over the horizon to the northeast.

Four different attributes of the Pleiades were reported. Two attributes are directly related to the relative clarity of transparency of the sky: the brightness of the cluster and the timing of the heliacal rise (the date of the first appearance in the eastern pre-dawn sky). The third attribute, the apparent size of the Pleiades, may also be related to atmospheric clarity. On nights when the dimmest starts are visible, the Pleiades will appear to be 25% larger in diameter than on less clear nights (figure 1). The fourth attribute, the relative position of the brightest star in the Pleiades, is reported in various ways in different villages. Our interpretation of this attribute is uncertain, but the brightest star in the cluster may appear to shift its position when the dimmest stars are no longer visible.

The villagers use these attributes to forecast the timing and quantity of rains and to estimate the size of the harvest, concentrated between March and May of the following year. The attributes associated with clearer skies indicate earlier and more abundant rains and larger harvests, while the opposite is linked to less clear skies. If poor rains are predicted, villagers postpone the planting of potatoes. A shallow-rooted crop, potatoes are most vulnerable to drought at planting, when low soil moisture inhibits root formation,[17] and again a few weeks later when the sprouts have depleted the residual moisture in the seed tubers. Lack of soil moisture at that time reduces the number of stems per plant and the overall yield.[18] By delaying for 4–6 weeks after the usual October-November planting time, the farmers reduce these risks by starting the potato crop in months of higher rainfall.

This forecasting system is likely to be more than four centuries old. The Incas, who unified the central Andes in the fifteenth century and were in turn conquered by the Spaniards in 1532, worshipped and closely observed the Pleiades.[19] It is not established that they used its appearance to forecast weather, but several sources do document such forecasts soon after the conquest. In the late sixteenth century, some central Andean villages celebrated the Pleiades in June,[20] some noted the date of its heliacal rise,[21] and some made forecasts that linked a large apparent size of the Pleiades with good harvests and a small size with poor harvests.[2] The general importance of the Pleiades in Andean astronomy is suggested by its prominent position in a seventeenth-century cosmological chart.[22]

We now examine whether the visibility of the Pleiades from the central Andes in June is correlated with harvests in the following year. We use high cloud as a measure of atmospheric transparency. The International Satellite Cloud Climatology Project (ISCCP) nadir-viewing satellite cloud data set provides data on high cloud cover over the central Andes.[23] For a measure of harvests, we use yield for Puno department, located near the center of the region in which forecasts are made. Because of the low angle of the Pleiades at the time of observation, the relevant region is about 175 km to the northeast of the villages, where correlations are in the −0.5 to −0.6 range. In the five cases for which independent data on forecast and outcome are available, the forecasts have been accurate.

To account for this correlation, we examine the links of high cloud amount and potato harvest, as well as precipitation, to El Niño/Southern Oscillation (ENSO). ENSO is an interannual climate fluctuation originating from large-scale dynamical interactions between the ocean and atmosphere of the tropical Pacific, and has the largest effect on short-term global climate variability of any such fluctuation. ENSO influences a number of atmospheric variables in the central Andes. Atmospheric extinction data measured by the Stratospheric Aerosol and Gas Experiment II (SAGE II) solar occultation instrument show that tropic cirrus cloud cover increases in warm ENSO years relative to cold ENSO years over the central Andes.[24] At the representative altitude of 14.5 km, the cloud amount increased from around 35% in cold ENSO years to 50% in warm ENSO years. Though too much high cloud could totally mask out the Pleiades, the SAGE II data show that most tropical high cloud is subvisual (with optical thickness

Figure 1

A diagram of the stars in the Pleiades of visual magnitude 6.0 or brighter. Although human visual acuity is often reduced at high elevations above sea level, suggesting that a lower threshold would be appropriate in this case, we note that hypoxia, the cause of this diminution, is not a problem for the populations under study. [30] In this diagram, the size of each star is proportional to its intensity. We show three frames representing the Pleiades in steps of a 0.75 change in apparent magnitude, to show the effect of different observing conditions. The stars can be grouped into three brightness classes. The brightest group consists of only one star (Alcyone or 25 Tauri) of magnitude 2.90. There is a gap of 0.72 magnitude between this star and the intermediate group, of magnitude 3.62–4.30. A gap of 0.79 magnitude separates this group from the dimmest group, of magnitude 5.09–5.80. The axis of the six brightest stars in the Pleiades has an apparent breadth of 59 arcmin. For comparison, the moon's apparent diameter is less than 32 arcmin.

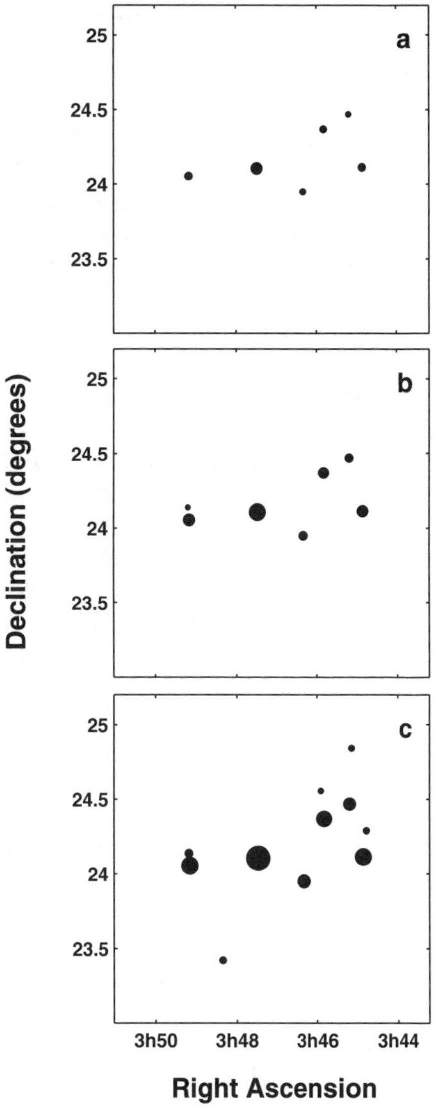

<0.03) from just over 50% of cloud amount at the 10.5-km level to almost 100% above 16 km. We estimate the average optical thickness of the 10–19 km cloud layer to be between 0.05 and 0.35, with the major uncertainty due to uncertainty in the extinction coefficients of the optically thicker clouds in this layer. Change in cloud amount between cold and warm ENSO years thus leads to an estimated optical thickness change between 0.01 and 0.1, yielding a change in Pleiades brightness of around 0.1 to 1 magnitude. This shift is sufficient to visibly reduce the apparent brightness of the Pleiades between cold and warm years.

Increase in cloud frequency in the SAGE II data set is corroborated by high-cloud data from the ISCCP dataset.[23] Optically thin (<0.1 at 0.6 μm) clouds are at the detection limit for the ISCCP,[25] but even if the optically thin clouds are not detected, the high-cloud correlation with ENSO implies more moist conditions during warm years and an increased likelihood of thin clouds.

We considered other factors that might influence atmospheric visibility in the central Andes in June. Using a reanalysis data set,[26] we found that upper-level winds increase in warm ENSO years. Though the accompanying decrease in vertical stability might lead to more turbulence, this change would have little direct effect on visibility. ENSO is also significantly correlated with total column-integrated precipitable water northeast of the villages, as estimated by mean monthly data from the Total Ozone Vertical Sounder (TOVS).[23] The increase in total precipitable water from cold to warm ENSO years is around 10–20% of the mean amount, and may contribute to the formation of thin high cloud. The reanalysis data set[26] indicates that the surface relative humidity of about 60–70% increases by about 5–10% in warm years. Standard formulas[27] indicate that this increase would alter apparent magnitude by about 0.1, a level too small to be appreciated by the naked-eye observer. We conclude that the significant changes in visibility are attributable to changes in high cloud alone. However, our confidence in the link between ENSO and shifts in cloud cover is bolstered by the consistent relationship found within independent data sets between ENSO and other atmospheric variables.

We note that synoptic variability in atmospheric conditions implies that a single viewing on 24 June at the festival of San Juan could be misleading. It is a common but not universal practice to make observations over a number of days, increasing the likelihood of registering the ENSO signal correctly. Additional research with a larger sample of villages would be needed to ascertain the range of observing practices. Are they near "optimal" for the purpose of prediction, or are they strongly shaped by social and cultural factors?

That drought conditions in the central Andes are associated with El Niño has been documented.[28, 29] To further analyze this relation, we examined precipitation data between July 1962 and June 1988 from the 4 stations with nearly complete records representative of the region occupied by the 12 villages: Ayacucho, Cusco and Juliaca in Peru, and La Paz in Bolivia. After removing the climatological monthly mean at each station, we normalized each time series by its standard deviation. We then averaged the four normalized anomaly time series to create an index of central Andes precipitation anomalies. When data were missing (about 9% of the time), we estimated the index as the average of the remaining available station values. Other indices (total rainfall; the first principal component) gave quite similar results.

Precipitation anomalies summed over the entire year (July to the following June) are likely to be lower during warmer El Niño years. Precipitation anomalies summed over the highest-precipitation months of December to February show an even tighter relationship. October precipitation is also suppressed during El Niño years, suggesting a later onset of the rainy season. In keeping with the type of forecasts made by the Andeans, we also divide ("bin") the data into high/low precipitation, and high/low NINO3, and apply χ^2 tests to measure the significance of the relations. (NINO3 is the sea surface temperature anomaly, averaged of 5° S–5° N and 150° W–90° W.) Our ability to test the significance of these relationships is limited by the relatively small amount of data; nevertheless, the test shows high significance (exceeding the 95% level) for the December-February precipitation relationship. The other two relationships are less significant (around the 75% level).

Given the sensitivity of potatoes to drought, this reduction in precipitation may account for part of the relationship between June high-cloud amount and potato harvests. A more complete analysis of the effect of climate on crops must include other climatic variables, most notably temperature. In fact, we find a strong monotonic relationship between ENSO and mean monthly temperatures in the central Andes region, with warmer mean temperatures in the central Andes during El Niño years. Though the effect of temperature on crop growth is not obvious, the consequence of ENSO for potato yields is convincingly demonstrated from preliminary analysis of potato-yield data from Puno department near Lake Titicaca. Significant reductions in potato yield are observed for warm ENSO years. A 2-bin χ^2 test shows significance at the 90% level. The linear correlation value is –0.6.

***

We thank G. Urton for insights into Andean ethnoastronomy, G. Rasmussen for discussions on visibility and cirrus cloud, G. Scott for providing potato yield data for Puno department, Peru, and R. Bishop, K. Cook, D. Dearborn, D. Helfand, A. Kaplan, G. Kiladis, J. Lenters, J. Sarazin and B. Schafer for comments. M.A.C. thanks B. D'Achille for first making him aware of the Andean forecasting scheme.

***

References

[1] Zimmerer, K. S. 1996. *Changing Fortunes: Biodiversity and Peasant Livelihood in the Peruvian Andes.* Berkeley: University of California Press.

[2] Salomon, F., & Urioste, G. L. 1991 [c. 1608]. *The Huarochirí Manuscript: A Testament of Ancient and Colonial Andean Religion.* Austin: University of Texas Press.

[3] Ballón Aguirre, E., Cerrón Palomino, R. O., & Chambi Apaza, E. 1992. *Vocabulario Razonado de la Actividad Agraria Andina: Terminología Agraria Quechua.* Cusco: Centro de Estudios Regionales Andinos "Bartolomé de las Casas."

[4] Urton, G. 1981. *At the Crossroads of the Earth and the Sky: An Andean Cosmology.* Austin: University of Texas Press.

[5] Grillo Fernández, E., Quiso Choque, V., Rengifo Vásquez, G., & Valladolid Rivera, J. 1994. *Crianza Andina de la Chacra.* Lima: Proyecto Andino de Tecnología Campesina.

[6] Mishkin, B. 1940. Cosmological ideas among the Indians of the southern Andes. *Journal of American Folklore,* 53, 225–241.

[7] Morote Best, E. 1953. La fiesta de San Juan, el Bautista. *Arch. Peruanos Folklore,* 1, 160–200.

[8] Orlove, B. S. 1979. Two rituals and three hypotheses: An examination of solstice divination in southern highland Peru. *Anthropol. Quart.,* 52, 86–98.

[9] Lira, J. A. 1946. *Farmacopea Tradicional Indígena y Prácticas Rituales.* Lima: El Condor.

[10] Camino, A., Recharte, J., & Bidegaray, P. 1981. *La Tecnología en el Mundo Andino: Runakunap Kawsayninkupaq Rurasqankunaqa* Vol. 1 (eds. Lechtman, H. & Soldi, A. M.), 261–281. Mexico City: Universidad Nacional Autónoma de México.

[11] Goland, C. 1992. *Cultivating Diversity: Field Scattering as Agricultural Risk Management in Cuyo Cuyo, Dept. of Puno, Peru.* Working paper No. 4, Research Project on Production, Storage and Exchange in a Terraced Environment on the Eastern Andean Escarpment. Chapel Hill: Department of Anthropology, University of North Carolina.

[12] Kolata, A. 1996. *Valley of the Spirits: A Journey into the Lost Realm of the Aymara.* New York: Wiley.

[13] Carter, W. E., & Mamani, M. 1982. *Irpa Chico: Individuo y Comunidad en la Cultura Aymara.* La Paz: Juventud.

[14] Mamani, M. 1988, in *Raíces de América: el Mundo Aymara* (ed. Albó, X). Madrid: Alianza.

[15] Yampara Huarachi, S. 1992, in *La Cosmovisión Aymara* (eds. van den Berg, H. & Schiffers, N.), 143–186. La Paz: UCB/HISBOL.

[16] Kraft, K. E. 1995. *Andean Fields and Fallow Pastures: Communal Land Use Management under Pressures for Intensification.* Thesis, University of Florida.

[17] Beukema, H. P., & van de Zaag, D. E. 1990. *Introduction to Potato Production.* Wageningen: Pudoc.

[18] MacKerron, D. K. L., & Jeffries, R. A. 1988. The distribution of tuber sizes in droughted and irrigated crops of potato, I: Observations on the effect of water stress on graded yields from differing cultivars. *Potato Res.,* 31, 269–278.

[19] Bauer, B. S., & Dearborn, D. S. P. 1995. *Astronomy and Empire in the Ancient Andes: The Cultural Origins of Inca Sky Watching.* Austin: University of Texas Press.

[20] de Arriaga, P. J. 1968 [1621]. *The Extirpation of Idolatry in Peru.* Lexington: University of Kentucky Press.

[21] Anonymous Jesuit priest. 1919. Misión de las provincias de los Huachos y Yauyos. *Rev. Histórica* (Lima) 6, 180–197.

[22] de Santillán, F., Valera, B., & Pachacuti, J. de S. C. 1950. *Tres Relaciones de Antigüedades Peruanas.* Asunción: Guaranía.

[23] Rossow, W. B. & Schiffer, R. A. 1991. ISCCP cloud data products. *Bull. Am. Meteorol. Soc.* 72, 2–20.

[24] Kent, G. S. et al. 1995. Surface temperature related variations in tropical cirrus cloud as measured by SAGE II. *J. Clim,* 8, 2577–2594.

[25] Liao, X., Rossow, W. B. & Rind, D. Comparison between SAGE II and ISCCP high-level clouds 1. Global and zonal mean cloud amounts. *J. Geophy. Res.* 100, 1121–1135 (1995).

[26] Kalnay, E. et al. 1996. The NCEP/NCAR 40 year reanalysis project. *Bull. Am. Meteorol. Soc.* 77, 437–471.

[27] Schaefer, B. E. 1993. Astronomy and the limits of vision. *Vistas Astron.* 36, 311–361.

[28] Thompson, L. G., Mosley-Thompson, E., & Arnao, B. J. 1984. El Niño-Southern Oscillation events recorded in the stratigraphy of the tropical Quelccaya ice cap, Peru. *Science* 226, 50–53.

[29] Aceituno, P. 1988. On the functioning of the Southern Oscillation in the South American sector. Part I: Surface climate. *Mon. Weath. Rev.* 116, 505–524.

[30] Frisancho, A. R. et al. 1995. Developmental, genetic and environmental components of aerobic capacity at high altitude. *Am. J. Phys. Anthropol.* 96, 431–442.

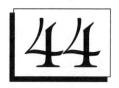

Sidney M. Greenfield recently retired from teaching anthropology at the University of Wisconsin (Milwaukee). His best-known books include English Rustics in Black Skin: A Study of Modern Family Forms in a Pre-Industrial Society, Structure and Process in Latin America (with A. Strickon), Entrepreneurs in Cultural Context (with A. Strickon), and Reinventing Religions: Syncretism and Transformation in Africa and the Americas (with A. Droogers).

Sociologists doing survey-research have long used "religion" as a demographic category, as if labeling someone "Protestant," "Catholic," "Jew," "Other," or "None" were a meaningful way of differentiating subpopulations with respect to such variables as morbidity, causes of mortality, attitudes, life-chances, and so forth. Some investigators insisted that further subdivisions were important, such as "ascetic," "fundamentalist," or "liberal" within Protestantism; "orthodox," "conservative," or "reform" among Jews; and so forth. Still others stress that self-described depth of commitment to any faith often appears to be more revealing than which faith one professes.

Anthropologists usually tend to be more flexible in terms of categorizing or classifying groups, posing more open-ended questions, and placing more reliance on context to ascertain what labels are described and important in the view of the subjects themselves. With specific reference to religion, it is increasingly evident that some people are far more flexible than others, trying one and then another, for different purposes at different stages of their lives, or even participating in more than one at a time.

Dr. Greenfield here succinctly shows not only the famous religious pluralism that is available in Brazil (including diverse Afro-Brazilian possession-cults and spiritism as well as Catholicism) but also, in case studies, how some individuals choose among them. If he were to do restudies, one would not be surprised to see some of the same individuals making different choices at other times.

The dyadic contract is important here (Foster, chapter 31), as is the distinction between folk- and formal-Catholicism (Canin, chapter 41). Although phrased very differently, the attractions of Protestantism in a religious marketplace are very similar in some respects (Arcand, chapter 36).

The Pragmatics of Conversion in the Brazilian Religious Marketplace

Sidney M. Greenfield

This paper addresses the subject of religious conversion in what is conceptualized as the Brazilian religious marketplace. The literature on religious conversion tends to focus on individuals consciously reacting to a belief system other than the one into which they were born and/or with which they are affiliated, and on examination of the process by which they choose to identify with and participate in it rather than the one formerly followed. Such analysis is generally presumed to be rational and intellectual, the subject matter spiritual and emotional, and the emphasis often otherworldly.

For many Brazilians, by contrast, I find instead that individuals regularly change their religious affiliation, some more than once during their lifetime. Such decisions are made, more often than not, for pragmatic, practical reasons. This is not to say that Brazilians do not feel passionately about religion. It also is not to say that those who change from one religion to another do not experience and express deep emotion. Instead it is to say that, for purposes of sociological or anthropological analysis, those who convert can fruitfully also be viewed as consumers choosing among alternative suppliers. Religious groups ranging from Roman Catholicism (in its popular form) to Candomblé, Xangô, Batuque, Umbanda and other African-derived traditions, to Kardecist Spiritism and even a number of Protestant denominations (mostly from North

Written expressly for *Contemporary Cultures and Societies of Latin America*, Third Edition

America) each offer, in addition to their beliefs about salvation and a better future in this and another world, a variety of services to help followers—and potential new recruits—with practical problems that range from material assistance to the healing of illnesses to domestic happiness. In times of personal crisis, individuals may be thought of as "shopping" among alternative religious groups until they find one that satisfies their needs. After finding a job, changing a mate, or recovering from an illness, often they convert to the religious group that facilitated that happening. This does not necessarily mean that they give up their affiliation with the religion they previously practiced. Multiple religious identities are not uncommon in Brazil. Should their new religion not be able to resolve their next crisis, they may re-enter the market, where they shop again until they find a provider that resolves their new difficulty. The imagery I offer is of individuals moving in and out of the marketplace in search of solutions to their personal problems. Help is offered by the many competing religious suppliers and the price is affiliation, implying conversion.

THE HISTORICAL AND THEORETICAL CONTEXT

For almost four centuries, from the time of its discovery in 1500 through the colonial period followed by independence as an empire beginning in 1822, Roman Catholicism was the official religion of Brazil. Only since the first Republican constitution (1891) and a series of revisions to follow (a period of a little more than a century) have Brazilians been free to worship in the religion of their choice. At present, numerous independent religious groups with their roots in the traditions of the indigenous peoples, the Africa of the slaves, pre-Reformation Iberian Europe, post-Reformation northern and western Europe and North America, Asia and other parts of the world (mixed, or syncretized in varying ways and degrees) are competing with Roman Catholicism, and with each other, for followers from a population that, in addition to becoming predominantly urban, industrial and modern in the second half of the twentieth century, has increased from approximately 17 million in 1900 to an estimated 170 million today.

"POPULAR" CATHOLICISM AND THE CULT OF THE SAINTS

Brazilian Catholicism, as Bastide (1951:346) observed almost half a century ago, is turned more toward the saints and the Virgin than to God. It is based on the ancient cult of the saints more than on the recent teachings of the official Church. As Freyre (1964) and others (Azzi 1978) remind us, religion in Brazil always has been a mostly private and personal matter. Individuals, many the founders of the great houses (and families) established around the production of sugarcane, the mining of gold and diamonds and other economic boom activities, and others across the socioeconomic hierarchy, had their own domestic shrines and chapels in which images of the Virgin and their personal saints were placed and venerated.

In its pre-Reformation or medieval form, the Catholicism that was introduced into Brazil and is still, for the most part, practiced there—as "popular" Catholicism, as it is in many other parts of Latin America—is part of a complex of understanding, central to which is a belief in and a reverence for saints, supernatural beings who at one time are believed to have lived as mortals on earth. "Reborn" and elevated to everlasting life in heaven by an all-powerful creator God believed to have control over all aspects of the universe, including the destinies of those on earth, they also are believed, as "friends of God," to be able to act as intermediaries with Him on behalf of supplicants on earth. As Wilson (1983:23) has phrased a position proclaimed in the official theology of the

Church, ". . . saint(s) might be seen as advocates pleading causes before a stern judge, as mediators, as go-betweens, as intriguers or wire-pullers at the court of Heaven . . ."

Through prayer the faithful may invoke the saints and petition their help with material as well as spiritual problems. Attaining this supernatural intervention in the material world is referred to as a miracle. Miracles, as Augustine of Hippo was so influential in maintaining, "were signs of God's power and proof of the sanctity of those in whose name they were wrought" (Woodward 1990:62).[1]

Vows to the saints, however, are made conditionally. They do not have to be fulfilled unless or until the petitioner obtains what has been requested. Only then is he or she obligated to fulfill the conditions expressed in the vow.

Because they once lived on earth, the saints are thought to understand and be sympathetic to human suffering and generally disposed to assisting those who invoke them. To increase the probability of obtaining a saint's help, a petitioner usually makes a vow,[2] or *promessa*, which will include some incentive or compensation (Azevedo 1963:76) for the saint, such as the promise to visit the saint's shrine and while there perhaps having masses said in his/her honor, lighting candles, performing acts of penitence such as walking the stations of the cross with rocks on the petitioner's head, or walking around the shrine on the believer's knees.

The ". . . relationship between a saint and a devotee," as Queiroz (1973:86) observes, "is one of reciprocity, or better of *dou ut des*: I give to receive something in exchange." The devotee and the saint, as Magnani (1984:123–149) writes in words that invoke the image of the marketplace, enter into a contract in which the worshipper offers the saint something of value to the saint in exchange for his or her intercession and help. This exchange, it should be noted, is what Foster (1963) and others (Greenfield 1972, 1977, 1979; Gross 1971; Hutchinson 1966; Roniger 1987, 1990) were referring to when they wrote about relations of patronage and clientage. These relationships and the efforts by the living to establish them with supernatural beings express, I suggest, the rules by which the religious marketplace in Brazil operates today.

NON-CATHOLIC ANALOGUES

I further contend that, in addition to their own specific histories, cosmologies, beliefs and ritual practices, the other religions that have undertaken to compete with Catholicism—and its popular cult of the saints—in Brazil's religious marketplace each offer potential converts access to supernaturals with whom relations of patronage and clientage can be established in ways analogous to the Roman Catholic practice of making and fulfilling a vow to a saint. If and when the request, *promessa*, or vow is fulfilled, an individual gets the help requested from the supernatural being, thereby establishing a relationship of asymmetrical exchange. Conversion often follows as part of the fulfillment of the "contract." Of considerable importance here is the convergence between the view of the supernatural that was brought by slaves from West Africa and is embedded in just about all the Afro-Brazilian religions, and popular Catholicism. Castro and Santos, for example, pointedly derive the etymology of the word *Candomblé*, the oldest and most generic of the Afro-Brazilian religious forms, from the proto-Bantu word *kò-dómb-éd-à*, which they say means "to ask the intercession of" (Castro and Santos 1977, cited in Harding 2000:45).

SOME ILLUSTRATIVE EXAMPLES

Case #1:   Marco Antônio is an educated young man who works as a bank clerk in a major Brazilian metropolitan center. Several years ago he began to experience nagging back pain, excessive fatigue and a loss of appetite. He went to his doctor, who sent him to a specialist after the medications he prescribed failed to ameliorate the condition. The tests the specialist ordered did not help him to diagnose and treat the ailment. In addition to his physical problems, conditions at work seemed to deteriorate. Furthermore, the young bank employee was constantly fighting with his girlfriend, whom he suspected of being involved with another man. Marco Antônio felt that his life was at an impasse.

One day a colleague at work mentioned Mãe Stella, the head of an Umbanda center, when relating a story about how medical doctors had been unable to cure his youngest child. After several traumatic incidents, a neighbor suggested that the Pomba-Gira, a spirit Mãe Stella "incorporated" (i.e., by whom Mãe Stella was possessed) might be able to help the child. The father then told Marco Antônio about the child's "miraculous" recovery after treatment at the Umbanda center. Not knowing what else to do about his own problem, the bank clerk attended a public session at the Umbanda center.

He remembered his skepticism when he first saw Mãe Stella and her *filhos-* and *filhas-de-santo* (saint sons and daughters) sing and dance and enter into trance. After all, he was an intelligent and educated person with a university degree. He "should have known better" than to participate in such *brucharia* (witchcraft), as his father called it when his son told him about his plan to attend the session.

Nevertheless, the still-suffering young man decided to go to the ritual session and consult with the Pomba-Gira—through Mãe Stella. As he moved forward in the line of people waiting to speak with her, he saw the *mãe-de-santo* for the first time. She was dressed in the attire of what to him seemed a nineteenth-century prostitute, smoking a cigarette in a long, black holder and gulping liquid from a champagne glass that was being refilled—for the fourth time since he had entered the room—by an attendant. When his turn to speak with her finally came, the spiritual leader greeted him in a deep, sultry voice, in an accent he could scarcely understand, and asked what his problem was and how she might help him.

In flirtatious, thickly accented tones, she promised to help rid him of his symptoms. She said that he would have to return for a private session and bring with him live chickens, a goat, some pigeons and other small animals. The work (*trabalho*) would cost the equivalent of several hundred dollars, close to a month's wages. Over the objections of his "very Catholic" father, Marco Antônio purchased the animals and returned to the Umbanda center at the designated time.

Already in trance when he arrived (and incorporating the Pomba-Gira), Mãe Stella informed Marco Antônio that his "paths were closed" and that her efforts would help to open them, leading eventually to his recovery. She took the animals he brought and sacrificed them, using the parts to prepare the Pomba-Gira's favorite foods—as an offering. She then informed her client that he had mediumship ability that would have to be developed if he wished to recover completely. The implication of this, as Marco Antônio came to understand, was that in order to be cured, he would have to learn to receive Umbanda's spirits: the *orixás*, *preto velhos*, *caboclos*, *exus*, and *crianças*. In brief, he would have to become an Umbandista and be possessed by its spirits.

In the days following the ceremony, Marco Antônio's pains, to his and his skeptical father's great surprise, gradually subsided. He had more energy and his appetite returned. He slept at night for the first time in months and he no longer felt depressed. That was three years ago. Since then he has become one of a growing number of "regulars" at Mãe Stella's Umbanda center. Recently he completed his first *obrigação* (obligation), beginning the initiatory cycle that will lead to his eventually qualifying to head his own center. In brief, in obtaining a cure for his still undiagnosed illness, Marco Antônio had become an Umbandista.

Case #2: Osamarina Budazi was an educated 61-year-old childless widow of a middle-class European immigrant when she was diagnosed as having breast cancer. Her doctor recommended surgery to remove the tumor, to be followed by radiation therapy. Mrs. Budazi, however, had a bad heart and had almost died during a previous surgical intervention. She doubted whether she could survive the recommended operation. Uncertain of how to proceed, she sought counsel from her relatives. A cousin in Recife, a city about 800 miles from her home, telephoned her with information about a Spiritist healer she had seen perform surgeries without chemical or any other visible anesthesia. The healer, himself a trained physician who, when in trance, was said to receive the spirit of a long deceased German physician who guided his body when treating patients, also used no antisepsis. On the basis of her relative's recommendation, and without telling her medical doctor, Mrs. Budazi went to Recife to have her tumor removed.

The surgery, performed at a Spiritist center, lasted about 45 minutes. Unlike most of the other patients treated by the healer that night, Mrs. Budazi experienced excruciating pain. She screamed uncontrollably for most of the time she was on the table. The tumor was removed and by the following day the pain had subsided, enabling Mrs. Budazi to venture out to a nearby shopping mall. The surgery and the pain she experienced had no negative effect on her heart.

After several weeks convalescing at her cousin's home, Mrs. Budazi returned to São Paulo. Less than a year later her cancer was back. She returned to Recife where she was told by the healer's wife that everything the spirits could do for her already had been done. Her treatment now could be finished by an earthly doctor. The healer then gave her the name of a friend in the city where she lived who specialized in cases such as hers.

Mrs. Budazi telephoned the doctor, who invited her to come to his clinic where he eventually removed the remainder of her breast and treated her with radiation therapy. The chemical anesthesia he used had no adverse effect on her heart; she soon was on the road to recovery. In Mrs. Budazi's mind she had been cured not by the medical techniques of her earthly physician but by the spirits, the deceased Dr. Fritz and his associates.

During the long waiting period before the healer in Recife arrived to attend to the patients at the Spiritist center, Mrs. Budazi and the others were instructed in Spiritist teachings and philosophy and told to read Allan Kardec, the codifier of the movement, and other Spiritist authors. They also were advised to visit a Spiritist center when they returned home, to take classes there and, most importantly, to participate in its program of doing charity, the *sine qua non* of the religion.

Mrs. Budazi did so. Soon she was participating in a pre-school program organized by the people at the center in a *favela*, as the many slums surrounding the city of São Paulo are called. She spent one full day per week working with and helping the children. During the 11 years I followed her progress after her first surgery, she said that she never missed a day working with the children. She organized her life, her visits to relatives in other states and everything else so that she would be with the children on Mondays. Although she still thought of herself as a Catholic, she had stopped attending church. Instead she participated exclusively in the Spiritist program. She was, she told me, giving to the children as charity what she had received from the spirits.

Cases #3 & 4: Maria was an eighteen-year-old immigrant from a rural part of Calabria in southern Italy who came to Brazil with her new husband in 1953. She was "a good Catholic" who grew up in the church and attended services regularly. Shortly after their first child was born and she was pregnant with a second, her husband deserted her. Maria stayed with a friend from her hometown who also had emigrated to the capital of Brazil's southernmost state. When her second child was two months old, he became very sick. Medical treatment did not help. Desperate, Maria followed the advice of the Brazilian wife of her Calabrian benefactor and took the boy to a *mãe-de-santo* (saint mother)—described by her as *bem pretinha* (very dark skinned) and a *filha de Xangô* (a daughter of Xangô).

When the infant recovered, Maria did something not unusual for an Italian woman who believed that she had received a miracle: she promised the boy to God—in this instance not to the God of the Roman Catholic Church (as a priest) but to the "gods" from Africa who had answered her appeal and saved her son.

Maria never told the boy of her vow, but she took him with her when, in response to being told that she had mediumship abilities, she undertook training and participated in ritual activities at an Umbanda center.

Until he was fourteen, Luiz said that he wanted to become a priest. At fifteen, however, he started to take training at an Umbanda center. At seventeen he went to live with the *mãe-de-santo* who, as is common in Porto Alegre, practiced both Umbanda and Batuque. By the time he was eighteen he was initiated in the latter. He then returned to his mother's home to devote himself to the religion. It was not until after he completed the first phase of his ritual initiation that Maria told him about his childhood illness and the promise she had made.

Today Luiz is *a pai-de-santo* and the head of his own center, where he practices both Umbanda and Batuque. Maria, in an interesting role-reversal, is a *filha-de-santo* devoted to Umbanda in his center. The two, interestingly, do not identify themselves as Brazilians, even though Luiz was born there. They see themselves as Italians living in Brazil who are devoted to the gods of Africa, or at least the syncretized Afro-Brazilian pantheon. Maria believes that those gods were responsible for her coming to Brazil so that she might learn about them. Worshipping them and helping them to help others in need is the goal to which mother and son have both devoted their lives.

Discussion and Conclusions

The four people discussed in these cases were all devout and practicing Roman Catholics before they experienced personal crises, the resolution of which resulted in their adopting a new religious identity and practicing its beliefs and rituals. At the suggestion of third parties, none of whom was a member of the religious group whose services they recommended, each sought out what for them was a new religion to which, in return for the resolution of their problem, they eventually converted. Along the way each entered into contracts with supernatural beings in the pantheon of the new religion, because they had successfully established relationships of patron-client exchange. In contrast with popular Catholicism and its cult of the saints, in the cases presented here a human intermediary facilitated the contractual exchange. Moreover, the supernaturals each manifested themselves materially through an intermediary. Mãe Stella, for example, incorporated the Pomba-Gira who cured Marco Antônio and in doing so informed him that the "price" of his full recovery would be his entry into Umbanda by developing his mediumship abilities. Edson Queiroz was the intermediary through whom Dr. Fritz became manifest to operate on Mrs. Budazi. His assistants taught her the importance of participating in the Spiritist dispensation of charity. The dark-skinned *filha-de-Xangô* incorporated the deity that cured Luiz, leading to a lifetime commitment to the gods of Africa by him and his mother.

In all these cases the parties entered the religious marketplace not necessarily looking for a new belief system but just seeking solutions to personal problems. All were fortunate in that they found them. As a result, however, after entering into a relationship of patron-client exchange with one of its supernaturals, each, on its urging, converted to the religion that helped them, with which they now identify, and in which they participate fully and believe with passion.

Notes

[1] A material representation of the miracle, or of a letter attesting to it, also may be promised in the vow and deposited as a votive offering at the shrine as testimony of the saint's abilities and accomplishments.

[2] "One feature, above all," writes Sanchis (1983:266), characterizes the devotion paid to [the] saints . . . and it is also a distinguishing feature not only of the [pilgrimage] festival but of popular religion generally, and that is the vow."

References

Azevedo, Thales de. 1963. *Social Change in Brazil*. Gainesville: University of Florida Press.

Azzi, Riolando. 1978. *O Catolicismo Popular No Brasil*. Petrópolis, R.J., Brazil: Editora Vozes.

Bastide, Roger. 1951. "Religion and the Church in Brazil," in *Brazil: Portrait of Half a Continent*, edited by T. L. Smith & A. Marchant. New York: The Dryden Press.

Castro, Yeda Pessoa de and Guilherme A. de Souza Santos. 1977. "Culturas Africanas nas Américas: Um Esboço de Pesquisa Conjunto da Localização dos Empréstimos." Paper presented at FESTAC [World Bank and African Festival of Arts and Culture], Lagos, Nigeria.

Foster, George. 1963. "The Dyadic Contract in Tzintzuntzán, II: Patron-Client Relationship," *American Anthropologist* 65:1280–1294.

Freyre, Gilberto. 1964. *The Masters and the Slaves*. Translated by Samuel Putnam. New York: Alfred A. Knopf.

Greenfield, Sidney M. 1979. "Domestic Crises, Schools and Patron-Clientage in Southeastern Minas Gerais," in *Brazil: Anthropological Perspectives*, edited by Maxine Margolis and William Carter. New York: Columbia University Press, pp. 363–378.

———. 1977. "Patronage, Politics and the Articulation of Local Community and National Society in pre-1968 Brazil, *Journal of Inter-American Studies and World Affairs* 19, 2:139–172.

———. 1972. "Charwomen, Cesspools and Road Building: An Examination of Patronage, Clientage and Political Power in Southeastern Minas Gerais," in *Structure and Process in Latin America*, edited by Arnold Strickon and Sidney M. Greenfield. Albuquerque: University of New Mexico Press, pp. 71–100

Gross, Daniel. 1971. "Ritual Conformity: A Religious Pilgrimage to Northeastern Brazil," *Ethnology* 10, 2:129–148.

Harding, Rachael E. 2000. *A Refuge of Thunder: Candomblé and Alternative Spaces of Blackness*. Bloomington: Indiana University Press.

Hutchinson, Bertram. 1966. "The Patron-Dependent Relationship in Brazil: A Preliminary Examination," *Sociologia Ruralis* 6, 1:3–29.

Magnani, José Guilherme. 1984. "Curas e Milagres," in *A Religiosidade do Povo*, edited by Lísias Negrão et al. São Paulo: Ed. Paulinas.

Queiroz, Maria Isaura Perreira de. 1973. *O Campesinato Brasileiro*. Petróplis, R.J., Brazil: Editora Vozes.

Roniger, Luis. 1990. *Hierarchy and Trust in Modern Mexico and Brazil*. New York: Praeger.

———. 1987. "Caciquismo and Coronelismo: Contextual Dimensions in Patron Brokerage in Mexico and Brazil," *Latin American Research Review* 22, 2:71–99.

Sanchis, P. 1983. "The Portuguese 'Romarias,'" in *Saints and Their Cults: Studies in Religious Sociology, Folklore and History*, edited by S. Wilson. Cambridge: Cambridge University Press, pp. 261–289.

Wilson, Stephen, ed. 1983. *Saints and Their Cults: Studies in Religious Sociology*. Cambridge: Cambridge University Press.

Woodward, Kenneth L. 1990. *Making Saints: How the Catholic Church Determines Who Becomes a Saint, Who Doesn't, and Why*. New York: Simon and Schuster.

Nancy Scheper-Hughes is a professor of anthropology at the University of California Berkeley, who sees her role "as that of an alarmist, reminding people of the utter abnormality of the normal and of the chronic state of emergency in which we are living." Her best-known books include Child Survival; Saints, Scholars, and Schizophrenics: Mental Illness in Rural Ireland; Death without Weeping: The Violence of Everyday Life in Brazil; *and* Small Wars: The Cultural Politics of Childhood.

Death is an important part of life in every culture, and the mother-child bond is usually close in emotional as well as other terms. Scheper-Hughes's account of mothers who do not grieve the death of their infant offspring is a sensitive and insightful portrayal of the interplay between social norms and what many people mistake for "human nature." Incidentally, this extract also shows how a dogged social scientist can ferret out significant data that people aren't even aware they control, without in any measure diminishing the empathy and sympathy she shows for her respondents.

Death without Weeping
The Violence of Everyday Life in Brazil
Nancy Scheper-Hughes

FOREBODINGS

"Why do the church bells ring so often?" I asked Nailza de Arruda soon after I had moved into a corner of her tiny mud-walled hut near the top of the Alto do Cruzeiro. It was a dry and blazingly hot summer of 1964, the months following the military coup, and save for the rusty, clanging bells of Nossa Senhora das Dores Church, an eerie quiet had settled over the town. Beneath the quiet, however, were chaos and panic.

"It's nothing," replied Nailza, "just another little angel gone to heaven." Nailza had sent more than her share of little angels to heaven, and sometimes at night I could hear her engaged in a muffled, yet passionate, discourse with one of them: two-year-old Joana. Joana's photograph, taken as she lay eyes opened and propped up in her tiny cardboard coffin, hung on a wall next to the photo of Nailza and Zé Antônio taken on the day the couple had eloped a few years before. Zé Antônio, uncomfortable in his one good, starched, white shirt, looked into the camera every bit as startled as the uncanny wide-eyed toddler in her white dress.

Nailza could barely remember the names of the other infants and babies who came and went in close succession. Some had died unnamed and had been hastily baptized in their coffins. Few lived more than a month or two. Only Joana, properly baptized in church at the close of her first year and placed under the protection of a powerful saint, Joan of Arc, had been expected to live. And Nailza had dangerously allowed herself to love the little girl. In addressing the dead child, Nailza's voice would range from tearful imploring to angry recrimination: "Why did you leave me? Was your patron saint so greedy that she could not allow me one child on this earth?" Zé Antônio advised me to ignore Nailza's odd behavior, which he understood as a kind of madness that, like the birth and death of children, came and went.

It was not long after that Nailza was again noticeably pregnant, and the nightly prayers to Joana ceased, momentarily replaced by the furtive noises of stolen marital intimacies. By day, Nailza's appetite and her normally high spirits returned, much to my relief. The peacefulness was, however, soon rent by the premature birth of a stillborn son. I helped Nailza dig a shallow grave in our trash-littered backyard, where pigs and stray goats foraged and where we hoped to dig a pit latrine before the start of the winter rains. No bells would ring for this tiny fellow, nor would there be any procession of angels accompanying his body to the graveyard. Stillbirths remained outside the net of public and medical surveillance. And when curious neighbors commented the next day on Nailza's flat stomach, she tossed off their questions with a flippant "Yes, free and unburdened, thanks be to God!" Or with a sharp laugh, she would deny having been pregnant at all. Even living with Nailza in our close quarters, I had a hard time knowing what she was experiencing in the weeks and months that followed, except that Joana's photo disappeared from the wall, and her name was never again mentioned as long as I lived in that house. The stillborn son returned Nailza to her senses and to an acceptance of the reality in which she lived. Neighbors would say approvingly that Nailza had learned to adjust to the unalterable conditions of her existence. But at what price I wondered, at what physical, psychic, and social cost to Nailza and other women like her and at what risk to their seemingly unbroken succession of "replacement" babies and subsequent angel-children?

THE OVERPRODUCTION OF ANGELS: KEEPING TRACK, LOSING COUNT

Throughout Northeast Brazil, whenever one asks a poor woman how many children she has in her family, she invariably replies with the formula, "*X* children, *y* living." Sometimes she may say, "*Y* living, *z* angels." Women themselves, unlike the local and state bureaucracies, keep close track of their reproductive issue, counting the living along with the dead, stillborn, and miscarried. Each little angel is proudly tabulated, a flower in the mother's crown of thorns, each the sign of special graces and indulgences accumulating in the afterlife. There are a great many angels to keep track of. It is just as well that so many women are doing the counting.

When I first began in 1982 to try documenting the extent of infant and child mortality, I was stymied by the difficulty in finding reliable local statistics. I was referred by various public officials of Bom Jesus to the office of the local IBGE, the national central statistics bureau. "No," I was told, "there are no statistics kept here—no numbers at all." Everything, I was told, was tabulated and sent off to the central office in Recife.

After I had begun, through various and sometimes creative means, to assess the extent of child mortality in Bom Jesus, I made a visit to the first and newly appointed secretary of health for the town. Responding to inquiries about the greatest health risks to the population, the debonair and energetic Dr. Ricardo offered without a moment's hesitation, "Stress." And he began to outline his proposals for a stress-reduction education program that would target the substantial business and professional class of the community. Heart problems and cancer were, he continued, the two greatest causes of death in the bustling little metropolis. When confronted with the data painstakingly culled from the civil registry office indicating that almost a half of all deaths in the *município* each year were of children under the age of five and that diarrhea, not heart disease, and hunger, not stress, were the main pathogens, Dr. Ricardo sighed and raised his eyes to the heavens: "Oh, child mortality! If we were to talk child mortality . . . an absurdity, surely. And unknowable as well."

"What do you mean?"

"When I took over this office last August, the municipal administration had no figures on child mortality, none whatsoever. I had to send for them from the state, and they were unusable: an infant mortality of 120 percent!"

"How can that be?"

"And why not? It's quite straightforward. The official figures said that of every 100 infants born in Born Jesus, 120 of them died before they reached the age of one year! What a disaster! No wonder we are so underdeveloped in Brazil—more of us die than are even born!"

"Surely there are other ways of counting the dead," I suggested. "For example, how many charity baby coffins does the mayor's office distribute each month?"

"Oh, there's no limit there, no limit at all. We give the people as many as they want. In fact, the more they want, the better! It's one of the things we take care of very efficiently and well."

The doctor was pulling my leg, of course, but his remarks captured both the social embarrassment and the bureaucratic indifference toward child mortality as a premodern plague in a self-consciously modernizing interior town.

Later that day I stopped in again to visit Seu Moacir, the municipal "carpenter"; what he "carpenters" for the city are poor people's coffins, mostly baby coffins. Nonetheless, he strongly objected to being called the municipal coffin maker or having his crowded annex to the back of the municipal chambers referred to as a coffin workshop. And so the discreet sign over his door read, "Municipal Woodworks." But even here there was some deception at play, for the media in which he worked were as much cardboard and papier-mâché as plywood and pine. His "product," he told me, cost the city between two and eight dollars apiece, depending on size.

Yes, he was quite busy, but he could answer a few questions. He has been the municipal carpenter 20 years, since it was decided that every citizen had the right to a decent burial. There were more than twice as many baby coffins requested as adult ones. February and March were the "busiest" months for his work. Why? Perhaps it was, he hazarded a guess, because people liked to marry in June after the holidays were over and boys and girls had begun to "pair up." A man of few words, his own curiosity in the matters I was raising was limited. But the craftsman in him readily agreed to pose for pictures, and he held up both an adult coffin and a baby one, pointing out that the style was similar for both—a cardboard top and a plywood bottom.

All adult coffins, regardless of sex, were painted a muddy brown ("Earth tone") and all children's coffins, males and females, to the age of seven were painted "sky blue, the favorite color of the Virgin." Moacir noted one detail: there were no fasteners on the children's coffins because parents preferred to put their angels into the ground as unencumbered as possible so that the children's spirits were free to escape their premature graves. He found it difficult to estimate how many coffins "left" the workshop each week: "Some days as many as five or six will leave the shop. And then there are days when there are no requests at all." But, he added, this doesn't affect my productivity. I just keep on working steadily so that coffins are never lacking. I don't like to fall behind in my work; even on a holiday a comrade can find me, and I will have a coffin in stock that will serve his needs."

I asked if he would be willing to go over his requisitions for the previous few weeks, and, somewhat reluctantly, he agreed. We moved over to a cluttered desk with slips of paper in small, untidy piles. "Here," he said picking up one pile, "I'll read them out to you. But I warn you, things are a little chaotic. Here's one: baby, female, three months, June 22, 1987." And he continued, "Newborn, male, June 17, 1987. Female, about six months, June 11, 1987. Male, four months, June 17, 1987."

Then something had him stumped, and he had a hard time reading the slip of paper. As I approached him to look at it myself, he put it down abruptly: "This has nothing to do with anything. It's an order for seventeen sacks of cement! I warned you that everything was all mixed up here."

When I learned that all the requisition orders were referred back to the mayor in town hall, I approached him for access to the records on all materials furnished by the *prefeitura*. Grumbling, the mayor got down the ledger books, but he warned me not to trust any of them: "If you want numbers," he suggested, "just double everything that's put down here—our inventory is incomplete." In the books that documented in neat columns the "movement" of all supplies in and out of the prefecture, the data on baby coffins were there, interspersed with data on Brillo pads, light bulbs, chlorine bleach, kerosene, toilet paper, cement, alcohol, and soap. In a six-month period in 1988, the prefeitura had distributed 131 free infant and child coffins.

ANGEL-BABIES: *VELÓRIO DE ANJINHOS* [WAKE OF ANGELS]

From colonial Brazil to the present the death of an infant or a very young child was treated as a blessing among the popular classes, an event "to be accepted almost joyfully, at any rate without horror" (Freyre 1986b:144). The dead baby was an *anjinho*, a "little cherub," or an *innocente*, a "blameless creature" who died unregretted because his or her future happiness was assured. The bodies of the little angels were washed, their curls were prettily arranged, and they were dressed in sky blue or white shirts, with the cord of the Virgin tied around their waists. Their little hands folded in prayerful repose, their eyes left open and expectantly awaiting the Beatific Vision, angel-babies were covered with wild flowers, including floral wreaths on their heads. Little petition prayers and messages to the saints were tucked into their hands to be delivered to the Virgin on arrival. Even the poorest were arranged on wooden planks laden with flowers or in large, decorated cardboard boxes "of the kind used for men's shirts" (Freyre 1986b:388). The *velório de anjinho* was immortalized in da Cunha's classic (1944), *Rebellion in the Backlands:* "The death of a child is a holiday. In the hut the poor parents' guitars twang joyfully amid the tears; the noisy, passionate samba is danced again and the quatrains of the poetic challengers loudly resound; while at one side, between two tallow candles, wreathed in flowers, the dead infant is laid out, reflecting in its last smile, fixed in death, the supreme contentment of one who is going back to heaven and eternal bliss" (113).

The festive celebration of angel wakes, derived from the Iberian Peninsula, has been noted throughout Latin America. All-night drinking, feasting, party games, courting rituals, special musical performances, and dances cross many culture areas in South America, where the infant wake may last for three or four consecutive days (Schechter 1983). Weeping is proscribed at the infant wake because a mother's tears make the angel-baby's path slippery and dampen its delicate wings (Nations & Rebhun 1988). Rather, the mother is expected to express her joy, as did the plantation mistress from Rio de Janeiro who exclaimed, "Oh, how happy I am! Oh, how happy I am! When I die and go to the gates of Heaven I shall not fail of admittance, for there will be five little children pressing toward me, pulling at my skirts, and saying, 'Oh, mother, do come in, do come in' (Freyre 1986b:388). In rural Venezuela, the mother of the dead baby generally opens the dancing at her child's wake so that her angel may rise happily to the kingdom of heaven (Dominguez 1960:31).

The body of the dead infant was fetishized during traditional angel wakes in rural Latin America. The little corpse was sometimes taken out of the tiny coffin and handled like a doll or live baby. The corpse could be displayed like a saint, propped up on a home altar in between candlesticks and vases of sweet-smelling flowers. Or the dead child might be seated in a little chair, elevated on a small platform, set up inside an open box, tied to a ladder placed on top of the casket (to suggest the angel's ascent into heaven), or even tied to a swing suspended on ropes from the house beam. The infant's flight on the swing was said to symbolize the baby's transformation into an angel. The custom of leasing out angel-corpses to enliven local fiestas was described for the late nineteenth through the twentieth centuries in the Argentine pampas as well as in Venezuela, Chile, and Ecuador (see Ebelot 1943; Lillo 1942). In all, the traditional infant wake was a grand pretext for "unbridled merrymaking," perhaps (some suggested) as a culturally institutionalized "defense" against grief and mourning in a context in which infant death was all too common.

But what of a situation where neither festive joy nor deep grief is present? My own startlingly different ethnographic observations of angel-babies and the *velório de anjinho* in that town today lead me to another set of conclusions, which I must touch on as a prelude to my final discussion of mother love, attachment, grief, and moral thinking. In Bom Jesus today, where an angel-baby is sent to heaven on the average of one every other day, infant wakes are brief, rarely lasting more than a couple hours, and dispensed with a minimum of ceremony. The *velório* of an infant younger than one is at best perfunctory. There are no musical accompaniments, no songs, no prayers, no ritual performances of any kind. Neither food nor drink is offered the casual visitor, most of them curious neighborhood children. Household life simply goes on as usual around the infant in her or his little casket, which may be placed on the kitchen table or across one or two straight-backed kitchen chairs. The infant's grandmother or godmother is in charge, in addition to the older woman who specializes in preparing the body for burial. There is neither great joy nor grief expressed, and the infant is rarely the focus of conversation.

The procession of the angels to the cemetery is formed on the spur of the moment from the children who happen to be present. No special clothes are worn. There may or may not be a small floral wreath carried in front of the ragtag little parade. Some adults, but never the infant's own mother, may follow the procession to the graveyard. On one occasion the father, godfather, and paternal grandfather attended the funeral of a firstborn child, and all were deeply and visibly affected. On another occasion the godfather (and uncle to the dead child) followed the children's procession at some distance while walking his bicycle. Although he came as far as the graveyard, before the baby was put into the grave, the godfather left to attend a previously scheduled soccer game.

The procession of the angels takes the main, and only paved, street, but once at the foot of the hill it veers away from the main plaza and bypasses the church of Nossa Senhora das Dores. The procession does not stop (as it once did) for the priest's blessing; consequently, the bells of Our Lady of Sorrows no longer toll for the death of each child of Bom Jesus da Mata. That way of counting the dead has gone the way of many other folk Catholic pieties, swept away by the reformist spirit of the Vatican Council and by the socialist philosophy of the new regime of liberation theology. And no priest accompanies the procession to the cemetery, where the body is disposed of casually and unceremonially. Children bury children in Bom Jesus da Mata today.

At the cemetery, the disabled and often ill-tempered municipal gravedigger and an assistant lead the children to the common space where pauper children are buried. The temporary space is normally already waiting, and in a few minutes the coffin is placed in the grave and covered over, thereby leaving a small, fresh mound to mark the space. No prayers are recited, and no sign of the cross is made as the coffin goes into its shallow grave.

DEATH WITHOUT WEEPING

And so I maintain that these women generally face child death stoically, even with a kind of *belle indifférence* that is a culturally appropriate response. No one in the area criticizes a mother for not grieving for the death of a baby. No psychiatrist, pediatrician, or social worker visits the mother at home or tells her in the clinic what she is "supposed" to be feeling at a particular "phase" in her mourning. She is not told that crying is a healthy (and womanly) response to child death or that it is "natural" to feel bitter and resentful (which reduces anger to a manageable medical "symptom") or that she must "confront" her loss and get over her unhealthy emotional "numbness."

Poor Brazilians "work" on the self and emotions in a very different fashion. Instead of the mandate to mourn, the mother is coached by those around her, men as well as women, in the art of resignation and "holy indifference" to the vagaries of one's fate on earth and a hopefulness of a better life beyond. In this cultural milieu a deficit of emotion is not viewed as unhealthy or problematic (as in the overly repressed Anglo-Saxon culture of the United States); rather, an excess is. To experience strong emotions and passions—of love and lust, envy and anger, ecstasy and joy, grief and longing—is for most Brazilians, rich as well as poor, urban as well as rural, the most "natural" and expected occurrence. It is what being human is all about. But if allowed to run riot, these emotions are understood as the harbingers of much misery and suffering. Excessive emotions can bring down large and powerful households as well as small and humble ones. They can ruin lives and livelihoods. They can destroy relationships. They can cause physical as well as mental sickness. The Brazilian folk ethnopsychology of emotion is based on a very different construction of the body, self, personhood, and society. One can, for example, contrast the once popular belief in American society that cancers were caused by the repressions of the inner self, by passion turned inward and feeding on itself (see Sontag 1979), with the popular belief in Brazilian culture that emotional outbursts can dissipate the individual, poison the blood, and cause tuberculosis or cancer.

The strong mandate *not* to express grief at the death of a baby, and most especially not to shed tears at the wake, is strongly reinforced by a local folk piety, a belief that for the brief hours that the infant is in the coffin, she is neither human child nor blessed little angel. She is something other: a spirit-child struggling to leave this world and find its way into the next. It must climb. The path is dark. A mother's tears can impede the way, make the road slippery so that the spirit-child will lose her footing, or the tears will fall on her wings and dampen them so that she cannot fly. Dona Amor told of a "silly" neighbor who was weeping freely for the death of her toddler when she was interrupted by the voice of her child calling to her from his coffin: "Mama, don't cry for me because my *mortália* is very heavy and wet with your tears." "You see," Amor said, "the child had to struggle even after death, and his mother was making it worse for him. The little one wasn't an angel yet because angels never speak. They are mute. But he was no longer a human child either. He was an *alma penanda* [wretched, wandering soul]."

"What is the fate of such a child?"

"Sometimes they are trapped in their graves. Sometimes when you pass by the cemetery, you can see little bubbles and foam pushing up from the ground where such infants are buried. And late at night you can even hear the sound of the lost souls of the child-spirits wailing."

In all, what is being created is an environment that teaches women to contain their affections and hold back their grief during the precarious first year of the child's life. The question remains, however, whether these cultural "conventions" actually succeed in producing the desired effects or whether the dry-eyed stoicism and nonchalant air of Alto mothers are merely "superficial" and skin-deep, covering up a "depth of sorrow," loss, and longing. Nations and Rebhun, for example, maintained that the lack of grief is mere facade: "The inner experience of grief may be hidden by the flat affect of impoverished Brazilians. This behavior is part of a culturally mandated norm of mourning behavior; rather than signify the *absence* of strong emotion at child and infant death, it reveals the *presence* of grief" (1988:158).

What they wish to suggest, drawing inspiration from the writings of Lifton and other psychologists of mourning, is that the "blankness" and "flat affect" that they observed in certain poor women of the Northeast "is the blankness of the shell-shocked" (160). They continued, "The loss is too great to bear, too great to speak of, too great to experience fully. . . Their seeming indifference is a mask, a wall against the unbearable . . . While flamboyantly open about such emotions as happiness and sexual jealousy, they adopt a generally flat affect when discussing painful topics" (158).

Although I have no doubt (and have gone to great lengths to show) that the local culture is organized to defend women against the psychological ravagings of grief, I assume that the culture is quite successful in doing so and that we may take the women at their word when they say, "No, I felt no grief. The baby's death was a blessing." One need not speak of "masks" or "disguises" or engage in second-guessing on the basis of alien and imported psychological concepts of the self. Nations and Rebhun assumed a "divided self" that conforms to our Western ethnopsychiatry: a split between a public and a private self and between a "true" and a "false" self-expression. Moreover, when they suggested that the "mothers' flat affect in response to infant deaths is due more to folk Catholic beliefs than to a lack of emotional attachment to infants" (141), they projected a very secular view of religious belief as a superficial feature of the interior life, rather than as a powerful force that penetrates and constitutes the person.

Until recently, most cultural and symbolic anthropologists tended to restrict their interest in emotions to occasions when they were contained within formal, public, collective, highly stylized, and "distanced" rites and rituals, such as in healing, spirit possession, initiation, and other life cycle events. They left the discussion of the more private, idiosyncratic feelings of individual, suffering subjects to psychoanalytic and biomedical anthropologists, who generally reduced them to a discourse on universal drives and instincts. This division of labor, based on a false dichotomy between collective, "cultural" sentiments and individual, "natural" passions, leads to a stratigraphic model of human nature in which biology emerges as the base and culture as the mere veneer or patina, as the series of carnival masks and disguises alluded to previously.

But the view taken here is that emotions do not precede or stand outside of culture; they are part of culture and of strategic importance to our understanding of the ways in which people shape and are shaped by their world. Emotions are not reified things in and of themselves, subject to an internal, hydraulic mechanism regulating their buildup, control, and release. Lutz (1988) and Abu-Lughod (1986), among others, understand emotions as "historical inventions" and as "rhetorical strategies" used by individuals to express themselves, to make claims on others, to promote or elicit certain kinds of behaviors, and so on. In other words, emotions are discourse; they are constructed and produced in language and in human interaction. They cannot be understood outside of the cultures that produce them. The most radical statement of this position is that without our cultures, we *simply would not know how to feel.*

In fieldwork, as in daily life, we often encounter radical difference, and we come up against things we do not like or with which we cannot immediately identify or empathize. These "discoveries" can make us supremely uncomfortable. As anthropologists with a commitment to cross-cultural understanding, we worry—as well we should—how our written materials will be read and received by those who have not experienced the pleasures (as well as the pains) of living with the complex people whose lives we are trying to describe.

References

Abu-Lughod, Lila. *Veiled Sentiments: Honor and Poetry in a Bedouin Society.* Berkeley: University of California Press, 1986.

DaCunha, Euclides. *Rebellion in the Backlands* (translated from original *Os Sertões*, 1904). Chicago: University of Chicago Press, 1944.

Dominguez, Luis Arturo. *Velorio del Angelito* (2nd ed.). Caracas: Imprenta Oficial Estado Trujillo, 1960.

Ebelot, Alfredo. *La Pampa: Costumbres Argentinas.* Buenos Aires: Alfer and Vays, 1943.

Freyre, Gilberto. *The Masters and the Slaves: A Study in the Development of Brazilian Civilization* (translated from original *Sobrados e Macombos*, 1936). Berkeley: University of California Press, 1986.

Lifton, Robert J. 1967. *Death in Life.* New York: Touchstone.

Lillo, Baldomero. "El Angelito," in *Relatos Populares.* Santiago de Chile: Nascimiento, 1942.

Lutz, Catherine. *Unnatural Emotions.* Chicago: University of Chicago Press, 1988.

Nations, Marilyn, and Linda-Anne Rebhun. "Angels with Wet Wings Can't Fly: Maternal Sentiment in Brazil and the Image of Neglect," *Culture, Medicine, and Psychiatry* 12:141–200, 1988.

Schechter, John. "Corona y Baile: Music in the Child's Wake of Ecuador and Hispanic America, Past and Present." *Revista de Música LatinoAmericano* 4(1): 1–80, 1983.

Sontag, Susan. 1979. *Illness as Metaphor.* New York: Farrar, Strauss and Giroux.

Jody Glittenberg is a professor of anthropology, nursing, and psychiatry at the University of Arizona. For a better understanding of the context of this article, see the author's To the Mountain and Back *(Copyright © Waveland Press, 1994).*

A sick child evokes unusually strong feelings, and Glittenberg—a nurse as well as an anthropologist—shows how this can be the case even in a setting where sickness, war, and misery are commonplace. Other aspects of the plight of Guatemalan Indians are discussed by Stoll (chapter 12); and strikingly different reactions to infant death occur in a Brazilian shantytown (Scheper-Hughes, chapter 45).

Empty Breasts and Empty Fields
A Mayan Subsistence Culture
Jody Glittenberg

INTRODUCTION

Land of Eternal Spring, or Land of Eternal Tyranny: both are phrases used to describe the culture of Guatemala, the largest Central American country. Since 1524 state oppression of the Mayan Indians of Guatemala has been persistently practiced (Simon, 1987). The events of the past are reflected in today's socioeconomic and political tapestry, even as the descendants of the great Mayan civilizations strive toward achieving peace and equality in the national arena.

From 1540, when local Indian communities lost their sovereignty, to the present day, the Indian peasantry has suffered from complex exploitation (Annis, 1987; Smith, 1990). "Peasantry" describes a relationship that is imbalanced by power; some deplore this unrelenting extraction of resources as forming castes that resist change (Stavenhagen, 1970). Clearly the system of peasantry creates a class or caste of very poor people. The Mayan subsistence agricultural family is an example of poverty in the highlands of Guatemala. Here the Mayan Indian family persistently devotes more and more time and energy to subsistence agriculture on less and less fertile land that they do not even own (Glittenberg, 1976).

Violent clashes between organized *campesinos* (farmers) and large landowners have marked the history of Guatemala, for the past fifty years in particular. Various local revolts and agrarian reform laws have attempted to reverse such maldistribution of wealth. None has been successful. Only in 1996 has hope sprung that peace may come at last, as a public display of unity and peace took place in the capital, Guatemala City. Rebels and national security guards alike laid down their arms with a mutual promise of peace-keeping. A national economic reform is in full swing (Smith, 1990); it appears that Guatemala may be entering a new epoch of development. Perhaps the country should be named The Land of Eternal Hope.

On the local scene, the effects of colonialism will take decades (or longer) to be modified or disappear. The following story illustrates the devastation that poverty imposes on the individual family when fields are empty and the people starve. Anthropologists study patterns of human activity in order to comprehend reasons why some events repeatedly occur.

Some profound issues can sometimes be uncovered in a slice of a story—a moment of time.

Written expressly for *Contemporary Cultures and Societies in Latin America*, Third Edition.

And, given this mysterious opportunity, further fieldwork and research will then follow, exposing further and further the many elements of the problem. The process of discovery is thorough, systematic, objective, yet compassionate, with honest reflection of the human beings involved. My account of the "Baby Rosa story" appears as a slice of such a problem—a moment of time—in the lives of a group of grieving Mayans and an anthropologist at the Behrhorst Hospital in Chimaltenango, Guatemala.

THE "BABY ROSA" STORY

Doc [Behrhorst] came running in, holding a small baby in his arms. "Help her," he called to me. "Give her oxygen, get her to breathe. I don't know if she'll make it . . . she's so malnourished." His eyes seemed filled with the pain of having seen too many babies lost. He put the small bundle into my arms, saying as he turned to run back to the clinic, "We have five emergencies right now. Do what you can." Later, much later, I would reflect on what it means in developing countries not to have enough health care providers—right then I needed to deal with the moment.

As I looked at her, I thought how small she was, a soft bundle dressed in pink. Yet only the whites of her eyes showed, and they were fixated. She lay with her head thrown back, limp and barely breathing. I knew she was nearly gone. "Oxygen," he'd said, "Give her oxygen."

Where was the oxygen? Oh, yes, I thought, there's a tank and a sort-of tent of plastic. I hurried through the motions. My hands were stiff as I tried to set up the makeshift oxygen tent. Now the baby, I thought—oh, she is so limp, but she's breathing. Barely.

I placed the limp little form on the table with some sheets underneath, motioning for the mother and Mike, the Peace Corps pal, to help me. We were all alone, just Mike, the mother and me. I knew she was the baby's mother—you could tell by her eyes. She, the mother, watched every move I made.

"What is her name?" I ask in Spanish.

"Rosa," came the soft answer.

"Help me, Mike, get the tank over to the table," I ordered. We worked fast, as Rosa's little face was still motionless, her color growing dusky, the breathing hardly detectable. We placed the plastic tent over the baby and around the sheets on the table and started the oxygen going. I tried to make a tight shield of the tent so that the oxygen couldn't escape. Somewhere in this makeshift emergency room I recalled the rows and rows of children with polio whom we had cared for in the 1950s when I was still a student nurse. We had so many oxygen tents then, too, and so many died. Some things don't change—like children dying.

With the makeshift oxygen tent in place, I gently massaged Rosa's tiny chest and lifted her frail arms. A gasp, a cry! Had I heard right?

"Look!" cried Mike. "Look! She's opening her eyes!"

Little Rosa's eyes began to focus. She saw me and now began crying harder and, wonderfully, harder. Her dusky face turned pinkish and then ruddy; Rosa's arms flailed about, reaching outward. The mother, by my side, began to cry . . . and so did Mike and I. The room suddenly became still, like a cathedral.

I had not noticed, but about twenty Cakchiquel Mayan Indians had quietly entered the room; they were watching intently. In a moment, all of them got down on their knees. They were praying. The whole room was full of praying Indians. Some moved closer to Mike and me and began to touch the hem of my uniform.

"Santa Blanca, Santa Blanca." I heard them mumbling.

"No, it can't be," I said with astonishment to Mike. "Do they think they are witnessing a miracle?" They must think I am a saint!"

"Yeah. They really do." said Mike with disbelief.

We were all quiet.

Little Rosa cried robustly; the sound shook the space. The mother, sobbing, pleaded to hold her little daughter.

"Please let me hold her; she is so hungry. I have milk [pointing to her breast]. Please let me hold her. She seems so strong, why not?" the mother begged.

"Wait a while," I said, as gently as I knew how. The stronger the lusty cry became, the more the mother begged to hold and breastfeed Baby Rosa. I could feel the tension: a mother's love, an infant's need, the reaching out. I thought, "I guess it's okay." Gently I took little Rosa out from under the makeshift oxygen tent and placed her next to her mother's breast.

Gasping, I saw the problem—the mother's abscessed breasts, the crusted nipples, her emaciated body. She herself was a skeleton—a starving being. How could she have any breastmilk? But the mother's cooing sounds seemed like music; it filled the quiet room as mother and baby became one. Eager sucking sounds came from Baby Rosa. But then, in only a few minutes, slowly—almost as if in a slow motion movie—I couldn't believe it: I watched as the grasp of Rosa's little hand loosened on her mother's breast; her rosy cheeks turned an ashen gray. Her body went limp as a rag doll. Rosa was gone—dead in her mother's arms, as I learned her other six brothers and sisters, who never lived to see their first birthday, had been. All of them gone, in just a few years. I could do nothing. Rosa's mother was sobbing, knowingly; the comfort of her abscessed, empty breasts was to have been little Rosa's last memory. Perhaps it was best; I wished I knew.

I turned off the oxygen tent; big Mike hugged me and then the mother; we all hugged. The Indians filed quietly out, into the courtyard and beyond—returning, I supposed, to their empty fields. As the lilies in the fields . . . so the winds passeth . . . knowing the place no more, I thought as I struggled not to cry but to maintain control. "I can't stand all of this death," I thought. I walked out into the woods behind the hospital, leaned against a sturdy tree, and sobbed.

"How can it be?" I asked the sky. "Isn't this just a perpetuation of death?" Empty breasts and empty fields—where does it end? How about my own well-nourished children so far away? Oh, how I missed them! I wished I were home. About then I heard a noise behind me, and I looked back and saw Doc. He came over to me and put his hand on my shoulder and said, "I know it hurts; it never stops hurting, but you did what you could. We never save them [at that age]. They don't have enough antibodies to fight the infections. And we don't have the right kind of Band-Aid to fight the poverty. The people need land to fight their hunger."

I was to learn many more lessons about poverty in the years to come, but the lesson of Baby Rosa will always be a painful part of me, and that pain has brought a curious strength and courage. I had much more to learn from these people of the mountains.

References

Annis, Sheldon (1987). *God and Production in a Guatemalan Town*. Austin: University of Texas Press.

Glittenberg, JoAnn (1976). *A Comparison Study of Fertility in Highland Guatemala: A Ladino and an Indian Town*. Unpublished doctoral dissertation, University of Colorado, Boulder.

Glittenberg, Jody (1994). *To the Mountain and Back*. Prospect Heights, IL: Waveland Press.

Simon, Jean-Marie (1987). *Guatemala: Eternal Spring, Eternal Tyranny*. New York: Norton.

Smith, Carol (1990). Introduction: Social Relations in Guatemala over Time and Space. In Carol A. Smith (Ed.), *Guatemalan Indians and the State (1540 to 1988)* (pp. 1–34) Austin: University of Texas Press.

Smith, Carol (1990). Conclusions: History and Revolution in Guatemala. In Carol A. Smith (Ed.), *Guatemalan Indians and the State (1540-1988)* (pp. 258–288). Austin: University of Texas Press.

Stavenhagen, Rodolfo (1970). Class, Colonialism, and Acculturation. In I. L.Horowitz (Ed.), *Masses in Latin America* (pp. 43–57). New York: Oxford University Press.

Joseph W. Bastien is a professor of anthropology at University of Texas (Arlington). He was a Catholic missionary/priest in Bolivia before turning to anthropology, with which he has done much to help us understand the ecology and cosmology of highland Indians, and the remarkable ethnobotanic knowledge and medical skills of native practitioners, some of whom are much in demand throughout the Andes.

This paper, as part of the corpus of Bastien's work, tells a little about how and why the author became an anthropologist. It also shows how profoundly the experience of close and sustained contact with members of another population can affect the worldview of an "observer," without interfering with that person's commitment to the scientific enterprise. Lessons learned in the field often can be applied in other contexts, especially when they have to do with something so fundamental as the meaning of social relationships. The reader may find it interesting to compare Glittenberg (chapter 46) and Scheper-Hughes (chapter 45), who very differently deal with human tragedy close at hand, and Robben (chapter 35), for whom a reflexive stance poses special problems.

The Healing Touch of Love

Joseph W. Bastien

I learned early in life that love heals. When I was three years old, I was stricken with polio, or infantile paralysis as it was called in 1938. My parents had just bought a new house, and we were moving into it. Instead of romping through the house, as any three-year-old would do, I went into a corner and cried. Later I was taken to the hospital and diagnosed with polio. My sister JoAnne also had polio. Treatment was slow and painful, with periodic spinal taps. Months later, my sister and I were delivered by ambulance to our new home. As we were carried by stretcher into the house, my mother asked the doctor if we would walk again. The doctor said that the paralysis was permanent—to which she replied, "Only God knows that!"

Mother wrote to Sister Kenney in Australia at the time to receive information on the therapeutic use of massages and hot baths. Mother bathed and massaged us until our muscles began to revive, and then she coached us to pick up marbles with our toes and later to crawl and to walk. Within two years, JoAnne and I both walked, ran, and swam as normal children. My memories have dimmed as to specifics except for periodic nightmares about the spinal taps and enclosure within the iron lung. But throughout my life there is an overwhelming sense of a mother, now an almost mythological figure of godlike proportions, taking care of me. It was, and still is, the love of my mother and my father, now long dead, that healed me—not only of polio but of a certain selfishness, in that I would come to dedicate a part of my life to the healing ministry of love.

Over time, throughout a long career—first as a priest and then as a religious layperson and medical anthropologist—the therapeutic love that my mother first taught me became secondary in importance to the marvels of psychiatric and biological medicine, and to the insistence on being objective and distant from the object-patient. For many scientists love implies emotions and emotional involvement, which hinder rationality and impersonal judgments. Fortunately, several people helped me to recall the lesson that my mother had taught me.

When I was 27, I was doing a chaplaincy internship at the Iowa State Mental Hospital near Independence, Iowa. I counseled patients with a variety of psychological ailments, from alcoholism to autistic behavior. After some time, I became very discouraged about my ability to help these patients, many of whom completely

Written expressly for *Contemporary Cultures and Societies of Latin America*, Third Edition.

rejected my visits with abusive remarks and behavior. At one point I was ready to resign, and I explained my feelings of ineptitude to a visiting psychiatrist from India (whose name I don't even recall). He put it simply: "These patients have not been loved; that is why they behave so poorly, and in turn people love them even less. To break the cycle of non-love, you should love them."

Later, after my ordination in 1963 as a Catholic priest, my mission of love became modeled after the life of Christ and his commitment to the sick, lonely, imprisoned, and homeless. That was during the sixties and seventies, when the message of love became so culturally important because of the Vietnam War and segregation, two social maladies that brought so much physical, emotional, and psychological distress to many. During the same years, love was also linked with a sexual revolution—but more recently it has been curtailed by increased fear of sexually transmitted diseases. During the 1980s and 1990s more sobering and sterile attitudes were adopted in my culture, such as "enlightened egoism" (*I'm Okay, You're Okay*) and the incessant demand for personal fulfillment.

I left the priesthood in 1969, was laicized, and studied to be an anthropologist. When I entered the academic job market in 1973, armed with a Ph.D. and several publications, I adopted the competitive practices necessary to "climb the greasy pole" to tenure. As one academic described it, "You have to claw your way to the top." Self-less giving and reciprocal relationships, such as are found in many societies that anthropologists study, were of little help in getting publications printed and maintaining positions in the university.

Anthropological fieldwork, however, again brought me back to the source of humanity that my mother and the Indian psychiatrist had revealed to me. Remote Bolivian shamans and doctors now began to reteach me the therapy of love. First, there was Florentino Alvarez, an herbalist, and next Oscar Velasco, a medical doctor and psychiatrist. Their philosophies and beliefs later helped me to find meaning and compassion in my relationship with a person dying of AIDS. Each of these three associations in turn revealed something vital about love in therapy: the cumulative wisdom imparted by these interconnecting modules of experience forms a subjectivity in relationship to patients.

LORD OF THE MEDICINE BAG: FLORENTINO ALVAREZ

Florentino Alvarez was the most famous Kallawaya herbalist of the twentieth century, one of the approximately thirteen thousand Kallawayas who live in the Province Bautista Saavedra, in the Department of La Paz, Bolivia. The Kallawayas are a well-known group of herbalists in the Andes. They follow a tradition of medical expertise more than a thousand years old. They performed brain surgery and used *Ilex guayusa loes*, a hollylike plant, as an anesthetic as early as A.D. 500, and they currently employ about a thousand medicinal plants (see Bastien 1987 for a list of some plants and ethnographic analysis). I began fieldwork with Kallawaya herbalists in 1978.[1] Although I observed fifteen herbalists in their practices, Florentino taught me the most about healing.

It was in the healing and caring context that we first met. When I first visited Florentino on June 26, 1978, he had been paralyzed by a stroke. Valentín, his adopted son, said that Florentino was slowly dying. He had suffered a blood clot in the brain a month earlier, could barely speak and walk, and some of his muscles had begun to atrophy. Since the stroke, Florentino had remained in bed, largely because Valentín did not have the time to help him since he needed to farm and take care of the sheep, pigs, burros, and chickens.

At sixty-seven years of age, Florentino was ready to die. I began helping him to live. For weeks, I massaged his muscles, helped him walk, and encouraged him to answer my endless questions about herbalism. I also gave him massive doses of vitamins to increase his appetite. When I left Bolivia in August, Florentino was walking with crutches and tending his store and herbal practice. His speech was still slurred, but he could be understood in Quechua, his native language.

One gratification of my research was that Florentino told his fellow Kallawaya herbalists that I had cured him. I told them that I was not a medical doctor and had healed Florentino by simple methods that could be used by anyone—I had cured him through a caring relationship. Nevertheless, Florentino felt deeply indebted to me and in return provided me with important information about the use of medicinal plants.

Moreover, Florentino repaid me by teaching me that this caring relationship extends to all of nature. Florentino believed that health came from a caring relationship among people, plants, and animals. Within all animals and plants—and even in the mountains, streams, and air—are "energies" that will heal us if we give ourselves to them in reciprocal exchange. This is a distinctly Andean view—within the equal dialogue with nature, as subject to subject, truths are revealed, harmony restored to the universe, and bodily disintegration restored. Within nature there are truths transcendental to the ephemeral disintegration of the body.

Florentino told me that he had received a divine call earlier in his life to care for the sick. Around 1935, he worked selling watches for a jewelry firm in Lima, Peru. He made a good profit and became wealthy until, as he said, "I read a pamphlet in church that said whoever sells useless things commits a sin. After reading this, I left the jewelry business." He learned the herbal trade with a religious fervor. He dedicated himself to helping others and became a person who, because of his "calling," established a spiritual relationship among animals, plants, and people, especially the sick. He realized that the disintegrating effects of sickness needed to be treated with a combination of empirical cures from herbs, cultural beliefs about Mother Earth (*Pachamama*) and Jesus, and caring relationships. Florentino never charged patients for his cures but only asked that they give whatever they could afford. Although his fame became widespread throughout South America, with patients coming from Chile, Peru, and Argentina, he remained humble, caring, and poor but rich in prestige and being loved.

Florentino enhanced the general reputation of all Kallawaya herbalists. In 1955, Victor Paz Estenssoro, President of Bolivia, commissioned him to prepare a display of Kallawaya medicines for the Museum Casa Murillo in La Paz. Victor wrote him a letter of commendation for his contributions to Andean medicine. Florentino cured in his clinic until 1981, when he died of unknown causes. In 1984, Kallawaya herbalists acknowledged Florentino Alvarez as an eminent herbalist by dedicating an herbal book to him.[2] They referred to him as *Nolla Kapachavuh* (Lord of the Medicine Bag).

Sometime before Florentino's death, I gave him a pair of binoculars. He said he would look at the distant and majestic peak of Aqhamani, about 20,000 feet high. He told me his eyes would travel the roads he once cured upon, and his heart would remember the suffering people he had cared for. Florentino's humility, simplicity, and caring inspired me to become more actively involved in Bolivian health projects.

PSYCHIATRIST AND SHAMAN: OSCAR VELASCO, M.D.

By 1981, I wanted to return to the Bolivian peasants something that they had given to me: a knowledge of their indigenous healing techniques. Although it may sound redundant to teach peasants about traditional medicine, many of their native curing techniques—especially the use of medicinal plants—were being forgotten from generation to generation. An old-time herbalist such as Florentino might know about medicinal uses of 300 plants, but a middle-aged herbalist may only know about 80, and aspiring herbalists might only learn about 40. My task was to write a Spanish herbal (Bastien 1983) and provide training courses for community health workers so that this important indigenous healing lore would not be lost.

I began working with Gregory Rake, director of Project Concern. A visionary and very caring person, Rake asked me to work with doctors and nurses of the Department of Oruro in articulating ethnomedicine and biomedicine (see Bastien 1992). It was then that I met Dr. Oscar Velasco, who taught me how the caring therapeutic session involves intuition and creativity.

Oscar tended a small hospital in Totora, a mining community on the road from Oruro to Potosí. The afternoon we met, I found him in a small herbal garden in back of the two-room hospital. He was harvesting herbs for an herbal tea intended for an elderly patient who lay in a metal, long-legged bed within the hospital dormitory. I accompanied him as he prepared the tea and then helped the Aymara Indian to drink it. As he held her up to drink, he spoke soothing words in broken Aymara. Afterward, as we walked through the rutted, dusty roads of Totora, Oscar described his life. Many of the details now escape me, but he said that he had received his M.D. from the University of Potosí and later specialized in psychiatry. He built up a small practice in La Paz. Later, he went to work with Jaime Zalles, an ex-Jesuit priest with extraordinary skills as a caring healer, in the altiplano around Tiahuanaco. Oscar became very knowledgeable about Aymara traditional medicine, and Rake later hired him to direct the hospital in Totora where I met him.

Oscar and I worked together for seven years. Never once did I see him become impatient with peasants as they continually stopped him wherever he was to ask for some cure. Nor did they pay him. I would sometimes become impatient, waiting in the jeep to travel somewhere, as Oscar carefully and caringly talked with each of them. Once, admitting that science was not my best area of study, I asked Oscar whether he thought I would have made a good medical doctor, and he replied: "You would be a good doctor because you are intuitive, creative, and caring." This surprised me, because these are also the characteristics of successful anthropologists. I had misconstrued medical doctors as cold and clinically empirical scientists. Oscar reminded me that many of them still practice the art of caring and healing.

During the time we spent together, Oscar gave me many opportunities to learn from him as he practiced this valuable art. Once he and I were visiting a village in the altiplano when a woman beckoned to Oscar, asking him to cure her daughter. The daughter was crouched in the corner of a dark room with her face covered. She refused to leave the corner because she was ashamed of her disfigured face. Her mother informed us that Juana was about thirty years old and separated from her husband, who had left her with their small child after she had become disfigured from a burn. While having an epileptic attack, Juana had fallen into a fire, leaving her face badly scarred. People laughed at her. Her relatives, who were Protestant and had been told that her troubles were caused by her sinfulness and lack of faith, rejected her. The minister further victimized her, which separated her from the church as well as from her relatives. She retreated to the rural village where Oscar found her, living with her mother as a recluse, afraid to go out.

Over the course of several therapeutic sessions, Oscar was able to get Juana to look into a mirror and accept herself. He reminded her that she was a loving mother who cared for her infant, which helped her build up her self-confidence. He gradually helped her go out into the village and to accept the stares of bystanders until they came to accept her as one of them. Oscar also asked that a nearby diviner perform a ritual for her. Oscar and the diviner gathered members of the community to participate in the all-night ritual. During the ritual, the diviner symbolically removed the evil attributed to her by the minister, and the participants joined together in a meal. Oscar explained to me that usually members of the family participate in these rituals but in Juana's case, since they had rejected her, he gathered a substitute family whose loving care would replace that of her natural family. The ritual brought peace of mind to Juana. With Oscar's assistance, Juana has had plastic surgery and is now a much happier person, living a normal life.

On another occasion, a father and mother brought their fifteen-year-old daughter to Oscar for consultation, saying that she had nausea, fainting spells, and nervous tics (Bastien 1992). After examining her, Oscar realized that she was pregnant. (The daughter had attended a fiesta, gotten drunk, and been raped by a mestizo.) However, he didn't mention the pregnancy because she was unmarried, and he feared her parents would whip her and consider the child illegitimate. Instead, he referred them to a diviner, whom he informed of the situation. The diviner, who had cured several patients in cooperation with Oscar, performed an elaborate ritual with the young woman and her relatives present. He divined from the coca leaves that the girl had arisen during the middle of the night to urinate outside, and as she was doing so, Pachamama had impregnated her with a child.

The father became furious on hearing that his daughter was pregnant but was unable to do much, because the diviner had structured the behavior and illness within a ritual and social context. As the diviner continued throwing the coca leaves for divination, he implied that the father had been involved in promiscuous activity and therefore should judge himself before judging his daughter. During the ritual the daughter and her parents became reconciled, and they offered a llama fetus, coca leaves, and guinea-pig blood to Pachamama. Her father said that he would accept the infant into his family and give it his surname.

Oscar knew that Bolivian peasants prefer to deal with illnesses as symbols that make them endurable and acceptable to members of the community. Although some doctors equate these symbols with ignorance, Oscar understood how diviners use symbols and rituals as adaptive mechanisms enabling people to cope with maladies. He also knew that he needed the help of ethnomedical practitioners to deal with complex behavioral and social problems. This knowledge, collaboration, and caring prevented unwarranted suffering—such as victimizing the victims. Just as Florentino had shown me that practitioners affect patients' relationships with nature, Oscar made me realize that successful therapists must be aware of how their practices affect loving relationships among patients, relatives, and members of the community.

ANTHROPOLOGISTS AND AIDS

Mother, Florentino, and Oscar have never left me, even though Mother and Florentino are dead and Oscar is thousands of miles away. The way they cared for their patients is the way that I would like to care for others. But it is difficult to love someone who is dying, especially if the friendship is new and you know that you will soon lose that friend to death. There is a certain holding back for fear of losing a part of yourself through the death. The dilemma of loving and letting go became real to me when a fellow academician recently died of AIDS.

My chairman approached me in my office in mid-1992 to tell me that a colleague was stricken with brain tumors, could not speak, and lay partially paralyzed in the Presbyterian Hospital in Dallas. That afternoon I visited Stanley (a pseudonym). He stammered some words that I could not understand, thrashed his crooked arm sideways, and began to cry. I also cried, feeling the utter despair conveyed by Stanley. Two weeks earlier I had attended a faculty meeting with him, and we both received service pins: Stanley's for twenty years as a distinguished professor, and mine for fifteen years. It didn't seem possible that he could have been so quickly transformed from a functioning faculty member into someone deprived of voice and partially paralyzed. I surmised that Stanley had toxoplasmosis because he had "gone gay" (openly homosexual) eight years before.

Before this first hospital visit, I had talked with Stanley perhaps only fifteen times during the fifteen years that we taught together. We had somewhat of a social link due to our both being senior full professors, but apart from that I had always been afraid of Stanley's icy cold intellectual abilities. He was stand-offish, always complaining about how intellectually poor the students were. When he went gay, he subsequently went through a bitter divorce and a severed relationship with a grown daughter, but he also became a warmer person.

Throughout that summer, I visited Stanley once or twice a week. At first the visits were unpleasant, with Stanley crying out of desperation and stammering in an attempt to tell me something. Someone thought that perhaps he was trying to tell us about his living will to permit his early death. Stanley was a fan of the arts, so I brought him a radio that played classical music all day. As we listened to a Chicago Philharmonic broadcast one Saturday afternoon, he managed to tell me the name of the opera that was playing. I also brought him an oil painting of an ocean shore in which the waves were violently beating against jagged rocks, yet the sun was peacefully setting on the horizon. I told Stanley that this scene was an analogy of his life, with the turbulent ocean beating against the rocks—a destructive place for a "swimmer" trying to negotiate the perils of life and illness—yet farther out, in the depths of the ocean and beyond, was the tranquility of the sunset. I also prayed the 77th Psalm, in which the psalmist prays to Yahweh to stop the foreign forces that are besieging him—a memory from my Roman Catholic Breviary, long since abandoned after I was laicized from the priesthood. In comforting Stanley, I felt a priestly energy returning.

Later that summer, I went to Bolivia for fieldwork. By now, Stanley and I were friends. I looked forward to my visits with him and had somewhat overcome the obstacle that was holding back my love, namely, the fear that if I cared too much, my loss would be that much greater when he died. The day before I left for Bolivia, I explained to Stanley that I would be gone for a month and that, if he died before I returned, he should look up my mother in heaven—a more devout Catholic than the Pope—who would help him. He laughed at this, and as I walked out the door, he slowly waved his hand from the side of the bed.

I returned in mid-August, two weeks before Stanley's death. Someone had brought him an icon of Jesus. Because Stanley was asleep at the time of the visit, the person had left the icon with a note asking that whoever attended Stanley pray the 21st Psalm with him. I put the icon next to his bed so that he could see it on the wall. I prayed as best I could the 21st Psalm, "The Lord is my Shepherd, I shall not want, he leads me to green pastures. . . . " But that was all I could remember. The day before Stanley died, I looked into his eyes and they were as transparent as those of Jesus within the icon: they looked out, beyond, and through to eternity. In Stanley's eyes, much like the eyes of the icon, there was an intimacy of love and eternity that he shared with me. Stanley died the following night.

With Stanley it all came together: the basis of therapy is loving care, because this is what transcends death and physical maladies and makes every therapeutic session meaningful on a universal level.

REFLECTIONS

It seems redundant to add to these personally meaningful experiences, except to say that I have written about them under the influence of the emotion of love. I want to avoid sterile academic abstractions about them. Perhaps I never really left the priesthood. It seems to me that even at the greatest moments in what the world now recalls as clinical history, unrequited love is the refrigerant that cools the frigid machinery of modernism, empiricism, and medicine. I also know with a surety that the true love of caring therapy is not an acquired technique; rather, it springs from some intimate relationship—perhaps from what Martin Buber refers to as I-Thou relationship. Mother referred to Jesus and me; Florentino was one with Mother Earth, and Oscar seems centered with Inkari through an underground river that leads to Cuzco. This very special relationship goes beyond the individual and individualism (concepts and terms that are unknown to Aymara and Quechua Indians). It connects the earth, animals, plants, and community. Are we then, as healers, helping our patients make this universal and healing connection? We can only do this if we ourselves become connected. We can then foster the connection—the healing relationship—between ourselves and our patients and, in turn, between our patients and the world: this is the therapy of love.

Notes

[1] Since 1968, I had done research concerning Kallawaya diviners and their uses of ritual in healing (Bastien 1978). I became interested in ethnobotany and herbalists in 1979 following the death of Louis Girault in 1976 (see Girault 1984, 1987, 1988, 1989). Included in the references is a list of articles and books that Girault and I have published concerning the Kallawayas.

[2] This recognition is found in the herbal book, *Plantas y Tratamientos Kallawaya*, published by Servicios múltiples de tecnología apropriada, La Paz, Bolivia, 1984.

References

Bastien, Joseph W. 1973. *Qollahuaya Rituals: An Ethnographic Account of the Symbolic Relations of Man and Land in an Andean Village*. Ithaca: Cornell Latin American Studies Program.

———. 1978. *Mountain of the Condor: Metaphor and Ritual in an Andean Ayllu*. Monograph 64, American Ethnological Society, ed. Robert Spencer. St. Paul: West Publishing Company. (Reissued by Waveland Press, 1985).

———. 1980. "Rosinta, Rats, and the River: Bad Luck is Banished in Andean Bolivia." In *Unspoken World: Women's Religious Lives in Non-Western Cultures*, Nancy Falk and Rita Gross, eds., pp. 260–74. New York: Harper and Row.

———. 1982. "Herbal Curing by Qollahuaya Andeans." *Journal of Ethnopharmacology* 6:13–28.

———. 1982a. "Exchange Between Andean and Western Medicine." *Social Science and Medicine* 16:795– 803.

———. 1983. "Pharmacopeia of Qollahuaya Andeans." *Journal of Ethnopharmacology* 8:97–111.

———. 1983a. *Las plantas medicinales de los kallawayas*. Oruro: Proyecto Concern.

———. 1985. "Qollahuaya-Andean Body Concepts: A Topographical-Hydraulic Model of Physiology." *American Anthropologist* 87:595–611.

———. 1987. *Healers of the Andes: Kallawaya Herbalists and Their Medicinal Plants*. Salt Lake City: University of Utah Press.

———. 1987a. "Cross-Cultural Communication between Doctors and Peasants in Bolivia." *Social Science and Medicine* 24:1109–1118.

———. 1988. *Cultural Perceptions of Neonatal Tetanus and Programming Implications, Bolivia*. Resources for Child Health Project. Arlington: REACH, John Snow, Inc.

———. 1988a. "Shaman contra enfermero en los andes bolivianos." *Allpanchi* 31:163–197.

———. 1989. "A Shamanistic Curing Ritual of the Bolivian Aymara." *Journal of Latin American Lore* 15(1):73–94.

———. 1990. "Community Health Workers in Bolivia: Adapting to Traditional Roles in the Andean Community." *Social Science and Medicine* 30:281–288.

Girault, Louis. 1984. *Kallawaya: Guérisseurs Itinérants des Andes*. Paris: Mémoires ORSTOM.

———. 1987. *Kallawayas: Curanderos Itinerantes de los Andes*. La Paz: UNICEF.

———. 1988. *Rituales en las regiones Andinas de Bolivia y Perú*. La Paz: Don Bosco.

———. 1989. *Kallawaya: El idioma secreto de los Incas*. La Paz: UNICEF.

A Bibliographical Essay

The information that follows is intended as a guide for beginning students. It has never been easy to monitor the vast literature available on Latin America and subjects that relate to the people who live there. The intellectual breadth of such an effort would be problematic in any area; the linguistic diversity of source material poses another obstacle. It is also commonplace that some journals and publications are short-lived, some books are printed in only small numbers and are not widely publicized, and so forth. To minimize those obstacles and to avoid expensive duplication of effort, a group of librarians in the mid-1900s organized the Seminar on the Acquisition of Latin American Library Materials (SALALM), which publishes a wide range of bibliographical tools and maintains an extensive website (http://www.library.cornell.edu/colldev/salalmhome.html), both of which are helpful to researchers on a wide range of subjects.

In a sense, the suggestions for further reading that accompany each of the section introductions in this book comprise a brief topical bibliography. Furthermore, the footnotes and bibliographies of the majority of the individual readings are included in full. Neither of those resources will be repeated here. Used together, these three classes of suggestions should help any interested person to find a variety of source material[1] on most aspects of contemporary cultures and societies of Latin America. It seems appropriate to provide, in addition, a summary expansion of suggestions intended especially as a guide to students who may choose to do research for a paper or other presentation.

The discussion that follows is ordered in terms of major types of sources and in terms of regions. Categories include: research aids and bibliographies; journals; monograph series; general sources; Middle America (including Mexico and Central America); and South America.

Although authors from several disciplines are represented, there is a strong emphasis on anthropological perspectives. Space limitations disallow the inclusion of references to many specific books, much less to the numerous excellent articles available in periodicals, but the listed research aids and bibliographies will help the interested reader to gain familiarity with that sizable and significant part of the literature.

Electronic reference sources are also mentioned.[2] In developing a listing for such use, a number of decisions were made that differ from those governing the preparation of a bibliography for a typical scholarly monograph. Brief mention of some of those decisions may help readers by indicating the strengths and shortcomings of this as a means of getting into the vast, varied, and widely dispersed literature on contemporary societies and cultures of Latin America:

• In the expectation that most of the people who use this resource will be native speakers of English, I have listed translations, when available. A few books[3] in other languages are cited, nevertheless—some because they are of special importance and a few because they are virtually the only pertinent sources available.

• On the assumption that books are usually strengthened and updated by revisions, I have usually cited the most recent edition rather than the original.

• In general, too, I have not included unpublished material or publications of institutions, governmental or other, that are not readily available for purchase or interlibrary loan within the United States.

• Some print sources that may at first appear outdated remain valuable, because electronic sources generally have very limited time-depth, and because some classics still deserve attention.

RESEARCH AIDS AND BIBLIOGRAPHIES

There are a few individual books that, although they were not intended to serve as reference volumes, are likely to be of special usefulness to a busy undergraduate who wants quickly to find out more about some particular aspect of contemporary cultures and societies of Latin America. For example, a good general introduction to the geography, history, and politics of all of Latin America is T. E. Skidmore and P. H. Smith, *Modern Latin America* (5th ed., Oxford University Press, 2001). Earlier editions of *Contemporary Cultures and Societies of Latin America* are very different and deserve to be consulted: D. B. Heath and R. N. Adams (eds.) (Random House, 1965), D. B. Heath (ed.), (2nd ed., Random House, 1974/2nd rev., Waveland, 1988).

For the cultural history that set the stage, some good general introductions are H. M. Bailey and A. P. Nasatir, *Latin America: The Development of Its Civilization* (4th ed., Prentice Hall, 1992); G. Arciniegas, *Latin America: A Cultural History* (A. A. Knopf, 1967); L. Bethell (ed.), *The Cambridge History of Latin America* (9 vols. to date, Cambridge University Press, 1984–); and R. E. W. Adams and M. MacLeod (eds.), vol. VII: Mesoamerica, and F. Salomon and S. B. Schwartz (eds.), vol. VIII: South America, both multivolume parts of *The Cambridge History of Native Peoples of Latin America* (6 vols. to date, Cambridge University Press, 1996–). Probably the best single volume that deals with Latin America from a predominantly anthropological perspective is E. R. Wolf and E. C. Hanson, *The Human Condition in Latin America* (Oxford University Press, 1972) even if it is slightly outdated in some details.

In a more specifically bibliographic sense, there can be no question that the cornerstone of research on Latin America has long been *Handbook of Latin American Studies* (HLAS) University of Florida, 1935–) (website: http://lcweb2.loc.gov/hlas); annually there are various numbers of volumes by thematic area, including references to journal articles as well as books. It is remarkably thorough and well indexed. *Hispanic American Periodical Index* (HAPI) (University of California at Los Angeles Latin American Center, 1975–) (website: http://milton.mse.jhu.edu/dbases/hapi.html) is nearly as comprehensive and is also well indexed.

A. Gropp compiled a *Bibliography of Latin American Bibliographies* (2 vols., Scarecrow, 1969–71), to which several other authors have added supplementary volumes over the years.

In searching for earlier sources, it is often helpful to consult the catalogs of specialized libraries, such as: University of Texas at Austin Library, *Catalogue of the Latin American Collection* (31 vols. to date, G. K. Hall, 1969–); Tulane University Library, *Catalogue of the Latin American Collection* (9 vols. to date, G. K. Hall, 1970–); or Harvard University Library, *Catalogue of the Latin American Collection* (18 vols. to date, G. K. Hall, 1968–).

Seminar on the Acquisition of Latin American Library Materials (SALALM) publishes a frequent but irregular *Bibliography and Reference Series* (University of New Mexico Press) on various subjects. Similarly, the Columbus Memorial Library of the Organization of American States issues occasional bibliographies on different topics.

Other important sources for bibliographies on a wide range of topics concerning Latin America are Instituto Panamericano de Geografía, Harvard University Libraries, Hispanic Foundation of the Library of Congress, and individual bibliographers such as C. K. Jones, S. A. Bayitch, H. Piedracueva, L. V. Loroña, D. R. Cordeiro, and M. H. Sable. For individual nations, ABC-Clio publishes a *World Bibliographic Series* with individual titles according with the country treated, and by various authors.

Research aids other than bibliographies can be helpful both in providing authoritative summaries on topics that are of broad interest for study and in steering the reader to more detailed source material on anything that is covered there. For example, B. Tenenbaum (ed.), *Encyclopedia of Latin American History and Culture* (5 vols. to date, Simon & Schuster, 1996–), or S. Collier, H. Blakemore, and T. Skidmore (eds.), *Cambridge Encyclopedia of Latin America and the Caribbean* (8 vols. to date, Cambridge University Press, 1996–).

With specific reference to anthropological approaches and data, a number of indexes are available including *Anthropological Index to Current Periodicals* (Royal Anthropological Institute, 1963–), *Anthropological Literature* (Peabody Museum of Harvard University, 1979–), *Anthropology and Related Disciplines* (Routledge, 1990–), and *International Bibliography of Social and Cultural Anthropology* (UNESCO, 1955–). For earlier sources, the *Catalog of the Peabody Museum . . . Library* (53 vols. to date, Harvard University, 1963–) is remarkably thorough, indexed to include most journal articles and book chapters as well as books and monographs.

JOURNALS

It is both an advantage and a problem that anthropologists write on so many different subjects and publish in so many different periodicals.[3] Guides to the periodical literature have already been mentioned. Specific journals that are of special interest for students of Latin America include—but are by no means restricted to—the following: *Latin American Research Review* (1956–) has excellent review-articles on a wide range of topics; *Index to Latin American Periodicals* (1929–) is just what its title suggests; *Journal of Interamerican Studies and World Affairs* (1959–) tends to focus a little more on political and economic matters. *Latin America* (1967–) combines current events and a sociocultural perspective.

More specifically weighted toward the social sciences are: *Journal of Latin American Anthropology* (1995–), *Latin American Anthropology Review* (1964–95), and *Journal of Latin American Lore* (1975–); *The Americas* (1944–) and *Hispanic American Historical Review*, both emphasizing history; *Revista Interamericana de Ciencias Sociales* (1950–), *Review of Latin America and Caribbean Studies* (1966–), *Bulletin of Latin American Research* (1981–), *Journal of Latin American Cultural Studies* (1990–), and *Journal de la Société des Americanistes* (1914–).

Topically oriented periodicals that often carry articles of immediate relevance to this book include *Journal of Peasant Studies* (1973–), *Culture and Agriculture* (1977–), *Economic Development and Cultural Change* (1953–), and a host of others. Regionally oriented journals similarly often publish articles by anthropologists and on relevant topics, e.g.: *América Indígena* (1940–), *Boletín Bibliográfico de Antropología Americana* (1937–), *Estudios Andinos* (1970–), *Guatemala Indígena* (1961–), *Luzo-Brazilian Review* (1964–), *Mesoamerican Studies* (1969–), *Quaderni ibero-americani* (1946–), *Revista Española de Antropología Americana* (1966–), or *Revista Mexicana de Estudios Antropológicos* (1927–).

MONOGRAPH SERIES

There are a number of monograph series that deal with Latin America, some in very general terms and others in specifically anthropological terms. Among the former, readers may find useful a series of volumes, each entitled *Historical Dictionary of . . .* (Scarecrow Press); they usually combine entries of ethnographic interest with others, together with a bibliographical essay, all with reference to a particular country or area.

Another good starting point for those who want to learn about a country and its people is the Area Handbook Series, published by the U.S. Department of the Army (DA-Pam 550–N); almost every volume has a different author and the titles are usually just . . .: *A Country Study.* For some countries there are successive editions; earlier the series was called Special Area Handbooks, and Special Warfare Handbooks, with the country name as part of the title. A third series of books on *Culture and Customs of . . .* , with each title indicating a different country in Latin America, is published by Greenwood Press (1998–).

Other monograph series that include more detailed reports by various authors and often on specifically anthropological topics include: *Ediciones Especiales* and *Series Antropología Social* (Instituto Indigenista Interamericano), *Ibero-Americana* (University of California, Berkeley), *Latin American Monographs* (Pan American Union Dept. of Social Affairs), *Monographs* (University of Texas (Austin) Institute of Latin American Studies), *Publications* (Centro Latinoamericano de Investigaciones en Ciencias Sociales), *Publications* (Smithsonian Institution Institute of Social Anthropology), and *Studies in Comparative Development* (Sage). There are also a few monograph series that focus on specific regions in Latin America, and that often include anthropological contributions.

GENERAL SOURCES

Each of the essays on suggestions for further reading included in this book refers to several sources on virtually every one of the major points that are mentioned in the introduction to the section of readings that precedes it, usually in sequence.

It is remarkable how much is told, concisely and effectively, in E. R. Wolf and E. C. Hanson, *The Human Condition in Latin America* (Oxford University Press, 1972). Similar efforts were made by M. Olien, *Latin Americans* (Holt, Rinehart & Winston, 1974) and E. Willems, *Latin American Culture* (Harper & Row, 1975). A recent counterpart to the present book is M. B. Whiteford and S. Whiteford, *Crossing Currents: Continuity and Change in Latin America* (Prentice Hall, 1998).

In general, however, it must be recognized that the anthropological enterprise, which emphasizes long-term close and sustained study of social systems that a single investigator tries to comprehend, does not easily lend itself to the kind of broad generalizations that one finds in books about "the masses in Latin America," "elites in South America," or "hemispheric issues in development" and such. To be sure, anthropologists do often borrow ideas from such works by economists, political scientists, sociologists, and others who are comfortable dealing with macro-level societal analyses. But in terms of data it is more common for an anthropologist to focus on micro-level analyses—case studies that may deal with the same or similar issues locally, whether in a hamlet, town, city, or region, where people tend to know each other or at least to know what to expect when they have occasion to interact.

The research aids and bibliographies as well as the journals listed previously will be helpful in locating general sources; a faculty member or reference librarian may provide further suggestions or shortcuts.

Middle America

Edited by R. Wauchope, *The Handbook of Middle American Indians* (16 vols. to date, University of Texas Press, 1964–) has authoritative articles by major authors on various peoples, aspects of culture, languages, archeological periods, and other anthropological topics, covering Mexico and all of Central America.

As an introduction to the region, it is remarkable how much of the same range of information E. R. Wolf was able to condense, in truly elegant prose, in *Sons of the Shaking Earth* (University of Chicago Press, 1959). A collection of synthetic essays edited by S. Tax, *Heritage of Conquest: Ethnology of Middle America* (Free Press, 1952) was important at that time; such ventures have not been essayed in recent years.

Individual communities, local market systems, and so-called tribes are often studied, whether holistically or with special reference to some anthropological theme but, as with the section on General Sources, it would be an overwhelming and not very fruitful task to try to list them here. New books and new authors appear every year, and a faculty member or reference librarian to whom you can explain your interests is likely to be helpful in this respect.

South America

The situation for South America is very similar to that for Middle America. There is an encyclopedic reference source that is both important and useful, and there are myriad books and monographs that, however excellent they may be, do not warrant detailed listing in this context. The major source is J. H. Steward (ed.), *Handbook of South American Indians* (7 vols., Smithsonian Institution Bureau of American Ethnology, 1946–51), again with authoritative articles by major authors on peoples, aspects of culture, languages, and archeological periods as they were known then. Its geographic scope includes much of Central America and the Caribbean islands as well as continental South America. An interesting one-volume synthesis is J. H. Steward and L.C. Faron, *Native Peoples of South America* (McGraw-Hill, 1959).

T. J. O'Leary's *Ethnographic Bibliography of South America* (Human Relations Area Files, 1963) and G. P. Murdock's *Outline of South American Cultures* (Human Relations Area Files, 1959) were thorough at the time; such books are rarely attempted in recent years.

Happy hunting!

Notes

[1] As simplistic as they may sound, a few general guidelines can avoid frustration and save considerable time and effort when one is just beginning to investigate a topic. Keep in mind that any author who has written about something is likely also to have written more on the topic elsewhere, and at another time. Many of the books, articles, and monographs cited in something that sparked your interest are likely also to be relevant, or at least to contain other references that would be helpful. In a sense, each list of references can lead you to a host of others. And never underestimate the value of serendipity! Browsing through a library's stacks is often a good way to find things that you want to learn more about, especially within a few feet on either side of some item that you know is of interest.

Any student who does not feel comfortable in a research library would do well to get a preliminary orientation before beginning to hunt for sources on an interesting topic. Some college courses include this; more often, the library staff offers such sessions to small groups at the beginning of each term, or on request. Once you have a fairly good idea about what is to be the theme of your paper or presentation, it may be helpful to ask a reference librarian for some individual guidance; most people in such a position are both very knowledgeable and more than willing to help others share their enjoyment of what a library can offer to anyone who knows a few guidelines.

[2] Electronic or online resources are increasingly useful complements to the printed word. Each medium offers something of value that the other does not, but there is not as much overlap as some would imagine. Items available electronically are not necessarily available without cost; some can be accessed only through institutions that pay a subscription fee.

Without belaboring the point, this is probably an appropriate context in which to remind readers that an important portion of the anthropological and other scientific literature is not available online, and that printed sources should always be consulted if feasible. It should also be obvious that not everything online can be believed; the same lack of oversight and regulation that makes electronic communication so exciting a medium also poses serious problems in terms of accuracy and validation. Although the process remains less than perfect, traditional peer-review provides a greater assurance that in-print material is trustworthy. A reference librarian or faculty member can be helpful in evaluating source material.

[3] Many readers are not aware that the production of a scholarly book requires at least a year's investment of time, thought, and effort—and usually more. For that reason and also because we want to communicate promptly with large numbers of colleagues who share special interests and who might not buy or read all of our books, much of the most important communication in a discipline like anthropology takes place in professional and scientific journals, by means of articles such as those that make up most of this book. I strongly recommend that anyone who wants to pursue almost any topic in more detail be prepared to rely on journals at least as much as on books.

ABOUT THE EDITOR

Dwight B. Heath is Professor of Anthropology and former Director of the Center of Latin American Studies, both at Brown University, in Providence, Rhode Island. He earned his A.B. (magna cum laude) at Harvard University, and Ph.D. (in anthropology) at Yale University. He has done extensive anthropological fieldwork among tribal and peasant peoples in Bolivia, Costa Rica, Mexico, Spain, and the United States, and has served as consultant to the Peace Corps, World Health Organization, and various other national and international agencies. His writings appear in many books, professional journals, and encyclopedias around the world. His books include *Mourt's Relation: A Journal of the Pilgrims at Plymouth* (1963; reissued 1986), *Contemporary Cultures and Societies of Latin America* (with Richard N. Adams, 1965; editor, second edition, 1974; reissued 1988), *Land Reform and Social Revolution in Bolivia* (with Charles J. Erasmus and Hans C. Buechler, 1969), *Historical Dictionary of Bolivia* (1972), *Cross-Cultural Approaches to the Study of Alcohol* (with Michael W. Everett and Jack O. Waddell, 1976), *Cultural Factors in Alcohol Research and Treatment of Drinking Problems* (with Jack O. Waddell and Martin D. Topper, 1981), *Alcohol Use and World Cultures* (with A. M. Cooper, 1981), *International Handbook on Alcohol and Culture* (1995), and *Drinking Occasions: Comparative Perspectives on Alcohol and Culture* (2000).